Eighth Edition

PARTIES AND ELECTIONS IN AMERICA

THE ELECTORAL PROCESS

MARK D. BREWER
University of Maine
L. SANDY MAISEL
Colby College

ROWMAN & LITTLEFIELD
Lanham · Boulder · New York · London

Executive Editor: Traci Crowell
Assistant Editor: Mary Malley
Senior Marketing Manager: Amy Whitaker
Cover Designer: Jen Huppert
Cover Art: © iStock.com/shmell_c4.

Credits and acknowledgments borrowed from other sources and reproduced, with permission, in this textbook appear on appropriate pages within the text or in the credit section on page 471.

Published by Rowman & Littlefield
A wholly owned subsidiary of The Rowman & Littlefield Publishing Group, Inc.
4501 Forbes Boulevard, Suite 200, Lanham, Maryland 20706
www.rowman.com

Unit A, Whitacre Mews, 26-34 Stannary Street, London SE11 4AB

British Library Cataloguing in Publication Information Available

Library of Congress Cataloging-in-Publication Data

Names: Brewer, Mark D., author. | Maisel, Louis Sandy, 1945– author.
Title: Parties and elections in America : the electoral process / Mark D. Brewer, University of Maine, L. Sandy Maisel, Colby College.
Description: Eighth Edition. | Lanham, Maryland : Rowman & Littlefield, [2018] | Includes bibliographical references and index.
Identifiers: LCCN 2018024594 (print) | LCCN 2018026519 (ebook) | ISBN 9781538114353 (electronic) | ISBN 9781538114346 (paperback : alk. paper)
Subjects: LCSH: Elections—United States. | Political campaigns—United States. | Political parties—United States.
Classification: LCC JK1965 (ebook) | LCC JK1965 .M35 2018 (print) | DDC 324.973—dc23
LC record available at https://lccn.loc.gov/2018024594

∞ ™ The paper used in this publication meets the minimum requirements of American National Standard for Information Sciences—Permanence of Paper for Printed Library Materials, ANSI/NISO Z39.48-1992.

Printed in the United States of America

Brief Contents

Contents v
List of Figures and Tables xi
About the Authors xiii
Preface xv
Acknowledgments xxi

1 Elections and Political Parties 1
2 American Political Parties and Party Organization 21
3 Voting and Other Forms of Political Participation 63
4 Organized Groups in the Political Process 111
5 Campaign Finance 136
6 State and Local Nominations 180
7 State and Local Elections 204
8 Presidential Nominations 246
9 Presidential Elections 288
10 The Media and the Electoral Process 328
11 Party in Government 360
12 The Role of Political Parties 396

Glossary 415
References 425
Credits 471
Index 473

Contents

List of Figures and Tables xi

About the Authors xiii

Preface xv

Acknowledgments xxi

1 Elections and Political Parties 1
An Examination of Elections in the United States 3
The Role of Elections in Democratic Theory 8
Modes of Elections 9
Implications for Representation 9
Definitions of "Political Party" and "Party Systems" 12
Conclusion 15
Critical Thinking Questions | Key Terms 18

2 American Political Parties and Party Organization 21
The Development of American Political Parties 22
The First Party System 23
The Second Party System 28
The Third Party System 34
The Fourth Party System 39
The Fifth Party System 41
A Sixth Party System—Yes, But Defined How? 43
The Modern Party Organization 49
Local and County Organizations 49
State Party Organizations 52
Party Organization at the National Level 54
Critical Thinking Questions | Key Terms 61

3 Voting and Other Forms of Political Participation 63
Who Votes; Who Doesn't 67

Expansion of the Franchise 67
Decline in Voter Participation 74
Voters in Presidential Elections 82
Models of Voting Behavior: *The American Voter* 82
Critics of the *American Voter* Model 86
Presidential Voting Reviewed 92
Voters in Congressional, Senatorial, and State and Local Elections 94
Voting Behavior Theory Revisited 99
Participation in Politics in America 101
Political Participation in the Real World 105
Critical Thinking Question | Key Terms 105

4 Organized Groups in the Political Process 111
Organized Groups in American Politics 114
Political and Nonpolitical Associations 114
Politically Active Groups 116
Electoral Activities of Organized Groups 121
Working within the Party 122
Group Ratings 124
Political Action Committees 125
Interest Groups' Influence on Their Members 130
Critical Thinking Questions | Key Terms 134

5 Campaign Finance 136
The Long History of Campaign Finance Reform 138
The Climate for Reform 140
The Federal Election Campaign Act of 1971 and Efforts at Amendment 141
Buckley v. Valeo, 424 U.S. 1 (1976) and Its Impact 142
The Seven-Year Battle for McCain-Feingold and Its Demise 144
The Costs of Democracy and Who Pays for It 148
The Costs 149
Sources of Campaign Funds 153
Campaign Finance in a Post–*Citizens United* and Post-*McCutcheon* World 176
Critical Thinking Questions | Key Terms 177

6 State and Local Nominations 180
Political Context and Politicians' Decisions to Run 181
Development of the Direct Primary System 183
Primaries as a Response to One-Party Domination 184
Primaries as an Item on the Progressive Agenda 184
Varieties of Primaries 185
Who May Run 185

Who May Vote 190
Who Wins 194
The Politics of Nominations 196
Uncontested Nominations 196
Contested Nominations 198
Conclusion 201
Critical Thinking Question | Key Terms 201

7 State and Local Elections **204**
The Conventional Wisdom: Old versus New Politics 206
The New Politics: Campaigning in a Media Age 207
Redistricting and Reapportionment 207
The Role of Political Parties 211
The Role of Organized Groups 213
Media Politics 214
The Candidate's Personal Organization 217
The Structure of a Modern Campaign 219
Old-Style Politics: A More Prominent Role for Parties 224
Reexamination of the Role of Political Parties 226
Local Campaigns in the Absence of Party 227
Do Campaigns Determine Who Wins Elections? 228
Lack of Competition in American Elections 228
Incumbent Advantage in U.S. House and State Legislative Races 228
Competition in U.S. Senate and Gubernatorial Races 230
Credible Competition in American Elections 231
Third Parties in State and Local Elections 234
Conclusion 238
Critical Thinking Questions | Key Terms 243

8 Presidential Nominations **246**
The Post-1968 Reforms 247
The McGovern-Fraser Commission 248
The 1972 Nomination 250
The Reform Movement: An Assessment 253
Twenty-first-Century Presidential Nominations 255
Strategic Considerations in the Contests for Nominations 260
The Political Calendar 261
The Rules of the Game 265
Strategic Use of Campaign Resources 269
Evaluating Nominating Campaigns 275
The Conventions 276
Credentials Challenges 278
Rules Disputes 278

Party Platforms 279
Vice Presidential Nominations 281
An Evaluation of the Conventions 283
The Presidential Nominating Process as It Stands 285
Critical Thinking Questions | Key Terms 286

9 Presidential Elections 288
From the Convention to the General Election 290
Organizing for the General Election 292
Structuring the Campaign Organization 292
Functions of a Presidential Campaign Organization 296
Setting a Campaign Strategy 303
Strategies for the General Election 303
Geographic Determinations 304
Coalition Strategies 307
Issue Strategies 308
The Strategic Use of Incumbency 313
Tactics for the General Election 315
Tactical Considerations of Where to Go 315
Tactical Considerations of Media Use 316
Tactical Considerations of Which Issues to Discuss 317
The Tactics of Presidential Debates 318
Third-Party Candidates in Presidential Elections 319
The All-Consuming Nature of a Presidential Campaign 323
Critical Thinking Questions | Key Terms 325

10 The Media and the Electoral Process 328
The Media in the Contemporary Context 329
Free/Earned Media: Journalists' Presentations of Candidates and Campaigns 335
The Varieties of Free Media 335
The Role of the Free/Earned Media 338
The Actual Role That the Media Play 341
An Assessment of the Role of Free Media 347
Paid Media: The Candidate Provides the Message 349
Types of Paid Media 349
Controversies Caused by the Use of Paid Media 351
Impact of Paid Media on Election Campaigns 354
An Uneasy yet Necessary Relationship in Transition 356
Critical Thinking Questions | Key Terms 358

11 Party in Government 360
Theoretical and Historical Context: Is Strong Party Government Possible in the United States? 370

Measuring Party Strength in Congress 375
Party Organization in Congress: The Leadership Hierarchy in the House and Senate 378
House Leadership 379
Senate Leadership 388
The President as Leader of Party in Government 391
Critical Thinking Questions | Key Terms 393

12 The Role of Political Parties **396**
The Role of Elections 397
The Context of Federalism 397
Voters, Parties, and Elections 404
The Electronic Revolution: Television and Digital Media 405
The Parties in the Modern Election 408
Parties' Appeal to the Electorate 411
The Tone of Twenty-first-Century Politics 411
Concluding Remarks 413
Critical Thinking Questions 413

Glossary 415

References 425

Credits 471

Index 473

Figures and Tables

FIGURES

1.1a Two-Party Competition in Twentieth and Twenty-first-Century Presidential Elections 15
1.1b Two-Party Competition in the Twentieth and Twenty-first-Century Senate 15
1.1c Two-Party Competition in the Twentieth and Twenty-first-Century House of Representatives 16
2.1 Party Division Prior to Realignment on Slavery Issue 32
2.2 Stress on Party System Caused by Slavery Issue 32
2.3 Party System after Realignment on Slavery 33
3.1 Turnout in Presidential and Midterm Elections, 1948–2016 75
3.2 Voter Turnout by Race, 1964–2016 77
3.3 Voter Turnout by Age, 1964–2016 78
3.4 Voter Turnout by Sex, 1964–2016 79
3.5 Funnel of Causality 83
3.6 Electoral Success of Incumbent Representatives, 1980–2016 96
3.7 Electoral Success of Incumbent Senators, 1980–2016 97
3.8 Electoral Success of Incumbent Governors, 1980–2016 99
3.9 Turnout in Iowa Caucuses, 1968–2016 106
4.1 Nonparty Independent Expenditures in Congressional Elections, 1978–2016 129
5.1 General Election Spending by Major Party Presidential Candidates, 1952–2016 150
5.2a Mean House Campaign Expenditure by Party, 1974, 1984, 1990–2014 151
5.2b Mean House Campaign Expenditure by Candidate Status, 1974, 1984, 1990–2014 152
5.3a Mean Senate Campaign Expenditure by Party, 1974, 1984, 1990–2014 153
5.3b Mean Senate Campaign Expenditure by Candidate Status, 1974, 1984, 1990–2014 154

5.4 PAC Contributions to Congressional Elections, 1974–2016, in millions of dollars 164
5.5 PAC Contributions to Congressional Candidates by Candidate Status, 2016 165
7.1 Structure of a Modern Campaign 220
11.1 Party Unity Votes in Congress, 1954–2016 376
11.2 Party Unity Scores in the House, 1954–2016 376
11.3 Party Unity Scores in the Senate, 1954–2016 377

TABLES

1.1 Elections Held in Baton Rouge, Louisiana, 2010–2018 5
1.2 Term-Limited States 6
3.1 Black Voter Registration in Southern States, 1960–2016 70
3.2 Registered Voters and Percentage of Voter Turnout, 1988–2016 73
3.3 How V. O. Key Would Have Characterized Voters after the 2016 Election 87
3.4 Party Identification, 1952–2016 93
4.1 Types of Organizations and Examples of Associations 115
4.2 Growth of Political Action Committees, 1974–2016 118
4.3 Top Ten PACs in Contributions to Federal Candidates, 2015–2016 127
5.1 Funding Sources for Congressional Candidates, 1974, 1984, 1994–2016 155
5.2 PAC Contributions to Congressional Candidates by Party, 1998–2016 167
5.3 Top Ten Outside Groups in Federal Campaign Spending, 2016 Election Cycle 175
6.1 Electoral Context of Gubernatorial Elections 183
6.2 Offices at the Top of the Ballot 183
8.1 Number of Presidential Primaries and the Percentage of Delegates Selected in Them, 1968–2016 254
8.2 Money Raised by Major Party Candidates for Presidential Nominations, 2016 259
8.3 Sitting Senators Seeking Their Party's Presidential Nomination, 1968–2016 271
10.1 Americans' Main Source of News about 2016 Presidential Election, November–December 2016 332
11.1 Party Leadership in the House, March 2018 387
11.2 Party Leadership in the Senate, March 2018 387

About the Authors

Mark D. Brewer is Professor of Political Science and member of the Honors College faculty at the University of Maine. His research interests focus generally on political behavior, with specific research areas including partisanship and electoral behavior at both the mass and elite levels, the linkages between public opinion and public policy, and the interactions that exist between religion and politics in the United States. Brewer is the author or editor of a number of books and articles in academic journals, with the most recent being *Polarization and the Politics of Personal Responsibility* (with Jeffrey M. Stonecash, Oxford University Press, 2015), *The Parties Respond*, 5th edition (with L. Sandy Maisel, Westview Press, 2013), *Party Images in the American Electorate* (Routledge, 2009), and *Dynamics of American Political Parties* (with Jeffrey M. Stonecash, Cambridge University Press, 2009). He is also the editor-in-chief of the *New England Journal of Political Science*.

L. Sandy Maisel is the Goldfarb Family Distinguished Professor of American Government at Colby College, where he was also the founding director of the Goldfarb Center for Public Affairs. A former (unsuccessful) candidate for Congress and frequent adviser to party committees and candidate campaigns, Maisel is the author or editor of more than twenty books focusing on American political parties and elections; his most recent edited volume is *Trumping Ethical Norms: Teachers, Preachers, Pollsters, and the Media Respond to Donald Trump* (with Hannah Dineen). His scholarly articles, many of which emerged out of the path-breaking Candidate Emergence Study, have appeared in the *American Political Science Review*, the *American Journal of Political Science*, the *Journal of Politics*, and other political science journals and anthologies of research on American politics.

Preface

Two of the last three presidential elections in the United States have been among the most compelling contests of all time. The 2008 presidential election saw the election of the nation's first African American president, who won in part by running one of the most innovative campaigns of all time. Just when we thought we could not top the excitement and enthusiasm of 2008, we got the 2016 presidential election cycle, which will certainly go down in history as one of the most bizarre and combative episodes in America's presidential election soap opera. But conflict and controversy aside, 2016 was also innovative and groundbreaking in many ways. Additionally, much of great significance occurred in the other election cycles in between 2008 and 2016.

The elections in the period 2008–2016 provide us with the unique opportunity to study the two major parties during a period of both relative parity in the electorate in presidential and midterm cycles and an intense atmosphere of change and upheaval: How will Donald Trump affect the Republican Party? What will be the Democratic Party legacy of Barack Obama? How did the Democratic and Republican parties organize to maximize voter turnout and electoral success in these cycles? How important were the parties to the candidates running for office during this period? How important were party labels to the voters at the polls? What role will the parties play in governing in the 115th Congress? Are there other institutions developing that will challenge parties for their centrality in American politics? What about the media as we enter into the thick of the 2018 election cycle? Are daily newspapers irrelevant? If so, will the broadcast television networks soon follow suit? How can candidates, parties, and other interested political actors find their necessary audiences in today's fragmented media environment? Where will the digital revolution take us next? Finally, what about the increasingly restriction-free and chaotic world of campaign finance? What are the implications for representative democracy in a post–Citizens United and post-McCutcheon world? This book aims to provide students with the theoretical tools and historical background to answer these questions and more.

Chapter 1 is a conceptual introduction to the study of political parties and elections: Parties are defined, and their role in the electoral process is made clear. Chapter 2 recognizes that modern political parties are a distinctly American invention. Since the founding of our nation, politicians have taken an ambivalent position on the American party system, playing a role in its development while bemoaning its existence. This chapter explains the evolution of today's Democratic and Republican parties in terms of six distinct party systems in American political history. We examine how each system has contributed to the development of modern party organizations—their institutions, structure, and norms.

But just who participates in the parties, in the elections, and in the American political system? Chapter 3 examines who votes and who does not, and who participates in political activities beyond casting a ballot on election day. In this chapter we look at motives and incentives for political participation, providing a detailed examination and careful review of the voluminous professional literature on voting behavior. We also explore newly emerging cleavages within the American electorate. Chapter 4 expands our understanding of political participation to organized groups and the extent to which they influence the voting behavior of their members. Political observers from Tocqueville to V. O. Key Jr. have commented that Americans congenitally tend to join groups and that they often relate to the electoral process as members of their groups. It could even be argued that some interest groups fit our definition of political party almost as well as the Democratic and Republican parties do, and indeed better than some minor parties. Organized group behavior has long had an impact on American politics—a phenomenon perhaps more important today than at any other time in our history, as groups vie for influence over policy outcomes in 2018 and beyond, on issues ranging from health care to greenhouse gas regulation and climate change, in a world where money continues to flow freely into political life.

In the twenty-first century, no one doubts the importance of money in electoral politics. Campaign finance is such an important topic that an entire chapter has been devoted to exploring the current situation. Chapter 5 examines the evolution of campaign finance reforms, from the 1970s to the Supreme Court's decisions in *Citizens United v. Federal Elections Commission* (130 S. Ct. 876, 2010), *McCutcheon v. FEC* (134 S. Ct. 1434, 2014) and their aftermath. Data are presented that summarize the costs of maintaining our democracy. In addition, we examine the sources to which politicians turn for campaign funding and the implications of the central role money plays in American electoral politics.

Chapters 6, 7, 8, and 9 examine nominations and election campaigns in the United States, the former two dealing with gubernatorial, senatorial, congressional, and state and local elections, and the latter two with the presidential election. Chapter 6 begins with a discussion of common views on the nominating process and then examines how reality differs from these views. We also explore the development of the direct primary as a means of securing partisan nominations, the variety of primaries that exists in various jurisdictions, and the politics of securing party nominations.

Chapter 7 examines general election campaigns below the presidential level. The conventional wisdom holds that politics has changed dramatically as the age of television and computers has evolved. The argument presented in this chapter is that "new politics" is very much in evidence in some campaigns but that the "old politics," the politics of personal contact and detailed organization, remains essential for many local politicians. In addition, the chapter explores the role of third parties, more specifically, what factors determine whether third parties are likely to have an influence in elections.

The American presidential nomination process is so complex that it is often misunderstood in the national media. In chapter 8, we explain changes to the nomination process and review recent presidential contests and the strategic considerations that determine how such contests were fought. We consider conflicting viewpoints on the role of national party conventions, the ultimate spectacle in American politics: Are they important elements of the electoral process or, as their critics would argue, useless vestiges from a bygone era, no longer worthy of serious consideration?

When many Americans think of election campaigns, they focus on the general election of the president. Chapter 9 considers how such an election is organized, what the recent strategies were (and what tactics were used for implementing those strategies), and what impact the campaigns ultimately had. While the topic would seem to be a familiar one, many of the nuances of presidential campaigns are obscure except to the most practiced observer.

Chapter 10 highlights another distinct aspect of the electoral process: the impact of the media—both paid and unpaid—on American elections. Constraints on the ways in which newspapers and television cover politics explain some of such media's apparent shortcomings. The controversy over negative advertising composes an important aspect of the discussion of paid media, as does the use and possible misuse of issue advocacy advertising. We also explore the growing importance of the Internet in American campaigns and elections, with a particular focus on social media and the democratization of news.

Chapter 11 examines the role of parties in government. The American political system is not a parliamentary one; it is not structured to encourage strong and responsible party governance. Instead, the American democracy is one of checks and balances in which separate institutions share legislative power. Parties are clearly the most dominant organizing element in Congress, but their leaders are constrained in how much they can control policy outcomes. Members of Congress owe their seats to their constituents, not to party leadership. This chapter explores congressional constraints to partisan governance, within and across both the House and the Senate, and the impact such constraints have on policies in the 115th Congress.

Finally, in chapter 12, we return to the themes raised in the introductory chapter: How well does the electoral process function? What role do parties play in the modern American democracy, and how does that differ from their traditional function? What are the consequences for our political system of (1) candidate-oriented campaigns, (2) the influence of soft money provided by outside groups, (3) Obama's innovative 2008 and 2012 presidential campaigns and Trump's highly unconventional 2016 campaign, and (4) America increasingly becoming a nation networked with the possibility of instantaneous communication? What do these phenomena mean for (1) parties as the organizing structure of elections, and (2) parties as the organizing structure of our governmental institutions? Can and should this process be reformed?

NEW TO THE EIGHTH EDITION

Our goals for this text remain the same as in previous editions, and are threefold: first, to give students the tools to analyze the political world around them, empowering them to be astute political analysts in their own right; second, to get students to see that the outcomes of the electoral battles waged in 2016 and beyond affect their lives—whether the contests are between the Democratic and Republican parties or between candidates and challengers at any other level of government; third, and most important, to get students excited about politics. Of course, we do not expect you to wait by your mailbox in the freezing rain for the next issue of Congressional Quarterly Weekly Report, nor do we anticipate that you will change your Friday night plans to watch Robert Costa's *Washington Week* on PBS, log on to realclearpolitics.com first thing every morning, or check your customized Reddit feed every five minutes. Rather, we simply hope you will be an interested, informed, and educated participant in and analyst of our exciting electoral process.

Understanding modern politics means understanding political history —today's parties and electoral processes did not emerge full grown. This new edition reflects our continuing emphasis on the foundations of our modern political system by providing a historical context where appropriate throughout the text. However, we have also thoroughly revised every chapter as needed. The revisions to chapters 5, 9, and 10 are substantial. Readers will engage in fully up-to-date discussions of changes to presidential campaigns and elections, the ever-evolving world of campaign finance, the rapidly changing media environment in the United States, and much more. The events of the 2016 election cycle are fully incorporated into the text, and we look to the 2018 cycle as best we can.

Acknowledgments

In preparing the eighth edition of this text, we both realized how many people truly merit our sincere thanks and recognition. First, we are indebted to all of the colleagues with whom we have discussed our mutual concerns about how to teach political parties and elections for their advice on improving this work. We want to begin by thanking all of those who have aided this work in that way.

Similarly, this book has benefited from the comments of those for whom it is intended, student readers. Sandy Maisel is grateful to generation after generation of Colby students—and to those students he has taught at the University of Melbourne, at Monash University, at Harvard, and at Stanford. One of the real joys of teaching is to have the opportunity to test one's ideas on the palette of relatively unpainted young minds and to learn from the ways in which the colors are reflected. For more than four decades Maisel has tested his ideas about elections and politics on Colby students. Their insights have helped to shape and refine those ideas; their reactions have led to a better understanding of what works and what does not work in a teaching environment, of how complex ideas can be effectively communicated, of how concern and enthusiasm can be transmitted to those who will carry the political banners in the years ahead. Brewer feels the same way about the students he has had the opportunity to work with, first at Colby and now for going on fifteen years at the University of Maine. For Brewer one of the biggest rewards of teaching is witnessing his students' passion during campaigns and elections. In a very real sense this book is written for students and because of students; any success it enjoys as a teaching tool is a direct result of what has been learned from them.

This edition, like previous ones, has benefited from research assistance from particular students. Much of the work of students cited in earlier editions is still in evidence in this work. Rye Powell served as the sole research assistant for the eighth edition, and did a phenomenal job. Andrea Berchowitz, Kate Gould, Julia Hidu, Brooke McNally, Kevin

Price, Justin Rouse, Abe Summers, Claire Walsh, and Sarah Whitfield all did exceptional work as research assistants on previous editions.

As one finishes work on a text, one almost automatically thinks back to those who have influenced the book's development in less specific ways. We feel fortunate to be part of a very special community, the community of scholars—in this case the specific community of scholars of American politics. Our work has been influenced over the years by conversations with and encouragement from literally scores of fellow political scientists. We want to mention specifically those close friends and colleagues who have influenced our professional development—John Bibby, Dave Brady, Chuck Bullock, Joe Cooper, Linda Fowler, Paul Herrnson, Chuck Jones, Ruth Jones, Suzanne Mettler, the late Warren Miller, Eric Petersen, Ron Rapoport, Walt Stone, and Jeff Stonecash, among others—and those who have led and contributed to three groups in which we have been active and from which we have gained a great deal: the Political Organizations and Parties, the Legislative Studies, and the Religion and Politics organized sections of the American Political Science Association. Much of the material in this book is derived from the ideas and research of the colleagues and friends who have seen the importance of sharing ideas, working together, and growing as a cooperating community of scholars. We feel fortunate to work in a profession that so clearly sees growth as a community to be a critical common goal.

Traci Crowell was our editor for this edition and brought great energy and advice to the project. We also want to thank the others at Rowman & Littlefield who have worked on this book: Jon Sisk, vice president and senior executive editor; Mary Malley, extremely helpful assistant editor; Alden Perkins, senior production editor; and copyeditor Catherine Bielitz Fitzgerald, who saved us from many errors.

Finally, we want to thank our family and friends—who support us in all that we do. Mark would like to thank in particular his daughter Megan and sons Jack, David, and Gabriel for understanding why Daddy often worked late nights and weekends toward the end of this project. This book is dedicated to Sandy's wife, Patrice Franko, and Mark's wife, Tammy Tetreault Brewer. Only authors know how important support from a spouse is as one struggles to finish a work such as this. We are both grateful that our spouses have been patient and supportive of our efforts.

Mark D. Brewer and L. Sandy Maisel

Chapter 1

Elections and Political Parties

President Donald J. Trump delivers his acceptance speech to the 2016 Republican National Convention in Cleveland, Ohio. While often criticized as outdated and empty rituals, national party conventions still fulfill important functions, not only for parties and their candidates, but also for the electoral process overall.

Let's begin by talking about the three most recent presidents of the United States—George W. Bush, Barack Obama, and Donald J. Trump.

George W. Bush was America's forty-third president, serving from 2001 to 2009. Bush's father, George H. W. Bush, held a number of high-ranking political positions in the United States, culminating of course in his own presidential term from 1989 to 1993. George W. Bush's grandfather, Prescott Bush, was a wealthy Wall Street banker and a U.S. senator from Connecticut. Grandfather, father, and son all graduated from Yale University, where they were all members of the prestigious Skull and Bones secret society. George W. Bush grew up in an intensely political, and privileged, setting. That George W. Bush went on to achieve political success at the highest level is certainly not shocking given his background.

Next consider the forty-fourth president, Barack Obama. Obama was born in Hawaii to parents who met as students at the University of Hawaii. His mother—Ann Dunham—was a white woman from Kansas and his father—Barack Obama Sr.—was a black Kenyan studying in the United States. Obama's father left the family when he was only two years old. Obama's mother remarried, and the new family moved to Indonesia, where Obama lived from ages six through ten. At ten Obama returned to Hawaii to live with his maternal grandparents. He spent two years at Occidental College in Los Angeles, before transferring to Columbia University in New York, where he finished his bachelor's degree. There is nothing in this story to suggest even a minor political career, much less attaining the presidency of the United States. Yet that is of course exactly what Barack Obama did, serving two full terms as president from 2009 to 2017.

Finally, consider the current president, Donald J. Trump. He was born in Queens in 1946. His father—Fred Trump—was a New York City real estate developer, and his mother—Mary Trump—was a homemaker born in Scotland before immigrating to the United States and becoming an American citizen. After graduating from the Wharton School at the University of Pennsylvania, Donald Trump took over his father's real estate business in 1974 and dramatically expanded its scope. Trump first became a billionaire in 1988 (or 1989, depending on the source) and became a fixture in the New York City tabloids. He also published his best-selling book *The Art of the Deal* during this period. In 2004 Trump expanded his celebrity even further when he began starring in the hit television series *The Apprentice*, for which he was eventually paid $1 million per episode. Trump has been married three times (all to fashion models) and divorced twice. Trump toyed with the idea of running for president multiple times before finally doing so in 2015. In an outcome that shocked many, Trump won the 2016 presidential election. Upon taking the oath of office on January 20, 2017, Trump became both the first person elected president of the United States without any previous governmental or military service and the first billionaire to occupy the White House. What can we learn about American elections by looking at these three examples?

Under the American system of government, elections are used to ensure popular support and **legitimacy**—acceptance of the right of public officials to hold office and make public policy because of the means by which they were chosen—for those who make governmental decisions. In his classic study *The Theory and Practice of Modern Government*, Herman Finer (1949) summarizes this connection between democracy and elections: "The real question . . . is not whether the government deigns to take notice of popular criticisms and votes, but whether it can be voted out of office or forced by some machinery or procedures to change its policy, above all against its own will" (219).

The examples cited here illustrate that the process is a most complex one. To even begin to understand American politics, one must know something about the political history and **political culture**—norms, expectations, and values concerning politics and government in a particular polity or region—not only of the nation but also of various regions. One must understand the kinds of choices that individuals make and the political contexts in which they make them. One must look at the role of political parties, individual voters, policy issues, and money. And one must always remember that politics is not only about power but also about personalities; the importance of how different people react to situations should never be underestimated. George W. Bush, Barack Obama, and Donald J. Trump are very different men who have lived very different lives. But they have all been elected to the office of president of the United States.

AN EXAMINATION OF ELECTIONS IN THE UNITED STATES

The contest for office is the machinery used by Americans to change policy and to change those who govern, often against the will of the officeholder in question. And the American electoral process is clearly different from that in other countries. A number of aspects distinguish how we use this machinery from how other countries do so. First, Americans are expected to go to the polls more frequently and to vote for more officeholders. Table 1.1 shows the elections in which citizens of Baton Rouge, Louisiana, were asked to vote from 2010 to 2018. In some of these elections, citizens were asked to vote for local, state, and federal offices. Critics of American democracy complain about low turnout rates in our elections, but they rarely note how often we are asked to vote. As one can see from Table 1.1, residents of Baton Rouge were asked to vote often from 2010 to 2018, and this was despite Louisiana not having the practice of statewide referendum or initiative. It does have elections to recall officials elected statewide, but there was no such recall effort in the time frame under discussion. The implications of a higher frequency of elections in the United States relative to most other countries are worth contemplating.[1]

Second, our elections are held at regular intervals, regardless of the flow of world events, and their scheduling is never changed because of particular national crises. President Bush did not have the luxury that, say, former British prime minister Tony Blair had, to call for a reaffirming election at a time when one's popularity is high (as Bush's was in 2002), nor could he postpone the regularly scheduled 2004 election when opposition to the war in Iraq was on the rise. Our presidential elections are held on the first Tuesday after the first Monday in November of every fourth year, without exception. Not even the Civil War could change the date of the 1864 presidential election; indeed, no one even thought of trying.

Third, the terms of various offices in our system are not all the same; thus, though elections are held at regular intervals, exactly which offices are contested varies not only from election to election but also in a particular election, from state to state and from locality to locality. For example, while all members of the U.S. House of Representatives are up for election every two years, only one-third of Senate seats are contested in any one national election (this is apart from special elections that are held to fill vacancies).[2] Similarly, while the president and most governors are elected for four-year terms, some governors are elected for two-year terms. Moreover, most of the four-year gubernatorial terms do not end when the president's term ends. This complexity is further compounded by the varied terms of office in state legislatures and local offices.

Fourth, the rules in different states and for different offices vary significantly. The U.S. Constitution specifies that states have the right to control the times and places of elections, even national elections, except when special provisions apply. The states also control most aspects of their own political systems, again with a few exceptions; one exception is the "one man–one vote" provision imposed on drawing district lines, through a Supreme Court interpretation of the **equal protection clause** of the Constitution, the phrase in section 1 of the Fourteenth Amendment that guarantees that no state shall deny any person within its jurisdiction "equal protection of the laws."[3] One recent controversy that illustrates this point relates to **legislative term limits**. In an effort to limit the power of entrenched incumbents, a number of states have imposed limitations on the number of terms their state legislators can serve.[4] States that have

Table 1.1. Elections Held in Baton Rouge, Louisiana, 2010–2018

2010	March 27	Municipal primary
	May 1	Municipal general
	August 28	Party primary
	October 2	Open primary
	November 2	General election
2011	April 2	Municipal primary
	April 30	Municipal general
	October 22	Gubernatorial primary
	November 19	Gubernatorial general
2012	March 24	Presidential preference and municipal primaries
	April 21	Municipal general
	November 6	Presidential general and open congressional primary
	December 8	Open congressional general
2013	April 6	Municipal primary
	May 4	Municipal general
	October 19	Open primary
	November 16	Open general
2014	April 5	Municipal primary
	May 3	Municipal general
	November 4	Open congressional primary
	December 6	Open congressional general
2015	February 21	Special primary
	March 28	Special general and municipal primary
	May 2	Municipal general
	October 24	Gubernatorial primary
	November 21	Gubernatorial general
2016	March 5	Presidential preference and municipal primaries
	April 9	Municipal general and special primary
	May 14	Special general
	November 8	Presidential general and open congressional primary
	December 10	Open congressional general
2017	March 25	Municipal primary
	April 29	Municipal general and special primary
	May 27	Special general
	October 14	Open primary
	November 18	Open general
2018	February 17	Special primary
	March 24	Special general and municipal primary
	April 28	Municipal general
	November 6	Open congressional primary
	December 8	Open congressional general

Source: State of Louisiana, Office of the Secretary of State.

imposed such limitations and the variation among states in how this concept has been implemented are shown in Table 1.2. Most states (though not all) restrict their governors to two terms, paralleling the federal example of the president.

In some states it has been possible to run for more than one office in the same election. Joseph Lieberman (then a Democrat; he eventually became an independent) was reelected to the Senate from Connecticut on the same day in 2000 that he lost the election to be vice president of the United States as the running mate of Al Gore; Lloyd Bentsen, Michael Dukakis's running mate, had the same experience in 1988. In Pennsylvania, it is possible to run for the party nomination for more than one office on the same day. At the opposite extreme, in Hawaii, a state officeholder must resign if he or she seeks another office. Vacancies in some offices are filled through an automatic succession. On the national level, the vice president becomes president upon the death, resignation, or declared disability of the president. Other vacancies are filled by appointment; in

Table 1.2. Term-Limited States

		House		Senate	
State	*Enacted*	*Limit*	*Effective*	*Limit*	*Effective*
Arizona	1992	8	2000	8	2000
Arkansas	1992	6	1998	8	2000
California[c]	1990	12	1996	12	1998
Colorado	1990	8	1998	8	1998
Florida	1992	8	2000	8	2000
Louisiana	1995	12	2007	12	2007
Maine	1993	8	1996	8	1996
Michigan	1992	6	1998	8	2002
Missouri[a]	1992	8	2002	8	2002
Montana	1992	8	2000	8	2000
Nebraska	2000	n/a	n/a	8	2006
Nevada[b]	1996	12	2010	12	2010
Ohio	1992	8	2000	8	2000
Oklahoma[c]	1990	12	2004	12	2004
South Dakota	1992	8	2000	8	2000

Source: National Conference of State Legislatures (www.ncsl.org).

Note: In four states (Massachusetts, Oregon, Washington, and Wyoming) term limits have been declared unconstitutional by state courts, and in two states (Idaho and Utah) term limits have been repealed by the state legislature.

[a]Due to special elections, term limits were effective in 2000 for eight current members of the House and one senator in 1998.

[b]The Nevada Legislative Council and attorney general have ruled that Nevada's term limits cannot be applied to those legislators elected in the same year term limits were passed (1996). They first apply to persons elected in 1998.

[c]The limits for California and Oklahoma are twelve total years in both chambers. This rule went into effect in California in 2012. The previous limit in California was six years in the House and eight years in the Senate.

thirty-six states, governors appoint senators to fill vacant seats until the next general election; in ten states, governors are allowed to appoint a senator until an election is required; and in four states, the seat must stay vacant until a required special election is held.[5] Still other offices, such as U.S. representative, can only be filled by election and remain vacant if an incumbent dies, resigns, or is removed from office until a special election can be held.

Generally speaking, well-known state laws and party rules structure most contests for office, but this can and does change, and it is important that we assess proposed and enacted changes. We will also ask whether the role that parties play is a good one or a bad one, in the process concerning ourselves with the standards that should be used to answer that question. This text also assumes, in line with Finer (1949), that the electoral contest provides a mechanism for expressing popular support or disapproval and for granting legitimacy. We will examine if this part of our democracy is working to our satisfaction. Indeed, we will ask you to consider the following two questions over and over again throughout this book: How well does our system work? And, to the extent that we are not happy with its functioning, what can be done to make it more effective?

One important feature of contemporary politics is that intense partisan competition does not exist everywhere in the country. In 2016, 21 winners

in the House of Representatives ran completely unopposed in the general election, and another 148 faced opponents who spent under $10,000 (many spent no money at all).[6] These numbers are not atypical. When 169 House races offer no real choice (and many would say that far more offer no real contest), how can the public express popular support in these "contests" for office?

It is our goal to examine the process through which **partisan elections** are contested in the United States.[7] Partisan elections are those in which the candidates on the ballot are identified by their political party affiliation. Nonpartisan elections lack such designations. This text addresses a tension, as it emphasizes the role of political parties as well as the more broadly defined electoral process. Partisan elections are, by definition, elections contested by nominees of political parties. For much of our nation's history, the parties dominated the contest for office (see Silbey 1998, 2002a). Citizens typically supported candidates of one party or the other with great loyalty. In order to understand elections in the contemporary context, we must understand this background.

Thus, this text looks at the history and development of the role played by parties in structuring American elections. It also examines the current role of parties in the contest for office. But this is not all that this text will consider. In the chapters to follow, we will also explore ways in which other groups may now be sharing the role that parties once played exclusively and, if so, with what impact. This is important because, while parties have played and continue to play an important role in elections, they do not constitute the sum total of the electoral process.

The clear theme of this book is that the contest for office is the most crucial element of representative democracy to be examined. Political parties play an important role in that process, but they are not the entirety of the process. It is not possible to understand the contest for office without understanding parties. But merely understanding how parties function does not tell the student much about how elections are fought. Our goal is to reach the latter understanding.

THE ROLE OF ELECTIONS IN DEMOCRATIC THEORY

Scholars are fond of pointing out that modern political parties are an American invention, even though such parties are never mentioned in the Constitution. In *Federalist* 10 (1787), James Madison warned of the mischief of faction, arguing that many groups must be allowed to flourish so that no one group becomes too powerful. Such was the concept of "party" at the time the Constitution was drafted.

The Founding Fathers, moreover, defined democracy in a somewhat limited way: the masses were not to be trusted with political power. Thus, while the House of Representatives was to be popularly elected (certainly a necessity, given the history of our Revolution and its most famous slogan, "Taxation without representation is tyranny!"), the Senate was indirectly elected by state legislatures, and the president was even more indirectly elected through the cumbersome mechanism of the electoral college.

Modes of Elections

Direct Elections

What general principles guided these rules for contesting offices? For direct representation in the House of Representatives, two were primary: districts with small populations so that the voters could "know" their representatives, and frequent elections so that citizens had the opportunity to express their views on how the government was working. The Founding Fathers would have been appalled by contemporary calls to extend congressional terms to four years. They envisioned an intimate connection between a congressman and his constituents. He would be one of them, one who was just like his neighbors and thus best suited to serve them. He would do his duty and return home to be replaced by another. If he became too headstrong in support of his own alien ideas, frequent elections would guarantee that the violation of trust would not go on for too long.

Indirect Elections

The other elected officials of the federal government were to be chosen through a filtering process. Only the "best of the best" were supposed to make the grade and be chosen to represent the interests of the people. Only those who really understood what was best for the masses would be chosen to serve in the Senate. Further, the elaborate mechanism for choosing the president can be understood best if one realizes that all those at the Constitutional Convention assumed that the towering figure of his time, the "father" of the new nation, George Washington, would be the first president. The mechanism was designed to pick the "right" leader, that is, someone like Washington.

Implications for Representation

Representatives' Perspectives

However, this system of elected representatives—or any other system yet devised—faces an inherent conflict. On the one hand, elected representatives should accurately represent the views of the people who choose them. On the other hand, they must have enough freedom to act on what they determine to be in the best interest of the people. One need not long debate the merits of the two theories of representation implied by these statements to see that a conflict exists. The American solution to this problem has been to give representatives a good deal of freedom to act, but to hold elections frequently in order to keep them accountable for their actions. One of the basic questions raised in this text is: How does such a system work?

The Public's Perspective and the Role of Parties in Representation

Democratic theory also requires a citizenry that has the ability to convert its views on the issues of the day—certainly the pressing, salient issues—into public policy. Frequent elections do not serve their intended purpose if the electorate is not given a choice nor if, after that choice is expressed, public policy does not reflect that preference.

The role that political parties have traditionally played in this context has been to structure the contest for office so that elections can perform their role most effectively. One of the key questions facing the American polity concerns how effectively that role is played (Brady, Bullock, and Maisel 1988; Brady and Stewart 1986). Brewer and Stonecash (2009), Gerring (1998), Pomper (1972), and Sundquist (1983), among others, have demonstrated that the Republican and Democratic parties differ from each other on major policy questions. But the links among differing party platforms, elections, and subsequent public policies are less clear in the American system than they are in parliamentary democracies.

V. O. Key Jr. (1964) highlights the important distinctions among **party in the electorate, party organization**, and **party in government**. The term "party in the electorate" refers to voters who generally align themselves with a particular party, the party's supporters at the polls. "Party organization" is the formal structure of the party, the elite that leads the party in election campaigns. Finally, "party in government" is comprised of the individuals who serve in the government as a result of having run on a party label or having been appointed by someone who ran on a party label.

This text is mainly concerned with party in the electorate (i.e., the extent to which party determines how citizens vote) and with party organization (i.e., how political parties are structured as institutions), but we cannot ignore the governmental context either. We elect members of Congress in individual districts and stress their electoral independence, but we should not forget that these individual representatives often consider the position of their party when deciding how to vote once in office.

For many years *Congressional Quarterly* has reported **party unity scores** for members of Congress each year. A **party unity vote** is one in which a majority of one party votes together against a majority of the other party. A member's party unity score is the percentage of time he or she votes with his or her party on those votes. During the Clinton administration, a bit more than half of the votes in each session in each house of the Congress were party unity votes, and party unity scores for both parties in both chambers routinely exceeded 80 percent. Both of these metrics have consistently increased since the 1990s. According to *Congressional Quarterly*, in 2017 a little more than three of every four House votes were party unity votes, while the same was true of two of every three votes in the Senate. In terms of party unity scores, both Senate Republicans (97 percent) and House Democrats (93 percent) set new records, while Senate Democrats and House Republicans were also very high, at 92 percent each.[8] This period of extremely high party unity covers periods in which each party has been in the majority. Thus it seems clear that party affiliation is far from unimportant as a linkage between citizens as they cast their votes and policies that are eventually adopted (see chapter 11).

Similarly, the extent to which recent presidents have imposed partisan tests on their principal appointees is without precedent. Beginning with President Reagan and continuing with all the presidents who have followed him, party affiliation is clearly the single most important criterion for staffing the executive branch, especially the most important positions (Mackenzie 2013). Thus, while the takeover of the national government by committed conservatives hailed as the Reagan revolution in 1980 might not have changed the role of government as completely as its perpetrators might have hoped; while Clinton's recapturing of the White House for the Democrats might not have reversed all trends started in the previous twelve years of Republican rule; while George W. Bush's winning the White House even as the Republicans controlled the Congress did not presage as many policy changes as his supporters would have liked; while the two terms of the Obama presidency were not as far-reaching as some Democrats, especially liberal Democrats, had hoped for—each of these presidencies did lead to significant changes in who populated the government. They just as surely led to changes in the philosophy of governing espoused by those in appointive as well as elective office. A little more than a year into his presidency, Trump has pursued a similarly strong partisan path in terms of his appointments. Trump has been aggressively partisan in his appointments to the federal judiciary (Rucker 2017), even going beyond the very strong partisan approach adopted by the Obama administration (Kimel and Randazzo 2012; Peters 2014). For our purposes, the importance of those appointments is also that they demonstrate another link between elections and subsequent government policies.

That political parties would serve as the linkage mechanism between electorate and governing officials was not envisioned by the nation's founders; in fact, it has evolved quite slowly (see chapter 2). Historically, the effectiveness of parties as the bridge between citizens and those they elect to govern has not been judged with universal acclaim, nor has that role remained constant in the face of a changing political environment. In order to understand this role, we must more carefully define what is meant by "political party" in the American political context.

DEFINITIONS OF "POLITICAL PARTY" AND "PARTY SYSTEMS"

French political scientist Maurice Duverger (1951, 62–71), in a classic study titled *Political Parties*, drew an important theoretical distinction between **cadre parties** and **mass membership parties**. Cadre parties rely on a small number of elites to set party policy, recruit candidates, and direct and fund elections; they have very few actual members, according to Duverger's definition. Mass membership parties, on the other hand, are grassroots organizations where power and direction flows from the bottom up; in Duverger's analysis mass membership parties have a large number of dues-paying supporters who effectively direct and support the party.

Duverger's distinction between cadre and mass membership parties works better in theory than in practice—a fact that he himself admits. This is especially true in the American context, where no pure cadre or mass membership parties have ever existed, at least none of any importance. In fact, Duverger never does arrive at a concise definition of what constitutes a political party, though he identifies a number of important considerations—membership, level of activity, type of activity, type of leadership, relationship to the government—that help to make comparisons and distinctions between different parties as they exist in the real world of practical politics. Several scholars studying American parties have used these considerations, along with others, in an attempt to define exactly what constitutes a political party:

> We may define "political party" generally as the articulate organization of society's active political agents, those who are concerned with the control of governmental power and who compete for popular support with another group or groups holding divergent views. (Sigmund Neumann 1956, 396)
>
> A political party is a team of men seeking to control the governing apparatus by gaining office in a duly constituted election. (Anthony Downs 1957, 25)
>
> Pat definitions may simplify discussion but they do not necessarily promote understanding. A search for the fundamental nature of party is complicated

> by the fact that "party" is a work of many meanings. . . . The nature of parties must be sought through an appreciation of their role in the process of governance. (V. O. Key Jr. 1964, 200)

> Any group, however loosely organized, seeking to elect governmental office-holders under a given label. (Leon D. Epstein 1967, 9)

> A party is any political group that presents at elections, and is capable of placing through elections, candidates for public office. (Giovanni Sartori 1976, 64)

> The major American political parties exist, as do other political organizations, to organize large numbers of individuals behind attempts to influence the selection of public officials and the decisions these officials subsequently make in office. . . . The differences between parties and other political organizations are often slender. (Frank J. Sorauf 1980, 17)

A number of themes emerge from this group of definitions. First, as Sartori claims, a minimal definition of contesting for office emerges. Second, as Neumann, Downs, and Epstein state, some type of organization is assumed. Third, as Key and Sorauf imply, "party" is a multidimensional term. Defining party too narrowly excludes organizations that ought to be included. Defining party too broadly takes in organizations that would be excluded by general consensus. The student almost has to fall back on the classic test, "If it looks like a duck, swims like a duck, flies like a duck, and quacks like a duck, then it probably is a duck." Thus the Republican party is a party; the American Federation of Labor and Congress of Industrial Organizations, even though it does many of the same things, is not.

For most purposes this definition is sufficient, but for others, often very important ones, it is not. For instance, when John Anderson ran for president as an independent, or third-party candidate, in 1980, the Federal Election Commission (FEC) had to rule on whether John Anderson's "party" in the 1980 presidential election constituted a party in any meaningful sense.[9] The FEC ruled that it did, thus making Anderson eligible for federal campaign financing in 1984.[10] The FEC ruled similarly on Ross Perot's "party" in the 1992 presidential election, even though the party under whose label he ran in 1996, the Reform party, did not exist in 1992. What definition is appropriate in that context?

This text adopts a fairly restrictive definition of *political parties*. Political parties are organizations, however loosely organized, that (1) have, for a period of time, run candidates for public office in the hope of controlling government and making public policy; (2) have earned the support of a significant following in the electorate for those candidates because of their allegiance to the organization; and (3) must be taken into account by other similar competing organizations. Did Anderson's party meet this definition in 1980? Remember that it disappeared by 1984. It did not meet the definition, then, because it did not meet the test of time. Did Perot's Reform party meet the definition?

This definition also implies acceptance of the concept of **party systems**, at least in its simplified form.[11] In democracies, if parties are to contest for public office, they must take into account others who are also competing for office. William N. Chambers (1975, 6) defines a party system as "a pattern of interaction in which two or more political parties compete for office or power in government and for the support of the electorate, and must therefore take one another into account in their behavior in government and in election contests."

Party systems are characterized on two different axes. First, they are distinguished by the number of parties competing. Second, they are distinguished by the intensity of competition. The American national party system is generally classified as a **competitive two-party system**. The Democratic and Republican parties compete with each other for national offices; each has a chance of winning. Minor or third parties may be on the ballot from time to time, but they neither persist nor have a chance of winning. In the 1992 presidential election (and to a lesser extent in the 1996 campaign) Ross Perot's third party threatened the hegemony of the Democratic and Republican parties. But in the final analysis, his effort to undermine the two-party system fell short (Bibby and Maisel 2003; Rapoport and Stone 2005). Thus our national system remains the competitive two-party system it has been since the election of 1828, though the parties have changed during that period.[12]

Figure 1.1 (a, b, c) shows a number of different measures of national electoral competition in this century. The pattern is clear: Democrats compete with Republicans for control of our national government. Other parties can and do contest for federal offices, but real competition is restricted to two parties. It is in this sense of structuring the contest for national power that the role of parties in the electoral process must be evaluated.

For all that, it is very misleading to look only at national politics. American politics is perhaps most notably characterized by its decentralization; local and state politics are not totally controlled by national forces. An observer cannot stop after saying that the American party system is a competitive two-party system. At the very least, one must look at the fifty separate state party systems. The domination of a single party within certain states can be veiled by a claim that we have a competitive two-party system nationally. Similarly, changes in national politics can reflect either trends across the entire nation in one direction or asymmetrical offsetting trends in a number of directions in a number of states or regions (Brunell

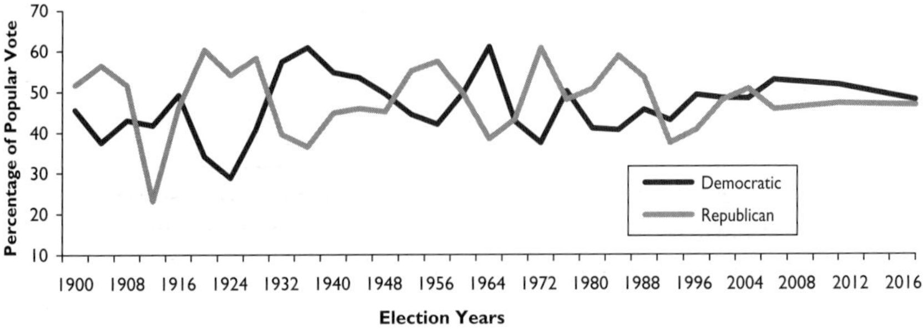

Figure 1.1a Two-Party Competition in Twentieth and Twenty-first-Century Presidential Elections

Note: Percentages are of total vote; other parties not shown.
Sources: 1900–2004, *Vital Statistics on American Politics* (Stanley and Niemi 2006); 2008, 2012, and 2016, Federal Election Commission.

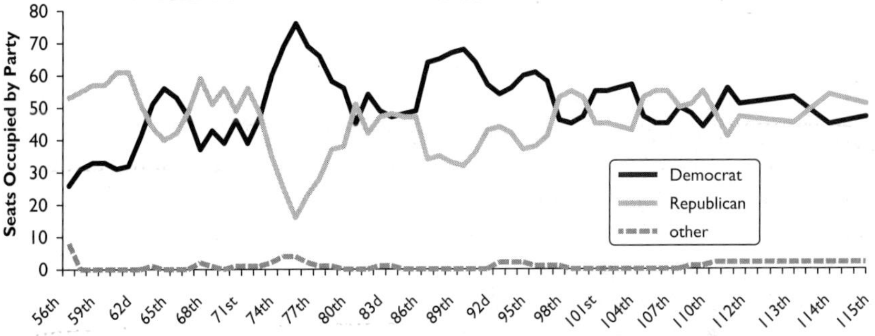

Figure 1.1b Two-Party Competition in the Twentieth and Twenty-first-Century Senate

Note: Figures for the 115th Congress accurate as of March 12, 2018. The two Senate independents in the 113th, 114th, and 115th Congresses caucus with the Democrats.*Sources*: *Vital Statistics on American Politics* (Stanley and Niemi 2006); data for 110th–115th Congresses compiled by authors.

and Grofman 1998). The reality is that in some instances we have fifty-one party systems—one federal system, and fifty state systems.

CONCLUSION

This text is not intended to be a workbook. However, if one homework exercise were to be assigned, it would be to have you call your state representative and ask, "What is the dimension of the party system that I should examine in order to understand the role that party plays in structuring your own electoral contest?" Merely posing the question should

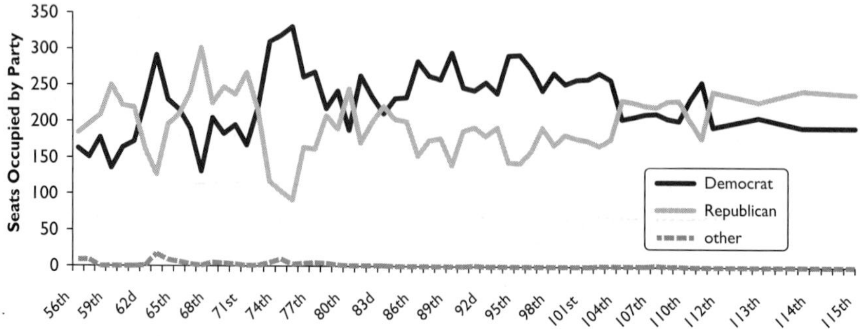

Figure 1.1c Two-Party Competition in the Twentieth and Twenty-first-Century House of Representatives

Note: Figures for 115th Congress accurate as of March 12, 2018 (reflecting four vacancies). The size of the House of Representative was set at 435 members by law in 1911, and took effect in the 63d Congress in 1913.

Sources: *Vital Statistics on American Politics* (Stanley and Niemi 2006); data for the 100th–115th Congresses compiled by authors.

be sufficient to demonstrate how ludicrous it is. While it is important to understand "the role of party," "structuring the contest for office," and "party systems" in order to analyze elections in America, these abstract terms are not in the working vocabulary of most politicians. Therefore this text regularly steps back from the analytical world of the student of politics to the practical world of the politician.

In that regard, it is important to understand that politicians only rarely look beyond the next election. Elections serve as their link to the people in a very concrete way. If the people vote for them, they are in office; if the people vote for someone else, they are out. The questions that politicians ask relate to what they must do in order to ensure their continuation in office or their advancement to the next office.

Important questions immediately arise. Are elections in America an effective way for the citizenry to control politicians? That is, do politicians lose because of the dissatisfaction of their constituents? This question can be answered empirically by looking at incumbent losses and the reasons for them, at the knowledge that constituents have of their officeholders' positions, and at major swings in the fortunes of the two parties (see Brewer and Stonecash 2009; Jacobson 1980; Maisel and Cooper 1981; Sundquist 1983).

However, equally important is how politicians think the electoral process works. Do politicians change their positions because they fear electoral reprisals? The late senator Henry Jackson (D-Wash., 1952–1983), sometimes referred to as the senator from Boeing (because the aircraft manufacturer is located in Washington State and Jackson saw it as part of his job to represent the interests of the thousands of his constituents who were Boeing employees), early in his Senate career explained the apparent contradiction between his "liberal" views on social and economic policies and his "conservative" views on defense matters. Jackson contended, "I have to be a senator before I can be a statesman." His winning percentages in four reelection campaigns for the Senate were 72 percent, 82 percent, 72 percent, and 69 percent; consequently, his fear of electoral reprisal might have been slightly exaggerated. But it was real nonetheless.

Anyone who has worked closely with an elected officeholder facing another election knows that nearly all such officeholders consider public opinion very important.[13] Politicians panic if their margin of victory goes down from one election to the next; they fret over the effects on their popularity of votes on controversial, salient issues. Study after study has emphasized how safe most incumbent legislators are from electoral defeat, in both the Congress and in the state legislatures (Herrnson 1998a, 2000; Jewell 1984; Jacobson 1992, 1996, 2001; Holbrook and Tidmarch 1991; Weber, Tucker, and Brace 1991). Although few incumbents are thrown out by constituents because of their stand on public policy issues, elections do work as a means of public control because politicians act as if they might be thrown out by the voters if they do not heed perceived voter opinion. In this case, a politician's perception of reality is more important than reality itself.

Similarly, just as it is important to understand how politicians view elections, it is important to know how they view party. In this case, the answer is very simple: It all depends.

Politicians may not understand abstract notions of party system and electoral environment, but they certainly do understand what the party—whether it is defined as the label or the formal organization—means for their election or reelection chances. In all but a very few cases, office seekers need a major party nomination in order to get on the ballot and stand a chance of success. However, that generalization is perhaps the only one that can be made.[14] Beyond a means of access to the ballot and perhaps some legitimacy in the eyes of the voters, major party designation means different things to different politicians. The key variables are the office being sought and the strength of the party, in terms of both organizational resources and voter identification, in the particular district. The importance of "party" varies a great deal from office to office, location to location, and even year to year.

What role do politicians see party playing in the elections? Again, it all depends. The biggest mistake a political analyst can make in writing about elections is to overgeneralize. We must distinguish election from election by constituency and by geography. Campaigns for local office are, for example, different from those for congressional or statewide offices. And no other election compares to a race for the presidency. In much the same way, campaigns in the East are different from those in the Midwest, and each of these is different from campaigns in the South or the Far West. Significant variations exist among geographic areas within these regions. The history of a particular area—particularly its political history—must always be taken into account. As noted here, the single most salient feature of the American political system is its decentralized nature. Unfortunately for the social scientist, much more is lost in accumulating what should be kept separate than is gained by trying to generalize about a series of diverse experiences.

For a political analyst to state at the outset of a text that generalizations about the electoral process might prove imprecise seems blasphemous, but the key point is that practicing politicians do not base their judgments on such academic generalizations. They base them on instincts, often faulty ones, about individual situations in particular circumstances. It might be argued that politicians are foolish to do so, but that does not change the reality. All too often politicians and political scientists seem to be operating in different worlds. But one thing that perhaps both groups can agree on is that electoral politics in the United States, at least at the federal level and in most cases at the state level too, is partisan politics. The role that parties and partisanship play certainly varies by time and circumstance, but party always matters somehow. The overwhelming majority of candidates for federal and state office run as partisans in a partisan context, which can either assist or constrict them (or both), depending on circumstances.

CRITICAL THINKING QUESTIONS

1. Why is legitimacy so important in a representative democracy?
2. What are the possible strengths and weaknesses of legislative term limits?
3. Does America's two-party system limit the effectiveness of Americans' voices on election day?
4. Do you prefer direct or indirect elections? Why?

KEY TERMS

legitimacy
political culture
equal protection clause
legislative term limits
partisan elections
party in the electorate
party organization
party in government
party unity scores
party unity vote
cadre parties
mass membership parties
party systems
competitive two-party system

NOTES

1. Sarah Anzia's (2014) study convincingly demonstrates that many American localities and even some states have long been home to a variety of interests attempting to manipulate the timing of elections for their benefit.

2. As each state has two U.S. senators, this provision means that senatorial elections are held in roughly two-thirds of the states and not in the other states during each national election.

3. In a series of cases from 1962 through 1964, the Supreme Court decided that the drawing of election district lines was in fact reviewable by the courts and that all election districts within the same legislative body (the U.S. Senate excluded, of course) must be roughly equal in size. Failure to do so resulted in one person's vote being worth more or less than another's, which violated the equal protection clause of the Fourteenth Amendment. The relevant cases are *Baker v. Carr*, 369 U.S. 186 (1962), *Gray v. Sanders*, 372 U.S. 368 (1963), *Wesberry v. Sanders* 376 U.S. 1 (1964), and *Reynolds v. Sims* 377 U.S. 533 (1964).

4. Some states have also attempted to impose limitations on the number of terms their representatives and senators can serve in Congress, but these efforts have been deemed unconstitutional.

5. Information obtained from the National Conference of State Legislatures website: http://www.ncsl.org/research/elections-and-campaigns/vacancies-in-the-united-states-senate.aspx. The four states that do not allow any form of gubernatorial appointment are Oklahoma, Oregon, Rhode Island, and Wisconsin.

6. Figures are from OpenSecrets.org and are accurate as of May 18, 2017. Some candidates had not filed complete reports by this date.

7. Most of the prominent elections in the United States are partisan elections—that is, contests between nominees of political parties. However, when all contests for office are considered, including local contests for positions such as city council, selectman, and even less prominent positions, such as trustee of the local library, nonpartisan elections outnumber those in which party is involved. This text will only deal with partisan elections, though a wide variety of those will be mentioned.

8. "CQ Vote Studies: Party Unity." *CQ Magazine* (February 12, 2018).

9. The distinction between independent candidacies and third-party candidacies is an important one and will be discussed in chapters 8, 10, and 11. In Anderson's case, the situation was further complicated because his designation on the ballot differed from state to state. See Bibby and Maisel (2003).

10. Anderson eventually decided that he would not run in 1984, preferring to build the organizational base for his "party," a task that proved fruitless.

11. Party systems are described, classified, and criticized in many scholars' works, for example, Chambers and Burnham (1975), Sartori (1976), and Sundquist (1983).

12. Silbey (2002a) applies a very different definition of party system, emphasizing the centrality of parties to the electoral process. See chapter 2.

13. Richard Fenno (1978, chap. 1) writes at length of how politicians judge public opinion and about the ways in which they reach their judgments. Jacobson (1980, 108) suggests that this process might well be a natural act, even for seemingly safe incumbents.

14. And even the necessity of party nomination does not apply in some states for some offices. Although Nebraska's state legislature is the only such body with nonpartisan elections, Louisiana has a "nonpartisan" primary for Congress and statewide offices. See chapter 6.

Chapter 2

American Political Parties and Party Organization

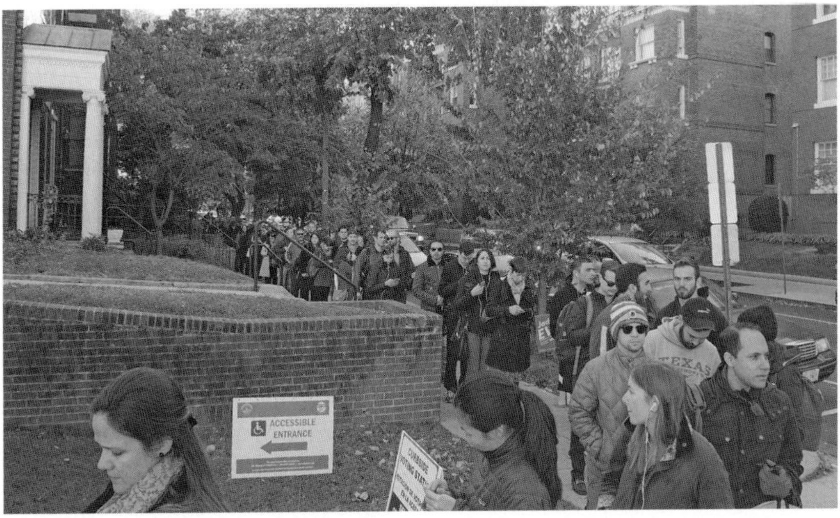

Voters wait in line to vote in Washington, D.C., on Election Day 2016. American voters now cast their ballots in a number of different ways, on a number of different days, and in a very diverse array of settings.

Modern political parties are a distinctly American invention. They did not appear fully formed; rather, they evolved slowly, the product of experimentation and innovation by the leaders of the nation's new form of government, at the end of the eighteenth and beginning of the nineteenth centuries. The first of the American parties, the **Federalist party**, was shaped largely by Alexander Hamilton, George Washington's treasury secretary, and favored a strong central government heavily focused on economic development. It was Hamilton's controversial economic proposals and his efforts to cultivate support for the administration's program in Congress that essentially gave rise to the first legislative party. Ironically, Hamilton is often credited with drafting Washington's Farewell Address, the theme of which was to warn of the *dangers* of party:

> In contemplating the causes which may disturb our Union, it occurs as a matter of serious concern, that any ground should have been furnished for characterizing party by *geographical discriminations*. . . . To the efficacy and permanency of your Union, a Government of the whole is indispensable. . . . Let me now take a more comprehensive view, and warn you in the most solemn manner against the baneful effects of the spirit of party. (Sparks 1840, 221–24)

Likewise, James Madison, in *Federalist* 10, warned his contemporaries of **factions**—divisions within the population driven by self-interest—that he saw as by nature "adverse to the rights of other citizens, and to the permanent and aggregate interest of the community." Yet it was Madison who pressured a reluctant Thomas Jefferson to join him in organizing an opposition party to Hamilton's Federalists. Jefferson's Democratic-Republicans formed as a reaction to the rising tide of Federalist policies gaining support in Congress, policies that favored New England merchants and manufacturers at the expense of Southern and Western farmers and tradesmen.

THE DEVELOPMENT OF AMERICAN POLITICAL PARTIES

Why did these early political leaders, virtually all of whom took pride in their stand against parties, play such critical roles in creating them? Clearly, Washington, Hamilton, Madison, and Jefferson recognized the negative power of factions—the Constitution, which Madison, Washington, and Hamilton all played large roles in drafting and getting ratified, never explicitly mentions parties, but its structure reflects its authors' fears. The very blueprint for the American political system is deliberate in its separation of powers and in its system of checks and balances. These early American political leaders were all too aware of the European experience with parties, and hoped to avoid a similar situation in their new nation. The antipartisan feelings of many of the founders were reinforced by the troubles during the French Revolution, when factions divided the French citizenry and when parties formed on the basis of economic self-interest and organized in opposition to the common good. Yet, even as most political leaders in the early years were keenly aware of the potential dangers associated with factionalism and were loath to endorse the concept of political parties, they did recognize the need to organize those who shared their views in order to succeed with this new form of government. In their efforts to make American democracy work, they invented the political institution that suited their needs: the party.

This chapter describes the birth as well as the development of American political parties and their organization within the framework of the five (arguably six) party systems in American political history. Each of these eras is marked by a new national issue/set of issues or crisis that polarizes the party elite; divides the electorate; increases turnout at the polls; and, in some cases, fuels the rise of third parties. The electoral eras are sometimes separated by **critical elections**, a term first used by political scientist V. O. Key Jr. to describe elections in which "there occurs a sharp and durable electoral cleavage between the parties" (Key 1955). The change brought about by a critical election is called a **critical realignment**. In other instances, the transition between electoral eras occurs more gradually, as "the rise and fall of parties may to some degree be the consequence of trends that perhaps persist over decades and elections may mark only steps in a more or less continuous creation of new loyalties and decay of old." Key termed this type of change **secular realignment** (Key 1959).[1] It must be noted here that the idea of critical realignments triggered by critical elections has come under increasing criticism within the discipline and no longer holds the sway it once did (see Mayhew 2002). But regardless of whether change is dramatic or gradual, labeled critical or secular, as the major parties adopt distinct positions in response to the divisive national issue or set of issues, the groups that support each party oftentimes reorganize, or "realign," along the new line of cleavage or division. Thus, by examining the evolution of American parties from their inception to modernity in terms of distinct party systems, we can explain how and why party coalitions have shifted over time and how American parties respond to change.[2]

The First Party System

One commonly held view about the founding of American political parties is that they were born of the battle over the ratification of the

Constitution—the Federalists versus the anti-Federalists. Surely the new nation was divided over ratification, but, as Washington said in addressing the First Congress, "The fight over the Constitution is over." Instead, it was the economic program of the first administration that drew new and polarizing battle lines that encouraged and in fact necessitated party organization. Although the first session of the First Congress went smoothly as the mechanics of governing were worked out, by the time Alexander Hamilton presented his economic agenda to the second session of that Congress, President Washington's "honeymoon" period was clearly over.

Hamilton felt that the strength of the new government would depend on its ability to demonstrate economic stability. Thus, the keystone of his program, which Washington adopted, was full funding of the entire federal debt and the assumption of all state debts by the national government. Others disagreed. On the question of funding, Madison and his followers felt that only notes held by original lenders, the true patriots, should be fully paid off. Notes held by speculators should only be repaid in part so that individuals did not profit from the war effort. Essentially, political leaders were divided into two groups on assumption of each state's debt—those from states that stood to gain, supported; those who stood to lose, opposed. In other words, these two issues—funding and assumption—led to a new line of division, a line that paralleled the political and theoretical divide on how one stood on the expansion of the central government.

Whereas the fight over the Constitution pitted large states against small states, economic issues presented to Congress in 1790 divided the nation along sectional lines. Broadly speaking, the North was for Hamilton's funding plan; the South opposed it. Similarly, the North was for assumption of state debts, but the South opposed it. Indeed, according to Jefferson's later recollection, the only reason Hamilton's funding plan was ultimately approved was a deal to bring the nation's capital to the South (see Banning 2004 for the full text). The other major issues of Hamilton's economic program—the charter of the Bank of the United States and the imposition of an excise tax—crystallized and invigorated public opinion and hardened the new lines of division.[3]

Parties, in the sense of permanent entities with well-developed organizational bases, had certainly not yet formed; however, the national issues of funding and assumption marked the start of enduring new divisions. Leaders in Washington's administration were uncertain about how to deal with these political differences. The overriding factor for most was success of the new government. A close second was personal loyalty to Washington, who, it is said, reigned more than ruled. The first president allowed his cabinet secretaries considerable autonomy, intervening only when they disagreed. Hamilton aggressively took the initiative and gained Washington's support for his program of economic growth. Adams, who disliked Hamilton personally and opposed some of his programs (feeling, for instance, that banks helped only the moneyed class), went along for the good of the nation. Jefferson also believed that his hands were tied: despite his strong objection to Hamilton's program, he remained in the cabinet until 1793, demonstrating his intense loyalty to Washington.

These divisions carried over into Congress, reaching new heights with the debate over ratification of the Jay Treaty with Great Britain. Hamilton, the Anglophile, led the Federalist party in support of the treaty that Ambassador Jay had consummated, a treaty that leaders such as Madison and the Francophile Jefferson denounced as a complete concession to the British. The Senate ratified the treaty before the opposition had time to focus its efforts, but the battle waged on in the House over appropriations to fund the economic compromise with Great Britain. The battle over the Jay Treaty marked the first—and perhaps only—time in our history in which an issue of foreign policy divided the legislature strictly on party lines. Those who opposed the administration realized that they had to organize their supporters if their vision of a new American society was to be fulfilled; to defeat the Federalist policies, they had to recruit candidates for Congress. Thomas Jefferson, overcoming his sense of loyalty to Washington and his fear of dividing the nation, assumed the leadership of the opposition, the **Jeffersonian (or Democratic) Republican party.** The Jeffersonians favored a more limited central government, more powers reserved to the states, and an America marked more by smaller, agrarian communities.

This marked the rise of two-party competition, from the inside out—that is, from the halls of Congress to the limited electorate, limited due to low suffrage, due to a relatively small and remote national government, and due to the difficulty of information dissemination to voters. Given that presidents and senators were not popularly elected, the Federalists and Democratic-Republicans had to extend their efforts to the states to woo potential presidential electors and to recruit state legislators who were supportive of their respective parties' national candidates. It was largely the legislative leaders who met, planned strategy, and sought and decided upon candidates. The parties in Congress came to be the scene of partisan maneuvering.

The Elections of 1796 and 1800

Two elections were particularly important in the development of the first American parties. In 1796 John Adams defeated Thomas Jefferson to succeed George Washington, who had stepped down, declining to seek a third term. Washington's action provided for orderly succession in a way virtually unknown until that time; in other words, Washington established the important two-term precedent, which has been violated only once in American history (by Franklin D. Roosevelt of course, although Ulysses S. Grant desperately wanted to run for a third term in 1876) and is now written into the Constitution. While partisan ties were strong enough to carry Adams into the presidency, the votes for vice president were widely scattered. By virtue of the electoral system of the time, second-place finisher Jefferson became vice president. Jefferson agreed to serve under Adams, who thus accepted the legitimacy of his political opposition.

Four years later the two leaders would run against each other again. In 1800 the Federalists chose President Adams to seek reelection against the Democratic-Republican's choice, Vice President Jefferson. By this time, partisan allegiance was much more firmly established. Jefferson and his running mate, Aaron Burr of New York, each received seventy-three **electoral votes,** the votes cast by state electors in America's indirect election process that decides the presidency (see chapter 9). Adams and his vice presidential nominee, Charles Cotesworth Pinckney of South Carolina, received sixty-five and sixty-four votes, respectively. Because Jefferson's copartisans each cast their two electoral votes for both of the party's candidates, the election ended in a tie and went to the Federalist-controlled House of Representatives. Rumors of possible Federalist action to prevent Jefferson's election were rife: Hamilton devised a strategy to secure concessions from Jefferson, and Adams met with Jefferson for the same purpose. The House meanwhile cast thirty-five inconclusive ballots. Finally, after several desperate Federalist caucuses, Thomas Jefferson was elected the third president of the new republic (see Chambers 1963, 162–69).

The new governmental system had thus demonstrated remarkable stability: the House had ratified as the new president the man the nation had elected, despite the fact that he epitomized the political opposition. The peaceful transfer of power from Adams to Jefferson marked a most critical step in legitimating the new system of government and the role of opposition parties within that government.

The election of 1800 marked the high point of partisan conflict during these early years. The Federalist party soon became a New England sectional party, promoting policies too conservative to appeal to the greater electorate. Never able to develop the national following that the Jeffersonians enjoyed, they became politically irrelevant. The Democratic-Republicans dominated the political scene for twenty-four years, without serious opposition during the administrations of Jefferson, Madison, and Monroe. Gone was the intense party competition in Congress; gone was the party competition for electoral support.[4] With the virtual disappearance of the Federalist party, the first American party system essentially collapsed.

While the elimination of a major party may seem incredible from today's perspective, we must remember that parties were weak and fragile in the early years of the nineteenth century. Partisan loyalties were not well established; political leaders themselves shifted frequently. In his inaugural address in 1800, Jefferson reflected not on the acrimony of the presidential campaign but on the commonalities shared by the two parties: "Every difference of opinion is not a difference of principle. We have called by different names brethren of the same principle. We are all Republicans, we are all Federalists" (Blum et al. 1993, 176). By the end of the first party system, Jefferson's figure of speech was a matter of reality as the Federalist party became eclipsed.

Even in Jefferson's administration, few legislators identified themselves according to party. James Young's (1966) renowned study of early American party politics demonstrates that boardinghouse ties—the congressional "fraternities" in which members lived in Washington, essentially social units that formed primarily along regional lines—were as strong as party and that President Jefferson's personal appeals through carefully planned dinners were necessary to gain supporters for his legislation. Coalitions were built from the center out, not from the grass roots into the political arena. Consequently, when the Federalists adopted unpopular policies, they failed to respond to popular protest and quickly lost support. No stable organization saved them from their decline.

Finally, the patrician politicians of the Federalist party had few incentives to save their national party. They viewed themselves as political amateurs, content to return to their prosperous farms and businesses once their service was over. The first "professional" politicians did emerge in this era—lawyers such as Aaron Burr and the first clerk of the House, John Beckley—but these men were thought to be morally inferior to such "true" leaders as Washington, Adams, Jefferson, and Hamilton.

Contributions of the First Party System

The most important contributions of the first party system were the invention of the modern political party and the provision of an orderly means of settling political disputes and legitimating the victory of the winner. Instead of being antigovernment, parties became integral to government. In other words, parties became the mechanism through which it was possible to legitimately oppose the policies and leaders of the government without seeming to oppose the form of government itself.

Parties as political institutions developed as enduring organizations during this period.[5] The first party system grew from the center out, the parties at first being elite associations without **grassroots** support—rank-and-file voters or party members. The Democratic-Republican party originated in opposition to administration policy; then legislators realized that they had to find a means to induce the election of like-minded colleagues if their policy preferences were to be adopted. The Democratic-Republicans began to develop a party structure based on the congressional caucus, and they began to recruit candidates for all offices. To secure the election of these candidates, the parties had to develop popular followings; and to do so, they had to enlist party workers—that is, adherents who would carry their cause to eligible voters. In sum, American politics was born at this time. During this relatively short period, the groundwork was laid on which subsequent politicians were to build.

The Second Party System

With the dissolution of the Federalist party, legislators in Congress were essentially nominal members of the Democratic-Republican party. With little opposition to speak of, James Monroe was reelected in 1820, his two terms so lacking in party conflict that the pundits deemed it the "era of good feelings." But the lack of another party to compete with in the electoral arena did not mean a lack of conflict within the dominant party (Courser 2007). Party competition would emerge again from within the ranks of the Democratic-Republicans, as copartisans competed for the presidency.

Campaigning for the 1824 presidential election began shortly after Monroe's reelection in 1820. Today's political analysts may complain about the length of presidential campaigns and the number of candidates vying for the party nomination, but long campaigns and large presidential candidate pools are not a strictly modern phenomenon. John C. Calhoun, the secretary of war, declared himself a candidate in 1821. Within the next two years, the names of Secretary of State John Quincy Adams; Secretary of the Treasury William H. Crawford; Speaker of the House Henry Clay; and the hero of the battle of New Orleans, General Andrew Jackson, had all been put forward by their supporters.

Crawford might well have been the front-runner, but he suffered a paralyzing stroke in the fall of 1823 and had to stop campaigning. Calhoun withdrew when he was promised the vice presidential nomination by both Adams and Jackson. In the election itself, Jackson led both the popular vote (in the eighteen states in which electors were chosen by popular vote) and the electoral vote, but he lacked the majority of the electoral vote needed to gain election. Once again, as had been the case in 1800, the election was thrown to the House of Representatives, where each state's delegation cast one vote.

The House had to choose among the top three finishers—Jackson, with ninety-nine electoral votes; Adams, with eighty-four; and Crawford, with forty-one. Clay, whose power came from the House, had been eliminated by finishing fourth, with thirty-seven electoral votes; but his allies in the House guaranteed him influence. After careful consideration, Clay threw his support behind Adams, who was then chosen by the congressional caucus. When the new president subsequently made Clay his secretary of state, cries of **"corrupt bargain"**—an allegation that Clay had traded his support of Adams for the position of secretary of state—were heard throughout the land. No clear evidence of such a trade-off exists, but the "coincidence" of events permanently scarred Clay's reputation. The results also angered Jackson, who felt he had been deprived of what was rightly his.

The election of 1824 created a violent split in the Jeffersonian Republican party, between the backers of Adams (the National Republicans) and those of Jackson (the Democratic-Republicans). Jackson's men organized furiously, and the personal competition increased national interest in politics. By 1828 all but two of the twenty-four states selected their electors by popular vote. The popular vote in 1828 more than tripled that of 1824; thus, Andrew Jackson had his revenge. He defeated John Quincy Adams, the **King Caucus** (as the congressional nominating caucus came to be known) and the elite rule with a populist "revolution." More important, Jackson's election marked the beginning of a series of maneuvers that were to solidify the shape of American politics from that date onward.

Jackson's victory in 1828 put a premium on party organization to mobilize voters. The successful grassroots organization by Jackson's supporters was due much in part to the leadership of Martin Van Buren (Silbey 2002b). Often referred to as the "father of parties," Van Buren was the chief architect of the first American mass party and the chief defender of the **patronage or spoils system**—the practice of rewarding your party members with material benefits after they help win an election—that supported it. True believers in the adage "to the victors belong the spoils," Jacksonian Democrats doled out jobs and government contracts as rewards for party loyalty, securing a dependable and motivated voting base in the electorate. Supported by a loyal following, Jackson readily won reelection in 1832, having been renominated by his party at the first **national party convention**—a gathering of party delegates from each state for the purpose of selecting the party's presidential nominee, among other matters—with Van Buren on the ticket as vice president. The establishment of the national convention for the purpose of nominating presidential candidates was a deliberate reform to democratize the selection process, by stripping nomination power away from Congress and the King Caucus and giving it to the party rank and file.

As Jacksonian Democrats continued to build support, a new opposition party led by Henry Clay and Daniel Webster, the **Whig party**, was formed to oppose Jackson. The traditional view is either that the Whig party represented the prosperous classes or that the split echoed ethnic heritage, but such easy answers do not explain why New Hampshire was heavily Democratic and why Vermont was heavily Whig or why adjacent areas in New York State often differed in partisan allegiance. The simple truth is that the Whigs united those who opposed Jackson and tended to favor a strong Congress over a strong presidency. "Old Hickory"—Jackson—had honed the spoils system to a fine point, rewarding legions of friends who helped him politically. Those who lost jobs (or sought and did not get jobs) became "King Andrew's" enemies and joined the political opposition.

By the election of 1836, competition between the Democrats (as the Jeffersonian or Democratic-Republicans came to be called) and the Whigs was intense, and this level of competition lasted into the 1850s. The Whigs learned much from the Democrats, mimicking their mobilization efforts as well as their electioneering style, and even "out-Jacksoning the Jacksonians" in 1840 by nominating a war hero for president—William Henry Harrison, victor against a coalition of Native Americans in the Battle of Tippecanoe and victor against the British in the Battle of the Thames.

The acrimonious presidential campaign of 1840, between Harrison and Van Buren, was run by a new breed of professional politicians; by the mid-nineteenth century, skilled politicians had raised the practice of their profession to an art. Political rhetoric incited the people; parades stoked their emotions; and catchy slogans, such as the Whigs' "Tippecanoe and Tyler Too" and "Van, Van Is a Used Up Man," simplified their views. Bringing out the vote meant bringing politics to the "common man." Strong party organization on both sides yielded a record number of voters at the polls: 78 percent of adult white males voted in the 1840 presidential election, up from the record set previously by Jackson in 1828 (the 56 percent turnout in 1828 was more than double the 1824 percentage). Politics had emerged as the true national pastime, and the spoils system retained its place as a powerful tool in the arsenal of nineteenth-century party warfare. Once in office, even the Whigs, who criticized the Democrats' use of patronage as corrupt, proved to be as adept as their counterparts in utilizing the spoils of success to their maximum electoral advantage (Blum et al. 1993, 231, 252–53). Indeed, those who view the current intensity of partisan conflict and competition in American politics as unique would be well served by an examination of this time period.

By the 1850s, it was clear that the leaders of the two major parties could no longer sidestep an inevitable political time bomb: the slavery issue. The slavery question had been a latent source of political conflict within the parties since the Missouri Compromise of 1820, which attempted to "resolve" the intense debate within Congress over the spread of slavery into the new territories. Recognizing the balance between the Union's eleven slave states and eleven free states (a balance that was difficult to change in the evenly apportioned Senate), the compromise allowed for Missouri to be admitted as a slave state whereas Maine would gain admission as a free state. In all other territories above latitude 3630′ north, slavery would be "forever prohibited." Not only did the new law fail to resolve the issue, but it also solidified the growing sectional division in Congress between the Northern and Southern wings of the two parties.

By the 1850s the slavery issue was front and center, igniting the passions of citizens and politicians throughout the country. With the outbreak of war with Mexico in 1846 and the debate over the Wilmot Proviso to prevent slavery in any newly acquired territory, the proslavery and antislavery divisions raged on in the House and Senate. While the Compromise of 1850 secured the admission of California as a free state and abolished the use of the District of Columbia as a depot in the interstate slave trade, it also opened the door to slavery in the New Mexico and Utah territories by granting popular sovereignty on the issue. Neither of the two major parties was willing (or able) to take a definitive stand on slavery, fearing that the inevitable alienation of one wing of their party would result in electoral losses. Yet slavery would prove too difficult an issue for political leaders to straddle. By the election of 1852, the Whig party was in shambles, with the "cotton" Whigs of the South bent on preserving slavery for their economic survival and the "conscience" Whigs of the North bent on eliminating it. In their last election as a national party, the Whigs received a majority of the votes in only one state.

While the major parties tried to skirt the most crucial question of the 1850s, other parties—that is, third parties in a two-party system—were willing to stand (or fall) on slavery alone. One of the important roles that nonmajor parties play in two-party systems is that of raising and debating the controversial issues of the day (Bibby and Maisel 2003; Sundquist 1983). New parties—first the Liberty party, then the Free Soil party—brought the slavery issue to the political forefront. Each of these antislavery factions drew significant numbers of votes in presidential elections and thereby elected their supporters to Congress and the state legislatures. The shape of the political system was changing (see Figures 2.1 and 2.2).

A coalition of antislavery parties united in opposition to the Kansas-Nebraska Act of 1854, which overturned limits on the expansion of slavery into the new territories. The **Republican party** emerged out of this coalition, and focused on gaining support based on its antislavery and

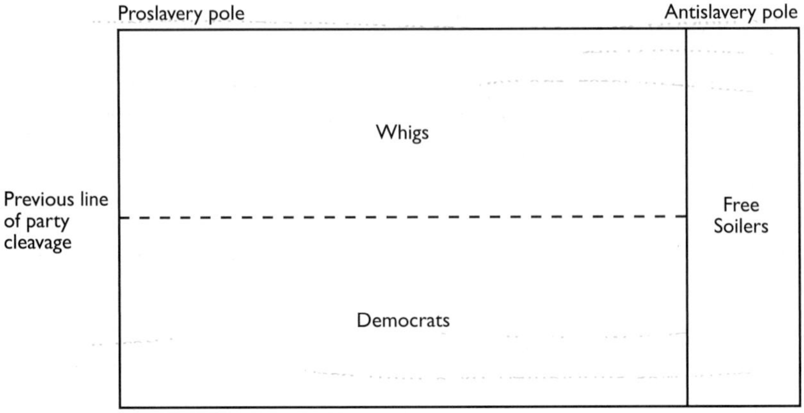

Figure 2.1. Party Division Prior to Realignment on Slavery Issue

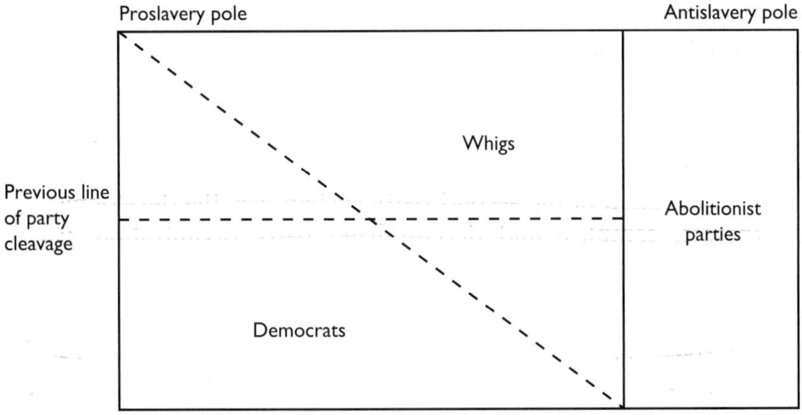

Figure 2.2. Stress on Party System Caused by Slavery Issue

anti-immigrant positions.[6] In 1856 the new Republican party held its first national nominating convention. The nominee, General John C. Fremont, called for the admission of Kansas to the Union as a free state and advocated a policy that upheld congressional authority over slavery in the territories. The Republican party was a sectional party from the start. Drawing on "conscience Whigs," antislavery Democrats, old Free Soilers, and some former "Know-Nothings" (nickname of the nativist anti-Catholic American Party), Fremont got nearly 40 percent of the vote in

1856 (a majority in the North), but he was not even on the ballot in most of the Southern states.

But four years later, the Republicans would take the presidency. Gone were the Whigs, and divided were the Democrats—the Northern and Southern wings each nominated their own presidential candidates. In the election of 1860, Abraham Lincoln, only the second Republican candidate to seek the presidency, defeated Democrat Stephen A. Douglas as well as Southern Democrat candidate John C. Breckinridge and the Constitutional Union party's John Bell, thereby realigning the electorate and ushering in the third party system. Figure 2.3 depicts the realignment at the time of the Civil War. For the only time in American political history, a major party was supplanted by a third party, a new party that served virtually no "apprenticeship" but immediately achieved major party status.

The Civil War, of course, meant much more than a change in the party system. The entire political system was threatened, and it nearly collapsed. What emerged was a badly torn nation, divided on the issue of slavery—an issue that was resolved by bloodshed, not political debate. The politics of the post–Civil War period reflected the split of the nation and a whole new way of resolving conflict.

Innovations of the Second Party Period

The key innovation of the second party system was the development of an elaborate, complex, and decentralized party organization. Parties

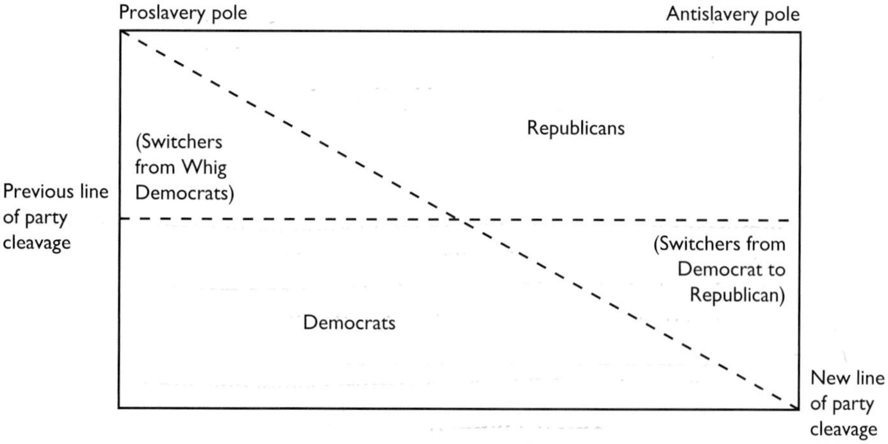

Figure 2.3. Party System after Realignment on Slavery

began to organize followers and workers at the local, grassroots level, establishing autonomous local units to see to the business of elections. National conventions drew on these local units, emphasizing citizen participation. By the 1830s, politics involved true two-party competition in every region—in fact, in every state except, perhaps, South Carolina. Unlike the first party system, in which policy differences were front and center, the electoral aspects of party were critical in this second party system.

The changing attitude toward politics was accompanied by equally significant changes in the law, changes that encouraged the spread of popular participation. Presidential electors came to be chosen by popular vote, with a whole slate of electors running at large in each state. As the Constitution leaves the method of choosing electors to the states (Article 2, Section 1), state politicians soon realized it was to their state's advantage if the winner received all the electoral votes, not just a share. Thus, the "winner-take-all" system was born, and it is still in place in every state except Maine and Nebraska. In addition, the need for a closer link between representatives in Washington and their constituents back home was recognized and actuated by district elections (as opposed to at-large elections) as early as the Jacksonian period, and it was eventually written into law as part of the reapportionment legislation following the Census Act of 1840.

Similarly, the populace began to participate in other elections during this time. More and more governors, previously selected by state legislatures, were now popularly elected. Many local officials, heretofore appointed, had to stand for election. All federal, state, and local elections were conducted according to new democratic rules designed to encourage increased participation. Some of these new election procedures were basic, such as the provision of printed ballots by the state. Some seem only logical, such as holding all elections on the same day and drawing small voting districts (to decrease unneeded and difficult travel). Taken together, these regularized procedures had an enormous impact. Although change came slowly during the second party period, the long-term effect was profound. By 1850, the basic features of the American political system were not unlike those in place today.

The Third Party System

The contributions of the second party system—party organization and popular participation—became the foundation for the next. The third party system roughly coincided with the "Gilded Age of parties" (Dobson 1972; Keller 1977; McCormick 1986; Silbey 1994), the period following the

Civil War to the mid-1890s, when political parties achieved unprecedented levels of power and organization. It remains the most competitive period in American history, characterized by intense electoral competition in districts across the country and popular votes in presidential elections so extremely close that pundits of the day called it "the era of no decision." Political historians argue that this competitive atmosphere put a premium on party organization (Silbey 1994; Jensen 1971; Keller 1977). Winning marginal elections required discipline, coordination, and energy; thus, the parties organized and mobilized like "armies drawn up for combat" (Burnham 1970, 72). As a result, this period had the highest turnout of any in American history; from 1868 to 1892, almost 80 percent of all eligible voters showed up at the polls for presidential elections (Silbey 1994, 219), although certainly these figures were inflated somewhat by various forms of election fraud (Rusk 1970, 1974). During the 1870s and 1880s, American political parties became more finely tuned and more fully developed vote-mobilizing institutions than ever before (McGerr 1986; Silbey 1994, 221–22).

While the nation as a whole was very competitive, rare was the state that was not dominated by one party or the other (Ware 2006). For example, consider the instances when Republican James Garfield won the election of 1880 and when Democrat Grover Cleveland won the election of 1884; in each case, with a popular plurality of less than 1 percent, the winning candidate had at least a 10 percent margin of victory in more than half the states. The Republicans would have dominated this period more convincingly had not a series of seemingly unrelated events hurt Republican political fortunes—namely, the economic depression in 1873, the scandals of the Grant administration, a decline in agricultural production in 1884, and the depression of the 1890s. The Democrats, after Reconstruction, made political gains in the South, where resentment by whites toward Republican domination of their region after the Civil War was high and when Southern blacks were prohibited from active participation in politics by the notorious Jim Crow laws. The Democrats won some political skirmishes, but the Republicans were the well-financed and powerful party of the captains of American capitalism. Both national parties were captured by the industrialists, but it was the Republicans that sponsored governmental programs favoring industrial growth and westward expansion.

In addition to being a time of rapid industrialization, the last quarter of the nineteenth century was also a period of significant immigration. Newly arrived immigrants would play an important role in the development of the most significant political innovation of this period: the urban **political machine,** which is a group of elites that controls the activities of a political party. In many ways, it is logical that political machines grew up during an era dominated by business growth. As Banfield and Wilson argue, the party organization of this period was essentially "a business organization in a particular field of business—getting votes and winning elections" (1963, 115). Urban political machines survived by heavily exploiting the patronage system.

Each machine was organized as a structured hierarchy: a dominant leader, the political boss; ward leaders beholden to the boss; precinct captains beholden to their ward leader; and those who worked the streets beholden to those organizing the precinct. The glue that held these machines together was material incentives, tangible rewards for work well done (and the withdrawal of those rewards if the work was not done). Patronage jobs were the reward for electoral success. Aid—to the newly arrived immigrant, the unemployed, or the underemployed—ensured loyalty to the machine. The political system proved an effective means for immigrants to assimilate themselves into American society. The political machine provided jobs, lodging, extra groceries, and a means of socialization for new groups of citizens. In return, the immigrant groups provided votes for the machine. Historian Richard Hofstadter went so far as to characterize this third party system as being fueled by these rewards for loyalty: "The parties of the period after the post–Civil War were based on patronage, not principle; they divided over the spoils, not issues. Although American political parties are never celebrated for having sharp differences of principle, the great age of the spoilsmen was notable for elevating crass hunger for office to the level of a common credo" (Hofstadter 1948, 169). Material rewards secured loyalty and maintained discipline among the ranks, both of which were necessary to win closely fought elections.

Perhaps the classic example of an urban political machine during this era was Tammany Hall, the Democratic New York City machine and its notorious ringleader, Boss William Marcy Tweed. The excerpted material below (after the next paragraph) explains the electoral success of the Tammany machine through the astute and frank insights of one of their own, George Washington Plunkitt, ward boss of the Fifteenth Assembly District in New York.

In these comments, the importance of patronage, material goods, and constituent services in securing party loyalty to the machine is clear; as Plunkitt acknowledges, "You can't keep an organization together without patronage. Men ain't in politics for nothin'" (Riordon 1995, 37). It is important to note, however, that machines' success was built on more than just patronage. Machines emphasized politics of personal contact, and they often provided a welcoming place for newly arriving immigrants in an otherwise hostile society (see Handlin 1951; Merton 1957).

These extended comments from Plunkitt provide great insight on how patronage was used by urban party machines.

> Who reads speeches, nowadays, anyhow? It's bad enough to listen to them. You ain't goin' to gain any votes by stuffin' the letter boxes with campaign documents. Like as not you'll lose votes for there's nothin' a man hates more than to hear the letter carrier ring his bell and go to the letter box expectin' to find a letter he was lookin' for, and find only a lot of printed politics. I met a man this very mornin' who told me he voted the Democratic State ticket last year just because the Republicans kept crammin' his letter box with campaign documents.
>
> What tells in holdin' your grip on your district is to go right down among the poor families and help them in the different ways they need help. I've got a regular system for this. If there's a fire in Ninth, Tenth, or Eleventh Avenue, for example, any hour of the day or night, I'm usually there with some of my election district captains as soon as the fire engines. If a family is burned out I don't ask whether they are Republicans or Democrats, and I don't refer them to the Charity Organization Society, which would investigate their case in a month or two and decide they were worthy of help about the time they are dead from starvation. I just get quarters for them, buy clothes for them if their clothes were burned up, and fix them up till they get things runnin' again. It's philanthropy, but it's politics, too—mighty good politics. Who can tell how many votes one of these fires brings me? The poor are the most grateful people in the world, and, let me tell you, they have more friends in their neighborhoods than the rich have in theirs. . . . The consequence is that the poor look up to George W. Plunkitt as a father, come to him in trouble—and don't forget him on election day.
>
> Another thing, I can always get a job for a deservin' man. I make it a point to keep on the track of jobs, and it seldom happens that I don't have a few up my sleeve ready for use. I know every big employer in the district and in the whole city, for that matter, and they ain't in the habit of sayin' no to me when I ask them for a job.
>
> And the children—the little roses of the district! Do I forget them? Oh, no! They know me, every one of them, and they know that a sight of Uncle George and candy means the same thing. Some of them are the best kind of vote-getters. I'll tell you a case. Last year a little Eleventh Avenue rosebud, whose father is a Republican, caught hold of his whiskers on election day and said she wouldn't let go till he'd promise to vote for me. And she didn't. (Riordon, 1995, 27–28)

A different type of patronage fueled the predominantly Republican state party machines—financial support from business interests. The state and regional machines were frequently run by a U.S. senator, and, as a consequence, the Senate of the 1880s resembled a "sort of federation of state bosses" (Dobson 1972, 33). For example, in return for party contributions (and personal gifts of new corporate shares), Pennsylvania Republican senators Simon Cameron and Matt Quay advocated high tariffs in

Congress, prevented industry strikes, and kept local and state authorities out of the affairs of business (Dobson 1972, 25; Reichley 1992, 143–45).

The machine bosses—Democratic and Republican, urban and state—directed the party activity, reinforced partisanship, and knew how to mobilize the masses and win elections. "Part skilled, part professional, part tribal chieftain, the boss flourished in a time when a complex industrial society outstripped the instruments of governance" (Keller 1977, 541–42).

Not only did the Gilded Age parties control patronage jobs, but they were the gatekeepers to elected offices as well. During this period, the parties controlled the nominating procedures for all elected offices—that is, a candidate could not get on the ballot without the backing of a party. Parties printed and distributed their own ballots, and in most states, the parties listed their candidates for national, state, and local elections all on one ballot. Such a system encouraged straight party voting, making it difficult for voters to cross party lines and split their tickets. The different appearance of the party-printed ballots (strategically varied in color and size) made it easy for party workers to spot both loyalists and defectors as they stood in line to cast their votes (McGerr 1986).

In the Gilded Age of parties, the bosses dominated politics, and the industrialists dominated society. As immigrants found jobs in the expanding factories, their employment symbolized a period of transition in American life, from an agricultural economy to an urban industrial economy. The political system reflected this shift.

But not everyone was satisfied. With the rapid industrialization of the country and the domination of politics and government by the business community, the farmers of the Midwest discovered that they were the consistent losers. As neither major party took up their cause, they soon set out on their own, forming a series of organizations to challenge the existing power structure. The Granger movement spread rapidly in the 1870s, founding a range of cooperatives (from buying and selling grain, to banking and manufacturing) to stop business interests from reaping profits at the expense of farming communities. By the 1880s the Farmers' Alliance emerged as the most powerful of the farmers' organizations to succeed the Grange as a strident voice of agrarian discontent. By the 1890 election, the pressure of the alliance was felt by Democratic candidates across the West and South as they were called upon to "stand up and be measured" against the yardstick of agrarian demands (Blum et al. 1993, 522–23). Finally, the Populists took the frustrations of the farmers into the political realm, their new party raising concerns that threatened the continuation of the existing two-party system. These groups signaled splits that were to lead to a significant change in the context of American partisan politics (Goodwyn 1978; Hicks 1931).

The Fourth Party System

Before 1896 both parties favored industrialization, and both parties sought to appeal to urban populations. Things changed, however, in 1896. First, the Democratic party had to carry the burden of the 1893 economic panic during the Cleveland administration, which led to a huge Republican landslide in the congressional elections of 1894: Republicans gained 132 seats and completely controlled twenty-four state delegations. Second, the Democratic party became associated with a charismatic leader who attacked business interests, called for softer money and a silver standard, and appealed to the farmers of the nation in a way that alienated urban workers. None could deny the powerful rhetoric of quasi-Populist Democrat William Jennings Bryan:

> The great cities rest upon our broad and fertile prairies. Burn down your cities and leave our farms, and your cities will spring up again as if by magic; but destroy our farms, and the grass will grow in the streets of every city in the country. (from Bryan's "Cross of Gold" speech ["You shall not press down upon the brow of labor this crown of thorns. You shall not crucify mankind upon a cross of gold."] quoted in Hofstadter 1955, 34)

But many doubted the economic effectiveness of the cause. The campaign of Republican William McKinley—led by perhaps the first modern campaign manager (Marcus A. Hanna) and financed by the nation's industrial leaders—was efficient and effective. Bryan was portrayed as a radical enemy of urban workers. Virtually all the cities came into the Republican fold. The new issue that divided the nation, the silver standard versus the gold standard, caused new regional splits—West versus East, rural areas versus urban—and the Democrats had defined for themselves a losing coalition.

The realigning election of 1896 signaled the end to the "era of no decision." The Republicans would hold the White House for sixteen consecutive years and for twenty-eight of the next thirty-six years. Although Democrat Woodrow Wilson won the presidency in 1912 and 1916, the electoral coalitions did not change: the Republicans remained the majority party. Wilson won the 1912 election because Teddy Roosevelt split the Republican vote, running on his own third-party ticket, that of the Progressive Bull Moose party. Wilson barely won again in 1916, as many old Progressives marched back to the Republicans. By 1920 the Republican coalition had regained prominence.

With the realignment of the electorate after 1896, Republicans dominated the North and Midwest, while Democrats maintained a stronghold in the Southern states and border states. The regional dominance of each party eliminated many of the marginal districts of the Gilded Age

(Brewer and Stonecash 2009; Burnham 1965; Price 1971; Schattschneider 1956, 1960). The decline in competition between the two major parties would take its toll on party organization; that is, no longer were the tightly run, vote-mobilizing institutions of the Gilded Age needed to win (McGerr 1986).

The Era of Reform

Party organization was dealt another blow by the antimachine movements, which were gaining speed at the end of the third party system and which reached their peak in the fourth. The most notable reform movements to target the "graft and corruption" of the powerful party machines were the Populists and, after their defeat in the 1896 election, those of the Progressive movement. The antiparty battle cry of the Populists is captured in the preamble of their platform:

> Corruption dominates the ballot box, the legislatures, the Congress, and touches even the ermine of the bench. The people are demoralized. Most of the states have been compelled to isolate the voters at the polling-places to prevent universal intimidation or bribery. . . . We have witnessed for more than a quarter of a century the struggles of the two great political parties for power and plunder. (quoted in Fink 1983, 182)

Popular momentum for the first of the antimachine reforms was provided by Charles J. Guiteau, the deranged, disappointed office seeker who shot President Garfield. His crime and Garfield's death focused popular criticism on the spoils system and indirectly created the **civil service system**, a process of filling government positions based on expertise and tests of merit rather than allegiance to a political party. The Pendleton Civil Service Reform Act of 1883 was the first step in the decline of the urban machines, depriving them of their very lifeblood: patronage jobs. The new restriction on patronage positions and the eventual replacement of the spoils system with a merit-based system for government jobs meant voters had less incentive to work for, or remain loyal to, the party machines.

Progressive reforms in the electoral arena had more immediate impacts. The first was the **Australian ballot**, a state-printed ballot cast in secret and listing all candidates for a particular position (not one party's candidates for all positions). The new ballot, adopted in all but two states from 1889 to 1891, enabled **split-ticket voting**—voting for candidates of different parties in the same election—and reduced voter intimidation at the polls. The second Progressive reform to reduce the powerful hold of the Gilded Age parties over the electoral arena was the adoption of **direct**

primary elections, a preliminary election in which party delegates or candidates are chosen directly by voters. The mandated primary, which most states instituted from 1905 to 1910, stripped the parties of a critical source of power: control over nominations. Candidates no longer needed the party nod to get on the ballot. In addition, many cities at this time introduced nonpartisan elections, in which party names do not even appear on the ballots, further reducing the stronghold of parties at the local level.

These Progressive reforms sapped the strength of the parties by limiting their resources (the "spoils" of nineteenth-century politics) and by restricting their control over nominations and elections. Other reforms of the Progressive Era that were primarily aimed at reining in the powerful corporate interests of the industrial revolution also had a long-term impact on the American political system. For example, in a revolt aimed primarily at politicians who represented the interests of the formidable Southern Pacific Railroad, California governor Hiram Johnson and the new state legislative majority in 1911 passed twenty-three amendments to the California state constitution. Aptly nicknamed by political historians as the "Camelot of California Progressivism," Johnson, with the support of his colleagues, empowered the populace with such electoral ammunition as the **initiative**—a process by which citizens can bring a proposed law directly to the electorate without the involvement of the legislature; the **referendum**—a method where the legislature asks citizens to vote directly on a proposed law; and the **recall**—a procedure through which citizens by petition can call for a vote on removing an elected official from office before the scheduled end of his or her term.

Lastly, the **Seventeenth Amendment**, adopted in 1913, would further rein in the power of the parties. With the mandated direct election of U.S. senators, no longer would the choice of a state's senators be left to the state legislature and, ostensibly, to the dominant state party.

Thus, the fourth party system was marked by declining party competition after the election of 1896 and by rising Progressive reforms. Given the new rules of the game, American political parties would never again attain such levels of organizational strength and electoral control as they had achieved in the latter half of the nineteenth century.

The Fifth Party System

The regional dominance of the major parties and the economic and social groups that supported each since 1896—rural interests for the Democrats, industry and business interests for the Republicans—remained in place for over thirty years. The context of electoral battles shifted during the Progressive Era, but the line of cleavage dividing the parties did not. However, the stock market crash in 1929 and the Great Depression changed everything, shattering the allegiances of the fourth party system and recasting the shape of electoral coalitions for decades to come.

In simplest terms, the American public blamed the Great Depression on Republican president Herbert Hoover and his party. In 1932, Franklin Roosevelt gave hope to the millions who had been hurt by the Depression; they responded by giving their allegiance to the Democratic party. In perhaps the perfect example of a critical election, FDR swept into office with 57 percent of the popular vote and carried the electoral college 472 to 59. In addition to the traditionally Democratic Southerners, the **New Deal coalition** that brought Roosevelt to office and whose support ensured Democratic electoral dominance for the next thirty years were urban workers, minorities (African Americans, ethnic Americans, Jews, Roman Catholics), and farmers—all of whom were attracted to the increased role of the federal government through the New Deal's public works, pro-union legislation, social welfare programs, and farm supports. This diverse collection of groups of voters consistently supported the Democratic party from 1932 to 1964, allowing the Democrats to be the majority party throughout this period. Throughout the New Deal era, the two major parties were aligned roughly along class lines: The Democratic party supported the working class and the poor; the Republicans represented business interests and the more affluent. There was also a religious element to the division between the parties in this era, with the Democrats attracting high levels of support from Catholics, Jews, and other religious minorities while the Republicans dominated among white Protestants, outside of the South of course (Brewer 2003).

The divisions outlined here defined the cleavage in the American political system for an unprecedented period of time. Most analysts believe that a description of electoral coalitions accurate to the mid-1930s would have been similarly accurate into the 1960s. Even though the Republicans won Congress in 1946, and despite President Eisenhower's defeat of Democrat Adlai Stevenson in both 1952 and 1956, these elections were seen as deviations—Eisenhower's success was more a result of a war hero's popularity than it was the result of an electoral shift to the GOP. The majority of Americans still owed allegiance to the Democratic party, and the issues dividing the electorate were still the New Deal issues. For more than three decades the political agenda would be defined primarily by the same question: Does the federal government have a responsibility to serve as the employer of last resort, to intervene actively in the economy, and to help those who are unable to help themselves?

While this question remains an important one today, it has been joined by new questions having to do with issues of race (Carmines and Stimson 1989) and, more recently, culture (Brewer and Stonecash 2007; Layman

2001; Leege et al. 2002). As these new issues assumed their place on the national agenda, the New Deal coalition began to show signs of strain.

A Sixth Party System—Yes, but Defined How?

Political journalists and political scientists have spent a substantial amount of time and effort debating if and when the fifth party system ended (see, e.g., Brunell and Grofman 1998; Ladd 1978, 1991; Silbey 1991; Burnham 1991; Aldrich and Niemi 1990). The best answer seems to be that no one critical election can be isolated as a point to define a critical realignment; instead, the American political system underwent a gradual transformation (Abramowitz and Saunders 1998; Burnham 1991; Ladd 1978, 1991; Ladd and Hadley 1975; Shafer and Spady 2014; Silbey 1991), although the years in which this transformation occurred are in dispute. If 1932 was the quintessential example of Key's theory of critical realignment, then perhaps the period from the late 1960s through the present is exactly what Key had in mind in his theory of secular realignment (Brewer and Stonecash 2009; Stonecash 2006). Although most in the field now believe we moved into a sixth party system, there is a fair amount of disagreement about how exactly we arrived at this new system and about its particular contours. In the wake of Donald Trump's successful 2016 presidential run, there is now emerging debate as to whether we are about to enter a new party system as Trump fundamentally reshapes the

Republican Party (Catanese 2017; Drutman 2016; Warren 2017). In our view it is too early to do much more than speculate on whether the sixth party system continues or is in the process of transitioning to a new, seventh party system. But it is more certainly the case that there has been significant change in American electoral politics since the 1960s, and that four changes are particularly important to understanding the contemporary electoral universe in the United States: the realignment of the South into a Republican bastion, the emergence of cultural issues as important factors in elections, the development of a close division between the parties, and the decline and resurgence of partisanship.

Realignment of the South

The first noticeable tension in the New Deal electoral coalition was provided by the South (see Aistrup 1996; Alt 1994; Brunell and Grofman 1998; Bullock 1988). Abundant evidence exists that a realignment has happened in the South since the 1960s (Abramson, Aldrich, and Rohde 1998, 2007; Abramowitz and Saunders 1998; Black and Black 2002; Glaser 1996; Green, Palmquist, and Schickler 2002; Jacobson 1996; Mattei and Niemi 1991; Miller 1998). But the irreconcilable regional and ideological division within the ranks of the Democratic party that would result in the Southern abdication to the GOP had deep historical, social, and economic roots. Slavery, the Civil War, and Reconstruction not only pitted "the party of Lincoln" against Democrats but region against region: Within the Democratic party, these were difficult historical obstacles to overcome.[7] The prominent issues of the 1960s—civil rights and the Vietnam War—further drove the wedge in the Democratic party between conservative Southerners and their more liberal copartisans in the North. The result would be the loss of the South to the Republicans.

The divides between the Northern and Southern wings of the Democratic party were evident even in the early years of the New Deal. What electoral coalitions brought together in the New Deal era, policy coalitions drove apart. In 1938, a group of conservative Southern Democrats voted with Republicans to block passage of Roosevelt's Fair Labor Standards Act. The act would have increased union membership and equalized wages, stripping the South of its major economic advantage over the North: cheap labor. Thus was born the Conservative Coalition, a dominant force in Congress from 1938 to 1965. Conservative Democrats (nearly all Southerners during the New Deal period) continued to vote with Republicans against a majority of the rest of the Democrats on a range of social issues, stopping (or seriously watering down) the passage of Medicare, civil rights, and fair housing legislation; increases in government management of the economy; and welfare policies such as food stamps and Aid to Families with Dependent Children (Brady and Buckley 2002; Patterson 1967).

But the primary issue that would initially force conservative Southern Democrats into the Republican party was race (Carmines and Stimson 1989). The presidential election of 1948 can be seen as a precursor of this shift. In that campaign, Southern Democrats walked out of their party's national convention in protest over the party platform on civil rights; Conservative South Carolina governor Strom Thurmond, then a Democrat, ran for president under the label of the States' Rights party (the segregationist "Dixiecrats") throughout the South, and he won enough states to garner thirty-nine electoral votes. At the presidential level, the South never returned to the Democratic party as a monolithic bloc (Frederickson 2001). But for state and local offices, Democratic loyalties remained strong for two more decades.

The realignment of the South that began in the 1960s was precipitated by certain critical events: the lunch counter sit-ins that began in Greensboro, North Carolina, in 1960; the freedom rides in 1961; the forced integration of the state universities of Mississippi in 1962 and of Alabama in 1963; the protests in Birmingham, Alabama, and other Southern cities; Martin Luther King Jr.'s march on Washington, which was the stage for his powerful "I Have a Dream" speech in 1963; and the march from Selma to Montgomery, Alabama, in 1965. Responses by political leaders to those events included passage of the **Civil Rights Act of 1964**, which prohibited discrimination in employment and in public accommodations and which penalized educational systems that discriminated against minorities. Also of great impact was the **Voting Rights Act of 1965**, which protected the voting rights of blacks by outlawing literacy tests and other methods of keeping blacks from voting (Weisbrot 1990). These events accelerated a redefinition of voting allegiances among Southern voters. Black voters registered and turned out to vote in numbers never before seen (see chapter 3). White voters began to look for conservative Republican alternatives. While they initially had difficulty finding such Republican options below the presidential level because the GOP as an organization was so moribund throughout the South that it ran few credible candidates for any office, this eventually changed as the Republican "farm team" developed and grew. Over time conservative Republican options were available up and down the ballot all through the South (Black and Black 2002).

It is important to note that while the issues surrounding race were of critical importance to change in the South, Southern realignment to the GOP was not based solely on race. Class too played a significant role. Until relatively recently, the South was the economic backwater of the United States. Most Southerners—black and white—were poor. However, as Key (1949) notes, class conflict was stifled by the dominance of issues surrounding race. If one was white, one was a Democrat, end of story. As the South began to develop economically after World War II, questions of class began to assume new importance in the region. As early as the 1950s, more affluent white Southerners began to vote Republican in presidential elections. As the region grew more prosperous, Americans from other parts of the country began moving south, and some of them brought Republican partisanship with them. By the 1960s class concerns, along with race, were clearly moving wealthier Southerners toward the GOP. This trend has continued ever since, and the South now exhibits patterns of class and partisanship similar to those that exist in the rest of the nation (Shafer and Johnston 2006; Stonecash 2000; Stonecash, Brewer, and Mariani 2003). The rise of cultural issues has also been important to the South's move into the Republican coalition. More will be said on this below.

At first the Republican rebirth in the South was for the most part confined to presidential elections. By 1996, however, the picture had radically changed. The Republican party was flourishing throughout the South: After the 1996 election, eight of the eleven Southern governors were Republicans; eight of the ten senators up for reelection from the South in that year were also Republicans, and all were reelected; and of the 125 Southerners elected to the House in that election, 71 were Republicans. Republican strength in state legislatures throughout the South reached new post-Reconstruction peaks. This pattern has continued. After the 2016 elections, the Republicans hold eight of eleven Southern governorships; all twenty-two state legislative chambers, eighteen of twenty-two Southern Senate seats; and 99 of the 138 Southern House seats (the total number of Southern House seats keeps growing due to population movements and decennial redistricting). Given these figures, along with Southern patterns in presidential voting, it is difficult to argue that the South has not realigned and that this realignment has not affected national politics.

The Rise of Cultural Issues

As noted above, one of the engines driving Southern realignment has been the rise to prominence of cultural issues like abortion and gay rights. From the New Deal through the early 1960s, economic issues and class concerns were the primary source of cleavage in the American party system. But by the late 1960s, this had begun to change. In a series of cases beginning in the 1950s, the Supreme Court gradually relaxed prohibitions on pornographic material. In the early 1960s, the Court banned prayer and Bible reading in public schools. The late 1960s saw the second wave of the feminist movement in the United States, along with the full flowering of the counterculture and the sexual revolution. Increasingly, social conservatives became concerned about the direction in which American society was headed. Then in 1973 the Court produced the biggest factor in the chain of events that thrust social issues onto the political agenda, declaring abortion legal throughout the United States in *Roe v. Wade*.

After *Roe* American electoral politics changed, and this change is still being felt today. Initially, the parties took somewhat ambiguous stands on the new hot-button cultural issues, unsure of where they stood. By the 1980s, however, each party had determined its stands and made them clear for all to see. The Republicans, due in no small part to Ronald Reagan, declared themselves consistently conservative on cultural issues. The Democrats delineated themselves as liberal on these same issues. American voters noticed, and responded. Since the 1980s, cultural issues have become much more important in which party an individual chooses to identify with and which parties' candidates he or she votes for on election day. It is not that these issues have replaced class concerns, but rather that cultural issues have joined class issues in shaping electoral outcomes (for more, see Brewer and Stonecash 2007; Edsall 2006; Frank 2004; Hunter 1991; Layman 2001; Layman and Carsey 2002b; Leege et al. 2002).

The Parties and the Closely Divided American Electorate

Today one often hears the United States referred to as a "50/50 nation." What does that mean? It means that in terms of politics, the American electorate is almost evenly divided between the two major political parties. There is a certain amount of truth to this description. It is certainly the case that neither party holds a commanding edge over the other—measures of partisanship in the electorate regularly show almost parity between the Democrats and Republicans, and the presidential elections of 2000 and 2004 were decided by slim margins. Some believed the Democrats' impressive performances in 2006 and 2008 signaled the rise of a new Democratic majority. The 2010 election cycle abruptly ended such talk. Barack Obama easily won reelection in 2012, but Republicans held the House comfortably and retook the Senate in the 2014 elections. In early 2018 Republicans hold the presidency and both chambers of Congress, but control of at least one chamber if not both is in question as the 2018 elections approach. According to Gallup, as of December 2017 Democrats hold a 7 percentage point advantage over Republicans in the American electorate, mirroring what has generally been a Democratic advantage going back a number of years (Jones 2016; 2017). However, this Democratic advantage is much less impactful than it might seem due to generally higher turnout levels among Republicans and legislative district lines that have been drawn to benefit Republican candidates (more on this in chapter 7). The bottom line is that the Republicans and Democrats are relatively evenly matched, and have been for quite a while.

What does this mean for American politics? At the very least it means that it will be very difficult for either party to attain the dominance that the Democrats held during the New Deal era or that the Republicans possessed after 1896, at least barring some dramatic event. It also means that elections will be more closely fought, as control of government could hinge on a handful of races in any given election. Under conditions like these, partisan political conflict becomes more pervasive and intense, and tensions rise accordingly. It is as if the parties have battled to a tough and bitter draw. Neither side is willing to concede any advantage to the other, and each side is relentless in its respective search for such advantage. While there is considerable debate as to whether this current divide is deep or shallow (Abramowitz and Saunders 2005; Fiorina, Abrams, and Pope 2011), there is little doubt that the divide is real (Brewer and Stonecash 2007; Bougher 2017).

The Decline and Resurgence of Partisanship

There is one final phenomenon that has marked the last thirty to forty years of American politics, one that is perhaps more important than any other. That is the decline and resurgence of partisanship in the United States. During the 1970s and 1980s it was commonplace to read works that basically amounted to being obituaries of American political parties (e.g., Broder 1971; Crotty 1984). Parties no longer structured the electorate, they no longer served as issue shortcuts for voters, they no longer activated and mobilized voters on election day, and they were no longer relevant to candidates for or holders of public office. Elections now, it was argued, are all about individual candidates, personalities, and perhaps, if we were lucky, issues (Beck 1984; Nie, Verba, and Petrocik 1979; Shea 1999; Wattenberg 1998).

Perhaps these views held some validity for a time, particularly in the 1970s as the American polity (including its parties) recovered from the Vietnam era and Watergate and struggled to find its footing. But views of parties as in decline or somehow losing relevance have no place in contemporary American politics. Wherever they may have been a few years ago, political parties are certainly back now. While the parties do not control nominations as they did during the late nineteenth and early twentieth centuries, the presence and power of parties and partisanship is ubiquitous in the United States of the early twenty-first century. Partisanship structures individual vote choice today at levels not seen since the 1950s. Split-ticket voting is decreasing, and the number of strong partisans is on the rise (Bartels 2000; Hetherington 2001; Stonecash 2006). Partisanship extends across a broader range of issue areas than at any time since the advent of modern survey data (Brewer 2005; Layman and

Carsey 2002a, 2002b; Layman et al. 2010). The levels of intraparty unity and interparty conflict in Congress are higher than at any time since the nineteenth century, and have been now for a number of years (Rohde 1991; Sinclair 2006; Stonecash, Brewer, and Mariani 2003). Put simply, parties matter.

THE MODERN PARTY ORGANIZATION

The modern American party is no longer one that controls its candidates, no longer the sole keeper of the keys to nomination and ballot access, and no longer the only route to political office and electoral success. In the modern political system it is the constituents, not the parties, who hire and fire candidates. Thus, the Democratic and Republican national parties have had to adapt to this new political environment or risk obsolescence. Overcoming their collective action problem—how to influence individual voting behavior to win elections and implement party policy—required incentives for candidates to commit to the Democratic or Republican label. Parties had to make themselves of use to their candidates—a task that demanded well-funded, well-staffed, and well-coordinated party organization to provide candidates with a gamut of services, from campaign assistance to vote mobilization. Thus, in the latest American party system, a new type of party has emerged. The Democratic and Republican parties are no longer parties that are in control of their candidates; rather, they have evolved into parties that are in service of their candidates (Aldrich 1995, 273), and that service is provided right from the local level. Interestingly, as these services have become more crucial to electoral success, the parties have regained a good deal of the importance that they may have lost from the 1950s through the 1970s (Herrnson 2009). Parties are once again key players in American elections.

Local and County Organizations

Organizing party workers, energizing local support, and mobilizing voters to get to the booths are certainly not new to the latest party system. Recall Tammany Hall and the Gilded Age machines, the quintessential local political organizations, and their bosses, the masters of grassroots politics. Lest one think the topic of local party organization dry, just think of the infamous Boss Tweed or of Frank Hague of Jersey City, New Jersey; or of the four O'Connell brothers of Albany, New York, dominant bosses for most of the first half of the last century; or of James Michael Curley of Boston, the engaging rogue on whom Edwin O'Connor patterned *The Last Hurrah*; or of Tom Pendergast of Kansas City, Missouri, the local boss who started the career of President Harry Truman; or of Ed Crump of Memphis, Tennessee; or of Anton Cermak, Pat Nash, and Richard Daley of Chicago, Illinois; the list goes on and on. Even after the reforms of the Progressive Era sapped the strength of the urban party machines and weakened party organization in general, some "political bosses" and their local organizations managed to thrive as late as World War II (Mayhew 1986). Their stories are the stuff of legend, their seventy-five-year life span marking a time of colorful, if corrupt, politics in America (Banfield and Wilson 1963; Bridges 1984; Erie 1988; Rakove 1975; Riordan 1963; Steinberg 1972; Tolchin and Tolchin 1971; Wilson 1973).

But even at their height, organized machine politics did not dominate all of American politics—their operating prowess was not standard procedure across the United States. Political machines existed in approximately two-thirds of the largest American cities during at least a part of this period, but they did not all exist at the same time, nor did they maintain the same level of dominance.[8] And surely, by the last quarter of the twentieth century, traditional political machines had been changed by new moralities and reforms and by new styles of politics and political communications. Gone are the days when local party organizations relied on material incentives—goods, services, patronage jobs—to cement support in the community.

Theoretically, the Democratic and Republican parties are organized in each of the roughly 190,000 precincts in the United States. But in practice, a wide variety is the norm—searching for the phone numbers of the Democratic and Republican precinct committees across the United States would prove to be an exercise in futility. Oftentimes, only one party has a precinct committee, and even then, it would be a bonus to have an interested contact person willing to act as a precinct committee chair. But this apparent lack of a comprehensive party structure at the precinct level—the level at which parties are geographically the closest to the electorate—can provide opportunities for influence as well. For example, in the 1980s and into the 1990s, the Christian Right motivated their members to show up for local precinct committee meetings in their areas and to attend the nominating caucuses to promote conservative candidates. This grassroots strategy eventually led to conservative control of local Republican party organizations in states such as Texas and Minnesota and has continued to provide a critical base of electoral support for GOP candidates (see Rozell and Wilcox 1995; Green, Rozell, and Wilcox 2006). Similarly, supporters of Vermont independent senator and unsuccessful 2016 Democratic presidential nomination candidate Bernie Sanders—angered and motivated by what they saw as unfavorable treatment of their candidate by Democratic Party elites—have been actively attempting to exert more influence over the party from the bottom up (Epstein and Hook 2017).

It is unclear at this point how successful their efforts have been and/or will be.

The county, however, is the more consistent organizational presence for the Democrats and Republicans at the local level. Each party is organized to some credible degree in most of the three thousand counties across the United States. Large enough for a "critical mass" of politicians to form, county committees tend to have formal rules and officers and are often much more politically active than precinct and ward committees. County committees (and their chairs) are usually elected by meetings of the party faithful—the precinct committee members or, in large urban areas, the ward committees. Elected county committee members are in large part self-selected, with real competition a rarity; they are mostly volunteers. There was a point in the 1970s and 1980s where the vast majority of county organizations were weak, and in many areas that is still the case. However, more and more county organizations are beginning to actively raise money and hire at least some professional staff.

County organization remains an important building block in the overall party structure: many officials are elected at this level. What few patronage jobs remain in the nation are often county jobs, and state legislative districts often fall within county lines. The most active and "professional" county organizations work year-round, building local organizations, recruiting desirable (or discouraging undesirable) candidates, and raising money. But during campaign season, activity heats up in counties for both parties across the nation. The county organizations help register voters, work on get-out-the-vote drives, and coordinate field campaigns for all the candidates running within their jurisdiction, focusing on candidates for local office or on local candidates for state office.

How important are these locally driven activities in the age of modern campaigns, with polling, television, the Internet, and relatively little grassroots campaigning? Many local races are far from "new style" campaigns; often candidates cannot afford the cost of modern campaigning. Local candidates remain dependent on labor-intensive efforts, still heavily reliant on the foot soldiers of American politics—the organizational volunteers at the precinct and county levels. In addition, a good deal of evidence suggests that strong local party organizations do indeed contribute to larger numbers of votes for the national party (Bibby and Holbrook 1996; Frendeis, Gibson, and Vertz 1990; Gibson 1991). Strong county-level organizations can coordinate the various campaigns in an area and thus recruit "better" candidates—functions that the Republican and Democratic national parties have seen as important enough to fund, especially in presidential election years, when each party invests millions of dollars in local and county organizations. Frendeis and colleagues (1990) demonstrate that the ability of a local party organization to recruit candidates to run for office under the party's label is indicative of its strength—the more full the slate on election day, the more likely the county has an actively functioning party organization. When this recruitment function is added to the more traditional grassroots roles that party organization plays, the total impact of a strong local party organization on vote totals is still significant.

State Party Organizations

The storied past of the incentive-based, patronage-fueled party "machine" was not limited to the cities or to local party organization. Many notorious and powerful state-run party machines dominated the politics of the Gilded Age as well as the Progressive Era. Generally, the "machine" of the dominant party in a state was headed by one of its two U.S. senators, as in the prevailing tradition of the day (and today as well), **senatorial courtesy** granted majority party senators control of most federal patronage in their home state. Put simply, the practice of senatorial courtesy meant that if a senator in the president's party objected to an appointment, the other senators would refuse to confirm the prospective appointee. The existence of this potential veto thus made it possible for senators to determine who in their state would get federal appointments, providing the necessary material incentives to cement a strong state party organization. Furthermore, senators had their own self-interested incentives for utilizing patronage to build and maintain strong state party organizations and for supporting candidates of their party to the state legislature. Until the passage of the Seventeenth Amendment to the U.S. Constitution (passed in 1912 and ratified in 1913 as part of the Progressive agenda), U.S. senators were appointed by state legislatures, not elected by the people. Their own reelection was dependent on maintaining their party's majority status back home.

For a period of time, however, state party organizations seemed ready to disappear not only from public view but also from any place of significance in the political process (Key 1956). State party committees were largely shadow organizations, their only possible function being to serve the will and the cause of a few elected politicians. Over the last fifty years, however, state-level organizations have made a remarkable comeback.

The Structure of the State Party

Today, state party central committees operate for both parties in each of the fifty states, and the means of choosing committee members is set by state law. The chairpersons of the state party committees play critical roles.

Effective state party chairs not only lead the state committee—defining its tasks and setting its goals—but they also act as the linchpin between the grassroots party and the national party. Each state party chair coordinates state, county, and local organizations, directing an increasingly complex and electorally involved state headquarters—the engine of the success or failure of the state party organization. Surely, state party machines of the pre–World War I period had headquarters and workers on a payroll; but for many years, from the administration of Franklin Roosevelt through that of Dwight Eisenhower, little was known about what went on in state headquarters.

The rejuvenation of state headquarters seems to have begun in the early 1960s—ironically at the same time that the candidate-directed campaign replaced the traditional, party-directed one. At that time, only a few state chairs occupied full-time paid positions. By 1990, however, nearly every state party was administered by either a full-time paid chair or a full-time paid executive director, or both. Whereas once the headquarters of the state committee "traveled" from city to city as the hometown of the state chair changed, now virtually all state committees are housed in permanent headquarters, almost always in the state capital. These headquarters contain the most up-to-date campaign technology, allowing for sophisticated campaigning for candidates for state and local office (Appleton and Ward 1997; Reichley 1992; Bibby 1990, 1998; Sabato 1988).

Concomitant with this strengthened presence has come a sizable increase in the budgets for state headquarters. The Party Transformation Study revealed that the average budget for state parties rose nearly five times (to nearly $300,000 annually) between 1961 and 1979. By 1984, the average had risen to nearly $350,000, with the largest state budgets reaching $2.5 million and with only a quarter of the party committees operating with budgets of less than $100,000. Impressive as these increases are, they have been dwarfed in recent years by the sheer amount of money that state party organizations are now raising. According to the Institute on Money in State Politics, the one hundred state party committees (fifty for each party) raised $457.6 million in 2000, and followed that with $571.6 million in 2002. In 2004, even after losing access to millions in soft money contributions from the national parties (see chapter 5), the state party committees still pulled in an impressive $296.7 million. In the 2015–2016 cycle, state Democratic and Republican Party committees (not counting state legislative party committees) raised $367.6 million. Clearly, even with the loss of soft money from the national parties, state party organizations are not starved for cash.[9]

The Role of the State Party

Professionally staffed with increased budgets and a permanent headquarters, the modern state party organization is a service-oriented entity continually engaged in building the state party and in supporting candidates for local and state offices. Not only do the state organizations raise funds to meet their own budget projections, but the state parties also directly support their candidates through individual contributions, a factor that can make all the difference in campaigns with smaller expenditures (such as that of a state representative). The state party organizations actively recruit (and even "decruit"—convince potential candidates not to seek the party's nomination) candidates for local and state offices to ensure the strongest party candidate in the general election. Endorsement by a strong and effective party organization can have a great deal of impact because primaries are typically characterized by low voter turnout. State parties are continually at work to increase turnout in both primary and general elections, identifying potential supporters and registering new voters well in advance of election day. They conduct public opinion polls to identify issues important to state and local residents, and they get out the word to the rank and file through newsletters and communiqués. Last but certainly not least, the state party organizations exercise their influence on the national party by selecting delegates to national nominating conventions (for elaboration on these activities see Huckshorn 1991, 1061–63). State party organizations have grown and developed in recent decades, in part because of an infusion of funds and influence from the national level. At the same time, state organizations stand as a cogent reminder of an organization's ability to adapt to a changing environment (Maisel 1998; Bibby 1998). Three decades ago, candidates could safely ignore most state party organizations if they were interested in running for office. Analysts could be ignorant of the functioning of the state party and miss little of what was important in a state's politics. Neither is true today.

Party Organization at the National Level

In 1964 Cotter and Hennessey called their important study of the two **national committees**—the pinnacle of the national party organizations, comprised of delegates from the states and from groups important to the political parties—*Politics without Power*. Their title aptly caught the significance of what transpired at the two national committee offices. Politics was everywhere; politicians were everywhere; intrigue was everywhere. But no one cared. The national committees had no resources, they had no influence, and they had no power. Nearly three decades later, Paul Herrnson wrote that "national party organizations in the United States are now financially secure, institutionally stable, and highly influential" (1990, 41). Virtually every aspect of party organization has been transformed in recent years, but in no case is this change more apparent than in the national party organizations, the major components of which are the

Democratic National Committee (DNC) and the Republican National Committee (RNC), the pinnacle of the party hierarchy, and the so-called **Hill committees**, the congressional and senatorial campaign committees of the two major parties.

The National Committees

The DNC has existed continuously since 1848; the RNC since 1856. Each was structured as a means of coordinating national election campaigns. (For an exhaustive history of the national committees and their chairs, see R. Goldman 1990, in addition to Cotter and Hennessy 1964.) Formation of the national committees was an important step in changing the parties from loose and totally autonomous confederations of state party activists to more federalized organizations with a unified purpose (Herrnson 1990, 41–42). For the first century of their existence, the two national committees were involved principally with presidential elections. Only in recent decades have their roles expanded.

Although each party's national committee is composed of representatives from the various states, the RNC follows a principle of equality among the states in determining membership. The RNC is composed of three representatives from each state—a national committeeman, a national committeewoman, and the state party chair.[10] The DNC, however, begins with state representation—a national committeeman, a national committeewoman, the state chair, and the highest-ranking officer of the opposite gender from each state—and expands from there. Two hundred additional members are apportioned among the states according to a formula weighing population and Democratic vote in the last presidential election. Others are added ex officio because of positions they hold—the officers of the DNC (who need not otherwise qualify as members); three governors, including the chair of the Democratic Governors' Association; the party leaders in the House and Senate and an additional member of each body; representatives of the Young Democrats and the National Federation of Democratic Women; representatives of Democratic mayors, county officials, and state legislators; and up to twenty other at-large members to accommodate groups still underrepresented. The DNC in 2017 totaled 447 members, including vacancies. Because each committee is too large and unwieldy to work as an efficiently functioning body, each meets only twice a year. Thus, it is the RNC's and DNC's respective executive committees that serve as the actual decision-making bodies within the organizations.[11]

RNC chair Ronna Romney McDaniel and DNC chair Tom Perez each have substantial influence among respective copartisans. They are in some instances the spokespersons for their parties and, in the case of the "in-party chair," spokespersons for the president on party matters. For the Republicans, the chair and the cochair (one man, one woman) are elected by the full RNC in January of each odd-numbered year for a two-year term, as full-time paid employees of the committee. Typically less precise, the Democratic party rules call for a chair, five vice chairs, a secretary, a treasurer, and "other appropriate officers." The "old tradition" allows for the successful Democratic presidential candidate to name the DNC chair, but competition is more open when Republicans win the White House, although Donald Trump played a large role in the installation of Romney McDaniel as the current RNC chair (Peters 2018).

For professional politicians, the national committee chair—the most important position for setting and coordinating the electoral strategy of the party—is a position of status and career value. Because of its high visibility within the party rank and file and because of its importance to the electoral careers of fellow copartisans in, and aspiring to, Congress and the White House, serving as the national committee chair can be not only a rational, hierarchical career move to the pinnacle of the party organization but also a stepping-stone for those aspiring to elected federal and state positions.

But the high visibility and responsibility of the position also mean that the party faithful and the pundits alike point their fingers first and foremost at the national party chair when the party suffers at the polls. The position of national party chair can be a lightning rod in times of electoral loss. For example, then DNC chair Terry McAuliffe took much of the heat for the historic midterm Democratic losses in the 2002 election; he was blamed for the lack of cohesive party strategy to defeat the GOP and to prevent unified Republican control of Congress and the White House.

The "Hill Committees"

Composed of House incumbents, the National Republican Congressional Committee (NRCC) and the Democratic Congressional Campaign Committee (DCCC, or "D triple C") have been in existence since the end of the Civil War, growing out of members' typical insecurity concerning the majority status of their party. The Hill committees of the Senate are the National Republican Senatorial Committee (NRSC) and the Democratic Senatorial Campaign Committee (DSCC), both created by Senate party leaders after the passage of the Seventeenth Amendment. During most of their existence, however, the Hill committees were of little consequence. They did not have access to the resources—specifically grassroots organization and volunteers—that were critical to winning campaigns. As campaigns moved into the electronic media age and candidates began to take more responsibility for directing their own campaigns, the most important resource became money, not party workers. The Hill committees have proven very adept at raising money, and thus have become far more important players in recent years (Dwyer and Kolodny 2006; Kolodny 1998).

The National Parties Respond

At the dawn of the modern electoral era, parties as significant contributors to electoral politics appeared to be a threatened species. With candidates taking greater responsibility for directing their own campaigns and the use of "wholesale" techniques of reaching voters (radio, television, and computer-generated mailings) rather than the "retail" techniques of traditional parties (personal relationships and loyalty), the Democratic and Republican party organizations appeared to be heading toward obsolescence. Instead of becoming the dinosaurs of American politics, however, the parties responded to change, adopting a new role in an evolving political reality (Aldrich 1995; Maisel 1990c, 1998).

The initial impetus for organizational change in the Democratic party was the 1968 party convention. From riots outside to fighting within, it was clear that the party was unraveling. After the election of President Nixon, the Democrats undertook a period of intense party reform with the goal of making the party more open, more representative, and more democratic. To achieve this goal, the party became more centralized, with reform commissions operating out of national headquarters and stipulating rules that governed state and local party procedures.

For the Republicans, the catalyst for change was the Watergate debacle, the disastrous 1974 congressional elections, and Jimmy Carter's defeat of Gerald Ford in the 1976 presidential election. One veteran GOP operative explained this turning point in the party's organization as such: "You almost have to roll over and be dead before you can revive. We had to do new things because we had one foot in the grave" (Clymer 2003a). Former Tennessee senator William Brock, an advocate of **party renewal**—an effort to change the way in which political parties operate so that they can play a more important role in the political process, won the election to head the RNC in 1977. At approximately the same time, two other strong party advocates—Representative Guy Vander Jagt of Michigan and Senator Robert Packwood of Oregon—were chosen to head the NRCC and the NRSC, respectively. These three leaders saw it as their mission to build their organizations into effective campaign support mechanisms for Republican candidates, focusing on party building for the long haul—the benefits of which GOP candidates are reaping today.

First and foremost, a rigorous program for building the party's financial base was developed. The Republican party's finances increased dramatically after Brock, Vander Jagt, and Packwood took command—

notably, through direct mail fund-raising, which provided a reliable and steady flow of checks to the party, however small the donation. With a sound financial base, the Republicans moved all their national organizations into a party-owned national headquarters and hired a sophisticated staff to serve the campaign needs of Republicans throughout the nation.

The RNC's long-term electoral strategy was to groom candidates at the local and state level to ensure the depth of the GOP candidate pool in future elections. Fostering this GOP "farm team" placed a premium on candidate recruitment for local offices and state legislatures. Campaign training schools were established, and local liaisons put in place. The GOP national committees worked with regions and states, appointing policy directors, organizational consultants, and fund-raising advisers to fan out across the country. Computer services were made available for all party candidates to assist, for instance, with compliance with campaign finance regulations, research on public opinion, compilation of voting lists, and analyses of opponents' records. In short, the RNC provided a full-service campaign consulting organization for Republican candidates (see Herrnson 1990, 1998b).

The Republicans did not stop there. The RNC and their two Hill committees developed truly awesome fund-raising capabilities so that they could support Republican candidates for federal office to the full extent permitted by law. The NRCC and the NRSC entered into "agency agreements" with state party organizations, empowering the national offices to pay the state parties' share of campaign contributions and coordinated expenditures in House and Senate races (Herrnson 1988, 1990, 1998b; Jacobson 1985a).

The Democrats were caught napping—they fell far behind in their fund-raising and organizational efforts. While their party's initial reforms may have conformed to a philosophical need to democratize the party, greater organizational change and party renewal would be essential for the DNC and the Democratic Hill committees to begin to support Democratic candidates in ways even remotely similar to the Republican model. As with the Republican party, the impetus for Democratic party reorganization was massive electoral defeat. The 1980 election saw President Carter's landslide loss to Ronald Reagan, the loss of the Democratic majority in the Senate for the first time since 1954, and the loss of thirty-four House seats (half the margin the Democrats held before the election).

Charles Manatt, a longtime Democratic activist and fund-raiser, was elected chair of the DNC after the 1980 debacle. At the same time, the enterprising and ambitious Representative Tony Coelho of California took over the DCCC (Herrnson 1988; Jackson 1988). And in rapid succession, two senators committed to party building, Lloyd Bentsen of Texas and George Mitchell of Maine, were elected to cochair the DSCC.

Although the Democratic national party was still organizationally behind its GOP counterpart, party efforts finally began to pay off. Task forces of consultants were established to aid Democrats in about a third of the states—double that number by 1988—with the same kinds of services the Republicans were supplying throughout the nation. The Democrats even moved all their organizations into a new party-owned building, complete with an impressive media studio. But catch-up is a difficult game to play, and for many years the Democrats were simply unable to match Republican efforts in terms either of supplying services or of helping candidates and parties with significant infusions of funds (Herrnson 1998b). To paraphrase George Washington Plunkitt of Tammany Hall, the Republicans saw their opportunities first and they took them, and the Democrats have been swimming upstream ever since. However, by some measures the Democrats appear to have drawn even for the first time since the rejuvenation of the national party organizations began in the 1970s (more will be said on this in chapter 5).

Both parties have used knowledge and experience gained at the national level to improve state and local organization. While the national Democratic party has imposed rules on its local party units—that is, "sticks" to compel action—the Republicans have refused to do so. However, the Republican party has used money and services as financial inducements to entice its state and local units to professionalize their operations, or "carrots," also used by the Democrats but in much smaller amounts. Thus, though in different ways, the "nationalization" of party organization goes on in both parties, affected more by the recognition of the sources of funds and of expertise than by philosophical concerns. The parties have adjusted to new situations, realizing that they are primarily electoral institutions and that they have to find a means to make their contribution significant to those running for office. They have successfully done so, and the parties are once again key actors in the drama of American elections.

Party Organizations and the Drive to Get Out the Vote

"Getting out the vote" (GOTV) has traditionally been the forte of one party in particular—the Democrats. By November 2002, it became clear that vote mobilization was no longer a cornered market. When an RNC study of the 1998 and 2000 elections revealed Democratic candidates consistently gaining ground from union vote drives in the final hours before the polls closed, the GOP created its own turnout machine to counter the Democratic advantage. The 72-Hour Task Force—spearheaded by the RNC, with White House GOP strategist Karl Rove—sent fifteen hundred operatives across the country with one mission: to mobilize Republican voters, especially those who tended to avoid voting in nonpresidential election years (such as evangelical Christians). Supervisors and their field operatives recruited volunteers—from churches to rotary clubs—to make phone calls and canvass neighborhoods. Volunteers were bused from safe GOP districts to neighboring ones in need of assistance—a program credited to future majority House leader Tom DeLay. Tested in governors' races in 2001, the task force was deployed in over thirty states to help GOP candidates beat their challengers in the 2002 midterm elections (Halbfinger 2002; Clymer and Rosenbaum 2002).

In Georgia, the new vote-mobilizing arm of the RNC proved a formidable one. Led by GOP state party chair Ralph Reed, a proven master of grassroots politics after years as head of the Christian Coalition, the 72-Hour Task Force was put in place well in advance of election day. In the summer of 2002, Reed deployed three thousand volunteers and five hundred paid workers to knock on 150,000 doors in six hundred target areas across Georgia. President Bush's visit three days before the election signaled the final push for GOP votes. After the president's pep rally for Republican senate and gubernatorial challengers Saxby Chambliss and Sonny Perdue, five hundred volunteers boarded buses to canvass thirty thousand GOP homes in just five hours. The results were record breaking, with the organizational prowess of the task force undeniable. For the first time since Reconstruction, the Republican party won the governorship and held a majority in the state senate. Even the Democratic Speaker and senate majority leader in the state house were defeated. As Reed explained, "The story of 2002 is not that Democrats stayed home. . . . It was that Republicans came to the polls in historic numbers" (Halbfinger 2002).

Thus the "story of 2002" is really one about the modern American party and its adaptability. Even in this age of candidate-centered elections and personal-vote bases, the RNC (and Karl Rove) emerged as the MVP of the 2002 midterms, while the DNC and Democratic House leader Richard Gephardt were held accountable for Democratic defeat at the polls. In other words, Republican victories and Democratic losses in Georgia were less about individual candidates and more about the power of party organizations in determining the outcome of the elections. In an era of heightened party competition, party organizations offer invaluable services to their candidates, which can be the difference between victory and defeat. The critical role of the parties and their GOTV efforts was on display once again in 2004—many attributed President Bush's reelection to the yet again superior seventy-two-hour strategy of the GOP (especially in the critical state of Ohio) (Edsall and Grimaldi 2004)—and in 2006 the Democrats, with a big assist from organized labor, responded to the recent

Republican edge with an impressive effort of their own (Balz and VandeHei 2006; Greenhouse 2006). The Obama campaign had a very impressive GOTV effort in 2008 as well, built at least in part on unprecedented and highly skilled use of social networking media. The DNC attempted to reactivate this machinery for the 2010 election cycle, but was unable to do so to its previous level (Dickinson 2010). Obama's 2012 campaign once again did very well in getting out the vote, but in a repeat of 2010 this success did not carry over for Democrats in 2014. Both Hillary Clinton and especially Donald Trump executed less vigorous than Obama's GOTV efforts in 2016, with Trump apparently suffering little in the way of ill effects. Much more will be said on the 2016 presidential general election in chapter 9.

The American party may not be on a historical trajectory from development to dominance to decline to disappearance, as some political historians have argued.[12] An electoral system where candidates are prominent and take active roles in directing their own campaigns need not be void of strong and relevant party organizations. The strength of the modern-day parties rests not in the controls they wield over their candidates but in the services they can provide them. In today's closely divided polity, those services are sometimes the difference between election night celebration and a sleepless night wondering what could have been.

CRITICAL THINKING QUESTIONS

1. Can American politics and government work without political parties?
2. Who is better equipped to make decisions for political parties—grassroots party members or the party elites?
3. Which is a better way to fill government positions—the spoils system or the civil service system?
4. Which future issues do you believe have the best chance of forcing partisan change or realignment?

KEY TERMS

Federalist party
factions
critical elections
critical realignment
secular realignment
Jeffersonian (or Democratic) Republican party
electoral votes
grassroots
"corrupt bargain"
King Caucus
patronage or spoils system
national party convention
Whig party
Republican party
political machine
civil service system
Australian ballot
split-ticket voting
direct primary elections
initiative
referendum
recall
Seventeenth Amendment
New Deal coalition
Civil Rights Act of 1964
Voting Rights Act of 1965
senatorial courtesy
national committees
Hill committees
party renewal

NOTES

1. Using Key's concepts, political scientists have been able to refine their classifications of various presidential elections. Angus Campbell and his associates classified elections according to whether the majority party won the election and whether the existing line of cleavage prevailed or was changed (Campbell et al. 1960, 531–38). They identified three types of elections—maintaining elections, deviating elections, and realigning elections. Seeing a logical gap in this reasoning and referring particularly to the election of 1896, Gerald Pomper (1973, 104) added a fourth category, the converting election.

2. James Sundquist (1983, 41–47) maintains that the interaction of five variables determines when and in what ways established patterns of political behavior will change. The five variables are (1) how strongly a new issue divides the nation; (2) the capacity of those supporting the status quo to resist change; (3) the skill of the political leaders; (4) whether the new cleavage cuts across existing differences or mirrors them; and (5) the strength of existing party attachments in the electorate.

3. It must be noted that Washington's Neutrality Proclamation early in his second term in 1793 also produced strong reactions and was especially problematic for Jefferson and Madison (Hamilton and Madison 2007).

4. Recall William N. Chambers's (1975) definition of a competitive party system: "A pattern of interaction in which two or more political parties compete for office or power in government and for the support of the electorate, and must therefore take one another into account in their behavior in government and in election contests" (6).

5. The two parties in this period also developed clearly distinguishable national ideologies. As early as 1792, a noticeably partisan James Madison wrote of these differences in the Philadelphia *National Gazette*:

> One of the divisions consists of those, who from particular interest, from natural temper, or from the habits of life, are more partial to the opulent than to the other classes of society; and having debauched themselves into a persuasion that mankind are incapable of governing themselves, it follows with them, of course, that government can be carried on only by the pageantry of rank, the influence of money and emoluments, and the terror of military force. Men of those sentiments must naturally wish to point the measures of government less to the interest of the many than of a few. . . . The other division consists of those believing in the doctrine that mankind are capable of governing themselves, and hating hereditary power as an insult to the reason and an outrage to the rights of man, are naturally offended at any public measure that does not appeal to the understanding and to the general interest of the community, or that is not strictly conformable to the principles, and conducive to the preservation of republican government. (Cunningham 1965, 11)

Not only were the ideologies clear, but politicians were already beginning to bring the American art form of rhetorical overstatement into the public eye.

6. William E. Gienapp (1987, 1991) provides a detailed analysis of the formation of the Republican party. His account makes note of the importance of temperance and of nativism as well as of the antislavery movement in describing, as opposed to other anti-Democratic parties, the demise of the Whigs and their replacement by the Republicans. While his discussion of realignment and of the decomposition of the Whig coalition is consistent with that provided here, he gives a much more detailed, state-by-state account of the strategies followed by Republican politicians and of the role of pragmatic politics and ideology in the decisions they made.

7. Southern voters, nearly all of whom were white, were Democrats for a variety of reasons; but it is not too much of a stretch to say that this allegiance dated back to the Civil War and to Reconstruction and was unaffected by the issues that led to realignments in the rest of the nation in the 1890s and again in the 1930s. It is also accurate to say that the Republican party, as an ongoing organization that ran candidates and claimed the allegiance of a significant number of voters, did not exist in much of the South during the first decades of the New Deal party system.

8. As David Mayhew (1986) has observed, machine politics was much more likely to exist in those states that had existed by the beginning of the second party system, the Jacksonian party system, when the spoils system came into existence. Although the spoils system established a base and gave rise to a political culture that persisted for some time, the other areas never followed suit.

9. These data come from the National Institute for Money in State Politics, https://www.followthemoney.org/assets/Uploads/PartyCmteAnalysis6.16.17 BauerGinsberg.pdf

10. The addition of representatives from American Samoa, the District of Columbia, Guam, the Northern Mariana Islands, Puerto Rico, and the Virgin Islands brings the total membership of the RNC as of March 2018 to 168.

11. The RNC's executive committee is made up of thirty members as laid out in Rule No. 6 of the Republican National Committee: https://prod-cdn-static.gop.com/docs/2016-Republican-Rules-FINAL.pdf. The DNC's executive committee is selected according to Article 4 of the Charter and Article 3 of the Bylaws of the

Democratic Party: http://s3.amazonaws.com/uploads.democrats.org/Downloads/DNC_Charter__Bylaws_9.17.15.pdf.

12. Joel Silbey (1991, 1998, 2002a) claims that American political history can be divided into four periods, distinguished by the importance of the role of political parties and the different kinds of political institutions, norms, and behavior that have predominated in each era. The period from the 1790s to the 1830s—the pre-party period (Formisano 1974)—was a period of party development, not electoral prominence, as parties were resisted by many in politics. The only time in American political history when parties totally dominated the political landscape (Silbey 1991) was from 1838 to 1893—the Gilded Age, or the party period. From the 1890s until the 1950s—the post-party period—parties were on the decline. And, according to Silbey, from the latter half of the twentieth century to today, the American political system has been dominated by candidates, not their parties; thus, he characterizes the present period as the nonparty period.

Chapter 3

Voting and Other Forms of Political Participation

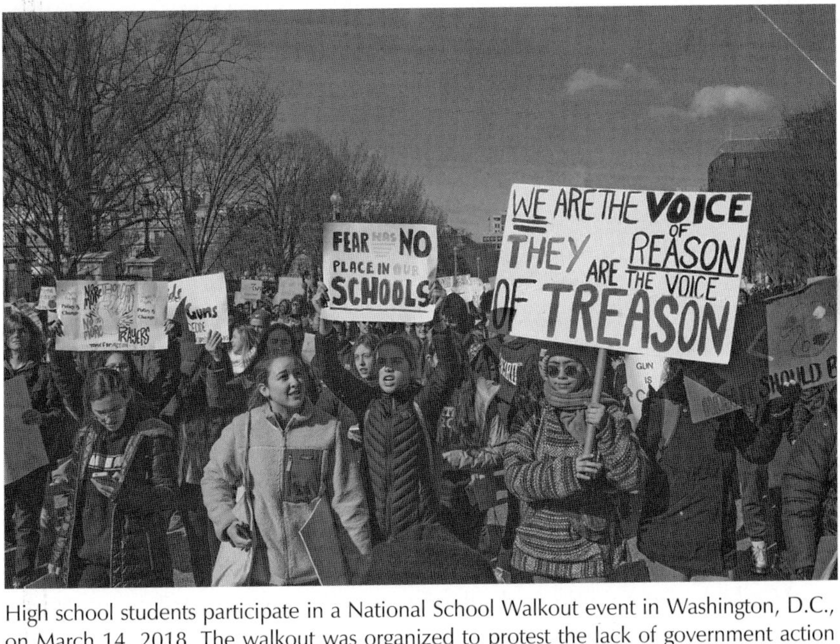

High school students participate in a National School Walkout event in Washington, D.C., on March 14, 2018. The walkout was organized to protest the lack of government action on gun control in the aftermath of the school shooting at Marjorie Stoneman Douglas High School in Parkland, Florida. While many are concerned over what they see as Americans' low voter turnout levels, Americans engage in other forms of political participation at relatively high levels.

If you travel abroad and talk to your hosts about American elections, the most often heard complaint about our system of government is that so few citizens turn out to vote. According to the United States Census Bureau, 64 percent of voting age citizens (a high for recent elections) bothered to go to the polls in the 2008 presidential election. In the 2010 congressional elections, about 46 percent voted. In 2012 and 2014, these figures dropped to 62 percent and 42 percent respectively. Even in the incredibly intense presidential election of 2016 voter turnout was 61 percent. Citizens of "less developed" democracies—ironically, countries with voter turnout of over 75 percent—ask incredulously, "How can you say the United States is a model we should follow when so few bother to take part in your democratic processes?"

When you think about the razor-thin margin by which President Bush carried Florida and thus won the presidency in 2000, think about how many Floridians did not even bother to vote. The 2000 election showed everyone that the question "Who votes and who does not?" is more than just a question of how one evaluates American democracy: it is often crucial to who wins.

Extremely close races are not all that rare. In Connecticut's Second Congressional District in 2006, Democrat Joe Courtney won by an eighty-three-vote margin over incumbent Republican Rob Simmons. The issue is not just how many turn out to vote but which voters go to the polls. Simmons was left to wonder whether the Senate race in Connecticut—a race in which incumbent Senator Joe Lieberman lost his party's primary but then ran and won in the general election as an independent—led some Republicans to stay home. A stronger Republican candidate might have brought more Republicans to the polls, saving Simmons's seat.

The closest Senate race in 2008, between incumbent Norm Coleman and challenger Al Franken in Minnesota, had no declared winner until seven months after the polls closed. Franken eventually won by 312 votes out of nearly 2.5 million cast. In 2010 six congressional races were so close that incumbents returned for the lame duck session of the 111th Congress not knowing if they had been reelected or not. In 2014, the closest race in the House (Arizona's Second District) was decided by 161 votes, while the 2016 U.S. Senate race in New Hampshire was decided by 743 votes. In 2017 the race in District 94 of the Virginia House of delegates was declared a tie after the panel of judges threw out a disputed ballot, resulting in the winner being decided by the drawing of one of the two candidates' names out of a pitcher (Gabriel 2017; Jarvie 2018; Vozzella 2017). Americans do not have to look very hard to find real-world examples of the old saw that every vote counts.

Voting is only one aspect of political participation, albeit the only type of activity in which most citizens participate (see Verba, Scholzman, and

Brady 1995). It is perfectly legitimate to question whether other forms of participation are more important than voting or whether any participation at all is better than none. This chapter begins with an examination of voting, exploring the expansion of the **franchise**—the right to vote—and the exercise of this right. Then we turn to the question of how people decide for whom they will vote, a complex question that political scientists have worked on for decades. Finally we look at other forms of political participation, activities that require more commitment by citizens and are therefore the choice of fewer Americans. We also raise questions about nontraditional forms of participation, some of which are viewed as acceptable in other nations but not ours.

WHO VOTES; WHO DOESN'T

Expansion of the Franchise

In 1789, only white males who owned property, about one in thirty Americans, were generally eligible to vote (Bone and Ranney 1976, 35). Today, legal limitations keep very few citizens from voting. The history of this aspect of electoral reform in America has been one of continuous expansion of the franchise. This history has four phases: increase in white male eligibility, enfranchisement of black citizens (done in two separate parts), enfranchisement of women, and enfranchisement of those between the ages of eighteen and twenty-one. More recently, reformers have turned from asking who is eligible to vote to asking what impediments keep those who are eligible to vote from actually exercising that constitutionally mandated right.

Property Requirements

The first step in expanding the franchise involved state-by-state action to eliminate the property requirement for white males, replacing it with the requirement that only taxpayers could vote. The property qualification finally disappeared when Virginia eliminated it in 1850.

A taxpayer requirement persisted for some years, often being fulfilled with the payment of a nominal **poll tax**, a tax paid by each person as he or she exercised the right to vote. The poll tax, employed mainly in the South to keep blacks from voting, affected poor whites as well. The poll taxes that persisted into the 1960s were rendered void for national elections with the ratification of the **Twenty-Fourth Amendment** in 1964; two years later, the Supreme Court held poll taxes to be unconstitutional in any election (*Harper v. Virginia State Board of Elections*, 383 U.S. 663, 1966).

Black Suffrage

The **Fifteenth Amendment** to the Constitution, ratified in 1870, forbade states from denying or abridging the right to vote based on "race, color, or previous condition of servitude."

However, that seemingly broad prohibition did not end the problem of racial discrimination in voting. Post-Reconstruction Southern legislators were extremely inventive in creating ways to prevent, or at least discourage, blacks from voting. The so-called **Jim Crow laws** (laws designed to restrict the activities of blacks in the South) included literacy tests, tests on interpreting the Constitution, **"whites only" primaries** (allowing only white people to vote in party nominating elections), poll taxes, and **residency requirements** (a stipulation that a person reside in a community for a certain period of time before she or he is eligible to vote). Social and economic pressures as well as administrative decisions, such as locating polling places in remote areas or in areas that had been the site of black lynchings, further restricted black voting. In 1960, fewer than 10 percent of the African American citizens of Mississippi were registered to vote.

The first important attack against Southern restrictions on black voting was the landmark Supreme Court decision in *Smith v. Allwright*, 321 U.S. 649 (1944). Southern states had established in law that political parties were private organizations that could decide their own membership, which meant that they could include a provision excluding blacks. Democratic primaries were then activities of "whites only" private groups. Since the Republican party was all but nonexistent throughout the South, receiving the Democratic party nomination was tantamount to election. Thus, Southern states effectively eliminated blacks from the political process. In *Smith v. Allwright*, the Court ruled that the primaries were part of one electoral process, during any part of which the exclusion of blacks would violate the Fifteenth Amendment. The "whites only" primary was thus ruled unconstitutional.

Black enfranchisement was an important goal of the civil rights movement of the 1950s and 1960s (see Weisbrot 1990; McClain and Stewart 2010). But as Table 3.1 shows, such efforts had little effect on black suffrage in many states. The Voting Rights Act of 1965 addressed this problem head-on, suspending literacy tests, a provision upheld by the Supreme Court in *Oregon v. Mitchell*, 400 U.S. 112 (1970), and empowering federal registrars to replace local or state officials in areas in which fewer than half of those eligible had registered and voted in 1964 (in a total of seven states). That act, most recently renewed for twenty-five years in 2006, has been credited with causing the dramatic impact on black registration. However, the future of the Voting Rights Act is cloudier than at any point since its initial passage in the wake of the Supreme Court's decision in *Shelby County v. Holder* 570 U.S. 193 (2013), which held that requiring jurisdictions to seek preclearance for any changes to voting laws and procedures under Section 4b of the VRA was unconstitutional. The Obama Justice Department responded by attempting to more vigorously enforce the remaining sections of the Voting Rights Act (Fuller 2014), but thus far the Trump DOJ has done exactly the opposite (Newkirk 2017a).

The 1970 extension of the Voting Rights Act also dealt with the question of residency requirements, frequently used by local officials to keep mobile populations from voting—namely, blacks in the South and others such as young people. The 1970 Voting Rights Act set thirty days as the maximum residency requirement permissible for presidential elections. In *Dunn v. Blumstein*, 405 U.S. 330 (1972), the Supreme Court ruled that the thirty-day residency limit should be used for all elections.

Legal restrictions on black voting have been all but eliminated, through a long series of constitutional amendments, congressional actions, and Supreme Court decisions. The path to this goal has been long, but legal limitations on black suffrage no longer keep black Americans out of polling places in the South or anywhere else in this country, at least not explicitly on the basis of race. However, it is clear to some—including a three-judge panel of the U.S. 4th Circuit Court of Appeals—that some recent changes in voting laws in some states are meant at least in part to reduce black voter turnout (Graham 2016; Newkirk, 2017a).

Women's Suffrage

In the early years of the abolition movement, the call for women's suffrage was closely linked to cries for rights of blacks. However, male leaders of the abolition movement soon found it in their interest to separate the two causes (for a full history of the struggle for women's suffrage, see Catt and Shuler 1969). While not abandoning their participation in the movement to free those who were enslaved, women came together in the famous conference at Seneca Falls, New York, in 1848 to assert their own rights. From that point until the successful adoption of the **Nineteenth Amendment** in 1920 allowing women to vote, women suffragists waged a valiant, prolonged, often brilliant, and frequently frustrating battle to win the right to vote.

The suffrage movement had to fight on a state-by-state basis while pursuing a national strategy. A variety of tactics were used. In states in which women had the right to vote, they pressured congressmen and senators to push for a national amendment. When the Democratic party proved recalcitrant, women demonstrated their power by organizing a campaign against all Democratic congressmen in suffrage states and defeated many of them in their bids for reelection.

Table 3.1. Black Voter Registration in Southern States, 1960–2016

State	*1960*	*1964*	*1970*	*1976*	*1980*	*1984*	*1992*	*1996*	*2000*	*2004*	*2008*	*2012*	*2016*
Ala.	13.7	19.3	66.0	58.4	55.8	71.4	71.8	69.2	72.0	72.9	69.9	68.5	72.2
Ark.	38.0	40.4	82.3	94.0	57.2	71.2	62.4	65.8	60.0	63.7	53.2	61.3	71.9
Fla.	39.4	51.2	55.3	61.1	58.3	57.3	54.7	53.1	52.7	52.6	63.5	56.3	47.2
Ga.	29.3	27.4	57.2	74.8	48.6	58.0	53.9	64.6	66.3	64.2	73.4	69.3	66.8
La.	31.1	31.6	57.4	63.0	60.7	74.8	82.3	71.9	73.5	71.1	75.4	77.1	71.1
Miss.	5.2	6.7	71.0	60.7	62.3	85.6	78.5	67.4	73.7	76.1	81.9	90.2	80.9
N.C.	39.1	46.8	51.3	54.8	51.3	59.5	64.0	65.5	62.9	70.4	72.2	83.7	73.3
S.C.	13.7	37.3	56.1	56.5	53.7	62.2	62.0	64.3	68.6	71.1	76.7	75.1	73.8
Tenn.	59.1	69.5	71.6	66.4	64.0	78.5	77.4	65.7	64.9	63.9	62.5	66.8	63.8
Tex.	35.5		72.6	65.0	56.0	65.3	63.5	63.2	69.5	68.4	73.7	70.9	70.2
Va.	23.1	35.5	57.0	54.7	53.2	62.1	64.5	64.0	58.0	57.4	72.3	68.1	68.7
Average of Total	29.7	33.2	63.4	64.5	56.5	67.8	66.8	65.0	65.7	66.5	70.4	71.6	69.1

Sources: U.S. Census Bureau, *Statistical Abstract of the United States: 1982–1983*. Data for 1984, "Population Characteristics," *Current Population Reports*, series P-20, no. 397, issued January 1985. Other data collected by Voter Education Project, Inc., Atlanta, Ga. Data for 1992, "Voting and Registration in the Election of November 1992," *Current Population Reports*, series P-20, no. 471, issued September 1993. Data for 1996–2012, U.S. Census Bureau, www.census.gov.

Note: All figures are percentages of the eligible, voting-age population. Figures for 1964 are based on the recorded voting-age population for 1960.

Faced with this show of power, both national parties included women's suffrage in their 1916 platforms. In 1917 women turned to more militant actions, picketing the White House and delivering petitions to the president. Some were jailed; others replaced them. Those in jail demonstrated for the cause of prison reform; some engaged in hunger strikes. When female prisoners were force-fed, the press had a field day. More women came to Washington, and the jails became increasingly crowded. The effect of the pressure was telling.

The women's suffrage amendment passed the House in the second session of the 65th Congress, but it failed to achieve the two-thirds vote necessary in the Senate. More women came to Washington, more picketed, more were jailed, and more hunger strikes ensued. Finally President Wilson was won over to the cause. When the Republican-controlled House repassed the measure in 1919, Wilson pressured his fellow Democrats in the Senate to enact women's suffrage. At long last, in August 1920, the Nineteenth Amendment was ratified by the requisite three-quarters of the states, and women won the right to vote in all elections.

This abbreviated description of the battle for women's suffrage points to a number of important conclusions. First, the tactics of the suffragists deserve much more attention than they are traditionally given. The suffragists' ability to gain their end, without the stimulus of a cataclysmic event like the Civil War or the threat of electoral reprisal in most states, is a tribute to the skills of the women as politicians.

Second, political participation is most often defined as voting. The suffragists demonstrated that less-traditional political participation (e.g., the hunger strike) can be equally effective in the American polity.

Third, the contrast with black suffrage is instructive. Black men won the right to vote through a constitutional amendment that forbade certain disenfranchisements by the states, but many states found ways around that amendment. Women won their right to vote first on a state-by-state basis, after decades of struggle at the national level; yet, once that battle was won, no further legal impediments stood in women's way. However, social pressures did keep women from voting in numbers equal to men for many years; the difference between legal eligibility and actual voting requires further examination.

Lowering the Voting Age

For much of American history, twenty-one was the traditional voting age. During World War II, when eighteen-year-olds were conscripted into military service, many people believed that the voting age should be lowered to eighteen. In 1943, Georgia, exercising the right of states to control the manner and means of elections, lowered its voting age to eighteen; but only Kentucky and the newly admitted states of Alaska and Hawaii had voting ages below twenty-one well into the second half of the twentieth century.

However, during the Vietnam War, once again, one heard the cries: "Old men send young men to die in foreign wars" and "Old enough to die but not old enough to vote." In response to this agitation and to the general public dissatisfaction with the war in Vietnam, one provision of the Voting Rights Act of 1970 made eighteen-year-olds eligible to vote in all national, state, and local elections. In *Oregon v. Mitchell*, however, the Supreme Court struck down this provision, asserting that Congress could not constitutionally take such actions for state and local elections. As a response to this ruling, Congress passed—and the requisite thirty-seven states ratified—the **Twenty-Sixth Amendment** to the Constitution, making eighteen the minimum voting age for all elections. Over the past few years a few small municipalities have lowered the voting age in only local elections to sixteen. In 2016 an attempt to amend San Francisco's city charter to lower the voting age in city elections to sixteen failed 52 percent to 48 percent. There is also an effort under way in Hawaii to lower the voting age there to sixteen for all state and local elections, but at this point its chances for success appear low. In addition to allowing sixteen- and seventeen-year-olds to vote, and thus possibly instilling the voting habit at a younger age, recent research indicates lowering the voting age to sixteen would also increase turnout among the parents of sixteen- and seventeen-year-olds (Dahlgaard 2018).

Additional Regulations: Residency and Registration

With few exceptions, the potential voting population in the United States today includes all citizens over eighteen years of age. Even citizens who had once been prevented from voting because of their inability to read and understand English can now vote; the 1975 extension of the Voting Rights Act requires bilingual ballots in areas of the country with large non-English-speaking populations. A Native American tribe with no written language is even permitted to vote orally.

Voting participation is a function of three factors: eligibility requirements; registration laws (that is, how one gets one's name on the voting roster); and the decision to vote, to turn out on election day. Table 3.2 shows how each of these factors affects the number who actually vote. Turnout is usually expressed as a percentage of the voting age population—that is, those who have reached the age of eighteen in a given area who actually vote. But, as the table demonstrates, many of those who do not vote do not do so because they have never registered.

Robert Erikson (1981) has demonstrated that the biggest reason citizens do not vote is that they are not registered. A number of other studies have examined the relationship between registration laws and the number of people registered (Teixera 1992, 23–38; Timpone 1998; Powell 1986; Squire, Wolfinger, and Glass 1987; Wolfinger and Rosenstone 1980).

States vary significantly in their registration procedures. Three states—Maine, Minnesota, and Wisconsin—have allowed so-called instant registration for many years: citizens may register to vote up to and on the day of an election. Eleven additional states have added same-day registration in recent years; North Dakota, alone among the states, does not require voter registration at all. In 2015 Oregon became the only state that would automatically register its citizens to vote when they renewed or applied for a driver's license (individuals can opt out). Critics believe that eased voter registration procedures can lead to voter fraud, but no evidence of efforts to subvert the system has been uncovered in states that use it. And registration in those states has increased.

In 1993, the Congress passed and President Clinton signed the so-called **Motor Voter Bill**, an effort to address the registration issue on the national level. The Motor Voter Bill requires states to allow citizens to register to vote when applying for a driver's license, to permit mail-in registration, and to provide registration forms at certain public assistance agencies. Passage of this law has led to continued assessment of the

Table 3.2. Registered Voters and Percentage of Voter Turnout, 1988–2016

Year	Voting Age Population (VAP) (in millions)	Percentage of Eligible VAP Reporting They Registered	Percentage of VAP Reporting They Voted	Turnout as a Percentage of Reported Registered Voters
1988	178.1	66.6	57.4	86.2
1990	182.1	62.2	45.0	72.3
1992	185.7	68.2	61.3	89.9
1994	190.3	62.0	44.6	71.9
1996	193.7	65.9	54.2	82.2
1998	198.2	62.1	41.9	67.5
2000	202.6	63.9	54.7	85.5
2002	210.4	60.9	42.3	69.4
2004	215.7	65.9	58.3	88.5
2006	220.6	67.6	47.8	70.8
2008	225.5	71.0	63.6	89.6
2012	235.2	71.2	61.8	86.8
2016	245.5	70.3	61.4	87.3

Sources: 1988–1998, *Statistical Abstract of the United States 1999*; 2000–2016, www.census.gov.

impact of easier registration laws on voting turnout (see Highton 2004; Knack 1995).

The debate on voter registration laws continues today. On the one hand, the issue poses a normative question about public policy: Shouldn't a democracy encourage its citizens to vote? Shouldn't all restrictions on voting be eliminated? On the other hand, the question is a pragmatic one: Is there evidence that restrictive voter registration laws significantly decrease participation? Do those whose names are added to the rolls by eased registration requirements necessarily turn out to vote? (See Bennett 1990; Bennett and Resnick 1991; Cassel and Luskin 1988; Gans 1990; Hill 2006; Jackman 1987; McDonald and Popkin 2001; Piven and Cloward 1988, 1989, 1990, 2000; Powell 1986; Rosenstone and Wolfinger 1978; Squire, Wolfinger, and Glass 1987; Teixeira 1987; Wolfinger and Hoffman 2001; Wolfinger and Rosenstone 1980).[1]

But the issue is also a political one. Surely Republicans and Democrats did not split on the motor vehicle registration bill because of differing views on the questions raised here, nor because of the cost, nor because of states' rights—though each of these arguments was made. The crucial question was the political one: If people were encouraged to register and they turned out to vote, for whom would they cast their ballots? Democrats and Republicans alike believed that more of these newly registered voters would vote Democratic; thus, each party dug in its heels and fought hard for its position on this seemingly innocuous change in electoral law. In January 2014 the Presidential Commission on Election

Administration issued a lengthy report calling for a number of reforms that it claimed would make it significantly easier for Americans to register and vote efficiently and accurately (Persily et al. 2014). Vigorous conflict is still ongoing in many states on voting issues such as being required to show photo ID to vote, early voting, absentee voting, voter registration requirements, and purging of voter lists, among others (Brennan Center 2017). The parties fight over these issues so heatedly because they believe the rules that determine voter eligibility affect election outcomes. They are correct in such a belief.

One final matter that must be noted here is state policies regarding voting rights for convicted felons. According to the National Conference of State Legislatures (NCSL), two states always allow felons to vote, even when they are incarcerated (Maine and Vermont), four states permanently bar felons from voting (Florida,[2] Iowa, Kentucky, and Virginia), and the other forty-four states and the District of Columbia have varying policies in place, although this latter group all allow felons to get the franchise back at some point.[3] According to the criminal justice reform group The Sentencing Project, laws related to felons and voting prohibit 6.1 million Americans from casting ballots, including one out of every thirteen African Americans.[4] There is no doubt that this can affect election outcomes. In March 2015 Maryland senator Benjamin Cardin and Michigan representative John Conyers Jr. introduced a bill titled "The Democracy Restoration Act," which they claim if enacted into law would re-enfranchise 4.4 million felons (federal voting only) who have been released from prison.[5] So far this bill has been unable to advance beyond the committee stage. Cardin submitted the bill again in the 115th Congress, and it was referred to the Senate Judiciary Committee, where it currently sits.

Decline in Voter Participation

Figure 3.1 shows the historical pattern of low voter turnout in the United States. Turnout declined for more than three decades before showing slight increases in the most recent elections.

Neither the decline nor recent increases have been precipitous. The pattern of low turnout relative to other nations has been persistent. States vary tremendously in their turnout rates. In the 2016 election, four states and the District of Columbia had turnout rates greater than two-thirds of the voting age population (led by Maine, at 71.3 percent); at the other extreme, four states had turnout rates less than 50 percent of the voting age population (with Hawaii the lowest at 43.3 percent).[6] If the United States has become "one big country," with state and regional differences blurred because of our mobile population and our reliance on a national media for setting so many standards, why do states vary to the degree that they do?

The rather simple reason is that the degree of nationalization has been overstated (Mellow 2008). The populations of the fifty states vary in all sorts of ways, some of which have implications for voting turnout. In addition, state election laws vary, and these too impact voting turnout rates.

Voting by Blacks

Figure 3.2 shows the impact of the registration and voter turnout efforts aimed at black voters, such as those led by the Reverend Jesse Jackson in the mid-1980s and renewed efforts in recent years. The gap in turnout between blacks and whites disappeared in the 2008 election, as black voters turned out to support Barack Obama, the first major party African American candidate. In 2012 black voter turnout rate nationally exceeded that of whites, marking a first in American history (Taylor and Lopez 2013). In 2016 white turnout exceeded black voter turnout by 2.3 percentage points.

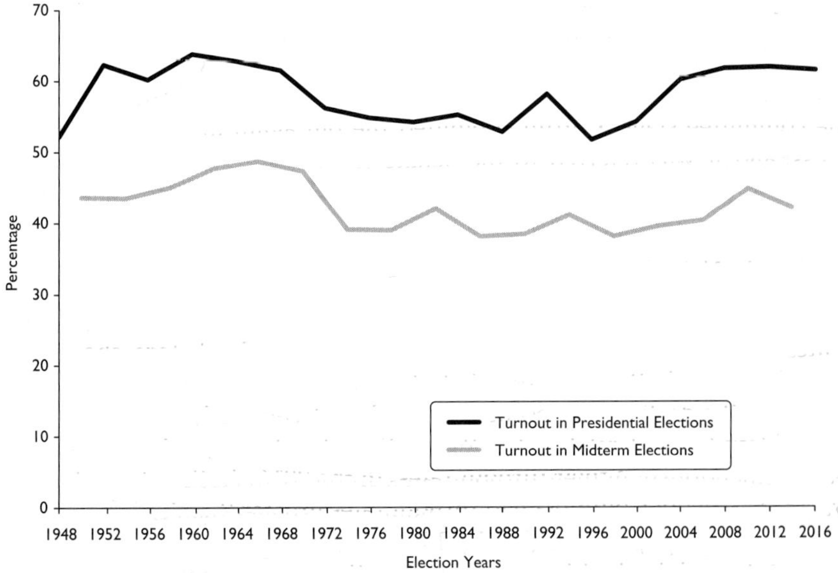

Figure 3.1. Turnout in Presidential and Midterm Elections, 1948–2016

Sources: Data for 1948–2008 provided by Michael McDonald, United States Election Project, George Mason University; Vital Statistics on Congress, 2008. Data for 2010–2016 obtained from the U.S. Census Bureau.

Hispanics are the fastest-growing group in the United States today; however, the Hispanic turnout is even lower than the black turnout, and the gap between Hispanic turnout and that of blacks and whites has not decreased significantly, even with the significant efforts taken by Democrats in the last three presidential election cycles. The barriers to effective Hispanic participation, including language and education level, remain serious obstacles; indeed, many Latinos living in the United States are not even eligible to vote, about as significant a barrier as one can get. But in certain geographic areas, Hispanic voters have become powerful forces (McClain and Stewart 2010). And even with their low turnout percentages, the raw total of Latinos voting continues to rise each election cycle as the number of Hispanic voters increases rapidly (Abrajano and Alvarez 2010; Lopez and Gonzalez-Barrera 2013). This development is almost certain to spread and gain additional strength. At present, Latinos tend to favor the Democrats over the Republicans, although not at levels as high as African Americans. Given that analysis by the Pew Research Center shows that Latinos will be 31 percent of the population by 2060, up from 17 percent today (Taylor 2013b), it is clear that both parties will have to carefully consider and address Hispanic voters going forward (Shear 2010).

Voting by Young Voters

For many years political scientists have known that the youngest voters vote in the smallest proportion (see Figure 3.3; Timpone 1998, 145–58; Miller and Shanks 1996; Wolfinger and Rosenstone 1980, 37; Converse and Niemi 1971; Campbell et al. 1960). Since the passage of the Twenty-Sixth Amendment, the young have constituted an increased portion of the total electorate; therefore, their unwillingness to vote contributes increasingly to the overall decline in voter turnout.

Political scientists disagree on the cause of this trend. Basing their findings on data from the late 1970s and early 1980s, some scholars have suggested that voters who came of political age in an era during which political activity was not an expected norm would not increase their participation rate with age, as had been the case in the past (Tarrance 1978, 12). The "negative" trend in overall voter participation, which was evident in the late 1970s, was attributed to a replacement of the age cohort that reached voting age before the New Deal, one with a consistently high turnout rate, with a cohort that first voted during the Vietnam War, a group discouraged by the politics of their time (Miller 1992; Teixeira 1987). The fear was that this younger cohort of voters would never increase in participation rates as had the generation before them.

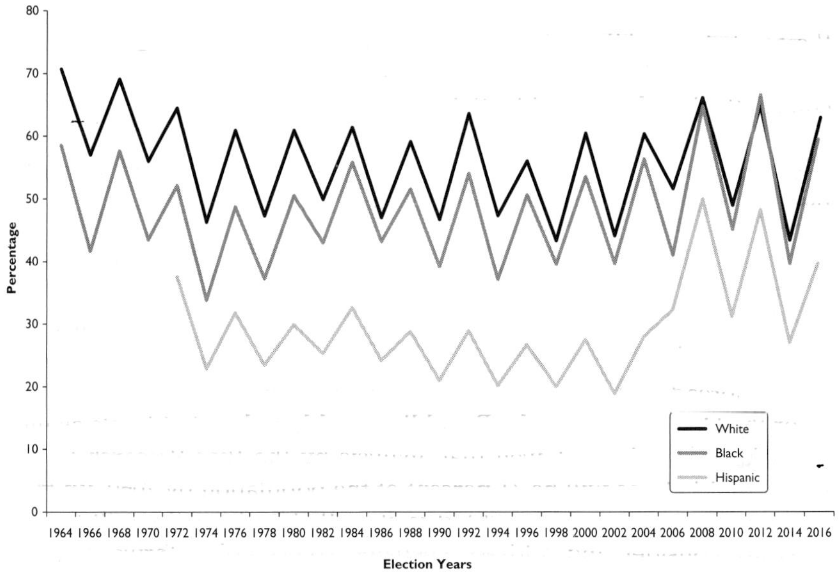

Figure 3.2. Voter Turnout by Race, 1964–2016
Source: United States Census Bureau.

However, the pattern of youthful voters participating in numbers much lower than their elders continued. As each cohort has aged, their participation rate has increased (Miller and Shanks 1996). With an increase in age expectancy and with older Americans constituting a larger share of the population as the baby boomer generation ages, the oldest segment of the population has become the most overrepresented. To the extent that they share opinions on the issues of the day, their views might well also be overrepresented by those whom they elect. In 2008 the turnout gap between young voters and older Americans narrowed (but was still considerable), as President Obama's 2008 campaign was particularly adept at attracting and mobilizing young people, as was that of Republican congressman Ron Paul during his run for the GOP presidential nomination in 2008. According to the U.S. Census Bureau, 44.3 percent of Americans eighteen to twenty-four years old voted in 2008. This figure was 38 percent in 2012 and 39.4 percent in 2016. In summary, it can be said that voting by the young continues to lag behind voting by older Americans, and nonvoters as a group tend to be significantly younger (as well as less affluent and less white) than voters (Doherty et al. 2014).

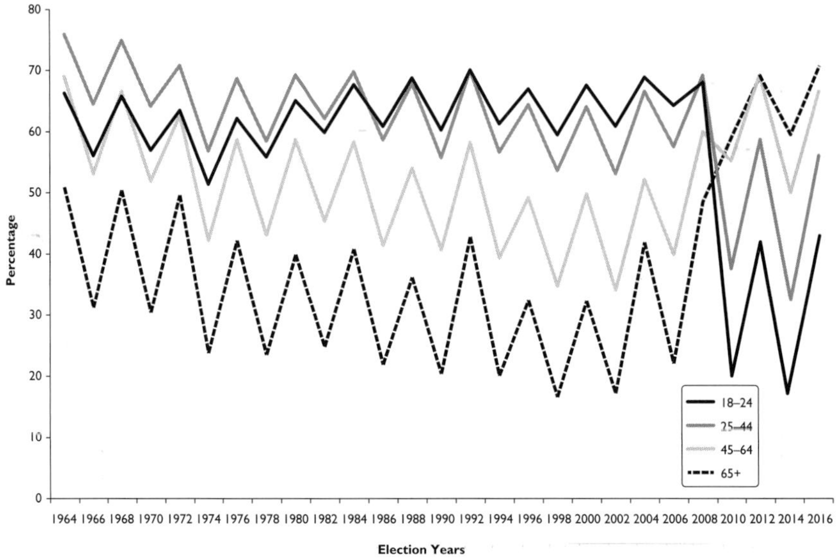

Figure 3.3. Voter Turnout by Age, 1964–2016
Source: United States Census Bureau.

Voting by Women

Turnout among women was quite low in the years immediately after enfranchisement; however, the number of female voters steadily increased until it leveled off by 1972, at a turnout level only slightly below that of men (see Figure 3.4).

The rejuvenation of women's political awareness, spurred by the women's movement in the 1970s, led to another increase in participation, and turnout rates of women voters have exceeded the rates for men in every national election since 1980. Because more women than men are eligible to vote, women now constitute a majority of the electorate. Women in the South participate in politics less than women in other regions because of regional cultural norms; therefore, it is clear that women in other regions now participate in significantly higher percentages than men in those areas (Pomper 1975, 88).

Politicians understand this phenomenon. In the 1996 election, political strategists explored how issue after issue would appeal to the so-called soccer moms, a subgroup never before seriously considered. In the post-9/11 world, women's concern for personal security—their own and that of their families—has led to directed appeals during campaigns. Similar

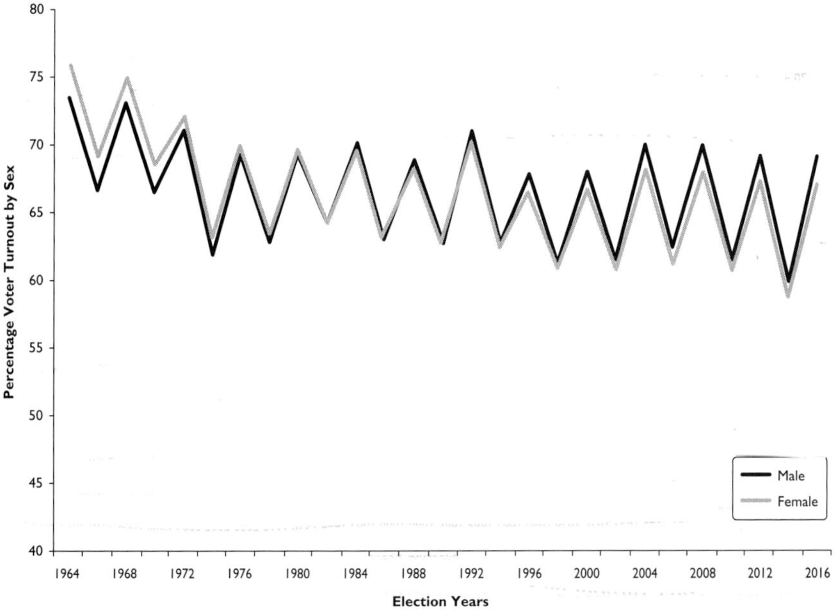

Figure 3.4. Voter Turnout by Sex, 1964–2016
Source: United States Census Bureau.

strategies will undoubtedly mark future campaign efforts. Nevertheless, we must go beyond mere demographic characteristics in distinguishing voters from nonvoters.

What Distinguishes Voters from Nonvoters?

For more than three decades, social scientists have been examining the American electorate in some depth. Despite a variety of research techniques, scholars have come to a remarkable consensus on what distinguishes voters from nonvoters. None of these conclusions is surprising, but some of the more important ones should be noted.

First, voting is a function of the "rules of the game." If it is easier to vote and if fewer roadblocks are put in the voter's way, more people vote. Thus, the expansion of the franchise, the easing of registration requirements, and the continued efforts to open the doors to black and Hispanic voters have increased the number of individuals voting (Campbell et al. 1960; Hill 2006; Milbrath and Goel 1977, chap. 5; Piven and Cloward 2000).

Again, state experiences demonstrate this point. One claim is that requiring citizens to go to a voting booth during set hours on election day decreases turnout and unfairly disadvantages some citizens. Proposals have been floated to have twenty-four-hour voting days and to make election day a national holiday (or to hold elections on Sundays, when fewer people are at work). These proposals have been rejected for a variety of reasons, including expense and legitimate questions of whether they would have the desired impact. However, state experiments have demonstrated that changing election procedures can increase turnout.

In Texas, since 1991, citizens have been permitted to cast ballots during a designated period before election day at sites in their communities or on election day. Votes are not tallied until the polls close on election day, but citizens are given many more options about when to cast their vote. Voter turnout has increased significantly (Robert Stein and Garcia-Monet 1997, 657–71). Other states have followed this model; in 2018, thirty-seven states plus the District of Columbia offered the opportunity for early voting; twenty-seven states (including most of those with early voting) plus the District of Columbia allow for absentee voting, with no reason necessary for requesting an absentee ballot (all states allow absentee voting in at least some instances).

In Oregon, state officials began experimenting with mail ballots for certain elections as early as 1987; the state now accepts mail ballots for all elections. Citizens can vote from their own home; they can review material carefully before they vote. Turnout has clearly increased. While this voting technique causes considerable difficulty for campaign strategists (see chapter 7), the goal of increased turnout has evidently been achieved (Southwell and Burchett 1997, 53–57). Colorado and Washington vote by mail as well, and both are relatively high-turnout states.

Second, social position distinguishes voters from nonvoters. "Citizens of higher social and economic status participate more in politics. This generalization . . . holds true whether one uses level of education, income, or occupation to measure social status" (Verba and Nie 1972, 125; see also Berelson, Lazarsfeld, and McPhee 1954; Campbell et al. 1960; Dahl 1961; Lane 1959; Milbrath and Goel 1977). Wolfinger and Rosenstone have refined this commonplace notion by isolating the effect of the various components of a voter's socioeconomic status. They conclude that "even after controlling for all other variables, education has a very powerful independent effect on the likelihood of voting" (Wolfinger and Rosenstone 1980, 24). Education has the greatest effect on those with low-income or low-status jobs, but it has a continuing effect at all levels, a finding attributed to the increased information made available to more educated voters, their ease of acquiring more information, and their decline in anxiety because of greater political knowledge (Wolfinger and Rosenstone 1980, 18–22).

Third, certain attitudes about politics distinguish voters from nonvoters. Those who have the strongest feelings toward one political party or the other are much more likely to vote than those without such intense partisan affiliation. We also know that people who are more interested in politics tend to vote more frequently than those who are less interested. Partisans tend to be more interested than nonpartisans and hence vote in higher percentages. Even in the 1992 and 1996 presidential elections, when third-party candidate Ross Perot attracted attention with his rhetoric decrying major party politicians, self-proclaimed independents voted at a lower rate than Republicans or Democrats.

We also know that certain elections, such as those with compelling candidates (e.g., Obama versus McCain in 2008) or those in which the outcome is in doubt (e.g., 2000), stimulate increased turnout; others seem to depress turnout—for example, the seemingly predetermined presidential election of 1996, between a flawed President Clinton and a boring challenger Bob Dole (Berelson, Lazarfeld, and McPhee 1954; Campbell et al. 1960; Hill and Luttbeg 1980, chap. 3; Milbrath and Goel 1977, chap. 3; Verba and Nie 1972).

So far the discussion has focused on turnout in presidential elections. As noted in Table 1.1 (p. 5), Americans are asked to go to the polls frequently. Turnout is much lower for elections that do not include a presidential race. Congressional elections are held every two years, whereas presidential elections take place every four years; thus, half of the congressional elections take place in off-presidential years (e.g., 2018). Turnout in these years is typically under 40 percent and has always been lower than that in adjacent presidential election years.[7]

Voters are also distinguished from nonvoters by the number of political stimuli to which they are exposed. We would expect those most interested in politics to receive the most political communication and, in fact, to seek out such contacts. Similarly, those less interested would doubtless not go out of their way to look for political information. Those expectations are supported by empirical evidence.

Yet we do not always control the information we receive, and campaign managers know that those who receive more information vote more frequently. Therefore, one of their goals is to bombard citizens with political messages, trying to penetrate the defenses of those who seek to avoid politics. Why? The more people are reminded about politics, the more they are reminded of their civic duty to vote and the more they feel guilty about not voting. Thus, one clear campaign strategy is to work hard to stimulate the participation of those most likely to support one's cause. If people are not interested in politics, the office seeker must stimulate that interest among his or her likely supporters, must appeal to their sense of civic duty, and must turn nonvoters into voters (Almond and Verba 1965;

Berelson, Lazarsfeld, and McPhee 1954; Campbell et al. 1960; Lazarsfeld, Berelson, and Gaudet 1944; Milbrath and Goel 1977, chap. 2).

Finally, in a number of different ways, scholars have demonstrated that those who are more knowledgeable about politics, more ideological, or more concerned about one particular issue participate in greater numbers than those who are less knowledgeable, ideological, or issue-committed. Certainly, many of these factors are interrelated, but the clear implication of these data is that frequent voters are becoming more knowledgeable and are distinguishing themselves more from nonvoters who are less informed (Gant and Luttbeg, 1991, chap. 2; Hill 2006).

VOTERS IN PRESIDENTIAL ELECTIONS

We turn now from the question of "Who votes?" to the questions of "For whom do they vote?" and "Why?" How many times have you heard someone say, "I am not a Republican or a Democrat; I vote for the person." What exactly does that mean?

When you ask friends about their choice for a certain office—say, whether they supported Barack Obama or Mitt Romney in 2012 or how they decide to vote for any particular candidate—how do they normally respond? Do they begin elaborate discussions of different candidates' stands on different issues? Do they talk of one issue that is most important to them? Do they talk about party only? Or do they talk about a candidate's personal characteristics?

The individual voter is, after all, the basic building block of the political world. We really want to know how each individual votes, but we cannot know this factor for every one of the millions of people who vote, and so we often group individuals together and look at their voting patterns. We begin with a brief examination of works that have laid the groundwork for current scholarship on voting behavior.

Models of Voting Behavior: *The American Voter*

Few books have dominated an area of study in the way that *The American Voter* (Campbell et al. 1960) has influenced the study of electoral behavior, for a period of five decades. Angus Campbell, Philip Converse, Warren Miller, and Donald Stokes, the authors of this classic study, were not the first to study voting behavior in depth. They owed and acknowledged a debt to earlier students of voting behavior in local communities, particularly to Bernard Berelson, Paul Lazarsfeld, and their associates at Columbia University (Berelson, Lazarsfeld, and McPhee 1954; Lazarsfeld, Berelson, and Gaudet 1944), who had earlier hypothesized that social characteristics determine political preference. What they focused on was two questions that had held the attention of a good segment of the research community: First, who decides to vote, and who opts not to participate in this way? Second, once a citizen has decided that he or she will vote, how does that citizen decide for whom to cast a ballot?

The authors of *The American Voter* and their colleagues at the University of Michigan Survey Research Center refined the national survey as a research instrument for social scientists, and they presented their findings in such a clear and coherent way that their work essentially became the model against which all others compared their results. All students of electoral behavior need to be aware of the book's conclusions.

Oversimplification in presenting the findings of *The American Voter* risks masking the sophistication and richness of the analysis. Campbell and his associates were engaged in a study of the psychological and sociological determinants of voting behavior. They looked to the end of what they called a funnel of causality: At the narrow end of the funnel was the variable they sought to understand, an individual's vote (Figure 3.5). Leading into the funnel were factors that caused an individual to either vote or not vote and, with respect to an individual who voted, factors that caused the individual to vote for a certain candidate; these factors—for example, socioeconomic status, parents' partisan leanings—were deemed to be the determinants of voting behavior. But there were intermediate steps along the way. The authors of *The American Voter* studied, first, how

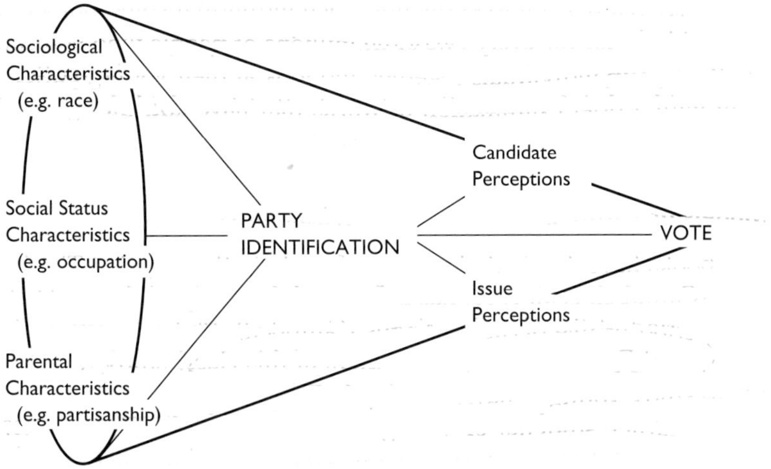

Figure 3.5. Funnel of Causality
Source: Authors, derived from *The American Voter*.

voters perceived parties, candidates, and issues; and, second, why they perceived them as they did.

Their first conclusion was that voter perception is a mixture of cognition and evaluation, of perception and affect. How the voter perceives politics is a mixture of what that voter chooses to know and how that voter feels about a political situation. The average voter is concerned about politics, but not all *that* concerned. While the average American does vote, he or she does not think about politics a great deal, does not become involved in many other political acts, and does not spend a good deal of time keeping informed about politics.

A number of conclusions follow from this finding. First, the average American has an extremely unsophisticated view of politics. Campbell and his associates note the inability of the voter to view politics in abstract terms, to develop a coherent **ideology**, a set of beliefs that structure one's thinking about politics. Rather than make judgments based on a sophisticated view of the issues, voters view candidates as representatives of the two major parties; the parties in turn are viewed as feeling certain ways on issues and toward certain groups in society. Whether these views are accurate, the voters use their perceptions in making decisions by fitting or ordering their view of politics to the outlines of the perceptions. Because most people do not care much about politics, it is fairly easy to manipulate their views.

According to *The American Voter* model, most Americans have developed a strong, long-term commitment to one or the other of the major political parties, and this commitment is a most significant guide to voting behavior. How is this tie to a political party developed? Campbell and his associates conclude that the individual's home is the most important source of partisan affiliation. The two most influential factors seem to be the parents' partisanship and their level of political activity. If both parents are strongly involved with one party, the children are likely to follow the same course. If the parents' **party identification**—the party one sees oneself as belonging to—is not the same or if the commitment of the respondent's parents to politics is not strong, then the likelihood of the children affiliating with one of the parties declines commensurably.

Other elements also influence the choice of party, particularly when parental pressure is not strong. Among these influences are other important **socializing elements of American society**—the school, the work group, the church. These socializing elements are institutions that teach those in them their norms, expectations, values, ideas, and so on. Once partisan affiliation is confirmed, it is quite difficult to change; however, factors such as marriage, increased education, changes in job, social status, and neighborhood can each have an impact. More significantly, cataclysmic events such as the Great Depression can affect the partisan political affiliation of entire generations.

Most important to remember is what this view says about the role that the voter plays in democratic theory. This is essentially a pessimistic view of the American electorate's ability to control its own destiny. Voters are not capable of making decisions based on a rational consideration of issues. To cast "issue-oriented" votes, the citizen must have an opinion on an issue (or "cognize" the issue, as per *The American Voter*), must have knowledge of current governmental policy on the issue, must have some information about the competing party's position on the question, and then must feel strongly enough to vote according to the perceived differences between the parties on that issue.

According to Campbell and associates, voters meet none of these criteria. Rather, partisanship is determined by socializing instruments in society. Voters follow partisan cues for voting. When they stray from these partisan predilections, it is not because of opinions on issues but because of appeals based on the personality or media image of the particular candidate or because of a particularly compelling short-range issue—such as a scandal or the appeal of a demagogue.

The American Voter also concludes that **independents**, those who do not identify with a political party, tend to be those least involved in politics, least interested, and least committed. Independents are the voters most likely to be swayed by emotional appeals, by charismatic candidates. Given that the Democrats' lead in voter allegiance constituted less than a majority in the 1950s, at the time this study was done, these least attractive voters—in terms of a democratic model—are often the ones who determine election results.

Not a very optimistic picture. Remember, this summary is an exaggeration of what Campbell and his associates actually wrote. After analyzing the American electorate in great depth, they did not set out to paint such a bleak picture. Rather, they seemed to predicate standards for performance that the electorate, taken as a whole, was unable to meet. Campbell and his coauthors asked for an electorate that was able to order complex political issues, one that was able to make voting decisions based on comparative stands on particular issues, and one that demonstrated qualities such that elections were in fact viewable as **mandates**—direction from or approval by the electorate for a party's or candidate's policy proposals.

They found instead an uninvolved, unconcerned, unsophisticated electorate, voters making decisions based largely on partisan affiliations, which in turn were handed down from generation to generation. This partisanship was, in the first place, often based on issues that were perhaps no longer relevant, an oversimplification that led citizens to view American political dialogue in often unrealistic ways. The element of this electorate that usually held the balance of power between the two parties was the group that met the tests of "good" citizens least well; that was most responsive to emotional appeals; and that was least well informed, least concerned, and least involved.

Critics of the *American Voter* Model

Any review of the voting behavior literature will demonstrate that even basic understandings of significant aspects of American political behavior can and do change over time. The fact that "revealed wisdom" of political analysis is overhauled is not a negative comment on those who have explicated the original model; rather, it is a testament to the progressive way in which we learn, drawing on and going further than those who preceded us.

The views presented in *The American Voter* were not accepted without controversy. Two schools of criticism stand out. V. O. Key Jr. and others maintained that Campbell and his associates placed too heavy a burden on the American electorate and that the view presented was far more negative than the actual situation warranted. The second group claimed that the heavy reliance on data from the 1950s led the authors to draw certain conclusions about the electorate that would not hold true over longer periods of time, even when applying the same theories to data gathered in the same manner.

Criticism by V. O. Key Jr. and His Followers

V. O. Key Jr. was a passionate believer in American democracy. While not refuting the data presented by Campbell and his associates, Key insisted that an expert could reinterpret those data and still arrive at the conclusion that the American electorate was responsible and trustworthy. Key's slim volume *The Responsible Electorate,* published posthumously with the assistance of Milton Cummings, is dedicated to the theme that the "voters are not fools" (Key 1966, 7).

Rather than divide the population by partisan affiliation, awareness of issues, concern over politics, and ability to conceptualize ideology, Key used survey data to categorize citizens according to how they voted in sets of elections. Looking at presidential elections, Key characterized those who vote for the same political party in two consecutive elections as "standpatters"; those who voted for one party in one election and the other party in the subsequent election as "switchers"; and those who voted in one election after not having voted in the preceding one as "in-and-outers," or "new voters" (see Table 3.3).

Key then examined the behavior of voters in each of these categories, trying to determine if their behavior could be understood as rational.

Most of the voters in any election are standpatters, those who vote the same way in consecutive elections. However, these voters are rarely numerous enough to determine a winner. The next largest group is the new voters. These voters tend to side heavily with the winner. In the time Key studied, switchers constituted between 13 and 20 percent of the electorate.

Key's findings about the relative positions of the two parties was important, particularly given the conclusion offered in *The American Voter* about party affiliation and its determining effect on vote. Key discovered some shifting between elections, even though most voters maintain stable party allegiance. Although the maintenance of the relative strength of the two parties between elections implied that a static situation existed, the supposed immobility was in fact the net result of a dynamic flow, "a complex process of interaction between government and populace in which old friends are sustained, old enemies are converted into new friends, old friends become even bitter opponents, and new voters are attracted to the cause" (Key 1966, 30).

Key further maintained that membership in certain cultural, economic, and social groups was an important factor in deciding how an American voted, as Campbell and his associates had maintained, but not in an irrational or predetermined way. Group pressure or group membership becomes important only for issues affecting that particular group. The fact that a voter is a member of a racial group or a religious group only affects that person's vote if and when that person believes that his or her racial or religious affiliation has an impact on how one distinguishes among candidates. This kind of analysis is significant in viewing the high percentage of blacks who vote Democratic or the Catholic voters' switch to Kennedy in 1960.

Perhaps Key's preeminent conclusion was that the most admirable, most rational voters were the switchers. He maintained that individuals switch based on their perception of the government's treatment of them in the intervening period between elections. If they are happy with what

Table 3.3. How V. O. Key Would Have Characterized Voters after the 2016 Election (major party supporters only)

		2016 Presidential Vote		
		Clinton	*Trump*	*Did Not Vote*
2012 Presidential Vote	*Obama*	standpatter	switcher	new voter/in-and-outer
	Romney	switcher	standpatter	new voter/in-and-outer
	Did Not Vote	in-and-outer	in-and-outer	

Source: Authors, derived from *The Responsible Electorate* (Key 1966).

the incumbent has done, regardless of whether they voted against him in the past, they will support him in the next election. In a parallel way, supporters of an incumbent in one election will turn against him—and, more important, against a subsequent nominee of his party—if they are unhappy with the effects of policies adopted during the intervening four years.

Similarly, Key maintained that standpatters are rational voters. Those voters who support the same party in consecutive elections do so either because they like what their party's winner has done or because they dislike what their party's competition has done. "Like" and "dislike" in this context are defined according to how those policies affect the individual in the areas that are of most concern to him or her.

Key's view of those who voted in an election after having not voted in the preceding election was not so sanguine. He viewed the two subcategories of this category of voters—first-time voters and "in-and-outers" (those who vote in one election but not in the next)—as distinct. First-time voters tend to go along with the tide. Nonregular voters are similar to the independents described in *The American Voter*: uninformed, unconcerned, and uninvolved. This group that tends toward trendiness is not the group that ultimately determines the winner in elections. Key maintained that the switchers play this role in American politics.

Two other conclusions follow from Key's analysis. First, he explicitly rejected the cult of personality. One need not have been a charismatic figure like Franklin Roosevelt to convince the Republican voters of 1928 to vote Democratic in 1932. Voters switched because of how they felt about the policies of the Hoover administration.

The other conclusion that follows from Key's analysis has served to structure much of the debate over voting behavior in the last four decades. Key (1966, xii) maintains that voters respond to the past, not to the future. He draws an explicit distinction between **prospective (future) voting**—casting a vote based on what the voter thinks candidates are likely to do in the future—and **retrospective (past) voting**—casting a vote based on the voter's evaluation of how the candidate or her or his party has performed in the past.

Modern scholars are quick to criticize Key's methods, particularly his reliance on recall data (voters' remembering their past actions). However, few underestimate his instinctive knowledge of politics and of the important questions to be examined. Key's influence persists more than five decades after his death.

The American Voter maintained that voters fail to vote prospectively because they are not sufficiently informed or concerned.

Key claimed that evaluation is the most important element in rational voting. Key's responsible voters evaluate what has happened in the past four years and make judgments. They are concerned with results only, not with policy promises. They do not give mandates; rather, they respond to results of past performance. In this understanding, to vote rationally, one does not need to understand issues thoroughly, recall where the party stands on those issues, and know precisely what the government has been doing. A rational voter only needs to know if "the shoe is pinching" and, if so, who is causing it to pinch. According to Key, this much easier test is also a perfectly appropriate test.

Scholars have expanded on Key's concept of retrospective voting. Drawing on the theoretical writing of Anthony Downs (1957), Morris Fiorina has developed a carefully crafted conceptual model of individual voting behavior (Fiorina 1977b, 1981; see also Franklin 1984; Franklin and Jackson 1983; Jackson 1975). Fiorina claims that the electorate makes rational choices. Citizens vote retrospectively because doing so is patently more manageable. Human beings simply find it easier to get information about what has gone on in the past than to evaluate what may happen in the future. Retrospective information, in fact, is acquired without effort. Furthermore, it is much more reliable than evaluative projections. Who, as a rational actor, believes politicians' promises?

For retrospective voting to be rational, voting citizens must see some tie between candidates and parties; they must understand that parties are consistent on the issues that most affect them. Thus, in this context, a vote for Barack Obama in 2008 was a rational vote if one believes that voters opposed George W. Bush's policies and linked Senator John McCain, the Republican candidate, with those policies.

An extension of this logic also holds that it is perfectly rational for a citizen to vote for a presidential candidate of one party and a congressional candidate of the other—if one does not want policy to move too far toward one party's view or if one was satisfied with the policies produced by divided government (Fiorina 1996).

Criticism from Successors in the Michigan School

The second line of criticism for *The American Voter* came from scholars at the Survey Research Center, who sought to explain changes they noticed in voter behavior while analyzing the series of National Election Studies (NES) subsequent to the ones on which *The American Voter* is based. Many articles published in the 1970s provided new interpretations of the American electorate's behavior (Brody and Page 1972; Miller 1978; Miller and Miller 1977; Miller et al. 1976), but it was left to another group of scholars, using NES data from the 1960s and 1970s, to question some of the basic findings of *The American Voter.*

In *The Changing American Voter*, Norman Nie, Sidney Verba, and John Petrocik explicitly acknowledged their debt to the authors of the earlier classic work by dedicating it to Campbell, Converse, Miller, and Stokes, "on whose coattails we ride." In calling the paradigm laid out in *The American Voter* into question, the authors of *The Changing American Voter* stated that such criticism "does not imply criticism of the paradigm makers" (1979, 8).

However, they most definitely did call the conclusions into question. The basic criticism was that the model constructed by the authors of *The American Voter* was based largely on the NES's 1956 survey and that the year 1956, a time of placidity in American politics, was hardly a baseline on which to construct a sound hypothesis. The task of *The Changing American Voter* was "to separate the time-bound from the timeless in political attitudes" (7). Which characteristics of voting behavior are indeed truly timeless? Which are time bound and therefore in need of reinterpretation? Attempting to answer these questions demonstrates how knowledge accrues.

The first of *The Changing American Voter*'s major findings was that the electorate it studied was much less committed to party than the electorate studied in *The American Voter*. Evidence was found in a rise in the number of independent voters, in a decline in strong partisans, in increased dissatisfaction with the two major parties, and in an increase in ticket splitting. Nie and his associates found that voters use two kinds of measures in presidential voting: first, the personal characteristics of the candidates; second—and this is the one emphasized—the issues.

Parties as institutions had weakened in the time since *The American Voter* was published. Following Walter Burnham (1970), the authors of *The Changing American Voter* argued that this weakness may well represent a long-term trend. Whatever the length of the trend, its significance was clear. Parties as organizations were feebler. Citizens might not oppose parties, but their commitment to parties was wavering; therefore, parties were less relevant to electoral behavior.

The authors of *The Changing American Voter* went further. They argued that the new independent voters fell into two groups. One group was the same as those Campbell and his associates identified nearly twenty years earlier; the other group, quite different. While the original group of independents constituted the least involved, least concerned, and least informed voters, Nie and colleagues found the new group to be well informed, concerned about politics, involved in every way, people who charge the two major parties with irrelevance but take politics seriously and choose a candidate based on their perception of the candidate's stand on issues (see also Miller and Wattenberg 1985; Wattenberg 1998). Thus, these authors claimed that the way in which Americans decided how to vote had changed because the times had changed. Issues had become more important in people's lives.

Which issues? The new and important issues of the day, a new set of issues that distinguish this time from the 1950s. War and peace in Vietnam, lifestyle, and race relations were important concerns for the American electorate of the late 1960s and early 1970s. Voters formed coherent political ideologies based on these issues; they could vote on issue preference.

Nie, Verba, and Petrocik claim that these issues have not led to a realignment because parties are so weak and inconsistent in policy that retrospective voting is impossible. The individual candidates are more independent of party; they run on the basis of their own characteristics and programs, not as representatives of continuing party institutions. Thus, electoral choice can no longer be retrospective. Voters are less able to vote on the basis of past performance because the candidate cannot be held responsible for what others in his party have done while in office—unless, of course, the incumbent is the candidate (Nie, Verba, and Petrocik 1979, 346–47).

How does one know that the elections of 1964, 1968, and 1972, those on which *The Changing American Voter* is based, are not as atypical in terms of their being elections determined by highly salient issues as 1956 was atypical in terms of being a low-saliency election?

According to Nie, Verba, and Petrocik, the election of 1964 was the one that best defined the parties in terms of issues. This election was perhaps the most ideological of the late twentieth century. Senator Barry Goldwater (Ariz.), the Republican candidate, was referred to as "Mr. Conservative" by friend and foe alike.

During the election of 1968, the nation was torn apart by the Vietnam War. Try as he might, Hubert Humphrey, the Democratic candidate, could not separate himself from Lyndon Johnson, whom he had served with utmost loyalty as vice president. Johnson was generally perceived to be the architect of our military involvement in Vietnam.

Finally, the election of 1972 was the one in which the Democrats chose an extremist candidate, perhaps more in appearance than reality but certainly in the perception of the voting public. Senator George McGovern (D-S.Dak.) was viewed as the candidate of "acid, amnesty, and abortion." That the McGovern election was tainted on the Republican side by Watergate and dirty tricks and that McGovern was not so far to the left as he was often depicted does not negate how easy it was for the public to see this election in ideological terms as well.

When the authors of *The Changing American Voter* enlarged their book to include the 1976 election, they began to see a trend that called some of their findings into question. They assumed that the 1976 election would be different, as it was an election that pitted two centrist candidates as opponents: Gerald Ford, the Republican incumbent who had succeeded to the presidency when Richard Nixon resigned amid the Watergate scandal; and former Georgia governor Jimmy Carter. But some of the differences turned out to deserve further analysis. This was particularly true of the voters' tendency to move away from voting without reference to a candidate's partisan affiliation and back to their previous allegiance, to candidates of one political party (see Table 3.4). Again, we are left asking which of the findings are timeless and which are time bound.

The controversy over how one decides if the American public votes prospectively or retrospectively, over how much issues matter, over what circumstances are important, and over whose interpretation of the same data is correct may well be a case of political scientists too involved with controversies over their research methods. At times it may be appropriate to reject the most sophisticated research methodology and go with one's instincts, to use the old Studs Terkel method—sit down in an Irish pub and ask people how they decided. If an analyst had done that for the 1980 election, the answer should have been clear: Ronald Reagan had his finger on the pulse of the people. He asked them to ask themselves a series of simple questions:

> Next Tuesday is election day. Next Tuesday all of you will go to the polls; you'll stand there in the polling place and make a decision. I think when you make that decision, it might be well if you would ask yourself, are you better off than you were 4 years ago? Is it easier for you to go and buy things in the stores than it was 4 years ago? Is there more or less unemployment in the country than there was 4 years ago? Is America as respected throughout the world as it was? Do we feel that our security is as safe, that we're as strong as we were 4 years ago? And if you answer all of those questions yes, why then I think your choice is very obvious as to who you'll vote for. If you don't agree, if you don't think that this course that we've been on for the last 4 years is what you would like to see us follow for the next 4, then I could suggest another choice that you have. (Carter 1982, 250–51)

Presidential Voting Reviewed

Where does this review leave the question of how Americans decide for whom to vote? Certainly the professional social science community is not of one mind. Parts of the model developed by Campbell, Converse, Miller, and Stokes have been rejected; other parts remain intact. Portions of the criticism of Nie, Verba, and Petrocik have been accepted; other portions might well need reexamination. The theory of retrospective voting, propounded by V. O. Key Jr. as a defense of the American electorate against the implied view of *The American Voter* and amplified by Morris Fiorina and others, has attracted some strong adherents.

Table 3.4. Party Identification, 1952–2016

Identification	*1952*	*1956*	*1960*	*1964*	*1968*	*1972*	*1976*	*1980*	*1984*	*1988*	*1992*	*1996*	*1998*	*2000*	*2002*	*2004*	*2008*	*2012*	*2016*
Democrat	47	44	45	52	45	41	40	41	37	35	36	37	37	34	33	32	34	35	34
Independent	23	23	23	23	30	34	37	34	34	36	38	35	36	40	36	39	39	38	32
Republican	28	29	30	25	25	23	23	23	27	28	25	27	26	24	30	28	25	27	29
Apolitical	3	4	2	1	1	1	1	2	2	2	1	1	2	1	1	0	0	0	0

Source: National Election Studies.
Note: "Democrat" combines those who identify themselves as strong or weak Democrats; "Independent" combines those who identify themselves as Independent Democrats, Independents, and Independent Republicans; and "Republican" combines those who identify themselves as strong or weak Republicans.

In a significant book, *The New American Voter*, Warren Miller and Merrill Shanks revisited the entire question of determinants in individual voting behavior (Miller and Shanks 1996; see also Miller 1991). While we cannot review the findings of this entire book, Miller and Shanks reaffirmed the importance of party identification in determining voters' choices. They claimed that the much discussed dealignment of the American electorate misrepresented the actual situation. According to the Miller and Shanks analysis, younger voters entering the electorate are not aligning with either party, but voters in older-age cohorts have maintained their party identification (certain caveats applying only to Southern white voters).

What was impressive about *The New American Voter* is the extent to which it drew scholars back to a reexamination of a fundamental set of questions: Who votes, and who does not? How do voters decide for whom they will vote?

The link between party identification and voting/rationality of voters has consumed political scientists' attention for decades. Human behavior is complex and difficult to comprehend. No clear consensus has emerged, as research questions abound (see Gant and Luttbeg 1991, 29–82; Niemi and Weisberg 1993, 2001). Among the most recent issues under examination are an ongoing debate over the role of cultural issues as opposed to economic issues in determining citizens' votes (Bartels 2008; Frank 2004; Gelman 2008; Layman 2001), the role of authoritarianism in electoral politics (Hetherington and Weiler 2009), the possible resurgence of regional divisions in partisan divides (Mellow 2008); and the question of whether American electoral politics is polarized (Abramowitz 2010; Brewer and Stonecash 2007; Fiorina, Abrams, and Pope 2011). The necessity of examining the context of each particular election is absolutely clear (see Miller and Wattenberg 1985). In the final analysis, it is important to supplement scientific examinations with common sense, with the knowledge of politics, and with a feel for people—not just numbers.

To this point, we have considered only presidential voting. Only the president and vice president run in elections that have a visibility approaching that discussed in the literature reviewed to this point. How do voters decide in cases different from those at the presidential level?

VOTERS IN CONGRESSIONAL, SENATORIAL, AND STATE AND LOCAL ELECTIONS

Almost all the research into American voting behavior has focused on presidential voting. In 1958, and again in 1978, studies were done of the electorate and how they voted in congressional and senatorial elections during a nonpresidential year. In other years, questions have been asked about congressional elections, but the total amount of research is much less than that on presidential elections.

The most often cited analyses of the data generated by the 1958 study of congressional voters describe an electorate not very concerned or knowledgeable about congressional politics (Miller and Stokes 1963; Stokes and Miller 1962). Nearly half the respondents replied that they had neither read nor heard anything about either candidate. For every one respondent who knew something about the challenger, more than two knew something about the incumbent, but few had any sense of how their representative stood on issues. With so little knowledge, voters relied heavily on party affiliation to determine their congressional choice. This view of electoral behavior is consistent with the *American Voter* model, only more so.

The 1978 study produced a wealth of literature on congressional elections that reevaluates the Stokes and Miller view (see Abramowitz 1981; Hinckley 1981; Jacobson 1980; Maisel and Cooper 1981; Mann and Wolfinger 1980). The most noticeable change is that most voters have an increased awareness of congressional candidates. Depending on the measure used, voters are able to express an opinion on over 90 percent of the incumbent candidates and on nearly half the challengers.

For some years, scholars had noted that an extremely high percentage of congressional leaders who were seeking reelection were in fact reelected (see, e.g., Fiorina 1978; Mayhew 1974a, 1974b). The 1978 data afford scholars the opportunity to explore the reasons for this phenomenon. What they find is that partisanship has been replaced by incumbency as the key voting cue. Further, voters support incumbents because they have more positive information about them, resulting in large part from the incumbents' skillful use of the resources available through their offices.

Some of the data are particularly striking. Nearly 90 percent of the respondents report having had some contact with their congressional representatives; almost a quarter had personally met their representatives; and almost three-quarters had received mail from their representative in Washington. These associations, all structured by the incumbent and virtually all positive in content, build a favorable image that is all but impossible to overcome. Typically, challengers are not known at all; voters do not choose between two candidates on equal footing but between one who is well known and positively viewed and another who has to fight to be viewed at all. These findings hold for the 2004 election—and even for the 2006 election in which control of the House switched hands but over 90 percent of the incumbents running for reelection did so successfully—as much as they did nearly three decades earlier. In 2016,

97 percent of House incumbents seeking reelection were returned to office by voters. (See Figure 3.6.)

Just as scholars are interested in incumbent advantages in House elections, they are also interested in why incumbent U.S. senators are frequently defeated. The data from 1978, again data that has not changed greatly in the ensuing years, show that senatorial incumbents do not have the advantages over their challengers that House incumbents have. Senatorial challengers are well known, and they contact voters frequently. Incumbents also cannot "control" all their contacts with constituents as well as members of the House can. Senators are more frequently covered by the news media in situations they cannot control; in most states, their jobs make them more prominent politicians. Most senators cannot build the personal relationships with constituents that representatives in the House can because of the size of their constituency. That combination—

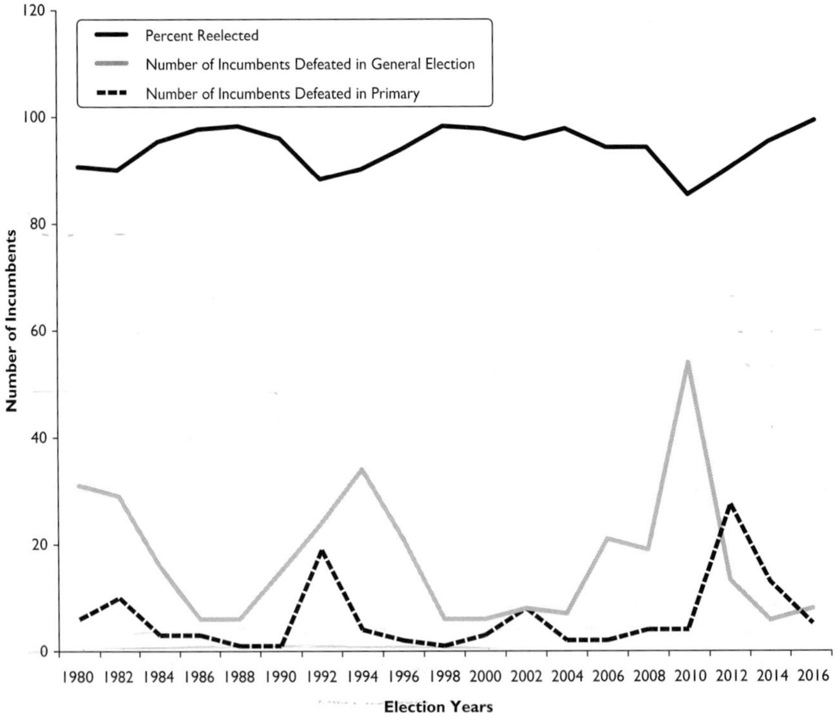

Figure 3.6. Electoral Success of Incumbent Representatives, 1980–2016

Sources: 1980–2012, 2016, Vital Statistics on Congress, 2017; 2014, compiled by authors using CNN.com and Roll Call.

the "balanced" image building, the challengers with better name recognition, and the challengers' ability to spend money to become even more widely known—has significantly reduced the advantage of the incumbent in Senate races. The variation in the number of incumbents winning reelection demonstrates that other factors are clearly at work in these elections (see Figure 3.7). But even with all of this being said, 2016 saw 93 percent of those senators seeking reelection win their contests.

Some of you reading this analysis of how citizens vote in congressional and senatorial elections might well be asking: How can this analysis explain the elections of 1994, when the Republicans took over Congress on the back of the influential Contract with America document, 2006, when the Democrats regained control by running against the war in Iraq, and 2010, when the Republicans regained control of the House after running a national campaign? The short answer to that question is that the theories of voting behavior still hold.

Those elections were not "normal" elections. In each case the party out of power, in both the Congress and the White House, took advantage of

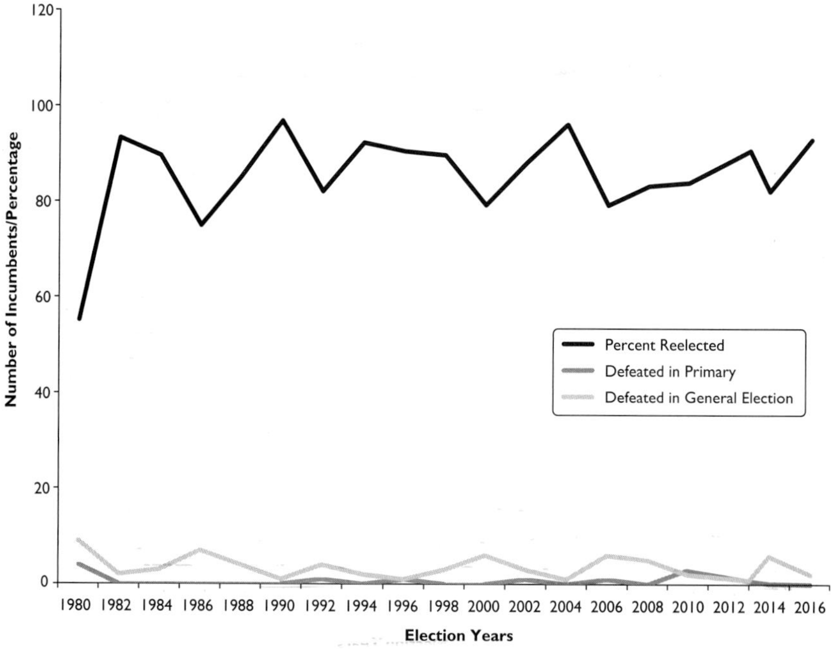

Figure 3.7. Electoral Success of Incumbent Senators, 1980–2016

Sources: 1980–2012, 2016, Vital Statistics on Congress, 2017; 2014, compiled by authors using CNN.com and Roll Call.

widespread public dissatisfaction and blamed the "ins." Normal election momentum turned into what analysts described as an electoral tsunami, with all close elections going to the Republicans in 1994, Democrats in 2006, and many—though not all—to the Republicans in 2010. Virtually all open seats—and there were many, particularly in 1994 and 2010, when a number of Democrats retired rather than face tough campaigns—went to the out party. The incumbent return rates were lower than those for most recent elections; but they only seem low because of the extraordinarily high rates in the other years. As we complete this edition in early 2018 there is much discussion about whether or not the 2018 congressional elections will fit this model.

Finally, the cases of 2006 and 2008 essentially prove the rule. In essence these were competitive elections only in the districts that were closely contested, about 15 percent of all House seats. In the others, the normal pattern was evident. In the few highly competitive seats, voters focused on the national issues of the day; most voters in the other districts voted for the incumbent knowing little of the challenger. In 2010, however, the Republicans were able to expand the number of competitive districts significantly, to more than a hundred; and thus they were able to nationalize the entire election. This election cycle too represented an aberration, as multiple ratings services found about only 15 percent of House races to be even somewhat competitive in the last three congressional cycles.

What of electoral behavior in elections for statewide offices or local offices? Until recently, political scientists have not produced systematic studies of elections at these levels (see Cox and Morgenstern 1993, 1995; Garand 1991; Gierzynski and Breaux 1991; Jewell and Breaux 1991; Weber, Tucker, and Brace 1991). However, some conclusions are inescapable. Races for governor, for instance, feature voting behavior parallel to that seen in races for senator. Governors are well known, but so are their opponents. Their accomplishments in office are examined in detail in the press. Gubernatorial opponents spend a good deal of money portraying the negative parts of incumbents' records. Voters decide based on these appeals—on party, image, and record. Figure 3.8 shows the electoral success of incumbent governors seeking reelection in the last three decades.

State legislators and others running in smaller constituencies face an electoral environment similar to that faced by members of Congress, with one notable exception—districts in many states are small enough that a significant percentage of the voters know their legislator on a personal basis. When this is the case, particularly in the smaller states, partisanship and issues become less important; however, when the personal relationship does not exist, partisanship and name familiarity again dominate (Garand 1991; Weber, Tucker, and Brace 1991).

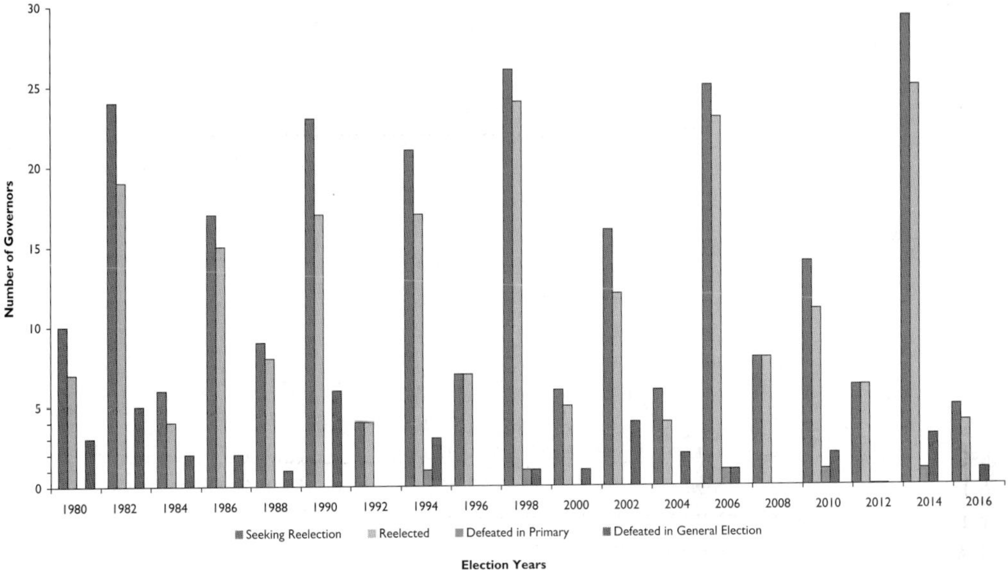

Figure 3.8. Electoral Success of Incumbent Governors, 1980–2016

Note: One of the incumbent governors seeking and obtaining reelection in 2012 was facing a recall—Wisconsin's Scott Walker.

Sources: 1980–2010, CQ Sources; 2012–2014, *New York Times*; 2016, Vital Statistics on Congress, 2017.

VOTING BEHAVIOR THEORY REVISITED

The picture that emerges of the American electorate is not a clear one. As Table 3.4 shows, a bare majority of Americans identify with one major party or the other; movement toward more independents and fewer party identifiers, particularly fewer with strong party identification, is evident. Questions have arisen about the strength of party allegiance and about the significance of that strength (see Converse and Pierce 1992 for a discussion of means of measuring partisanship; Miller 1998; Mattei and Niemi 1991; Finkel and Scarrow 1985).

The research community has been watching elections for signs of a new partisan realignment for decades. After the 1988 presidential election, Warren Miller (1990, 110–15) described a two-stage realignment:

> My analysis of the 1988 elections thus supports the thesis that a significant first phase of the 1980–1988 realignment occurred between 1980 and 1984 among the less experienced and less sophisticated voters who responded to Reagan's personal leadership with an increase in Republicanism. A smaller

> but perhaps more meaningful second phase then occurred between 1984 and 1988, particularly among the older and better-educated voters who ultimately responded favorably to the Reagan administration's emphasis on conservatism. (Miller 1990, 114; see also Miller 1991; Shanks and Miller 1989, 1990)

But those conclusions did not go unchallenged. In the 1990s, scholars had continued to debate such topics as the extent to which the most recent realignment was regional, rather than national, in scope (Black and Black 1987); the question of whether voters' identification with party is different at the national and state levels (Hadley 1985; Niemi, Wright, and Powell 1987); the group composition of the two parties and its significance (Stanley, Bianco, and Niemi 1986; Stanley and Niemi 2010); and the extent to which dealignment is merely a reflection of "unrealized partisanship" (Carmines, McIver, and Stimson 1987) or the degree to which the apparent dealignment is in fact a reflection of the nonalignment of the newest voters (Miller and Shanks 1996). In the early part of the twenty-first century, political scientists are once again reexamining seemingly basic questions regarding parties and elections in the attempt to make sense of the contemporary electoral environment (e.g., Abramowitz 2013, 2010; Brewer and Stonecash 2015; Fiorina, Abrams, and Pope 2011; Noel 2013; Shafer and Spady 2014).

Two concerns drive this research: how citizens make voting decisions and what is happening to the American electorate as a whole. How one views the role of *party* in the electoral decisions reached by voters in the modern context depends on what theory one espouses. Parties are still important to many; the Democrats' advantage in party identification over the Republicans has narrowed and, at times, even disappeared. We also know that many people eschew party allegiance, identify with neither party, and vote based on other cues.

What else enters into that decision? As *The Changing American Voter* shows, when issues seem to play a crucial role in election races or when the parties clearly differentiate themselves on ideological grounds, issues and ideology can have a large impact on voting behavior.

However, voters are most concerned about their overall well-being and how politicians—in their role as government officials—have contributed to that well-being. Voting based on the evaluation of an incumbent's performance, rather than promises of future action, is the most common explanation of the Reagan and Bush victories in 1980, 1984, and 1988 (Pomper 1981, 97); the Clinton victories in 1992 and 1996 (Arterton 1993; Quirk and Dalager 1993; Elshtain and Beem 1997); the George W. Bush win in 2004 (Abramson, Aldrich, and Rohde 2005; Nelson 2005); the Obama wins in 2008 and 2012 (Balz and Johnson 2009; Nelson 2009), and even of congressional elections in 1994, 2006, 2010, 2014, and 2016.

One school of thought even claims that voters are casting rational, considered votes when they choose to support a presidential candidate of one party and a congressional or senatorial candidate of the other. These scholars say that voters want to hedge their bets. They might favor one candidate for president, but he or she might be a little too liberal than they really want; they will thus temper their vote by choosing a congressional candidate who is more conservative, to keep the president from going too far (Fiorina 1996; Jacobson 1996).

Given what we know about the level of information citizens have concerning their representatives in Washington or concerning the issues of the day, it is difficult to imagine citizens thinking in this way; but perhaps it is not too difficult to imagine them doing so intuitively. If they believe the government has gone too far in one direction or not far enough in another, they can cast their vote accordingly.

PARTICIPATION IN POLITICS IN AMERICA

Voting is the most prominent form of political participation, but it is far from the only form. Social science research into political participation has consistently emphasized voting, since it can be measured easily. Official returns show how many go to the polls; census data provide a demographic breakdown of the electorate; and survey research reveals something about the voters' opinions, attitudes, motivations, backgrounds, and affiliations.

Finding out about other activities involves carefully identifying them, grouping them, and analyzing them. Few are dichotomous variables. An individual either votes or not. But what about talking about politics? Or trying to tell others how to vote? If a woman casually tells her friend that she finds the improper sexual behavior of David Vitter (senator from Louisiana) offensive, is that discussing politics? How should we measure that activity against a long discussion of President Obama's Afghan war policy? Should an individual who gives $25 to a friend running for school board be grouped with an individual who gives $1,000 to ten congressional candidates, listing both as "those who contribute to campaigns"?

Finding out about political "passivists" is also difficult. Probably half the nonvoters in this country tell survey analysts that they vote. Who are they? Why do they lie about it? Why don't they vote? If it is not easy to ascertain what low voter turnout means for the American system, it is even more difficult to evaluate political behavior that is nonconventional or even illegal. How many individuals who have been involved in burning abortion clinics would discuss their reasons for doing so in response to a scholar's open-ended questions?

Thus, our knowledge about political participation is not as extensive as we would like, but we still do know a good deal. The most extensive research on this subject is found in an important study by Sidney Verba, Kay Lehman Schlozman, and Henry Brady (1995). What they studied was the political and voluntary activities of a large sample of American citizens. We can only highlight some of the findings of this monumental study.

Social and economic resources influence not only the ways in which citizens participate in voluntary political and other organizations but also the extent to which they participate. The views of those who are active in these types of organizations are not representative of the views of inactive minority group members, whether examined by race or ethnicity. Political activity is more skewed by demographic and socioeconomic factors than activity in either religious or community organizations. The implication of these conclusions—those who are socially and economically less privileged are not heard as well as those more privileged when they participate in voluntary groups (especially political voluntary groups)—is laid out in the book *Voice and Equality*.

Earlier studies found that it is possible to break the American electorate's political behavior down into certain modes of participation (Verba and Nie 1972; Milbrath and Goel 1977). Citizens were classified as *active*, or as *passive but supportive*, or as *inactive*. The active group includes those who are identified as party and campaign workers, those who are community activists, those who frequently contact officials about particular problems, and those who are involved in a communications network that discusses political matters (a group identified only by Milbrath).

Not many Americans fit into these groups, ranging from about 4 percent who contact officials about particular problems, to 20 percent who are community activists, to over 30 percent who engage in some form of campaign activity, such as contributing money, wearing a button, or putting a bumper sticker on their car. Although most of these "active" individuals also vote, voting is a separate style of participation.

By far the largest group consists of those identified as passive supporters—individuals who pay taxes, who rise and sing the national anthem at ball games, but whose active involvement in politics is limited to voting. Large numbers of Americans support the system, at least passively. More than three in five Americans claim to vote regularly, though that number exaggerates actual turnout.

The group of citizens defined as inactive, or apathetic, is the smallest group, constituting less than a quarter of the population. We know little about why they are not involved. While they are uninterested and uninformed, most are supportive of the system and patriotic enough to fly the flag on the Fourth of July. They cheer for American Olympic medalists, and they grieved for the victims in New York, Washington, and Pennsylvania on September 11, 2001. If these citizens maintain their love of country, even though they do not participate in politics, perhaps their apathy really does not hurt the political system.

This group can be compared with those unconventional activists labeled "protesters."[8] Milbrath and Goel (1977, 14–19) gather into this category those who would "protest vigorously if the government does something morally wrong (26 percent)," "refuse to obey laws (16 percent)," "attend protest meetings (6 percent)," "join a public street demonstration (3 percent)," and "riot if necessary (2 percent)." These findings should be viewed as tentative because they were derived from one city at a time of considerable urban unrest (1968), but they also reinforce the conclusion drawn here, because protesters, by and large, participate in all forms of political activity. They did not withdraw from politics and thus "[voted] with their feet." They were active in politics and saw protesting as an extension of their activity. We should note that this type of activity has played a critical role at key moments in the history of this country. What were our nation's founders, if not violent protestors against the British? The nonviolent protests of the civil rights movement led to the Civil Rights Act of 1964 and the Voting Rights Act of 1965. Student protesters were instrumental in changing the nation's policy in regard to the Vietnam War. The Tea Party movement and Black Lives Matter are two more recent examples of American political protest.

Although the number of citizens involved in protests of these types is typically small, especially compared with the number who vote, the impact of their actions has at times been far-reaching. Critics of the American political system say that our politics are ineffective because, to use an analogy from football, everything happens between the forty-yard lines. When people want to change a situation drastically, they have to act in a totally different way. These means are nontraditional and are not much discussed in books on elections and the electoral process. But shouldn't we be concerned about a system that often fails to address such important problems in a way that defuses these kinds of protests? Does the need to protest signal a failure in the electoral system?

Are there signs that the system is not working for a significant group of citizens today? The militia movements active in some states generally are composed of Americans who are extremely unhappy with the system, with the intrusion of government into their lives, with the loss of independence and individual freedom. Some have taken their protests to an extreme, arming themselves and resisting all forms of government intervention. Do you think that makes them so anathema that they should be ignored by the media and government officials? Might ignoring them play into their hands? How should our system treat those who hold extreme views and choose to participate in the most nontraditional ways? This question has confounded elected officials throughout our nation's first two centuries.

When rights clash, the government generally intervenes. Everyone agrees that those opposed to abortion have the right to protest. But what level of protesting at abortion clinics is permissible? Most would agree that marching outside a clinic is a permissible exercise of First Amendment free speech rights. What about blocking clinic entrances? Some might claim that preventing abortions is so important that restricting other people's freedom of access, requiring intervention by local police to open the doors, is a legitimate action. Others would disagree.

What about bombing an empty clinic? That would shut it down without hurting anyone.

What about bombing a clinic that is open? Some people might be hurt, but abortion protesters might find that price acceptable for ending abortion.

What about shooting a physician who performs abortions? Is that level of violence permissible? Most people would draw a line well short of this type of violence. But clearly others disagree, and it is important to understand that their actions, while not considered traditional political participation, are participation of an important kind that cannot be ignored.

Is it possible to draw a profile of political participation among Americans? First, most Americans only engage in voting, not in any other political activity. In any given election, 30 to 80 percent of the electorate does not vote, but these nonvoters do not make up a stable group. Most Americans describe themselves as regular voters.

Beyond voting, political participation falls way off. Only one in ten Americans either belongs to a political club or an organization or contributes money to political campaigns; only a slightly larger number ever wear a button or display a sticker; and only one in four tries to convince others to vote for specific candidates.

Other modes of behavior have been distinguished from those that some believe are in political decline (R. Putnam 2000). Nearly a third of all Americans are involved in community activities, and many more make certain they are involved in communicating about politics. A much smaller number contact public officials about their personal problems with the government, regardless of their level of participation. Furthermore, some evidence points to the thesis that a small group of people are actively involved in political life in an unconventional way—that is, they are people willing to protest (and even riot, if necessary) to accomplish their political ends. These protesters do not view their activity as illegitimate but as the ultimate expression of their patriotism.

Finally, a small but relevant number of Americans are inactive and apathetic. They rarely even vote; however, they remain patriotic citizens. It appears that they truly are unconcerned yet not turned against the system.

POLITICAL PARTICIPATION IN THE REAL WORLD

A county chairman, along with his friend, walked up the stairs and into the first meeting of the county committee after the state convention. The chairman had been something of a hero at that convention, defending a gay rights plank against an attack from the religious right. This meeting would be a mere formality; he would be reelected, discuss plans for the upcoming election year, and adjourn the meeting in time to catch the last few innings of the Red Sox game. As he opened the door into the meeting room packed with people, he turned to his friend and said, "We're in for a long evening."

"What do you mean? Who are these people?"

"I don't know, but they sure didn't get elected to the county committee to come to vote for me." The about-to-be-ex-county chairman had learned an important political lesson.

For practicing politicians, the most important part of citizen political participation is predictability. If only 50 percent turn out to vote, no one is bothered, as long as it is always more or less the same 50 percent. If a few people complain when an officeholder takes a controversial stand, she will not get upset—if that reaction was expected. But the unpredictable reaction—the large turnout, the new faces, the massive protests—doesn't just worry politicians. Unpredictable participation gives politicians nightmares.

The county chairman mentioned here lost because he took a stand that caused people who had never been concerned before to take an interest in party politics. When he saw a sea of unfamiliar faces, he knew only too well why they were there. His opponents took advantage of the meeting to get rid of an unacceptable "radical."

Voter turnout, particularly in primary elections, is difficult for politicians to predict accurately. Figure 3.9 shows the turnout in Iowa presidential caucuses from 1968 to 2016. In 2004, more than twice as many caucused as had in 2000; in 2008, it was nearly three times the highest previous total. In each case turnout was stimulated by candidates spending vast sums. In 2012 the turnout numbers were down, primarily due to the fact that Barack Obama did not face an opponent in the Democratic contest. Caucus participation rebounded strongly in 2016 as both parties

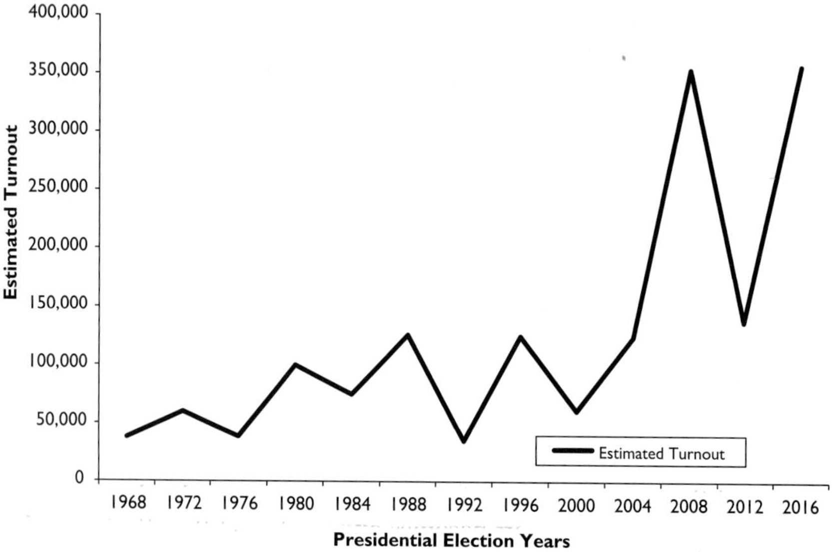

Figure 3.9. Turnout in Iowa Caucuses, 1968–2016

Sources: 1968–1996, Various CQ sources; 2000 and 2012, *Des Moines Register*; 2004, United States Election Project; 2008, compiled by authors using CNN.com; 2016, reported by Michael McDonald on *Huffington Post*.

had competitive races, and the Republicans had the celebrity power of Donald Trump.

In 2010 Tea Party supporters overwhelmed traditional Republicans in nominating contests in states across the nation. In Maine and Kentucky, in Nevada and Utah, no one predicted the extent of their influence. The system turned in ways few saw coming. In 2012 the so-called Republican establishment was much more effective in out-maneuvering the Tea Partiers. In 2016, even as the anti-establishment Donald Trump steamrolled to the GOP presidential nomination, the establishment held control in nonpresidential contests.

How then have practicing politicians viewed the changes in the electorate presented earlier in this chapter? First and foremost, they view it as unfamiliar terrain that they have to cross. When the electorate has expanded, politicians have dealt with that expansion, making appeals to new voters as they have seen fit. Those who have predicted accurately how the new voters would react have prospered, such as the Southern politicians who have softened their formerly racist rhetoric. Those who have guessed wrong have lost, often badly. Others learn for the next electoral round. For instance, today's politicians are faced with an expanding

Hispanic electorate, and they are faced with an electorate divided on social issues. How do they appeal to those voters?

It is evident to most politicians that an individualized sales approach is the most effective. As one member of Congress put it, "I love going door-to-door. When I talk to someone in their living room, and when they say they'll support me, *I know* I have their vote. No question about it."

But consider the problems of bringing one's campaigning to individual voters. According to the U.S. Census Bureau, the average congressional district has approximately 711,000 people. Maybe 450,000 of those are potential voters, who live in 200,000 households. If a candidate spent twenty minutes in each living room, assuming everyone was home and that no time was needed between stops, that candidate would have to have put in nearly 5,500 twelve-hour campaign days. Candidates accomplishing 1 percent of such a schedule in a two-year cycle feel that they have developed the common touch. Even with surrogates and volunteers, the enormity of "personal" effort becomes apparent, and the effort must be multiplied many times over for senatorial, gubernatorial, or presidential campaigns. Campaigning for individual votes might well work in local elections, but most politicians must use other means to approach the electorate.

Rather than see voters as individuals, politicians tend to see them as members of groups to whom appeals can be made. Once the decision has been made to group individuals, a number of options are open, some of which can complement one another; some others, however, seem to preclude possible strategies.

The religious right remains influential in Republican politics today (see Wilcox and Robinson 2011). This group of citizens, defined in various ways, agrees that certain moral principles they share should be important in political decision making (see chapter 4). Among the issues most important to this group are banning gay marriages, outlawing abortion, and permitting prayer in schools. In some areas of the country, those who believe that they are the most important issues on the political agenda constitute a majority of the Republican party, maybe even of the population. In other areas, however, if Republican candidates appeal directly to these voters, they might well be hindering their chances of winning over other voters for whom Republican stances on economic issues are more important. According to recent studies from the Pew Research Center, Republicans face similar difficult choices on issues related to women, immigration, and perhaps even legalization of marijuana.[9]

Each candidate must define his or her constituency by grouping the potential electorate in ways that are meaningful to his or her campaign. Some groupings preclude others; it is not possible to appeal to both the religious right and to activist women's groups. Other strategies are less limiting; a candidate can appeal to the elderly on social security or health care issues without ruling out ardent environmentalists.

But politicians can also look at their constituency as a whole and break it down into groups of people who are concerned with particular issues. Which groups seemed to favor President Bush in 2000 and 2004? In 2000 candidate Bush talked of being a "compassionate conservative" and someone with a strong moral sense. He sidestepped the issue of his conservatism and tied Vice President Gore to the questionable personal moral code of President Clinton. In 2004, Bush, as incumbent president, emphasized that he was a decisive leader, needed at a time of danger symbolized by the constant reference to a post-9/11 world. He appealed to those who wanted security and portrayed his opponent, a decorated war veteran, as wishy-washy and indecisive.

A second strategic approach groups voters by geographic region, not by interests or similar categorizations. Candidates for statewide office in Massachusetts look at how their campaign is doing in Boston—and then the rest of the state. In Colorado, at Denver and at those areas on the western slopes of the continental divide and at the arid plains on the eastern slopes; in California, at liberal Northern California versus conservative (yet changing) Southern California. In some congressional districts, the geographic distinctions are almost as pronounced. Connecticut's Fifth District is divided between poor mill towns and affluent bedroom suburbs of New York City. California's Forty-Fifth District includes not only Palm Springs and other wealthy suburbs of Los Angeles but also lush farmlands and nearly unirrigatable desert. Politicians are acutely aware of their geographic surroundings.

Note the distinction. In this case the politicians are appealing to those who live in a certain area because politicians assume—justifiably, it turns out (Bishop 2008)—that citizens relate to others in that area. This strategy is quite different from that appealing to groups based on shared issue concerns. But in a broader sense, the theory is the same. Electoral strategies do not normally involve appeals to individuals. Individuals vote, but candidates appeal to them in groups, groups defined by the candidates and their strategists according to their strengths and perceptions of what will work. The larger the constituency, the more this is the case.

Tip O'Neill (D-Mass., 1953–1987; Speaker of the House 1977–1987) has been quoted as saying, "All politics is local." Politicians still believe Tip, decades after his death. Many started out as local politicians, and they know the effectiveness of one-on-one campaigns. Their goal is to make national or statewide politics local by defining smaller groups into which voters fall and then seeking to appeal to these groups. Elections like the 2010 midterms in which national forces outweighed local efforts remain the exception, not the rule. Many techniques are available for candidate appeals—mass media directed at a certain audience, targeted mailings, the Internet, speeches to certain groups. But in the end, the political strategy is the same: make an appeal, in any way possible, to the largest number of people so that it will seem personal to each voter. Campaigners sell the product by figuring out what the voters want to buy.

Whereas political scientists seek to explain voting behavior with some degree of precision, politicians—with the souls of artists, not scientists—try to mold the electorate into the shape they want. The skills of both the scientist and the artist deserve attention.

CRITICAL THINKING QUESTIONS

1. Why is the right to vote so hotly contested?
2. Is there any reason why an American citizen should forfeit her or his right to vote?
3. Should voting in the United States be mandatory?
4. Is there a legitimate reason for a citizen to not vote?

KEY TERMS

franchise
poll tax
Twenty-Fourth Amendment
Fifteenth Amendment
Jim Crow laws
"whites only" primaries
residency requirements
Nineteenth Amendment
Twenty-Sixth Amendment
Motor Voter Bill
ideology
party identification
socializing elements of American society
independents
mandates
prospective (future) voting
retrospective (past) voting

NOTES

1. This debate also points to the cumulative way in which a discipline informs itself. A careful review of this literature reveals concern with normative questions, with pragmatic consequences of those normative questions, and with methodological controversies over how to answer important questions posed.

2. On November 6, 2018, Floridians will vote on a constitutional amendment that would restore voting rights to felons who have fully completed their sentences. This would affect 1.5 million Floridians (Brennan Center 2018; Lemongello 2018).

3. The four states that permanently bar felons from voting allow restoration of voting rights by gubernatorial action. National Conference of State Legislatures, http://www.ncsl.org/research/elections-and-campaigns/felon-voting-rights.aspx.

4. The Sentencing Project, https://www.sentencingproject.org/issues/felony-disenfranchisement/

5. Brennan Center for Justice at New York University Law School, http://www.brennancenter.org/legislation/democracy-restoration-act

6. All figures from the U.S. Census Bureau.

7. A few states still hold statewide elections in odd-numbered years that do not include either presidential or congressional elections. Many cities hold municipal elections in those years as well. Turnouts for them are typically lower than that for congressional elections—though highly salient state or local issues can stimulate larger turnout from time to time. Primary elections see the lowest turnouts of all. For example, although Maine typically comes close to leading the nation in turnout in presidential and off-year general elections, fewer than 12 percent of the electorate turned out to vote in the Maine primary elections in 1998.

8. Verba and Nie do not ask similar questions and thus do not identify this group.

9. See various 2015 Pew studies reported in their "Fact Tank" feature. http://www.pewresearch.org/fact-tank/

Chapter 4

Organized Groups in the Political Process

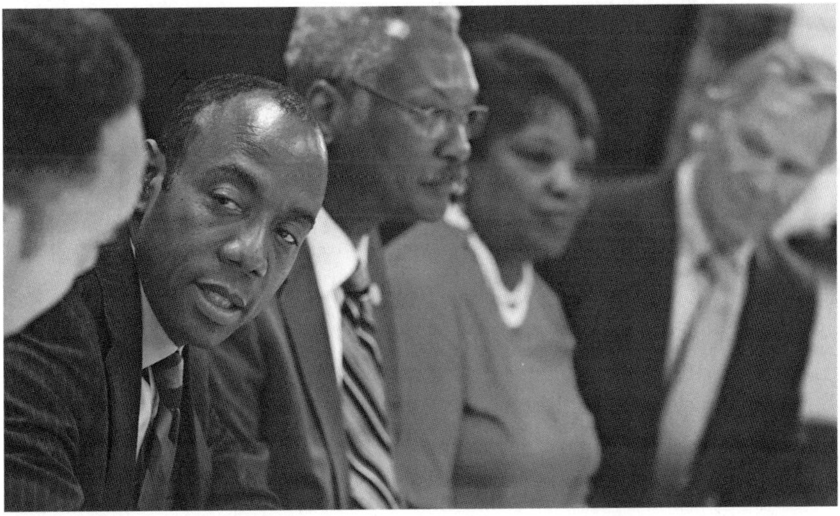

NAACP President Cornell Brooks, left, and other activists and officials speak in St. Paul, Minnesota, in the aftermath of Philando Castile being shot and killed by a law enforcement officer in a neighborhood outside of the Twin Cities. Organized groups, such as the NAACP, play critical roles in the American electoral process, providing information and voting cues to their members, campaign resources to political parties and candidates for public office, and extensive efforts aimed at getting out the vote on election day.

Think about yourself and the others in your class. In what ways are you the same as the others? In what ways are you different? Many, if not most, college campuses regularly have had discussions revolving around issues of diversity, inclusiveness, and tolerance. Is your class a diverse group or a homogeneous group? What are the relationship dynamics among the groups you see as present on your campus? What do those terms mean to you? How do you think these questions relate to politics?

Since 1964 the *American National Election Study* (ANES), now jointly administered by the University of Michigan and Stanford University, has routinely asked respondents to rate their feelings toward various groups using a "feeling thermometer" that runs from 0 to 100, with 0 representing negative feelings toward the group and 100 indicating a positive evaluation. The groups respondents are asked to rate include labor unions, feminists, civil rights leaders, people on welfare, women, conservatives, poor people, Catholics, big business, blacks, Christian fundamentalists, the federal government in Washington, liberals, the Tea Party, Black Lives Matter, illegal immigrants to name just a few. Obviously, the designers of this question believe that Americans respond to political messages by filtering those messages through reactions that they have as members of a group. But aren't there really different types of groups, as the partial list provided above would seem to indicate?

If you are a careful reader, you probably are troubled by the conceptual inconsistency in applying the concept "group." The groups cited in the ANES questions were different kinds of groups—social groups, ethnic groups, racial groups, ideological groups, occupational groups, political groups, and others. Not only are these groups not mutually exclusive (e.g., one could certainly be a black teacher who is a union member), but they are also generically different. This serves to complicate the analysis of groups in politics.

Americans, like citizens of many other nations, divide themselves "automatically" into certain types of groups, through a process of **self-identification**, in which the individual places himself or herself as a member of a group. The electorate can be divided by race/ethnicity (blacks, whites, Hispanics, Asians, etc.), by religion (mainline Protestants, evangelical Protestants, Catholics, Jews, Muslims, etc.), by age (the elderly, the middle-aged, young adults, etc.), by sexual orientation (gay, straight, etc.), or by occupation (farmers, teachers, construction workers, lawyers, etc.). As mentioned in chapter 3, politicians often treat the electorate as a collection of such groups, appealing to voters to react through their **group consciousness**, a phenomenon where certain attitudes and opinions are adopted by the individual because they are reflective of a group with which the individual associates. In this regard it is important to find out which groups voters principally self-identify with (as the survey asks) and how candidates will appeal to "their" social groups and those of their rivals. But what commentators have long noted as a distinguishing characteristic of the American populace is not the ability to identify with demographic, occupational, or social groups but rather a long-lived tendency to join organized groups. Until very recent times, analysts, from the authors of the *Federalist* papers through V. O. Key Jr., have focused their attention on the impact of organized groups on the policymaking process, not the electoral process. In the last edition of his classic text *Politics, Parties, and Pressure Groups*, published in 1964, Key wrote:

> A striking feature of American politics is the extent to which political parties are supplemented by private associations formed to influence public policy. These organizations, commonly called **pressure groups**, promote their interests by attempting to influence government rather than by nominating candidates and seeking responsibility for the management of government. Such groups, while they may call themselves non-political, are engaged in politics; in the main theirs is a politics of policy. (18)

Key (1964, 19) acknowledges that "pressure groups may campaign for party candidates and may even become, in fact if not in form, allied with one or the other of the parties." However, the emphasis in his five chapters on pressure groups is most decidedly on how these organizations seek to effect policy changes *after* elections have been held.

Within a decade of Key's death in 1963, even much less perceptive observers of American politics had come to realize that the role of interest groups (the term "pressure groups" has been all but dropped because of its pejorative connotation) has been drastically altered. Although they continue to play an important role in all aspects of the policymaking process, organized interest groups acting as organizations, not merely associations with which voters identify, now play a central role in the electoral process as well (see, e.g., Berry and Wilcox 2009; Cigler and Loomis 2007; Herrnson, Shaiko, and Wilcox 2005; Schlozman and Tierney 1986; Wright 1996). Indeed, much recent work focuses specifically on how intimately connected some groups and political parties have become (Cohen et al. 2008; Grossman and Dominguez 2009; Herrnson 2009; Koger, Masket, and Noel 2010; Skinner, Masket, and Dulio 2012, 2013).

This chapter focuses on the role of organized groups in the electoral process. Two aspects of this role will be examined separately: (1) the ways in which these organizations enter into the campaigns of various candidates, and (2) the effectiveness of these groups in controlling their members' votes. As you read these sections, you should be asking yourself about what role you think groups should be playing in the process. What were once referred to as "pressure groups" have become "interest groups." But political journalists talk all the time about the pressure put on politicians by those groups whose support they seek. Is that good or bad, in your view? What is the relationship between interest groups and political parties? The Democrats are often viewed as the party of labor unions, and the Republicans as the party of big business. What do those connections entail? How often do parties and interest groups work together? When are they at odds? Are such characterizations accurate? Before turning to these questions, however, we need an explicit understanding of the types of groups to be examined.

ORGANIZED GROUPS IN AMERICAN POLITICS

Table 4.1 lists a sampling of organized groups in the United States today. Organized groups cover a wide array of interests, from those concerned with more general topics, like the AFL-CIO, to those concerned with very specific subjects, like the National Rifle Association. They come in a variety of sizes, from a few hundred members, like the National Football League Players' Association, to tens of millions, like AARP (formerly the American Association of Retired Persons). They engage in a variety of activities, from sponsoring agricultural fairs like 4-H Clubs to sponsoring presidential candidate debates like the League of Women Voters. Only some of these groups are involved in the political process as groups, though members of virtually every group are involved in politics and any group can become involved in politics if it wishes to do so.

Political and Nonpolitical Associations

Americans form associations for various reasons: camaraderie, education, charitable work, economic advancement (Walker 1983; Verba, Schlozman, and Brady 1995). Some of these groups have an obvious stake in the political process. For example, the National Federation of Independent Businesses clearly is concerned with legislation affecting small business establishments. Some of these organizations were formed for political purposes, the liberal Americans for Democratic Action standing as one such group. Other groups were formed for purposes unrelated to politics, but they became politically involved as the government began to involve itself in matters relating to that group's purpose. For most of its first hundred years, the American Medical Association (AMA) tried to stay out of organized politics. But for the last sixty years or so, the AMA has monitored national legislative action and has frequently lobbied and campaigned to protect its perceived interest. Finally, some groups have stayed

Table 4.1. Types of Organizations and Examples of Associations

Health and Medical	American Medical Association
	AIDS Research Alliance
	American Council on Pharmaceutical Education
	American Dental Association
	March of Dimes Foundation
	National Council on Aging
	National Kidney Foundation
	Society of Gastrointestinal and Endoscopic Surgeons
Religious	American Zionist Movement
	Christian Coalition of America
	Equestrian Ministries International
	Interfaith Alliance
	Islamic Center of America
	Lutheran Historical Conference
Cultural	American Quilters Society
	American Society of Marine Artists
	Authors Guild
	Business Committee for the Arts
	National Public Radio
	National Trust for Historic Preservation
	United States Chess Federation
Scientific, Engineering, and Technical	American Chemical Society
	American Political Science Association
	American Society of Landscape Architects
	Association of Public Data Users
	Experimental Aircraft Association
	International Linear Algebra Society
	National Space Club

Source: Encyclopedia of Associations, 55th edition.

above the political fray, despite the expanding role of government. Phi Beta Kappa, the academic honor society formed in the year of our Revolution, has never entered the political realm in over 240 years and remains removed from politics today.

When the leaders of an organization see that their group's interest is affected by governmental action, they must make an important decision regarding whether they would like to play a more active political role. The decision of whether to become involved in politics—through either the policymaking process or the electoral process, or both—is a significant one for an organization. Politicization may make fund-raising more difficult for other groups. However, if they stay out of politics, the group's members may decide that the group has become irrelevant to the issues around which it has formed; this perception may erode the group's membership and support as well.

If they decide to become politically involved, they take on a new status. If they decide to lobby Congress for legislation, they must register as a **lobbying** organization. Lobbying entails taking action to persuade policymakers to pursue the policies favored by one's group. If they decide to directly support candidates for office, they must form a separate **political action committee (PAC)**—a separate political committee that can raise money specifically for and donate money directly to candidates or political parties, at least in most instances. This is not an easy decision for a number of reasons. For instance, organizations that have been granted tax-exempt status by the Internal Revenue Service may well lose that status.

At times these decisions are easy for leaders to make; at other times they are not. Environmental groups are an interesting example. In the early years of its existence, the only political activities engaged in by the Sierra Club involved efforts to create more national parks. In the late 1960s, however, as environmental concerns heightened, the club became involved with lobbying on more issues. In 1975, for the first time, the Sierra Club opened a Washington office in order to focus its political efforts. It began to use paid advertising to extend its message of environmental concern to a wider audience. Because the Sierra Club spent more than 10 percent of its revenues for political purposes, the Internal Revenue Service revoked its status as a tax-exempt foundation.

Obviously, the leadership of the Sierra Club was aware of the implications of the decision to expand its political activities. The Audubon Society, an organization with a similar perspective, has decided to forgo this approach and has remained a foundation exempt from federal taxes and eligible for tax-deductible contributions.

Politically Active Groups

Our concern is with groups (or individuals representing groups) that have decided to become involved politically. According to the Center for Responsive Politics (West 2017) there were 9,182 registered lobbyists in Washington in the third quarter of 2017,[1] and certainly many more who lobby only infrequently and thus are not required to register. While this figure is down from a recorded high of almost 15,000 in 2007, it is still quite large. Over sixteen hundred political action committees contributed to candidates in the 1978 congressional elections; more than four thousand had registered with the Federal Election Commission by the end of 1988. This number held relatively steady through 2006, before beginning a rapid increase that continued through 2016; the reasons why will be discussed in chapter 5 (see Table 4.2). In the face of these awesome numbers, we should look carefully at the rationale behind the formation of such a farrago of interest groups.

Economic or Noneconomic Interests

One way to analyze interest groups is on the basis of their membership. If the members are motivated by *primarily* economic interests, they can be distinguished from other groups whose members have fewer (or at least less obvious) immediate tangible concerns.

A preponderance of the groups active today exists in order to defend their members' economic interests. Why do people find this economic defense so crucial? As the American economy diversified, our citizens increasingly felt that they needed to band together with people of similar interests to defend themselves against those who seemed to be more powerful. Thus farmers' cooperatives and labor organizing began at various times in the 1800s. As these groups diversified further—and thus developed separate interests—more groups were formed. At present, groups with very specific interests have registered themselves with the Federal Election Commission (FEC). Indeed, a quick glance at the list of PACs registered with the FEC reveals a remarkably diverse array of economic interests.[2]

The number of economic interest groups also increased rapidly when the federal government became more and more involved in regulating the daily life of most Americans. As government played an increasingly intrusive role in regulating economic matters, greater numbers of Americans came together to advance or defend those interests. Similarly, as the American economy became more and more diversified, the associations

Table 4.2. Growth of Political Action Committees, 1974–2016

	Corporate	Labor	Trade Membership/ Health[d]	Non-connected	Cooperative	Corporation w/o Stock	Independent Expenditure Only Committees	Political Committee with Non-Contribution Accounts	Leadership	Total	Contributions to Congressional Candidates ($ millions)
1974[a]	89	201	318	—	—	—				*608*	12.5
1976[a]	433	224	489	—	—	—				*1,146*	22.6
1978	785	217	453	162	12	24				*1,653*	34.1
1980	1,206	297	576	374	42	56				*2,551*	60.2
1982	1,469	380	649	723	47	103				*3,371*	87.6
1984	1,682	394	698	1,053	52	130				*4,009*	113.0
1986	1,744	384	745	1,077	56	151				*4,157*	139.8
1988	1,816	354	786	1,115	59	138				*4,268*	159.2
1990	1,795	346	774	1,062	59	136				*4,172*	159.1
1992	1,735	347	770	1,145	56	142				*4,195*	188.9
1994	1,660	333	792	980	53	136				*3,954*	189.6
1996	1,642	332	838	1,103	41	123				*4,079*	217.8
1998	1,567	321	821	935	39	115				*3,798*[b]	219.9
2000	1,545	317	860	1,026	41	118				*3,907*	259.8
2002	1,528	320	975	1,055	39	110				*4,027*	282.0
2004	1,622	306	900	1,223	34	99				*4,184*	289.1
2006	1,582	273	937	1,254	37	100				*4,183*[c]	372.1
2008	1,598	272	995	1,594	49	103				*4,611*	408.3
2010	1,642	283	978	1,605	39	98				*4,639*	413.8
2012	1,654	286	961	1,626	40	105	504	44		*5,220*	421.3
2014	1,804	288	965	1,723	41	114	796	79		*5,618*	435.9
2016	1,803	289	973	1,981	42	104	2,722	180	*572*	*8,666*	441.3

Source: Federal Election Commission.
[a]These numbers represent all other PACs; no further characterization is available.
[b]During the first six months of 1997, 227 PACs were administratively terminated because of inactivity.
[c]During the second six months of 2005, 189 PACs were administratively terminated because of inactivity.
[d]In July 2011 the FEC began reporting trade and membership groups separately and dropped the specific health group category. They are reported together here for the sake of continuity.

became more and more specialized. Examples of economic interest groups abound. Some are quite well known, such as the United Auto Workers or the National Association of Manufacturers. Others are considerably more obscure, like the Coalition for Government Procurement or the Joint Labor Management Committee of the Retail Food Industry.

Noneconomic groups, sometimes called **public interest groups**, pursue goals that their members view as good for the entire society, even if those goals do not serve the economic interest of one particular segment of society. The individual most closely associated with the formation of public interest groups is **Ralph Nader**. He first made his reputation by crusading against General Motors for producing unsafe automobiles (Nader 1965). He was instrumental in forming a cadre of public interest groups concerned with consumer issues, government reform, health care, and other issues. Currently active "Naderite" organizations include Public Citizen, Congress Watch, Critical Mass, Public Citizen Litigation Group, Tax Reform Research Group, Health Research Group, and various state and local public interest research groups (PIRGs).

Others associate public interest groups with Common Cause, an organization of nearly a quarter-million members formed by former health, education, and welfare secretary John Gardner in 1970 (McFarland 1984). Common Cause bills itself as the "citizens' lobby" and concentrates heavily on issues of government reform.

However, many other groups—some older, some younger; some larger, some smaller; some more effective, some less effective—have formed around noneconomic issues and remain active in politics today. These include the environmental groups mentioned earlier, civil rights organizations, ideological groups of the left and the right, religious groups, groups interested in government reform, and many more. Their impact on public policy and on elections is often just as great as that made by their economic counterparts.

Although the distinction between economic and noneconomic groups is a useful one, it should not be overemphasized. The line can become blurred and can change over time. The organized women's groups that formed around the issue of suffrage are a good example. Suffrage, once achieved, gave way to certain other rights, culminating in the unsuccessful drive for ratification of the Equal Rights Amendment (ERA). Along the way, however, women's economic rights were recognized as being as clearly involved as their other rights. One important goal of the women's movement became "equal pay for equal work." The goal was symbolized by the "59 cents" button, signifying that women earned only fifty-nine cents for every dollar a man earned. Although equal pay is now mandated by law, "equal pay for comparable work" has remained a goal of the women's movement. The economic concerns of organizations like the

National Organization for Women (NOW) have spread to include the allegedly discriminatory practices of the insurance industry, compensatory pay for past discrimination, and many other important issues. NOW is not primarily an economic interest group, but it cannot ignore women's economic concerns.

Multipurpose or Single-Purpose Groups

The discussion of the women's movement raises another possibility for categorizing groups active today. Some groups—**single-purpose groups** —are organized for a single purpose; others—**multipurpose groups**— lobby on a whole range of issues of interest to their membership. The size of each division depends on how narrowly or widely the term "single interest" is defined. Again, some examples are self-evident; others, however, cannot be so clearly defined.

During the first two decades of the last century, the Congressional Committee of the National American Women's Suffrage Association was organized for the sole purpose of achieving women's right to vote. Similarly, today's National Pro-Life Alliance and NARAL Pro-Choice America (previously the National Abortion Rights Action League) are associations whose purpose relates to only one issue—women's ability to control the choices surrounding their sexual and reproductive lives. On the other hand, groups such as NOW, the League of Women Voters, and the American Association of University Women are concerned with a whole array of women's issues.

The distinction between single-purpose and multipurpose organizations has important implications for the effectiveness of these groups. When Ilyse Hogue, the leader of NARAL, speaks on the question of abortion, she speaks authoritatively for the approximately five hundred thousand dues-paying members of her group. They joined the group, combining their financial investment often with a personal investment of time, because they feel a strong commitment to one side of the issue of abortion. No one can question the firmness of their stand on this issue.

On the other hand, if Deborah Frett, the CEO of the Business and Professional Women's (BPW) Foundation of America, were to speak on the same question, despite the fact that she "represents" that group's members (thirty thousand members in two thousand local organizations), her audience could certainly question the commitment of her members to a strong stand on this particular issue. BPW's views on this issue are not self-evident. The same questions regarding commitment are also important in trying to determine how important membership in a group is to the members' other political activities.

Federal or National Groups

A distinction like the one made above differentiates **federal groups** from **national groups**. National organizations are ones in which members, be they individuals or groups, belong directly to the national organizations. The National Association of Manufacturers is a national organization to which various corporations belong individually. Decisions in these organizations are made directly, with the leaders of the national organization responsible (in ways that are often difficult to define) to their members (see Eismeier and Pollock 1984).

Federal organizations are ones whose national organization is a joining together of state or local organizations, each of which is itself autonomous or semiautonomous. The AFL-CIO is the obvious example of such a group, but it is only one of many that could be given. In organizations of this type, lines of authority are much less distinct. If the various constituent units split on a particular issue, how can the federal leadership speak authoritatively, particularly if the local units are permitted to retain their autonomy? Thus federal organizations may spend a good deal of time on internal politics, assuring that stands taken in Washington do not cause problems out in Pocatello.

The same distinction between national and federal organizations affects the input they make to the electoral process. When the Grocery Manufacturers of America, a national organization, decides to back a candidate for U.S. Senate in Illinois, it is clear that the organization has spoken. However, before the Americans for Democratic Action decides to take a similar stand, the leadership in Washington has to consult with the local Illinois affiliate. The problems of federal organizations multiply when the autonomous members disagree. The power of such a group is diminished when politicians perceive that it does not speak for "all."

ELECTORAL ACTIVITIES OF ORGANIZED GROUPS

The purpose of drawing the distinctions noted above relates to the varying impact that groups have on the electoral process. The groups became involved in electoral politics in the first place in order to effect changes in public policy. For many years "interest group" or "pressure group" was used as a synonym for "lobbyist." Only *after* the lobbying role was firmly established did organized interest groups become involved in the electoral process in a meaningful way. Today it is not far from the truth to assert that most people who think of interest groups assume that they are synonymous with PACs. Although this connection is not absolute, the role of interest groups in campaigning has indeed become prominent.

Even though their role has expanded, it is still distinct from the role played by political parties. Parties run candidates for office and seek control in order to organize the governing process. The parties stand for certain principles, but they use these principles chiefly as a means to attract adherents. Interest groups, contrarily, became involved in the electoral arena *only* to put forward their policy preferences. Put simply, instead of taking positions to attract followers, they support candidates who support their positions—or oppose candidates who do not favor their positions. This last point is important. Political parties field candidates in order to *win* positions; interest groups at times support one candidate simply to bring about the defeat of another.

How do interest groups affect the electoral arena? In the following section, which deals with the group's impact on the voting behavior of group members, we will examine the activities through which these groups seek to have an impact in the broadly defined political environment (see Berry 1999; Berry and Wilcox 2009; Wolpe and Levine 1996, 48–54; Wright 1996; Schlozman and Tierney 1986, 200–20).

Working within the Party

Many interest groups attempt to maintain some degree of bipartisanship because they do not want to alienate, in either party, public officials who favor their policy preferences, although there are more groups today that work mostly or exclusively within one party than there were in the past. However, even for those groups attempting to remain "above" the partisan battle does not mean removing themselves wholly from the internal operations of both parties. Traditionally, interest groups have attempted to effect changes in the two party platforms.

Many groups have been actively involved in the platform-writing process. Before most recent conventions, each party has held a series of platform hearings. The stated goal has been to reach out for the opinions of rank-and-file Republicans and Democrats. To a great extent the effect was to reach out for the views of organized groups. The groups send their leaders to testify; they prepare their own "miniplatforms," and they "lobby" with members of the platform committee. The most involved groups even campaign, often successfully, to have their followers made members of platform committees. Although debate continues over the importance of platforms in the policymaking process (see Pomper with Lederman 1980, chap. 8; Wayne 2008), interest group leaders unquestionably see the platform as one place in which they can have an impact.

In the 1998 election cycle, antiabortion forces went one step further in trying to influence the Republican party. Instead of seeking to have their position inserted in party platforms, they attempted to make adherence to their position a sine qua non for receiving campaign funding support from the national Republican party, essentially applying a litmus test that GOP candidates had to pass in order to receive support. The effort, put forth at an RNC meeting by committee members from states with strong religious right delegations, was narrowly defeated after the intercession of RNC chair Jim Nicholson, who argued that he did not want to exclude candidates from the party who would be potentially strong in some regions. This example also demonstrates the sometimes conflicting needs of interest groups and of parties. Parties certainly want the support of members of important interest groups (and party leaders court the leaders of various groups who are thought to be influential in gaining that support), but at the same time, the parties do not want to be captured by the interest groups. Party leaders must look to a broader audience with a wider range of views than is true of group leaders.

While groups try to maintain ties in both parties, no one doubts that many groups are closer to one party than the other. The more feminist-oriented women's groups—NOW, NARAL, The Sister Fund—certainly feel more at home in Democratic party circles than they do in Republican circles. The same can generally be said for black organizations. While these groups maintain contact with Republicans and attempt to influence the positions of Republican party candidates, they have been more successful with the Democrats. And, of course, the opposite can be said for groups such as the National Rifle Association or the National Federation of Independent Businessmen, whose allies are mostly Republicans.

The relationship between organized labor and the Democratic party brings this tie to the extreme. Labor's involvement in the Democratic party has been strong and steady with few exceptions since the early years of the New Deal. When the DNC was elected in 1980, party leaders felt that too few of the members were labor leaders. Consequently, the chair of the DNC used fifteen of his twenty-five at-large appointments to name union officials to the party's ruling body. To cement its ties with the Democratic party further, organized labor formed an advisory committee to help with party fund-raising and strategy setting immediately before the 1982 elections. Union-represented groups have contributed substantially to the DNC each year since.

Labor leaders have also been important in the internal functioning of many state and local Democratic organizations. They have played key roles as Democrats plotted strategies for congressional and senatorial elections. They took the lead in the effort to recapture the House of Representatives after the Republican takeover in 1994. They did this not only through financial contributions, but through working with Democratic strategists in planning attacks on the freshman Republicans seeking re-election throughout the nation. Organized labor continues to be very active in its support of the Democratic party and (most of) its candidates for public office. The extent and openness of organized labor's commitment to the Democrats is unique. That being said, an increasing amount of research is demonstrating that more and more groups are thickening their ties with party elites, blurring the lines between parties and groups, or perhaps even forcing us to rethink our definitions (Cohen et al. 2008; Herrnson 2009; Skinner, Masket, and Dulio 2012, 2013). Research by Smith and Kimball (2012) shows that outside groups are also increasing their interaction with individual candidates and their campaigns in the wake of *Citizens United* (much more will be said on this matter in chapter 5). Attempting to bring influence to bear on internal party matters is clearly one technique that interest groups use to reach their goals.

Group Ratings

Increasingly, organized groups are "rating" representatives and senators in terms of the degree to which they support or oppose legislation favored by those groups. These ratings, which usually range from 0 (no support) to 100 (total support), are computed by the groups after they select the issues most important to them (Fowler 1982).

Group ratings differ in terms of which issues are chosen (those deemed appropriate to the group's concern), how many votes are chosen (all or only the most important on the selected issues), and how scores are computed (how absentee or proxy votes are counted). For example, the Chamber of Commerce of the United States constructs an index of how members vote on a series of issues on which they take a position and communicates that position to members in advance of a vote (Gugliotta 1998). Other groups choose issues after the session is over and rate members without regard to whether the group's position was known in advance. Whatever means are chosen, the ratings are identical in intent: They identify friends and enemies of the groups for the group members to see and for others interested in the group's opinions to weigh in judging incumbents.

Some of the ratings are more prominent than others. *The Almanac of American Politics* and *Politics in America*, two widely circulated books that give basic information on every representative and senator, list how various groups rate the officeholders. Two of the more widely used scores are attempts to rate legislators ideologically across a range of issues. Americans for Democratic Action (ADA) uses a series of votes—on both domestic and foreign policy issues—which it asserts are litmus tests for liberals. In 2016, nine senators and fifty-nine members of the House scored a perfect 100 (all liberal votes).

At the other ideological extreme, the American Conservative Union (ACU) uses a sophisticated system to show how frequently members of Congress vote "for safeguarding the God-given rights of the individual" (Malbin 1981, 126), that is, to determine how conservative legislators are, according to the ACU's definition. Unsurprisingly, those who score high on the ADA scale frequently score low on the ACU scale, though the two scales are not exact opposites because of different issues chosen and different ways of handling absences. In 2016 the ACU gave perfect scores to only two senators and twenty-one members of the House. While the ACU ratings demonstrate a bit more fluctuation than those of the ADA, the ratings given by both groups indicate that both houses of Congress have members willing to be categorized as having ideologically extreme positions, even with the 2016 numbers being down from those seen more commonly in recent years. However, the ratings of incumbents can sometimes have direct electoral implications. Although few citizens, and not even most members of the involved groups, monitor these group ratings closely, many interest groups weigh them heavily in determining whom to help financially in upcoming campaigns. In addition, groups take particular care to identify those on the "extreme" as special friends or enemies, of whom members should be aware.

Since the 1970s one group, the League of Conservation Voters (LCV), has in each election year identified the twelve "worst" candidates for public office (this has been expanded from congressional candidates only at the outset) according to their rating on environmental concerns. The group dubs these representatives the "dirty dozen" and targets them for defeat. Besides wishing to avoid being dubbed one of the twelve "worst" candidates on environmental issues, incumbents want to avoid being targeted for defeat by this particular group. In 2016 four of the twelve "dirty dozen" candidates lost, a figure that is a bit lower than it usually is. Clearly, the rating systems perform an important function for the politically involved interest groups and, by implication, for candidates as well.

Political Action Committees

The use of PACs by interest groups has been highly controversial. While much of the discussion of PACs will occur when the financing of campaigns is considered at length in chapter 5, a short preview of the rise and significance of these committees is appropriate at this point. The year 1974 was critical in terms of changes in campaign finance laws affecting groups. Before that year (or, more accurately, before 1971, when the Federal Election Campaign Act was passed, even though that year's provision did not affect groups), the difference between legality and reality was extreme.

Before 1971 the financing of federal elections was governed by a series of outmoded and largely ignored laws—the 1907 Tillman Act, which prohibited corporate contributions; the 1925 Corrupt Practices Campaign Act, which set limits on expenditures in House ($2,500 to $5,000) and Senate ($10,000 to $25,000) campaigns but not on presidential campaigns; the 1939 and 1940 Hatch acts, which put limits on contributions and involvement of federal employees; and the 1944 Smith-Connally and 1947 Taft-Hartley acts, which prohibited labor unions from contributing directly to campaigns. All of these laws will be discussed at greater length in the next chapter. But for our purposes here the most important thing to know about these laws is the ease and impunity with which they were ignored (Epstein 1980; Sorauf 1988, 28–33).

The reality of campaign financing as America entered the decade of the 1970s revealed a picture of significantly increasing expenditures, corporate influence, and union activity, all sidestepping the intent, if not the letter, of the law, and all far removed from public view. The Federal Election Campaign Act (FECA) of 1971 marked the first step in the attempt (to this point largely unsuccessful) at reforming these practices. But in terms of the role organized groups play in the electoral process, it is the 1974 amendments to the FECA of 1971 we need to pay attention to. The 1974 amendments limited individual contributions to $1,000 per campaign but permitted the establishment of PACs, which could contribute up to $5,000 in each campaign. The amendments specifically allowed corporations or unions to use money for the "establishment, administration, and solicitation of contributions to a separate, segregated fund." The weight carried by this action was made all the more clear when, in a 1975 case involving Sun Oil Company, the Federal Election Commission ruled that corporations could use general treasury funds to establish PACs. This ruling was opposed by organized labor, since the AFL-CIO foresaw the rapid expansion of corporate PACs (Epstein 1980). Table 4.2 shows that these fears of labor unions had a firm foundation.

Organized labor unions formed PACs shortly after they were legalized; the number peaked at 394 in 1984 and has declined somewhat since that time. Similarly, trade, membership, and health associations—the organized interest groups with which we are concerned—saw the opportunity quickly. While we can list many more PACs in this category than in the labor category, their growth also slowed after the early 1980s, except for one brief spurt in the mid-1990s. Corporate PACs, to the contrary, are another phenomenon. From the time of the SUN PAC decision in 1975 until the election of 1988, the number of corporate PACs expanded more than twentyfold. In absolute numbers, there are approximately five times as many corporate PACs as labor PACs, and twice as many corporate PACs as PACs representing trade associations, membership groups, or health associations.

Why do we discuss corporate PACs in a chapter on organized group activity? The answer should be evident. To a large extent corporate PACs are an extension of trade association PACs. Each PAC is limited in the amount it can contribute to any one campaign. However, corporate members of trade associations can form their own PACs and then give as separate entities, thus becoming the functional equivalents of interest groups (Schlozman and Tierney 1986, 9–12). Table 4.3 lists the ten largest PACs in the 2015–2016 election cycle in terms of dollar contributions made to candidates. Five of the ten are membership or trade associations, four are corporate PACs, and one is a labor PAC.

Another type of PAC is the so-called independent, or nonconnected, PAC. These PACs do not grow out of a parent organization but are formed for specifically political purposes. The prototype of this form of organization is the National Conservative Political Action Committee (NCPAC). These PACs can contribute to individual campaigns, and they also take advantage of a provision in the Federal Election Campaign Act that maintains that PACs can make independent political expenditures as long as they are not coordinated with a particular candidate. The Supreme Court in *Buckley v. Valeo*, 424 U.S. 1 (1976), the suit that challenged the constitutionality of the Federal Election Campaign Act, had ruled that limitation on such independent expenditures was an abridgment of the freedom of speech. In 1976 the FECA was amended to correct this constitutional fault. Nonconnected PACs were first registered with the FEC in 1978; today more than 2,700 such PACs register and contribute to federal campaigns.

Using sophisticated direct mail techniques, independent PACs have raised a substantial amount of money. As early as the 1981–1982 election

Table 4.3. Top Ten PACs in Contributions to Federal Candidates, 2015–2016

	PAC	*Contributions*
1	National Association of Realtors	$3,973,350
2	National Beer Wholesalers Associations	$3,322,700
3	AT&T Inc.	$2,953,750
4	Honeywell International	$2,861,364
5	National Auto Dealers Association	$2,659,250
6	Lockheed Martin	$2,612,750
7	Blue Cross/Blue Shield	$2,573,398
8	IBEW	$2,570,650
9	American Bankers Association	$2,444,007
10	Credit Union National Association	$2,380,350

Source: Center for Responsive Politics, based on data released by the Federal Election Commission.

cycle, NCPAC raised over $7 million. By the 1995–1996 cycle, the amount spent by nonconnected PACs had reached $22 million; in the 2001–2002 election cycle, the amount rose to $165.7 million; in 2003–2004, the total amount spent by nonconnected PACs was $255.2 million; and by 2015–2016 the figure reached a truly staggering $2.9 billion (all data from the FEC). This increase is dramatic (much more will be said on campaign finance in the next chapter). How was this money spent? On whose behalf? It was spent as the directors of the fund wished, on behalf of or against any candidates they chose. As John T. Dolan, head of NCPAC, said, "I am responsible to absolutely no one." NCPAC and other nonconnected PACs have run extensive campaigns *against* particular candidates. At times they have advertised against certain incumbents well before the surfacing of an opponent. In 1980 NCPAC's use of this technique was deemed successful in contributing to the defeat of liberal senators Birch Bayh (D-Ind.), John Culver (D-Iowa), Frank Church (D-Idaho), and George McGovern (D-S.Dak.). NCPAC was a feared opponent and an actor others sought to emulate as well. Now independent PACs cover the entire political spectrum.

The success or failure of specific interest groups does not alter the two most important basic questions about independent PACs: (1) Unlike labor unions, trade associations, or even corporations, these groups represent leaders who are not held accountable in any way to their constituency. (2) These groups influence elections in ways that are by their very nature not connected with the candidates who are running but are very effective. Let's deal with these two points separately.

First, these PACs have no members per se. Individuals are contributors; they can fail to contribute again. But talented fund-raisers will tell you that there is no dearth of small contributors, which raises the key defense for independent PACs as well as other PACs and relates to participation in politics, by individuals and individuals acting as groups. A salient goal of campaign reform has always been to increase the number of small contributors. The objective is to get "big money" out of politics. PACs do indeed increase the number of small contributions. These contributors know the causes they are supporting. But do PACs get the big money out of politics? That conclusion is more doubtful. For years Common Cause and other reform-minded interest groups have waged a vigorous (but so far unsuccessful) campaign against PACs. Those who oppose the ability of PACs to contribute to campaigns, at least without further restrictions, argue that PACs hinder the political process by giving undue influence to powerful groups. PAC defenders argue that these organizations get individuals involved—just as has always been desired. To a large extent one's stand on this debate depends on where one sits. If you sit in Congress as a recipient of PAC money, you are unlikely to oppose PACs. But if you are a challenger on the outside—or one who is not likely to receive PAC money—PACs look much more evil.

Second, these groups use independent expenditures, often spent on **issue advocacy advertisements**, which are advertisements created to advocate for or against an issue rather than for or against a specific candidate[3]—to influence elections. Figure 4.1 depicts the amount of money

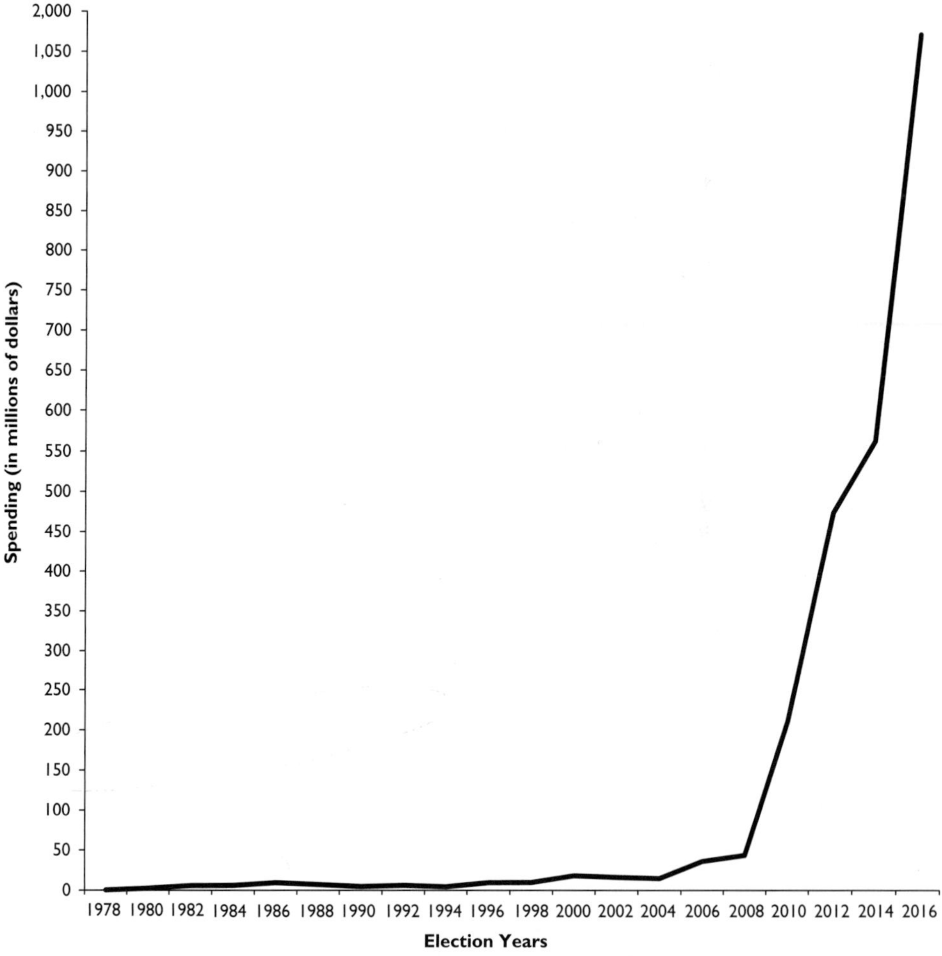

Figure 4.1. Nonparty Independent Expenditures in Congressional Elections, 1978–2016

Sources: 1978–2008, Campaign Finance Institute based on data from the Federal Election Commission; 2010–2016, Center for Responsive Politics, based on data provided by the Federal Election Commission.

spent on congressional and senatorial campaigns through nonparty independent expenditures since 1978. Readers should note that not all independent expenditures come from PACs. The amount of money spent has risen consistently since the 1995–1996 election cycle (although that may be difficult to see here), until it exploded upward in the 2009–2010 cycle. There are reasons for this. First organized labor and then interest groups representing more conservative causes, such as the National Federation of Independent Business, spent millions of dollars in attempts to influence congressional campaigns. They did so by targeting individual representatives and attacking their records, often pointedly and sometimes (some would claim) unfairly. The result was the creation of a negative impression of the candidates under attack; their opponents, however, did not bear responsibility for the attacks. NCPAC's successful technique of twenty years ago has been used by other PACs—labor, association, corporate, and nonconnected PACs—and more recently by Super-PACs and 527 and 501(c) groups (more on these groups in chapter 5) and the parties themselves. Many observers believe that the extent of these expenditures in 1995–1996 fundamentally altered the political process in a deleterious way; the continued high levels of spending, particularly in the subsequent presidential campaigns, did nothing to lessen that concern. The Bipartisan Campaign Reform Act (BCRA) of 2003 (more on this in the next chapter) aimed to address this concern, but the large jump in independent expenditures since 2004 (the first election after reform) indicates the failure on this front. Now that Supreme Court decisions—most recently *Citizens United v. Federal Election Commission* (2010, No. 08–205)—has largely gutted BCRA, it once again seems like the Wild West when it comes to financing in American elections. Indeed, one should be sure to note the huge spike in spending in the wake of the *Citizens United* decision. These issues and questions are discussed at length in chapter 5.

INTEREST GROUPS' INFLUENCE ON THEIR MEMBERS

As stated above, interest groups try to affect the electoral process in two distinct ways. In addition to attempting to influence the ways in which candidates and parties present themselves, and the ways in which those campaigns are perceived by the electorate at large, interest groups try to influence the voting behavior of their own members.

Leaders of interest groups try to exert this influence for two distinct reasons. The simplest, most direct reason is that they believe their choice of candidates is the best for those sharing their interest; it is logical to try to convince others that Senator X is *their* candidate. A less direct reason is that the influence of interest group leaders with political figures varies with the extent to which politicians feel that the group leaders have influence with their members. That influence is demonstrated in two ways—getting members to give money to a campaign and convincing members to support a candidate with their votes.

In this context we should separate interest groups in a way that is distinct from those ways already mentioned. Some interest groups—referred to as trade associations earlier—are actually confederations of other *organizations,* most frequently corporations. The leaders of these parent groups can speak to the leaders of their member groups; they can convince lesser officials to support candidates with their dollars, but in fact few votes are involved. This type of association is, however, not unimportant. In fact, the unanimity of corporate PAC support for candidates who are also favored by their trade associations is a testimony to the effectiveness of this kind of network. However, the influence of this partnership is different from that of a union leader who claims to speak for tens of thousands of his members. In the latter case, politicians are increasingly distrustful of the effectiveness of these spokespeople. It is important, therefore, for interest group leaders to demonstrate that they can distinctly influence their members.

How is this influence achieved? Interest groups use a number of techniques to persuade their members to support the candidates their leaders have identified. One technique has already been identified: the group rating. Interest group leaders make certain that their members know the politicians who supported them in the past and the ones who did not. They clearly identify friends and enemies for their members. But few citizens follow politics closely enough to keep up on group ratings. These ratings can be used as evidence for identifying friends and enemies, but persuasion must come about through other means.

A second technique is producing a newsletter, in print and/or electronic formats. Various groups use newsletters of varying levels of sophistication. The express purpose of communicating with group members through a newsletter is educational. The staff of an interest group wants the members to know what and how much they have been doing for the group, how various issues affect the group's interests, and which political officials have been helpful in their efforts to support favorable legislation or oppose that which is harmful. Using this technique, interest group leaders frequently try to counter the "generalizing" effects of the mass media. The popular media give a general audience a particular view of a political issue and/or a political leader. Through interest group mailings, interest group leaders try to teach their members that they are a specific segment of the public and that issues and leaders affect them in a *particular* way.

Specialized approaches to a particular audience distinguish other techniques used by group leaders as well. Many groups use direct mail and/or telephone and/or e-mail campaigns to inform their members about specific pending issues in which they have a stake. Similarly, they make certain that their members know when the leaders feel that they have a pressing interest in a particular candidate, when one of their favorites is in trouble, or when they have an opportunity to beat one of their enemies.

Groups vary tremendously in terms of their effectiveness in reaching members. Some groups, like realtors, have a reputation of reaching members with persuasive messages in a very short time. Some labor union leaders, on the other hand, seem to be increasingly far removed from the opinions of the rank and file. Certainly during the Reagan years the leaders were more liberal and more clearly tied to the Democratic party than were their members; in recent years labor leaders seem more in touch with the views of their followers. Most recently, more and more groups have concentrated their efforts on educating their members. Labor unions began to use cable television as a means of reaching their constituencies in the 1980s; other groups soon followed suit. Teleconferencing has become a common means of bringing group leaders in Washington into touch with their constituents across the nation. The Internet marks the latest phase of the communications revolution to attract widespread interest group attention (Andres 2009; Berry and Wilcox 2009; Patterson 1990; Coval 1984).

The effectiveness of interest groups in influencing the political opinion of their members has frequently been explored by political scientists. Nearly six decades ago, David B. Truman published his seminal interpretation of American politics based largely on group influence. Truman's book *The Governmental Process* (1951) dealt with much more than the influence of organized groups. Truman's explanation of competing group influences is as persuasive today as it was when first presented.

Imagine the predicament of a certain hypothetical citizen: a Catholic woman who is a union member and, along with her husband, an ardent hunter. Many years ago they joined the National Rifle Association (NRA) and have become active members. Their children have learned about gun safety at NRA workshops. She is faced with a choice in a congressional election between a Democrat who is very much a union supporter but a firm advocate of gun control, and his Republican opponent, a woman who is supported by the local business community, at least in part because of her anti-union stands, and backed by the NRA because she opposes any further restrictions on handgun ownership. Our hypothetical voter is urged by her union leaders to support the Democrat; her economic interest seems to lie in that direction and, after all, good union members *should* vote for pro-labor Democrats. But she is torn. Her NRA friends are for the Republican because of the contrast between that candidate's stand on gun-related issues and the Democrat's hard-line approach, which they see as a step toward taking their guns away. She is puzzled and confused. Clearly, neither the union leader nor the NRA leader can speak authoritatively as her representative.

The issue gets even more complicated. Let us suppose that our hypothetical voter has become something of a feminist in reaction to the way women are treated in the workplace; in fact, she has become active in certain women's organizations. Her deep religious beliefs lead her to oppose abortion. Her feminist friends urge her to look at the predicament in which many working women, facing unwanted pregnancies, find themselves. She is frankly not certain about her own feelings on the abortion issue. The Democratic candidate is also a Catholic and states quite frankly that he is morally opposed to abortion. She agrees. The Republican candidate says that women often find themselves in untenable situations, that abortion is a terrible alternative, but it is one that many women need. Our hypothetical voter agrees with that assessment as well.

Truman presents exemplary cases of competing group demands, and his book demonstrates that group membership does not always determine a voter's choice on election day. Our hypothetical voter's dilemma reflects these competing influences. The position in which she finds herself, although exaggerated, is typical of many real situations. Her quandary shows us how difficult it is for group leaders to claim that they can speak for all the members of their association.

One case stands out, however, in which group membership seems to be a determining factor. Let us assume that our female Catholic union member is not just interested in women's issues but is a member of NARAL Pro-Choice America. She has had an unwanted pregnancy and has gone through the painful process of examining her own beliefs. She has emerged from this examination with the firm view that a woman must be able to control her own body, that her religious doctrine must be put aside in this instance, and that it is wrong for others to let their moral convictions dictate her actions. She did not arrive at these decisions lightly. The process that led to her decision was the most difficult she ever had to undertake. Further, she had to back up her conviction with action, undergoing an abortion, a step she had always been taught was against the law of God. In reaching the decision that an abortion was right for her, she also reached the very strong conclusion that no one should dictate what another may do. After all, anyone who asserted the right to make those decisions for all in society was directly calling into question the very process and the very decision in which she had been so intimately involved.

For this voter, only the candidates' stand on the abortion issue mattered. If the Democrat was pro-choice and the Republican was for restricting a woman's right to have an abortion, our hypothetical voter would have cast her vote for the Democrat. If the candidates held the opposite opinions, her vote would have changed accordingly.

The interest group leaders who are most effective at claiming to represent their members' views and the leaders who are most effective at convincing their members how to vote are the leaders of single-issue groups whose members care more about that one issue than any other. These groups are few and far between. Over the past twenty to thirty years, in some geographic areas, the groups representing the two sides of the abortion question or the gun control issue have been in that situation. More recently groups dealing with issues surrounding homosexuality have assumed a similar importance, and groups dealing with immigration have the potential to do so in the very near future. In close elections, those who vote on the basis of only one issue may in fact determine the result. Certainly it is in the interest of the group leaders to make it appear that they and their members can tip the balance. Single-interest groups seem to be most effective in multicandidate primary fields (Maisel 1986). However, in closely contested elections, no candidate can ignore the appeal of these groups with impunity.

In a very real sense, interest group leaders are politicians too. They try to influence who is elected to office, attempt to affect policy outcomes, and deal with other politicians in striving for these goals. But they themselves do not seek office and do not vote on policy outcomes; the effectiveness of their advocacy for the interests they represent depends on how they are perceived by elected and appointed government officials.

In the final analysis the question of how politicians respond to interest groups and their leaders becomes a question of how effective these leaders are at representing the views of their members, mobilizing their members during campaigns, and deploying their group's resources for or against its selected targets. If a group leader can perform effectively in these areas, he or his group can most certainly affect elections, and therefore influence public policy. And for interest groups, that is ultimately what it is all about.

CRITICAL THINKING QUESTIONS

1. Why do economic groups predominate in the American interest group universe?
2. Is there such a thing as the public interest or the common good?

3. Should interest groups be prevented from spending money on election campaigns?
4. Alexis de Tocqueville famously called the United States "a nation of joiners." Why do Americans belong to so many groups?

Key Terms

self-identification
group consciousness
pressure groups
lobbying
political action committee (PAC)
public interest groups
Ralph Nader
single-purpose groups
multipurpose groups
federal groups
national groups
group ratings
issue advocacy advertisements

NOTES

1. This number almost certainly increased due to late filers.
2. This information is available at www.fec.gov.
3. This line is often very blurry.

Chapter 5

Campaign Finance

American election campaigns have become extremely expensive affairs, causing alarm among many political observers. The Supreme Court's decision in *Citizens United v. FEC* increased both costs and concern.

Money and politics. This is a pairing with a long history in American politics, and anyone who claims that the importance of money in American elections is a recent development is simply ignorant in terms of U.S. political history. However, it is clear that the amount of money spent on campaigns in the United States has grown exponentially over the past sixty years. In 1952, political scientist Herbert Alexander calculated that approximately $140 million was spent on political campaigns nationwide (Alexander and Bauer 1991). In 2016—like 1952, a presidential election year—$6.5 billion was spent on campaigns for federal office alone, according to the Center for Responsive Politics, with an additional unknown amount spent on state and local races across the nation. The 2014 elections also set the record for an off-year cycle, with figures compiled by the Center for Responsive Politics indicating that total spending on federal races in 2014 came up just short of $4 billion, an increase of more than $1 billion from 2006 but only a slight increase from 2010. The amounts spent on some individual races are enough to move even the most laissez-faire observer to raise an eyebrow—for example, $118.1 million was spent on the 2014 Hagan-Tillis Senate race in North Carolina and $23.1 million was spent on the 2014 Bera-Lungren congressional race in California (both records). In the 2010 California gubernatorial election, billionaire and former eBay CEO Meg Whitman spent over $178.5 million, $144 million of which was her own money (Chang 2011). Whitman spent $2.6 million on election day alone, when everyone in their right mind knew she was going to lose.[1] Barack Obama raised over $721.4 million in his successful 2012 bid for reelection.[2]

But what exactly do the dramatic general rise and specific examples of seemingly out-of-control spending imply? Does the rising cost of campaigns necessarily distort election outcomes in the direction of moneyed interests? Does undue influence accrue to those who give large sums of money to successful politicians' campaigns? In other words, how do the escalation in campaign costs and the politicians' search for sources of money affect the government? Does the regulation of campaign finance help or hinder American democracy, and more specifically, what impact does regulation have on free speech? These are the basic questions in the ongoing debate over the role of money in federal elections and the ones to which we turn in this chapter.[3]

This chapter in the fifth edition of this text opened with a photo of Senator John McCain flanked by Representative Marty Meehan and Senator Russ Feingold descending the steps of the Supreme Court. The chapter also contained more than eight pages discussing exclusively what was in many ways their (along with Representative Chris Shays) crowning legislative achievement—the **Bipartisan Campaign Reform Act (BCRA)**, known simply as **McCain-Feingold**. It took over seven years for McCain and his colleagues to get BCRA through Congress and signed by the president, and after it survived a Supreme Court challenge in 2003 (*McConnell v. Federal Election Commission*, 540 U.S. 93, 2003) many believed that meaningful changes were about to take place in the way American elections are funded—that perhaps once and for all the concern with money's influence in American campaigns and elections had been addressed. Seasoned observers should have known better. Sweeping changes in campaign finance have indeed occurred, but not at all along the lines envisioned by supporters of McCain-Feingold. In fact, this chapter no longer needs eight-plus pages on BCRA because the law has been largely gutted by a series of Supreme Court decisions and efforts by outside interests to take advantage of administrative loopholes in U.S. campaign finance and tax law. Some **hard money**—money raised and spent by parties and candidates under strict **Federal Election Commission** (FEC) guidelines—limits (indexed to inflation, presented here for the 2017–2018 election cycle) established by BCRA—$2,700 per candidate, per campaign and $33,900 per national party, per year—remain in place, and therefore still effectively regulate hard money contributions. But even here boundaries between money and campaigns are coming down. In *McCutcheon v. FEC*, 572 U.S. 193 (2014), the Supreme Court declared unconstitutional a longstanding cap on the total amount that an individual could give to federal candidates. Indeed, many (including the authors) would argue that the only other significant element of BCRA that remains in effect—a ban on national party organizations raising **soft money** (money that is raised and spent largely or entirely outside of FEC guidelines), limiting their fundraising to hard money only—has had a negative impact on the regulation of campaign finance in the United States, at least as compared to the practices that have developed in the wake of this ban.

One statement we made in the fifth edition regarding McCain-Feingold still holds true: Even after the Supreme Court initially upheld the law, it was clear that BCRA was not an endpoint in the fierce conflict surrounding the issue of campaign finance in the United States. It was simply one point in a continuing, uncertain, and fluid process. It is to this process that we now turn.

THE LONG HISTORY OF CAMPAIGN FINANCE REFORM

The battle cry to reduce the power of money in American politics is not a new one. In fact, it resonates back over at least the past century. Since the days of Teddy Roosevelt, there has been a national consensus that corporate contributions have no place in our federal election system. In 1907,

Roosevelt signed into law the **Tillman Act**, banning direct campaign contributions from corporations and banks to those running in federal elections. The law was intended to cut the ties between special interests and politics by curbing the influence of corporate money on the outcome of federal elections. Roosevelt's efforts were a response to the success that Republican boss Mark Hanna had in soliciting campaign money from big corporations in the 1896 election (Keller 2003). Indeed, if the estimates of $7 million raised by Hanna are correct, that would translate to $193 million in 2017 dollars. But even with the passage of the Tillman Act, corporations remained active in financing political activity through indirect means—most notably, election year "bonuses" to executives, which often found their way quickly to the appropriate campaign coffers—and through visible and generous contributions by well-known corporate presidents and chief executive officers.

The first actual restrictions on spending were imposed under the aptly named **Federal Corrupt Practices Act of 1925**, the principal means for regulating campaign financing for almost fifty years. The 1925 act called for disclosure of receipts and expenditures by candidates for the House and the Senate and by political committees that sought to influence federal elections in more than one state. (The law was silent, however, on the campaign activities of presidential and vice presidential candidates.) But the act could be circumvented by simply establishing a large number of committees in support of a particular candidate; multiple committees made it nearly impossible to find out who was giving how much to a candidate and how much was being spent on behalf of a candidacy.

The first limit on the amount an individual could donate to a candidate was established in the **Hatch Act of 1940**, which also prohibited political activities by certain federal employees. The cap was meaningless, however, because the law was interpreted to allow contributions to a number of different committees all supporting the same candidate. With nobody to enforce the early regulations—no one was ever even prosecuted under the Federal Corrupt Practices Act—campaign finance regulations held little weight for politicians and parties and held little public attention.

This would all change in the 1960s, with the rise of costly media-dependent campaigns and candidates taking more responsibility in conducting and financing their own campaigns. Once campaigning entered the television age, the first impetus for reform came from President Kennedy. Sensitized to the issue by claims that his father had "bought" the Democratic nomination for him, Kennedy appointed a bipartisan Commission on Campaign Costs, which was charged with examining ways to both reduce the costs of presidential campaigns and finance necessary costs. The commission's recommendations, which were endorsed by Kennedy and his two immediate predecessors, Presidents Truman and

Eisenhower, set the agenda for future reformers, though few of the recommendations were immediately enacted (President's Commission on Campaign Costs 1962). (For histories of campaign finance and reform efforts before 1970, see Corrado et al. 2005, chap. 2; Heard 1960; Mutch 1988, chaps. 1–2; Overacker 1932; Sorauf 1988, 16–34; for a more journalistic account, see Thayer 1973).

The Climate for Reform

Concern over the cost of campaigns and the impact of media advertising reached a crescendo after the gubernatorial elections of 1966. Two of those elections stand out. First, in Pennsylvania, millionaire Milton Shapp, an ambitious man with no previous political experience, decided that he wanted to be governor. He hired media consultant Joseph Napolitan to design an advertising campaign to sell "Shapp for governor" to the Pennsylvania voters. Napolitan spent millions of dollars to help Shapp win the Democratic nomination, though he lost the general election (Agranoff 1976, 9). In the next election, however, Shapp, again spending his own money quite heavily, became Pennsylvania's chief executive.

In neighboring New York State, incumbent governor Nelson Rockefeller was thought to be out of favor with his constituents as the 1966 election approached. He mounted a successful multimillion-dollar campaign to win reelection, relying heavily on paid media to transform the Rockefeller image and the public perception of his tenure as governor. Other examples abound. Politics seemed to be leaving the realm of political parties and entering the suites of advertising executives. The impression was that those who could afford extravagant media campaigns won the privilege of governing.

After Richard Nixon outspent Hubert Humphrey by two to one in the 1968 presidential election, the problems of campaign financing were given renewed attention. The election presented the nation with a "new" Nixon, carefully packaged to rectify an unfavorable image that had emerged from the former vice president's first two decades in public life—a phenomenon not lost on Joe McGinniss, in his chronicle of Nixon's transformation and electoral success, the title of which—*The Selling of the President 1968* (1969)—was borrowed from the well-known series of books by Theodore White (*The Making of the President* 1961, 1965).

Despite a general dissatisfaction among the populace with the system in existence, reform would not come easily. As has been oft stated, the rules of the game are not neutral—a truism particularly applicable to campaign finance laws where members of Congress must legislate the rules that govern their own reelection campaigns. In this case, reform gains momentum when change is in members' best electoral interests.

Thus, it was the congressional Democrats that pushed for reform in the early 1970s. The Democratic party was heavily in debt after its defeat in 1968, and Democrats had much to gain in closing the gap with such reforms as **public financing** (use of tax payer dollars) of presidential elections.

The Federal Election Campaign Act of 1971 and Efforts at Amendment

In 1971 Congress passed two significant pieces of legislation related to campaign finance.[4] The more comprehensive piece of legislation, the **Federal Election Campaign Act (FECA)**, attacked three perceived problems. First, it dealt with the problem of extremely wealthy candidates "buying" their own elections by limiting the amount of money a candidate and the candidate's family could spend to win federal office. Second, it dealt with the "Madison Avenue approach" to politics by placing a limit on media expenditures. And, third, it dealt with the sources and uses of campaign funds by tightening the requirements for disclosure of receipts and of expenditures by candidates for federal office (Corrado 1991a; Corrado et al. 2005; Sorauf 1988).[5] For the next thirty years, meaningful disclosure of campaign expenditures and receipts, as well as the impact of media advertising and the influence of personal wealth, would remain front and center for reformers.[6]

The second piece of reform legislation to pass in 1971 was the **Revenue Act**. This law encouraged small contributions to political campaigns by allowing a tax credit or (alternatively) a tax deduction for limited contributions to campaigns. In addition, the Revenue Act provided for a **tax checkoff** (box on IRS tax forms that citizens can use to indicate whether or not they want to contribute to the public financing arrangement) to subsidize future presidential campaigns. The tax checkoff has been used for the Presidential Campaign Fund, which has been used to fund presidential campaigns since 1976. As we discuss further below, many have come to see the Presidential Campaign Fund as outdated and irrelevant (neither major party candidate took any public financing in 2012 or in 2016). In 2014 President Obama signed legislation to eliminate the public financing of parties' nominating conventions and there is legislation working its way through the 115th Congress to eliminate the program (Garrett 2017).

The 1972 election was the first to be regulated under the new FECA provisions, and with considerable understatement one can conclude that the 1972 experience was not one that would convince reformers that all was in order. When Richard Nixon's reelection campaign spent over $60 million, more than twice the amount spent on his 1968 campaign, analysts began to focus serious attention on the fact that the costs of campaigns were escalating out of sight. The unethical and illegal practices of the Committee to Reelect the President (and, to a lesser degree, some of the Democratic campaigns in 1972) have been well documented, not only by the General Accounting Office (GAO, now known as the Government Accountability Office) but also by two special prosecutors (Archibald Cox and Leon Jaworski); by the Senate Select Committee on Presidential Campaign Activities (the Ervin Committee); by the House Committee on the Judiciary, as it considered impeachment proceedings in the summer of 1974; and by journalists and scholars too numerous to list. Pressure mounted to enact additional reform, and Congress responded by enacting the **1974 amendments to the FECA**, over the veto of President Nixon.

The 1974 act totally revised the 1971 FECA, fundamentally changing the ways in which all federal campaigns were funded for the next thirty years (Corrado 1991b; Corrado et al. 2005; Sorauf 1988). Presidential elections (including the prenomination phase) were to be publicly financed, at least in part. Candidates who accepted public financing also had to accept a cap on their total spending, so as to halt the runaway inflation on the cost of running for president. While the cap on media spending for congressional elections that was imposed in 1971 was lifted, much stricter limits were placed on

1. *Individual contributions:* $1,000 to any campaign—primary, runoff, or general—in a single election, with a total cap of $25,000 to all campaigns in any one year; and
2. *PAC contributions:* $5,000 to any campaign in a single election but with no cumulative limitation.

Additionally, reporting and disclosure requirements were improved. Even the amount that an individual could spend on electoral activities independent of an organized campaign was limited. Finally, an independent, bipartisan Federal Election Commission was established to oversee the reporting and enforcement requirements.

Buckley v. Valeo, 424 U.S. 1 (1976) and Its Impact

Shortly after the 1974 amendments became effective, a curious coalition of liberals and conservatives joined in a lawsuit challenging the constitutionality of the FECA. The law was attacked because it allegedly limited free speech and discriminated against presidential candidates of minor parties. The judicial branch of the government was asked to define the line between the guaranteed rights to free speech and free association and the obligation of the polity to protect the integrity of elections.

In the landmark case *Buckley v. Valeo* 424 U.S. 1 (1976), the Supreme Court ruled that some aspects of the 1974 act were unconstitutional; other provisions, deemed separable, were permitted to stand. The Court permitted the disclosure requirements and campaign contribution limits to remain in place. But with regard to the question of free speech, the Court held that limits on campaign spending, on **independent expenditures** (money spent that is not controlled by or coordinated with a candidate's campaign), and on the amounts individuals could contribute to their own campaigns restrained the interchange of ideas necessary to bring about social change and were therefore unconstitutional. Put simply, the Court ruled that in political campaigns, money equals speech. Understanding all of the complexity of American campaign finance begins with this premise. The spending limits were constitutional, however, if presidential candidates accepted public funding (Gottlieb 1985, 1991; Lowenstein 1991a). The Court also struck down the way in which the FEC was appointed, requiring that all appointments be made by the president with the advice and consent of the Senate, essentially ruling the existing FEC unconstitutional.

Buckley v. Valeo was handed down in January 1976, right in the middle of the 1976 presidential campaign. The decision effectively closed down the FEC for four months; it wasn't until May 11 that President Ford and Congress "fixed" the problems with the FEC to comply with the Supreme Court ruling. In the meantime, there was no commission to provide the much-needed matching funds to the major parties' presidential candidates, funds they had been counting on to finance their campaigns. Jimmy Carter was the only Democratic contender able to secure loans from a sympathetic bank until the matching funds were available. Meanwhile, his rivals for the Democratic nomination were broke by the time the primaries were held in Michigan and Pennsylvania, two states critical to Carter's success (Clymer 2003b). While the election of 2000 may have been the first time the Supreme Court was accused of "electing a president," the Supreme Court's ruling in *Buckley v. Valeo* in 1976 played an unexpected role in the nomination of soon-to-be president Jimmy Carter. We will return to the significance of *Buckley* momentarily.

When the FECA was eventually revised and passed in May 1976, the new amendments reflected the recent Supreme Court decision. The changes brought on by the amendments included reconstitution of the FEC, caps on contributions, public disclosure of all donations above $200, partial public financing for presidential primaries, and complete public financing for presidential elections for candidates who voluntarily accepted campaign spending limits. (Notably missing from the final version was any provision for public funding of congressional elections.) But the amendments didn't stop with these changes. In 1979, concerned that

FECA was stifling grassroots politics at the state and local level, Congress amended the act to permit state and local parties to solicit unlimited contributions for "party-building" activities. In addition, state and local party committees were allowed to contribute volunteer time to individual campaigns so that the traditional role of local party organizations in federal elections was not lost in the rush to reform. (On the role of campaign finance legislation in the revival of political parties, see Adamany 1984; Aoki and Rom 1985; and Jacobson 1985b, 1985–1986).

But when one venue is closed, another will open. "Money in politics is like water"—it finds its way through the cracks. The major unintended consequence of the new FECA limits on contributions was the proliferation of PACs, which were free to raise and spend as much money as possible in the name of "party building." As a result, soft money grew exponentially. From the 1980s on, there was much talk of an overhaul to the system by both parties and by both chambers of Congress, but little action ever came of it—proposals fell victim to Senate filibusters, presidential vetoes, and conference committees that either failed to deliver or, in some cases, never met.

Clearly, incumbency presented a formidable obstacle to reform. For example, President Clinton included campaign finance reform as an important part of his platform when he sought the presidency in 1992. During the first Congress of his administration, both the House and Senate passed separate versions of campaign finance legislation that dealt with voluntary spending limits and restrictions on PAC contributions and soft money. But the "Democratic majority allowed the legislation to languish until the final days of the 103rd Congress, when Senate Republicans used a filibuster to block a conference with the House" (*Congressional Quarterly Almanac* 2001, 64; *Congressional Quarterly Almanac* 1994, 32). It would take more than a presidential priority to motivate a majority of members to overhaul a campaign finance system that contributed to their electoral advantage over their challengers.

THE SEVEN-YEAR BATTLE FOR MCCAIN-FEINGOLD AND ITS DEMISE

The "seven-year odyssey" of McCain-Feingold—beginning in 1995 and culminating in the BCRA of 2002—highlights the formidable obstacles not only to campaign finance reform but also to any sweeping reform measure that is proposed in Congress and which aims to significantly shift policy away from the status quo. The act itself also illustrates the incredible difficulty in keeping money out of American elections. But here we get ahead of ourselves. First we need to look briefly at the passage of BCRA and also at what the law actually did, or attempted to do.

Senators John McCain and Russ Feingold first introduced their campaign finance bill in 1995, with the major goals of banning soft money, restricting "issue advocacy ad" contributions to PACs, and granting free television time to candidates willing to limit spending. Supporters argued that the bill would put an end to the corrupting influence of big money contributions in American politics. Opponents, led by Senator Mitch McConnell (R-Ky.), at the time chair of the National Republican Senatorial Committee and so-called Darth Vader of campaign finance reform, argued that McCain-Feingold would infringe on free speech, weaken political parties, and give more power to outside special interests operating independently of candidates and parties. McConnell and his fellow Senate Republicans successfully filibustered the first version of McCain-Feingold; it never came up for a vote in the 104th Senate. The House companion legislation to McCain-Feingold—introduced by Representatives Chris Shays (R-Conn.) and Marty Meehan (D-Mass.) and aptly named Shays-Meehan—met a similar fate in the 104th House.

The election of 1996, however, provided greater momentum for change. Five months before the 1996 presidential and congressional elections, the Supreme Court ruled that parties could spend unlimited amounts to promote positions on issues so long as they did not coordinate directly with candidates—that is, so long as they were "independent" of candidates (*Colorado Republican Federal Campaign Committee v. FEC*, 518 U.S. 604, 1996). Taking advantage of the Court's decision, parties raised then record-breaking amounts of soft money in 1996: $260 million, three times the amount raised in 1992—money widely used for individual campaigns.

After the much-publicized excesses in fund-raising techniques during the 1996 elections—including reports of major donors sleeping in the Lincoln bedroom, allegations of foreign money being donated to the DNC, and photographs of Vice President Al Gore accepting "gifts" at a Buddhist temple—campaign finance reform was given new impetus during the 105th Congress (1997–1998). Public pressure was clearly mounting for some congressional attention to be devoted to the problem. The Clinton White House, reeling under charges that the president's 1996 campaign had violated the spirit if not the letter of the existing law, supported the Bipartisan Campaign Reform Bill. But ultimately this support meant nothing. Efforts to enact something like BCRA failed in both the 105th and 106th Congresses.

John McCain's emphasis on campaign finance reform in his failed bid for the 2000 Republican presidential nomination did improve the chances of enacting reform somewhat during the 107th Congress, and reform advocates slowly but surely made progress during 2001. But even with this progress, passage of reform still appeared unlikely. Then in October of 2001 the supporters of the Bipartisan Campaign Reform Bill suddenly acquired an unforeseen ally—the Enron Corporation. The Enron bankruptcy scandal essentially provided the final push to passage (Foerstel 2002). The company's collapse exposed $3.6 million in soft money contributions to both parties since 1990, and the consequent media frenzy added to the pressure for real reform. Supporters of McCain-Feingold and its companion, Shays-Meehan, could not have asked for a better example to promote their cause in Congress, as stories of Enron's corporate contributions potentially buying political influence and disproportionate access to lawmakers flooded the media. The bill passed both chambers in the spring of 2002, and was reluctantly signed into law by President George W. Bush.

The seven-year odyssey to final passage was over. Members of Congress had voted for what many political observers believed to be the impossible—they had voted to change the very system that had elected them. To the American public the solution seemed an obvious one: Reform the system before campaign spending spiraled out of control. But the fight over reform was far from over, as opponents moved from the congressional arena to the courts. Knowing the inevitability of a court challenge, BCRA's sponsors included a provision in the new law that provided for an expedited judicial review process, ensuring a hearing by the Supreme Court. That hearing came in September 2003. The critical question before the Court was essentially whether the BCRA curbed corruption or violated the right to free speech, much the same question the Court faced in *Buckley*.

On December 10, 2003, the Supreme Court answered that question. In a narrow five–four decision on *McConnell v. Federal Election Commission*, 540 U.S. 93 (2003), the Court ruled that BCRA's ban on soft money contributions to political parties and candidates did not violate rights delineated in the U.S. Constitution. Writing for the majority, Justices John Paul Stevens and Sandra Day O'Connor spoke directly about the corrosive nature of soft money:

> Just as troubling to a functioning democracy as classic *quid pro quo* corruption is the danger that officeholders will decide issues not on the merits or the desires of their constituencies but according to the wishes of those who have made large financial contributions. . . . The best means of prevention is to identify and remove the temptation. The evidence set forth . . . convincingly demonstrates that soft-money contributions to political parties carry with them just such a temptation. (*Congressional Quarterly Weekly* 2003, 3078)

McConnell v. FEC seemingly secured the safety of the reforms included in McCain-Feingold. But this has not been the case, and within the last decade BCRA has essentially been gutted. In 2007, less than four years after upholding the core provisions of BCRA in *McConnell*, the Court essentially declared the ban on the groups using a candidate's name in issue advocacy ads thirty days before a primary election or sixty days before a general election unconstitutional. Writing for the majority in a closely divided five–four decision, Chief Justice John Roberts stated: "Discussion of issues cannot be suppressed simply because the issues may also be pertinent in an election. Where the First Amendment is implicated, the tie goes to the speaker, not the censor" (*Federal Election Commission v. Wisconsin Right to Life, Inc.*, 551 U.S. 449, 2007). In 2009 the U.S. Court of Appeals for the District of Columbia Circuit invalidated some FEC guidelines that governed how nonconnected groups must allocate their money in federal elections (*EMILY's List v. Federal Election Commission*, 581 F. 3d 1, D.C. Cir. 2009).

Both of these decisions weakened BCRA, and campaign finance regulation overall. However these two decisions could almost be seen as irrelevant when compared to ***Citizens United v. Federal Election Commission*** (130 S. Ct. 876, 2010), a decision seen by many campaign finance experts as the Court's most significant action since *Buckley*. This case dealt with a documentary titled *Hillary: The Movie*, a scathing attack on then New York senator and candidate for the Democratic presidential nomination Hillary Clinton. The documentary was produced by Citizens United, a nonprofit group dedicated to conservative causes. Citizens United aimed to broadly advertise the documentary and make it available via video-on-demand, presumably in the hopes of damaging Clinton's presidential bid. Concerned that doing so would violate various FEC regulations, Citizens United petitioned the federal courts for a preliminary injunction barring the FEC from blocking the ads and/or the video-on-demand availability. The group eventually got far more than just a preliminary injunction. In its decision in *Citizens United* the Supreme Court not only removed BCRA restrictions on corporate- (and, presumably, union-) funded **electioneering communications**[7] but also struck down FECA restrictions on the use of money directly from corporate (again, presumably, union as well) treasuries to explicitly campaign directly for or against candidates for federal (and likely state as well) office, so long as such efforts were done independently. The rationale behind the Court's decision in *Citizens United* was the same as it was in *Buckley* over thirty years prior—restrictions on the use of money in election campaigns is a restriction on freedom of speech, and thus a violation of the First Amendment.

The federal courts have extended the reach of *Citizens United* in important ways. In March 2010, the Washington, D.C., Circuit Court of Appeals

held that preventing SpeechNow.org—a nonprofit **527 group** (more on such groups later in this chapter) that made independent expenditures to influence federal election outcomes—from accepting donations from individuals in excess of $5,000 was an unconstitutional violation of free speech rights (*SpeechNow.org v. FEC*, 599 F. 3d 674, D.C, Cir. 2010). And as noted previously in this chapter, the Supreme Court eliminated the aggregate limit on money that individuals can give to federal candidates in *McCutcheon v. FEC* (572 U.S. 193, 2014). It is clear that the impact of *Citizens United* on the financing of American elections has been very large, and also that the full implications of this ruling have yet to be seen (Hansen, Rocca, and Ortiz 2015; Levitt 2010; Ruprecht 2015).

THE COSTS OF DEMOCRACY AND WHO PAYS FOR IT

To more fully understand the potential pros and cons of campaign finance regulation, it is necessary to take a more detailed look at the actual costs of American democracy—that is, how much money is raised and spent by parties, candidates, and outside groups, and where the money is coming from, at least to the extent that we can answer these questions. In the following section, we first explore the price tag of federal, state, and local elections since the enactment of FECA in 1971. What patterns in campaign expenditures have developed in response to previous regulations? Then we look at the sources of campaign funds, more specifically at the contributions of individuals, PACs, and political parties, as well as the controversial roles of soft money and public funding in American elections.

The Costs

As we have discussed, concerns over the rising costs of campaigns first manifested themselves at the presidential level, particularly after the elections of 1968 and 1972. Figure 5.1 shows the rapid rise in the costs incurred directly by presidential candidates during the general election phase of the campaign and the disparity that existed between the two major parties before 1976, the first election in which costs were contained through the use of public funds.[8] Figure 5.1 also shows relatively large disparities between the parties returning in 2008, 2012, and 2016, differences due in large part to Barack Obama's fund-raising prowess in 2008 and 2012 and the unorthodox nature of Donald Trump's fund-raising in 2016. But even as steep as the increase shown in Figure 5.1 is, in many ways it dramatically underrepresents the true amount of money that is spent on presidential campaigns today. The totals in Figure 5.1 only include funds spent directly by the candidates' campaigns during the general election. If one also considers the money spent by the campaigns during the nomination phase, and some additional independent expenditures by the parties and other outside groups, the figure for the 2016 presidential campaign rises to $2.4 billion according to the Center for Responsive Politics, an increase from $1.2 billion in 2004 and $671 million in 2000 but a decrease from the $2.6 billion spent in 2012.

Dramatic increases in spending are not limited to presidential campaigns. House and Senate campaign spending has exploded as well, as revealed in Figures 5.2 (a and b) and 5.3 (a and b), respectively. No matter how these data are read, the pattern is clear: increasingly large sums are being spent to finance campaigns. In 1974, the mean expenditure (all amounts in Figures 5.2a, 5.2b, 5.3a, and 5.3b are adjusted for inflation and reported in 2014 dollars) for all candidates for the House of Representatives was slightly over $256,000; in 1990, it was just under $583,000; in 2014, it reached almost $1.1 million. The gap between incumbents and challengers widened as well.[9] The mean expenditure for incumbents rose from approximately $271,000 to $755,000 to $1.5 million for the same years; and for challengers, from $192,000 to $243,000 to $498,941. For open

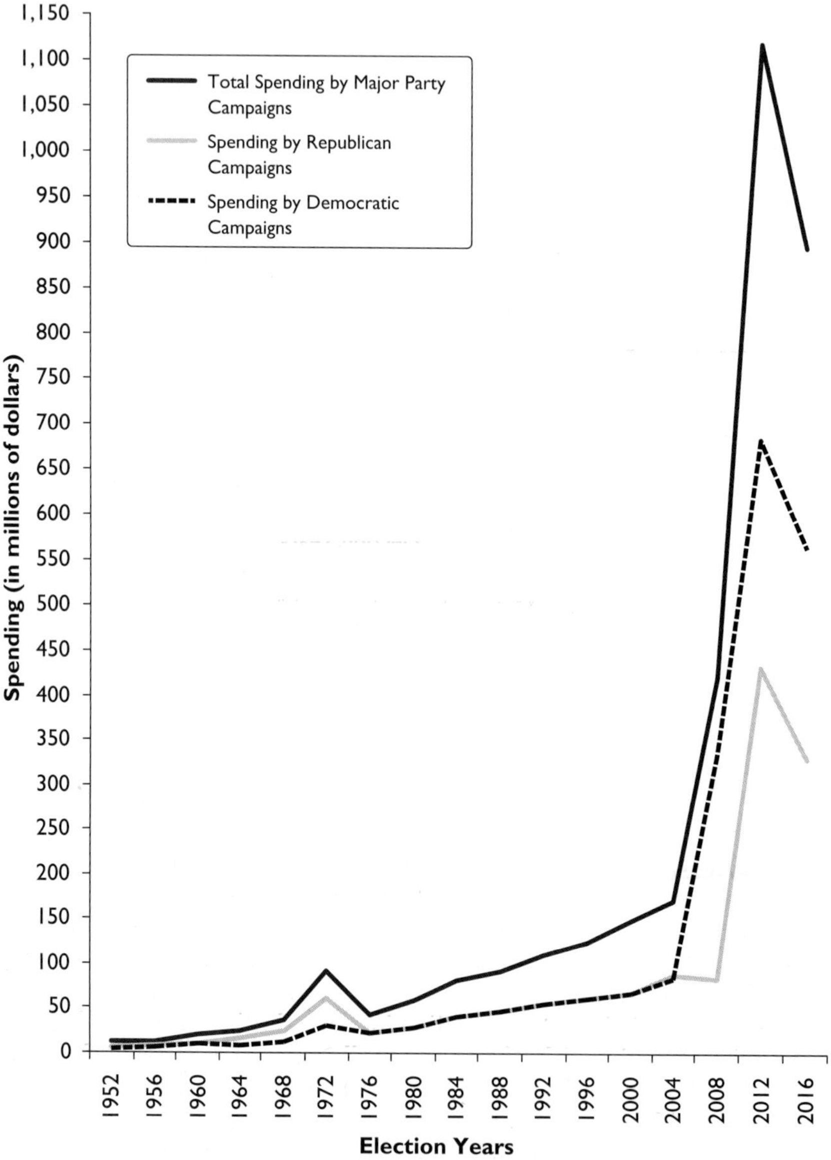

Figure 5.1. General Election Spending by Major Party Presidential Candidates, 1952–2016

Sources: Federal Election Commission and Center for Responsive Politics.

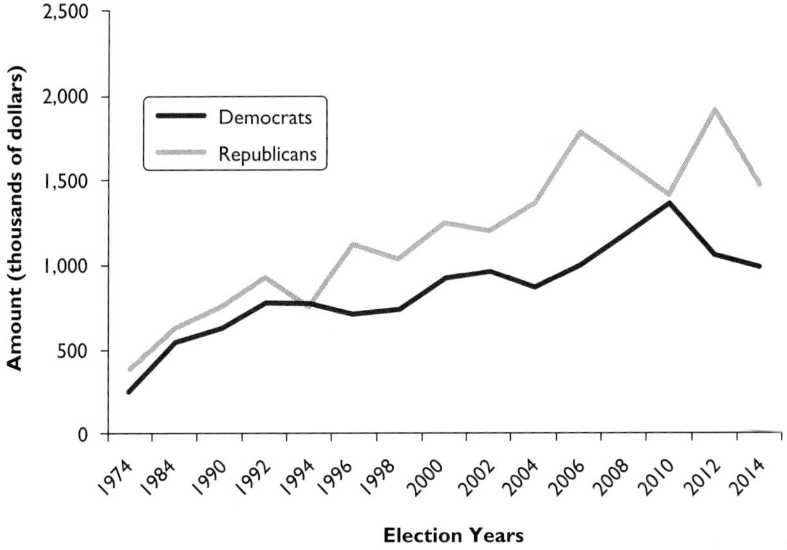

Figure 5.2a. Mean House Campaign Expenditure by Party, 1974, 1984, 1990–2014
Note: These amounts are adjusted for inflation and reported in 2014 dollars.
Source: Brookings Institution, *Vital Statistics on Congress*, based on data reported by the FEC.

seats, the mean expenditure rose from about $434,000 to $973,000 to almost $1.4 million.

In the Senate, the mean expenditure for all candidates went from approximately $2.1 million in 1974; to $4.7 million in 1990; to $7.8 million in 2014. For incumbents the mean expenditure surpassed $10.9 million in 2014; for challengers, the mean was still a daunting $5 million. The mean expenditure in the open-seat races was $7.2 million. Because only one-third of the Senate is up for reelection in every election year, year-by-year comparisons can be misleading—especially open-seat data—as the same states do not necessarily have open seats. However, spending has clearly risen, even without taking spending by outside groups into account. This trend is stronger in the Senate than in the House, likely reflective of the fact that the Senate tends to have a greater percentage of competitive races than does the House.

Despite the limitations of the data available, those who study state and local elections have concluded that the same escalating campaign costs seen at the federal level are present at state and local levels. In 1980, Herbert Alexander of the Citizens' Research Foundation estimated that $265

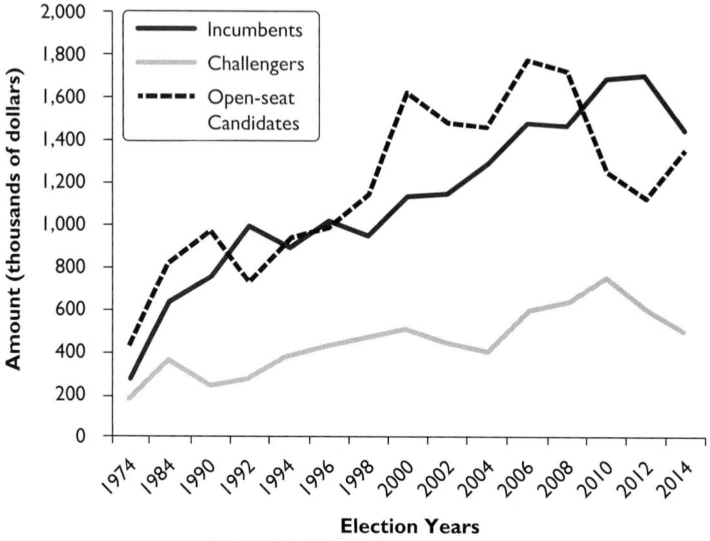

Figure 5.2b. Mean House Campaign Expenditure by Candidate Status, 1974, 1984, 1990–2014

Note: These amounts are adjusted for inflation and reported in 2014 dollars.
Source: Brookings Institution, *Vital Statistics on Congress*, based on data reported by the FEC.

million was spent on state elections and $200 million on local elections (Alexander 1984, 104). A decade later he estimated that $540 million was spent on state elections and $365 million on local elections, an amount that constituted 45 percent of the total spent on all elections in 1990 (Alexander and Bauer 1991, 3).[10] After the 1996 campaigns, Alexander's estimates rose to $650 million for state elections and $425 million for local elections, just under 25 percent of the total amount spent. It should be remembered that more state and local elections are held in nonpresidential years than in presidential election years and, further, that some of these elections (e.g., New Jersey's or Virginia's) are held in odd-numbered years.

Ruth Jones (1984) and Anthony Gierzynski and David Breaux (1991) found significant increases in spending by candidates as well as significant variance across states in the years after the first campaign finance reform act. Michael Malbin and Thomas Gais, in their study of spending in state house races from 1982 to 1992, found that "after controlling for inflation, total campaign expenditures in Kansas House elections grew by 66 percent . . . in Kentucky House elections by 45 percent . . . in Oregon

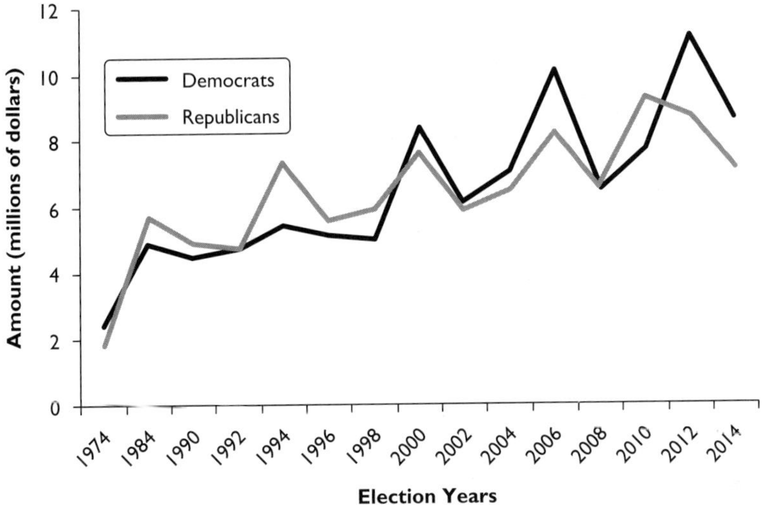

Figure 5.3a. Mean Senate Campaign Expenditure by Party, 1974, 1984, 1990–2014

Note: These amounts are adjusted for inflation and reported in 2014 dollars.
Source: Brookings Institution, *Vital Statistics on Congress*, based on data reported by the FEC.

House elections by 225 percent . . . and in Maine Senate elections by 292 percent over the same period" (1998, 15). More recent data on spending on state and especially local elections are hard to come by, but it is certain that spending on these elections has increased significantly from the late 1990s. According to the National Institute on Money in State Politics, $3.6 billion was raised for state and local elections in 2016, a figure that is almost certainly lower than the real amount raised and spent on nonfederal elections.

Sources of Campaign Funds

For a long time many Americans have believed that campaigns in America cost too much money. These same people, and often many others, are concerned about where the money for campaigns comes from and what strings, if any, are attached to political contributions. These concerns are what led to the campaign finance regulations that we discussed at the beginning of this chapter. The presumption is that individuals, groups, and corporations do not donate campaign funding out of the goodness of their hearts, but rather contribute huge sums in reward for past action and in hope of some later benefit. Although little empirical evidence supports the assumption of a link between contribution and

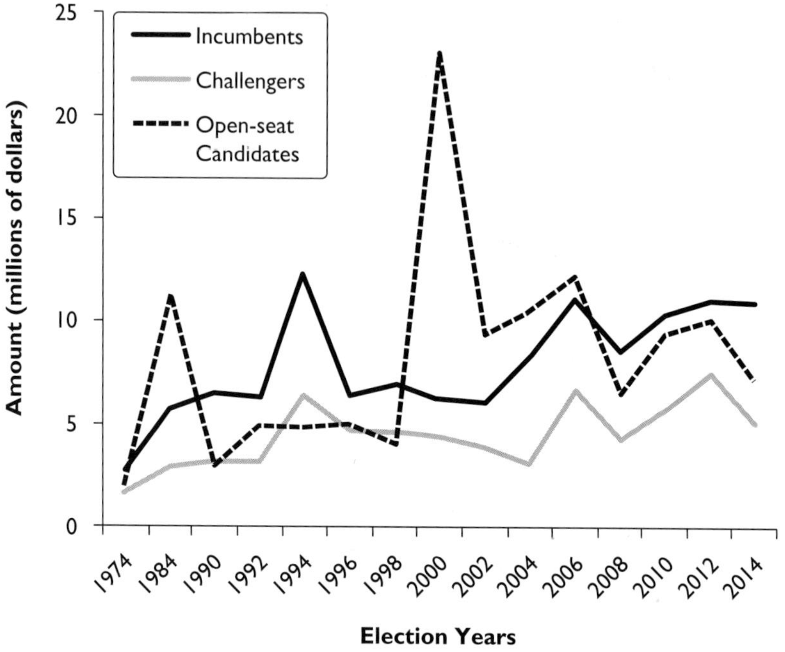

Figure 5.3b. Mean Senate Campaign Expenditure by Candidate Status, 1974, 1984, 1990–2014

Note: These amounts are adjusted for inflation and reported in 2014 dollars.
Source: Brookings Institution, *Vital Statistics on Congress*, based on data reported by the FEC.

payoff, the general perception—if not the reality—is that few people give something for nothing. In the sections that follow, we examine the five primary sources of money (one of which is now largely irrelevant, at least in federal races and likely soon in state races as well) and the questions that accompany each funding base.

Although the FEC has changed the ways in which it categorizes the sources of campaign contributions to federal campaigns, we can nonetheless discuss relative contributions with some historical perspective—for both congressional and presidential elections. Generally, campaign funds come from the following sources: the candidate, individuals, PACs, political parties, and public financing—the last of which is only available to presidential candidates and some state and local candidates, and is also the one already far down the road to insignificance.

As shown in Table 5.1, the majority of contributions to House and Senate candidates come from individuals (for more on individual donors to

Table 5.1. Funding Sources for Congressional Candidates, 1974, 1984, 1994–2016

	Amount Raised by Candidates and Party Expenditures on Behalf of Candidates (in millions)	Percentage Distribution				
		PACs	Party (contributions and expenditures)	Individuals	Candidate to Self (contributions and unrepaid loans)[a]	Other
House						
1974						
All candidates	45.7	17	4	79[b]	—	—
Democrats	23.9	22	1	77[b]	—	—
Republicans	21.7	10	7	83[b]	—	—
1984						
All candidates	203.8	36	7	47	6	5
Democrats	107.2	41	3	44	6	6
Republicans	96.6	30	11	49	6	5
1994						
All candidates	371.3	34	5	49	8	4
Democrats	196.7	43	5	43	5	4
Republicans	174.6	24	6	56	11	3
1996						
All candidates	460.8	33	4	53	6	4
Democrats	211.6	35	4	48	9	4
Republicans	249.2	30	4	57	4	4
1998						
All candidates	436.1	35	3	51	6	4
Democrats	199.6	38	3	49	6	4
Republicans	236.5	33	3	53	6	4
2000						
All candidates	533.6	36	2	53	7	5
Democrats	266.6	37	2	51	8	6
Republicans	267.0	35	2	55	6	5
2002						
All candidates	537.8	38	2	50	9	4
Democrats	267.7	38	2	46	12	5
Republicans	272.0	38	3	52	6	5
2004						
All candidates	622.6	36	2	56	5	4
Democrats	279.8	35	2	57	5	3
Republicans	342.8	36	2	55	4	4
2006						
All candidates	777.8	35	1	54	5	5
Democrats	375.5	33	1	58	4	4
Republicans	402.3	38	1	51	5	5

(Cont.)

Table 5.1. Funding Sources for Congressional Candidates, 1974, 1984, 1994–2016 (Cont.)

	Amount Raised by Candidates and Party Expenditures on Behalf of Candidates (in millions)	Percentage Distribution				
		PACs	Party (contributions and expenditures)	Individuals	Candidate to Self (contributions and unrepaid loans)[a]	Other
2008						
All candidates	983.8	31	1	54	11	0
Democrats	539.6	34	1	54	8	0
Republicans	440.8	26	2	54	14	0
2010						
All candidates	949.3	33	2	57	6	2
Democrats	469.9	40	2	54	2	2
Republicans	479.4	27	2	60	9	3
2012						
All candidates	970.9	35	1	56	5	3
Democrats	414.4	35	1	57	5	2
Republicans	556	34	1	56	4	4
2014						
All candidates	901.8	37	1	53	5	3
Democrats	400.4	37	1	56	3	2
Republicans	501.4	37	1	50	7	5
2016						
All Candidates	900.1	39	1	52	5	4
Democrats	413.9	35	1	56	6	2
Republicans	486.1	41	1	47	4	6
Senate						
1974						
All candidates	28.2	11	6	83[b]	—	—
Democrats	16.2	13	2	85[b]	—	—
Republicans	11.6	7	13	80[b]	—	—
1984						
All candidates	157.7	18	6	61	10	4
Democrats	73.1	18	6	56	16	4
Republicans	84.6	18	6	65	5	4
1994						
All candidates	291.7	15	8	54	19	4
Democrats	124.9	18	10	55	12	5
Republicans	166.7	13	6	53	24	4
1996						
All candidates	242.1	17	9	58	12	4
Democrats	116.2	13	8	59	16	4
Republicans	125.9	21	9	57	8	4

(Cont.)

Table 5.1. (Cont.)

	Amount Raised by Candidates and Party Expenditures on Behalf of Candidates (in millions)	*Percentage Distribution*				
		PACs	*Party (contributions and expenditures)*	*Individuals*	*Candidate to Self (contributions and unrepaid loans)*[a]	*Other*
1998						
All candidates	265.9	18	7	58	11	7
Democrats	126.1	16	8	58	9	9
Republicans	139.8	19	7	57	12	4
2000						
All candidates	366.7	14	4	56	25	6
Democrats	203.4	9	3	42	44	6
Republicans	163.3	19	6	73	1	6
2002						
All candidates	281.90	20	5	65	8	6
Democrats	136.2	17	2	69	8	6
Republicans	145.7	22	7	62	8	7
2004						
All candidates	373.90	16	5	72	4	7
Democrats	194.8	14	5	77	3	5
Republicans	179.1	19	6	67	5	9
2006						
All candidates	530.90	13	3	67	13	5
Democrats	275.5	11	2	70	13	3
Republicans	230.2	16	4	60	15	6
2008						
All candidates	436.2	18	3	62	7	2
Democrats	239.5	14	3	63	7	4
Republicans	196	23	3	61	8	0
2010						
All candidates	597.6	13	6	61	13	7
Democrats	242.3	15	6	70	3	7
Republicans	355.3	12	5	55	21	8
2012						
All candidates	491.8	13	3	67	13	4
Democrats	287.1	14	3	77	2	4
Republicans	204.7	11	3	57	25	4
2014						
All candidates	399.8	13	4	71	6	6
Democrats	289.9	15	3	73	4	6
Republicans	109.9	10	7	66	9	8

(Cont.)

Table 5.1. Funding Sources for Congressional Candidates, 1974, 1984, 1994–2016 (Cont.)

	Amount Raised by Candidates and Party Expenditures on Behalf of Candidates (in millions)	*Percentage Distribution*				
		PACs	*Party (contributions and expenditures)*	*Individuals*	*Candidate to Self (contributions and unrepaid loans)*[a]	Other
2016						
All candidates	551.4	16	5	68	2	10
Democrats	297.2	10	3	76	3	8
Republicans	254.2	22	7	59	0	12

Sources: 1974–1994, Ornstein, Mann, and Malbin (1998), table 3-9; 1996–2004 and 2008, FEC sources; 2006, Campaign Finance Institute analysis of FEC data; 2010–2016, Campaign Finance Institute analysis of FEC data.

Note: "All candidates" includes major party candidates only.

[a]The FEC did not report the contributions of candidates to themselves separately.

[b]Includes the contributions of candidates to themselves, unrepaid loans, and individual contributions up to $500.

congressional campaigns, see Francia et al. 2003). The next most important source of direct contributions to candidates is PACs, though it should be noted that PACs are more important to House candidates than they are to candidates in Senate elections. Although the amount that candidates contributed to their own campaigns was not reported in the early 1970s, House candidates tended to give just under 10 percent in the earlier period and much less in more recent campaign cycles. There is wide variation, however, with some candidates financing much of their own campaigns and with others contributing relatively little (Wilcox 1988).

The same variations hold for Senate candidates, but because so few Senate elections are held in each election year, no pattern emerges. For instance, when John Heinz (R, 1973–1991) spent a large amount of his own money to win the Pennsylvania Senate seat in 1976, his expenditures raised the average for all Senate races in that year. The same would hold true of races in New Jersey in 2000 (John Corzine) or North Carolina in 2002 (Erskine Bowles) or Nebraska in 2006 (Pete Ricketts) or Connecticut in 2010 and 2012 (World Wrestling Entertainment [WWE] mogul Linda McMahon both times). It should be noted that all of these candidates, with the exception of Corzine, lost. Individuals have even proved willing to spend large sums of their own money in Senate primary contests; Blair Hull spent almost $29 million of his own money to lose the Illinois Democratic Senate nomination to Barack Obama in 2004, and Texas Lt. Gov. David Dewhurst spent over $11 million of his own fortune to lose the Texas Republican Senate nomination to Ted Cruz in 2012. It is important to reiterate that the figures presented in Table 5.1 and discussed in these last two paragraphs reflect hard money contributions only and thus significantly underreport the total amount of money raised overall for congressional campaigns.

The sources of presidential campaign funding is a somewhat more fluid picture over time. Before FECA and its later reforms, not much was known about where presidential campaigns got their money, although many had heard stories of Richard Nixon and money stuffed into brown paper bags. This of course was one of the concerns that FECA was designed to address. The public financing component of the 1970s reforms was also meant to "level the playing field" in presidential elections: Each campaign was supposed to spend the same amount of money; each candidate received the same federal grant; and each national committee was allowed to spend the same amount of money directly on each campaign. And while some would argue that public financing did equalize things to a certain degree, the total amounts spent by presidential campaigns have varied considerably since the inception of the program.

During the 1980s, the major source of this variation was independent expenditures. Nearly $13 million in independent expenditures was spent on behalf of the Reagan-Bush campaign, compared to only $1.7 million on behalf of Carter-Mondale. In 1984 the total spent by independent groups exceeded $17 million, with the bulk of it spent on behalf of the Reagan-Bush ticket. When the Supreme Court ruled that these expenditures could not be limited, it formalized a new, unregulated source of funding for the two major party candidates' presidential campaigns (*Federal Election Commission v. National Conservative Political Action Committee*, 470 U.S. 480, 1985). However, despite fears that the sums spent independently could skyrocket—and that they would cause an imbalance between the campaigns—the amount actually spent in 1988 declined to about $10 million, though the Republicans did hold a three-to-one advantage (Alexander and Bauer 1991, 82–85).

From 1992 to 2000, the major source of variation—and the major factor in the escalation of the total costs of presidential campaigns—was soft money. In 1992, the Republicans raised nearly $50 million in soft money, compared to $36.3 million for the Democrats. In 1996, total soft money receipts reached $263.5 million, with the Republicans having an advantage of approximately $20 million over the Democrats. The amount raised in the 2000 campaign was nearly double that total, with the two parties' shares about equal. With the BCRA's ban on soft money, many were interested to see what the 2004 presidential election would produce in terms of equity in spending. The answer, once again, was an uneven playing field, although in this case a field that tilted in favor of Democratic candidate John Kerry. The Kerry campaign outspent the Bush campaign in the general election by a little over $100 million. Most of this difference was accounted for by spending on behalf of Kerry by the Democratic party and interest groups (including 527 groups) in the form of independent expenditures (Corrado 2006b). It is overwhelmingly likely that the 2004 presidential election was the last of this system of public financing. What is clear is that the 2008 presidential campaign was unlike anything ever seen before, at least in terms of how it was financed and the overall levels of spending. As noted earlier in this chapter, the Center for Responsive Politics placed the total price tag for the 2008 presidential election at $3.1 billion. Total spending in the 2012 presidential race—where no major party candidate took any public money—went down to $2.8 billion, according to the Center for Responsive Politics, although it is almost certain that not all money spent was accounted for. The final official Center for Responsive Politics figure for the 2016 presidential cycle was $2.4 billion, with the decline almost certainly due to the unconventional campaign ran by Donald Trump.

Individual Contributions

Although early reformers focused their attention on large contributions by individuals, that concern has been tempered in the last decade, at least if one looks only at hard money (the question of large soft money contributions by individuals is causing more concern than perhaps ever before, as we will discuss below). If the campaign finance reforms of the 1970s have been successful in any one area, it has been in curbing significant hard money contributions by wealthy individuals and thus limiting the alleged abuse caused by such huge donations. Gone are situations, as in 1972, when Stewart R. Mott contributed nearly half a million dollars to various Democratic presidential candidates in the prenomination phase of the campaign and over $800,000 to all campaigns in that year; or, in that same year, when fifty-one multimillionaires contributed a total of over $6 million to political campaigns, with more than $5.5 million to Republican candidates. The *McCutcheon* case discussed earlier in this chapter once again allows wealthy individuals to contribute a virtually unlimited amount of hard money funds in the aggregate in a particular cycle, but the limits on contributions to individual candidates, PACs, and party committees remain in place.

With the advent of the campaign finance reforms, the amount that individuals could give to a single campaign was set at $1,000, and the total amount that they could contribute to all campaigns was restricted (with the exception of contributions to their own campaigns and independent expenditures). The clear result of this change has been that large, individual contributions play a smaller role in politics—at least in terms of direct hard money contributions to candidates and parties—and smaller contributions play a larger role.[11] Indeed, the Obama campaign relied on small donors to an incredible degree in its record fund-raising performance. According to analysis done by the Campaign Finance Institute, 30 percent of Obama's 2008 campaign contributions during the primary season came from individuals who gave $200 or less, as did 34 percent of his general election contributions. Obama's 2012 reelection campaign followed a similar pattern as it raised $233.2 million—33 percent of all hard money funds raised—from small donors, according to the Center for Responsive Politics. In 2016, Trump raised 27 percent of his hard money from small donors compared with 18 percent for Clinton, again according to the Center for Responsive Politics.

A second implication of this change has been that candidates have had to work at developing a broader base of smaller contributors to fill their campaign coffers. Candidates have had to develop new techniques for raising money. The Goldwater campaign of 1964 and the George Wallace campaign of 1968 demonstrated the power of direct mail as a tool for raising large amounts of money (and for cementing the allegiance of a massive number of voters). The techniques used in those campaigns have been emulated and improved on by all politicians in the ensuing decades. In the most recent election cycles, presidential candidates John McCain, Howard Dean, and especially Barack Obama have demonstrated the effectiveness of the Internet for raising money. Many congressional, senatorial, and gubernatorial candidates hope to copy these success stories.

Most would agree that increased reliance on small donors is a good thing. It serves to bring more people into the process, and it also reduces the likelihood that any one individual or group will be able to achieve outsized influence due to a large direct contribution of hard money. But there is a downside here as well. As is always the case in American politics, those with the resources and desire to make large contributions have found other avenues through which to contribute their money.

Political Action Committees

Among the recipients of such money are PACs. Much has been written about PACs, so it is important to understand clearly what is meant by a political action committee. As is not atypical when one scrutinizes commonly used terms, one finds that the term *political action committee* does not appear in the statutes of the federal government. However, the statutes do refer to *political committees*, which are distinct from either *party committees* or *candidate committees*. A political committee, according to the U.S. Code (26 U.S.C. 9001[9]) is "any committee, association, or organization (whether or not incorporated) which accepts contributions or makes expenditures for the purpose of influencing, or attempting to influence, the nomination or election of one or more individuals to Federal, State, or local elective public office."

The U.S. Code further defines **multicandidate political committee** as "a political committee which has been registered . . . for a period of not less than six months, which has received contributions from more than fifty persons, and, except for any State political party organization, has made contributions to five or more candidates for Federal office" (4 U.S.C. 441 [a]).

Finally, PACs, as we normally think of them, are separate from their parent or sponsoring organization (if there is one). Campaign finance legislation has long prohibited direct political contributions by labor unions or corporations; however, provisions have been made for establishing a **separate segregated fund** for political purposes. The law specifies how money for this fund may and may not be raised. PACs with parent organizations, then, are the committees set up to administer these "separate segregated funds" (Sorauf 1984, chap. 1; 1991). The acronym PAC is thus commonly used to refer to a nonparty, noncandidate committee that funds more than one candidate and may or may not be affiliated with an established corporation, union, or interest group (Sabato 1985).

The FEC identifies seven major types of PACs: labor, corporation, trade, membership, nonconnected, cooperative, and corporation without stock. The first four types identified can be defined as multicandidate political committees that are administering campaign funds that have been raised from, but kept separate and segregated from, a parent organization—be that a labor union; a corporation; or a trade or membership organization (such as the American Bankers Association or the American Medical Association). The nonconnected PACs tend to be ideological multicandidate political committees that have come together for specific political purposes and that do not draw on an established parent organization. Cooperative and corporation without stock PACs are relatively minor players compared to the first four types listed here.

While their rise to prominence was a 1970s phenomenon, political committees came on to the American political scene prior to that decade. From the 1940s, until its merger with the American Federation of Labor (AFL) in 1955, the Congress of Industrial Organizations (CIO) operated a separate fund to receive and dispense voluntary contributions from labor unionists to political campaigns. The AFL-CIO Committee on Political Education (COPE), established after the 1955 merger, has been described as "the model for virtually all political action committees" (Epstein 1980, 100). In the late 1950s and early 1960s, some of the larger membership and trade professional organizations, such as the American Realtors and the American Medical Association, formed political committees (Alexander 1979, 559–66; Sorauf 1984, 33).

However, the factors that initially caused the most concern regarding PACs were the massive increase in their numbers and the corresponding increase in the magnitude of the role they played in the elections (as measured in the dollars they contributed) that took place in the 1970s and early 1980s. These increases developed directly out of the campaign finance reforms of the 1970s. The FECA amendments of 1974 put a more stringent limit on individual contributions than on contributions by multicandidate political committees. This followed naturally from the fact that reformers were more concerned about huge contributions by individuals than by group contributions.

The 1974 amendments also lifted the restriction that had prohibited government contractors from setting up separate segregated political committees. The public financing of presidential elections, effective for the 1976 election, led PACs to switch their emphasis from presidential to congressional campaigns. But, because the viability of PACs under the FECA was initially unclear, there was only cautious movement toward establishing new PACs. This situation changed in 1975. The FEC, in response to an inquiry from the Sun Oil Company, issued an advisory opinion in which it informed Sun Oil that the corporation could legally establish a separate segregated fund for the purpose of contributing to political campaigns and that it could solicit voluntary contributions from its employees to support that fund. As a result of all these actions, many corporations decided to form PACs, and these committees as a major force in funding congressional elections became a most visible aspect of electoral politics. Hundreds of other corporations eventually followed Sun Oil's lead (Epstein 1980).

Look back at Table 4.2 (p. 118), which depicts the rapid growth of PACs. The total number of PACs grew from slightly over six hundred, in 1974, to well over 4,200, by 1988. This figure reached over 8,666 in 2016. PAC expenditures have also continued to rise. From $12.5 million in 1974, PAC expenditures topped $100 million in 1983–1984, exceeded $392 million in 1993–1994, and reached $3.97 billion in 2015–2016 (all data from the FEC).

It should be noted further that this growth has not been constant among the various types of PACs. While organized labor was quick to see that PACs could increase their influence—nearly all major labor unions organized PACs—the number of labor PACs has never doubled the number that existed in 1974. It has also declined from its high point in the mid-1980s, and has held steady at around 300 for roughly the past decade. In contrast with organized labor, corporations were slower to realize the potential influence they could wield through PACs. But the number of corporate PACs eventually increased to far exceed that of labor unions, with major jumps coming after the **SUN PAC** opinion and again during the Reagan administration. (See Eismeier and Pollock 1985a, 1985b; Malbin 1984a, 1984b.) The number of corporate PACs has continued to grow and in 2016 the number of corporate PACs was more than five times the number of labor PACs. In the late 1980s, growth was also seen in the nonconnected PACs, as more "political entrepreneurs" came to view this avenue as a viable way to increase political influence. The number of nonconnected PACs has continued to grow as well.

The growth in the number of PACs and the amount they contribute to political candidates, more specifically to congressional candidates, has led to a number of concerns: the necessity of PAC support to secure electoral victory, the link between PAC support and legislative behavior, the ideological imbalance of present and future PACs, and the responsibility of PAC leaders to contributors.

The influence of PACs on electoral outcomes. Some things are clear. Examining recent elections for the U.S. Congress shows that, by and large, winners spend more money than losers. Although it is appropriate to be concerned about who gets money from each source, attention has been focused on PACs because PACs are contributing an increasingly large amount of money, as indicated by Figure 5.4. Additionally, Figure 5.5 shows that PACs do not distribute their money equally among all candidates. Incumbents are able to raise PAC money much more easily than their challengers. While PACs flirted with supporting more challengers in the early 1980s (see Eismeier and Pollock 1985b, 1986; Jacobson 1985–1986; Sabato 1985; Wright 1985), in the last decade PACs have typically given a minimum of 70 percent of their contributions to incumbents and less than 15 percent to challengers.[12] Ironically, money is more significant

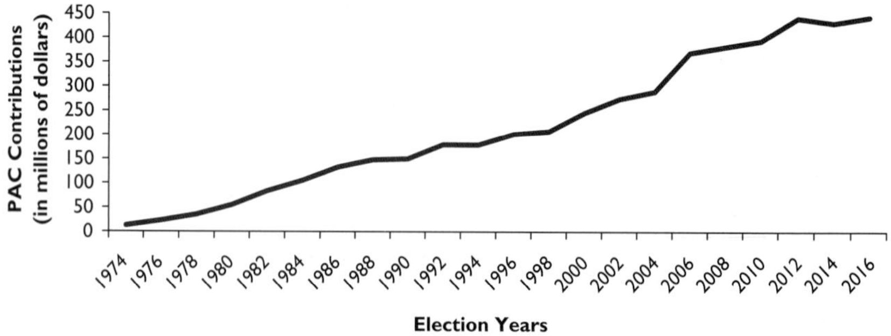

Figure 5.4. PAC Contributions to Congressional Elections, 1974–2016, in millions of dollars

Sources: Federal Election Commission and Center for Responsive Politics.

for challengers than it is for incumbents (Jacobson 1980, chap. 5) in terms of running a serious campaign, so the imbalance in PAC giving can be viewed as problematic.

The influence of PACs on legislative outcomes. PACs are connected to specific groups that have a direct interest in legislative decision making. The funds may be separate and segregated, but the connection is there in the minds of all involved. One does not have to stretch one's imagination too far to see that the directors of the BP political action committee have certain views on issues affecting the oil industry or that those deciding on the allocation of funds from the Machinists Nonpartisan Political League care greatly about the level of governmental support for the aerospace industry. PAC leaders know this and candidates know this. This connection raises concerns among some that PAC contributions can buy policy outcomes. Still others feel that while PAC money does not directly buy outcomes, contributions do buy access, and access can lead indirectly to influence and desirable policy outputs.

Another view notes that PACs contribute to individuals likely to support their cause in any case, and individual PAC contributions are not significant in terms of the total amounts spent on campaigns. Incumbents have tremendous electoral advantages, regardless of PAC actions or intentions, and they face an array of pressures; thus, they cannot listen to PAC leaders only.

Still, members of Congress do accept large amounts of money from groups with a direct stake in legislation. Increasingly members of Congress have leadership PACs as well, a vehicle that allows them to effectively double the amount of hard money that members can receive from

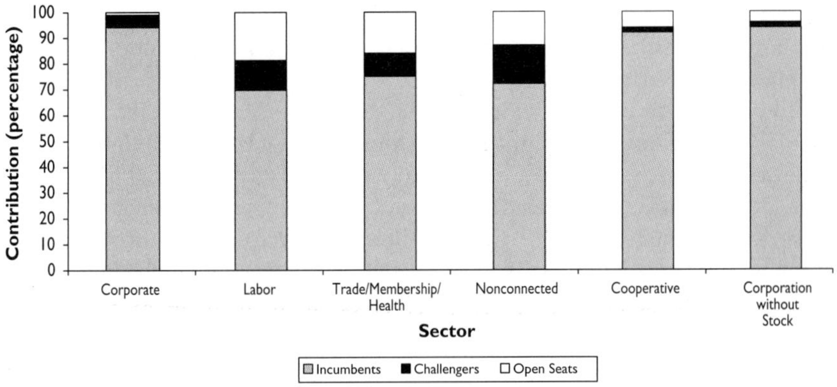

Figure 5.5. PAC Contributions to Congressional Candidates by Candidate Status, 2016

Source: Federal Election Commission.

an individual or group (although they cannot spend leadership PAC money on their own campaign) (Goldmacher 2013). The total contributed by like-minded groups might well represent a sizable percentage of a candidate's campaign funds, and interest group representatives are often quite overt in exercising pressure when key decisions are pending. There is, in the words of the Supreme Court, "the appearance of impropriety," which may well be as detrimental to the system as the reality.

Alleged PAC influence on legislation tarnishes the reputation of PACs (Common Cause 1986; Drew 1983; Jackson 1988; Stern 1988). PAC supporters argue persuasively that citizens should have a right to associate with others of similar views to maximize the likelihood of having their views heard. PAC detractors point to the number of cases in which large PAC contributions have been funneled to incumbents facing no challengers; they cite it as evidence that PACs are polluting the system by setting up an assumption that legislative behavior is for sale to the highest bidder. Political scientists have searched for evidence of PAC influence on legislative behavior, but their conclusion is that hard evidence of the corrupting influence of PACs is all but absent (Evans 1986; Frendeis and Waterman 1985; Grenzke 1989, 1990; Schroedel 1986; Wright 1985). But the concerns remain nonetheless.

The ideological imbalance of PACs. Labor leaders were among those most interested in writing legislation allowing for the formation of PACs in the early years of the 1970s reform movement. They saw tremendous advantages in trying to exert influence over the electoral process. However, these labor leaders were shortsighted, as the trends in the increases in PACs show. Labor PACs are as well organized and about as effective as they are likely to be, and in terms of number and influence, corporate PACs and trade association PACs have far outstripped those formed by labor unions. Now, labor leaders, Democrats, and other liberals worry that PAC influence will increasingly become more conservative, business oriented, and Republican.

This argument can be dealt with on two levels. First, Table 5.2 shows that PACs have not given significantly more to Republicans than to Democrats, but rather PACs have tended to support incumbents (Figure 5.5). The Democrats controlled the House (and the Senate, except for the period between 1980 and 1986) for the first twenty years of the FECA. Since incumbents have received more PAC support, the Democrats benefited. When the Republicans regained control of Congress in 1994, PAC money began to be split more evenly between the two parties, reflecting the fact that nearly equal numbers of incumbents of both parties have been seeking reelection and also that the Republicans were the new majority party.[13] The GOP exhibited its largest advantage in PAC money over the Democrats in 2004, a likely reflection of Tom DeLay's infamous

Table 5.2. PAC Contributions to Congressional Candidates by Party, 1998–2016

	Republican Party	*Democratic Party*	*Other*	*Total*
1998				
Corporate	67.9%	32.1%	0.0%	$78.0 million
Labor	8.8	90.9	0.3	44.6
Trade/membership/health	62.3	37.6	0.1	6.2
Nonconnected	60.5	39.3	0.2	28.0
Other	56.0	43.9	0.2	4.4
Total	52.9	46.9	0.2	220.0
2000				
Corporate	67.7	33.3	0.0	91.6
Labor	7.7	92.0	0.3	51.9
Trade/membership/health	61.6	38.2	0.2	71.5
Nonconnected	59.2	40.6	0.2	44.6
Other	57.8	42.2	0.1	6.5
Total	52.2	47.6	0.2	274.3
2002				
Corporate	66.7	33.3	0.0	71.3
Labor	9.3	90.5	0.2	46.6
Trade/membership/health	60.9	39.1	0.0	56.5
Nonconnected	55.5	44.5	0.0	22.5
Other	58.7	41.3	0.0	6.9
Total	51.4	48.5	0.0	203.9
2004				
Corporate	67.7	32.3	0.0	104.3
Labor	12.2	87.6	0.2	50.3
Trade/membership/health	63.2	36.8	0.0	78.2
Nonconnected	64.5	35.5	0.0	49.8
Other	56.5	43.9	0.0	6.5
Total	56.0	43.9	0.0	289.1
2006				
Corporate	66.6	33.4	0.0	122.0
Labor	11.1	88.9	0.0	53.9
Trade/membership/health	61.8	38.1	0.0	95.1
Nonconnected	62.1	37.9	0.0	66.7
Other	55.3	44.7	0.0	7.6
Total	55.5	44.5	0.0	345.3

(Cont.)

Table 5.2. PAC Contributions to Congressional Candidates by Party, 1998–2016 (Cont.)

	Republican Party	*Democratic Party*	*Other*	*Total*
2008				
Corporate	51.9	48.1	0.01	56.5
Labor	7.5	92.5	0.0	62.3
Trade/membership/health	48.5	51.5	0.0	112.5
Nonconnected	46.7	53.3	0.0	64.9
Other	47.5	52.5	0.0	12.2
Total	40.4	59.6	0.0	408.3
2010				
Corporate	46.7	53.1	0	141.4
Labor	6.1	93.8	0	62.1
Trade/membership/health	49.6	50.3	0	118.1
Nonconnected	49.7	50	0	64.5
Cooperative	35.3	64.7	0	4.2
Corporation without stock	53	47	0	7
Total	41.7	58.1	0	397.3
2012				
Corporate	63.6	36	0.4	166.2
Labor	9.8	89.5	0.8	56.7
Trade and membership[a]	62.2	37.3	0.4	115.7
Nonconnected	54.2	45.4	0.4	70.5
Cooperative	58.1	41.5	0.4	5.1
Corporation without stock	60.4	39.2	0.5	6.8
Total	54.3	45.3	0.4	421
2014				
Corporate	64	36	0	178
Labor	10.8	89.2	0	50.6
Trade and membership[a]	55.9	44.1	0	119.2
Nonconnected	49.5	50.5	0.03	76
Cooperative	52.5	47.5	0	4.9
Corporation without stock	61.3	36.7	0	7
Total	56.2	43.8	0.01	435.7

(Cont.)

Table 5.2. (Cont.)

	Republican Party	*Democratic Party*	*Other*	*Total*
2016				
Corporate	67.4	32.0	0.01	181.8
Labor	14.3	85.3	0	46.4
Trade and membership[a]	65.3	33.8	0.01	122.8
Nonconnected	60.6	38.9	0	78.1
Cooperative	56.4	42.5	0.01	4.7
Corporation without stock	61.3	38.1	0.01	7.5
Total	59.8	39.5	0.01	441.3

[a]In July 2011 the FEC began reporting trade and membership groups separately and dropped the specific health group category. Trade and membership groups continue to be jointly reported here for comparability with past data.

Source: 1998–2006, 2010, 2016 Federal Election Commission; 2008, 2012–2014, Campaign Finance Institute

"KStreet Project." But once the Democrats recaptured Congress in the 2006 elections, the split (excepting labor) returned somewhere close to even. It appears that on the whole incumbency matters more to PACs than does partisanship, although Republicans do generally attract more funds than Democrats. Finally, readers may be wondering why we have not yet mentioned so-called Super PACs. The reason is because they are fundamentally different from regular PACs. We discuss Super PACs under soft money below.

Political Parties

The conventional wisdom in the 1970s was that parties did not play a major role in campaign finance. The Nixon campaigns of 1968 and 1972 raised substantial amounts of money independent of the Republican National Committee. The major financial effort on behalf of the Democrats was to retire the debts incurred by the Humphrey and Kennedy campaigns of 1968. In other words, the Democratic National Committee expended most of its fund-raising efforts in paying off debts, not in aiding candidates. This changed. Party national committee money can be of vital importance to a presidential campaign, as it was for John Kerry in 2004 and John McCain in 2008. However, the future of the parties' significant role in presidential campaigns has become less clear in the post–*Citizens United* world as Super PACs and 501(c) groups (more below) raise and spend ever-growing amounts to influence the presidential contest. But if the past is any indication of the future, the parties will figure out a way to play an important role in financing presidential races.

The parties most certainly remain key players at the congressional level. Congressional and senatorial campaigns of the past did not cost the large amounts that are in evidence today. The national parties were not active in raising large sums for these campaigns, and the state and local parties did not have sufficient resources to make significant differences. However, as Gary Jacobson (1983, 49; 1985–1986), Frank Sorauf (1988, 127–49), Paul Herrnson (1995, 1998a, 1998b), and others have shown, the biggest change in campaign financing since the 1980s has been the significant role played by the political parties, first that of the Republican party with the Democrats eventually catching up, on behalf of congressional and senatorial candidates (Jackson 1988; Arterton 1982).

The 1980s saw the emergence of the Hill committees—the National Republican Senatorial Committee (NRSC), National Republican Congressional Committee (NRCC), Democratic Senatorial Campaign Committee (DSCC), and Democratic Congressional Campaign Committee (DCCC) —as important forces in congressional politics. For many years, at each of these levels, the Republicans were much more active than Democrats and much more successful. This is no longer the case. In recent election cycles the Hill committees of each party have been quite successful in terms of raising money, and in some reporting quarters the Democrats come out on top. The Hill committees are crucial in allowing the parties to boost the chances of their more promising candidates who are challenging incumbents and also in aiding in the defense of some of their incumbents who might be vulnerable to defeat. Party money can also be critical in open-seat races. If you want to know if a party considers a certain House or Senate race competitive, watch what the Hill committees do. If they send money, they believe the race is competitive. If there is no money forthcoming, they do not.

Soft Money

This chapter has frequently referred to soft money, which in some ways became the tail that wagged the dog. So much soft money was spent in the last few campaigns pre-BCRA that all of the restrictions on existing campaign finance laws seemed useless. The authors of the McCain-Feingold bill were so obsessed with controlling soft money that they were willing to make a whole series of compromises to achieve that goal.

What exactly is the problem with soft money? Put in the bluntest terms, individuals and corporations could give as much as they wanted to campaigns through soft money. Even though these amounts were reported, the result was that influence could be purchased, or at least it seemed to be purchased, in much the same way as it was before the reforms of the 1970s. The soft money loophole eviscerated the effect of the restrictions on large contributions, thought by most to be the principal accomplishment of the FECA.

How serious was the problem? According to Public Disclosure, a watchdog group that monitors FEC filings, the problem was exploding out of control. The amount raised and spent in the 2000 election year approached $500 million, nearly double the amount raised and spent in 1996. Stephen Weissman (2005) of the Campaign Finance Institute put the soft money figure for the 2002 election cycle—the last in which the national parties were allowed to accept soft money—at $556 million (remember, 2002 was a nonpresidential year). The money did not come equally from all rungs of American society. Businesses and trade associations gave more than ten times the amount contributed by labor unions. Extremely wealthy individual contributors reentered the system in significant numbers, contributing tens of millions of dollars. Think about who can give money in this way, in six- and seven-figure checks. Public Disclosure claimed that twenty-three of the twenty-five individuals who gave at least a quarter of a million dollars in 2000 were either chairpersons, or presidents, or CEOs of well-known corporations. Facts like these contributed to the drive to eliminate soft money.

Why did these individuals give, and why did they give to the extent that they did? Direct linkages between motivation for giving and legislation that is pending are difficult to confirm, but the appearance of impropriety is not hard to imagine. During a Congress in which tobacco regulation and telephone-access legislation were high on the legislative agenda, Philip Morris contributed $2.1 million in soft money, and RJR Nabisco contributed $900,000; Bell Atlantic, MCI, and AT&T each contributed nearly $1 million. Cynical citizens were given a substantial amount of ammunition to fuel their concerns. Given this level of spending, and the lack of restrictions in the law and in FEC regulations, it is small wonder that reformers claimed that if Congress could only get a hold on soft money spending and fail to do anything else, that sole accomplishment would still represent significant progress. BCRA was their effort to do just that.

Of course, passage of BCRA did not end the soft money debate. In some ways, concerns about soft money and its impact have intensified post McCain-Feingold. Even while the political community awaited the Supreme Court decision regarding the constitutionality of the law, many political players were already looking for ways around it. In September of 2003 (months before the Court would ultimately uphold the ban on national parties accepting soft money), hedge fund billionaire and philanthropist George Soros, whose foundation, the Open Society Institute, was among the leaders in pushing for campaign finance reform, announced that he would give $15 million to two liberal organizations—MoveOn.org and America Coming Together—whose primary goals in the 2004 election cycle were to advocate on behalf of liberal causes and register nonvoters and get them to vote—ideally, against the incumbent president, George W. Bush. In announcing the gifts, Soros said that he was willing to do anything within the law to defeat Bush in 2004 (for more on Soros see Carlisle 2004).

Even those who agree with Soros's goal fear that his methods undermine the campaign finance reforms about which he feels so strongly. The history of political money is that it finds a hole in the law and fills it, and with his large donation Soros pointed out for all to see the gaping hole in BCRA. America Coming Together and MoveOn.org are examples of 527 groups—the name comes from the provision of the tax code that governs the activities of these types of organizations (MoveOn.org also has a 501(c) component—see below). A 527 group is a political organization with a primary purpose of affecting elections. Such groups are tax exempt (except for investment income) and are not subject to any limits in terms of the amounts of money they raise or spend, or the size of donations they receive. Although 527 groups existed before BCRA, when the law banned soft money donations to parties but was silent on 527 groups, interest in and attention to the groups soared. Previously, wealthy individuals and interests who wanted to make large donations in the hope of affecting an election often gave soft money to the parties. With this door closed by BCRA, much (but not all) of these large soft money donations went to 527 groups. According to the Center for Responsive Politics, 527 groups spent $432.8 million on federal races in the 2003–2004 election cycle, the first election cycle in which national party organizations were prohibited from accepting soft money. The vast majority of the donations (over 80 percent) that generated this spending were $250,000 or more, including fifty-two individuals who gave over $1 million (Weissman and Hassan 2006). Soros himself eventually donated almost $23.5 million to 527s in 2003–2004 (in support of Democratic efforts), while Texas billionaire Bob Perry (one of the primary donors to the infamous Swift Boat Veterans for Truth) was the top giver to Republican-supporting 527 groups at a little over $8 million (according to the Center for Responsive Politics).

Senators McCain and Feingold, and many other supporters of campaign finance reform, were aghast at the way in which 527 groups were able to take advantage of loopholes in election law and keep the massive amounts of soft money flowing. Congress considered new legislation to shut down 527s, but ultimately did nothing. Reform advocates urged the FEC through its rule-making process to force 527 groups to follow the same soft money guidelines that parties were forced to adhere to. The FEC refused to take this step, but it did issue some rulings that somewhat reduced (but certainly did not end) the attractiveness of 527 groups as destinations for soft money in some cases. This is reflected in the amounts spent on federal races by 527 groups since the 2003–2004 cycle: $204.8 million in 2005–2006, $253.9 million in 2007–2008, $200.9 million in 2009–2010, $199 million in 2011–2012, $196.7 million in 2013–2014, and $250.9 million in 2015–2016 (Center for Responsive Politics). But these figures still represent significant amounts of money, and 527s spent still more in state races.

A large part of the reason for the declining use of 527 groups is the emergence of two far more attractive options for big donors. As is always the case with money and elections, where one door closes (even partially) another one (or in this case, two) opens. The first door is the **Super PAC**. Super PACs developed in the wake of the post-BCRA court decisions discussed earlier in this chapter. Traditional PACs that we discussed earlier in this chapter are bound by fund-raising and contribution limits. This is not the case with Super PACs. Super PACs are independent expenditure-only committees. This means they are not allowed to contribute directly to candidates or parties—in other words, they only raise and spend soft money. However, unlike regular PACs, Super PACs are allowed to raise unlimited amounts of money from unlimited sources. They must disclose the identity of their donors, the same as a traditional PAC. And Super PACs are supposed to be entirely separate from the candidate or party they support, although most would say such separation is porous at best and a joke at worst (Carney 2014). Some Super PACs also have affiliated 527 groups. The Center for Responsive Politics indicates that Super PACs spent $609.4 million on federal races in the 2012 cycle, $346.9 million in the 2014 cycle, and $1.06 billion in the 2016 cycle. Super PACs have become especially important in presidential campaigns (Gold 2015a). Most recently we have seen the rise of an entity called a hybrid PAC, a cross between a regular PAC and a Super PAC. Hybrids can raise unlimited soft money funds like a Super PAC but can also raise dedicated hard money like a PAC, so long as the hard money is kept in a separate account (Allison 2011; Backer 2012; Levinthal 2012). These developments trouble many campaign finance watchers, and there is little doubt that the importance of Super PACs and their hybrid cousins will continue to increase.

The second newly opened door for big money in American elections is represented by **501(c) groups**, which are also named after the provision of the IRS code that governs such groups. The 501(c) groups are social welfare organizations or labor unions or trade associations that have tax-exempt status. Of particular concern here are 501(c)(4)—civic league, social welfare, and employee association—groups and 501(c)(6)—business league and chambers of commerce—groups. Under current tax and election law, these 501(c) groups can raise and spend soft money in virtually unlimited fashion, as long as campaign activity is not their "primary activity" or "major purpose." In other words, as long as these groups keep their electioneering secondary (defined by the IRS as less than 50% of their activity) to their social welfare or labor or business purposes, they can operate without soft money constraints. For many donors, 501(c) groups are clearly preferable to 527 groups. While each type of group can for the most part raise and spend soft money without restriction, 527 groups are required to disclose the identities of their donors; 501(c) groups are not. In many cases 501(c) groups are also not required to disclose expenditures. Given these facts, it is obviously difficult to know for sure how much 501(c)(4) and 501(c)(6) groups are actually raising and spending, but the Center for Responsive Politics put the figure at $311.3 million for the 2012 election cycle, $179 million in the 2014 contests, and $177.3 million in 2016, with the recognition that these figures are underestimates of true spending and the actual totals are likely much higher. Money moving through 501(c)(4) and 501(c)(6) groups is the "dark money" that so many speak of in ominous tones, claiming it is highly corrosive to American campaigns and elections (Aronsen 2012). The IRS (Flynn and Bade 2015) and many states (Carney 2013a) are looking to tighten the rules on the electioneering activities of nonprofits. But so far such efforts have gone nowhere.

BCRA clearly did not eliminate soft money from American elections. This is made clear by Table 5.3, which presents the top ten outside groups in terms of federal campaign spending in the 2016 election cycle. The bottom line on soft money in federal elections is this: Despite the intentions of McCain-Feingold, soft money is still very prevalent and very important in American elections. Many would say that the situation today is far worse than it was in the days before BCRA. At least when soft money was flowing through political parties, one knew where it came from and where it was spent. That is not the case today.

Public Financing

The reformers of the 1970s proposed public financing as the way to take the taint of money out of politics. If political campaigns were funded by the mass public, politicians would not have to deal with those seeking to buy influence.

Since 1976, public financing has been an important part of presidential campaigns. During the prenomination phase of the presidential election, after reaching a qualifying plateau, candidates for the two parties' nominations can receive matching funds for all contributions of $250 or less received from individuals. Of course, the number of active candidates for the nomination can affect the amount of public money spent on the campaigns, as can individual candidate decisions on whether to accept public money.[14]

Table 5.3. Top Ten Outside Groups in Federal Campaign Spending, 2016 Election Cycle

Group	*Total Spent*	*Super PAC*	*527*	*501(c)*
Priorities USA/Priorities USA Action	$133,407,972	X		
Right to Rise USA	$86,817,138	X		
Senate Leadership Fund	$85,994,270	X		
Senate Majority PAC	$75,413,436	X		
Conservative Solutions PAC	$55,443,483	X		
National Rifle Association	$54,398,558			X
House Majority PAC	$47,470,121	X		
Congressional Leadership Fund	$40,125,691	X		
Emily's List	$33,167,285	X		
Freedom Partners	$30,024,803	X		X

Source: Center for Responsive Politics, based on data provided by the Federal Election Commission.
Note: "Outside groups" refers to nonparty and noncandidate organizations.

Each major party is granted public funds to run its nominating convention. Each party's nominee is granted public funds for running a general election campaign; other candidates for the presidency qualify for public funding according to the success they achieve.[15] The system of public financing appeared to work well in the 1980s and 1990s, but cracks in the system began to appear as we moved into the twenty-first century. Neither George W. Bush nor Steve Forbes took advantage of public financing as they pursued the 2000 Republican presidential nomination. Bush refused public funding again in 2004 and was joined by Howard Dean and John Kerry on the Democratic side. In all instances, these candidates did very well raising money privately and were subject to many fewer restrictions on what they could do with their money. However, both Bush (in 2000 and 2004) and Kerry did use public money to run their general election campaigns once they had secured the nomination. John McCain did the same in 2008, but as noted earlier Barack Obama did not accept public money for his nomination race or for the general election. The 2008 presidential election was the first since public financing was made available in 1976 in which one of the major party candidates did not accept any public money. None of the major party contenders took public money in 2012 or 2016, and under the current rules it is unlikely that any will ever again. Some states still have some form of public financing for state elections, but it is likely that many of these programs will have to be modified or scrapped altogether given recent court rulings.

Proponents of public financing say that public financing worked for presidential elections (at least it did until 2008) and will do so at the congressional level as well. They hold that using public funds to finance elections is fairer; less susceptible to corruption; and, in the long run, the only way to reduce the costs of elections, especially given the Supreme Court ruling that only those who accept public financing can be restricted in the amounts they spend.

Opponents of public financing argue from a number of different points. Some argue that any public financing bill would automatically protect all incumbents because challengers must spend huge sums of money to overcome the advantages of incumbency. This argument is especially important in the House, as its incumbents are rarely defeated.

Others argue that public financing would be impossible to implement for congressional and senatorial elections because congressional districts (and even states) are so different that the amounts of money needed to campaign effectively in different districts would vary substantially. They are further concerned about candidates who receive public funds when no serious challenger exists.

Still others argue that public funding would create opposition to popular incumbents where none currently exists. Some incumbents are forthright enough to state that they will not support public financing, because it is against their best interest. Others hedge this argument, stating that it is not in the interest of the nation to force people to pay for unwanted campaigns. Challengers and those eager to support competitive elections see this as an advantage of public financing because it encourages competition. But the level of public funding must be sufficient so that challengers can run credible campaigns. There is significant disagreement about what that level of funding is—and whether it is the same from district to district for House elections.

There are other points to consider as well. Should people be forced to pay for the campaigns of candidates they oppose? Can fair competition ever be imposed through law? Is there anything wrong with the current situation, and if not, why change it?

CAMPAIGN FINANCE IN A POST–*CITIZENS UNITED* AND POST-*MCCUTCHEON* WORLD

Any elected official at the federal level, and increasingly at the state and sometimes even local level, will tell you that winning an election costs money—in many cases, a lot of money. This has been the case for some time now, and seemingly becomes more set in stone with every election cycle. Spending on elections continues to rise, no matter what Congress does or what the courts decide. But how money enters the system and where it comes from is very fluid, and adapts to both changes in the laws and technology, as we have shown in this chapter.

Elected officials bemoan the amount of time and effort they have to devote to raising money to fund their campaigns. This undeniably takes time away from the tasks we send them to office to perform. Reports of wealthy donors such as the Koch brothers or Tom Steyer spending millions of dollars of their own money to influence election outcomes appall many Americans. However, it is difficult to see this changing in any meaningful way any time soon. The stakes of American politics are high, and individuals and groups are willing to spend heavily to increase the likelihood that the game plays out in their favor. The hard truth is that money always finds its way into elections. No matter how the rules are changed, it is likely impossible (short of amending the Constitution) to keep money out of campaigns.

CRITICAL THINKING QUESTIONS

1. Should there be limits on how much money political actors (candidates, parties, interest groups, etc.) are allowed to spend on political campaigns and elections?
2. Do you support or oppose a system of full public funding for all federal elections?
3. When it comes to campaigns and elections, does money equal speech?
4. Do you agree or disagree with the following statement: money corrupts American politics.

KEY TERMS

Bipartisan Campaign Reform Act (BCRA), or McCain-Feingold
hard money
Federal Election Commission (FEC)
soft money
Tillman Act
Federal Corrupt Practices Act of 1925
Hatch Act of 1940
public financing
Federal Election Campaign Act (FECA)
Revenue Act
tax checkoff
1974 amendments to the FECA
Buckley v. Valeo
independent expenditures
Citizens United v. Federal Election Commission
electioneering communications
527 group
multicandidate political committee
separate segregated fund
SUN PAC
Super PAC
501(c) groups

NOTES

1. As we put the finishing touches on this edition the 2018 gubernatorial race in Illinois is on pace to surpass California 2010 as the most expensive gubernatorial race in American history (Burnett and O'Connor 2018).

2. All figures here other than the 2010 California gubernatorial race are from the Center for Responsive Politics.

3. Those who have come of political age in the last four decades might think that the problems of campaign finance are new and associated with the advent of television as a means for communicating campaign messages. Nothing could be further from the truth, and there is a vast literature of previous reform efforts. For more than four decades the research into campaign finance practices and reform has been dominated by a small group of political scientists. Alexander Heard of Vanderbilt University set the agenda for much of the work in this area (see Heard 1960), and Herbert Alexander, former director of the Citizens' Research Foundation, gathered and analyzed a great deal of early data on the financing of federal elections. Since the Federal Election Commission has been gathering data, more political scientists have begun to look systematically at the ways in which American elections are financed, with Anthony Corrado, Ray LaRaja, and Michael Malbin being among the most active. Relatively little work has been done on elections at the state or local level, largely because the experiences differ so widely from state to state and data are difficult to gather (but see Gierzynski and Breaux 1991; Gierzynski 1992; Jones 1984, 1991; Malbin and Gais 1998).

4. The recent history of campaign finance reform can be traced through many of the sources mentioned in this chapter. The first congressional response to pressure to reform campaign finance laws was the passage of an act regulating political broadcasts; however, this bill, which passed Congress in 1970, was vetoed by President Nixon.

5. The congressional response dealt only with candidates for federal office (and thus would not have impacted the Shapp or Rockefeller campaigns discussed previously) because of perceived limitations of congressional jurisdiction. Various states responded in different ways at different times (Alexander 1976; Jones 1984, 1991).

6. It should also be noted that this law did have a significant impact on campaign finance practice. Despite the fact that the Government Accounting Office, which was assigned enforcement responsibilities for presidential campaign compliance with this law, had very little time to gear up for its new role, it did investigate and prosecute some major violations of the law, including the "laundering" of campaign funds by President Nixon's Committee to Reelect the President during the 1972 campaign.

7. According to the Federal Election Commission,

> An electioneering communication is any broadcast, cable, or satellite communication that fulfills **each** of the following conditions: (1) The communication refers to a clearly identified candidate for federal office; (2) The communication is publicly distributed shortly before an election for the office that candidate is seeking; (3) The communication is targeted to the relevant electorate (U.S. House and Senate candidates only).

8. It should be noted that the public financing of presidential elections, called for in the 1971 act, was not to go into effect until the 1976 election; this provision was part of the agreement necessary to prevent a veto of the legislation by Richard Nixon, who was, of course, a candidate for reelection in 1972.

9. These data do not deflate the averages by including uncontested seats. The data used in this discussion are drawn from FEC reports on the elections over this period. These data, for the period from 1974 to 1990, have been summarized in various sources, including Malbin (1984b) and Ornstein, Mann, and Malbin (1998).

10. Ruth Jones, an expert on the cost of state and local campaigns, feels that Alexander's estimate is low; on this topic scholars must speculate because of the lack of systematic data. Election officials in a majority of states do not publish aggregate figures on receipts and expenditures for those offices (Sorauf 1988, 288).

11. This rosy conclusion should not be accepted casually. In point of fact, a small number of individuals still manage to give large sums of money, much of it to the political parties in soft money. In addition, wealthy individuals often play the role of broker, bringing their wealthy friends in contact with candidates they support in order to add significantly to those candidates' war chests.

12. The remaining money, of course, went to candidates in open seats.

13. When the Republicans controlled the Senate, between 1980 and 1986, there was some evidence that PACs were giving more to the Republicans than to the Democrats. Upon careful scrutiny, it was revealed that this finding reflected the larger number of incumbent Republicans than Democrats whose seats happened to be contested in the years studied (Magleby and Nelson 1990, 82, table 5–3).

14. In 1988, neither party had an incumbent running, so both parties had spirited primary campaigns. In 1992, President Bush was challenged by Patrick Buchanan, but the campaign was not one in which large sums were spent. In 1996, though he was without a challenger in his own party, President Clinton spent extensively to jump-start his reelection effort. The Republicans also had a spirited campaign in that race.

15. For example, H. Ross Perot received $29 million in 1996, which is just under half of what the major party nominees received; the amount was determined because he had received just under half of the average major party vote in 1992.

Chapter 6

State and Local Nominations

Then Virginia governor Terry McAuliffe, left, and lieutenant governor Ralph Northam celebrate Northam's victory in the 2017 Virginia Democratic Primary for Governor. Some contests for state and local nomination are sleepy and uneventful, while others are hard-fought and high-energy affairs. Either way, the nominating process determines whom voters get to choose from in the general election.

We know a great deal about how presidents receive their party's nomination (chapter 8). For months on end we follow the candidate parade through the fields of Iowa and the snows of New Hampshire all the way to the national party **conventions**—a gathering of party members to endorse or nominate candidates for office, adopt platforms, and establish party rules—in late summer. We complain that the process is too long and the rules too complex, but much of it is public and open. It is certainly well documented in the political science literature (e.g., Aldrich 1980; Buell and Sigelman 1991; Kessel 1992; Lengle and Shafer 1980; Orren and Polsby 1987; Polsby, Wildavsky, and Hopkins 2008; Wayne 2008).

What do we know about the ways in which the thousands of other elected public officials are nominated for office by their parties? Back in the days of party bosses and dominating political machines, Boss Tweed of Tammany Hall is reported to have claimed, "I don't care who does the electing, just so I do the nominating." When machines dominated American politics, one of the most important aspects of their control was the ability to control political nominations. We know that machines no longer dominate our politics as they once did. But what has replaced them?

Ask yourself! What do you know about how your U.S. senators were nominated? Your representative in Congress? Your state representative (do you honestly even know who he or she is)? What about county commissioners? How are these candidates chosen?

These questions are particularly important when we realize the significance of the decisions that many of these individuals make or when we understand that many holders of more prestigious positions have used lower offices as stepping-stones for higher office. Recent research indicates that we must begin looking very, very early in the life cycle if we are going to fully understand why some individuals choose to seek public office while the vast majority of Americans do not (Fox and Lawless 2011; Lawless 2012). This chapter will look at how potential candidates decide whether to run. It will then turn to the question of how state and local officials gain party nominations. Finally, it will move to an examination of the politics of the nomination process.

POLITICAL CONTEXT AND POLITICIANS' DECISIONS TO RUN

Politicians often think in terms of career progression: Is this the time for me to move up? Should a state legislator run for Congress? Should a U.S. Representative run for governor? (Schlesinger 1966).[1]

How do politicians decide to risk seeking a higher office? Jacobson and Kernell (1983) have posited an important theory—that politicians weigh the value of the office for which they strive and the probability of winning against the risk involved in giving up the office they currently hold. Politicians weigh the public climate in determining whether they will run. The decisions made by **qualified candidates**—candidates who are thought by experts to have the characteristics to run a strong campaign—about whether they will seek a higher office are very important (Maisel, Stone, and Maestas 1999; Stone and Maisel 2003; Stone, Maisel, and Maestas 2004; Maestas et al. 2006; Stone et al. 2008, 2010).

One reason for incumbent reelection success, at least in House elections, is that qualified candidates, in the aggregate, decide that the political climate is not right for moving up. When candidates with the greatest likelihood of winning decide not to run, challengers of lesser quality frequently step up to fill the void (Abramowitz 1981; Hinckley 1981; Jacobson 1981; Maisel and Cooper 1981).

Looking more deeply into the reasoning of individual candidates, Jacobson and Kernell (1983) review two competing sets of theories that are used to explain electoral results. One body of speculation stresses the impact of economic conditions on electoral outcome (Bloom and Price 1975; Kramer 1971; Tufte 1975, 1978). The other theory uses survey data to explain electoral results in terms of individual voter attitudes (Arsenau and Wolfinger 1973; Fiorina 1978, 1981; Kernell 1977; Kinder and Kiewiet 1979; Mann and Wolfinger 1980; Mondak and Mitchell 2008). In either case the operating assumption is that voters cast their votes for *some* offices based on their overall assessment of the political and economic situation in which they find themselves. Politicians certainly think in these terms, but they also think in terms of specific salient issues of the day, such as our military commitments in Afghanistan or the issue of immigration.

In making the decision about whether to run for higher office, politicians are very concerned about what else is going on at the time of that election. Potential candidates are aware that voters give most attention to the top of the ballot. In a presidential election year, electoral hopefuls must consider whether their party's presidential candidate is going to help or hurt them. If it is an off-year election, one in which no presidential election is being held, what other elections are most likely to capture the voter interest (e.g., senator, governor)? Politicians are very concerned about insulating themselves from the fate of other politicians or taking advantage of the coattails of a popular candidate higher on the ballot.

Changes in state election laws demonstrate this trend. In the early 1950s, the governors of nineteen states were elected for two-year terms. Virtually every state that has changed from two-year to four-year terms has decided to hold gubernatorial elections in nonpresidential election years, insulating state elections from national politics (see Table 6.1). Candidates for office below governor are aware of this trend as well. In considering a run for the state senate, for instance, a political candidate is confronted with one political environment if the upcoming election year is a presidential election year in which there is also a gubernatorial and senatorial race in his or her state, and another if it is a nonpresidential election year that features neither a senatorial nor a gubernatorial election. Table 6.2 lists the various electoral environments that might confront potential candidates, all possible because U.S. senators serve six-year terms and thus no senatorial seat is contested in any state in one out of three national elections (barring vacancies due to death, resignation, etc.).

DEVELOPMENT OF THE DIRECT PRIMARY SYSTEM

While historically most nominations were decided in party conventions, the most common means of nomination in American politics today is the

Table 6.1. Electoral Context of Gubernatorial Elections

	1951–1952	*2015–2018*
TWO-YEAR TERMS	19	2
FOUR-YEAR TERMS		
Elected with president	10	10 (2016)
Elected in off year	14	34 (2018)
Elected in odd year	5	5 (2015 and 2017)

Source: National Governors Association (www.nga.org).
Note: The 2016 gubernatorial election in Oregon was a special election. Gubernatorial elections in Oregon are normally held in an off year.

Table 6.2. Offices at the Top of the Ballot

	Number of States						
Offices	*2006*	*2008*	*2010*	*2012*	*2014*	*2016*	*2018*
P-G-S-R	—	6	—	9	—	10	—
P-G-R	—	4	—	2	—	3	—
P-S-R	—	28	—	24	—	26	—
P-R	—	12	—	15	—	11	—
G-S-R	22	—	27	—	26	—	22
G-R	17	—	10	—	14	—	15
S-R	8	—	9	—	8	—	9
R	3	—	4	—	1	—	4

Source: Compiled by the authors.
Note: P = president; G = governor; S = senator; R = representative.

direct primary election. In a direct primary system, the citizens of a particular area who are permitted to vote in a party's primary election vote directly to choose the party's nominee. The direct primary is distinguished from any indirect means of nominating, the most notable example being the national conventions that nominate the presidential candidates based on votes by **delegates**—party members who are selected by other party members or by party leaders to make decisions for the party, mostly regarding the party's nominees for office. Some delegates are chosen directly and some are chosen indirectly in caucuses, but they are delegates in either case.

Direct primaries were not always the most common means used for nominating state and local candidates. Chapter 2 traced the history of party systems in the United States and made the point that in the second party system the nominating system moved away from a legislative caucus system to a convention system; this move was seen as a democratizing reform. The further movement from the convention system to the direct primary system had two distinct impetuses.

Primaries as a Response to One-Party Domination

At the end of the Reconstruction era, following the Civil War, the Democratic party totally dominated Southern politics. The Republican party for all intents and purposes did not exist in the South. In an era of one-party politics, when nominations were determined only by party officials, no mass participatory democracy existed. Citizens were given the opportunity to vote for only one candidate nominated by an elite faction of the dominant party. The primary election was first used, in the Democratic party, as a means to extend some modicum of democracy into this heavily one-party system.

Primaries as an Item on the Progressive Agenda

Shortly after the turn of the twentieth century, primaries began to appear as part of the nominating process in states with Progressive movement influence for ideological reasons. Seen as a response to boss domination of the political process in many Northern cities and states, primaries spread rapidly; the direct primary was used to nominate candidates for at least some offices in all but a few states by the end of the second Wilson administration in 1920.

In contrast to the ebb and flow of the use of primaries in the presidential nominating process (see chapter 8), direct primaries as a means for choosing nominees for state and local office have had a more steady history of development and expansion. Few states that adopted direct primaries as the means for nominating candidates in the early twentieth century have taken the nominating process out of the hands of the voter; today direct primaries are used as the means for nominating candidates for some offices in all states and for *all* offices in thirty-eight states plus the District of Columbia.

It should be noted, however, that nominating conventions have not totally disappeared. A number of states still use conventions, either for nominating purposes or to endorse desired candidates, or merely to build party solidarity. While state nominating conventions are a rarer and rarer phenomenon, they remain among the most interesting aspects of politics for those able to participate in or observe them.

VARIETIES OF PRIMARIES

Stating that the direct primary is the means used for nominating party candidates in most states is not the same as saying that an identical system is used in all states. Some state laws mandate that a primary will be used and set very specific rules for that primary. In other states the decision on how to nominate is left to the parties. If a primary is used, the rules for that primary may be determined by the party, not by state law. In some states the primary is used for all offices; in others it is used for only the more prominent offices (see Epstein 1989, 1991).

A systematic examination of the state and local nominating process is difficult because of the variety of systems in place. The variety of primary types does not trouble candidates for statewide office, however; whatever particular system is in place for a particular political party in any one state is the only system relevant for candidates for that party's nomination. Still, each candidate must be acutely aware of how his or her state's system works.

States using the direct primary differ in terms of who is eligible to vote in a particular primary, of whether parties can endorse—in an official way—in advance of the primary, of how such endorsements are made if they are permitted, and of whether a **plurality** (more votes than any other candidate) or a **majority** (50 percent plus one of all votes cast) is necessary to nominate (see Jewell 1984; Jewell and Olson 1988; Jewell and Morehouse 2001).

Who May Run

One would think that the question of who may run in a party's primary would be a simple one to answer. Democrats run in Democratic primaries; Republicans run in Republican primaries. If only it were that simple!

Party Membership and Petition Requirements

The most prevalent rules call for candidates to run in their party's primary if they meet certain fairly simple criteria. First, the prospective candidate must be a registered member of the political party whose nomination he or she seeks (or in some other way demonstrate allegiance to that party in states that do not have official party registration).

Second, candidates must meet some sort of "test," often gathering a certain number of signatures on a petition, to gain access to the ballot. The ease or difficulty candidates have in meeting this requirement varies with who is eligible to sign the petition and how many signatures are required. If the number is small and if anyone can sign any number of petitions, then access to the ballot is quite simple. For example, in Tennessee only twenty-five signatures are required for most offices. By contrast, if the number of signatures required is large and if some restrictions apply as to who may sign petitions, then access to the ballot is more restricted. In Maine, candidates must acquire a fairly large number of signatures (a percentage of those voting in the last election); only registered party members may sign petitions; and they must sign a petition that contains only the names of party members from the signers' hometown.

In states with easier requirements many more candidates frequently qualify for the primary ballot for the same office. Is this good or bad? "Good," one hears often, "because anyone can run." But what if one candidate appeals to a relatively small, but extremely dedicated, group of voters whose views are on the fringe of public opinion, and election law requires only a plurality to nominate? Would the extremist nominee represent the voters' opinions in these districts? Is democracy served?

If access to the ballot is relatively restricted, then fields of candidates tend to be smaller. All the candidates tend to be serious contenders, but groups out of the mainstream have less influence. Moreover, lesser-known individuals are prevented from testing their views in primary campaigns. Is democracy better served?

The Role of Parties

Access to the ballot can be even more restricted than it is in those states that require a large number of signatures. Eight states—Colorado, Connecticut, Delaware, New Mexico, New York, North Dakota, Rhode Island, and Utah—have party conventions that play a significant role in determining access to the primary ballot for at least some offices. The philosophy behind systems like these is that, while the party voters in the state should have the final say, those most involved with party affairs—that is, those willing to go through the process of selection as delegate to a convention—should have increased influence.

The significance of these relatively obscure rules were on display for all to see in May 2010 when three-term senator Bob Bennett did not finish among the top two at Utah's Republican nominating convention. Only the top two finishers at the state convention move on to the primary ballot. Thus Bennett was denied nomination for a fourth term. In Utah, if one candidate wins 60 percent of the convention votes, he or she is declared the nominee without a primary. In Colorado, New Mexico, and New York, anyone who receives a specified percentage of the votes at the state convention has his or her name placed on the primary ballot. In Delaware, North Dakota, and Rhode Island, the person endorsed at the state convention—or by local committees for local offices—automatically appears on the primary ballot, but others must follow the petition route.[2] Preprimary conventions—conventions held in advance of the party's primary—tend to be used in competitive two-party states with relatively strong party systems.

Connecticut, which was the last state to adopt a direct primary, implemented a system called a **challenge primary** in 1955. New York State adopted a similar system, for statewide offices only, in 1967. In the challenge primary system, the convention nominee is automatically the party nominee unless he or she is challenged in a primary after the convention is over. The assumption that there has to be a primary election is reversed. Losers at the convention with a certain percentage of the delegate votes have an automatic right to challenge, but they have no obligation to do so, and many opt out. The Connecticut challenge primary system was itself challenged in the courts, and it was declared unconstitutional by a U.S. District Court in 2003 (242 F.Supp.2d 164). The New York State challenge primary system (for statewide offices only) remains on the books (New York State Board of Elections 2017, Article 6, Section 104).

While party endorsement has official status in the eight states mentioned above and a "semiofficial" status in Massachusetts (where failure to do well at the convention often leads candidates to drop out), in a number of other states (e.g., Illinois, Minnesota, and Wisconsin) party organization or other party groups endorse candidates and work for their election without that action having an official role.

The quintessential example of this would be Cook County, Illinois, the Greater Chicago area. For many years the vaunted Cook County Democratic party machine was headed by "Hizzonah" the mayor, Richard J. Daley. The first Mayor Daley's (as opposed to his son, Richard M. Daley, who also served as Mayor of Chicago) organization stands as the last of the classic urban machines (see Rakove 1975; Royko 1971; Tolchin and Tolchin 1971). When Daley endorsed a candidate, that candidate became a prohibitive favorite. Few challenged the machine because a challenge was fruitless. However, reform clubs did eventually emerge in Chicago (Wilson 1962) to present an alternative to Daley. These clubs served as a base for political activists interested in a different type of politics in Chicago, working outside of the formal party structure to present alternatives.

Can one generalize about how effective party endorsements have been? As is so often the case, the experience among the states varies widely. Malcolm Jewell and Sarah Morehouse (2001, 109) have examined the history of party endorsements. Between 1960 and 1998, 57 percent of the endorsees in states with legal endorsement procedures were nominated without opposition; this figure compares with 26 percent in those states with informal endorsement procedures. Jewell and Morehouse note that some state parties are most effective, with endorsees rarely challenged (e.g., Connecticut and Delaware, Democrats and Republicans; Colorado, Democrats; New York, Republicans); other states' endorsees are sometimes challenged but rarely upset (e.g., North Dakota, Republicans; Utah, Democrats); and still other states' endorsees are usually challenged and sometimes upset (e.g., New York, Democrats; Utah, Republicans). The history of the party organizations helps explain this difference, as it does many such discrepancies among states. Recent evidence suggests that California's adoption of the top two primary system (see immediately below) has dramatically increased the importance of party endorsements there (Cahn 2013).

The Top Two System

On June 8, 2010, the voters in California approved Proposition 14, which holds that all candidates for office should appear on one primary ballot (with or without party designation as the candidate chooses) and that only the top two candidates in the primary election, regardless of party affiliation, should appear on the November ballot. This system is currently in use in Washington State and, in a slightly different form, in Louisiana. Nebraska also uses a top two system for the state's non-partisan legislative races only.

For many years Washington and Alaska used a unique system called the **blanket primary**; California moved to this system beginning with the 1998 election, as a result of a citizen initiative. Citizens voting in a blanket primary could cast votes in the Republican primary for one office, the Democratic primary for a second and third office, the Republican primary for a fourth office, and so on. The only restriction was that they could only vote in one party's primary for each office. The winners of the primary are those affiliated with each party who draw the largest number of votes.

This type of primary is extremely detrimental to party organizations. A coalition of parties—the Democrats, Republicans, Libertarians, and Peace and Freedom party members—challenged the law in California, claiming it violated their associational rights. This challenge was upheld, and the blanket primary was ruled unconstitutional in June 2000, in the case of *California Democratic Party v. Jones*, 530 U.S. 567. Washington pursued legal action to keep its blanket primary, but that state was ultimately denied in federal court as well (*Washington State Grange et al. v. Washington State Democratic Party*, 541 U.S. 957).

First Washington (by legislation) and then California (by referendum) adopted the **top two system**—as a means around the Supreme Court rulings. While the top two system is billed as a means to increase competition and to nominate more centrist candidates by mitigating the influence of ideologically extreme partisans who were thought to dominate party primaries, their actual effect is less clear. The major parties oppose the system because it clearly takes power away from them. Minor parties also oppose the system, because it is highly unlikely than any minor party candidate will achieve the first- or second-place finish required to qualify for the November ballot. California is still very early in its top two experiment, but it is already clear that this system differs significantly from what we are used to and that these differences are having substantive political implications (Beck and Henrickson 2013; Myers 2016). There have been efforts to present California voters an opportunity to repeal their top two system and return to more traditional party primaries, but so far these efforts have not been successful (Myers 2017).

Cross-Filing: Another Exception to Party Allegiance

Cross-filing represents an exception to the rule that party nominees must be registered in or hold allegiance to the party whose nomination they seek. In New York State, a candidate may be the nominee of more than one party if the state party committee of the second party accepts that nominee. New York State has a tradition of strong third, fourth, and even fifth parties. While these parties do not win many offices on their own, they frequently hold the balance of power between the Democrats and the Republicans.

One tactic used by the Conservative and Workers parties in New York is to endorse the candidate of one of the major parties. The minor parties know that they will not win office; however, they are very concerned about certain issues. Similarly, the candidates of the major parties know that minor party candidates will not win. However, they are concerned that these minor party candidates might draw votes from them and swing the election to their opponents. Thus the major party candidates are willing to accept certain issue positions of the minor parties in exchange for that party's nomination and another line—literally another listing—on the ballot and some advertising and organizational support from the minor party's followers.

In congressional elections in New York in 2016, Democrats ran candidates in all of the state's twenty-seven districts; the Working Families party endorsed eighteen of these nominees. Three Democratic nominees also ran on an Independent line. Republicans ran candidates in twenty-three congressional districts; twenty-one of those candidates had Conservative party backing and ten Republicans also ran on Independent lines.

Who May Vote

Just as states and localities differ in who may run in partisan primaries, so too do they differ in who may vote in primary elections.

Closed, Open, and Hybrid Primaries

Nine states currently use **closed primaries,** and Nebraska uses a closed primary for federal offices. Closed primaries are defined as primary elections in which only those who declare allegiance to a party in advance may vote. There is some variation among these states in terms of the manner in which citizens are required to declare their partisan allegiance.

At the other extreme are states that use **open primaries**. In open primaries, those voting in the primary elections are not required to publicly choose one party or the other. Rather, they enter the voting booth and choose the party ballot on which they will vote in secret. No records are kept of these decisions. Fifteen states currently use the open primary model.

Finally, twenty-two states use some form of a **hybrid primary**, a somewhat less than satisfactory category that denotes a system somewhere between completely open and completely closed. There is a great deal of variation among the states that currently use a hybrid model.[3]

The rules governing state elections are generally specified in state law; those wanting to change these rules set by statute have to work through state legislatures (or in the case of California, through a ballot initiative to impose the blanket primary and court action to eliminate it) to alter state law. However, in 1984, the Republican party of Connecticut challenged that norm, not for philosophical reasons but for purely political ones. For some time Connecticut has been a heavily Democratic state and has had a closed primary system. Independents, a large group in Connecticut, have not been permitted to participate in primaries. By allowing them to vote in Republican primaries, Republicans hoped to attract the allegiance of independents to Republican nominees. After unsuccessful attempts at changing state law, the state's Republican party challenged the closed primary law in the courts. In the case of *Tashjian v. Republican Party of Connecticut*, 479 U.S. 208 (1986), the Supreme Court ruled that the Connecticut law failed to meet the First Amendment guarantee of freedom of association because it did not permit the Republican party to define its own membership. The law was thus ruled unconstitutional. Connecticut Republicans—and potentially other state parties—were permitted to define their own membership and have an open primary if they decided to do so (Epstein 1989; Maisel et al. 1990). Presently party nominating processes are determined in part by the state government and in part by the state parties.

Political scientists use the traditional categories—closed or open—to distinguish among primaries. In truth, it is more meaningful to view the variety of primaries as constituting a continuum from those in which party affiliation is the most fixed to those in which it is the least fixed. These distinctions have important consequences, whether they are viewed in terms of the theory of how politics should work or in the most practical political terms, as the Connecticut example demonstrates (Carr and Scott 1984; Finkel and Scarrow 1985).

Theoretical Arguments regarding Primary Voter Eligibility

The question of who should be eligible to vote in a primary revolves around the theoretical debate over what role the political party should play in the electoral process. The more restrictive primary eligibility is, the greater the role that party plays.

If, on the one hand, the major political parties are viewed as distinct, as presenting differing philosophies from which citizens should choose, then it follows that adherents of those philosophies should make the choice of who will carry their banner into the general election. Thus only those to whom the party is important and truly meaningful should decide the party's nominee. If, on the other hand, one feels that the parties are really two sides of the same philosophical coin, then the primary is merely a way to pare down the field of eligible candidates. In this case, voters should be able to support the candidate most closely linked with their views.

This assertion is an extension of the argument about who should be able to run. Those who favor stronger parties want more of a role for party organization in determining who can seek a party's nomination; they favor systems that call for preprimary conventions and endorsements of one sort or another. In contrast, those who view party as an unnecessary intermediary between citizens and their elected servants want anyone to be able to run; they favor no role for party regulars in determining primary contestants.

Pragmatic Considerations regarding Primary Voter Eligibility

The student of politics who looks at the systems in place in various states and then talks to politicians in those states is led to conclude that politicians generally feel that their state systems reflect the needs of their constituents quite well. Many, indeed, cannot understand why other states do not do things the way they do. Two conclusions follow from this observation: Either state politicians have been incredibly astute in creating systems that correctly match the political culture of their state, or politicians are happy with a system they understand.

Very few politicians in the United States have expert knowledge of campaign laws beyond the boundary of their own state. Why should they? What they need to know is how to play the game in which they are currently involved. They approve of the rules that are in effect because they know how to play by and win under those rules. Reformers, conversely, tend to be those who are out of power, who have not managed to win with the rules in place. The efforts by Connecticut Republicans to open their primary stands as a case in point. More recently, Democratic, Republican, and minor party leaders in California opposed Proposition 14. They knew how to play the political game under the old rules and were uncertain of the consequences of the new.

Strategic Consequences of Different Primary Rules

Imagine the most basic problem facing a candidate in a primary: To whom must I appeal for votes? In a closed primary state, with recorded party enrollment, the constituency seems easy to determine. Candidates and their campaign managers simply obtain lists of potential voters—that is, lists of people who are enrolled in their party and are eligible to vote in their party's primary.

In a closed primary state without permanent enrollment, the only comparably available lists are rosters of those who voted in the party's last primary (if the party had workers compile such a list at the polls). Even where such lists are kept, they tend to be highly inaccurate, ignoring those who think of themselves as members of the party but did not vote in the last primary or any new voters.

But those lists, as flawed as they are, are preferable to the lists that can be obtained in open primary states. The only voting lists that candidates can collect in open primary states are lists of eligible voters and/or lists of those who did in fact vote in the last primary. Candidates have no way of knowing with certainty which ballot a particular voter marked.

Think of the consequences of these differences for campaign strategy. In the first case direct mail, targeted Internet communication, and/or door-to-door campaigning are possible and efficient. Campaigns can reach those who are eligible to vote. In the second case these techniques of contacting voters are much less efficient, though still possible. In the open primary scenario, if one does not want to contact all voters, it is necessary to rely on much less accurate methods of deciding on whom to concentrate—for example, targeting areas in which a high percentage of the voters seem to favor one's own party.

Crossover or Strategic Voting

Politicians are also very concerned about **crossover or strategic voting**. Let us assume that a Democratic incumbent is running unopposed for his party's nomination in an open primary state. We further assume that there is a contested primary in the Republican party. No legal barrier prevents supporters of the Democratic incumbent from crossing over to the Republican primary and voting for the weaker of the two contestants in that primary, in an effort to nominate a weaker opponent for their favorite in the general election.

Hypothetically this scenario could happen easily enough. In practice, however, it is difficult to document instances of this kind of perfidy. First, an orchestrated campaign to nominate the weaker candidate in the other party would require a level of sophistication unknown to most American political organizations.

Second, voters who participate in primaries most often are concerned about more than one race. Even if an incumbent lacked a Democratic opponent in one race, still other offices would very likely feature contested Democratic primaries. In open primary states, Democrats crossing over to influence the outcome of a Republican primary would forfeit their rights to vote in these Democratic races, which presumably would be of more interest to them than other Republican primaries.

Third, the American voting public believes in fair play. It is very unlikely that enough voters would engage in this type of behavior to have an impact on any particular election. A political party that openly promoted such a strategy would run the risk of a moral backlash and thus lose more than it hoped to gain. Empirical research on this subject is difficult to come by, but one study examining a call for strategic voting in a real world environment found no evidence that the practice took place (Stephenson 2011).

The fact that behavior of this type is unlikely to happen does not diminish the paranoia of politicians who worry about perfidy. Be that as it may, the true importance of voter eligibility rules relates much more closely to impact on election strategy than it does to the loyalty of the voters to the party in whose primary they participate.

Who Wins

Plurality Rule

Despite the lip service given to our "basic principle" of **majority rule**, majority rule is the exception in American politics. Most elections in America—and certainly most primaries—are determined by **plurality rule**. That is, the person with the most votes (not necessarily 50 percent plus at least one) in the primary wins the nomination.

Plurality rule has important consequences, particularly in elections with large fields of candidates. For example, in 2002, in California's Thirty-Ninth Congressional District, Linda Sanchez emerged victorious in a six-person primary, with only about one-third of the vote. The sister of Loretta Sanchez, who was already a House member from California, Linda Sanchez beat Hector de la Torre by only 4 percent of the vote, in a very negative campaign, to win the nomination in a new district, drawn to favor the Democrats. Many of the two-thirds of the Democrats who did not vote for Sanchez might well have been voting against her, preferring any of the other candidates, because her campaign drew a great deal of criticism. But the system does not recognize intensity of feeling behind a vote, nor does it allow voters to indicate a second choice. Sanchez won a narrow plurality and went on to win her seat in the 108th Congress.

Variations from Plurality Rule: Runoff Primaries

Plurality rule is not in effect in every electoral jurisdiction. The major exception to the plurality winner rule is found in eleven states[4] that require a majority vote to receive the nomination; if no candidate wins a majority, a runoff or second primary is held.

Runoff primaries were instituted in the South shortly after the beginning of this century, during a period of Democratic dominance in the South. Party officials viewed the **runoff primary** as a means of guaranteeing continued party strength, of assuring that the party was united behind one candidate and could thwart any independent challengers. Some, however, including most vocally the Reverend Jesse Jackson, have argued that runoffs were instituted to reduce the likelihood of blacks winning Democratic party nominations.

Jackson's attention was directed to this issue by H. M. "Mickey" Michaux Jr., an African American who lost the Democratic party nomination in North Carolina's Second Congressional District in 1982 after having captured 44 percent of the vote against two white candidates in the first primary. In the runoff Michaux polled 46 percent and lost to Tim Valentine, who went on to capture the seat. Using the Michaux contest as an example, some have claimed that blacks and other minorities would have ten to fifteen more seats in the Congress if the runoff primary were eliminated. This claim is based on two premises. First is the assumption that whites vote for whites and blacks for blacks in primary elections. Thus, in districts with large black populations but not black majorities, blacks can lead in the first primary but lose when the whites all vote together in the runoff. The second premise is that voters stick to party lines in the general election, regardless of the candidates. These two assumptions seem to be at odds with each other and with recent experience, certainly the experience in the 2008 presidential election.

If the first assumption is accurate, then runoff primaries are discriminatory against minority groups only in those districts in which they constitute a large bloc but not a majority. In districts in which blacks or Hispanics constitute a majority, the runoff primary would seem to work in their favor. For instance, African American candidates can be helped in districts with African American majorities.[5] In neither case is it evident that the system is discriminatory, only that one electoral system out of several possible ones has been chosen.

Turning to the second assumption, would it help minority candidates to get the nomination if they were then to lose in the general election? If voters follow racial lines, wouldn't it be logical for white voters to desert the Democratic party in the general election and support white Republicans? Some argue that this is the case regardless of the primary laws (see McKee 2010; Bullock and Johnson 1992; Lamis 1984; Stanley 1985).

Variations from Plurality Rule: Instant Runoff Systems

In recent years a number of election experts have begun to explore more fundamental alternatives to plurality rule. A number of reform groups, including FairVote: The Center for Voting and Democracy, www.fairvote.org, have been advocating for the **instant runoff voting (IRV)**—also known as **ranked choice voting (RCV)**—or **single transferable vote (STV)**, used in a number of European countries. IRV/RCV is used when there is a single winner for a single seat, while STV is used when there are multiple winners for multiple seats (e.g., multimember districts).

IRV/RCV/STV systems allow voters to rank candidates in order of preference. If no candidate receives a majority of the vote, the candidate with the fewest votes is dropped, and his or her votes are reallocated to the candidates who were those voters' second choice candidate. Votes are then retallied. This process is repeated until a winner emerges.

IRV/RCV/STV systems are used for municipal elections in a number of communities across the country, including San Francisco. They are referred to as "instant runoffs" because they permit a result with a majority winner to be achieved as a result of the votes cast in one election. Their key advantage is that they eliminate the situation in which a minority winner in a multicandidate field is the least favored candidate of the voters who cast their ballots for all of the other candidates. Extreme ideologues and single-issue candidates are disadvantaged; centrists are advantaged. The argument against implementing a system such as this one is that it would be confusing to voters, though those in cities that have adopted it would counter that point. As we go to press with this edition it appears that the United States will see its first statewide test of an RCV system in our home state of Maine. Maine voters approved the use of RCV for all state elections except for presidential elections in November of 2016. Before the system could be used, the Maine Supreme Court found in 2017 that the use of RCV in state legislative and gubernatorial elections violated the Maine Constitution, and eventually the Maine Legislature passed a law delaying RCV until at least 2021 or indefinitely if the state constitution was not amended. But Maine RCV supporters gathered enough signatures to force a people's veto, and a statewide ballot question in June 2018 will ask voters to approve or reject RCV. This ballot question also preempts the state law delaying RCV implementation, meaning that primary elections in June 2018 will be decided by RCV. If Maine voters approve RCV, Maine will have two different election systems in place for November 2018: RCV for U.S. Senate and House of Representatives, and plurality election for Maine state legislative races and the gubernatorial election (DeCosta-Klipa 2016; Maine Department of the Secretary of State 2018; Seelye 2017; Thistle 2018).

THE POLITICS OF NOMINATIONS

Uncontested Nominations

Recall the offices listed at the beginning of this chapter. How much competition is there for water district commissioner or other minor offices? Compare the interest in those offices with that for a U.S. senator or governor. Or compare the attractiveness of serving as a state legislator in Vermont—where the legislature sits for four to five months a year, where there are 180 state legislators, and where the weekly salary while in session in 2018 was $707.36, plus $115.00 (if staying overnight) or $74.00 per day (if commuting) for lodging and meals plus mileage—with the attractiveness of the same position in California, where serving in the state legislature is a full-time job and the base annual salary was $105,118 plus a per diem of $183 while in session in 2018.

These kinds of comparisons point to the difficulty in analyzing nominations at the state and local level. The situation varies from office to office and from state to state. Obviously, more seats are contested for the more prestigious offices. Nominations for the U.S. Senate are uncontested much less frequently than nominations for state assembly. Further, state offices in larger states are more likely to attract contested primaries than are similar offices in smaller states.[6] This thesis follows quite naturally from the fact that such offices are more likely to be full-time, highly paid, and prestigious in larger states.

Other conclusions about contested primaries have been found to be similarly predictable. Incumbents win nominations without the necessity of contesting a primary more often than do challengers. Contested primaries are more likely to occur for open seats, those without an incumbent running, particularly in the party of the retiring incumbent, than for seats in which incumbents are running. Primaries are always more likely to occur in dominant parties than in minority parties. One basic rule seems to apply: The more valuable the party nomination, the greater the likelihood of a contested primary. The value of the party nomination, in turn, relates to two variables—the prestige of the office sought and the likelihood that the party's nomination will result in victory in the general election.

How do candidates get nominated in situations in which there is no contested primary? No systematic research has addressed this question, and most students of politics would answer it based on their personal experiences. The process is seemingly simple. Each candidate follows whatever procedure is necessary to have his or her name placed on the primary ballot. No one else does so. The nomination then goes by default. But that analysis begs the question: Who is the individual who presents himself or herself as a candidate?

One working assumption is that incumbents normally want to succeed themselves, even for the less prestigious offices. Few people desire or are more qualified to serve as water district commissioner than the individual holding that position.

If no incumbent is running, or if the incumbent is in the other party, then party officials have the responsibility of finding candidates for office.[7] For less prestigious offices and thus less valued nominations, party officials must identify potential candidates and convince them to run.

Party organizations traditionally controlled access to the ballot. This power was lost for prestigious offices with the advent of the direct primary and with increased popular participation. However, the party's role persists for lesser offices. Some party organizations are quite successful in playing this role; others much less so.

In congressional elections in the 1980s, one major party or the other did not field a candidate for the House of Representatives in about one district in six. The major parties were more successful in guaranteeing competition in the early 1990s, when control of the Congress was hotly contested; but the number of incumbent representatives running without major party opposition increased until 2008, when fifty-six House incumbents ran without major party opposition. That trend was reversed in 2010, when the Republicans fielded a near record number of candidates (430) and the Democrats were not far behind. All eligible gubernatorial and all, save for a very few, Senate seats have been contested by both parties in every recent election.

Contested Nominations

When most analysts talk about primary elections, they are actually concerned with *contested* primary elections, a subgroup that is a minority of all primaries.[8] Contested primaries receive the most attention because they provide campaign watchers with something to watch. They also play an important role in weeding out contestants for office. Any discussion of contested primaries needs to emphasize differences by office and locale.

Incumbent Advantage

Political observers have again been able to make some generalizations about these contested primaries. The first generalization is that incumbents win a high proportion of the primaries in which they are challenged (recall Figures 3.6–3.8, pp. 96–97, 99). Second, incumbent victories are increasingly the rule for lesser or more local offices. Incumbents have an advantage over opponents in that they have already built up support within the party (Fenno 1978). Unless they have acted in a way that undercuts their own support, they are rarely beaten in a primary.

Since 1980 only eleven U.S. senators have lost in a primary or at a convention, and two of those losers—Joe Lieberman of Connecticut and Lisa Murkowski of Alaska—went on to retain their seats in the general election as an independent and a write-in candidate, respectively. Incumbent losers are so few that analysts can almost always explain each case as idiosyncratic. As the most recent example, longtime Indiana Republican Senator Richard Lugar lost in a primary in 2012 as the Tea Party gained influence within the state GOP and it became known that Lugar hadn't actually lived in Indiana in over thirty years.

Similarly, House defeats are few and far between (five in 2016), but the 1992 election stands as an exception: Nineteen House members lost primaries in that one year. However, this exception can also be explained. Every ten years House districts change. After reapportionment, which determines the size of each state's delegation, the states must undergo redistricting to account for added or subtracted seats when their relative population has changed significantly or to account for population shifts within the state, so that each district contains the same population, meeting the constitutional mandate of one person–one vote. As a result of reapportionment and redistricting, many House members faced substantially new districts in 1992; in fact, in a number of cases two members found themselves representing the same district. When this decennial phenomenon was combined with the House bank scandal, in which many members were tainted as frequent abusers of a congressional privilege, the result was an unusual number of incumbents defeated in primaries. Even in that record year, however, 95 percent of the incumbents seeking renomination to the House were chosen by their party.[9]

The experience of 2006 is more common. Only two House incumbents lost. One, Republican first-term Representative Joe Schwarz of Michigan, was a moderate Republican who had won the 2004 primary in a plurality election against five conservative candidates, who split the mainline GOP vote. Schwarz lost to a conservative candidate who coalesced the opposition in a way impossible two years earlier. The other, Georgia Congresswoman Cynthia McKinney, was a controversial figure who had lost the seat once before and was involved in a much publicized brouhaha with Capitol Hill police in the spring before her primary loss. The norm is clearly for incumbents to win with relative ease.

Contests without Incumbents

What about races in which incumbents are not running? Conclusions in these cases are more tentative. Winners tend to be those who make best use of the resources necessary to win election, chief among them, name recognition. The candidate who is much more widely known than his or her opponent(s) is likely to win. How is such recognition achieved?

Some candidates have it when they enter a race. For instance, a state senator who is entering a congressional primary may have represented many of those who are eligible to vote in the primary, an eventuality likely to happen in large states, such as California or Florida, with sizable state senate districts. Such a candidate would start with an advantage over a political neophyte.

Or a candidate may be known for other reasons. Arnold Schwarzenegger was well known as an actor before he ran for governor of California; Al Franken as a comedian before he returned to his native Minnesota to run for the U.S. Senate. Athletes, actors, media personalities, astronauts, and others with similar fame start with a name recognition advantage when they enter the political arena (Canon 1990).

Yet many candidates do not start with these advantages, particularly candidates for local offices. How do they get known? Three key ingredients contribute to successful campaigns—candidate effort, campaign organization, and money. In smaller districts candidates themselves may well be able to "get around," to shake hands with a large portion of the potential electorate. Candidates for sheriff go into high schools and talk about drug and alcohol abuse. Candidates for state representative address the Rotary or the Lions clubs in town after town. All candidates for these offices attend party meetings and picnics, town meetings, PTA meetings—any meeting at which they can be certain that they will be introduced. They go door-to-door and discuss mutual concerns with voters. Candidate after candidate will attest that there is no better campaign technique than actually talking to a potential voter. If a district is small enough and if a candidate can commit enough time, nothing is more effective.

Many districts are too large, however, for a candidate to have any chance of meeting even a sizable proportion of the potential electorate. Although candidates campaign personally to the extent possible, they must rely on an organization to extend their outreach. A candidate's campaign organization uses various techniques to serve as surrogates for personal contact. Workers go door-to-door seeking support for their candidate. They carry literature that describes the candidate's views and qualifications. They telephone potential voters and discuss why they favor the candidate for whom they are working. They put up lawn signs, hand out buttons and bumper stickers, speak on behalf of their candidate at functions she or he cannot attend. An effective organization reaches out for candidates farther than they themselves can reach.

Campaign organizations in smaller districts are frequently volunteer organizations. Friends and neighbors of a candidate will offer their assistance. But even these campaigns need some money in order to function effectively. Buttons and bumper stickers, brochures and balloons all cost money. As the size of the district expands, the cost of the campaign rises. In many of today's primaries, money has become a sine qua non for success. As recently as 1974, when the FEC began keeping these records, only ten congressional campaigns spent $200,000 in the primary and general elections combined, and expenditures of $100,000 in primaries were all but unknown. A decade later a congressional primary that was won on a budget of $100,000 has been cited as evidence that "a congressional seat can still be won without spending a fortune" (*Congressional Quarterly Weekly Report* 1984, 1119). Since 2000, particularly in open seats in the party with a partisan electoral advantage, spending a million dollars in a primary is no longer considered unusual (see chapter 5).

The precise combination of candidate effort, organization, and money that is necessary to win any primary is difficult to ascertain with precision. The ability to arrive at that combination is what separates winners from losers. Still, the imprecision of the calculation is why politics remains more art than science. If one formula worked for every campaign, then every campaign manager and every candidate would do the same thing. Candidates and their campaign managers start with a certain amount of knowledge of how to campaign (most of it gained from experience), with an understanding of their districts, their candidacies, and so forth, and with a certain amount of resources. Working with these, they devise tactics and strategies. They play on their strengths and try to exploit the weaknesses of their opponents. They play down their weaknesses and try to undercut the strengths of their opponents. Politicians seek to find the formula that will give them the largest number of votes in the primary while doing the least harm to their chances in the general election (Jacobson 1983). That, after all, is what the primary campaign is all about (Maisel 1986).

CONCLUSION

State and local nomination procedures are quite diverse across the United States, not only in terms of the specific processes used but also in terms of how hotly contested the nomination. This variation extends further across time and location. A congressional district or state that has witnessed little nominating conflict for years may suddenly find itself at the center of a bruising and bloody nomination fight, while a district or state that has consistently exhibited high levels of vigorous competition for party nominations may become the scene of significantly less activity as the population of the district or state changes or if a very popular official obtains the seat and scares off competition. But the one thing that is consistently true regarding state and local nominating processes is that you cannot get to the general election without them.

CRITICAL THINKING QUESTIONS

1. In your opinion, what constitutes a qualified candidate for public office?
2. Which is the best method for a party to use in selecting its nominees for office—convention, caucus, or primary?
3. Who should be allowed to vote in a party's primary?
4. What makes incumbents so difficult to defeat?

KEY TERMS

conventions
qualified candidates
delegates
plurality
majority
preprimary conventions
challenge primary
blanket primary
top two system
cross-filing
closed primaries
open primaries
hybrid primary
crossover or strategic voting
majority rule
plurality rule
runoff primary
instant runoff voting (IRV) or ranked choice voting (RCV) or single transferable vote (STV)

NOTES

1. Certainly, how politicians view career progression can change during an individual's career as a result of political decisions or personal decisions. See Stone, Maisel, and Maestas (1998) and the work evolving from the Candidate Emergence Study.

2. To further demonstrate the variety of state experiences, the Democratic party charter in Massachusetts requires that a candidate receive 15 percent of the vote at the convention to appear on the primary ballot; despite the fact that this provision is *not* in state law, the Massachusetts courts have upheld the provision, so it has the same impact as if it were law. (See Jewell and Olson 1988, 97.)

3. All information on state primaries is obtained from the National Conference of State Legislatures. Attentive readers will note that the state total for closed, open, and hybrid primaries is forty-six, forty-seven if one counts Nebraska. This is because of three previously mentioned states that use the top-two model. Nebraska uses the top two model in non-partisan state contests.

4. According to the National Conference of State Legislatures, these eleven states are Alabama, Arkansas, Georgia, Louisiana, Mississippi, North Carolina, Oklahoma, South Carolina, South Dakota, Texas, and Vermont.

5. In 1989 North Carolina amended its runoff primary law to lower the threshold to 40 percent. Furthermore, the second-place finisher must request a runoff. In 1992, in the newly created majority minority First District, Walter Jones, the only white candidate in a six-person field, led the primary field with 38 percent of the vote. The runner-up, Eva M. Clayton, won the primary runoff with 55 percent of the vote, beating Jones by eight thousand votes. Three of the primary candidates openly endorsed Clayton. Jones was on the defensive for most of the campaign, accused of trying to thwart black political aspirations. He denied this and yet tried to get on the ballot the following November as an independent, an action deemed illegal under North Carolina law.

6. It should also be noted that there are fewer Republican primaries than Democratic primaries for similar offices in similar states. This phenomenon deserves further study.

7. Party officials—county chairs, state and county committee members, ward and precinct leaders, and the like—are frequently not well-known. Why they seek and accept such positions is a most interesting question, the answer to which varies significantly from locale to locale and individual to individual. In any case, one of the principal responsibilities they undertake is to ensure that their party is represented on the general election ballot.

8. One could make the subgroup smaller still. Primary contests could be divided into those involving serious opposition and those in which the opposition is marginal or frivolous. Candidates have a sense of this distinction in advance, but analysts have trouble determining who is serious and who is frivolous until some additional information is added—for example, how much money a candidate can raise, what kind of organizations or endorsements a candidate can attract, and so on. Because these judgments are essentially subjective, this differentiation will not be pursued in this discussion.

9. It should be noted that ten or more incumbents were defeated in primaries in 1982, 1972, and 1962 as well.

Chapter 7

State and Local Elections

Texas governor Greg Abbott speaks in Forth Worth, Texas, during his 2014 campaign. While presidential elections routinely get the bulk of our attention, state and local elections are also important exercises in American representative democracy with important policy implications.

Compare the experiences of two politicians at the Washington County Fair. Thirty-one states in the Union have Washington counties. Their experiences could happen in any of them. The first politician is a candidate for the county board of supervisors. His district encompasses about one-fifteenth of the county. He has long been active in county politics and government. The second candidate is a member of Congress; she is running for U.S. senator. Washington County is one of over sixty counties in the state; she is from the other end of the state and has been in Washington County perhaps twice.

The candidate for board of supervisors has been looking forward to the county fair, one of the most important social events on his annual calendar, for months. Since most of the people in the county attend the fair at least once during fair week, this is also an important political event. Our candidate is in charge of his party's voter registration booth at the fair, making sure that the decorations are in place and that the booth is always open. He sees to it that his signs are in evidence. He has set the entire week aside so that he can spend as much time at the fair as possible. After all, what could be a better way to campaign among likely voters?

The Senate candidate will attend the fair too. She will put in one appearance, for about an hour, at a time that the local people tell her will be quite busy. She is not looking forward to the fair with eagerness. In fact, one day before, she is not even aware that she will be attending. Her staff arranged for the visit. Someone else will be certain that her signs are in place, that she is introduced to the right people, and most important, that the media know she is there. She probably will attend every county fair in the state.

The senatorial candidate's visit is a major event for the local candidate's campaign. He is filmed introducing her to local folks; that scene is on television at eleven, and everyone sees it. He makes sure that someone takes candid pictures to use in his campaign flyer; maybe the photographer will even get the best one autographed.

The Senate candidate squeezed the visit to the fair into a busy day. She was up at dawn, shaking hands at a factory gate. She flew halfway across the state to have lunch with a union leader whose PAC had promised, but not delivered, financial support. After lunch she did a brief radio interview and stopped in at the local newspaper to talk with the editor. On the flight into Washington County Airport she conferred with her campaign manager and her pollster about the impact of her recent statements on Afghanistan. At multiple points in the day she posted on Twitter. After the appearance at the fair, she was driven a hundred miles south for a fund-raiser. She did not even see the speech she was to give until an hour before the dinner. She did not know where she was staying that night but hoped she would have time to make some calls before she went to bed.

One call would be to dictate some letters to her secretary; she would remember to tell her to write a note thanking that guy who introduced her at the fair. "Can't remember his name or where he's from. Find out from someone."

These two politicians are engaged in the same enterprise—winning the votes of enough people to gain election. To win these votes, they must identify likely supporters and figure out some way to get those supporters to the polls. Both candidates have to set strategies aimed at accomplishing these goals. They must devise a strategy that involves identifying likely supporters and determining how they can structure a candidacy that will reach these voters. Each candidate must also come up with tactics aimed at carrying out the strategy.

But what do they do on a day-to-day basis? How do they structure an organization, and what does that organization do? As the hypothetical scenario just depicted demonstrates, these two candidates on a day-to-day basis are actually involved in very different enterprises.

THE CONVENTIONAL WISDOM: OLD VERSUS NEW POLITICS

Under the old politics, campaigning was person-to-person and door-to-door; candidates were individuals representing the political parties that structured both the campaigns for office and the institutions of government. Supporters gave allegiance to the parties because they agreed with their stand on issues or because the parties' candidates would do certain things for voters if elected. The candidates of the party in control of government, as a group, were held accountable for the performance of the government.

New politics, however, is media and image-oriented, not person-to-person. It is the politics of television and increasingly digital (especially social) media (see chapter 10). Political party organization has been replaced in part by **candidate-centered** organization. Partisanship and party organization certainly still matter, but modern candidates, at least those for federal and in many cases state office, have assumed much more control over their own campaigns. Individual candidates call the shots, and they have much more freedom to do things without the consent of their party, or things that might be contrary to the interests of their party.

The reality of campaigning for office in the early years of the twenty-first century is, like so much else in this text, dependent on context. New politics has replaced old politics, in some areas, for some offices. Often the change is more subtle than bold. Consider again the Washington County Fair. The Senate candidate was running a "new politics," candidate-centered campaign. She was concerned about the perception of *her* position on foreign policy, about raising money from the union PAC for *her* campaign, about the media coverage of *her* appearance at the Washington County Fair.

But the candidate for county supervisor was involved in an "old politics" campaign. The booth at the county fair was a party organization activity; it was part of a party voter registration drive. All the party candidates together put up their posters. He used the senatorial campaign for party and personal publicity, but such events were not part of his overall tactics or strategy. He spent much of the week at the fair because that was where he could greet and talk to the greatest number of people. Even the Senate hopeful was engaging somewhat in "old politics" with her appearance at the fair. She was appearing as a partisan, at her party's booth, hoping to improve both her (primarily) and her fellow partisans' (secondarily) election chances in a partisan context.

Old politics and new politics exist hand in hand in America today. New politics gets more attention because it is designed for getting attention—and because the campaigns for more visible offices are often run using state-of-the-art new politics techniques. But that does not mean that all campaigning has changed. In this chapter we show how the two coexist.

THE NEW POLITICS: CAMPAIGNING IN A MEDIA AGE

Let us assume that a politician is making a fully rational decision about seeking office.[1] A politician considering stepping up to a larger constituency, a more prestigious office, will seek some information:

1. What voters am I going to need to appeal to?
2. What is the partisan distribution of voters within the new district?
3. What is the normal voting strength for candidates of my party in this district? Conversely, what are the strengths of the opposition candidate and his or her party?
4. What kinds of techniques will work in appealing to the voters whose support I will need?

This list could easily be expanded, but it serves as a starting point for the discussion of so-called new politics. Candidates for all offices ask the same questions about how to get the support of a plurality of all voters. They ask the same questions about their party and/or personal support and that of their opponents.

Redistricting and Reapportionment

It is important to put this discussion of voters in a candidate's district into context, in this case the constitutionally mandated context of **redistricting** and **reapportionment**. Article 1, Section 2, of the Constitution requires that representatives in Congress be apportioned among the states according to population, as determined by a census, to be conducted every ten years.

Actually, two processes are involved. Not only is the number of seats that each state is allocated in the House determined by the census (the process of reapportionment), but the boundaries of individual districts and of state legislative districts are also redrawn to reflect shifting population patterns (the process of legislative redistricting).

During much of the nation's history, the process of reapportionment was politically painless because Congress continuously voted to expand the size of the House of Representatives. Thus the House grew from its original 106 members to nearly 400 by 1900. In 1910, however, in part at least because of the size of the chamber, Congress voted to set the size of the House permanently at 435. As a result of the cap on the size of the House (exceeded only between the admission of Alaska and Hawaii as states and the next census) and of shifting population panels, reapportionment has led to some states gaining seats in Congress and other states losing seats. Since the 1930 reapportionment, a formula has been used, an attempt to remove politics from the process. However, the recently announced plan by the Trump Commerce Department to reintroduce a question on U.S. citizenship to the Census puts politics squarely back in play, and could have substantial reapportionments and redistricting implications (Blake 2018).

Politicians have never shown much of an appetite for removing politics from decisions regarding legislative redistricting. Traditionally, district lines have been drawn to accomplish political purposes. **Gerrymandering**, drawing districts, often of strange shapes, to advantage one party or candidate over another, is a revered part of American political folklore.

Judicial intervention has led to less blatant gerrymandering. In *Baker v. Carr*, 369 U.S. 186 (1962), the Supreme Court, responding to extreme cases of malapportionment and reversing an earlier decision in which it had held that redistricting was a political issue beyond its reach, decided that it could intervene in a case in Tennessee where state legislative district lines had not been redrawn in sixty years, despite massive population shifts that resulted in some legislators representing a hundred times more citizens than others.

In subsequent rulings (especially *Gray v. Sanders*, 372 U.S. 368 [1963] and *Wesberry v. Sanders*, 376 U.S. 1 [1964]), the Court established a criterion of **one person–one vote**—the idea that districts for seats in the same body should have roughly the same population so that each person's vote counts equally—against which apportionment schemes would be measured (Ansolabehere and Snyder 2008; Brunell 2008; Butler and Cain

1991; Cain 1984; Cain and Butler 1991; Grofman 1990; Lowenstein 1991b; Polsby 1971; Schuck 1987).

However, judicial regulation does not mean that reapportionment has become apolitical. Political scientists have spent a good deal of time and effort looking at the extent to which redistricting favors incumbents and impacts subsequent electoral chances (Abramowitz, Alexander, and Gunning 2006; Basehart and Comer 1991; Born 1985; Cain 1985; Forgette and Platt 2005; Forgette and Winkle 2006; Galderisi 2005; Gelman and King 1990; Glazer, Grofman, and Robbins 1987; King 1989; Maisel, Maestas, and Stone 2005; Niemi and Jackson 1991). The conclusions reached by these scholars convincingly demonstrate that redistricting does not affect one political party adversely and does not make the ultimate difference in reelection bids by incumbents. Yet there can be no doubt that politicians work very hard to be certain that district boundaries are redrawn in a way that meets the judicial criteria but also brings as much benefit as possible to those drawing the lines, and most (but not all) research indicates that incumbents do tend to benefit when politicians rather than the courts or an independent commission draw the district lines. It has also become increasingly apparent that while both major political parties are eager to gerrymander, when one party controls the process for a long period of time concerns over gerrymandering become much more important.

The Court has moved cautiously into the area of reviewing partisan gerrymandering. In *Davis v. Bandemer*, 478 U.S. 109 (1986), the Court seemed to rule that partisan gerrymandering could be a violation of the equal protection clause of the Constitution but that the case before the Court did not appear sufficiently egregious to merit judicial intervention (Cain and Butler 1991, 32; Lowenstein 1991b; Schuck 1987). However, after a very controversial redistricting by the Texas legislature, a second redistricting after the 1990 census, the Court ruled that the actions of the Texas Republicans were constitutional (*League of Latin American Citizens v. Perry*, 548 U.S. 399, 2006), a majority holding that redrawing district lines for nothing more than partisan advantage was an acceptable practice. In 2015 the Supreme Court ruled in *Arizona State Legislature v. Arizona Independent Redistricting Commission* (135 S. Ct. 2652, 2015) that taking redistricting out of the hands of state legislatures and placing line drawing in the hands of independent commissions was not a violation of the times, places, and manner clause of the Constitution of the United States, potentially allowing for greater change down the road. As we go to press with this edition, the Supreme Court is considering two gerrymandering cases, one (*Gill v. Whitford*) considering whether overtly partisan line drawing is a violation of the equal protection clause and the other (*Benisek v. Lamone*) asking if partisan gerrymandering was a violation of individual voters' free speech rights (Barnes 2018; New York Times 2018). The implications of these decisions could be huge. State courts are getting involved as well. In January of 2018 the Pennsylvania Supreme Court declared that state's congressional map an unconstitutional gerrymander and ordered the map to be redrawn. When this was not done, the Pennsylvania Supreme Court created its own map for use in the 2018 election cycle (Wines and Gabriel 2018; Ingraham 2018). The Supreme Court of the United States has now twice refused to intervene in the Pennsylvania case, taking the view that the issues here are entirely matters of state law (Liptak 2018). At both the federal and state levels, courts seem to be increasingly willing to involve themselves in the drawing of legislative district lines, although what exactly the Supreme Court will do (if anything) remains unclear as we go to print (Barnes 2018).

All of this is to say that redistricting may be a more exact art than it once was, and certain democratic principles must be considered. But in essence the act of redistricting today is just as political as it ever has been, if not more so. The tools that boundary drawers have at their disposal to manipulate district lines are more powerful than ever. The stakes are high because the House of Representatives is so closely divided, and citizens do not seem to be well served by the machinations of their elected officials' seeking to gain or retain partisan advantage.

Based on an often impressionistic analysis of the district, they decide if they can win the election they are considering. Rarely does victory seem certain. If victory were certain, others with similar qualifications would be seeking the office, thereby removing the apparent certainty because of the presence of a primary election (Stone and Maisel 2003).

If preliminary analysis leads to a conclusion that victory is unlikely, experienced politicians holding other elective office, generally stay put.[2] It is almost always easier to retain a seat than to move up the ladder (Jacobson and Kernell 1983, chap. 3).[3] If, however, they feel that victory is possible, that they have a legitimate chance, then they begin to analyze how to get the votes.

At this stage, they must look at party strength in detail, at the potential for a personal organization, and at the potential for a media campaign (Gibson et al. 1983, 1985). A candidate who is considering a campaign for Congress or for statewide office, or even for state senate in some of the larger states, must realize that he or she cannot personally reach all the voters. Also, voters no longer use party affiliation as the only cue in deciding how to vote. What techniques will be successful in convincing voters that they should cast their ballot for this particular candidate?

Let us now assume that the candidate, a nonincumbent, has decided to run.[4] Our candidate is either challenging an incumbent or running in an open seat. In either case the tactical problems, if not the difficulty of the task, are the same (Maestas et al. 2006; Stone and Maisel 2003; Stone, Maisel, and Maestas 2004). The candidate must match available resources with necessary tasks in the most effective way.

The first jobs are to identify likely supporters and to ascertain what other voters are possible converts to the candidate's side. After identifying these two groups, the candidate must set a strategy for reaching both groups in a way that will solidify their support and increase the possibility that they will turn out to vote in droves. That might sound simple, but it certainly is not. The most important resource that any candidate has is personal time (Mann and Wolfinger 1980). In some local races nothing more is necessary. The candidate can identify supporters and potential supporters and talk to them all. Many politicians in their first campaign went about seeking support in this way. They are thus used to directly contacting people and have difficulty realizing that this strategy will not work in all campaigns.

"Pressing the flesh" of all the voters is not possible in a campaign for the House of Representatives, in which the average member represents over seven hundred thousand people; nor is it possible in a campaign for statewide office, when over forty states have populations exceeding a million. Thus the candidate must learn how to use personal time in a new way, not merely contacting individual voters but maximizing the number of voters on whom that candidate can have an impact. Surrogates for the candidate are necessary in order to best use the results of time spent, essentially by "expanding" the amount of personal time (Morehouse, McCally, and Jewell 2003).

The Role of Political Parties

Many candidates have experience in using party as a surrogate. Some voters will vote for a candidate because of party affiliation. For these voters, the candidate need only be certain that party affiliation is well known. Little candidate time is necessary to make this connection. Party, then, is one resource on which politicians are used to relying.

But political party is not a resource that is equally available to all candidates, nor is it a resource with which all candidates are equally comfortable (see van Erkel, Thijssen, and Van Aelst 2017 for an interesting analysis of Belgian candidates' decision-making calculi here). Candidates must weigh the impact of party in the district. Is the organization efficient? Is the degree of partisan affiliation strong among voters? Is the candidate perceived to be in line with most of the others in the party? Or is the candidate an outsider to whom party people will not automatically flock? Is the candidate's party a majority or not? Is party strength spread equally throughout the district or concentrated in some areas? What is it that party organization can and cannot do in a particular campaign? How important is the campaign for the party organization? Are party activists likely to work hard for this campaign, or are they more concerned about another race?

Merely posing these questions demonstrates how complex tactical campaign planning can be. Return for a moment to the question of what other offices are on the ballot. If John Doe is a candidate for Congress, in all likelihood his congressional district does not have the same boundaries that districts designed for other elective offices have. Most party organizations are structured around the county unit. In rural states, and in rural districts in some of the more urban states, congressional districts tend to encompass a large number of counties. For example, the First Congressional District in West Virginia includes all or part of twenty counties; the First Congressional District in California, in the northwestern corner of the state, includes all or part of eleven counties. On the other hand, in urban areas many congressional districts fall into single counties. The five counties that compose New York City contain all or part of seventeen congressional districts.

County organizations are often unconcerned about congressional politics. Members of Congress deal with issues far away in Washington. Party people care more about issues closer to home; they are more likely to campaign hard for the candidates who can do something for them. The local sheriff may have more immediate impact on these politicians than do their representatives in Washington. Similarly, they are more likely to work hard for candidates for executive office than they are for candidates for legislative office. All this theorizing assumes, of course, that the party organization exists and is capable of doing effective campaign work, an assumption that is far from clear in many areas of the country (Eldersveld 1982; Epstein 1986; for a more positive view of the role of county organizations, see Gibson 1991).

On the other hand, in recent decades the national parties have become more active in local campaigns. First the Republicans in the late 1970s and in response the Democrats have built professional campaign organizations that concentrate on recruiting good candidates for office—at the congressional level and even at the level of state senator and state representative in some instances—training local candidates and their staffs in basic campaign techniques, and supplying support services, including polling, fund-raising, and opposition research. Between 2004 and 2008, under DNC chair Howard Dean, the Democrats implemented the 50-State Strategy, aiming to create a robust party organization at every precinct in the nation (see Kamarck 2006). Recent research has shown that party organizations and extended networks can be important to congressional candidates, especially to candidates challenging incumbents (Desmarais,

La Raja, and Kowal 2015; Nyhan and Montgomery 2015). Both parties, with the Republicans in the lead, have sought to nationalize voter mobilization drives on behalf of their candidates, efforts thought to be critical because of the closeness of the division between the parties (see Adamany 1984, 78–92; Bibby 1986, 1991; Herrnson 1988; Reichley 1985; Stewart 1991; and the discussion in chapter 2).

With all these caveats, what can be expected from party as a resource? First, in any geographic area some citizens will vote for a candidate because of party label. The number of die-hard party loyalists varies from area to area, but candidates should know the history of party loyalty in a district (Petrocik 2004). Similarly, some citizens use party label as a negative voting cue: "I could never vote for a Republican" (Sabato 1988, chap. 4).

Second, some jobs are better accomplished by party than by any other political organization. Some tasks benefit all candidates who are running under a party label. Thus candidates frequently call upon party organization to run voter registration drives. Party organizations can often be counted on to organize get-out-the-vote drives on election day, or at least to monitor the polls on election day, to be certain that votes are not lost owing to error or fraud.

In sum, party is a resource that candidates have to be aware of, but must also beware of. One cannot expect too much from an organization that might not be that strong and almost certainly will have at least some interests that differ from those of a single candidate. But candidates must use such a resource for all that it has to offer.

The Role of Organized Groups

Organized groups often work hard in a particular candidate's campaign. Group involvement in political campaigns was discussed in chapter 4. From a candidate's perspective, questions involving organized groups are like those that must be asked of political parties. Which groups can provide active support? How can they help reach out to supporters or potential supporters? How effective are they going to be at that task? How concerned are they going to be about supporting this candidate as opposed to other candidates?

Groups can be very effective surrogates for candidates. The techniques that groups use in the political arena have already been noted (chapter 4). All of the techniques that attempt to influence the voting behavior of group members are important for candidates because the group replaces the candidate as the prime contact to the voter. Groups attempt to ensure that the supporter remains a supporter and actually votes and that the potential supporter comes over to the candidate's side.

However, group support does not come automatically to a candidate. Our hypothetical candidate must expend blocks of time to garner group support and more time to ensure that group support stays firm and is mobilized. Furthermore, candidates must recognize that groups have multiple interests that extend beyond any one campaign and are engaged in activities other than politics. Thus group activity is also a limited resource.

Candidates must recognize that the very same groups that are most likely to generate a good deal of support for a candidacy from their followers are the ones that also alienate other voters. A candidate who is not firmly committed to the views of a particularly controversial group might view that group's support as something of a mixed blessing. For many years Democratic candidates worried whether vocal support from very liberal groups hurt their chances; Republicans have asked the same question about vocal advocacy by culturally and religiously conservative groups.

Like political parties, special interest groups can be very effective at convincing their members to turn out to vote, when voting for a particular candidate is clearly perceived as in the members' interest.

Media Politics

The discussion to this point has purposefully avoided the major surrogate for personal contact by a candidate: media campaigning. A candidate who cannot reach the voters personally can surely reach them through the media. In the middle of the second decade of the twenty-first century, media campaigning has become a way of life for all of us. Shouldn't that be obvious? Don't all successful candidates use television and now social media to reach voters?

Again, reality is not quite what it might appear. Certainly television and politics have blended in familiar ways in recent years—and the Internet has become the tool of choice for many campaigns, especially social media, which allow candidates to precisely target voters and in some instances speak directly to them without a media filter. Using the media to carry political messages has become familiar to all viewers; a vast majority of Americans receive most of their political information from television. But that does not end the discussion.

While we discuss media and politics in more detail in chapter 10, we will provide a context for that discussion here. A number of different cases suggest themselves. First, consider a candidate for Congress from the Eighth Congressional District in Maryland. The media market for Maryland 8 includes the District of Columbia and the Virginia suburbs of Washington as well as the Maryland suburbs. The voters and the media follow national politics, not local. How can a candidate for Congress in this situation attract attention in the D.C. media market? Advertise effectively? Use the media as a surrogate for personal contact?

For a second scenario, imagine a candidate running for state senate from a district in Portland, Maine. Most voter attention will be centered on the top of the ticket—either a presidential election or a gubernatorial election. In two out of every three election years, there will also be a U.S. Senate election. The local media blankets the Portland state senatorial districts, but over ninety cents of every television advertising dollar for state senate candidates is wasted because messages are also beamed to voters who reside in other districts. The same is true of radio and newspaper advertising. What role, then, should the media play in this state senate campaign?

Contrast these two cases with a third scenario, the race for Congress in North Dakota. North Dakota elects its governor in the same year the president is elected. Thus, in "off-year" elections, if neither of the two Senate seats happens to be up that year, the congressional race is on top of the ballot. North Dakota is a sparsely populated state with slightly more than 750,000 people spread out over a vast area; the state's citizen density is less than ten citizens per square mile. Although citizens expect to meet the candidates personally (an expectation in many smaller states), North Dakota is perfect for a media campaign because the state has only two dominant media markets—Fargo and Bismarck, neither of which is an expensive market and neither of which beams to many voters out of the state.

These three examples point to the first conclusion about the role of mass media in general, and television in particular, in modern campaigns. Mass media advertising as a surrogate for personal contact is very important in today's campaigns. However, the electoral context determines the extent to which such campaigning can replace personal campaigning as a way to reach the voters.

Campaigning through electronic or digital media, which can be targeted more precisely than television, radio, or newspapers, can be more effective. "Narrowcasting" on cable television and reaching citizens through social networking sites on the Internet have played expanding roles in campaigns in recent election cycles; a recent Pew (2014e) study found that 28 percent of registered voters used their phones to access political or campaign content in the 2014 election cycle, more than double the 13 percent who did so in 2010. Pew did not even ask this question regarding the 2016 election cycle, likely reflecting the ubiquitous nature of the usage of cell phones to access campaign information. While there is no question that these techniques have great potential, their effectiveness has varied from candidate to candidate. Enough experience has not been accumulated to assess when these techniques work better and when they are less effective; however, a number of variables can be isolated. First, the quality of the campaign team is important. It is difficult for candidates and campaign managers to give up key campaign roles to those often half or a third their ages; but in fact, the best Internet campaigns are run by those most familiar with how young citizens use the Internet—and those tend to be young people.

Second, in order to activate a group of voters through the Internet, they must be motivated. Voters must decide to go to an Internet site; the information does not come to them automatically. Potential voters and activists are most likely to do this when either a compelling issue or a charismatic candidate motivates them. The inability of Organizing for America to sustain the momentum built during the Obama presidential campaign for the 2010 midterm demonstrates both the potential and the limitations of this still emerging media tool. Twitter has changed this calculation. Once a voter signs up to follow a candidate or office holder on Twitter, they receive tweeted material from this party unless they decide to unfollow this person. Donald Trump used Twitter masterfully—something we discuss more fully in chapter 10.

In any of these forms, media are used by candidates to define their image and to portray their opponents. But that tactic is only successful to the extent that the chosen media penetrates the voters' consciousness. The use of media of various types that we see in presidential campaigns and in large statewide campaigns is often very different from that accessible to candidates running for not only local office but also more prominent state and federal office for which citizen attention to an effective mass medium is lacking (Goldenberg and Traugott 1984).

Even in districts in which media advertising plays a dominant role, only certain kinds of messages can be transmitted through thirty-second commercials. These messages can convey impressions and images, but they cannot present and analyze issue positions very well. Nonetheless, in those districts such advertisements play a crucial, perhaps even critical, role in many campaigns. Candidates like former eBay executive Meg Whitman, who ran unsuccessfully for governor of California in 2010, can go from virtual unknowns to household names through repeated appearances on television. In districts and states in which media advertising is an expected part of campaigning, citizens use television as a prime means of evaluating candidates.

Since 1996, political parties and interest groups (through so-called issue advocacy advertisements [see chapter 4]) have used electronic and digital media to convey pointed messages to the electorate. These have supplemented the candidates' own media campaigns and in some cases have been intense enough to overwhelm the candidates' own efforts. Freed from earlier constraints by the *Citizens United* Supreme Court decision, various groups dominated the airwaves in 2010, drastically affecting the result according to some critics. The accuracy of these messages has been debated frequently, but their impact has not. Candidate images have been built—and more often destroyed—through these efforts.

Since 2000, ample evidence leads to the conclusion that parties and interest groups have played a clearly defined role. They run the negative campaigns, attacking their candidates' opponents, leaving their own candidates to take the high road. Often, more media dollars are spent by these surrogate groups than by the candidates themselves. The Bipartisan Campaign Reform Act (BCRA) of 2003 was aimed, at least in part, at curtailing these roles, by limiting the amount of soft money that parties can raise and spend and by limiting others' independent expenditures. The 2010 campaign experience clearly demonstrated that the Supreme Court's decisions on BCRA ended any hope of reducing the influence of these groups and of advertisements whose sponsors' identities are not revealed (see chapter 5).

The charge is often made that the media consultant, the political equivalent of a Madison Avenue adman, makes or breaks a candidate. The implications of this charge for the role of campaigning in the political process are obvious and serious (cf. McGinniss 1969). Candidates must consider whether media advertising is appropriate for their particular campaign and must determine whether an impersonal message, often quick and slick, is the vehicle they want to use for presenting themselves to those whose support they seek.

The Candidate's Personal Organization

Parties, groups, and media are frequently used as surrogates for personal campaigning in races for higher office. The fourth surrogate, the most common one, is the candidate's personal organization. When commentators speak of candidate organizations, they mean a number of different things. For the purposes of this discussion, they are volunteers who go out and campaign on behalf of a candidate. They function as the candidate's eyes, ears, and mouth, a necessity in those districts in which a candidate cannot reach every voter personally.

This type of campaigning is done in a number of different ways. Where possible, campaigners go door-to-door, talking to individual voters and seeking their support for a particular candidate. If an organization is sophisticated enough, these volunteers then compile lists of the voters they have visited, commenting on the likelihood that those voters will support the candidate. On election day the likely supporters are called again and urged to go to the polls. The voters who are likely to vote for another candidate are left alone. One congressional candidate claims to have contacted 31,000 households in this way during the fifteen weeks before the 1998 election (Moberg 1998), but analysis and follow-up of this sort require a sophisticated organization with a large number of trained volunteers.

Other campaigns use volunteers in less complex ways. Some campaigns merely "drop" literature at every door, letting the brochures speak for themselves. Still other campaigns use volunteers, usually young volunteers, to distribute leaflets at shopping centers, malls, ball games, or other locations where large numbers of potential voters are to be found. Many areas have their own typical modes of reaching voters—"human billboards" along congested commuter routes, door holders at subway stations, refreshment providers at factory gates, and so on.

Still other campaigns employ telephone banks, phoning perspective voters with messages about the candidate. Telephone campaigns vary tremendously in sophistication, depending on how well trained the callers are and how organized the entire operation is. At one extreme these campaigns can be as effective as door-to-door campaigning, especially for rural districts; at the other extreme they resemble the scattershot technique of shopping mall leafleting.

One of the keys to establishing a volunteer organization is to have workers who will campaign for just one candidate. In some ways this service is inefficient. If a volunteer is to go door-to-door, why not carry propaganda for a group of candidates? Many volunteers will do this. The difference in effort extended is minimal. However, from a candidate's perspective, the difference is important. If a worker carries material or campaigns for more than one candidate, the potential effect of the volunteer contact on the voter is certainly diminished, and it might even be negated. What if the voter has not heard about one candidate but has a negative view of the other candidate, and using only that opinion, discounts both candidates? A New Hampshire candidate for state representative reported that one voter told her on election day that the only reason he bothered to vote at all was because of a call he received on the Sunday night before the election. He voted for one candidate on the whole ballot, the candidate from whose organization he received that call (Crosby 1998).

Although scenarios can be imagined in which combined efforts would help a candidate, if they had their choice, most candidates would want volunteers to work for them and them alone, a far cry from the days when political parties did this kind of campaigning on behalf of an entire ticket.[5] Strong individual candidates who are supported by large numbers of dedicated volunteers eschew combined campaign efforts; weaker candidates with fewer supporters are the most eager to have a "team" approach to campaigning.

The ability of candidates to form their own volunteer organization is another factor that varies with what other races are being held at the same time. However, once a winning candidate has a personal organization in place, maintaining it over a period of years is not difficult. Some supporters drop out; new supporters are recruited for each new campaign. But a core of candidate-inspired activists remains as a powerful resource (Fenno 1978).

The Structure of a Modern Campaign

Volunteer organizations such as the one just described have been an important part of American politics for some time, at least since the spread of direct primaries. In recent years, however, as major campaigns have become more expensive and more complex, candidate organizations have taken on a different meaning.

Figure 7.1 depicts a possible organizational chart for a modern, well-funded general election campaign. The coordination of various means of contacting voters, using traditional and modern techniques, defines the extent to which the new politics has come to dominate campaigns for many offices.

The candidate sits atop the organization. Or at least one hopes the candidate does. Too often campaigns run so efficiently that the candidates seem to be all but unimportant, merely the product to be packaged. However, in this case, let us assume that the candidate is in charge, selecting the campaign manager and approving strategy and tactics. (See Agranoff 1972, 1976; Hershey 1984; Johnson-Cartee and Copeland 1997; Kayden 1978; Luntz 1988; Maisel 1986; Rothenberg 1983; Salmore and Salmore 1985; Shea 1996.)

The campaign manager runs the day-to-day campaign. Campaigns for statewide office routinely require budgets in the millions of dollars and require professional management. In the last two decades a corps of "professional" campaign managers has emerged. Some work as individual entrepreneurs, working one campaign at a time and then waiting for the next biennium to begin again. More and more, however, the pattern is for political managers to form companies that take over the management of a number of campaigns at the same time, handling many of the tasks from a central headquarters. Political campaign management is indeed a growth industry these days.[6] Different firms have different expertise and/or are willing to handle different aspects of a campaign. But they all combine some of the functions we will now describe, with advice on how the campaign should proceed (see Thurber and Nelson 2000; Luntz 1988; Sabato 1981).

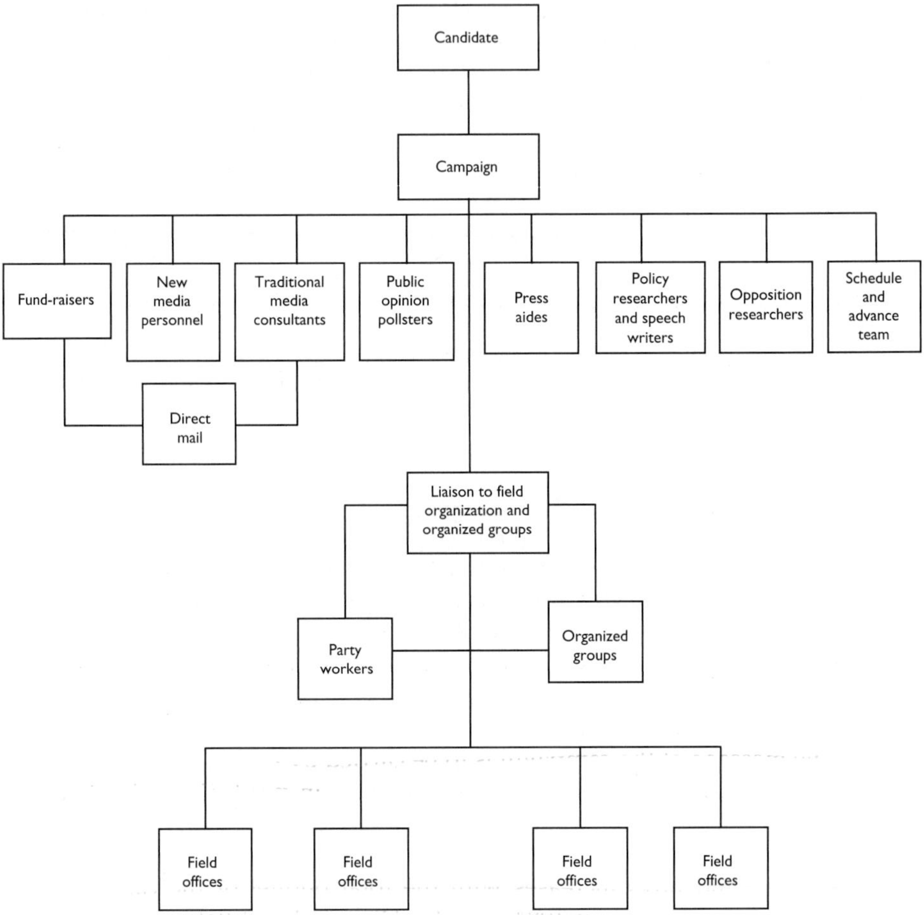

Figure 7.1
Structure of a Modern Campaign

Public Opinion Polling

Modern campaigns do not rely on hunches to determine what the public is thinking or to evaluate how different approaches to campaigning are working. Public opinion polling has acquired a prominent role in modern campaigns. In some cases the campaign management firm handles the public opinion polling; in other cases a polling firm plays a major role in campaign management; in still other cases two firms work together. Prominent pollsters like GarinHart-Yang Strategic Research Group; the Tarrance Group; Penn, Schoen, and Berland; Greenberg Quinlan Rosner Research; and Fairbank, Maslin, Maullin, and Associates are sought after as key figures in major campaigns. Pollsters play major roles in ascertaining what issues concern the public, how the candidate is perceived, how the opponent is perceived, and what approaches will and will not work.

More elaborate campaigns do continuous polling during the campaign period. In lower-budget campaigns, a pollster takes a first poll, called a benchmark poll, to determine a candidate's position and the views of the public at the beginning of the campaign and then polls occasionally throughout the campaign, to measure attitudes and changes in opinions in response to specific events or to determine the impact of specific strategies. Professional pollsters not only provide and analyze the data, but they also interpret what those data mean in light of other campaigns around the country (see Crespi 1988, 1989; Hillygus 2011; Stonecash 2003).

Media Consultants

The campaign manager and the pollster also work closely with the media expert on a campaign. Some large management firms take care of designing media strategies, making commercials, and buying time for campaigns. Some firms, primarily advertising agencies, specialize in political advertising and only that. Because media expenditures constitute such a high percentage of total campaign expenditures, the role of the media consultant is central to most campaigns (Goldenberg and Traugott 1984, chap. 6; Johnson 2011; Medvic 2001, 2003; Pfau and Kenski 1990).

If the message of the campaign is to be carried by paid media, then the media consultant has to be involved, not only in producing advertisements and buying time and space but also in setting strategies. The percentage of total campaign budgets spent on media consultants and ad production and buys increases with the total budget of the campaign (Goldenberg and Traugott 1984; see also Diamond and Bates 1984; Pfau and Kenski 1990).

Internet and Social Media Consultants

As recently as 2006, few campaigns would have had a senior staff member in charge of Internet strategy and tactics—and a few still do not. However, it is now the norm for campaigns to have individuals and firms on board whose job is to devise and implement a broad Internet and social media strategy. Social media specialists have become increasingly common as well, and are rightly seen as a necessity for campaigns for higher office. These strategies involve a web presence, advertising over the Internet, fund-raising through the Internet, and the use of social networking sites and other social media to energize and mobilize supporters (Druckman et al. 2010; Karpf 2013; Vaccari 2013). The advantage that the

Internet and social media have for microtargeting an audience and for gaining nearly instantaneous feedback means that its use in various ways as campaign strategy and tactics evolve can only increase.

Fund-Raisers

Polling, media advertising, and effective web presences are expensive. Million-dollar campaigns were cause for concern in the late 1960s; multimillion-dollar campaigns are commonplace today. In order to run campaigns of this magnitude, candidates must spend a good deal of time and effort on fund-raising (recall chapter 5). At this point it is sufficient to state that one important part of any campaign organization involves raising the money necessary to conduct the campaign and monitoring how that money is spent.

Many campaigns now hire professionals to handle these tasks (Cummings and Cummings 2004; Herrnson 1991). They must begin well in advance of the start of actual campaigning for two reasons. First, fund-raising requires a good deal of candidate time. It is difficult to convince a donor to make a major contribution if that donor cannot sit down and actually talk with the candidate. Second, most campaign expenditures require payment in advance. Few of those enterprises used to dealing with campaigns will do so on a credit basis; all too often campaigns end up with unpaid bills.

Therefore, candidates have to raise money in advance in order to start effective campaigning. A number of observers have commented that raising money early can have important strategic consequences for dissuading effective opposition (Goldenberg and Traugott 1984; Green and Krasno 1988; Jacobson 1990b; Jacobson and Kernell 1983; Sorauf 1984). This lesson is not lost on politicians. One group interested in assisting more women who are running for office has based its entire strategy on this premise. Many think that EMILY's List is named after its founder, but in fact it is an acronym for Early Money Is Like Yeast—because it makes the dough rise. The group supports female candidates early in the process so that those candidates will be able to demonstrate viability to others who might give them money later on.

Until quite recently, **direct mail** was undeniably the most effective technique for raising money from large numbers of donors, and it is still heavily used (Hassell and Monson 2014). It was first employed on a national level by the Republican party under Chairman Ray Bliss and perfected by Richard Viguerie, a kind of direct mail guru who developed lists and raised money for a series of conservative candidates. Viguerie's success spurred others to copy his techniques, though none quite duplicated his early success in raising large sums of money from small donors. Today liberal and conservative candidates, as well as interest groups, use computer-generated lists of potential donors and/or potential voters. They appeal to these voters directly based on certain known characteristics or preferences—therefore the term direct mail. Although Viguerie's inflammatory techniques have not always been successful (in fact, declining response rates led him to cut back his efforts [Edsall 1986]), these techniques continue to reach many voters in each election cycle.

In the last decade the Internet has become the fund-raising tool of choice for many candidates. Recognizing the success of presidential candidates in raising unheard-of sums of money over the Internet, candidates for Congress and the Senate, for governor and other state offices have turned to this tool as well. Internet fund-raising firms now compete effectively with direct mail firms for campaign budget allocations.

As fund-raising tools, neither direct mail nor the Internet knows political boundaries. Appeals flow to potential donors throughout the country as campaigns attempt to convince those who have donated to campaigns in the past that they should donate to similar campaigns now.

These fund-raising tools are equally effective as campaign tools. Once mailing or e-mail lists have been developed, campaigns can direct "personalized" appeals to groups of voters who share certain characteristics. All environmentalists in a state might receive a mailing or e-mail that stresses the candidate's record on environmental matters, and all members of the National Rifle Association might receive one that describes the candidate's opposition to gun control legislation. The environmentalist mailing will not mention the candidate's position on gun control, and the NRA appeal will not mention environmental issues, lest anyone be offended.

Scheduling and Advance Work, Press Relations, Field Organization, and Liaison to the Political Party and Organized Groups

Other parts of the campaign operation work to coordinate the use of candidate time and to link the candidate to various other actors involved in the electoral arena.

For instance, candidates for statewide offices, even in smaller states, frequently have more calls for personal time than they have time available. How to use the limited time of the candidate is not a trivial question. Every major campaign has one person—or even a staff of people—whose job it is to see that the candidate's time is used most effectively. Before a candidate arrives at a political event, someone has to be sure that the event will run efficiently; otherwise, the whole effort might be a waste of time. That is the role of the advance team (Bruno and Greenfield 1971).

Another important campaign function involves establishing ongoing relations with the working press. The extent of press coverage varies from campaign to campaign depending on how important the individual campaign is for the geographic area covered by the various media. Thus a congressional race in Nevada is important for the print and electronic media in Las Vegas and Reno, since Nevada has only three representatives in Congress. On the other hand, the *New York Times* and the electronic media in New York do not pay much attention to congressional races because more than two dozen members of Congress represent the metropolitan area served by the *Times* and the New York television stations.

Press aides to candidates in major campaigns deal with the press, but they do not do so in a vacuum. Press relations are part of an overall strategy. Press aides work with all of the major players in a campaign to coordinate the press strategy with the overall message of the campaign.

Field organization plays an essential role in almost any campaign. The campaign needs some way to reach out into the geographic area covered by the districts. Campaign managers talk about the need for a physical presence, a ground war; voters need to know that there are real people behind a campaign. This physical presence takes the form of district offices; of volunteers on the street; of leaflet drops and brochures; of bumper stickers, buttons, and lawn signs. The field organization gives supporters the feeling of joining a vibrant organization.

In any campaign, the campaign manager and the candidate must determine what effective role political party organization will play. However, even in those areas in which political party organization is not strong, someone in a campaign must have the responsibility of coordinating campaign efforts with those of the party leadership. Whatever party officials can do for a campaign to garner the support of their loyal followers is a plus. Whatever extra activities the party can undertake is a plus.

In a large campaign organization, staff coordinate the work of the organized groups that are supporting the candidate. This work involves a number of different problems. In some cases there must be coordination with the fund-raisers; in others, with direct mail or Internet providers; in still others, with scheduling. At times it is appropriate to set up separate committees to demonstrate group support—Lawyers for Jones or Teachers for Miller. These efforts might require coordination with the press aide or with the media consultant. If organized groups aid a campaign by providing volunteers, their work should be coordinated with the field organization or with political party machinery.

OLD-STYLE POLITICS: A MORE PROMINENT ROLE FOR PARTIES

Look back at Figure 7.1. The entire organization is directed toward getting in touch with as many voters as possible in as many effective ways as possible. Voters are informed about the candidate through the news media, through paid media, through sessions with the candidate, through mail and the Internet, or through the campaign efforts of others. An efficient campaign organization will reach each prospective voter a number of times in a number of different ways; most of these appeals will be directed specifically at individual voters. Once voters have been informed about a candidate, they will be asked to support that candidate with their help, their money, and their votes. They will be asked, again and again, to help in whatever ways are possible. All the efforts of the campaign staff and organization, the professionals, the consultants, and the volunteers are aimed at this goal.

This campaign chart represents "new politics" because of the techniques used. Modern technology has, in fact, replaced older techniques that relied upon person-to-person contact and party allegiance. Now computers, not precinct committeemen, are used to identify and categorize voters, to analyze polling data, to monitor the progress toward reaching certain campaign goals, even to make telephone calls.

Television, radio, and increasingly the Internet are used to reach large numbers of voters with messages that were carried by volunteers on foot in an earlier time. Direct mail, e-mail, and social networking sites and apps allow for "personal" contact with significant numbers of voters. Campaign budgets have multiplied to amounts that would have been beyond belief even twenty years ago. Professionals are called in to monitor these huge organizations. No candidate can personally manage a major campaign; the two functions (candidacy and management) are separate, and each is full-time during a big campaign. However, it is important to keep in mind that the job of the campaign in the modern era is not fundamentally different from what it was in the days before modern techniques changed politics.

Remember the candidate for county supervisor described at the beginning of this chapter? He staffed the voter registration booth; he put up posters; he scheduled his own time. He was the one shaking the hands of voters at the fair, creating the media event by introducing the Senate candidate, probably with remarks that he himself had labored over. Why was *he* doing all these things himself? Where was *his* organization?

The answer probably is that he doesn't really have one. How many people can he expect to get excited about working for a candidate for county supervisor? How many people are likely to contribute large sums of money to candidates who are running for county supervisor? For clerk of courts or water district commissioner? Or even for state representative or state senator in any of the smaller states?

Think about the people who hold these offices in any community. Who are they? What do they do? For such low-visibility offices, do most people really care enough to become involved with active campaigning?

For most of us, our reaction to the campaigns for these offices is a resounding, "Who cares?" When we do care, the reasons are quite obvious. Most often the "organization" of candidates for local offices is made up of friends and neighbors who are friends and neighbors first and become involved in politics secondarily.

Similarly, these campaigns often involve local issues. A parent who is concerned about a particular item on the city council's upcoming agenda—closing the public pool or granting a liquor license to a bar in his neighborhood—might become involved in a campaign. Often local campaigns are the most intense because the issues strike closest to home. Issues and personalities are familiar. Neighbors work with and against neighbors.

But even when one is involved in these campaigns, the campaign is not of the same scale as a congressional or statewide campaign. Most candidates for city council or county commissioner represent an approachable number of people. The candidate can personally touch those people. Large budgets, surrogates, and complex organizations are not necessary. Many of the important campaign functions that help one candidate help all candidates of the same party. Political parties play important roles.

Reexamination of the Role of Political Parties

This is not to say that local politics, campaigns for "less major" offices, is a throwback to a time when political parties dominated our political scene. However, party plays a much more prominent role, and the style of campaigning is much more susceptible to party organizational efforts than is the case in larger campaigns.

Candidates for state and local offices face the same strategic questions that other candidates face. Who are one's likely supporters? Who are those who might be convinced to become supporters? How can these people be convinced? What will draw supporters to the polls? However, these candidates often face these questions in an environment marked by public inattention and apathy.

Most campaigns for state and local office involve candidates seeking to represent districts that fall within one county, the most common party organizational unit (Eldersveld 1982). County party activists are familiar with the candidates; and candidates need only deal with one party committee. Party organizations work best in districts in which the boundaries coincide with existing party structures. County parties were central in the formation of the first party organizations in the United States (DeWitt 2013), and they remain important today in areas as diverse as structuring state and local elections (Streib et al. 2007) and mobilizing (or not) Latino voters (Lehman 2013).

Furthermore, party organizations work best at stimulating activity by regular party supporters. When candidates are looking for likely supporters, all other things being equal, voters who share their party affiliation are obvious targets. Think about your own decisions on voting. You are probably saying, "I don't vote for the party! I vote for the best candidate." But consider specific examples. You vote for the presidential candidate you think is best, for the best candidate for governor and U.S. senator, maybe even for representative in the House. But what about the candidate for registrar of deeds, for probate judge, for clerk of courts? Do you honestly know who they are? How do you judge who you think is the "best" candidate?

You need some other means to make a judgment. Party is often that voting cue. You might not be a "member" of a political party, but you probably have different feelings about the two major parties, feelings that often determine votes for local office. Thus candidates are interested in party efforts to register copartisans and to get them out to the polls. Those are precisely the kinds of tasks that party organizations still perform quite well.

Local Campaigns in the Absence of Party

Campaigns using the party organization work well, if there is a party organization. How does a candidate run when the party organization is nonexistent or inactive, as is the case in many counties throughout the country? Or how does a candidate run if the opposition party is stronger in his or her district, making it necessary to appeal to those in the other party? In these cases it is necessary to return to the original form of "old politics," person-to-person campaigning.

For some candidates, this is what politics is all about, getting to know those who live nearby. In city after city and town after town, autumn evenings and weekends see scores of candidates knocking on neighbors' doors. **Canvassing**—talking directly with individual voters and asking for their votes—is king in these elections. No kind of campaigning is more time-consuming, but none bears greater fruit.

If candidates are willing to devote the time, frequently they can cover an entire district. An early morning breakfast in a country store is more important for a candidate for sheriff than any paid advertisement. Five minutes over coffee in an elderly man's apartment pays more dividends than literature distributed in a shopping center. Politics at these levels is intensely personal, rarely substantive. These kinds of politics also raise all sorts of questions about the functioning of our democracy. Why do we have such long ballots? Why are these kinds of positions filled by elections and not appointments?

DO CAMPAIGNS DETERMINE WHO WINS ELECTIONS?

We have already presented conflicting theories about what determines the results of elections. One theory accounted for election results on the basis of aggregate economic conditions. The second theory related electoral results to individual citizens' opinions about conditions in the country. Although these theories were developed to explain the results of congressional elections, they should cause anyone reading this chapter to pause for a moment. Do campaigns—at whatever level—matter?

Lack of Competition in American Elections

The answer is that they do. Jacobson and Kernell (1983) take some pains to demonstrate that the quality of a candidate is an important factor in determining the results of an election. The better candidates, identified as those who have previously achieved electoral success, are more likely to run credible campaigns and, as a consequence, to win (see Fowler and McClure 1989; Jacobson 1987a, 1987b; Maisel 1989, 1990a; for a different perspective on candidate quality, see Maisel, Stone, and Maestas 1999; Stone, Maisel, and Maestas 2004). The problem is that there are not many of these better candidates running for office.

In describing campaign structure, what we were really describing was how these things are done in well-run campaigns. For most campaigns, reality does not approximate this ideal. In campaign after campaign, year after year, candidates' names appear on ballots and then they are never heard from again. They lose. And they do not provide significant competition for the winner.

Most frequently they lose to an incumbent or, if no incumbent is running, to the candidate of the dominant party. That they lose is less important than the fact that they never really run a campaign. Without effective competition, the citizens of a district are denied the opportunity to choose. Even if two or more names appear on the ballot, electoral choice is effective only when the citizens are presented with candidates who appear serious to them.

Incumbent Advantage in U.S. House and State Legislative Races

For years political scientists have noted that incumbents running for reelection to the Congress have won in large numbers. Many explanations have been offered for the observed phenomenon of incumbent advantage (Abramowitz 1975; Cover 1977; Ferejohn 1977; Fiorina 1977a, 1978; Herrnson 1998a, 2000; Mayhew 1974b; for a different view see Stonecash 2008).

The scholarly analyses of the 1978 midterm election were among the first to demonstrate what Jacobson (1981) has aptly called "the vanishing challengers" (see also Abramowitz 1981; Hinckley 1981; Maisel and Cooper 1981; Mann and Wolfinger 1980). Whether measured in terms of dollars spent, voter perception, even voter recognition, challengers were basically invisible; incumbents won because no one knew who was running against them.

The rate of incumbent success in races for the House of Representatives surprises many casual observers (see Figure 3.6, p. 96). In only seven elections since World War II have fewer than 90 percent of those seeking reelection been reelected. But one of those elections occurred recently in 2010, when more than fifty incumbents, almost all Democrats, lost bids for reelection. Why?

Scholars have identified many causes that contribute to incumbent advantage, but no single cause—or even most prominent cause—has emerged. A number of scholars are now examining the supply side of incumbent advantage, seeking to understand why stronger challengers do not run (Jewell and Whicker 1998; Maestas et al. 2006; Moncrief, Squire, and Kurtz 1998; Stone and Maisel 2003; Stone, Maisel, and Maestas 1998; Stone, Maisel, and Maestas 1998, 2004; Williamson 1999; Gaddie and Bullock 2000). One interesting and unexpected conclusion is that strong challengers often choose not to oppose an incumbent because they think the incumbent is doing a good job and value his or her public service (Stone, Maisel, and Maestas 2004). To the extent this is the case, we can worry less about the high rate at which incumbents get reelected.

In 2010 the Republicans recruited many strong candidates, because both the national party and local candidates saw incumbent Democrats—many of whom had taken over previously Republican seats in either 2006 or 2008—as vulnerable, particularly given popular frustration over the state of the economy. Despite vigorous campaigns by these threatened incumbents, an unusually large number of challengers prevailed. Why? First, the playing field was tilted toward the Republicans because so many Democrats were defending seats in districts that favored the GOP. Second, as a result, Republicans fielded strong candidates in many districts. Third, anti-Obama feelings, invigorated in many states by Tea Party movement activists, energized Republicans more than Democrats. Fourth, the Republicans were able to nationalize the election, turning it into a referendum on Obama's stewardship of the nation and especially the economy, not a vote on the particular representative seeking reelection. And fifth, Republicans were better able to exploit the freedom given to individuals and groups to run advertisements without restriction than the Democrats. The 2012, 2014, and 2016 House cycles more closely resembled the norm, with 90, 95, and 97 percent of those incumbents seeking reelection keeping their seats respectively. A recent analysis by Charlie Cook of *The Cook Report* says that the number of truly competitive House districts has dropped dramatically since 1998 (Cook 2013). Heading into the 2018 cycle, Cook rates eighty-two House races as competitive, a total that accounts for 19 percent of the seats in the U.S. House of Representatives.

State legislators seeking reelection also win virtually all of the time, again mostly without serious opposition (Jewell and Breaux 1988; Calvert 1979). Analysis by Ronald Weber, Harvey Tucker, and Paul Brace (1991) demonstrates that the number of **marginal seats** (i.e., seats in which contests are so close that either party has a legitimate chance of victory) and the number of contested seats in a group of twenty state lower houses declined between 1950 and 1986 (but see Garand 1991; Jacobson 1987a). However, again the 2010 election broke the pattern. The Republican party gained over six hundred seats nationally, although many of those were open seats, vacated because of **term limits**. Things have returned to a more "normal" pattern since.

Competition in U.S. Senate and Gubernatorial Races

Researchers who hypothesize that incumbent advantage is due to lack of quality challengers point out that incumbent U.S. senators, although frequently reelected, are not sent back to the Senate in anywhere near the same proportion as are House members. Incumbent senators are often challenged by well-known politicians who run impressive campaigns, spending significant amounts of money, reaching and recognized by voters throughout the state. These conclusions were recognized at the same time that the advantages of House members were under exploration (Abramowitz 1975, 1981; Hinckley 1981; McAdams and Johannes 1981; see also Mondak 1995; Zaller 1998). Figure 3.7 (p. 97) shows that there has been tremendous variation in the percentage of incumbent senators winning reelection.[7]

Data on gubernatorial elections are less easily obtained than those on House and Senate elections (but see Jewell 1984). Figure 3.8 (p. 99) shows the success rates for gubernatorial challengers in recent elections. Not all incumbent governors are eligible for reelection because of state laws restricting the number of consecutive terms some governors may serve, and so the percentage of incumbents seeking reelection is not as large as it is for senators. Nonetheless, the data still show that governors seeking reelection lose more frequently than do members of Congress, seemingly in numbers more comparable to those for unsuccessful incumbent senators. The parallel to senators is quite close. Many incumbent governors seeking reelection have attracted credible challengers. At times, elections are quite competitive, and many incumbents lose; at other times, this seems less so. The variables at play seem to be peculiar to one election year and, often, to one election. Analysts were hard put to explain, for instance, why an anti-incumbent mood in the electorate in 1990 led to the defeat of more incumbent governors than in any other election in two decades, while only one incumbent U.S. senator was defeated and more than 96 percent of the House members seeking reelection were victorious. Similarly, in 2010, gubernatorial and senatorial elections showed important gains for the Republicans, but mostly in open seats: twenty-one of the twenty-three incumbents on the general election ballot for the U.S. Senate (including Alaska Republican Lisa Murkowski, who was running as a write-in candidate after having lost a primary) and eleven of the thirteen incumbent governors running for reelection in that election. Gubernatorial and senatorial incumbent safety rebounded significantly in 2012 and have remained strong since, although not as strong as for House incumbents.

Credible Competition in American Elections

One obvious conclusion from this review is that what has been happening at the congressional level has been happening at other levels as well. Incumbents are winning because challengers are poor campaigners (Jewell and Breaux 1988; Holbrook and Tidmarch 1991; Weber, Tucker, and Brace 1991). When challengers run good campaigns, incumbents can lose (Garand 1991). But good challengers appear too infrequently for too many important offices.

The lack of good challengers and good campaigns insulates incumbents in congressional races; in all probability, the same factors insulate those incumbents seeking reelection to other less visible and less attractive offices as well.

Campaigns do matter. The low number of credible campaigns for many offices, and the invulnerability of many incumbents because of the scarcity of these credible campaigns, points to a major flaw in the way our electoral system operates.

Is this flaw correctable? Some feel the system has failed and that the only way to remedy the flaw is to impose term limits for more offices. Those who advocate term limits argue that because incumbents cannot be beaten it is necessary to remove them from office by limiting the number of terms they are permitted to serve. The term limit movement spread widely in the early 1990s; Table 1.2 (p. 6) lists term limitations for state legislators now in effect. Term limits have been proposed for members of Congress. The constitutionality of states imposing such limits on their representatives is dubious; the likelihood of the Congress passing an amendment to do so, even less likely.

It is not our purpose here to debate the merits of the term limit movement. The question for this discussion is whether or not term limits would increase electoral competition. To this question, the answer seems clear. When a legislator is forced out of office because he or she is not legally eligible to seek reelection, a high level of competition is likely in that district.[8] We know from long experience that competition in congressional elections is strongest when seats come open due to death, retirement, or an incumbent's leaving to seek another office. We have found the same experience to follow when a seat becomes open because an incumbent was forced out by statute.

On the other hand, we have also found *less* competition when a legislator is eligible to run for reelection. Here the reasoning of a potential candidate is quite different. Why should a potentially strong candidate run against an incumbent when he or she knows that that incumbent will shortly be forced to retire? The incentive to wait for an open seat is enhanced if it is known for certain when that seat will become open. Thus the effect of term limits on competition is most likely to be to increase competition in one election in every cycle (i.e., one in four if the limit is four terms; one in six if it is six terms, etc.), but to decrease competition or leave it unchanged in the other years. Whether this result is good or bad and (if it is judged to be beneficial) whether other results from the imposition of term limits merit such a change in the political system are value judgments, not matters that can be explored empirically.[9]

Are there other means to enhance competition? What is necessary to run good campaigns? In major elections, the answer that is most often given is money (e.g., Gierzynski and Breaux 1990, 1991; Jacobson 1981, 1985–1986). A good campaign could be run, an incumbent could be seriously challenged, if the opponent's campaign were adequately financed. But this explanation may well beg the question. A challenger's campaign *would* be adequately financed if the challenger were viewed as serious. Serious challengers always appear when the risk of running for office is offset by the attractiveness of the office and the perceived chances of winning.

Can this circle be broken? Two answers seem possible. The congressional elections of 2006, 2008, and 2010 provide hints of one possible answer. In 2006, the electorate was dissatisfied with the policies of the Bush administration and with the degree to which the Republicans in Congress followed it. That dissatisfaction was widely perceived, and quality Democratic challengers emerged. In 2008, once again Democrats fielded strong challengers and secured strong majorities in both houses of the Congress.

But dissatisfaction with the policies of the Obama administration and with the Congress as an institution followed that election. By the summer of 2010, according to the Gallup Poll, public confidence in the Congress had dropped to an all-time low, with only 11 percent voicing a positive evaluation of the national legislature. The Republicans saw this dissatisfaction as an opportunity. In the 2010 midterm elections, strong Republican challengers to incumbent Democrats emerged in district after district, bringing more seats into competitive play and leading to the Republicans reclaiming the majority in the House and picking up six seats in the Senate. Republicans continued to build on Americans' unhappiness with President Obama and their own momentum by recapturing control of the Senate as well in 2014. Republicans kept control of both chambers in 2016 (in addition, of course, to winning the White House), but appear to be in some danger of losing significant seats and possibly even control of one or both chambers in 2018.

This pattern is not very different from that seen in the 1990s, when first the Democrats (in 1990 and 1992), then the Republicans (in 1994) and then again the Democrats (in 1996) responded to perceived public dissatisfaction by fielding strong slates of challengers. In the last two elections before the post-2000 census redistricting, however, and in the first two elections after redistricting (2002 and 2004), incumbents emerged virtually unscathed. Why? The reason deals with strategic choices made by potential candidates once again. The most vulnerable Democrats had been defeated in 1994. The most vulnerable Republicans, especially of those first elected in 1994, had been defeated by Democrats in 1996. Most of those who remained were strong candidates for reelection. Most analysts viewed the 1998 election as a great victory for the Democrats because they held even in the Senate and picked up five seats in the House of Representatives, the first time a president's party had gained House seats since 1934 and only the second time since the Civil War. The correct interpretation is that these were victories for the incumbents: 98.5 percent of the incumbents who ran in November 1998 won reelection.

A second possible answer, clearly related to the first, may well be through a rejuvenation of political parties. Traditionally, as we have seen, political parties controlled nominations and access to the ballot. When they lost control over nominations, they also lost an important role in the recruiting process. We know surprisingly little about how individuals are recruited to run for office today (Canon 1990; Cotter et al. 1984; Eldersveld 1982; Gibson et al. 1985; Maisel 1991; Maisel et al. 1990; Seligman 1974; Snowiss 1966). We do know that many candidates are self-starters, that they themselves determine if and when they will seek office (Maisel 1986).

However, in the most recent elections, both national parties, through their congressional campaign committees, have played a more active role in candidate recruitment at all levels (Adamany 1984; Bibby 1981, 1991; Bumiller and Sanger 2002). When the parties have made gains in recent elections, it has been because they ran very attractive candidates. These candidates did not simply emerge; they were recruited and supported by the national party.

Both national parties have also increased their efforts to provide needed services to their candidates. They raise money for their most competitive candidates; they help them in other fund-raising endeavors. They provide training and political support throughout the cycle, intervening directly in the races they see as most crucial. This nationalization of congressional politics, evident in the elections of 2006, 2008, 2010, and 2014 (but not necessarily 2012) is an important trend to watch in the future (Herrnson 1988; Bumiller and Sanger 2002). Early indications are that 2018 will present another cycle of nationalized congressional elections, but it is too early to say definitively as we go to press.

But more than that, the successful party efforts on the national level have set a precedent for both parties' state-level organizations to follow (e.g., Cotter and Bibby 1980; Cotter et al. 1982, 1984; Gibson et al. 1983; Huckshorn et al. 1986). As the national party staffs have moved into fund-raising and polling, into issue research and speechwriting, into strategy setting and media advising, state party organizations have seen opportunities to provide services as well.

For some years parties have been looking for a role to play in the era of new politics. The role of the party may well be to recruit these candidates and support their efforts so that elections in America can become more competitive, with incumbents not being guaranteed victory in every election. It is becoming increasingly clear that parties have a greater role to play if our electoral system is to become competitive at all levels of government. It must be noted, however, that stronger parties will not necessarily result in more competitive elections. It could end up that stronger parties produce stronger partisanship among both voters and politicians, which could in fact result in less competitive elections depending on the distribution of the American population (Carney 2013b).

THIRD PARTIES IN STATE AND LOCAL ELECTIONS

What is the role of "third parties" in a two-party system? Would it surprise you to know that forty-one different parties ran at least one candidate for federal office or for governor in the 2016 general election?

The electoral system in the United States is described as a competitive two-party system because, all other things being equal (which in this case they usually are), only the Democratic or the Republican candidate for office in a partisan election anywhere in the United States has a realistic chance of winning. In the 115th Congress (2017–2018) ninety-eight of the one hundred U.S. senators were either Republicans or Democrats (and both independent senators caucus with the Democrats); all 431 of the representatives in the House of Representatives as of March 2018 (4 seats were vacant) were affiliated with one of the two major parties; so too were 49 of the state governors and almost 7,300 of the approximately 7,400 state legislators elected in partisan elections in 2015 or 2016.[10] In plotting strategy, except for in the most unusual circumstance, major party candidates only need to consider the candidacy of the individual running on the other major party's ticket.

But this is not always the case. An examination of some of the exceptions is a good way to come to an understanding of the general rule. Bernie Sanders (I-Vt.) is one of two independents in the Senate. Senator Sanders, a former mayor of Burlington and a longtime member of the House of Representatives, has had a long and colorful career in Vermont politics. At one point he was the only avowed socialist mayor of any American city. When he ran for Congress, he drew support mostly from liberal Democrats; in both the House and the Senate he has caucused with Democratic members, who treat him as one of their own in awarding committee assignments. The Democrats have not run a candidate against Sanders, who has been elected and reelected with relative ease since first winning his House seat in 1990. Sanders, of course, sought the Democratic Party's presidential nomination in 2016 and is currently trying very hard to reshape the party to be more in his image.

Angus King, who served two terms as the independent governor of Maine (1995–2003) and is now serving his first term and seeking reelection as an independent senator from the same state (2013–present), came to office in a very different way. King entered politics as a Democrat, serving on the staff of William Hathaway, who represented Maine in the House from 1965 until 1973 and then for one term in the Senate. Leaving politics and government service, King followed two careers simultaneously, as a very successful owner of a small business and as the host of a statewide television program examining Maine politics on the state's public television network. In 1994 he decided to run for governor. He made two key decisions: that he would run as an independent, and that his campaign would be largely self-funded. Maine has had a long history of supporting independent candidates. Since James Longley was elected governor in 1974, every gubernatorial election has seen a serious third-party candidate (Maisel and Ivry 1998). At the time King sought office, the Democrats and Republicans were engaged in a bitter feud in the legislature; at one point state government had been shut down over a budgetary impasse. Partisan animosity had turned many citizens sour on the two major parties. King narrowly defeated the Democratic candidate, former governor and former congressman Joseph Brennan, the very personification of a career politician, having run one office or another for more than twenty years. The Republican candidate was a then untested former senatorial aide, Susan Collins. King did not run against the two major parties so much as he ran as a conciliator, one who would work with leaders from both parties. For four years, he governed in that manner, gaining credit for the state's economic recovery. In 1998, he won reelection with 60 percent of the vote. Neither the Republican nor the Democratic candidate polled even one-third of his total. When longtime Maine senator Olympia Snowe unexpectedly announced that she would not seek another term in 2012, King quickly entered the race as an independent and showed that he still had what it takes to win in Maine, defeating his Democratic and Republican challengers with 53 percent of the vote.

But then there was the candidacy of Jesse "The Body" Ventura, who surprised virtually everyone by winning Minnesota's gubernatorial election as the Reform party candidate in 1998. Ventura won, in many ways, not because he represented a national emergence of the Reform party started by Ross Perot, but for the same reasons, though in a very different manner, that King had won. The public was dissatisfied with the major party candidates, who were rather colorless, traditional, career politicians. The alternative, Ventura, a former professional wrestler and radio talk show host, was a character. His very physical presence drew attention. His name drew attention. His willingness to be outspoken on his radio program drew attention. His campaign gained momentum late; neither major party candidate was able to mount a significant reply to his advances.[11]

When King won in Maine and governed successfully for four years, he did so without forming a "third party." He dealt with the Democratic and Republican leadership in the Maine legislature and sought compromise. The citizens of Minnesota watched Ventura for four years. While he continued to gain a good deal of press attention, he did not build a new, third-party base and chose not to seek reelection in 2002 (see Bibby and Maisel 2003).

The exceptions are always interesting, but it is also important to look at the norm. By any measure, the impact of the overwhelming majority of third-party or independent candidates is limited. In only a few of the 435 races for Congress did the winner poll less than 50 percent of the vote. That means if all of those who voted for the third-party candidate had voted for the losing candidate, the losing candidate still would not have polled enough additional votes to win the election. And of course the assumption that all who voted for the minor party candidate would have voted at all, much less for one particular candidate, is difficult to justify.

But once again, it is valuable to look at cases in which the minor party candidate might have had an impact. Let's compare experiences in two elections held in the Third Congressional District in New Mexico, a special election in 1997 and the 1998 general election. In each case, the Green party ran a candidate in opposition to the Republican and Democratic nominees.

In the special election Republican Bill Redmond won the seat by a margin of 3 percentage points. The Green party candidate in that special election, Carol Miller, polled 17 percent of the votes. It is logical to conclude that many of her votes would have gone to the Democratic candidate, who shared many of her views, had she not been in the race.

In the 1998 general election, too, Miller was the Green party candidate. In that election, opposing Redmond, now the incumbent, was the new Democratic candidate, Tom Udall, the state attorney general. The Udall name is well known in environmental circles in the Southwest; his father, Stewart, had been a congressman from Arizona before serving as President Kennedy's secretary of the interior; his uncle, Mo, was a leading environmentalist during his own long congressional career. Tom Udall drew on his reputation as a defender of the environment. He appealed directly to Green party leadership not to undermine his campaign against Congressman Redmond. Although Miller remained on the ballot, about six weeks before the election, nine leaders of the Green party sent out a letter to their supporters asking them to support Udall over Miller. Their argument was that support for Miller would virtually ensure a victory for Redmond, a conservative Republican whose environmental record was such that he was among the dirty dozen identified by the League of Conservation Voters (see chapter 4; Ayres 1998). In the November election Miller drew less than half of the support she had received only one year earlier; Udall was one of five Democrats to unseat incumbent Republicans in the off-year election.

Certainly, examples such as this are not common, but they are not all that uncommon either. In the 2014 gubernatorial elections, one independent candidate, Bill Walker of Alaska, won. Six other governors won with less than 50 percent of the vote, raising the possibility that minor party or independent candidates held the balance of power. Walker is seeking reelection as an independent in Alaska in 2018, and campaign watchers are keeping a close eye on the role of independent candidates in Maine's 2018 gubernatorial election.

These examples demonstrate both the potential and the problem for third-party and independent candidates. They have the potential to force the major party candidates to take a stand on issues that are most important to their followers. But they also have the potential to divide the vote in such a way that the candidate they least favor wins. And they rarely have the opportunity to win an election. Thus, as campaigns draw to a close, third-party candidates face the argument that a vote for them is at best a wasted vote and at worst counterproductive. As the case of New Mexico's Third Congressional District demonstrates, that is an argument that can be decisive even for leaders of a relatively strong third-party movement.[12] The effectiveness of this argument is likely to restrict the importance of third parties in state and local elections for the foreseeable future.

CONCLUSION

Recall the two candidates with whom we began this chapter. The candidate for county supervisor rearranged other aspects of his life so that he could concentrate on the county fair. For the Senate candidate, the campaign was her life. That defines a critical difference, not only between the two individuals but also between the two jobs.

Think about candidates for different offices. At the more local levels, candidates serve in part-time positions and run limited campaigns to get there. Many of these candidates like campaigning. They have the opportunity to meet interesting people, to observe how people live and what they do for a living, to talk to them about their concerns and about their opinions of government. When the campaign is over, they have the opportunity to serve, to work on some of the problems they have learned about, to make their community a better place. But they also have the opportunity to go back to a more normal kind of existence. They can have dinners with their families, spend weekends in the backyard, shop for groceries without shaking hands. The campaign is what they did for a while to win office; it is not their life's work and certainly not their life itself.

Contrast this normality with the existence—and we have chosen that word carefully—of a member of Congress from a marginal district. Members of Congress in this situation start one campaign the minute the last one ends. Many of them are at the plant gates the morning after an election, thanking those who voted for them and hoping that they will remember how appreciative he was when the next election comes around. Even those who do not start campaigning for reelection on day one of the new term are constantly campaigning. They come back to the district nearly every weekend. They continue with the same kinds of activities they did in the campaign: speaking to anyone who will listen, attending countless suppers, judging at county fairs. During the week they work hard in Congress, spending much of their time ensuring that their constituents are happy (Cain, Ferejohn, and Fiorina 1987; Fiorina 1978; Mayhew 1974a). On weekends and during congressional recesses, they are back in the district. They know that if they work hard, they might be able to squeak out another term (Fenno 1978; Taggart and Durant 1985). But what about the rest of their lives—vacations, outings with their children or grandchildren, leisure reading?

Put simply, for many members of Congress, such things do not exist. They rarely see their children or spouses; there is no "rest of their lives." Their only enjoyment is politics. This picture should cause concern. Do we really want to be governed by a group of individuals who are willing to give up their lives to campaign full-time? Even if we are not concerned about the mental health of such individuals, how much can they know about the problems facing their constituents, about the reality of ordinary day-to-day life?

Many have expressed concern that members of Congress represent a social and economic elite and cannot relate to the problems facing middle-class America. The problem may well be more serious than that. Many of today's politicians do not live a real life at all. Not only are they unrepresentative in terms of economic and social indicators, but even more so in terms of their ability to understand everyday problems.

Impressionistic evidence indicates that few members of Congress lead "normal" lives, even if normality is defined in as broad a way as is necessary, given today's heterogeneous world. Many are single and can imagine no time for a family; the divorce rate on Capitol Hill is very high. Competitive politics at this level has produced a group of officeholders unfamiliar with the daily experiences of most of the people they represent.

How do politicians react to this style of life? A number of responses are possible. Some politicians refuse to enter the arena. Every year political journalists speculate about likely candidates for office in a particular region. Every year some refuse to run; some say that they have enough to do where they are now; others are frank in saying that the sacrifices are not worth the honor.

Others immerse themselves in politics totally and then escape. In recent years many have been concerned about the number of members of Congress who are voluntarily retiring. In fact as of late May 2018, fifty-four members of the House and three members of the Senate have announced they will not seek reelection, breaking the previous record of fifty-two set in 1992. Many of these retirees state explicitly that they are leaving because the pressure to campaign is too heavy. Some of the most respected members of Congress have retired, often well before the age at which we might normally expect such officeholders to step down. Certainly we could list many reasons for such early retirements besides the exigencies of the two-year election cycle. However, as a matter of public policy, we must be concerned if some of the best officeholders feel that they cannot stay in office and serve because the electoral demands are too costly.

A third response is to avoid the pressure of constant election by seeking a different office. In 2016, thirteen representatives chose not to seek reelection in order to run for the Senate. One reason for taking this route is that senators face reelection every six years, not every other year. Senators campaign very hard in the two years before their term expires, but in the other four years, at least to some extent, they are able to concentrate on the policymaking aspects of their job (Fenno 1984).

Not all members of Congress face difficult elections every two years. Some of these members have reached accommodations with their jobs that are not unlike the positions of senators or others who do not feel they must campaign constantly. Consider the career choice that former Congressman Barney Frank (D-Mass.) made some years ago.

In 1984, when Massachusetts senator Paul Tsongas (D) decided not to seek reelection in order to spend more time with his family (he was diagnosed as having a serious illness), many speculated that Frank would be among the first in the race for the Senate seat. Frank was one of the more outspoken members of Congress; he won his seat in a hotly contested race in 1980 and was reelected in a very tough race after the 1980 census in which he had to face Margaret Heckler (R-Mass., 1967–1983) in one of those few races every ten years in which, because of redistricting in states that have lost seats in Congress, two incumbents must face each other. The 1982 Frank-Heckler race was the most expensive race in the country. Political journalists conjectured that Frank, fresh from two extremely difficult campaigns, would view the six-year term of a senator as a panacea for all his ills.

Frank saw it differently:

> I've got the best job in the world. Look, I can build up a relationship with this district. I won't have another tough campaign for ten years, when they might fool around with reapportionment again. I go back to the district every other weekend. I enjoy it. I can live a normal life here [in Washington]. How many Senators ever live a normal life? They are always in the spotlight. I don't need that. (Frank 1985)

Frank was satisfied with his life in the House. He, like others who gained the spotlight in the House of Representatives—men like Speaker

John Boehner (R-Ohio) or Henry Waxman (D-Calif.)—found the House to be a congenial home. In 1984 Frank had no desire to move on to the Senate. He was making a contribution and did not feel that the electoral pressure was burdensome because he had become comfortable with his district.

Frank's subsequent electoral experience demonstrates his point. In May 1987, Frank revealed that he is a homosexual, becoming only the second member of the Congress at that time to publicly announce that he is gay. After having won reelection without opposition in 1986, Frank faced a challenger in 1988 but won the election with over 70 percent of the vote. In August of 1989 the *Washington Times* revealed that Frank was involved with a male prostitute whom Frank had hired as a household assistant. The House Ethics Committee investigated to determine if Frank had violated any House rules, particularly in response to a charge that Frank had used his influence as a member of Congress to have parking tickets fixed. Even after cries for his resignation and weeks of bad publicity, Frank was easily able to weather another serious challenge, winning the 1990 election by nearly two to one. Massachusetts lost a seat in the House as a result of the 1990 census. But Frank was able to win easily in his reconfigured district and faced no serious opposition until he was targeted by Republicans in 2010, still winning his toughest race in decades by a margin of more than 10 percent. His analysis of the difference between House and Senate seats, at least in his case, seems as prescient as it was nearly a decade and a half ago. By 2010, he was one of the most influential congressmen, leading the reform of the financial markets industry through the House. Frank became the first sitting member of Congress to become married in a same-sex ceremony and retired from the House in January 2013 on his own terms. Those interested in learning more about Frank should check out his recently released memoir, *Frank* (2015).

Thus politicians have a number of different ways of responding to general election pressures, from letting politics dominate their entire lives to opting out of the system. How they respond over a period of time is different, however, from how they view general elections in the short run.

The question of how politicians view elections can be approached in two ways. The first is affectively: What do politicians think about the prospect of campaigning? The response varies from individual to individual and may vary as well from office to office and from time to time. Many share the sentiments of an extremely successful politician who said, "I like lots of it, but not the door-to-door stuff. I feel I am imposing. People are awfully nice, but I feel their home should be their home, not a soapbox for my views." An opposite point of view is represented by former senator William Cohen (R-Maine; House, 1973–1979; Senate, 1979–1997), who routinely asked people if he could spend the night in their home while campaigning. Cohen figured that people really feel that they know you if they open their home to you.

Some politicians like talking to big contributors and impressing them with the importance of their being elected. Others, like the late senator (1949–1964; 1971–1978) and vice president (1965–1969) Hubert Humphrey (D-Minn.), found that asking someone for money was the most distasteful part of politics. Some enjoy appearing before large audiences and debating; others are more reticent and seek to have their records speak for themselves.

The list of variations could go on. All that can be said with certainty is that campaigning is a highly personal experience. Some find it totally rewarding; others find it a necessary evil, withstood in order to hold office.

The second way in which politicians view elections is in a strategic sense: What does this election mean to me? Can I win? What are the costs to me personally? Professionally? If I win? If I lose? What are the benefits if I win? If I lose?

Were politicians rational men and women in reaching these decisions, they would weigh the costs and benefits carefully and reach judgments based on that evidence. Jacobson and Kernell (1983) lay out this model of electoral decision making and defend it persuasively (see also Maisel et al. 1990; Brady, Maisel, and Warsh 1994). On the other hand, Maisel (1986) demonstrates that politicians do not always behave rationally in reaching decisions about their electoral future. Very often office seekers look at all the facts (e.g., the fact that over 90 percent of the incumbent members of Congress seeking reelection are normally successful) and make seemingly irrational decisions.

Given this caveat, however, some strategies followed by candidates in the general election reflect their view of this process in the short run. The objective of the election is not merely to win, but to win by a wide margin. They always "run scared." No matter what the evidence says, no matter what one's instincts are, run scared. Do not appear to be complacent; do not take anything for granted. Build the margin. Ensure a big victory; it might frighten away opponents the next time (Goldenberg, Traugott, and Baumgartner 1986; Jackson 1988; Krasno and Green 1988; Maisel 1990b).

Analysts of campaigns describe a rational process. They present a process in which politicians weigh alternatives, reach rational decisions, set appropriate strategies, allocate resources effectively, appeal to the voters persuasively, and evaluate their campaigns logically.

The difficulty with this description is that, although the entire process viewed as a whole may be rational, individual politicians often act very irrationally. Two seemingly conflicting trends are in evidence. The first is represented by the incumbent member of Congress whose winning percentage has not fallen below 65 percent in ten years but is being confronted by one strongly organized group in his district on a particular issue. This politician "runs scared." All evidence from hundreds of campaigns for more than a decade indicates that as an incumbent he is safe. However, for a year he goes home every weekend, spending more time in the district than he has in years. He raises more money than has ever been spent on an election in his district. He has his campaign staff in place before any opposition has surfaced. He campaigns hard throughout the fall, despite the fact that his opponent is unknown and underfinanced.

The second trend could well be represented by his opponent. She believes that the group supporting her has widespread support throughout the district that will carry her to victory. All the evidence about incumbent safety does not deter her. She views this campaign through rose-colored glasses. Objective views of her chances do not mute her optimism. She is undeterred by the fact that she has little money and remains unknown to most in the district. She campaigns hard right up until the election, convinced that the justice of her cause will be sufficient to guarantee victory in the end.

The incumbent wins big. The process is understandable and rational in the overall picture. These two candidates and literally thousands like them campaigning for all sorts of offices all over the country have been acting irrationally, caught up in an amazing exercise in self-deception. However researchers eventually understand the results in congressional and state elections in 2010, those results will feed incumbent insecurity and challenger optimism.

Politicians invest so much of themselves in campaigns that they cannot believe that their experiences are not unique. The November campaigns are a critically important part of politicians' lives. For some, campaigns become too important. These politicians are not willing to put that much of themselves on the line and let others make a judgment about their merit. For others, the election is what their life is all about. Politics is not only a means to an end; it is an end in itself. Campaigning becomes not only their life's work but also their life. For all, it is a deeply personal experience. At whatever level the campaign, the candidate is aware that fellow citizens are making a judgment of him or her. Few can view that process in a detached way like objective analysts. Most are caught up in the election as one of life's crises, which can only be experienced in the most personal of ways.

CRITICAL THINKING QUESTIONS

1. Are so-called average people equipped to hold public office?
2. Should local elections be partisan or non-partisan? Why?

3. Do local elections matter?
4. Should all state and local elected offices have term limits?

KEY TERMS

candidate-centered	gerrymandering	canvassing
redistricting	one person–one vote	marginal seats
reapportionment	direct mail	term limits

NOTES

1. Before we proceed any further, we should recognize that this assumption is, in all likelihood, not supportable. Few politicians really understand the process into which they are entering; even experienced politicians make decisions about campaigns in spite of information that would lead a rational person to another conclusion (Hershey 1984; Maisel 1986).

2. Exceptions to this generalization include a politician's race for office in order to increase name recognition and visibility for a future race, politicians who might be "term limited" out of a seat in another two years and see the chance now, no matter how slim, as better than it will be in the future, and/or a politician's willingness to run a seemingly futile race in order to ensure that a respectable candidate is fielded. The candidate in the latter instance earns many IOUs from the party.

3. Obviously one key factor is whether one must give up a current office to run for another office. In most cases this is so, but exceptions exist. For example, as noted earlier, five states hold state elections in odd-numbered years and thus terms for state legislature do not expire when congressional elections are held.

4. The candidate is not an incumbent. But incumbents have all faced this problem at some point—when they first sought the office; although now they are in the position of a candidate seeking to stay in the same office. By and large, their campaign tactics were dictated by what worked well the last time.

5. In areas with strong party organizations, party volunteers still carry "sample ballots," urging supporters to vote for all candidates in their party. This technique is particularly effective in areas dominated by one party or the other, or in areas in which the organization can effectively target households in which their supporters live (Hicks 1998).

6. There is a growing literature on campaign consultants. See, as examples, Thurber and Nelson (2000); Johnson-Cartee and Copeland (1997); Medvic and Lenart (1997); Petracca (1989); Shea (1996); Sabato (1981).

7. As is always the case with data concerning U.S. Senate elections, it is necessary to interpret percentages with great caution. Although percentaging among 435 House elections makes good sense, presenting percentage data when the total number involved is generally less than thirty can lead to misinterpretation. The

number of incumbent senators seeking reelection in any campaign is small enough that analysis of individual races is often most appropriate.

8. The caveat that increased competition is not likely in strong one-party areas needs to be added, though it is rarely raised by those arguing for term limits.

9. It is worth noting that the momentum for term limits seems to have abated. After they captured majority status in the Congress in 1994, the Republicans attempted to pass a constitutional amendment mandating term limits, as they had promised in the Contract with America. That amendment did not pass; it was opposed by a significant number of Republicans. As the 2000 congressional elections approached, Republican representatives first elected on the Contract faced the inevitability of the self-imposed three-term limit on which they originally campaigned. Many had second thoughts but were faced with a dilemma—to leave the House or to risk giving an opponent a campaign issue, the broken term limit promise. None of those who "broke the pledge" was punished by the electorate to the extent of losing his or her seat.

10. Nebraska's state legislature differs from those in all of the other states in two regards. First, legislators are elected on nonpartisan ballots, that is, they do not run under a party label. Second, the legislature has only one house; it is unicameral, not bicameral, as are the other state legislatures as well as Congress. In reality, party lines are extremely clear in the Nebraska legislature. If we consider these Nebraska seats as in reality partisan and exclude the 62 state legislative seats that were vacant in mid-2018, there were a total of 39 nonpartisan state legislators.

11. In Ventura's case, the Minnesota campaign finance law, which restricted the amounts the major party candidates could spend, worked in the Reform party candidate's favor. He was unable to secure loans to spend money until late in the campaign. By the time Ventura was viewed as a serious candidate and had money to advertise, his opponents had already committed most of their money. Thus the playing field tilted to his advantage. We are indebted to former Congressman Bill Frenzel of Minnesota for this insight into his home state's politics.

12. State law can make a difference in the impact of third-party candidacies. In New York State, as discussed in chapter 6, candidates can run on more than one party label at the same time. If that is the case, their *total* vote is the one that is counted—that is, their votes on different labels are added together. In that situation, third parties use the leverage of either giving or refraining from giving an extra line on the ballot as a means to convince candidates to adopt certain policy positions. To counter the influence of third parties, or in some cases to supplement that influence, many candidates run as independents as well as on party lines, in the same election. Although the independent label might appear oxymoronic, candidates believe that some voters will support them on that label, rather than as a candidate of a party, in order to show lack of support for the parties themselves.

Chapter 8

Presidential Nominations

Donald Trump and John Kasich speak while other participants Mike Huckabee, Jeb Bush, Marco Rubio, and Ben Carson look on at a 2015 Boulder, Colorado, debate among those seeking the 2016 Republican presidential nomination. Many critics complain that the American presidential nominating process begins too early, takes too long, and costs too much money.

The political year 1968 must seem like ancient history, but it is the year you need to know about if you want to understand how Americans nominate their presidential candidates. That year, marred by the assassinations of Robert Kennedy and Martin Luther King Jr., saw President Lyndon Johnson challenged within his own party and eventually withdraw from the presidential contest, and Vice President Hubert Humphrey being nominated even as the American public watched frustration being vented on the convention floor and violence on the streets of Chicago. Events were set into motion that could not be reversed and that would fundamentally change the way in which presidential nominees are chosen.

Each nomination since 1968 has been played out under its own unique circumstances, but largely within the framework established in the aftermath of the 1968 contest. Even the seemingly highly unusual context of 2016 was fundamentally shaped by the 1968 reforms. The politics of the past forty-plus years of presidential nominations have played out in the long shadow of the post-1968 reforms. This chapter begins with an examination of these reforms, their implications, and how they have impacted recent nominations. Following that review, we will turn to an examination of the strategic questions that face potential candidates for major party presidential nods. Over the course of this chapter it will become clear that the process of nominating major party presidential candidates is a political animal unlike any other.

THE POST-1968 REFORMS

Democrats competed in fifteen **presidential preference primaries**—elections where voters make their choice as to who a party's presidential nominee should be—in 1968. Senator Robert Kennedy won eleven of the primaries; Senator Eugene McCarthy won the other four. Vice President Hubert Humphrey, the heir apparent after President Johnson announced that he would not seek reelection, followed a political strategy in which he avoided confrontation with McCarthy and Kennedy. He did not announce his candidacy until deadlines for filing intentions to run had passed in all states. Humphrey backers won just over 2 percent of the primary vote, but in 1968, votes in primaries did not convert directly to convention votes. For example, Senator McCarthy won nearly three-quarters of the votes in the Pennsylvania primary; Vice President Humphrey garnered 80 percent of the Pennsylvania convention votes.

In 1968 primaries were seen as a tool used to influence party officials about electability; they were not a means to "win" a nomination. Candidates used primaries to prove to powerful party leaders that they were in fact "electable," but that was all there was to these primaries. The conventional wisdom of party politicians was that the party bosses in the larger states had the power to control the nomination. They not only believed that this was true but also believed that this was as it should be. All of this was to change because of a series of events that culminated at the 1968 Democratic Convention.[1] Virtually no Democrats were pleased at how the 1968 convention played out, and many critics charged that the party was boss controlled and argued vehemently that the selection process was undemocratic and unfair.

The McGovern-Fraser Commission

Party leaders responded to this criticism; they saw the frustration of those who worked within the system. They saw the damage done to the party and the nation by the 1968 nominating process, which so obviously did not reflect the will of those who participated.

Shortly after the 1968 elections, Democratic national chairman Fred Harris appointed a commission to examine the nominating process. The Commission on Party Structure and Delegate Selection was chaired by South Dakota senator George McGovern, who had taken up the mantle of Senator Kennedy after his assassination. The McGovern Commission (which became known as the **McGovern-Fraser Commission** after the chairman resigned to run for president and was replaced by Congressman Donald Fraser of Minnesota) began by assessing the situation that existed in 1968. Their general assessment can be summarized succinctly: The "system" was disjointed across geographic lines; the procedures were unfair to many and undemocratic in the broadest sense of that term; and the end result did not represent the views of many of those who participated.

Some of the procedures revealed by the McGovern-Fraser Commission seem unbelievable from today's perspective. In two states (Georgia and Louisiana), governors appointed all members of the delegation to the national convention. State committees appointed all or most of the national convention delegations in eight other states. So informal was the situation that no one really knew how the delegations were appointed in many other states. The usual explanation was that party officials met behind closed doors and reached secret accommodations. None of these revelations was surprising to the professionals in either the Democratic or Republican parties, however, for they made the decisions. From their point of view, that was how it should be done.

Research by the staff of the McGovern-Fraser Commission defined the philosophical issues that have structured the debate of the presidential nomination process since that time. On one side are party professionals who believe that the most important criterion for an effective process should be the selection of a nominee who can win the general election and govern the nation. They feel that those who have worked most closely with active politicians and know the political scene well can best make that judgment. On the other side are those who believe that the process should be open and democratic and that the voters in a party should decide who their nominee will be. The debate has gone back and forth and is often the backdrop for arguments over obscure subissues. But the questions are fundamental: Should the process be elite-dominated or popularly dominated? Should the outcome of the process be more important or the means by which that outcome was reached?

The final report of the McGovern-Fraser Commission, titled *Mandate for Reform*, specified that nominating procedures must be changed to make the process *open, timely, and representative.* To the members of the commission and those who were distressed by the events leading up to Humphrey's nomination in 1968, these goals appeared to be at the heart of a democratic process and thus noncontroversial. However, the specific reforms that were suggested (and then accepted as mandatory for state parties for the 1972 nominating process by the Democratic National Committee) rocked the existing system so fundamentally that the ground has yet to fully settle.

Perhaps the most important guideline promulgated by the McGovern-Fraser Commission was to require that all state parties adopt procedures consistent with the principles it outlined. This requirement led to the establishment of one nominating process, with the rules set at the national level by the national Democratic party, thus changing the power structure within the Democratic party in a way that has not since been altered.

Remember, in 1968 presidential preference primaries had been held in only fifteen states. In some of those states, such as Wisconsin, Oregon, and California, the primaries determined the delegations to the national convention. In many of the other states, such as New Jersey, Pennsylvania, and Illinois, the connection between primaries and convention delegations was less clear. And in thirty-five states, delegates were chosen through some appointive means with no voter input.

In 1972, two procedures were permissible. States could run primaries under a variety of permissible rules, but regardless of the rules in place the result would determine at least 90 percent of the state's delegation. Or the states could continue to keep delegate selection a matter for party regulars, selecting delegations through series of meetings of party members and regulars in a series of local party **caucuses** and conventions organized under the new guidelines.

The differences between primary elections and a caucus/convention system are important and should be made explicit. In a presidential preference primary, party members go to their local polling place and cast a ballot for their preference, much as they do in a general election. In a caucus/convention system, party members go to a meeting; they all must come at the same time and stay for the duration of the meeting. At the meeting or caucus, those in attendance elect representatives to attend another meeting—usually at the county, congressional district, or state level—in proportion to the presidential preferences of those at the caucus. Those at the subsequent meeting (or perhaps a third-level meeting) elect the delegates to the national convention, again in proportion to the presidential preferences of those in attendance.

Does it sound complicated? Party leaders thought so. Many had preferred the caucus/convention system in the past because they could control the results. No public notices; no rules; no stated preferences. Just party leaders selecting themselves and their friends as convention delegates, fully understanding that they would be told for whom to vote by those leaders who really chose the nominees. But caucuses became more difficult to run under the new guidelines. Twenty-two states opted to hold presidential preference primaries in 1972; 65 percent of the delegates were chosen in these primaries.

The 1972 Nomination

Imagine that you wrote the rules for a very complicated card game. If hand A were dealt, one set of rules applied; if hand B were dealt, another set of rules came into play; hand C would be played in a different way. Don't you think you would have an advantage the first time you played the game?

George McGovern resigned the chairmanship of the Commission on Party Structure and Delegate Selection after most of the work of that group had been finished. He resigned to run for president—under the new rules, his rules. McGovern chose as his campaign manager and chief strategist a young fellow named Gary Hart, who had been a key staff member of the McGovern Commission. They knew the rules and played them to their advantage.

The front-runner in 1972 was Maine senator Ed Muskie, who had impressed the party leaders as Humphrey's vice presidential running mate four years earlier. Muskie followed the old conventional wisdom. He lined up all the party leaders, the opinion leaders in the big states, behind him. Then he lost because they could not deliver. Hubert Humphrey entered the race late, as he had done in 1968, but this time he was too late; party leaders could not deliver for him either. Delegates selected in primaries and caucuses remained loyal to George McGovern, not to local party leaders, and he won the nomination.

The openness of the process led to participation by activists interested in discussing controversial issues. The Democratic Convention showed the party for what it was, an amalgamation of differing and competing interests. All the warts were visible to the large national television audience. When McGovern lost the general election by a landslide to Richard Nixon, party leaders were quick to blame the new rules. McGovern had been an extremist; he was not the candidate of the traditional core of the party. He was not the candidate of the blue-collar, union, big-city Democrats. And he was not the candidate who would have been chosen by the party leaders who had dominated previous conventions.

In fact, the rules neither gave McGovern the nomination nor caused his defeat. But the rules did present something of a conflict between types of representation. As had always been the case, they called for **geographic representation**, specifying that states break delegations down to more local areas. They also called for **demographic representation**, at least of groups traditionally loyal to and underrepresented in the Democratic party—women, blacks, and youth. And they called for representation by candidate preference. Individuals supported presidential candidates based on their views of critical issues; this last type of representation approximated, in the view of many, to **ideological representation**, a system of representation based on how individuals stand on the issues under consideration and debate.

Critics claimed that the mixing of three kinds of representation, rather than the traditional reliance on geographic representation and domination by party leaders, led to the replacement of delegates who were concerned with winning by issue-oriented delegates who cared more about specific matters of principle than electoral victory. This conclusion has been actively debated ever since (see Kirkpatrick 1976, 1978; Norrander 2010; Polsby 1983; Polsby, Wildavsky, and Hopkins 2008; Ranney 1975; Sullivan et al. 1977–1978; Sullivan, Pressman, and Arterton 1976; Sullivan et al. 1977; Wayne 2008).

Between 1972 and 1988 the Democrats appointed a series of commissions that continually reexamined the nominating process. Each commission looked at the problems from the preceding election and sought to correct them. Changes to the nomination system were made as a result of each of these commissions, including some important ones such as the reinstitution of **winner-take-all primaries** after the 1976 nomination contest and the creation of so-called **superdelegates** after the 1984 election. In a winner-take-all contest, the candidate with the most votes gets all of the delegates being contested rather than having the delegates awarded proportionally based on the percentage of the vote obtained by each candidate. The winner-take-all primary at the state level had been eliminated by the McGovern-Fraser Commission; the justification was that such a system distorted the actual preference of those casting their votes (see chapter 9 for a discussion of the winner-take-all aspect of the Electoral College system). The distinction between winner-take all versus proportional primaries can be of critical importance. Indeed, it is very likely that if all the 2008 Democratic primaries had been of the winner-take-all variety, the party's presidential nominee would have been Hillary Clinton rather than Barack Obama. The creation of superdelegates was an attempt to return at least some influence over the nomination process to party elites. These individuals were to be prominent party and/or elected officials—for example, governors, senators, or members of Congress who had played key roles at conventions before the reforms but whose participation levels had declined. The superdelegates were to come to the convention officially unpledged. The theory was that they would bring practical experience to the convention and help nominate a winning ticket if the primary process failed to determine a clear nominee (Mann 1985). Indeed, the superdelegates played an important role in the 2008 Democratic nominating process; Obama would not have secured the nomination without the strong support he received from superdelegates (Norrander 2010, 80–81). Superdelegates received even more attention in

The primaries were a long slog of state-by-state contests, each with different sets of confusing rules and outcomes.
But at the end of the day, each candidate is trying to reach a seemingly straightforward goal: rope in enough delegates to win his or her party's nomination and move on to the general election.

the 2016 Democratic contest, as they overwhelmingly supported Hillary Clinton over Bernie Sanders, leading some—including then Republican nominee and now Republican president Donald Trump to claim that superdelegates cost Sanders the nomination. While fact-checking services such as Politifact declared such claims false (Qiu 2016), the role of superdelegates in 2016 became highly controversial within the party and led to many calls for reform. The DNC agreed to do so, but as of March 2018 the party has been unable to agree on what exactly to do (Bradner 2018; Sanchez 2018). But even with such changes and controversies, the Democratic party's presidential nominating process today is still for the most part the process established after the 1968 election cycle.

The Reform Movement: An Assessment

Compare the experience of the Democrats with that of the Republicans. Over the past forty years the Democrats have almost constantly reevaluated and readjusted their presidential nomination process. The Republicans by contrast have been blissfully happy with their system, or at least they were until the 2016 nominating cycle (see Peters 2016). This is not to suggest that they have not had reform commissions. But a number of factors distinguish Republican reform efforts from Democratic ones. First, Republicans, even when their nomination has been hotly contested, have not divided their party because of the nominating process. Even in the highly controversial 2016 nominating contest, most would say that in the end the party for the most part held together and supported Donald Trump (even if some did so uneasily and/or took a fair amount of time to come around) once he secured the party's nomination. Second, most Republican "reforms" have been suggestions, not mandates. Philosophically the Republicans do not believe that the national party should dictate to the states, or at least this was true historically, as this changed somewhat in the lead-up to the 2012 nominating cycle. The GOP then built on those changes for the 2016 nominating process, although in the end these changes did not make much of a difference in the final outcome (J. Putnam 2016).

However, the Republican process has changed significantly because some of the changes wrought by the Democrats have resulted in changes in state laws that also impact the Republicans. Look at Table 8.1. In 1968, sixteen states chose delegates to the Republican National Convention through the primary process, making up 34 percent of the delegates. By 1988, these numbers had changed to thirty-five states holding primaries and 77 percent of the delegates being chosen in that manner, and they have been relatively steady ever since. The Democrats instituted the

Table 8.1. Number of Presidential Primaries and the Percentage of Delegates Selected in Them, 1968–2016

	Democrats		*Republicans*	
	Primaries (#)	*Delegates (%)*	*Primaries (#)*	*Delegates (%)*
1968	17	38	16	34
1972	23	61	22	53
1976	29	73	28	68
1980	31	75	35	74
1984	26	63	30	68
1988	34	67	35	77
1992	39	77	38	80
1996	34	63	43	90
2000	40	86	43	93
2004	34	56	32	72
2008	38	72	40	77
2012	36	71	38	78
2016	41	86	39	82

Sources: 1968–2000 from Wayne (2000); 2004, 2008, 2012, and 2016 compiled by authors from RNC, DNC, and various state sources.

changes and caused states to change their election laws accordingly. Therefore, the Republicans were forced to follow suit.

The reforms begun in 1968 have fundamentally changed the ways in which the two parties nominate their presidential candidates. The conventional wisdom before 1968 was that party leaders in large states had the most influence over the nominations. The conventional wisdom since 1968 has been that the process is open and that demonstrated success in attracting voters will be necessary in order to win. The delegates to the national conventions are now representatives of those who have participated in the process, not stand-ins for party bosses.

Party leaders and elected officeholders still retain influence, but the change in their role in the last forty years may provide a perfect example of the difference between influence and power. The strategic premises of presidential contenders in 1960 were not very different from those of 1948, nor for that matter from those of 1928. But since 1968, the situation has been one of continual flux. Winning in the reformed system involves mastering the rules, reading the political lay of the land, and learning the right lessons from the most recent contests, including lessons about the timing of primaries.

Critics claimed that the reforms after 1968 were harmful to the parties, particularly to the Democrats (Kirkpatrick 1976, 1978; Polsby 1983). By contrast, we would argue that the reform process, begun after 1968 but continuing for two decades, had a positive effect on the parties. Although party leaders can no longer dictate who the nominees will be, the process involves many more people in the work of the parties and gives them a stake in the nominees. The process has evolved in such a way that party leaders themselves are now comfortable that successful nominees will emerge strengthened as candidates, not weakened, by the road taken to their nomination. In addition, work by Marty Cohen and his colleagues (2008) suggested that even with the post-1968 reforms in place, party leaders maintain a fair amount of control and influence over their parties' presidential nominating contests. This all being said, it is possible that the 2016 Republican nominating process (and perhaps the 2016 Democratic contest as well) represents a change from the norm, and could be indicative of increased ability for outsider candidates to secure their party's presidential nomination over the objection of party elites (Ceaser 2017; Cohen et al. 2016; Galdieri and Parsneau 2016; MacWilliams 2016).

Or it might not be. This is a good point to make clear a theme that all of us—authors and readers—should keep front and center in chapters 8 and 9. Certainly the 2016 presidential contest—both the nominating portion and the general election—was unusual in many ways. But there are also ways—as hard as this may be to believe—in which it was more or less par for the course (see Lucas et al. 2018 for some early takes here). Undoubtedly Donald Trump's election as president of the United States was not "normal," and thus far his presidency has been highly unconventional, to say the least. However, it is important not to go too far in how unprecedented Trump's election was and even more important to note that it is far too early to say whether the areas where Trump's campaign truly was different represent indicators of long-term change or are anomalies relevant to Trump and Trump alone. We have done our utmost to balance these matters in chapters 8 and 9 (and really the entire text), and we urge readers to do so as well.

TWENTY-FIRST-CENTURY PRESIDENTIAL NOMINATIONS

Given our discussion of reform and its implications, it is worthwhile to take at least a brief look at the most recent presidential nominating contests. In 2000 no incumbent president sought reelection. Both parties wanted a system that would permit their nominee to emerge without serious intraparty warfare, but despite efforts by the parties to rationalize the timing of the primaries and caucuses, no systematic changes occurred and the process remained incredibly **front-loaded**, a situation created when multiple states schedule their presidential primaries or caucuses very early in the process. The 2000 nominating calendar was decided by various state legislatures acting in their own interests, or in a way thought to improve the chances of candidates favored by state legislators, with California and New York moving their primaries much earlier in the process.

For the Democrats, Vice President Al Gore entered the nominating race as the prohibitive favorite, the heir apparent who had worked hard for the party for eight years, who twelve years earlier had sought his party's nomination, who was right on the issues of the day and clearly the candidate of the party elite. Gore's only serious challenge came from former New Jersey senator Bill Bradley, who had retired from the Senate in 1998 and spent two years building an organization of young activists. Bradley stressed that he wanted to bring a new style to national politics. Somewhat wooden as a campaigner, even in comparison to Gore, the former Rhodes scholar and NBA star attracted a wide following of liberals and environmentalists who felt that the New Democrats had compromised too much on fundamental issues. The press was attracted to Bradley's campaign, and he was able to raise nearly as much money as the vice president, but Gore's superior name recognition and organizational support proved too much for the outsider to overcome in a condensed process.

The Republican nominating process in 2000 was reminiscent of a prereform campaign. A large number of well-known Republicans were lining up to challenge Al Gore—former Tennessee governor and education secretary Lamar Alexander, Christian Right leader Gary Bauer, conservative commentator Patrick Buchanan, two-time cabinet secretary and wife of the 1996 nominee Elizabeth Dole, former candidate and magazine mogul Steve Forbes, Senate Judiciary Committee chair Orrin Hatch (Utah), House Budget Committee chair John Kasich (Ohio), former ambassador and conservative spokesman Alan Keyes, former POW and campaign finance reform advocate Senator John McCain (Ariz.), and former vice president Dan Quayle. But from the start, the Republican hierarchy, particularly the Republican governors and many large contributors, lined up behind Texas governor George W. Bush, the eldest son of the former president.

The key to Governor Bush's path to nomination was his early decision not to accept federal matching funds for the primary campaign, instead raising money from individual contributors. By refusing federal funds, Bush also freed himself from the state-by-state and overall spending limits. The Bush campaign proceeded to raise more money than ever before thought possible. By the "first-in-the-nation" New Hampshire primary, he had raised more than $70 million and had spent more than $37 million. Most of the other candidates soon saw that they could not compete—Alexander, Bauer, Dole, Hatch, Kasich, and Quayle left the stage. Buchanan left the Republican party and decided to seek the Reform party nomination. Forbes, who was also funding his own campaign, attracted no widespread support. The field of challengers to Bush's ascendancy was left to the ideologically pure but noncompetitive conservative Keyes and more significantly to John McCain, he of the compelling personal story and the "Straight Talk Express," his campaign bus to which he gave virtually unlimited access to any journalist.

McCain made the case that he was electable, that he was speaking to the issues that the American people wanted to hear. His strong showing in the New Hampshire primary led to an immediate infusion of campaign funds over the Internet, the first time the Internet had been used successfully to raise large amounts of money quickly. McCain appealed specifically to independents who could vote in open Republican primaries. Therein lay both the strength and the weakness of his candidacy. He did appeal to independents and did well in open primary states. But he was not acceptable to the Republican establishment. When the calendar turned from open primary states to closed primary states, the McCain threat to Bush dissipated. Like Bradley for Gore, McCain remained a nuisance for the Bush campaign, but little more. After **Super Tuesday** 2000, the inevitability of Bush's nomination, like that of Vice President Gore, demonstrated that the system had once again worked as party officials, if not the public, desired. Each party had settled on a mainstream nominee early enough in the process to begin planning for the general election. Each had been briefly challenged, but the party establishment had emerged victorious and ready to head for November before serious damage had been done.

Timing again was the major consideration as the 2004 process took shape. For the Republicans, the nomination was never in doubt. President Bush, unopposed for renomination, once again declined public funding for the nomination phase of the campaign, raising over $250 million to spend before the fall campaign actually began. The Republicans scheduled their convention much later than normal, from August 30 until September 2, enabling them to make the case for their candidate and against their opponent for as long a period as possible before they fell under the restrictions of the publicly funded fall campaign.[2]

For the Democrats, front-loading took on a whole new meaning in 2004. Iowa still held its caucus in January, and the New Hampshire primary was one week later. But then, twenty-one states scheduled primaries—and nine others, caucuses—before the middle of March, with five primaries and three caucuses on February 3. The conventional wisdom was that any candidate to be viable had to win something on or before that date. Nine states—including California, New York, and Ohio—held primaries on March 2, the date by which many pundits believed that the eventual nominee would be known. The rules for the nomination in 2004 might not have changed, but the calendar made a huge difference in strategies. Massachusetts senator John Kerry had plenty of money, allowing him to expend considerable resources in the early caucus and primary states, especially the first-in-the-nation contests in Iowa and New Hampshire. Even though Kerry was viewed as an underdog heading into these contests, his wins in both Iowa and New Hampshire, combined with favorite Howard Dean's third-place finish in Iowa (and of course, "the scream") largely cleared the path for Kerry to secure the nomination. Front-loading was crucial to Kerry's success.

The 2008 nomination process will be remembered for "firsts"—the first African American to receive a major party nomination, the first woman to be a serious candidate for her party's nomination, the first Hispanic, the first Mormon, the oldest candidate. However, in terms of process, 2008 represents an extension of the past. More candidates refused public funding—and those who accepted matching funds with consequential limitations were outspent to the point of being noncompetitive.

In the GOP process, John McCain, whose campaign nearly folded in late 2007, came back strong in New Hampshire and benefited from winner-take-all primaries in a front-loaded process to eliminate all of the opposition. His route to the nomination was eased by the failure of the leading contenders—Arkansas governor Mike Huckabee, former New York mayor Rudolph Giuliani, former Massachusetts governor Mitt Romney—to excite copartisans beyond their narrow bases. The establishment that had rejected McCain in 2000 now accepted him as their best alternative.

New York senator Hillary Clinton entered the Democratic fray as the front-runner. But her strategists didn't account for the Obama phenomenon. Illinois senator Barack Obama raised more money than anyone thought possible and started a movement whose momentum could not be stopped. Obama and Clinton overpowered the rest of the field early on. While Clinton held on for some time, once Senator Ted Kennedy swung to Obama's side, his candidacy became first acceptable and then inevitable. The 2012 nominating contests, while of course unique in some ways, once again represent more of the same in most ways. Barack Obama was unopposed for the Democratic party nomination, as is generally the case with sitting presidents. The Republican field totaled ten contenders for the presidential nomination, although there was never a point where all ten were active at the same time. Former Massachusetts governor Mitt Romney was always viewed as the front-runner and party establishment pick, and despite brief public infatuations with Georgia businessman Herman Cain and former GOP Speaker of the House Newt Gingrich and the dogged campaigning of former Texas congressman Ron Paul, Romney did indeed secure the nomination. Romney's financial advantage and establishment support was simply too much for his opponents to overcome. It is also important to note that not a single major party candidate accepted federal matching funds in 2016, the same as in 2012 (see Table 8.2).

The 2016 campaign began with a relatively popular two-term Democratic president—Barack Obama—preparing to leave office. After some very public equivocation Obama's vice president Joe Biden decided not to run. This seemingly left the Democratic field to former First Lady, Senator from New York, and Secretary of State Hillary Clinton. While Clinton did of course eventually get her party's nomination, it was much more difficult than virtually anyone imagined as she faced a spirited challenge from Vermont independent Senator Bernie Sanders. While Sanders electrified young voters and the more progressive wing of the party, strong

Table 8.2. Money Raised by Major Party Candidates for Presidential Nominations, 2016 (in dollars)

	Contributions from Individuals	*PACs*	*Self-Financed*	*Transfers*	*Other*	*Federal Matching Funds*
Republicans						
Jeb Bush	33,589,054	230,317	795,704	0	50,000	0
Ben Carson	63,461,403	5,588	25,000	0	649,471	0
Chris Christie	8,432,629	115,738	0	0	0	0
Ted Cruz	92,111,0603	101,095	0	250,013	8,086	0
Carly Fiorina	12,045,838	20,925	0	0	39,506	0
James Gilmore	104,396	2000	279,075	0	0	0
Lindsey Graham	3,741,437	71,750	0	1,975,000	8,730	0
Mike Huckabee	4,273,404	33,000	12,000	0	0	0
Bobby Jindal	1,432,464	10,000	0	0	0	0
John Kasich	19,053,420	275,871	0	0	9,966	0
George Pataki	510,332	1,000	20,000	0	0	
Rand Paul	10,229,422	47,171	0	1,735,263	212,501	
Rick Perry	1,329,276	7,040	0	0	0	
Marco Rubio	45,361,828	455,971	0	662,432	595,103	
Rick Santorum	1,364,537	7,350	24,000	0	75,237	
Donald Trump	36,959,858	0	49,950,643	2,201,314	0	
Scott Walker	8,210,190	53,100	0	0	350,529	
Democrats						
Hillary Clinton	231,158,512	1,339,118	997,159	33,940,000	32,864	0
Lawrence Lessig	181,812	0	32,000	0	0	
Martin O'Malley	4,573,815	115,002	0	0	500,000	
Bernie Sanders	230,670,406	5,622	0	1,500,000	44,029	
Jim Webb	771,578	5,000	0	0	0	

Source: Federal Election Commission, receipts reported through June 30, 2016.

support from the Democratic establishment and core elements of the party's base allowed Clinton to emerge victorious (Heersink 2017).

The Republican side was in many ways wide open in 2016. As Obama worked his way through his second term, no candidate emerged as the presumptive frontrunner for the Republican nomination. Eventually 17 candidates officially declared for the Republican presidential nomination, a figure that does not include hotly speculated-about runs from one or both members of the 2012 GOP ticket, Mitt Romney and Paul Ryan, both of whom ultimately declined to run. Early on, if anyone was seen as even a slight favorite it was former Florida governor Jeb Bush, son and brother of former presidents. But Bush struggled to raise money and attract support. The pundit class talked variously about Ted Cruz, Marco Rubio, Chris Christie, and Scott Walker, among others, but no candidate took off. This began to change in late 2015 as the candidacy of New York City real estate developer and reality TV star Donald Trump quickly gathered support and momentum. Widely viewed as entertainment-only when he declared his candidacy in June 2015, by the end of that year Trump had managed to build significant strength toward gaining the nomination. None of Trump's GOP opponents seemed to have any idea on how to handle him, and Trump methodically dispatched his Republican opponents one by one (Singer and Slack 2016). By early May 2016 Trump became the presumptive Republican nominee. By the end of May 2016 multiple media outlets reported Trump had secured enough delegates to be the GOP presidential nominee, and despite much handwringing among GOP elites, efforts by some to draft 2012 nominee Mitt Romney, and reports of possible attempts to deny Trump the nomination at the party convention and give it to someone else (possibly Ohio governor John Kasich), on July 19, 2016, Trump officially received the Republican Party's nomination for president. We have much more on the 2016 contests over the remainder of this chapter.

STRATEGIC CONSIDERATIONS IN THE CONTESTS FOR NOMINATIONS

The nomination process is, by its very nature, complex. The goal for the two major parties at this stage is to winnow the field of potential presidents down from all those eligible to two—one Democrat and one Republican. What criteria are used? Obviously a principal concern is to find an individual qualified to hold the office, but that concern is for naught if the individual cannot win the general election. Thus the parties are looking for the individual who will be the best candidate and the best president. Those are separate jobs that call for different skills. Why would one think, for example, that the person who is best at campaigning on television or at raising money for a campaign would also have the skills necessary to negotiate with the leaders of other nations or to craft compromises that could be accepted by a Congress controlled by leaders of the other party? How should those skills be combined?

Perhaps a group of politicos reasoning together could arrive at the perfect mixture of skills and seek the best-qualified individual. But that is not the nature of our political system. The individuals selected are selected through a political process. More accurately, they are chosen through different political processes in each of the fifty states (and the District of Columbia and various other areas). And they are chosen by a large number of participants, each of whom is free to choose based on his or her conception of how the choice should be made. It is small wonder then that the process is characterized most by complexity (Norrander 2010).

Presidential contenders must face a complex process, with uncertain dynamics. They do not control the order of events, though they do have some say in the importance they attribute to different events. They do not control others' perceptions of events. To a large extent they proceed by instinct; success or failure is often a function of the acuity of their political instincts and those of their advisers. Politicians as a group are firm believers in learning the lessons of the past.

Given that, it is somewhat unbelievable how many politicians have learned the wrong lessons from even very recent experiences. But others have clearly benefited from understanding what happened to others facing similar situations. In the following sections, we will examine some of the strategic considerations facing today's would-be candidates as they try to decipher the presidential nominating process.

The Political Calendar

Perhaps the most important lesson that candidates and their staff must learn is that the calendar of events is critical to success or failure. Past examples cannot be followed if those examples are drawn from contests run with different calendars. Three concepts dominate calendar considerations under the current system. Each must be understood if appropriate and effective strategies are to be adopted.

The Influence of Iowa and New Hampshire and Front-Loading the System

Front-loading refers to holding a large number of primaries and caucuses, contests in which a significant number of delegates are selected, early in the political year. Rules in both parties call for all contests to select delegates to the national conventions, to be held between the first Tuesday in

February and the first Tuesday in June of the presidential election year. New Hampshire and Iowa have traditionally been given exemptions from these rules, but only by one and two weeks, respectively.

A number of states—and some political reformers—have felt that Iowa and New Hampshire have more influence on the process than they should. After all, the citizens in these states are not representative of either party's voters, or of the nation as a whole. However, because they have been permitted to hold their contests first, when no other states compete for attention, candidates have spent an inordinate amount of time there. The media has devoted a disproportionate amount of attention to the contests in these states (Orren and Polsby 1987). Recent research has also shown that this media coverage has a powerful impact on Iowa caucus goers, with the effects differing by party (Winfrey 2017).

Partially in response to the prominence of Iowa and New Hampshire, and certainly as a means to increase their influence, a number of states decided to hold their primaries early in the 1984 nominating season, and the move to advance the calendar accelerated after that. But front-loading, like so many reforms, has had unintended consequences. Candidates cannot enter the race late; in fact, because so many states have moved their process up, states holding later primaries and caucuses feel they have no influence. So more and more moved up. The process was certainly accelerated, but the influence of Iowa and New Hampshire was not diminished. As a result, for the 2008 nominating season, a limited number of caucus states were permitted to begin their delegate selection process in the weeks immediately after the New Hampshire primary. In 2007, Florida's legislature voted to move its primary to late January, responding to the large number of states that had already moved their delegate selection process to February 5. The Democratic National Committee's dominance of the process was directly challenged by Florida's action. Ultimately Florida held its primary on the day of its choosing, but all of the major Democratic candidates pledged to not actively campaign in the state.

This change in the calendar might increase the influence of some more representative states, but no one sees it as a fundamental reform that will significantly improve the system. Indeed, most see such movement as more problematic than what came before. Front-loading remains a larger problem than ever; the calendar is determined by the whim of state legislators. And reformers remain uniquely unsuccessful in their efforts to rationalize the timing of the primary and caucus calendars. Both the Democrats and the Republicans attempted to deal at least somewhat with the issue of front-loading in 2012, with limited success. Iowa and New Hampshire were supposed to have had the first selection contests in early February. South Carolina and Nevada were then supposed to be the only other states allowed to hold their contests in that month. All other states were supposed to wait until at least March. These plans did not work, as Florida once again scheduled its primary earlier than it was supposed to, forcing the four traditionally early states to move their primaries to earlier dates. The RNC was determined to prevent this in 2016. The party once again changed the rules, stating that Iowa, New Hampshire, South Carolina, and Nevada are the only states allowed to hold contests in February, and that all other states must wait until March. This time the rule change had legitimate teeth—any state jumping ahead in the order will have its number of delegates slashed to nine, or one-third of its allotted number, whichever is smaller—and appeared to have the desired effect. Whether this change had any influence on the final outcome of the nominating process is much less clear.

Super Tuesday

Super Tuesday was originally invented to give more influence to the South. However, decisions on the timing of primaries and caucuses by various states have thwarted that goal. In 1992, March 10 was clearly Super Tuesday. Eight states held their primaries on that day—six Southern or border states, plus Massachusetts and Rhode Island. In 1996, eight states held primaries on March 5—five New England states plus Georgia, Maryland, and Colorado. Seven states, with more delegates among them, held their primaries one week later. In 2000 eleven states, including California, New York, and Ohio, as well as the New England states, held primaries on March 7; four other states had caucuses that week. The 2004 process followed a pattern similar to 2000, but five other states jumped ahead to February 3, reducing the influence of some of the bigger states that had selected their dates earlier.

Thus the concept of Super Tuesday is an evolving one. It is now closely linked with the concept of **regional primaries**. Regional primaries represent efforts by state officials to enhance the influence of a region by holding all of that region's primaries on one day—or within a week, if one includes the caucus states. Because candidates want to appear in as many places holding primaries as possible, regional primaries advantage candidates by cutting down on travel time and costs. Also, because many media markets cross state lines, campaigns piggyback advertising budgets for primaries in neighboring states, parts of which might well be in the same media market, when primaries are held on the same day. However, unless states out of the region defer the primaries to another day, the sheer number of states choosing to hold their contests on one day all but necessitates a national campaign—making the process extremely difficult for underfunded candidates. The advantages of a regional primary are lost. The Super Tuesday concept went away for three or four presidential election cycles, but Georgia led a charge to make March 1, 2016, Super Tuesday for the 2016 cycle (Reinhard 2015) and succeeded to a large extent. Eleven states held Republican contests on Super Tuesday 2016, while twelve states and territories did the same for Democrats, accounting for 661 GOP delegates and 865 Democratic delegates (Weiland 2016). Both parties' eventual nominees won big on Super Tuesday, with Trump and Clinton each winning seven states and Clinton adding the Democratic-only contest in American Samoa. But neither candidate was able to deliver the knockout blow they were hoping for, as Republicans Ted Cruz and Marco Rubio and Democrat Bernie Sanders also won states on Super Tuesday (Collinson 2016). Perhaps the most important thing about Super Tuesday 2016 was that it provided an early glimpse of the Clinton campaign's difficulty in generating the levels of enthusiasm among Democratic voters that Barack Obama was able to produce in 2008 and to a lesser extent in 2012 (Confessore 2016).

Filing Deadlines

Each state specifies how a candidate wins a place on its primary ballot. In some cases the decision is made by a state official. In other cases the presidential candidates must file slates of proposed delegates. In still other cases the delegates themselves must file petitions to be on the ballot. The variety of requirements is almost endless. But each state, according to its own laws, specifies a certain date by which those who seek a place on the ballot must have fulfilled whatever requirements exist. **Filing deadlines** are a necessity so that ballots can be printed in advance of an election. But filing deadlines also have strategic implications. Anyone who does not meet a state's filing deadline cannot win delegates in that state. In 1984, for instance, Gary Hart was unable to gain the momentum he might have from his New Hampshire victory over front-runner Walter Mondale because Hart's campaign had failed to file delegate slates in many of the districts in Florida, a delegate-rich state whose primary followed shortly after New Hampshire's. A national campaign organization is important for a prospective presidential nominee in that someone can keep track of approaching deadlines and alert state campaigners, who are often rank amateurs, to their approach. In most cases meeting state filing deadlines is a nonissue for the major candidates (no top-tier candidate missed a filing deadline in 2016), but their presence is something candidates and their organizations must account for.

Strategic Implications of the Political Calendar

Recent campaign experience has demonstrated conclusively that the political calendar has serious implications for campaign strategy. In 1992, for example, many of the first-tier Democratic candidates held back because they feared President Bush's strength as a candidate. Bill Clinton stepped into that void and became the front-runner. However, he looked like a flawed candidate, as his character and ethics were attacked during the New Hampshire primary. Many party leaders tried to convince one or more of those who had earlier decided not to run that it was time to step in. But it was too late to step in. By the time the New Hampshire primary was held, filing deadlines had passed in most of the states that would elect delegates in March and April. It was already too late to raise money and organize a campaign in those states that would hold primaries on the first two Tuesdays in March.

The concentration of many caucuses and primaries on the same day also has important implications. In the old system, when fewer states held primaries and when they were spread out over the political calendar, it was possible for a candidate's organization to get by with a skeletal crew, moving key campaign operatives from an important primary state, after the contest had been held in that state, to another such state. However, to be successful under the new rules and calendar, a candidate must build a national organization from the start. If not, he or she will be overwhelmed by an opponent who has. Bill Bradley and John McCain each faced that reality in the 2000 contests, despite the encouraging starts that their campaigns achieved. Despite some changes, nothing changed on this front in 2016.

The Rules of the Game

George McGovern's 1972 campaign will always stand as the example of a campaign that understood the rules and won because of how they were taken advantage of. But in interesting ways that lesson has been repeated over and over again in the reform era. If there is a real lesson here, it is that campaign strategists ignore the rules in effect at their peril. Although many rules were altered by state law changes in order to meet Democratic party mandates, there are still important areas in which the two parties' rules differ—with very significant consequences for the candidates.

Proportional Representation versus Winner-Take-All Systems

The Democratic party insists that delegates be apportioned according to the presidential preference of those voters participating in the process. While certain loopholes have been permitted, the basic concept of delegate strength reflecting proportional strength among the voters has been maintained. The Republicans did not follow the Democrats' lead, or at least they did not until 2010, a change we will discuss further below. But through the 2008 nominating process the GOP maintained a system that permitted states to run winner-take-all primaries should they choose to do so. Each system has strengths and weaknesses; decidedly each has strategic implications.

Consider the Democrats. If one is on the ballot in a system that gives delegates proportionately to the strength at the ballot box, a candidate can "lose" an election but still pick up delegate support. As the nominee is the person with a majority of the delegates, close losses can be important "victories." This is a method in which delegates are awarded under a system of **proportional representation**. In 1976, Jimmy Carter ran everywhere. He picked up some delegates everywhere. Even when Democrats seemed to be tiring of Carter, as the primaries drew to a close, he picked up delegates. Few recall that Carter lost five of the last seven primaries. What is remembered is that he had guaranteed himself a majority of the delegates at the convention on the day the primary process ended. He did so by winning delegates in primaries that he lost. Similarly, in 1992 Bill Clinton continued to gain strength when he lost primaries, with the result that unexpected victories by Jerry Brown as the process wore on did not encourage new opposition. In 2008, Senator Clinton could not overcome the Obama lead, despite late victories, because he kept winning delegates. In 2012, Obama was of course unchallenged within his own party. The importance of proportional representation in the Democratic nomination process was once again manifest in 2016. Under a winner-take-all system, Hillary Clinton would have dispatched Bernie Sanders far sooner than she was able to under the Democrats' complicated proportional representation system.

But proportional representation could work in another way, one much less beneficial to the front-running candidate. In recent contests the Democrats have had one leader and other candidates trying to make themselves into the one principal opponent. The leader has prevailed by successfully playing off other candidates against each other and amassing delegate support. Imagine a scenario in which there are two or three equally well-positioned candidates contesting for the nomination in a front-loaded system. If two or even three candidates emerge from the early round of primaries in competitive positions, with enough money and organization to see themselves through the process, or if their resources are equally depleted (see section "Strategic Use of Campaign Resources"), then proportional representation might well mean that no one candidate can garner the support of a majority of the delegates before the convention. Serious strategists and analysts must consider the possibility as they plan a nominating campaign.

What about the Republicans? When there is a front-runner with a strong financial and organizational base, a winner-take-all system allows that front-runner to dispense with pesky challengers quite easily. George H. W. Bush did it in 1992; Bob Dole did it in 1996; by Super Tuesday 2000 George W. Bush had all but guaranteed himself the nomination. The system benefits the leaders. It allows the eventual nominee to have more time to bring the party together, united behind his candidacy.

But what if the leader is not likely to be a winner in November? What if the early primaries reveal hitherto unnoted weaknesses or a lack of voter appeal? The same system makes it difficult to change course in midstream. The Dole example is a good one. Bob Dole was the favorite for the GOP nomination from early on in 1996, but the Dole candidacy looked weak at many points in the early caucuses and primaries. The political calendar worked in his favor; so too did the winner-take-all provisions in the rules of most states that held primaries in March of that year. In those primaries Dole never won more than two-thirds of the votes (albeit an impressive number) and on six occasions he won less than half of the votes, but in many states he won all of the delegates. The system exaggerated his strength and downplayed campaign weaknesses that would later become apparent.

But this changed for Republicans in 2012. In the summer of 2010 the GOP quietly made a dramatic change in its presidential nominating process, requiring for the first time the majority of states to award their convention delegates via proportional representation. Some have argued that this change was a preemptive strike against a possible Sarah Palin nomination. Whether this is true will likely never be known. But what is known is that the GOP introduced proportional representation into its nominating process in 2012 and kept it there in 2016, especially for states that go early in the cycle. This change allowed some of the candidates in the non-Romney category to stick around a bit longer in 2012, and certainly delayed Trump's securing the nomination in 2016 by allowing some candidates—particularly Ted Cruz and John Kasich—to hang around much longer than they would have been able to under a winner-take-all system.

Superdelegates versus Influential Party Leaders

Recall that the superdelegates were put back into the Democratic party process because influential party leaders and elected officials chose not to participate in the nominating process after the McGovern-Fraser reforms were implemented. These leaders refused to participate because they did not want their local reputations to be sullied by having backed a losing national candidate. Decisions not to back presidential candidates did not follow from lack of interest but rather from strategic considerations. Either an elected leader would beat some of his or her own constituents in a contest to be a convention delegate or he or she might lose. Neither was a good outcome. Thus many decided to opt out altogether; few party leaders were represented at the 1972, 1976, or even 1980 Democratic conventions.

The Republicans never faced the same problems. Because they allowed unpledged slates to run and because they did not require fair reflection of presidential preference, influential Republicans have continued to play a key role in their party's nominating process throughout the entire reform period. Most would argue that they have done so to the benefit of their party's candidates.

From the perspective of this discussion, what is important is the strategic differences that the two systems call for. The Republican process is not very different from what it has been in the past. Prospective candidates want party leaders and elected officials to support their candidacies. When all, save one, of the Republican governors came out for George W. Bush before the first primary vote had been cast, not only the national media but all of his opponents knew that he had a huge advantage. A Republican presidential candidate is wise to spend his time courting those who have influence in their own states because they can frequently turn that influence into delegate support.

Democratic party leaders tend to hold back support. Their role is supposed to be that of a broker, to be certain that popular participation in the convention does not run away with the party. Thus the superdelegates were extremely important in helping Walter Mondale secure the party nomination in 1984; those who had worked closely with Gary Hart did not see him as presidential material. Similarly, superdelegates worked against Jesse Jackson in his two bids for the Democratic nomination. He won support from the Congressional Black Caucus (though not from all of its members), but he was not able to attract a wider following among the party leadership. Democratic campaigns for party leader and elected official support are more subtle than those in the Republican party. Each individual is courted for his or her own support, not because he or she can necessarily translate that support to a wider following.

However, the support of the superdelegates viewed as a whole is an important element in the Democratic party process. In 2004 observers watched to see whether superdelegates would desert John Kerry for the early front-runner, Howard Dean; when many stayed with Kerry, the signal was that his candidacy still had life. When selected superdelegates declared for Barack Obama in 2008, they were essentially conceding him the race. Their support said that they knew who the winner would be and that they wanted to be on his team. As discussed earlier in this chapter, superdelegates were certainly important (but not determinative) for Hillary Clinton in 2016.

The superdelegates and the party officials who have been added to state delegations have never played the brokering role that was intended for them. Again, however, that is not to say that a scenario could not eventuate that would necessitate that role. The **brokered convention** is a thing of the past, according to most analysts. But if no nominee has a majority—or a near majority—of delegate support when a convention is called to order, no strategist and no contemporary analyst has a historical precedent to rely on to see what might happen. It seems very likely that the party elite would emerge as leaders in such a situation.

Strategic Use of Campaign Resources

Any serious candidate for president starts the campaign possessing certain resources. Others can be obtained. Still others must be done without. Campaign strategists are often in the business of resource management.

Office

The key resource to hold if one wants a presidential nomination seems to be the White House. Eligible incumbent presidents are normally renominated. Renomination may be semiautomatic, resembling coronations, as in the cases of George W. Bush in 2004 and Barack Obama in 2012. Or renomination may require a battle, as was the case for the first President Bush in 1992.

These latter cases are particularly instructive. As noted earlier, George H. W. Bush was challenged by Patrick Buchanan, who claimed that as president, Bush had not been a faithful successor in upholding Ronald Reagan's conservative agenda. Bush felt insecure about his own party base and was uncomfortable with the degree of strength Buchanan showed in some of the early primaries. Thus he responded to Buchanan, attacking him and positioning himself further toward the right on the political spectrum. Bush was able to use the power of his office to defeat Buchanan, but he was not secure enough in that power to dismiss him presumptively as others had done.

Other offices have also proved useful. The vice presidency seems to be something of a mixed blessing. Eight out of the last eleven vice presidents have either succeeded to the presidency or sought that office themselves.[3] For Vice President Mondale, his service under Jimmy Carter clearly cut two ways. He was considered an excellent vice president, gained a good deal of national exposure, and built a wide range of political contacts during his four years in office. However, he was also saddled with the legacy of a failed presidency and with defending policies for which he was not, in fact, responsible.

On the other hand, Vice President Bush, in 1988, had a tremendous advantage. His only problem was to convince Reagan supporters that he was not only a loyal lieutenant but also a worthy heir. That problem continued to plague him as president. In 2000, Vice President Al Gore was able to draw on the allegiance of loyal Democrats who appreciated the hard work he had done for the party over an eight-year period, but he also had to deal with the legacy of Bill Clinton and the residual consequences of the scandals that plagued the Clinton presidency. In addition to the vice presidency, having experience in the U.S. Senate or in a state governorship can also be an advantage for prospective presidential nominees (see Table 8.3). It is always important to remember, however, that context is always key in determining how useful (or harmful) office is in obtaining a presidential nomination. It is true, after all, that President Trump in 2016 became the only president ever elected without holding previous high level (on in his case, any level) public office or an officer position in the U.S. military.

Money

Running for a presidential nomination actually involves running more than fifty separate campaigns. In 2016, primary elections or caucuses were scheduled on twenty-seven different days, obviously with a number of different events held on some of those days. Candidates had to monitor the selection of the individuals who would serve as convention delegates from the caucus states and many primary states, as well as additional facets of the process. An enterprise this vast requires a complex organization, extensive travel by the candidate and staff, sophisticated information gathering and dissemination, and effective advertising. These require money.

Since the 1976 presidential nomination, all contenders for major party nomination have been eligible for federal matching funds. (See chapter 5 for a detailed discussion of campaign financing in all elections.) When Steve Forbes decided to forgo federal funding and finance his own campaign in 1996, he became only the second candidate in twenty years to do so.[4] In so doing, he launched a fundamental change in the way the nomination phase of the process is financed, a change that has yet to play out completely. Neither Forbes nor George W. Bush accepted federal funds in 2000, and Bush's huge war chest played a significant role in the outcome of the nominating contest.

As noted earlier, in 2004 President Bush again refused matching funds for the prenomination stage of the election; so, too, did Democrats Dean and Kerry. In 2008, Obama and McCain and the five most prominent challengers for the nomination all refused matching money, knowing that to

Table 8.3. Sitting Senators Seeking Their Party's Presidential Nomination, 1968–2016

1968	Robert F. Kennedy
	Eugene McCarthy
1972	Vance Hartke
	Hubert Humphrey
	Henry Jackson
	George McGovern
	Edmund S. Muskie
1976	Birch Bayh
	Lloyd Bentsen
	Frank Church
	Fred Harris
	Hubert Humphrey
	Henry Jackson
1980	Howard Baker
	Robert Dole
	Edward M. Kennedy
1984	Alan Cranston
	John Glenn
	Gary Hart
	Ernest Hollings
1988	Joseph Biden
	Bob Dole
	Albert Gore
	Gary Hart
	Paul Simon
1992	Tom Harkin
	Bob Kerrey
1996	Bob Dole
	Phil Gramm
	Richard Lugar
	Arlen Specter
2000	John McCain
	Orrin Hatch
	Bob Smith
2004	John Edwards
	Bob Graham
	John Kerry
	Joseph Lieberman
2008	Joseph Biden
	Sam Brownback
	Hillary Clinton
	Chris Dodd
	John McCain
	Barack Obama
2012	none
2016	Bernie Sanders
	Ted Cruz
	Lindsey Graham
	Rand Paul
	Marco Rubio

Source: Compiled by authors.

be competitive they would have to exceed the limits that would be imposed if they took the federal grant. In 2012 and 2016 none of the major party candidates accepted federal matching funds for their campaigns. Unless their public financing element is completely overhauled, the days of matching funds having any relevance in the presidential nominating process (and general election process as well; see chapter 9) are almost certainly over.

Whereas in the past a legitimate strategy was to concentrate on Iowa and New Hampshire and hope good showings there would lead to an infusion of the funds needed to contest later primaries, the front-loading of the calendar and the huge sums raised in recent years have made raising early money essential for viability for most candidates. We saw this clearly in the 2012 contest as Mitt Romney used his sheer financial might to drive his opponents from the race. Romney generated over $450 million for his nomination campaign in 2012, while Obama generated over $620 million in a contest where he was unopposed. While raising early money was important for most candidates in 2016, Bernie Sanders was a partial exception and Donald Trump a near total one. Sanders was able to build momentum and raise money relatively slowly early in the 2016 contest before catching fire in both areas as the nominating season progressed. Trump seemingly never had to worry about raising money, and indeed likely spent the least amount of time and energy raising money of any presidential candidate since the 1960s if not earlier. Part of this had to do with Trump's success with the media, which will be discussed further below and in chapters 9 and 10.

The Media

In many ways the press makes the presidential nominating process work. How many average citizens are thinking about presidential politics more than a year before an election, when the contenders are courting delegate candidates in Florida, Iowa, and Maine? Has the public begun to focus on the next election when scores of candidates and their staffs are trooping through the snows of New Hampshire? In most cases, the answer to these questions is a resounding "no!" But the working press is gearing up.

Initially one or two reporters will accompany a candidate on a campaign swing. If a candidate is lucky or if a press secretary is extremely good, a television crew may cover part of a campaign trip. Particularly at the beginning of the primary process, free publicity is the key. Odd as it seems, not all presidential contenders are necessarily well known to the general public.

In 2000 many people thought that the George Bush running for president was the same one who had been president before, until the media began to cover the Texas governor. John McCain was virtually unknown until the press began to cover his campaign. One "advantage" that the little-known Howard Dean had in the 2004 nominating process was that the other, better-known candidates, such as Senator Kerry, were not actually known by the public either. The situation was obviously very different for a candidate as well known as Hillary Clinton in 2016. But even with Clinton holding this significant advantage, the relatively unknown Bernie Sanders was able to attract significant media attention relatively quickly and close the gap with Clinton. At first the 2016 Republican field had low levels of attention and knowledge among the American public. Most Americans knew little about the Republicans believed to be considering a run, and even the best known of the bunch—former Florida governor Jeb Bush—was known mostly by last name as the son and brother of two former presidents. This all changed when celebrity Donald Trump entered the race. Trump brought national (indeed, international) name recognition and star power to the Republican field. The importance of this for Trump's eventual success cannot be overestimated. Indeed, the media could not seem to get enough of Trump, and coverage of Trump caused ratings to spike across network and cable television programming featuring Trump. This in turn allowed Trump to generate a huge amount of free/earned media (more on this in chapter 10)—estimated to be over $2 billion just in the nomination phase of the campaign—a figure that was much higher than his fellow Republican challengers and likely set records for a presidential nomination campaign (Confessore and Yourish 2016; Patterson 2016; Wells et al. 2016).

The goal in the early stages of a campaign is to be mentioned. Television advertising cannot be effective without the public focusing on the campaign, and so candidates court press attention. They play to local media wherever they go; more important, they seek mention in the national press, some positive reference as a real contender.

Consider Bill Clinton in 1992. Clinton had a difficult press problem. In 1991 his candidacy began to be taken quite seriously by Washington insiders because most of the Democrats who were more prominently mentioned had decided not to seek the nomination. Washington journalists knew that Governor Clinton had a reputation in Little Rock as a womanizer. That reputation made the rounds of Washington cocktail parties, but it was never reported in nationally syndicated stories on the upcoming campaign. Then the accusations of Gennifer Flowers, first reported in a supermarket tabloid, hit the newsstands. The national press had to decide how to play the story. Media leaders decided that the story, once reported, had legitimacy; the pack of journalists on the presidential campaign trail followed. As the New Hampshire primary approached, the Clinton campaign was on the ropes. Clinton's response was again to use the media—this time an interview on *60 Minutes,* in which he and his wife talked about their marital difficulties and how they had worked them out. Clinton had gone around the intermediary of the journalists and used the media to communicate directly to the voters.[5] His strategy was successful. His campaign halted what could have been a fatal plunge in his support.

Or look back at the McCain campaign in 2000. John McCain was first elected to the House of Representatives in 1982; four years later he moved up to the Senate. McCain is the son and grandson of navy admirals. He is a decorated pilot who was shot down over Vietnam and spent five years in a prisoner-of-war camp; he refused to be given special treatment because of his family connections. But he was largely unknown when he announced what many thought was a quixotic campaign for the Republican nomination. McCain used the press masterfully. In a campaign in which the front-runners were staying away from the press in order to avoid making mistakes, McCain made himself available at every opportunity. And he labeled his campaign bus the "Straight Talk Express," to differentiate himself from politicians who did not give straight answers. While his fellow senators found McCain acerbic and difficult to work with, the press loved him. They told and retold his compelling personal story and drew parallels between his military career and his political career. In the end journalists had to report that McCain's campaign could not overcome Bush's advantages; but the campaign went as far as it did largely because of the media attention it drew.

The media portrays images of candidates to the public—for good or for ill. At times, media delving into a candidate's personal life can have devastating effects. We can see this in Gary Hart's failed quest for the 1988 Democratic nomination. Hart was the clear front-runner for the nomination, but saw his chances go up in smoke after the media exposed an extramarital affair with a young model named Donna Rice. At other times, the portrait can be much more positive. The portrayal of Barack Obama in 2008 is a perfect example of this. Indeed, many of his opponents vociferously complained of the favorable media coverage Obama received. Candidates certainly understand that they are perceived by the public largely as they are portrayed by the media; they go to great lengths to be sure that the image that comes across is one with which they are comfortable. Recent experience leads to the conclusion that a key to gaining early press attention is to do better than is expected or to make a more positive showing than early reports would have predicted; but doing worse than expected can have a detrimental effect. In this regard the Iowa caucuses and the New Hampshire primary—and how candidates are presented as these events unfold—have been very important (Orren and Polsby 1987). The experience of Governor Dean in the 2004 Iowa caucuses, where he failed to meet expectations and then was pilloried for his emotional concession speech, is an obvious case in point. Senator Obama gained media attention with well-publicized early forays into New Hampshire; his upset win in Iowa provided momentum that carried on into the Super Tuesday states.

Surpassing expectations is not the only strategy for dealing with the media; demonstrating uniqueness—and thus newsworthiness—certainly works as well. In 1984 Jesse Jackson demonstrated that the press can be a crucial resource when used in this way. Jackson was newsworthy. He ran an entire campaign based on free media exposure. The press did not dare ignore him because he was the first serious black contender for a major party nomination—that was news. He was articulate and controversial, and he was drawing large numbers of blacks to the polls—again, news. When he challenged his opponents, when he slept in the ghettos, when he traveled to Syria, when he did not disavow the support of the controversial Louis Farrakhan, when he ran well in the South, Jesse Jackson was news. He knew how to use the media. His rhetoric was made for television; his dynamism demanded action photos; his place in history commanded attention. Despite his total inability to draw financial support, despite the fact that his Rainbow Coalition never really materialized, Jesse Jackson stayed on page one. He stayed on the nightly news (Barker and Walter 1989).

In 2000 the press wanted a contest. If Governor Bush and Vice President Gore won their nominations without contests, what story would there be to cover? The press did not invent the competition, but media analysts certainly played up the contests—Bush versus McCain, Gore versus Bradley—at times when many outside the media thought it would only be a matter of time before these challenges to the front-runners evaporated.

The role of the press in the nominating process has received a great deal of critical attention. That attention has been deserved because the national media, print and electronic journalists alike, have not done a very good job of defining their role in this process. The nominating process itself has come under scrutiny because it is so easily manipulated by the press (see Grassmuck 1985; Orren and Polsby 1987; Traugott 1985). But reform is not the immediate province of candidates for party nominations. They are concerned with winning. In reaching for that goal, they must learn to use the press as a resource. Free media attention has made and broken many presidential campaigns. This remains true even as the rise of digital media—in particular, social media—has given candidates and their campaigns greater control over how they are presented to potential voters (Pew 2013a). Some have argued that Trump has changed the equation here. We will more fully explore this matter in the next two chapters.

Evaluating Nominating Campaigns

Nominating campaigns are difficult to assess. Viewed with twenty-twenty hindsight, one can easily see that the Muskie strategy in 1972 was flawed; that the Carter strategy in 1976 was brilliant; the Dole strategy in 1996 pragmatic and effective; and so on. The evidence again points strongly to the conclusion that politics is more art than science.

Some of the most effective members of Congress—Wilbur Mills of Arkansas, Ed Muskie of Maine, Ted Kennedy of Massachusetts, Phil Gramm of Texas, Orrin Hatch of Utah, Joe Biden of Delaware, and Chris Dodd of Connecticut—proved to be poor presidential candidates. Skills are not always transferable. The corps of national campaign experts is very small, and these "experts" frequently learn the wrong lessons from their previous experience. New faces often have the clearest sense of how to attack the system—not only Hart as McGovern's strategist in 1972, but also James Carville for Bill Clinton in 1992, Karl Rove for George W. Bush in 2000, Joe Trippi for Howard Dean in 2004, David Plouffe for Barack Obama in 2008, and Corey Lewandowski, Steve Bannon, and Kellyanne Conway for Donald Trump in 2016.

All candidates show their strengths and weaknesses as they announce their candidacy. All understand the need for money, for an effective press strategy, for influential followers, for gaining and maintaining momentum, but few are successful in doing all these things. But the political terrain is difficult to read. In the preceding sections, many examples have been given that might seem to the reader in 2018 as if they are ancient history. Candidates have been mentioned of whom few reading these pages have heard. But presidential elections happen every four years. What happened in 1972 might be forty-six years ago, but today's presidential nomination process is still fundamentally shaped by the rules first used in that election cycle. If one is going to understand a process, as a student, as a researcher, or as a practitioner, it is necessary to study what history there is. New situations arose in 2016, but perhaps the only thing totally without precedent was candidate Trump himself; the precedents need to be understood for that reason. The process is so interesting precisely because those of us who are political analysts and members of the interested public can sit back and watch the contenders compete and test their strategies. We can know nearly as much about the past as do the strategists themselves. And we can judge the ways in which the campaigns are contested. Monday morning quarterbacks have no better process to kibitz about.

THE CONVENTIONS

The excitement was electric at the 1976 Republican National Convention in the Kemper Arena in Kansas City. Betty Ford came in from one end and the band struck up the University of Michigan fight song, "Hail to the Victors!" Nancy Reagan entered from the other end; the band responded with "California, Here I Come!" The crowds cheered loudly as Ford and Reagan supporters tried to drown each other out. Television commentators tried to gauge support for the two candidates by the intensity of the cheering. The convention was as thrilling as any college football game.

The excitement of conventions stirs the emotions in those of us who love politics. But the broader question to be addressed is whether national nominating conventions decide anything at all anymore. After all, no politician active today has ever participated in a convention whose nominee was not known before the opening gavel sounded.

The first party conventions were held in the Jacksonian period in the nineteenth century (recall chapter 2). Conventions were places to which delegates came in order to make decisions, to choose the presidential nominees. In fact, nine times delegates have had to cast ten or more ballots in order to choose their party's nominees. In 1924, the Democratic National Convention in Baltimore took 103 ballots before finally settling on the nomination of John W. Davis, the last true favorite son to gain a major party nomination. But since 1952, every presidential nominee has been chosen on the first ballot cast at his or her party's convention. While there is still the possibility that party conventions could indeed actually determine a presidential nominee—the political junkie's dream of a brokered convention where no candidate has the required number of delegates to secure the nomination, and horse trading and backroom deals have to be used to select the nominee—recent history suggests that they have become little more than rubber stamps for decisions reached by primary and caucus voters. Some claim that they are nothing but celebratory events—opportunities for the party faithful to unite behind their nominee (Nelson 1997). The television networks seem to reflect this view, as they provide fewer and fewer hours of live coverage (Kerbel 1998). The delegate selection process has worked in such a way that one candidate has a guaranteed first-ballot majority by the time the convention opens. Little else remains to be decided.

As much of the nation's attention still focuses on the nominating conventions every fourth summer, it is appropriate for us to examine whether this attention is warranted. If we admit that the conventions do not decide the nominee, what can we say about the relevance and importance of other decisions made in these political arenas (Davis 1983; Parris 1972; Shafer 1988; Sullivan, Pressman, and Arterton 1976; Wayne 2008; Polsby, Wildavsky, and Hopkins 2008)? National nominating conventions make four different kinds of decisions. In addition to deciding on the nominees for president and vice president, they rule on credentials disputes, changes in the party rules, and platform language.

Credentials Challenges

Credentials disputes are the most easily understood. In party rules and in the call to the convention, each party establishes the procedures through which delegates are to be chosen. In most cases no one challenges the delegates presenting themselves as representing a certain state. However, the procedures are not always simple. The political situations are not always unbiased, and challenges result. Each party appoints a Credentials Committee that hears challenges to proposed delegations and rules on the disputes. The report of the Credentials Committee is the first order of official business before the nominating convention.

While most **credentials challenges** are disposed of without major controversy, those that do attract attention are often critically important. Among the most noteworthy challenges was that of the Mississippi Freedom Democratic party in 1964 (White 1965). The appeal by Mississippi black Democrats was instrumental in desegregating Democratic politics in the South. But such credentials challenges are extremely rare in recent conventions, and those that have occurred have not been terribly important.

Rules Disputes

The national convention of each party is the ultimate rule-making authority for the national party.[6] Each party appoints a Rules Committee that examines proposed changes in party rules. In most cases party rules are sufficiently obscure and esoteric that few notice the workings of the Rules Committee. Often the real impact of rules changes will not be felt for four years; in the heat of an ongoing campaign, few are looking that far ahead.

On occasion, however, the work of the convention Rules Committee is seen as having immediate impact. In 1976, candidate Ronald Reagan tried a desperate ploy to wrest the nomination from President Gerald Ford. In an unprecedented move, Reagan announced, in advance of the convention, that he would choose Pennsylvania senator Richard Schweiker as his running mate if he were nominated for the presidency. Reagan's bold move was a reaching out toward the liberal wing of his party, toward those who felt he was too conservative. The battle was very close. Reagan hoped the needed delegates would swing to his side, but few budged.

As a second step in his strategy, Reagan sought a change in rule 5 of the Republican Party Rules, with his proposed amendment requiring that prospective presidential candidates designate their choice for running mate in advance. Reagan hoped that this rule change would force President Ford into a choice that would cost him support from the followers of the hopefuls who were not chosen and give the nomination to Reagan.

The ploy failed; the rule was not changed, although the vote on it was very close, and Ford secured the nomination (Pomper 1977, 18–27; Wayne 1988, chap. 5; Witcover 1977).

National political journalists have focused on disputes such as this one as pivotal events in nominating conventions. In some sense they were, but in a more realistic sense the results were very predictable. Delegates to conventions choose which candidate they will support early on, and then they work hard for that candidate. They are seeking two goals. Their principal goal is to help their candidate secure the nomination. Their secondary goal is to be a delegate for that candidate and share in the candidate's success. Rules disputes need to be viewed through such a lens. Convention delegates are not fooled by the intricacies of credentials or rules fights. The questions may be worded differently, but delegates know that the real question is: Which candidate for the presidency do you favor? In that sense, to the extent that one candidate has been guaranteed the nomination before the convention opens, credentials and rules fights are much less likely to assume importance.

Party Platforms

The **party platforms** are statements of the direction in which the two parties want our country to go. Their significance is frequently disputed, though Gerald Pomper (1972) demonstrated that they show real differences between our parties and that much of them are implemented and not forgotten. It is clear that they receive a lot of press attention at the time they are adopted.

The Democrats use the platform-writing process as a means to reach out to grassroots activists around the country. In many years, their Platform Committee, the composition of which reflects candidates' strengths, has turned into a traveling road show, seeking advice from Democrats around the country. The Republican Platform Committee, on the other hand, normally only meets in the convention city on the weekend before the convention itself. It is not a road show, but perhaps a sideshow before the main event.

Platforms serve different purposes for different individuals. For activists and ideologues they are often a means to gain a foothold into party dogma. For interest groups, they represent one way to gain support for particular views. For candidates, the platform process has served as a way to reach out to those in the party who did not support them.

Each candidate at a national convention has an extensive organization. Since the 1960 nomination of John F. Kennedy in Los Angeles (White 1961), each convention has seen increasingly sophisticated communications networks so that candidate organizations can reach their supporters on the floor. Each candidate sets up a "whip" organization so that delegates are instantly informed how they must vote on matters coming to the floor for votes.

The whips inform the delegates, and the delegates fall in line. Thus, in 1988, the Dukakis campaign operatives allowed votes on the platform planks dealing with increasing taxes on upper-income families and pledging to forgo the first use of nuclear weapons, but they also ensured that their candidate would not be saddled with a platform with which he was not comfortable (Pomper 1989). However, platform disputes are seen as matters of conscience more frequently than is the case for credentials or rules disputes. The delegates often are freed to vote as they choose. At times, winning candidates concede platform disputes to their vanquished foes so that the losers have some pride with which to return home and thus they retain some enthusiasm for the party.

That is not to say that the platform-writing and platform-adopting processes are not important. Never was this more clearly demonstrated than in 1992. The entire Democratic platform-writing process was controlled by the Clinton campaign. The platform was drafted by a Clinton loyalist. The drafting committee was chaired by Clinton supporter Bill Richardson, then a congressman from New Mexico and later Clinton cabinet appointee, the governor of New Mexico, and a candidate for his party's presidential nomination in 2008. The supporters of Paul Tsongas and Jerry Brown were allowed their say at platform hearings and were permitted to offer amendments on the convention floor, but the result was preordained. The Clinton campaign wanted to present the image of a new Democratic party; the platform was one vehicle for doing this. Controlling the process throughout ensured this goal and was thus considered to be very important (Maisel 1994). The Obama campaign was also quick to demonstrate its control of the Democratic platform in 2012, acting quickly to force the Convention to reinsert language regarding Jerusalem as the capital of Israel and a reference to God that had been struck from the document by the Platform Committee (Landler 2012). The 2016 platform-writing processes generated little attention outside of each party's inner circle.

At the other extreme, George H. W. Bush's campaign lost control of the platform-writing process at the Republican Convention. The platform battle became a symbol of an intense ideological struggle being waged within the Republican party. To oversimplify, three camps, each claiming to be true conservatives, were in evidence. Bush represented the traditional conservatives in his party; these were fiscal conservatives, concerned with balancing the budget and deficit reduction. Buchanan fought for the soul of the Republican party on moral and value-related issues; his backers were engaged in a cultural war with those who had deserted traditional American values. Buchanan supporters controlled key positions on the platform subcommittees that dealt with values issues such as abortion. Finally, lurking in the background were economic conservatives represented by Jack Kemp; they favored opportunity and growth policies, but they also supported the Buchanan definition on family values. The platform that emerged reflected the most controversial statement of conservative views, particularly on social issues. Many Republicans, particularly moderate Republicans from the Northeast, felt that it was a divisive platform, one that divided them from their own party. It certainly was not a centrist platform that could help President Bush in the November election (Maisel 1994).

It would be too much to argue that the differences between the two parties' platforms in 1992 determined the result of that very complex election (see chapter 9). However, one can surely claim that the Republican platform in that year did go far toward defining the public's view of the GOP.

Platforms, which do distinguish the two parties, clearly can still play a role in uniting a party for the November showdown or preventing party activists from coming together behind the nominee. They are important statements about party philosophy. Writing the platform is an exercise in defining a party. Platform construction is also an opportunity for various factions within a party to try to shift the party in their preferred direction. Controversy may or may not be apparent at a convention, but this part of the process remains critically important and should not be underestimated.

Vice Presidential Nominations

Vice presidential running mates for major party candidates are officially nominated by the two parties' conventions. But the choices, of course, are made by the presidential candidate. The last presidential candidate to leave the choice of running mate to the convention was Adlai Stevenson, for whom the Democratic National Convention chose Tennessee's veteran senator Estes Kefauver over a young Massachusetts senator named John Fitzgerald Kennedy in 1956.

Today's presidential nominees know that the choice of vice president is a most serious undertaking. From a political standpoint, the vice presidential nominee can help or hurt the ticket. Certainly the nominee is evaluated in part on this choice, the first important decision he has to make after confirmation as his party's standard-bearer. In 1972, George McGovern's campaign suffered badly when it was revealed that his original choice, Thomas Eagleton, a senator from Missouri, had undergone shock treatment for mental depression. Under intense pressure, Eagleton eventually withdrew. McGovern faced the embarrassing situation of having to find a stand-in and being turned down by a number of prominent Democrats before Sargent Shriver, President Kennedy's brother-in-law and the founding director of the Peace Corps, accepted McGovern's invitation.

But the choice is viewed as more than a political decision. The nominee is naming an individual who will be the proverbial "heartbeat away" from the presidency, should the ticket win. Since Harry S. Truman succeeded to the presidency upon the death of Franklin Roosevelt in 1945, political leaders have been confronted with the seriousness of the vice presidential decision. Truman was picked for a variety of reasons, none of them clear at the time (Phillips 1966). What was clear was that he was not included in the Roosevelt inner circle as the president directed Allied efforts toward ending World War II. As an extreme example, Truman was only vaguely aware of the project to develop the atom bomb when he became president. In a world in which the president of the United States is the most powerful single individual on earth, the choice of the person who is to succeed to the presidency should anything happen to the incumbent must be taken most seriously.

The process for choosing vice presidential candidates is not a formal one, but it has been a careful and organized one for each of the last eight elections. Candidate Jimmy Carter established a process that his successors as Democratic nominees have more or less followed since 1976. As it becomes clear that the nomination is in hand, each prospective nominee has asked a trusted adviser to begin to compile a list of possible running mates. These individuals are then screened in great detail, to make sure that none has any problems similar to that discovered with Senator Eagleton in 1972. The extent to which the names on the list have been public has varied from year to year. In part that is because being mentioned is a great political coup—and those seeking the nomination understand that they are involved in a political process. Eventually the list of many nominees is pared to a few, usually fewer than five. They are interviewed by the prospective nominee, again sometimes in secret and sometimes quite openly. The Republicans have not followed a process quite as formal as the Democrats, but their outline is basically the same.

The eventual decision rests with the nominee, but he consults widely, seeking opinions on the assets and liabilities of each of those under consideration. He wants to be certain that the nominee is someone with whom he is comfortable—personally, politically, and in terms of policy views. But he also wants to be certain that he chooses someone whom others respect—as a running mate, as a vice president, and potentially as a successor. When the choices have been announced, the nominee always hails his running mate as the person in the nation most qualified to assume the presidency should anything happen to the president.

The vice presidential nominees are certainly chosen to aid the national ticket. In the past, they were often selected to balance the ticket and balance some perceived shortcomings of the presidential nominee. George W. Bush's selection of Dick Cheney as his running mate in 2000 is in many ways a perfect example of this tactic. One of the primary criticisms of Bush in the 2000 campaign was that he was too inexperienced on the national stage, particularly in the arena of foreign affairs. In choosing Cheney, a veteran Washington hand with the extensive experience in national politics and foreign affairs that Bush lacked, Bush defused much of this criticism. Obama did a similar thing in naming Biden as his running mate in 2008. John McCain's selection of Sarah Palin in 2008 is another seemingly perfect example of selecting a running mate to address one's own perceived weaknesses. In 2008 many expressed the concern that McCain's age would work against him in the campaign. It was also widely noted that the evangelical wing of the Republican party did not particularly like McCain. In the choice of Palin—a young, energetic favorite of the religious right—McCain dealt with both of these criticisms and reenergized—at least temporarily—what was a lagging campaign. Similarly, many saw Barack Obama's selection of Joe Biden in 2008 as a way to add experience and foreign policy background to the ticket, while at the same time making it easier for Obama to appeal to members of the white working class. In 2012, Mitt Romney's selection of Paul Ryan can be interpreted as a way to signal the campaign's seriousness about fiscal responsibility while reaching out to Midwesterners and Catholics. For 2016, Donald Trump's selection of Mike Pence was almost certainly a way to reassure culturally conservative Republicans that he recognized their importance and shared their views, while Hillary Clinton's choice of Tim Kaine did not have as clear a reason. The importance of Kaine's home state of Virginia might have been part of the calculation, while Cassidy (2016) argued that Kaine's reputation as a consensus builder and his similarities with Clinton were important factors. It is also possible that Kaine's Roman Catholicism and missionary work in Honduras as a young man played a role in his selection.

An Evaluation of the Conventions

The national television networks have cut way back on their television coverage of the recent nominating conventions. They did this because the excitement was gone—because the ratings were not there. Obviously, they have every right to make that judgment.

But they are wrong. Conventions are important events. They are times for partisans to share and to celebrate. That is newsworthy. They are "comings together," which is what "convention" really means. Republicans and Democrats around the country can share this via television, if they are permitted to do so.

Television journalists define news as controversy. It is true that the last eight conventions of each party lacked that. But the rhetoric of Mario Cuomo and Jesse Jackson and Pat Buchanan and Barack Obama, the emotions caused by the nomination of Geraldine Ferraro and Joe Lieberman, the depth of feeling for Bob Dole and Fritz Mondale and Paul Tsongas, the humanness of photographer and outgoing Senate leader Howard Baker, the degree of unanimity behind and pride in Ronald Reagan and George Bush in 1984 and Bill Clinton and Al Gore in 1996—these too were important news events. So were the delegates' reactions to those individuals and their performances, but also their emotional reaction to the American flag and the National Anthem. Television misses a major opportunity for civic education by focusing on journalists interviewing journalists, when the public really wants to experience the thrill of a convention vicariously.

Conventions have not been forums for decision making in recent years. That is not to say they will not again become so. Delegates will continue to be pledged and bound (by conviction) to their favorite candidates. If one candidate has gained majority support before the opening gavel, the "competition" will be a charade. But if this does not eventuate, we may once again see real decisions made by conventions.

We can easily paint a scenario that would lead to the convention playing an important role for each party if the large number of states holding early caucuses and primaries do not produce a clear leader and more than two candidates remain viable. Others are free to hypothesize about how a convention faced with reaching important decisions would work, should the situation eventuate. The frank answer is that we do not know. Could candidates control their delegates? Would demographic representation—of women, blacks, Hispanics—become more potent? Would interest groups come to the fore? Would impressive rhetoric win the day? We just do not know. The old keys—domination by a few bosses—no longer fit, but it is unclear if anyone has yet cut the new ones.

Shortly before his death Walter Cronkite, the very epitome of a network news anchor in the heyday of convention coverage, nostalgically recalled conventions of another era, when the crowds and the demonstrations were important, when emotions swept the floor, when spontaneous excitement ruled the day. Conventions still have that potential. They are an important element of American politics and continue to deserve attention as potentially significant events, not as dinosaurs from another era.

(See Norrander 2010; Polsby, Wildavsky, and Hopkins 2008; Shafer 1988; Wayne 2008.)

THE PRESIDENTIAL NOMINATING PROCESS AS IT STANDS

Frequently how one views a certain situation depends on whether or not one benefits from that situation. Junior members of congressional committees like the seniority system less than senior members do. Five-foot-eight-inch point guards favor a wider lane under the basket more than do seven-foot centers. Such is human nature.

The same holds for how politicians view the nominating process. At one extreme perhaps is Walter Mondale in 1976. After testing the presidential waters for a number of months, Mondale withdrew. The reason: "I simply do not want it enough. I cannot face a whole year of nights in Holiday Inns." The process was dehumanizing. It was too long and too boring, and, in Mondale's case that year, offered too little hope for success.

Sometimes the criticism of the process deals with the rules. Thus losing candidate Morris Udall in 1976 became an advocate for regional primaries, to restrict the amount of time and money spent traveling. Others have advocated a national primary. Of course that would favor well-known candidates and hurt those seeking to make a name for themselves. Obviously how one stands on a reform like that would depend on where one sits. What is progressive reform to some is unfair to others. Politicians' ultimate view of the nominating system—other than complaints about how arduous it is—relates to whether they are helped or hurt by it. Jesse Jackson was hurt by the rules so he cried for reform (Norrander 2010).

The process will always be long. But its length does not seem to bother the winning candidates. Bill Clinton thrived on it in 1992. Bob Dole had no complaints in 1996, even though he traveled the length and breadth of the North American continent over and over. Bush and Gore thought the process worked just fine in 2000; it invigorated them. In many ways Barack Obama was at his best in the 2008 nominating process, speaking before large, rabidly enthusiastic crowds on the campaign trail. Both Obama and Romney seemed to rise to the occasion in 2012. Trump's success in 2016 has raised still more questions about the American presidential nominating system. The process will always be complex. It will always seem to favor some candidates over others. Some candidates will always be dissatisfied.

But the system can be viewed as successful if the citizens feel that the candidates have been tested fairly, in a variety of ways, under rules that were designed to be as fair as possible for all contenders. As the nation looks back on the 2016 nominating process it must ask itself if it believes these standards were met, regardless of its happiness or unhappiness with the eventual outcomes.

CRITICAL THINKING QUESTIONS

1. What is the best way to select presidential candidates?
2. Does the American presidential nominating process produce good presidential candidates?
3. Does the American presidential nominating process last too long?
4. Do vice presidential candidates matter?

KEY TERMS

presidential preference primaries
McGovern-Fraser commission
caucuses
geographic representation
demographic representation
ideological representation
winner-take-all primaries
superdelegates
front-loaded
Super Tuesday
regional primaries
filing deadlines
proportional representation
brokered convention
credentials challenges
party platform

NOTES

1. Much of this discussion focuses on the Democratic party because most recent reform efforts have been made by Democrats. Republicans have been more satisfied with their procedures but have had to change as well because many of the reforms implemented by the Democrats involved changes in state laws affecting both parties.

2. Partially in recognition of the Bush strategy, two candidates for the Democratic nomination, former Vermont governor Howard Dean and Massachusetts senator John Kerry, announced in November 2003 that they too would not take public money during the nominating phase of the campaign. Dean justified his decision as a necessary step to counter Bush after the nomination was won. Kerry said that he would not "unilaterally disarm," blaming Dean for forcing his decision. It should be noted that candidates who do not accept public funds can spend more in the early primary states than those who abide by the restrictions that are imposed on publicly funded candidates (see chapter 5).

3. Of the others, one resigned in disgrace (Agnew), one was an appointed vice president who had earlier sought the presidential nomination of his party (Rockefeller), and one has refused to seek the presidency, at least to this point (Cheney). Joe Biden chose not to run in 2016, but is considering a run in 2020.

4. John Connally, former governor of Texas who became famous when he was shot in the motorcade with President Kennedy and later switched to the Republican party (serving as President Nixon's secretary of the treasury), did so in 1976. Connally felt that his only chance for success was to outspend and thus outadvertise all his opponents. He felt, correctly, that he could raise a good deal of money from his Texas oil friends and the big business connections he had cemented during his tenure as treasury secretary. He was wrong in believing that he could parlay that money into a successful campaign. When Connally withdrew from the race, he had won only one delegate who, when interviewed on television at the Republican National Convention, was kiddingly referred to as the "$6,000,000 delegate."

5. The Clinton campaign used another extremely effective technique in the 1992 primary campaign, again seeking to communicate directly with the voters. The campaign mailed approximately thirty thousand campaign-produced videotapes to potential undecided voters in order to rebut personal attacks on the candidate. Polling results showed that those who in fact viewed these positive biographical tapes voted overwhelmingly for Clinton (Arterton 1993).

6. By any definition this is true in the Republican party. As mentioned earlier, in recent years the Democrats have permitted the National Committee and/or specially appointed commissions to change rules between national conventions. Whether these commissions in the DNC can overrule specific votes at a national convention is still in question.

Chapter 9

Presidential Elections

Donald Trump campaigns in Philadelphia, Pennsylvania, in the final weeks before the 2016 presidential election. No election in the world generates more attention or costs more money than the American presidential election.

As president-elect Barack Obama delivered his victory speech to approximately 125,000 ecstatic supporters in Chicago's Grant Park around midnight on election day in 2008, one had to appreciate what had truly been an outstanding campaign for the presidency. Whether one supported or opposed Obama, one had to accept that his presidential campaign was a masterpiece. Obama was able to raise money seemingly at will, far exceeding what previous presidential candidates had been able to accomplish. Campaign staff used advances in communications technology such as cell phones and social networking services on the web to build a grassroots network unparalleled in the history of modern presidential campaigns. The campaign was incredibly well organized in all fifty states and in the smaller jurisdictional units within those states, something many would have written off as impossible when the campaign began. This combination of skillful use of technology, grassroots strength, and nationwide organization allowed the Obama campaign to register millions of new voters, and a remarkably well-oiled get-out-the-vote machine turned out a high percentage of these new voters and other voters as well on election day. These accomplishments are even more impressive given that Obama was only forty-seven years old, a relative political neophyte involved in only his second campaign for federal office. Obama's successful 2012 reelection campaign mirrored these successes, and in many ways extended them even further. The Obama camp once again broke new ground and clearly demonstrated what a well-run presidential general election campaign looks like.

To see the opposite of a well-run presidential campaign, one only has to turn to the campaign conducted by Obama's 2008 general election opponent, John McCain. The McCain campaign was marred by vicious internal fighting and backbiting, forcing numerous personnel shake-ups. It never had enough money, a fact that limited what the campaign could do throughout the entire general election. McCain struggled to excite the Republican base, much less attract and register new voters. Even the selection of Sarah Palin as McCain's running mate—a choice that at least some lauded as genius when first made—backfired on the campaign as questions about Palin's qualifications and comments made by some supporters at Palin rallies caused many independents and undecided voters to support Obama. McCain's failures were all the more glaring given his experience as a candidate. McCain had run six successful congressional campaigns and had also conducted a well-regarded campaign for the Republican presidential nomination in 2000. But perhaps we should not be so surprised by the poor quality of McCain's 2008 effort. If anything, the Mondale-Ferraro campaign of 1984, the Dole-Kemp campaign of 1996, and the Kerry-Edwards campaign of 2004 were even more disastrous than the McCain-Palin effort. The 1988 Dukakis general election campaign, in terms of strategy and execution, paled in comparison to the battle for the nomination; so too did the reelection campaign of George H. W. Bush in 1992 (though many claimed his drive to nomination led to the difficulties in the fall). Mitt Romney's 2012 campaign was not a disaster by any means, but neither was it clearly an example that one would want to follow. It is important to note that none of these failed campaigns were headed by wet-behind-the-ears candidates.

This brings us to 2016. Donald Trump, who had never before run for any public office, defeated Hillary Clinton—who was central in her husband's two successful presidential campaigns, had run a very strong and credible campaign for the 2008 Democratic presidential nomination, and had won two elections to the U.S. Senate in New York—in what many described as the most shocking upset in U.S. presidential election history (Goldmacher and Schreckinger 2016; Healy and Peters 2016; Pilkington and Gabbatt 2016). Were the Trump and Clinton campaigns well run or poorly run, respectively? In many ways one can make a case for either, neither, or both, for each campaign. Part of this ambiguity has to do with the fact that to a certain extent the dust from the 2016 presidential election is still settling even as we write this in spring 2018. But part also has to do with the unconventional nature of the 2016 presidential race, where it often seemed as if nothing went according to script.

Why were the presidential campaigns of such experienced, seasoned candidates as John McCain, John Kerry, Bob Dole, and Walter Mondale plagued by problems? How were relatively inexperienced candidates such as Obama in 2008, George W. Bush in 2000, and Jimmy Carter in 1976 able to wage successful presidential campaigns against far more experienced opponents? What are we to make of the 2016 campaigns of Donald Trump and Hillary Clinton? How will the 2016 presidential election influence future contests? We will attempt to answer these questions as we look at how presidential election campaigns are run.

Before we begin, it is worth repeating our admonition from chapter 8 regarding the 2016 presidential cycle. Less than two years removed, it is difficult to say with any certainty what elements of the 2016 presidential election represent durable change and what elements are anomalous. Therefore we tread cautiously in this chapter, highlighting where the Trump campaign broke new ground (this was much less the case for the Clinton campaign) while at the same time not becoming overheated about the degree to which American presidential campaigns have entered a brand-new world.

FROM THE CONVENTION TO THE GENERAL ELECTION

Politicians at the national level spend a good deal of time complaining about the length of presidential campaigns. What they are really concerned with is the length of the campaign for nomination. For the candidates who win nomination, and for the advisers most closely involved with their campaigns, the break between the convention and the general election is almost seamless. They continue to campaign hard, to work on the same issues, to work at the same pace, with the same goal in mind. There is little time for relaxation or reflection.

What is lost in their fatigue is the realization that the general election is separate from the campaign for nomination. The opponent is different, the rules are different, the strategies are different, and the length of time one is campaigning is different. General election campaigns are in fact quite short. The party conventions are held in late summer. The general election is held on the first Tuesday after the first Monday in November. The general election campaign is over in about three months (although the general election phase of the 2016 presidential contest lasted about five months, as both Trump and Clinton had clinched their party's nomination by the first week of June).

In this short period of time, the candidates and their staffs must run a truly national campaign. The battle for the nomination involves a separate campaign in each state. Different states have different rules, and the political calendar extends through six or seven months. The general election campaign is different on all counts. Of the most significance is that the campaign must reach its peak in every state throughout the entire nation on the same date. Whereas during the preconvention period it was possible to run separate campaigns in each state and to reuse human resources by switching staff from one state in which the primary or caucus had been held to another state in which the contest was upcoming, in the general election the organization must cover the entire nation at one time. The logistics of an operation on this scale exceed anything that first-time campaign organizations have experienced.

Furthermore, the rules of the election contest make strategic planning intricate. The point in the general election is not simply to win a plurality of the votes. While vote maximization is desirable, in our presidential elections the winner is the candidate who is supported by a majority of the **electoral college**—the indirect means through which U.S. presidents and vice presidents are chosen. Therefore, each state is a separate contest. Campaign strategists must determine how much effort they should put into each of the states and which states to focus on. Because all states (except Maine and Nebraska) award the plurality winner of the **popular vote** with all of that state's electoral votes—the votes cast by delegates selected to serve in the electoral college—strategists not only focus on large states but also have to determine which states are lost (and therefore not worth additional effort), which states are safe (making further effort superfluous), and which states are competitive (and therefore worthy of increased effort).[1] These estimates must be evaluated and reevaluated as the campaign progresses.

Candidates for the presidency are interested first in winning, but they are also interested in winning with a large mandate. Therefore, even apparent winners cannot coast. They must be aware of their opponent's strategies and must counter them effectively. They must take into account the mix of voters throughout the nation as they respond to the events of the day. They are uniquely aware of the complexity and the magnitude of the job that they are seeking. They have reached the point at which they are not just among those considered for the presidency, but are one of two individuals who will hold that job. They must be certain that the conduct of their campaign does not make governing more difficult in the event that they win the election.

In the remainder of this chapter, we will look at the campaigns for the presidency, from after the conventions to the November election. We will begin by examining campaign organization and planning and proceed to look at the **strategy** (overall design and plan of a campaign) and **tactics** (specific techniques used to implement the overall strategy) used in these most important contests. (On presidential elections generally, see Kessel 1992; Polsby, Wildavsky, and Hopkins 2008; Wayne 2015. On specific campaigns see, e.g., Black and Oliphant 1989; Ceaser and Busch 1993, 1997; Drew 1981; Germond and Witcover 1985, 1989, 1993; P. Goldman and Fuller 1985; Jamieson 2013; May and Fraser 1973; Moore 1981; Moore and Fraser 1977; Runkel 1989; Schram 1977; Simon 1998; Thomas 2009; White 1965, 1969, 1973, 1982; Witcover 1977.)

ORGANIZING FOR THE GENERAL ELECTION

A presidential campaign is a highly complicated animal. Some aspects of the campaign are controlled in a centralized manner, but others are decentralized. Further, the magnitude of the tasks that can be handled centrally call for significant and sophisticated staffing.

Structuring the Campaign Organization

The Campaign Headquarters

A number of questions must be faced when a nominee and his closest advisers reassess their campaign organization after their national convention. A very basic question involves the location of the campaign headquarters. Should there be one national headquarters for the campaign? Probably yes. Where should it be located? Washington is the logical choice, but it is not the only choice. In 1992, for example, candidate Bill Clinton decided that his national headquarters would remain in Little Rock, Arkansas. For Clinton, Little Rock was a strategic choice. Like Jimmy Carter, the last Democratic Southerner elected president, Clinton wanted to emphasize that he was not part of the old Washington crowd. In 2008 Barack Obama also avoided Washington and maintained his headquarters in Chicago, largely to keep intact his successful primary team. Obama once again used Chicago as his headquarters in 2012. In 2016 both candidates set up shop in New York City, Trump at his eponymous Trump Tower in Manhattan and Clinton a mere seven miles away in Brooklyn.

Prior to the past few presidential cycles many candidates have chosen Washington as their national headquarters, a decision dictated, in part at least, because Washington is the seat of government and also the home of the Democratic National Committee (DNC) and Republican National Committee (RNC). The mere mention of these committees, however, raises another set of questions.

The National Committee

What should be the relationship between the candidate's personal organization and the staff of the national committee? This is not an easy relationship to work out. Obviously the national committee staff is a resource that a candidate should use. Once the nominee has been chosen, the national committees are dedicated to helping their candidate win. On the other hand, the national committee is an organization that is at least somewhat out of the candidate's direct control, and also an organization that has concerns beyond the presidential election. So campaigns do have to devote some time and attention to how they want to utilize the national committees.

This process is easier at some times than at others. When an incumbent president is renominated, the national committee staff is often pretty much under his control before the nomination is secure. Thus throughout 2012 it was clear that the staff of the Democratic National Committee was fully under the control of President Obama and was 100 percent committed to his reelection. But what if no incumbent president has a nomination in hand or an out-party nominee begins to organize for the general election? Then the national committees must bide their time and wait for a particular candidate to secure the nomination. This delay sometimes makes integrating the national committee fully into the efforts of the candidate's campaign more difficult. We saw this with the Romney campaign in 2012. Even in these situations, however, the national committees are still important resources for campaigns to tap. The national committees have connections to state and local party organizations across the country, connections that can be crucial to success on election day—as the Obama campaign demonstrated in 2008. The Clinton campaign also took advantage of DNC resources in 2016, even before securing the nomination, much to the dismay of Sanders supporters (Brazile 2017; Heersink 2017). The national committees can also raise large amounts of money that they can spend on their presidential candidates in the form of independent expenditures, as the RNC did for both McCain in 2008 and Romney in 2012. Although the specifics vary, every campaign must address how the national committee fits into its overall plan. This was a particularly fraught question for Trump's campaign in 2016. Trump ran as a party outsider, regularly deriding the party and its established leaders. In turn, many establishment Republicans viewed Trump with disdain. But once Trump secured the GOP nomination, the candidate and the RNC were in many ways stuck with each other. Moreover, they needed each other. The RNC obviously needed Trump in order to secure the White House for the party, and Trump needed the Republican Party apparatus for fundamentally important matters such as voter targeting, technological support, and get-out-the-vote (GOTV) efforts (Confessore and Shorey 2016; Pramuk 2016).

The Mobile Headquarters

But if the definition of campaign headquarters is where important decisions are made, then one must also consider the mobile nature of presidential campaigns in this era of crisscrossing the nation in a matter of hours. In a very real sense, the campaign headquarters is where the candidate is. Presidential campaigns travel in an airplane that is outfitted for the comfort of the candidate and the needs of his staff. In essence, the candidate's plane is a traveling office (Kessel 1992, 123–24). Those traveling with the candidate (not those in the permanent campaign headquarters) make many of the important strategic decisions, since decisions must often be made quickly. Thus candidates often insist that their most trusted advisers travel with them. However, those on the plane can lose sight of the fact that many important decisions need not be made instantaneously, but rather require planning and staff work and must be made back in the more permanent headquarters.

Campaign managers face a dilemma. On the one hand, they know that managing a national campaign with a multimillion-dollar (soon possibly to be multi*billion*-dollar) budget represents a major administrative challenge. To handle this task requires time for planning, staff assistance, and a complete organization. On the other hand, they need access to the candidate, and he needs their counsel on the road. Most managers divide their time between the permanent headquarters and the plane—the traveling headquarters of the campaign.

In 1992 the Clinton campaign came up with a new headquarters concept. While some of Clinton's principal advisers traveled with him, others, including strategist James Carville, typically remained behind in the Little Rock "war room." Carville was convinced that the Dukakis campaign in 1988 suffered from an inability to respond to the actions of the campaign of George H. W. Bush. He did not want to repeat that error. Thus, taking a page from military strategists, he organized a rapid response team in the Little Rock headquarters. These strategists were constantly in touch with what was happening throughout the nation, as well as with the presidential candidate and his wife; the vice presidential candidate, Gore, and his wife; and others on the campaign trail. The successful Clinton pattern has been followed by all campaigns since that time, although not all campaigns have followed it with equal skill, and each campaign maintains a somewhat idiosyncratic mix of who goes with the candidate and who works from the campaign headquarters.[2]

Division and Integration of Authority and Responsibility

Since a presidential campaign requires a tremendous amount of work, a large number of people, all of whom are quite powerful politically, are involved in organization and management. Authority is divided among the campaign manager, the chair of the candidate's campaign committee, and perhaps others with titles such as chief strategist, pollster, or simply adviser. The chair of the national committee is also often a powerful voice in the campaign. Each of these has access to the candidate; each came to the campaign with a certain power base; each hopes to leave with more power. Each definitely has a personal stake not only in the outcome of the campaign but in his or her own role in reaching that outcome.

In addition, various individuals assume authority over functional aspects of the campaign. They carve out their own space and either apply existing expertise or quickly develop expertise, so that they know the area in which they are working better than anyone else. In short, they make themselves indispensable. These individuals must be made to fit into the campaign organization. On the one hand, they are important cogs in a wheel that needs to be complete in order to function efficiently. On the other hand, they demand (and often require) a certain amount of autonomy. The juggling act is often difficult.

One test of a campaign organization is how well it all works together. With the stakes so high, for the candidate and for the individuals involved, with the time so short, and with the task so formidable, it is possible that integration of the campaign organization is never accomplished. A fragmented campaign often is the result of frustration when strategies are not working; that kind of fragmentation only compounds the problems that created it. Observers of the Dukakis campaign in 1988 believed that his problems came from an inability to listen to what his advisers said (Black and Oliphant 1989). The losing efforts by President Bush in 1992 and Bob Dole in 1996 both showed signs of leadership difficulties. The extremes of organizational quality can be seen in the 2008 race. Obama's campaign organization worked together almost flawlessly. Chief strategist David Axelrod, campaign manager David Plouffe, communications director Robert Gibbs, adviser Valerie Jarrett, and other key personnel were seemingly always on the same page, although there were numerous reports that Plouffe and Jarrett did not like each other very much (Kornblut and Wilson 2011; Thomas 2009). The McCain campaign was almost the complete opposite. McCain himself could not respect any type of chain of command, and regularly consulted advisers without the knowledge of his other advisers. The campaign infighting was so intense that it became a regular story in the media. McCain even went so far as to install a new campaign chief—Steve Schmidt—in July of 2008, a very rare move. All in all, the McCain campaign team did not work together well at all, and it was never able to design and fully embrace a coherent strategy for the candidate to follow (Nagourney 2008a; Thomas 2009). Obama's team once again jelled very well in 2012. While there were some reports of infighting among Romney's inner circle—most prominently surrounding chief strategist Stuart Stevens (Allen and VandeHei 2012)—these reports were disputed by many in the campaign. Regardless of whether there was truth in these assertions, one can say that Romney's 2012 campaign was not anywhere close to the level of dysfunction exhibited by McCain in 2008. By all accounts Clinton's campaign team worked very well together in 2016, while Trump's campaign was seemingly in constant disarray. Yet in this case Trump emerged victorious while Clinton went home disappointed. Generally disarray results in failure, but by now we are all well aware of how Donald Trump prefers to operate in chaos, and thus conducted his campaign accordingly (Schwartzman and Johnson 2015; Sullivan and Costa 2016). More will be said regarding the importance of staffing elsewhere in this chapter.

Functions of a Presidential Campaign Organization

In simplest terms, the function of a presidential campaign organization is to carry the candidate's campaign for the presidency to the length and breadth of the country. The structures adopted by various campaigns over the years to achieve this goal have had a number of similarities.

Grassroots Politics

After securing a presidential nomination, candidates and their top aides do not take time to rest; rather they are engaged in a different type of activity that is, though less visible, no less important. They are engaged in the task of building and cementing an organization that spans the nation, that draws in as many different types of people from different locales as is possible, and that is ready to jump into action, to perform the tasks necessary to campaign nationally, as soon as it is called upon.

These tasks involve the grassroots approach to politics. Friends and neighbors must be convinced to support the candidate. A campaign must be visible in area after area. There must be a feeling that it is right to support a candidate actively because many others are doing so. When the candidate or his running mate appears in an area, enthusiastic crowds must be in evidence. This enthusiasm breeds more enthusiasm, but the initial response does not occur spontaneously; it results from continuous activity on the part of the most active on board. This is one of the many areas in which the Obama campaigns excelled. Obama was able to match this level of success in 2012. Clinton's 2016 campaign was unable to come anywhere near this level of enthusiasm, while Trump's campaign generated Obama-esque levels of mass excitement, based primarily on the charisma and salesmanship of Trump himself. This was crucial for a campaign that lacked many of the traditional elements of a successful campaign.

Geographic organization. Basic to any presidential campaign organization is a national campaign committee that stands at the pinnacle of a pyramid of regional committees, state committees, and local committees. One test of the strength of an organization is its ability to find individuals willing to lead and serve on all these committees. Again, this is another area where the Obama campaign performed exceeding well, although it must be noted that here they were able to build on the 50-State Strategy put in place by former DNC chairman Howard Dean. This plan involved spending the money and putting in the effort to ensure that the Democratic party had an organizational presence everywhere in the country, even in places that were heavily Republican. Dean's strategy was controversial in the Democratic party at the time he first implemented it, but it paid off handsomely for Obama and other Democratic candidates in 2008.

Demographic organization. Further, campaign organizers must beware of the trap of thinking only in geographic terms. An activist woman from Pittsburgh might well relate more closely to women's groups supporting a candidate than to the Pittsburgh party organization. Consequently, campaign organizers frequently set up a series of committees based on demographic characteristics that are parallel to those based on geographic location.

For these committees to work, a number of conditions must be met. Group members must have a sense of unity and a sense that there is a reason for them as a group, not just as individuals, to back one candidate. Second, a key leader of the group must be willing to take a visible position, heading that group's efforts on behalf of the candidate. The leader must be aware of the internal politics within the group and of the ways to unify that group behind one candidate. Finally, the communications network between the campaign organization and the group organization must be extremely sensitive.

Establishing parallel organizations with overlapping responsibilities always creates the possibility of conflict. Every woman, every black, every Hispanic, every Jew, every member of every group lives somewhere. Most of these individuals are members of more than one demographic group. Many are members of other self-defined groups, for example, labor unions, teachers, and clergy. Their loyalty is often divided. They are undoubtedly part of a group for reasons other than electoral politics; members share a common interest but not necessarily a common political orientation. Group leaders in each group appeal for their support. These efforts, while all well-intentioned, can work at cross-purposes. Gaining the benefits of group efforts without losing support because of intergroup conflict or conflict between group organizations and geographically defined committees defines another test of the strength of a candidate's overall campaign organization (Kessel 1992, 125–33).

Staffing the Candidate's Mobile Operation

As mentioned earlier, one of the key decisions faced early in a campaign is deciding who should travel with the candidate. Many of the functions that are performed at a campaign headquarters for a local campaign are service functions for the candidate. It only seems logical that those who perform these tasks need to be near the candidate wherever he or she happens to be campaigning.

Press aides must accompany a candidate, since the press is traveling with the candidate. Speechwriters are similarly needed in a candidate's traveling entourage. For some time journalists have been aware that every candidate for national office develops a set speech that is given at virtually every campaign stop along the way. "The speech" is an important part of a candidate's campaign arsenal, but it is not the only public address given during a campaign.[3]

The speech is shaped and molded and improved along the way. Speechwriters come up with new lines for the candidate to try. If they receive a positive response, they are incorporated into the speech for future presentations. Some candidates work hard at the details of their set speech. Most leave that to the wordsmiths, staffers traveling with the candidate who are responsible for the candidate's spoken word.

"The speech" reflects the basic themes of a presidential campaign. A candidate must speak to a specialized audience or on a detailed or technical topic almost every day. The set speech is not appropriate for these occasions, and a speechwriter is called for. Many have marveled at the ability of candidates for national office to speak authoritatively on a wide range of subjects. Their real skill is to present the words of others as if they were their own.

When a speech to a group with a particular interest is called for or a new policy statement must be outlined, or a candidate must respond to an important event during the campaign, the candidate and his top advisers go over the general topic, refining the positions to be taken. The speechwriters then take over, converting some vaguely stated ideas into smooth-flowing prose that echoes the cadences and images thought to be unique to their candidate. If the speech is of particular significance, the candidate and top staff might review draft after draft, suggesting changes and calling for the amplification of some points or the downplaying of others. The test for a good speechwriter is the ability to write in the voice of the candidate. The true test for a candidate comes when he is asked to clarify points he has made in a speech that he has hardly had time to read.

Advance men and women make certain that a candidate's day runs smoothly. The plane carries logistical staff of various types. Campaigns employ teams of young staff members, many right out of college, whose job is to go into an area ahead of a candidate, plan all the logistics of the visit, and then remain for the candidate's visit in order to ensure that all goes as planned. Advance work has become an art, the art of knowing where a candidate should appear and when, the art of knowing which politicians to consult and which not, the art of knowing how to bring out the biggest crowd (or the crowd that appears the biggest), and the art of ensuring good visuals for the nightly news (see Bruno and Greenfield 1971 for a description of advance work by an acknowledged expert).

Key political advisers and strategists are another element of the campaign plane staff. Everyone with important responsibilities on a campaign must decide whether those responsibilities can best be carried out on the road with the candidate or at the national headquarters. Access to the candidate means influence, and those who view themselves as important often want to be traveling with the candidate at all times. Senior campaign advisers, in consultation with the candidate, must determine who should have instant access to the candidate and on whose counsel the candidate wants to be most dependent when key strategic decisions are called for. These decisions often change as a campaign progresses.

Staffing the Campaign Headquarters

Two functions, research and public relations, are a part of every presidential campaign. Speechwriters, as mentioned earlier, perform one type of research necessary for a campaign to function smoothly. But more is expected of a presidential candidate than the ability to turn a quick phrase. Speechwriters draw on the research performed by an array of issue specialists.

Some of these people are paid staff, professionals who are working on detailed presentations of a candidate's views. Others are supporters of the candidate, or of his party, drawn into the campaign for a particular purpose. Recent campaigns have used task forces of experts drawn from universities, research think tanks, and the private sector to work on a candidate's position in a certain area. For instance, Barack Obama relied heavily on a number of longtime associates from the Chicago area, along with individuals that he came to know during his short stint in the U.S. Senate. George W. Bush tapped those who had worked in his father's administration and scholars like Condoleezza Rice for expert advice. Bill Clinton used many friends and contacts. Most often a staff member coordinates the work of these groups and presents the material in a coherent way, ready for review by the candidate and his top staff and for eventual presentation to the public. Hillary Clinton in 2016 followed these models, building a team of longtime Democratic experts and operatives, many of whom she had known and/or who had worked for her for years. Donald Trump, on the other hand, ignored these models, and built his team primarily from family members and longtime personal friends and business associates, supplemented by the occasional experienced political operative who somehow managed to get into Trump's good graces. Again, Trump's approach here was not normal, but we cannot say whether this is a one-time anomaly or a harbinger of campaigns moving forward. It is simply too soon to say.

The general public is not very concerned about the details of the wide range of proposals presented by presidential candidates. However, one of the means that the press uses to assess the effectiveness of a campaign and the quality of a candidate is to evaluate the specific proposals floated by that candidate to handle the nation's problems. The press (as well as the most interested segments of the public) is also concerned about the quality of the individuals who are working for a candidate. A candidate's campaign advisers give some idea of the kind of people who will staff an administration should that candidate be elected. The press and the attentive public view these matters seriously.

Public opinion pollsters do an entirely different kind of research for presidential campaigns. Though the tasks and the methods are different from those researching specific policy issues, the results are put to surprisingly similar use. Public opinion polling has played an important role in presidential campaign politics at least since John Kennedy's campaign in 1960. However, as pollsters have become more sophisticated and as campaigns have become more sophisticated, that role has been changing.

Today every major party candidate for the presidency employs a professional public opinion pollster or a team of pollsters throughout the campaign. Candidates vie for the best pollsters. Public opinion firms are engaged in many campaigns in any cycle, but securing a presidential campaign is their most important prize.

Whereas pollsters once sampled public opinion a couple of times during a campaign, today that opinion is under scrutiny constantly. The latest polling technique involves a **rolling sample**: pollsters test public opinion continuously. They arrive at their latest judgments by replacing responses that are a couple of days old with ones coming in overnight, rolling over a third or a fourth of the sample each day. Thus the pollsters feel they can tell, on a day-to-day basis, how a campaign is moving, what appeals are working with what groups, and what ideas should be dropped.

In addition, public opinion experts rely on **focus groups** to supplement their polling data. Focus groups are smaller groups of citizens taken to be roughly representative of some subpopulation. Their views on a particular subject are probed in depth by a public opinion analyst. Focus groups are typically employed to see how people are likely to react to a new campaign initiative or to a proposed commercial.

The pollster of today is, almost by definition, a major adviser to a candidate. The pollster tests the political waters on new ideas, gauges how the public will respond to new issue positions or to the candidate's response to an emerging crisis, and advises how a campaign can present the best image to the public. Major party candidates for the presidency are too well known, and their positions are too well known, for any candidate to completely alter his or her views to fit the latest polling results. But that is not to say that these candidates are not capable of molding their views, and the data produced by their pollsters help them decide whether or not to do so. Today's pollsters are also bolstered in fine-tuning their designs by access to more data than ever before, and by the ability to analyze these data in ever-increasingly complex ways.

The press aides who travel with the candidate are not the only ones on a campaign concerned with public relations. They are only part of a larger public relations team. The public relations team works on many different fronts. Supplementing those traveling with the candidate are aides concerned with how the candidate is perceived by the press throughout the nation. The candidate on the road stimulates coverage in most of the nation's newspapers. The campaign headquarters staff concerned with press relations monitors this coverage and seeks means to ensure that the campaign is perceived in the best light. Campaign managers are very concerned about the image a candidate portrays in the daily newspapers, on the nightly news shows on television, and in the weekly newsmagazines. A good deal of effort goes into working with those responsible for the media (Adams 1982; Crouse 1973; Patterson 1980; Patterson and McClure 1976; Robinson and Sheehan 1983; Wayne 2008; chapter 10 discusses the role of the media in greater detail).

However, to an uncomfortable extent, how a candidate and a campaign are portrayed in the press is beyond the control of the campaign staff. Hard as they may work, the final decisions are made by those observing and interpreting their actions, not by campaign staff. In contrast, the campaign organization has direct control over paid media. A crucial part of the public relations effort revolves around producing paid media for the campaign. In modern presidential campaigns the media specialist has become a key political adviser. This situation was highly controversial when it was first revealed to the public in Joe McGinniss's popular book on the 1968 Nixon campaign, *The Selling of the President 1968* (1969), but it is now accepted as commonplace and unobjectionable. For many years, the primary concern of the media specialist was the production of television ads. While television is still critically important, the web has fostered a whole new breed of public relations experts on presidential campaigns, generally young politicos adept in designing websites and keeping them current, creating blogs, maintaining the candidate's Facebook page, and tweeting all material that requires tweeting. All contemporary presidential campaigns have to devote serious time and resources to ensure that they keep up with twenty-first-century information technology.

The public relations aspect of a campaign cannot be devised in a vacuum. What the candidate is saying on the road, what issues the candidate chooses to emphasize, how the candidate is perceived in the press, and the themes of paid media commercials and web-based information must all fit together in one harmonious package. In the 2000 election Vice President Gore was never able to define what he really stood for, to offset an image that he would say anything and do anything to become president. The job of coordinating and presenting a coherent message is the most important in the campaign. Its effectiveness is measured by public reaction, not by how critics respond to the way in which the message is portrayed (Buchanan 1991).

Setting a Campaign Strategy

The enormity of postconvention work cannot be overestimated. Certainly much of the organization was in place during the nomination battle, and the key advisers were all known. But the game has changed: the organization has to be expanded, the prenomination opposition must be co-opted and absorbed, and, most important, the new opposition has to be assessed and ultimately engaged.

Not only is setting a campaign strategy not glamorous work, but also it is not done in public. After the convention, candidates and their advisers are hard at work, devising a plan that will maximize chances of victory in November. The public is not privy to these plans, since their effectiveness would be limited if they were made known.

Chroniclers of recent campaigns have had access to some of these plans after the campaigns have ended (Caddell 1981; Drew 1981; Wirthlin 1981). Some are quite elaborate. The plan for Ronald Reagan's 1980 campaign filled two full volumes. Others have been little more than one-page outlines of what had to be accomplished. The sophistication of these plans says a good deal about the sophistication of the campaign organization. In fact, two sets of plans are put into motion. The first deals with the basic strategy of the campaign: What themes will be stressed? How will the candidate be portrayed? What issues will be spotlighted? Where will the necessary electoral votes be found? To whom will the candidate appeal? The second set of plans deals with tactics: How will the message be conveyed? What consideration will be given to **third-party candidates** (used to denote any candidates other than those of the two major parties), if any are relevant? When and how will debates be structured? The tactical matters deal with how the strategic elements will be implemented.

STRATEGIES FOR THE GENERAL ELECTION

Every campaign must deal with various types of strategies, and these can be categorized in a variety of ways. We will look first at geographic determinations. In this section the basic questions deal with how the campaign views the country. Where are the necessary votes likely to be found? From there we move to considerations of group dynamics. Just as the campaign organization must be built geographically and demographically, so too must strategies be set to appeal to specific groups as well as to specific regions. Finally, we will look at the way in which the candidate is to be perceived. What is the basic theme of the campaign? Why should citizens support this candidate and not the other one? What kind of person is the candidate? How has he or she demonstrated the qualities that Americans look for in a president? What will the candidate do once in office? What concerns are highest on her or his priority list? How does the candidate respond to the issues of the day?

Geographic Determinations

The basic goal of a presidential campaign is deceptively simple: garner 270 electoral college votes. Campaign strategists are all well aware that the popular vote is not the vote that counts in presidential elections. Each state has a number of electoral votes equal to the number of representatives plus the number of senators (always two) who represent that state in Congress. As mentioned earlier, in forty-eight states, plus the District of Columbia, the candidate who wins the plurality of the votes wins all of the electoral votes.[4] To win the presidential election, a candidate must win a majority of the electoral votes—270 electoral votes. If no one wins that number, the election is thrown into the House of Representatives for an election among the top three electoral vote recipients. Were such a contingency election to be held, each *state* would cast one vote—presumably cast according to the views of the majority of representatives from that state, though the procedures for such an election would be debated at the time. Again, a majority of the votes would be needed to win.[5]

In point of fact, the plurality winner in the popular vote normally wins a majority of the electoral votes. No election has been decided by the House of Representatives since that of 1824. But the results of the 2000 and 2016 elections demonstrate how important the rules of the presidential electoral game are. In the 2000 election Al Gore received more than half-a-million more votes than did George W. Bush. The outcome of the election was not determined, however, until the Supreme Court ruled that Governor Bush had won the disputed Florida electoral votes. Bush's slim margin in Florida gave him all 25 of Florida's electoral votes and put him over the magic number of 270. While the Democrats and the Gore campaign challenged the way in which votes were and were not counted in Florida, it is important to note that no one seriously challenged the legitimacy of the Bush victory because he had received fewer popular votes. The same is true of the 2016 contest. Hillary Clinton bested Donald Trump by just short of three million votes in the popular vote, but Trump defeated Clinton in the electoral college vote 304–227.[6]

Different campaigns have used different techniques to determine which states are secure (won), which are hopeless (lost), and which are marginal (possible). Increasingly, the techniques used to devise campaign strategies are more and more sophisticated, but sophisticated scientific precision is not a substitute for political judgment. As has been oft repeated, politics remains more art than science. Strategies must reflect changing political times, multiple perceptions of the stakes involved, and the chemistry of certain candidacies, as well as the more stark realities of political analysis.

Perhaps the best way to understand geographic strategies is to look at the Clinton campaign in 1992. By 1988 the concept of an electoral college "lock" was part of the everyday parlance of political analysts. The "lock" referred to states that seemed to be safe for Republican presidential candidates in recent elections. Twenty-three states (with over two hundred electoral votes) had voted for the Republican candidate in every presidential election since 1968. If the states that supported only Jimmy Carter among the Democratic hopefuls in this period were added, considering them aberrations because of his Southern candidacy, the safe Republican states contained more electoral votes than the number needed for victory—the Republicans had a lock on the election. Despite losing the 1988 election to George H. W. Bush, Michael Dukakis demonstrated to some that the Republican lock might be "pickable." He came close to winning in a number of states that had gone to the Republicans for many years.

The 1992 Clinton strategy grew from what he considered a desperate situation—he was running third behind President Bush and Ross Perot in the early spring. In order to have any chance of winning, he needed to find a combination of states to give him an electoral majority. His strategists started with states that had gone consistently to the Democrats, added those in which Jimmy Carter had shown that a Southern Democrat (and eventually in this case, one with a Southern running mate) could do well, and finally tacked on those in which Dukakis had done better than expected. California and New York—the two biggest electoral prizes with eighty-seven electoral votes between them—were key to his strategy. By August both states appeared safe. The Clinton campaign could then put extra effort into other states—trying to secure what they thought were winnable states in the South, the Far West, and New England and then concentrating major efforts on the industrial heartland—states like Ohio, Pennsylvania, and Michigan. The results of the election show the extent to which the strategy succeeded. In addition to New York and California and the traditionally Democratic states, he won four Southern states, most of the Far West, all of New England, and the rust belt states of Pennsylvania, Ohio, Michigan, and Illinois (Ceaser and Busch 1993, 160–61; for discussions of geographic strategies in earlier campaigns, see Black and Oliphant 1989; Germond and Witcover 1985, 1989; Runkel 1989; Pomper 1985; Ranney 1985; Drew 1981; Jordan 1982; Moore 1981; White 1982; Schram 1977; Witcover 1977).

What does it mean to follow a geographic strategy? Put simply, the question is one of campaign resources. A campaign has a limited amount of resources—candidate and surrogate time, money for television, staff—no matter how those are defined. All votes across the country are not of equal value. A campaign puts more resources into states (and therefore looks for votes) that are more competitive but where it feels it has a chance. If a state is definitely won, then it will receive fewer resources—the candidate, the vice presidential candidate, and their wives will visit less often; less money will be spent on television. It does not matter by how much a state is won. There is no benefit in building up the margin of victory. What is important is that the state is in the win column and that its electoral votes are tallied. Conversely, if a state is lost, if there is no hope of winning the electoral votes, then it too receives fewer resources. It does not matter by how much it is lost, if it is lost.

In the last five presidential elections, much of the talk by pundits dealt with the so-called **battleground states**, states that were too close to call and into which both campaigns poured enormous resources because each campaign believed it could win (Liasson 2012). The results of the election show that these resources were spent in the states that were in fact most closely contested—Colorado, Florida, Iowa, New Hampshire, North Carolina, Ohio, Pennsylvania, Virginia, and Wisconsin, among others. The goal is to concentrate efforts in winnable states in which the outcome is in doubt. Assessments of which states receive how much emphasis change over the course of a campaign. That is the nature of the dynamics of campaigning. And second-guessing is always possible—what if the Gore campaign had expended a little more effort in New Hampshire in the 2000 campaign? What if Kerry had concentrated more on Ohio in 2004? But the theory that campaigns seek electoral votes and emphasize states that are winnable but not assured never changes. In 2008 the Obama campaign was able to expand the number of states in play simply due to the amount of money that the campaign was able to raise. In doing so Obama was able to win a few states that had gone Republican in recent elections. Even in some states he did not win, by spending money in them Obama was able to force McCain to do the same. This made for some difficult choices in the cash-strapped McCain campaign (Thomas 2009). In 2012 the Romney campaign claimed that Michigan, Pennsylvania, and Wisconsin were truly in play for their candidate toward the end of the campaign, and thus made moves to take these states. The Obama campaign's internal models disagreed with such claims, and kept its focus elsewhere. In this instance, the Obama folks were right (Moschella 2012).

A similar dynamic unfolded in 2016, as Trump's campaign insisted these same three states were in play while the Clinton team viewed them as safely for their candidate (famously referring to these states as her "Blue Wall"). This time, it was the Republicans who were right, and Trump stunned Clinton and the nation by winning all three: Michigan, Pennsylvania, and Wisconsin.

Coalition Strategies

The election is contested in the states, but voters do not see themselves merely as citizens of states, and they do not receive campaign stimuli as citizens of states only. Thus another approach that campaign advisers use is to look at voters as people who can be grouped according to their views on politics and may logically be expected to either favor or oppose a certain candidate. Strategies using this premise are less explicit than those based on geography, but they are nonetheless important in campaign planning.

Let's look back to the 1992 and 1996 appeals of Bill Clinton, as they serve as excellent examples. As mentioned earlier, Clinton's 1992 nomination marked a triumph for the Democratic Leadership Council (DLC), a group started by Southern Democrats who were convinced that their party needed a new, more centrist appeal. In their view, Democrats had based too much of their appeal on issues favored by relatively small minorities—blacks, gays, civil libertarians. While defending these groups involved important stands of principle, such actions also depicted the party as one defending the fringes and not concerned about the vast majority. Al From, the president of the DLC, argued that the Democrats could be true to their basic principles but still strive to appeal to a majority. He defined this group as suburban housewives, concerned with bread-and-butter issues, with the economy, with safety, with responsibility. The 1992 Democratic platform stressed these issues; candidate Clinton never strayed from them in the campaign. To a large part they made him President Clinton.

In 1996 the term **triangulation** came into common parlance. Political consultant Richard Morris, an old friend of Bill Clinton who had worked for both Democratic and Republican candidates, was brought into the White House for advice after Democrats were badly beaten in the 1994 midterm election. Morris's advice was simple: If Clinton positioned himself between liberal Democrats and conservative Republicans in Congress, he would be able to form a winning coalition. By "capturing the center," he would take potential voters away from the Republicans while losing no Democrats, as they would have no viable alternative to whom they could turn. The strategy, exemplified by passage of a conservative welfare plan, worked admirably. The Republicans screamed because Clinton was usurping their issues. He did get credit for "Republican" programs passed on his watch. Liberal Democrats were distraught because they were forced to abandon some cherished programs, but they could not desert their president. And President Clinton was reelected with relative ease.

Polling and historical data can tell strategists how they are perceived by and have fared among groups of voters. Just as it is possible to set targets for states by analyzing election returns, so too is it possible to set targets for group support. It is also possible to base some parts of a candidate's appeal on group loyalties. However, with few exceptions, group members do not live in concentrated geographic areas. Most campaign appeals go out through the mass media, which is by and large geographically based. Therefore, appealing to group loyalties as separate from geographic location is a difficult task for a campaign to undertake and is, in fact, a tactical matter to which we will return.

Issue Strategies

In one sense, events define the issues of a campaign. President George W. Bush's 2004 reelection campaign centered on the war on terrorism, because he was in office when the 9/11 attacks occurred. But in a very important way, the candidate sets the tone for a campaign. He does so by the force of his personality, by his statements about why he wants to be president and what he would do if elected, and by the concerns that he chooses to emphasize as he campaigns throughout the nation.

Campaign Themes

In 1992, President George H. W. Bush was constantly criticized for not having "the vision thing." He never understood the term and never understood what was missing. In a very fundamental way, what was missing was any sense of why he should be reelected president of the United States. His campaign never had a theme. He never gave the citizens a sense of where he wanted to take the country. In turn, the citizens refused to give H. W. Bush a second term in office.

When a campaign begins, the opening theme needs to be presented often and forcefully. Consider the 2004 and 2008 presidential elections. One could make the case that both were won and lost primarily on themes. In 2004, George W. Bush's theme was simple—America is in danger and I will keep her safe; John Kerry will not. For his part, Kerry did not have a clear theme. Indeed, it seemingly changed multiple times throughout the campaign. Bush won and Kerry lost. The 2008 campaign is similar. Barack Obama ran on the very powerful themes of hope and change. John McCain's theme, what there was of one anyway, seemed to consist of claims that Obama was not up for the job of president. Obama came out on top. This is why candidates spend a great deal of time thinking about how to make their thematic statements most effectively. The messages conveyed in early speeches and television interviews, the ways in which those messages are delivered, the audiences to whom they are directed, the efforts made to disseminate them to the public: these are all part of a campaign's opening gambit. A candidate is most able to define his or her own message, to articulate his or her own theme, early in the campaign. After that, the candidate often must respond to challenges from opponents and to events as they unfold. Donald Trump in 2016 is a classic example of the importance of theme. From the outset of his campaign Trump articulated clearly and loudly the central theme of his campaign—Make America Great Again. His message resonated with voters, and Trump never missed an opportunity to hit on his Make America Great Again message, sometimes in very un–politically correct language, which only served to further excite his supporters. Hillary Clinton's "Stronger Together" (or was it "Forward," or "I'm With Her," or . . .) never had a chance.

Candidates must have a good deal of faith in their basic theme—in the ways in which they are presenting that theme to the nation. Their campaign is built on that foundation. But what if it is not working? Campaign strategies are not static; they are not set in cement. Situations change and the candidate must react. Pollsters, journalists, strategists, and the candidate all make assessments about "how it is going." All these observers see what is working and what is not. They know when it is time for a change, when it is time for a "strategic adjustment" (Kessel 1992, 75–76).

Changes in the basic theme of a campaign are not easy to make. First, it takes some time to realize that all is not going as planned. With modern polling and with candidates sensitive to the "pulse of the people," feedback is constant. Still, it takes some time to realize that a pattern of failure is appearing, that the campaign is not having its desired impact. Second, those who have made the initial decision about a campaign's theme, by and large, are the same ones who are assessing this new information. The team consensus about what should work is not easily disrupted, just as it was not easily arrived at. The more a candidate is invested in the theme, the harder it is to shift.

Changes in general election campaigns are much more difficult than changes in primaries, for a number of reasons. No events in a general election campaign are as decisive as a caucus or primary defeat to signal the need for change. The general election campaign team has experienced too much success together for the candidate to consider a change in senior advisers. The compressed fall campaign means that there will be little time remaining to articulate a new theme and to sell it to the American people. Doing so might appear hypocritical. Finally, the advisers on board have given the situation the benefit of their best analysis, and thus it is unlikely they will come up with anything different.

Thus, despite the fact that campaigns are not static events, major thematic adjustments are most difficult to make. More frequently, concerns are expressed and minor adjustments are made. Tactical decisions, not strategic decisions, are the order of the day. And the days slip by while these assessments and adjustments are being made. Soon it is time for the final push to election day. And by that time, as political scientist John Kessel has so aptly put it, "time's up" (Kessel 1992, 76). The push to election day might be very important in a close election, but what one does in those last days cannot represent a major change in the themes that have been set out in advance.

Character as a Campaign Issue

In most instances Americans hold their presidents to a high standard. The press examines candidates for party nominations in great detail, and those who are found wanting are often left by the wayside. Bill Clinton and Donald Trump are the two notable exceptions here, as both had well publicized personal shortcomings on the character front and were elected president anyway. But in most instances character is an important issue. Americans vote for a party; they vote for a set of ideas; but they also vote for a person—someone they can trust to lead the nation.

Character was undeniably crucial in both of George W. Bush's presidential victories. Bush appeared to many Americans as one of them in both of his campaigns, or at least as how they envision themselves—honest, hardworking, friendly, down-to-earth. Bush does not put on airs; what one sees is what one gets. There is no pretense. This was very different from Al Gore in 2000. While Gore's friends liked him and say that he is a funny man in private (and often in public now as well), in the 2000 campaign he often came across as stiff and calculating. During the campaign he kept changing his personality. During the three debates Gore seemed to switch persona, morphing to meet his handlers' suggestions. The overall impression was that he did not know who he really was. The late-night talk show hosts and *Saturday Night Live* had a field day imitating the changing character of Al Gore. Although not as extreme, much of the same can be said of John Kerry in 2004. In the final analysis, voters chose someone they liked—even if they were unsure of his positions and even of his abilities—over someone with whom they could not become comfortable, even though they liked the policies he stood for and knew he was very much up to the job. George W. Bush passed the crucial "who would you like to have a beer with" test, while Gore and Kerry did not. Similarly, Barack Obama was viewed as a much more likable guy than either John McCain in 2008 or Mitt Romney in 2012. Even many of Obama's Republican critics would start their attacks on Obama with something along the lines of "I admit Obama is a likable guy. . . ." Even the character-flawed Bill Clinton and Donald Trump were seen as likable, Clinton more broadly than Trump, but Trump's supporters do really like him. Likability is incredibly important, and campaigns must take note of this dynamic and attempt to act accordingly.

The Issues Raised during a Campaign

Candidates for the presidency must be responsive to the issues of the day. They attempt to emphasize those issues that work to their advantage and downplay those that help their opponents. At times, events dictate how issues will affect a campaign. At other times, candidate strategy concerning issue emphasis has the most impact.

When the nation is involved in a foreign crisis, international concerns tend to dominate the issue discussion during a campaign. If America's sons and daughters are in harm's way, the citizenry focuses on these concerns.

However, in times of peace, domestic issues, particularly the bread-and-butter issues relating to the economy, are more salient. The electorate's attention to these issues is broader than it is deep. Citizens care how the economy is affecting them personally, and they credit or blame the incumbent president for these effects. They are not sophisticated critics of particular economic policies; rather they evaluate results. Controversial issues like affirmative action, abortion, or same-sex marriage are viewed at an emotional level; citizens have general views on these policies but they do not want to examine programmatic details.

The 1992 and 1996 elections provide relevant examples of how issues play in presidential campaigns and of how they can be used for strategic purposes. The first President Bush was accorded record high poll ratings after the victory in the Persian Gulf War in 1991. However, when election time rolled around in 1992, the popular frenzy over the lightning-fast military victory had died down. The electorate was more concerned about the economy than what Bush had done more than a year earlier.

The Clinton campaign emphasized the economy. Recall the now famous sign on the desk of campaign press secretary George Stephanopoulos: "It's the economy, stupid!" Candidate Clinton stressed the economy at every opportunity. He talked about the problems caused by the expanding deficit; he talked about the need to create more jobs, "to grow the economy." He talked about the failures of the Bush administration to handle the perceived recession. Other issues also worked to Clinton's advantage. The Republican Convention had been dominated by those stressing "family values." But the stridency of the debate made many uncomfortable; it seemed as if the Republicans wanted to dictate what values should be important to all citizens. Clinton talked about health care, education, and the environment—noneconomic domestic issues about which the public clearly cared. Clinton came out ahead of Bush on the issues strategy. The one area in which Bush had an advantage—foreign and military policy—was the one about which the people cared least.

Fast-forward four years. By 1996 the recession had ended. The deficit was receding and the budget moving toward balance. More people had jobs, and they were more confident that they would retain jobs in the future. The voters credited Bill Clinton for these improving conditions. Even though many economists believed that the seeds for the economy's improvement had been planted in the Bush administration, that was irrelevant. It was irrelevant that Clinton's policies at times were forced on him by the Republicans. What was relevant was that the public credited President Clinton with these improvements. The country was at peace, the economy was healthy, and people were optimistic. That left Dole with nothing to exploit but Bill Clinton's character flaws. Voters clearly demonstrated that they were more concerned with their quality of life and their economic future than they were with assessments of the moral rectitude of the man sitting in the Oval Office.

The 2008 campaign stands in stark contrast. By mid-2008 the war in Iraq, the key issue as the primary season began, had been replaced by concern for a diving economy; Senator McCain was saddled with the economic downturn that gripped the nation under President Bush's leadership. These economic concerns grew by the day as election day grew closer and closer. Obama convinced Americans he would do something to deal with the economic crisis. McCain was unable to do so. We all know how this election turned out. In 2012 enough Americans believed Obama's claims—that things were getting better and would continue to do so if he was reelected—that he did indeed achieve a second term. In 2016 Donald Trump tapped into concerns surrounding the economic and cultural insecurity felt by many members of the white working and middle classes, groups that felt they had been ignored in recent years. Trump's talk on immigration, fair trade, reviving American manufacturing and other issues important to these voters were critical in building his support. Too often Hillary Clinton's campaign seemed to lack any meaningful issue appeal, instead relying on the fact that she was not Donald Trump. In the end that was not enough.

The Strategic Use of Incumbency

We might think that incumbent presidents would have enormous advantages in seeking reelection, as we have seen that members of the House do. Think about the advantages an incumbent president holds. First, he has the power and prestige of the office at his beck and call. No one speaks for the nation as does the president. Even the most cynical political observer realizes that "Hail to the Chief" quickens the heartbeat of many Americans. When the president travels, he travels in **Air Force One** (the U.S. Air Force plane that carries the president), with "United States of America" proudly emblazoned on its side. When the president speaks, the presidential seal adorns the podium. The basic premise is that the incumbent is "our" president, and anyone else is a pretender to the throne.

Whatever the president says or does is news. Thus an incumbent president is guaranteed front-page stories in the nation's press every day. More than that, his views are considered important and legitimate merely because they are the views of the president. Few are willing to put presidential statements under the same scrutiny they put the statements of a mere challenger to office.

Furthermore, presidential action shapes events. When a president travels overseas, he is the U.S. government negotiating with another power. When a challenger travels, he is gaining experience in foreign affairs. When a president signs a bill into law, the law goes on the books. When he vetoes legislation, Congress must address his veto. When a challenger says what he would do, there are no consequences. When a president says that he will not close an air force base or that he will push a public works project, the base remains open or the bridge is built. Citizens know too well the difference between wielding actual power and promising what might be done. Presidents for some time have used the advantages of their office to time grants, appointments, legislation, and travel for strategic political purposes.

Presidents do not have to prove that they are capable of handling the office or that they have the requisite background and experience; they have held the job for four years. What is better experience for being president than having been president?

Finally, incumbent presidents have a political organization in place. In most cases this is an organization that has already run and won a national election. But even in the case of incumbents who have succeeded to the presidency, the White House staff serves the president for political purposes as well as governmental purposes. Their job is to keep the president in a strong political position so that he can achieve his policy objectives (Neustadt 1976); one consequence of this job is to enhance his chances for reelection.

All these advantages would seem to make incumbent presidents seeking reelection invulnerable. But three of our last seven presidents have lost bids for reelection. Before President Obama won a second term in 2012, Clinton was the first Democrat to be elected twice as president since Franklin Delano Roosevelt. Among Republicans, only Dwight Eisenhower, Richard Nixon, Ronald Reagan, and George W. Bush have achieved reelection in the twentieth and twenty-first centuries. The advantages in favor of incumbent presidents might appear to be strong, but their record of winning reelection is not unblemished.

President Truman won with great difficulty in 1948;[7] and Truman in 1952 and Johnson in 1968 each decided not to seek their party's nomination, in part at least because it seemed they would succeed in doing so only at great political cost. Presidents Ford, Carter, and H. W. Bush have lost in recent years. How can their cases be distinguished from those of the presidents who sought and won reelection with relative ease—Franklin Roosevelt, Eisenhower, Nixon, Reagan, Clinton, George W. Bush, and Barack Obama?

There are commonalities among Ford, Carter, and H. W. Bush. For all the advantages of incumbency, one important consequence serves as a countervailing force. Incumbents are held accountable for what happens while they are in office, even if they do not cause those events. President Ford was an appointed vice president who succeeded to the Oval Office upon the resignation of his disgraced predecessor. His term was marked by continuing controversy over Watergate and his pardon of President Nixon and by a recession in 1975. President Carter presided when the nation's prestige was compromised as night after night the news programs emphasized that "America was held hostage" by a band of terrorists in Iran, a reference to the Iranian Hostage Crisis of 1979–1981. The actions of terrorists in Iran and a continuing sluggish economy led voters to reject his leadership for that of the charismatic Ronald Reagan.

Similarly, despite his foreign policy successes, President H. W. Bush was blamed for the recession that was being felt in 1992. His position was further hurt by the fact that he refused to recognize the recession and continued on a policy course that citizens felt was not working. The judgment of the voters can be cruel; their horizon is very short. That Bush's policies eventually proved effective did not counter the citizens' short-term view that their economic future was not bright.

The lessons for incumbents seeking reelection appear to be clear. The incumbency is a tremendous advantage in running for the White House if the first term has been a successful one and is perceived as such as it is ending. Only an incumbent can point to leadership ability, experience, and accomplishments in precisely the appropriate context. Only an incumbent can say to the American voting public, "Let's not rock the boat.

Things are going well because of me. Why change?" Successful presidents can run a Rose Garden campaign in which the candidate is always seen as the president, not as a campaigner.

However, if the accomplishments are not there, if the country does not have a positive view of the way in which the incumbent has run the country, if the four years since the last election have been troubled ones, the president is likely to be blamed. If the difficulties outweigh the accomplishments, the election is just as likely to be a referendum on the last four years and the outcome is not so likely to be a happy one for the individual in the Oval Office.

TACTICS FOR THE GENERAL ELECTION

The distinction between strategies and tactics is often a subtle one. The *strategy* that a campaign adopts is its overall plan to convince voters controlling a majority of the electoral college that a candidate deserves support. The *tactics* are the day-to-day means used to implement that strategy. A strategic decision involves identifying areas of the country to be emphasized; a tactical decision would be how to carry the message to the specified areas. This section will review four specific tactical considerations to which all campaigns must give attention—scheduling of the candidate and other campaign principles, the message that will be used in the paid media, the issues that will be emphasized, and the decisions concerning possible candidate debates.

Tactical Considerations of Where to Go

The scarcest resource in a presidential campaign, as with a campaign for state or local office, is the candidate's time. Strategic decisions about what areas of the country to stress dictate some tactical decisions about where the candidate should campaign.

But other factors must be taken into account as well. What image should be portrayed on the campaign trail? Thus, the Gore campaign in 2000 decided that Vice President Gore and Senator Lieberman should campaign together, particularly early in the campaign. The tactical consideration was that Lieberman, a person of irreproachable character, the first Democrat to be critical of President Clinton during the Lewinsky scandal, would symbolize that Gore had distanced himself from the president's moral problems.

Other tactical decisions regarding candidate appearances deal with scheduling surrogates. Who should appear with the candidate? When?

Who would be best for which areas? Or who would suffice in less important areas? The 2000 Bush campaign knew that it would be able to use General Colin Powell only on a limited number of occasions. How should this be done? Where should they campaign with John McCain? These tactical questions were aimed at implementing a strategy that determined where the candidate would have to do well in order to win.

Tactics, like strategies, can be changed over time. Demographic shifts and change mean that state electorates are constantly changing. Turnout machines can also affect the degree to which an individual state is competitive. As some states become more competitive or marginal, as some campaigners gain in appeal or effectiveness, tactical decisions can be reviewed. It is difficult to make broad strategic adjustments, but it is much easier to refine the strategies by changing tactics. Candidate and surrogate schedules require some advanced planning. However, they require neither the lead time nor the fundamental rethinking that changes in strategy necessitate.

Tactical Considerations of Media Use

Today it is a given in planning a presidential campaign that a large percentage of a campaign's budget will be spent on paid media. The general strategy of a campaign lays out how the campaign will appeal to the voters and how a candidate will be distinguished from his opponent. Tactical considerations include what specific messages will be emphasized on the media campaign at what times. Of particular importance is the opening message, for this sets the theme for a campaign. Just as important is the way in which candidates respond to changing situations.

In 1992, James Carville, Bill Clinton's chief strategist, established the much publicized war room at the Little Rock campaign headquarters with the express purpose of being able to respond to anticipated negative campaign ads, gaining the tactical advantage of the ability to respond quickly with new, countering advertisements. Modern media technology allows campaigns to design, cut, and air commercials overnight. In 2004 the Kerry campaign failed in part because its response to the attacks on the candidate's character by the Swift Boat Veterans for Truth was too slow. The Kerry campaign failed to benefit from the tactic Carville had pioneered.

There are many ways in which the Obama campaigns of 2008 and 2012 were highly innovative, but perhaps nowhere more than in the use of so-called big data to identify highly specific groups/types of voters and then target them with personalized messages placed in finely targeted media (Bimber 2014; Issenberg 2012; Scherer 2012). Nothing like the Obama campaigns' efforts in this area had ever been seen before. This being said, it is also important to remember that a huge element of Obama's success in both 2008 and 2012 was the large number of highly trained and coordinated boots-on-the-ground volunteers who were the backbone of a highly sophisticated ground game (McKenna and Han 2014). While Hillary Clinton tried to replicate the Obama model in 2016 (and failed to reach that level of success), Donald Trump eschewed the Obama model—and really all established models—for how presidential campaigns relate to the media. Trump used Twitter to speak to millions of his supporters directly, cutting the media out of the equation. At the same time, he made himself available to the media much more extensively than candidates generally have done, at the same time he engaged in regular doses of media-bashing. Trump had built his entire career on successfully marketing his personal brand, and he followed this model in his 2016 campaign. It worked (for a discussion of this, see Appelbaum 2016). More will be said on Trump and the media in chapter 10.

Tactical Considerations of Which Issues to Discuss

The questions of what issues a candidate should discuss and what the emphasis of television ads should be are closely related. Right from the start, the content of the speech repeated at each stop by a candidate is a tactical expression of his basic strategy.

The tactical aspects of the 1980 Reagan campaign have been used as models by candidates in succeeding elections. The basic tactic was first to establish a positive image of the candidate and then to attack the opponent.

Reagan's campaign began by disabusing voters of the notion that his views were out of the mainstream and that electing him would be dangerous. His early speeches emphasized that his views were not set in ideological stone and that he was willing to change. When President Carter was unsuccessful in his attempt to convince Americans that they had to be afraid of a Reagan presidency, the Reagan strategists knew that their tactic had worked. Poll results confirmed this assessment.

At that point, Reagan's tactics changed. His image was secure, so he could begin to attack Carter's image. He could begin talking about the four-year Carter record. The tactical decision was to switch to issues that reflected badly on Carter, once Reagan's own image was secure in the minds of the voters. The final weeks of the campaign saw Reagan repeatedly asking one question, "Are you better off now than you were four years ago?" The tactic was to change the focus of the debate from Reagan's image to Carter's record. It was a most successful switch.

The 1992 Clinton campaign portrayed an image of an outsider, "the man from Hope," someone who wanted to change the way things were done. Once he had set that basic picture in the electorate's eye, he turned to the message that the economy was in trouble, that Bush did not have the answer, and that he would "grow the economy" and provide jobs for the American people.

The same tactic was followed by Barack Obama in 2008, and it is an obvious ploy for any relatively unknown candidate. To pursue this tactic, the issues discussed by the candidate reflect the same concerns as those portrayed in television commercials. The basic strategy of theme and issues had been set; the tactic involved ways to portray that message forcefully and repeatedly to the voters.

The Tactics of Presidential Debates

Debates between (or among) presidential candidates have become a familiar part of the election process, but it was not always so. Until 1960 the television networks felt that they were restricted from presenting debates between the Republican and Democratic candidates for the presidency because of the **equal time provision**, which specified that if any candidate for an office was given free time on television, all candidates should be given equal time. The networks were concerned about how this applied to minor party candidates. In 1960 Congress suspended the equal time provision to allow for the famous Kennedy–Nixon debates (Kraus 1962; see also Ranney 1979). These set one agenda for campaign tacticians for the future. Should a candidate seek (or accept) a series of debates with his opponent(s)?

The legal questions about the viability of debates have been ironed out, and the debates have now become a much anticipated, institutionalized part of presidential campaigning. Since 1988, the debates have been sponsored by the Commission on Presidential Debates, a privately funded, bipartisan organization headed by the chairs of the two major political parties.[8] But every four years the candidates still face tactical decisions regarding the debates, in these cases questions of how many debates will be held, when, under what format, and with what participants. Candidates also must decide on the tactics they will use during the debates themselves. Millions of Americans watch the presidential and vice presidential debates every four years. A good debate performance can significantly improve a candidate's chance of winning the election. A bad debate performance, especially one that features factual mistakes or other gaffes, can prove disastrous.

The significance of presidential debates can be seen in the 2008 election. Before the 2008 debates many Americans had determined that while they did indeed like Barack Obama, they were not sure if he was experienced enough to be president. Was he up for the job? This concern was likely the only thing keeping John McCain even remotely in the race. The general consensus on the 2008 debates is that Obama performed very well, and clearly bested McCain in each of the three debates that were held. In these performances, Obama was able to remove the doubt that at least some Americans were feeling about his ability to serve as president. Indeed, *New York Times* reporter Adam Nagourney described the 2008 presidential debates as "a prolonged tryout for Mr. Obama" (2008b). By the end of the debates Obama had convinced enough Americans to give him the job. In 2012, Obama was widely viewed as having been bested by Romney in the first debate, and according to post-debate polling the contest quickly tightened. But Joe Biden soon turned in what was viewed as a strong performance in the vice presidential debate, and Obama dramatically improved his performance in the final two presidential debates, preventing Romney from building on his momentum. Much conventional wisdom claims that debates do little to affect election outcomes, but any time that many people watch an event the potential for impact is most certainly there. The 2016 presidential debates drew huge audiences—the first Clinton-Trump debate drew 84 million viewers, setting the record as the most watched presidential debate of all time (Kennedy 2016; Stelter 2016)—but most would say they did not do much to move the needle in the contest. Clinton was widely seen as having won the first debate, while Trump was seen as having done much better in the second debate. The third was mostly uneventful and could easily be viewed as a draw.

The debates have become an accepted part of presidential campaigning. It is difficult to see how debates will not remain a permanent part of presidential campaigns. But they will also continue to raise tactical questions that all campaigns must address as they view ways to implement their strategies. And debates will have an impact—not necessarily a decisive impact, but surely one about which every campaign manager must be concerned.

THIRD-PARTY CANDIDATES IN PRESIDENTIAL ELECTIONS

The American party system has been described as a strong two-party system. Yet in six of the last sixteen presidential elections more than two parties have fielded candidates who have had a significant impact on the strategies of the major party nominees (and perhaps on the outcome of the elections themselves).[9] However, at the same time, third-party candidates are rarely able to earn any votes in the electoral college (only Strom Thurmond in 1948 and George Wallace in 1968 have done so since the New Deal), and have virtually no chance of winning the election.

Third-party candidates in American presidential elections frequently suffer a loss of support as election day approaches. Candidates win electoral votes only if they lead a state's ballot on election day, not if they do better than expected. Many voters realize that a protest vote for a third-party candidate is, in fact, a wasted vote, because that candidate will not win enough votes in their state to capture any electoral votes. Thus they are convinced that it serves their interest better to vote for whichever major party candidate more closely reflects their views.

Ross Perot's 1992 campaign stands as the most successful challenge to major party dominance of presidential politics since former president Theodore Roosevelt ran on the Bull Moose party ticket in 1912. Perot's appeal was unique. Rather than splinter off from one of the two major parties, Perot denounced them both. He claimed that he stood as an alternative to business as usual in Washington. Using simple "down-home" language, Perot based his appeal on a simple premise: He had been fabulously successful in business and would do the same in running the government. He would not permit the kinds of sloppy business dealings that had been exhibited by the Democrats and the Republicans. He would butt heads and not permit partisan differences to obscure solutions to pressing problems. He was the pragmatist who could do it right.

His theme was clear, and despite its oversimplistic view of exceedingly complex problems facing the national government, he struck a responsive chord. He also had one unique advantage over previous third-party candidates:[10] he was capable of and fully prepared to finance his own campaign. In fact, during the 1992 campaign Perot spent approximately the same amount of money as did the two major party candidates. Financing was not an issue in this case.

Perot crossed the first hurdle—viability—by gaining access to the ballot in every state. That alone is no mean feat. Every state has its own requirement. Some are quite onerous, though challenges by previous third-party candidates have eased the burden somewhat. Still, the logistical problem of exploring legal statutes and meeting petition requirements by the deadlines that are imposed is a major one. Previous candidates have had to rely on volunteers to cross this hurdle. Perot was able to hire "volunteers" whenever he needed to do so.

Viability also involves continuous exposure. In this case, while Perot's money certainly helped, his genius for gaining the spotlight was equally significant. He first announced that he would explore the possibility of running on Larry King's CNN television show. At the time King was a flamboyant host with a large following. He was not a hard interviewer. Perot appeared on King's show over and over, garnering free publicity not only from his appearance but also from the news stories that reported on his appearance.

His genius for attracting attention carried over into the claim that he would only run if "the people" urged him to do so. They were to do this by calling his 800 line and volunteering to help in his campaign. He aptly named his organization United We Stand, clearly with the intent of implying a large following. And people did decide to follow him.

Perot pursued his campaign theme assiduously, never getting off message. His tactic was simple: to belittle his opposition and to pose solutions that everyone could understand. Whether those solutions were in fact practical, or if they were politically possible, mattered little to him or his followers. He implied that he would impose them on the system, seemingly ignoring the branches of government coequal to the one he sought to head. But again, none of this mattered. When Perot withdrew from the campaign in July, he was seen as running even with President Bush and Bill Clinton in most trial heat polls. When he reentered the campaign, he never quite achieved that position again, but he was always a strong contender.

Two other aspects of Perot's 1992 campaign should be noted. First, he was included in the presidential debates, and his running mate participated in the vice presidential debate. There is no question that his participation had an impact on how those debates were contested and on the election. His mere presence on the stage gave credibility to his campaign.

Second, Perot reintroduced a forgotten form of political media advertising, the **infomercial**.[11] Perot bought half-hour blocks of time and went before the cameras to explain his program. Political experts derided his effort when he announced his plans, arguing that no one would watch. They were wrong. The audience tuned in to see what this new phenomenon in American politics was all about. As Perot stood before the cameras with his charts and diagrams, millions watched. Many accepted his points—and many more understood that the complaints he had about the way the system was functioning were valid, even if his solutions might not be.

Perot did not crisscross the nation. He did not have an elaborate national campaign structure. He followed virtually none of the techniques we have laid out as typical of presidential campaigns. He had a dedicated corps of volunteers and enough paid staff to use them effectively. And he went his own way. He frustrated traditional politicians who simply did not know how to react to him. And in the end, he had an impact, forcing the two major parties and their candidates to pay attention to his message and his followers.

Ralph Nader's 2000 campaign on the Green Party ticket also merits mentioning here. While the party did not poll as many votes as its leaders hoped, Nader was a force throughout the election and may well have been the factor that determined the eventual winner. The Greens hoped to poll

5 percent of the vote in order to qualify for public funding in the 2004 election. Nader fell far short of that goal. Nader did, however, raise the Green banner throughout the country; his candidacy was extremely influential in close states, especially those with strong environmental movements. Nader's candidacy affected the campaign in two ways. Before we look at these, however, it should be noted that Nader drew two types of voters—those who were disenchanted with both parties and excited by Nader and who turned out to vote for Nader as opposed to sitting at home; and those who were taken with Nader's positions on environmental and anticorporate policies and who voted for Nader for those reasons but who otherwise would have voted for Gore. Very few voters chose Nader over Bush; thus, the net effect of his candidacy was to take votes from the Democratic camp.

For some time the Gore camp chose to ignore Nader, but as the campaign reached its crescendo, it was clear that Nader was affecting Gore's chances in some states, especially those with strong environmental movements, like Oregon. Thus, the first effect of the Nader candidacy was to force Gore to put more resources into some states that he should have won easily, in order to avoid a loss. The second effect of the Nader candidacy was in holding the balance of power between the two major party candidates. In Florida, for instance, while Nader polled "only 96,000 votes," if one assumed that 50 percent of those would not have voted at all except for the fact that Nader was contesting and that Gore would have won 60 percent of the remaining votes (a very low estimate), Gore would have won Florida easily, with no worries about undervotes or hanging chads. The same could be argued about New Hampshire. The presence of this third-party candidate—and the ways in which the major party candidates responded to him—clearly had a determinative effect on the winner in 2000. One could also make a case that Green Party candidate Jill Stein hurt Hillary Clinton in the three crucial states of Michigan, Pennsylvania, and Wisconsin (Rozsa 2016).

In presidential elections, third-party candidates have been of three types. First, the minor party candidates who run on ideologically pure platforms. Their goal is to express their views in the public forum. They expect to (and do) have little impact on the result of the election. But they play an important role by raising public debate on critical issues.

The second type of candidate represents a group that is splintering from one or the other of the major parties, or both. The 1948 Dixiecrats are a perfect example of this kind of third party. Generally, the major parties reabsorb these third-party candidacies after one election. But as demonstrated in chapter 2, other scenarios are possible. If the major parties do not respond, then a new party can come into existence, replacing one or both of the major parties.

Perot represents a third type of third-party candidate—one based on the individual. As individuals frequently act as catalysts for a split from the major parties, it is difficult to be certain that this category is in fact distinct. Was George Wallace's campaign a split within the party or the effort of one man? Perot's case can be differentiated in two ways, however. First, he had no previous allegiance to either of the major parties; nor did many of his followers. He was appealing to those who were disaffected with politics as usual. Second, he institutionalized what had been personal by establishing the Reform party. But the institution was not able to outlast the candidate. (For further discussions of the significance of the Perot campaigns, see Black and Black 1993; Abramson et al. 1995; see also Aldrich 1995; Abramson, Aldrich, and Rohde 1995; Bibby and Maisel 2003; Rapoport and Stone 2005; and Rosenstone, Behr, and Lazarus 1984.)

THE ALL-CONSUMING NATURE OF A PRESIDENTIAL CAMPAIGN

From a candidate's perspective, the key aspect of a presidential campaign is that it is totally consuming. If the incumbent president is running, he certainly has other duties to perform. But the emphasis is on winning reelection. The duties of the presidency are performed around the exigencies of the campaign. For the challenger (or if no incumbent is running, for the two presidential candidates), the campaign is everything. The race for the White House is the peak of any candidate's political career. There is no higher prize in the American system; no higher stakes exist.

Once the strategy is set and the active phase of the fall campaign begins, the two presidential candidates and their chief surrogates are on the road constantly. If the campaign is going well, then they continue what they are doing. If it is not going well, then they must figure out what to do with the feeling that they are not accomplishing their goals. But they cannot sit down and think about a new strategy. They must leave that to someone else. They simply do not have time. The candidate and his entourage can have input, but their fate is in the hands of the organization they have carefully molded over an extended period of time. And they must live with the results.

Think back on the career of Al Gore. Son of a senator, Gore first rejected politics for a career in journalism. However, clearly affected by his father's career, including the loss of his Senate seat in a bitter campaign, Gore turned to politics himself. He was elected to the House in 1976 and reelected three times. He was elected to the Senate in 1984. In 1988, he sought the Democratic nomination for president but was rejected by the voters. He was the first candidate to try the Democratic Leadership Council strategy of appealing to more moderate Democrats, not to the liberal wing of the party. Reelected to the Senate in 1990, Gore was tapped by Bill Clinton to run for vice president in 1992. For the next eight years, he was the hardworking number two. He did what he was asked. He was Clinton's partner in the White House. He was the loyal party man. And he waited his turn.

Gore was Clinton's heir apparent, and he was ready. He had served his apprenticeship. He had served the party. He won the nomination, beating a stubborn Bill Bradley, demonstrating that he could take on a fight. But during the general election, he never could resolve the Clinton problem. How did he accept credit for the accomplishments of the Clinton administration in which he had played such a key role without being tainted by the scandal mentality that pervaded Washington for eight years?

Gore struggled with this issue. How could he be his own man? How could he show the nation that he deserved to be president? To the end there were those in his campaign who urged him to let Clinton loose, to let Clinton save the Gore campaign. But Gore stuck with his own sense that he had to do it on his own. And then he and his family faced election night—and the night after, and the night after, and more than a month of counting in Florida. In the end, while a plurality of those who voted chose Gore, the electoral college majority went to George W. Bush. And Al Gore, as the sitting vice president, faced the unenviable task of announcing his opponent's victory before a joint session of Congress.

How did Gore react to this devastating defeat? He had put himself before the American public, asked the voters to weigh his lifelong commitment to service, and was rejected. And to many observers it was a rejection of Gore the man, not the policies he favored. Al Gore's reaction seemingly was one of equanimity. He had done the best he could. He would move on to something else—but he would decide later if he would run again. By 2006 Gore had reemerged as an important figure in the environmental movement, winning rave reviews and an Oscar for his film, *An Inconvenient Truth,* focusing attention on the earth's climate crisis. Followers urged him to run for president again. He thought long and hard on that course of action. All potential presidential candidates must focus on the personal costs that they will bear—and that their families will bear. In the end, he did not return to that arena.

As you think about Al Gore considering another presidential race, consider the amazing tenacity of Thomas Dewey, of Adlai Stevenson, of Richard Nixon, and of Hubert Humphrey. If you do not know about their careers, you should look them up. Their lives speak volumes about this nation's call to public service. How these men could receive the verdict of a nation regarding their candidacy and then come back to run again is difficult to comprehend. Each must have had a great sense of his own worth, of his ability to convince the nation that its decision had been in error, or of the inability of his strategists to convey the correct image and message. Nixon went on to victory and then to disgrace. Humphrey died as the Happy Warrior, seemingly always ready to have another go at the nation's highest office.

For most, however, one unsuccessful campaign for the presidency is enough. A number of candidates have tried in the prenomination phase more than once, but few have come back from a losing general election campaign to try again. Why? Because of the effort involved, because of the finality of the decision, because once one has campaigned throughout the entire nation, once one has presented his best effort to the electorate, and once one has been rejected, that verdict is enough.

In contrast, victorious presidential candidates want to have that experience again. There was never any doubt that Barack Obama was going to seek a second term in 2012. Harsh personal attacks did not deter Bill Clinton from seeking reelection; George H. W. Bush's health did not deter him; Ronald Reagan's age did not deter him; Jimmy Carter's lack of popularity did not deter him. In the last seventy-five years, only Lyndon Johnson, saddled with an unpopular war and dissent within his own party, and Harry Truman, in much the same situation, did not run for reelection when they were eligible (and each of these had served more than one full term, having first succeeded to the presidency). Victory in a national election seems to have nearly aphrodisiac qualities. "If the public loved me once, they will love me again. And I owe it to them to give them the chance." That very personal reaction is the essence of a candidate's evaluation of a presidential campaign.

CRITICAL THINKING QUESTIONS

1. Should the electoral college be abolished in favor of electing the president via the national popular vote?
2. It is often asserted that whichever candidate (of the two major party candidates) wins the "who would you rather have a beer with" contest wins the presidential election. Do you agree or disagree with this assertion?
3. Do presidential debates matter?
4. Should there be a recall procedure for the office of President of the United States?

KEY TERMS

electoral college	rolling sample	triangulation
popular vote	focus groups	Air Force One
strategy	third-party candidates	equal time provision
tactics	battleground states	infomercial

NOTES

1. In Maine the winner of the First Congressional District's popular vote receives one electoral vote, the winner of the Second Congressional District's popular vote receives one electoral vote, and the winner of the entire state receives two electoral votes. Since this provision went into effect (1976), Maine delivered all of its electoral votes to the same candidate every time until 2016, when it delivered three electoral votes for Clinton and one for Trump. Nebraska switched to a similar system for 1992, and split its electoral vote for the first time in 2008, four votes for McCain and one for Obama. A 2016 bill to switch Nebraska back to a winner-take-all system failed in the state's legislature by one vote.

2. The drama of the 1992 Clinton campaign experience was captured in the film *The War Room,* released in 1994.

3. "The speech" is as much a part of the arsenal of candidates when they are seeking the nomination as it is after they are nominated. In January 1988, the *New York Times* ran a series in which the set speeches of those seeking the nomination were reprinted. Similar series have appeared in various newspapers across the nation in each subsequent campaign.

4. Recall note 1 of this chapter.

5. The general procedure for the contingency election is spelled out in the Constitution, in Article 2 and in the Twelfth and Twenty-second Amendments. The specific procedures to be used in the House would be determined by the rules adopted by the House at that time. In a curiosity that has given pause to many analysts, the president would be elected by the House, but the vice president would be chosen by the Senate. In this age of divided government, it would theoretically be possible for the two individuals so chosen to be from different political parties.

6. As per election results Trump earned 306 electoral votes and Clinton earned 232, but in 2016 a record seven presidential electors voted for someone other than the candidate they were pledged to. Two Trump electors defected (voting for Ron Paul and John Kasich) while five Clinton electors defected (three voted for Colin Powell, one for Bernie Sanders, and one for Faith Spotted Eagle).

7. The 1948 election was the first time Truman had run for president on his own, but he had served all but a few months of the fourth term to which President Roosevelt had been elected in 1944.

8. The Commission on Presidential Debates took over this role from the League of Women Voters, which had sponsored presidential debates in 1976, 1980, and 1984. The commission itself is somewhat controversial because it is

made up of Democrats and Republicans and it makes decisions about whether third-party candidates should be involved in the debates.

9. In addition, a series of minor party candidates have qualified for the ballot in some states in virtually every modern presidential election. The role of minor party candidates in American politics is an interesting one, particularly in historical perspective, but these candidates do not have significant impact on either the strategies of the major party candidates or the outcome of the general election. For those reasons only, they are not dealt with in greater length in this text. (See Bibby and Maisel 2003; Mazmanian 1974.)

10. We have been using the term *third-party candidate* to refer to any candidate other than one of the two major party candidates. In fact, the individuals under consideration have been, more often than not, independent candidates, not third-party candidates, because the labels under which they ran were not those of political parties that meet the definition used throughout this text.

11. Obama revived the infomercial in presidential campaigns, airing a thirty-minute advertisement on three major broadcast networks and four smaller channels at 8:00 p.m. on October 29, 2008. The airtime for the infomercial cost a little more than $3 million, and was viewed by 33.5 million Americans. In contrast, Perot's eight infomercials averaged 13 million views, with a high of 16.5 million (Reuters 2008; Rutenberg 2008).

Chapter 10

The Media and the Electoral Process

The media environment in American politics changes on a seemingly daily basis, as social media becomes more and more important in terms of how voters, candidates, and parties engage in the American political process. This being said, more traditional campaign tools and media such as television spot advertising, direct mail, and free/earned media coverage by television broadcasters and daily newspapers remain critical as well.

How many of the candidates for president in 2016 did you see? We do not mean "see" as in seeing on television or the web. We mean "see" as in seeing face-to-face in person, whether across a room, in an auditorium, or even at a football stadium. We do not want to be too restrictive in our definition.

Let's take a step back from the top office in the land. How many of the candidates for governor, U.S. senator, or even member of the House of Representatives in 2016 in your state did you see (same sense of the word)? One? None? Well, if you didn't see these people often enough to form an opinion about them and their views, then how did you learn about them? Where did your political information come from?

A century ago the answer to that question would have been easy. Citizens did not know much about candidates for office. But they did know about political parties. And candidates were candidates of political parties. Today, candidates have greater control over their campaigns, and in many instances greater freedom from their parties. Citizens proudly claim (somewhat inaccurately) that they vote for the candidate, not the party. How do they find out about the candidate?

The short answer is that they find out from "the media." But that very answer begs the question. What do we mean by "the media"? How are political messages communicated through the media? How effectively does this institution serve our democracy?

THE MEDIA IN THE CONTEMPORARY CONTEXT

Sixty years ago, newspapers dominated the mass media that affected American politics. Citizens learned the news of the day through their daily papers; in major cities multiple newspapers competed for the public's attention, and both a morning and evening newspaper were standard. Newspapers lost their primacy with the emergence of television, and today newspapers face an uncertain future. By the late 1950s television sets had saturated the American landscape. Today 99 percent of American homes have at least one television, and two-thirds have three or more.

Thirty years ago, three major networks—ABC, CBS, and NBC—dominated television broadcasting. According to the Project for Excellence in Journalism (2010), in 1980 the three network nightly news broadcasts combined for a Nielsen rating of 42.3, meaning that 42.3 percent of all television households in the United States were tuned into one of the nightly news broadcasts. By 2013 this same Nielsen rating was 15.3. In terms of viewers, the network broadcasts have dropped from a combined 52.1 million viewers in 1980 to 23.8 million in 2016 (Pew 2017c), despite a national population increase of almost one hundred million people over this period of time (U.S. Bureau of the Census). The loss of viewers is staggering. Citizens first turned to cable or satellite outlets, means of viewing that were available to only a small minority at the time of the ratings first cited. Although many still do turn to cable for news, increasing numbers of citizens are skipping television altogether as they seek out information about politics and turning to the Internet, an act that would have been unthinkable thirty years ago.

It is becoming increasingly evident that we are currently at the dawn of yet another evolutionary period in the relationship between politics and the media. While television undoubtedly remains the most important media source in the political world, it is also true that the Internet is assuming a greater role in American politics, a role that seemingly grows exponentially by the day. In 2012, 46 percent of Americans went online for news three or more times a week; that compares with less than 2 percent in 1996 (Pew Research Center 2010b, 2012). For 50 percent of Americans in 2013 the Internet was a primary source for news (Pew Research Center 2013a), compared with only 3 percent in 1996 (Pew Research Center 2007a, 2007b). The web has passed newspapers as a main source of news for Americans, and is now second only to television (Pew Research Center 2013a). And the gap is narrowing. In 2016, 38 percent of Americans reported getting news *often* online versus 57 percent for television, a 19-point difference. By 2017 the gap had shrunk to 7 points, with the online figure rising to 43 percent and the television figure falling to 50 percent (Pew Research Center 2017c). The Internet is now an important source of news for millions of Americans, which is a development that is even more pronounced among the young and those with a college education (Pew Research Center 2014a, 2014f, 2013a, 2012). In what is perhaps the most impressive figure documenting the rise of the Internet as an important source of news, in 2017 93 percent of Americans reported getting news online at least some of the time (Pew Research Center 2017c). That figure is staggering, especially for a technology that is less than thirty years old (what we refer to as the World Wide Web came online in 1989). With some relatively inexpensive equipment, relatively little technical expertise, and a broadband or other high speed connection, any individual can produce video or other content and post it on the web. **Social media** services such as Facebook, Twitter, YouTube, and Instagram make it easier and faster than ever to disseminate such content across the web, and thus across the country. Seemingly everyone has a smartphone with a high-quality digital camera and video recording capabilities, and politicians now realize that today they are never truly off the record or safe from public view. Finally, Twitter allows politicians and institutions to communicate directly and instantly with those who choose to follow them, revolutionizing the way political actors communicate with citizens. We will have much more to say later in the chapter about the rise of the Internet. But at the outset we want to make two things clear: First, there is no doubt that the Internet has changed politics in important and sometimes dramatic ways. Second, no one knows where this development will end or where it will take us next. Even attempting to speculate runs the risk of looking silly and/or naïve in a relatively short period of time. Indeed, at least some of what was cutting edge when we last revised this text in 2015 is now seen as blasé and dated, and some has even ceased to exist.

What has been the effect of these changes on the impact of the mass media on politics? Put simply, it is more difficult to cut through the noise and also to control the message and content. Thirty years ago, politicians had a pretty good idea of what sources their constituents would turn to for news. National politicians were concerned about the major networks. At the state level, politicians tried to garner national media attention, but they concentrated on local outlets, television stations, and major newspapers. Local politicians had their sights lowered even more, hoping for some television coverage but trying to ensure that the local press covered them adequately.[1]

Today's politicians try desperately to find an audience wherever it might appear through the use of sophisticated data mining and statistical analysis. Table 10.1 presents the percentages Americans gave various sources when they were asked about their main source of news for the 2016 presidential campaign. The diversity and fragmentation in this list are impressive, and suggest how difficult it is for politicians to get their messages across. The political elite might open the *New York Times* or spend time watching CNBC or Fox News or listening to NPR or reading the Drudge Report online. Certainly many still watch the network newscasts and read their local daily newspapers. But others pay less attention to the news, or get their news from unconventional sources—and politicians must find their targets "where they live." Presidential candidate Bill Clinton was one of the first national politicians to recognize this when he appeared on MTV in 1992, and again as President Clinton in 1994 (where he famously informed viewers that he wore briefs rather than boxer shorts). Today all serious presidential candidates, and many congressional and state candidates, have followed Clinton's lead (in terms of where they appear, not necessarily underwear preference). Candidates appear on *The Tonight Show with Jimmy Fallon* on NBC or *The Daily Show* on Comedy Central (candidate Barack Obama's appearance in October 2008 remains the most highly watched episode of *The Daily Show* ever); they have elaborate websites (often more than one) and produce video and other content specifically for social media; they participate in conference calls with popular bloggers. And this only scratches the surface of what campaigns do today in the attempt to communicate their message. The primary message of Table 10.1 is that Americans use a highly diverse array of media to access news, and in today's fragmented media environment political consultants worry about where to communicate a message just as much as they worry about what message to communicate. There is at least the possibility that Donald Trump figured out how to guarantee

Table 10.1. Americans' Main Source of News about 2016 Presidential Election, November–December 2016

Source	*Percentage Used Regularly Watch/Read/Listen*
Fox News	16
CNN	14
Facebook	11
Local TV	7
CBS	4
ABC	4
NBC	4
NPR	4
MSNBC	2
New York Times	2
Local Newspapers	2
Google	2
Local Radio	2
Univision	2
Yahoo	1
YouTube	1
Twitter	1
BBC	1
Washington Post	1
Reddit	1
Drudge Report	1
MSN	1
Telemundo	1
PBS	1
Refused	7

Source: "Trump, Clinton Voters Divided in Their Main Source for Election News." Pew Research Center, Washington, D.C. Study released January 18, 2017. Study conducted November 29–December 12, 2016.
Note: Question asked: "Thinking specifically about the 2016 presidential campaign, do you get most of your news about this topic . . . ?" Respondents were given the randomized response options of "on television," "on news websites or apps," "through social networking sites," "on the radio," or "in print." A follow-up question was used to determine a specific source. Percentages here add up to more than 100 due to the fact that Pew allowed respondents to identify up to three main sources. Only responses of one percent or more shown.

himself an audience during his run to the presidency in 2016 as he seemingly dominated news coverage across multiple platforms throughout the campaign (Persily 2017). In the words of FiveThirtyEight's Nate Silver (2016): "Trump has been able to disrupt the news pretty much any time he wants, whether by being newsworthy, offensive, salacious, or entertaining. The media has almost always played along."

The types of media in existence is not the only major change that parties and candidates have had to deal with. Forty years ago—the date is arbitrary, for the process has been changing over time—reporters covered the news. Increasingly today, candidates for office take actions in order to be covered by the media, and preferably covered on their own terms. No clearer example can be found of this phenomenon than the national nominating conventions.

In the 1960s, presidential nominating conventions were major events on television. The networks competed with each other to provide the best "gavel-to-gavel" coverage. They were concerned about what was going on at the podium, what decisions were being made in the hall, and who was having what influence.

At the 1964 Republican National Convention, when nominee Barry Goldwater chided his vanquished moderate opponents that "extremism in the defense of liberty is no vice," the networks reported that his selection marked a defining moment for his party. The drama at the site of the convention, San Francisco's Cow Palace, was presented "live" for the entire nation to watch. Few who watched would forget the late John Chancellor's exit line as he was forcibly removed from the convention floor: "This is John Chancellor, NBC News, somewhere in custody!"

When the Democratic National Convention in Chicago broke into chaos in 1968, the networks covered the disorder as a major news event. Again, few who watched would soon forget the delegates barred from the floor, the protestors beaten outside delegate hotels, or the religious slur shouted by Chicago mayor Richard Daley at Connecticut senator Abraham Ribicoff, who was decrying the violent tactics of the Chicago police. The events were real; the reporting was real; the news was real.

But the parties could not stand the criticism. Internal schism, they felt, should not be viewed by potential voters. Not atypically, the Republicans learned this lesson before the Democrats. In 1972, Democratic nominee George McGovern accepted his party's nomination with a truly great speech, which was heard by nearly no one because it was delivered long after most people had gone to bed. Convention business had dragged on—viewed in all of its untidiness by a large television audience—and McGovern was not afforded his finest hour until well past midnight. By contrast, the Republican convention of that year was scripted down to the minute to guarantee that the viewing audience saw only what the party officials wanted them to see and saw it when they wanted it to be seen. President Nixon's renomination was as carefully orchestrated as a royal coronation, down to the minutest detail (Davis 1996, chap. 13).

It didn't take the Democrats long to learn the lesson of careful planning from the Republicans; their conventions came to be as carefully scripted as their opponent's. Once, national nominating conventions were widely anticipated events with huge television audiences, but by the time George H. W. Bush and Michael Dukakis were nominated in 1988, fewer than one in five households bothered to watch. The major networks abandoned the gavel-to-gavel coverage of which they had been so proud only a few short years earlier, leaving such coverage to C-SPAN, CNN, and PBS.[2] Even when the networks were on the air, they covered the podium only selectively, preferring to air their own versions of what was going on.

Network disenchantment with the extent to which the conventions had become a showcase for the parties as opposed to news reached a new height in 1996. Ted Koppel had moved his *Nightline* television show to California, the site of the Republican National Convention. After one night, he pulled up stakes and returned to New York with the disclaimer, "There is no news here." Little changed for the staged shows in the summer of 2016, even with the star power of Donald Trump. But it is important to note that while the networks are unhappy with how the party conventions have evolved, actions such as Koppel's are the exception rather than the rule. The networks may grumble, but they still devote extensive resources to covering the Democratic and Republican conventions (Stelter 2008). And Americans watch this coverage. Trump's acceptance speech at the 2016 GOP convention attracted 34.9 million viewers, while Clinton's speech at the Democratic convention drew 33.7 million. It is interesting to note that both of these figures were down from the record setting numbers of 2008 (Battaglio 2016a, b).

Recent national conventions demonstrate two points regarding the relationship between the media and politics in the United States. First, politicians try to use the media to "make the news" they want. Second, media coverage is no longer cast broadly; it is now cast narrowly. Each media outlet is aware of its audience, and programs accordingly. Thus the major networks reduced their coverage of the conventions, but the more news-oriented cable networks continued theirs. The media context for politics as we enter the twenty-first century is an extremely complex one. Politicians try to structure the ways in which they appear on **free or earned media**—media exposure that a candidate receives without having to pay for it. They continue to use **paid media**—exposure that a candidate's campaign pays for and therefore controls to present their message as they define it in a way most likely to impact the intended audience. The distinction between free media and paid media continues to be important. And both types of media have changed as a result of the Internet.

FREE OR EARNED MEDIA: JOURNALISTS' PRESENTATIONS OF CANDIDATES AND CAMPAIGNS

The Varieties of Free Media

There was a time when anyone who heard the phrase "free media" would have a pretty good sense of what was meant. In the early days of the republic, free media referred to pamphlets and early newspapers, the so-called **penny press**, newspapers and leaflets costing a penny that printed news for all to read. Frequently the news was slanted in one political direction or another because many of the early presses were funded and directed by persons having specific political agendas.

As the country grew and as technology advanced, free media came to mean newspapers, many of which were parts of national or regional chains, and eventually newsmagazines. In the first half of the twentieth century, radio and television—network and local—were added to the media mix. When free media was discussed in the context of political parties and elections, it meant news as covered in the free media.

In the contemporary context both the media and the ways in which political messages are communicated have changed. To be sure, the media still include newspapers and magazines, radio, and television. But none of these is the same as it was even a few decades ago. For instance, the number of newspapers—and the number of communities served by more than one major paper—has shrunk dramatically as the newspaper industry continues to suffer through rough times. Despite subscriber growth among the nation's largest newspapers in the last couple of years, overall newspaper subscriptions continue to decline (Pew Research Center 2017b). Many believe that in order to survive, newspapers have to figure out how to make money online, something that it appears the *New York Times* and *Washington Post* have finally figured out how to do (Ember 2017; Ingram 2017; Noguchi 2017; Pope 2016). Whereas once "newsmagazine" meant *Time, Newsweek*, or *U.S. News & World Report*, today more and more specialized magazines are filling part of the news picture. Indeed, *Newsweek* underwent an extensive makeover, briefly ceased publishing a print edition, and now faces questions regarding its continued viability; *U.S. News & World Report* has ceased to function as a newsmagazine in any sense of the word. Changes in television have already been noted. The trend is clear. Major network audiences are falling, and cable audiences are growing. Indeed, cable news outlets have been the only component of the so-called mainstream media to post growth in recent years, but that growth now appears to have plateaued (Pew Research Center 2017c, 2014a, 2013a). Cable networks aim at particular audiences, and the news that they provide is also often aimed at those audiences. Given this, it perhaps should not be surprising that the audiences for cable news outlets have become increasingly divided by partisanship. Republicans tend to heavily favor Fox News, while Democrats increasingly tune into CNN or MSNBC (Pew Research Center 2017a, 2014c). The same is true in the very important world of talk radio, although here conservative voices dramatically lead those of liberals in terms of audience share. Twenty years ago the Internet as a source of news was irrelevant; today it is the second most utilized source by Americans and continues to grow in importance. The American news environment has undergone a seismic shift, and the rate of change shows no signs of slowing down.

Entertainment programming informs the public as well. How many of you have seen the footage of President Clinton playing his saxophone on the *Arsenio Hall Show*? Clinton as musician is one way the politics and entertainment shows mingle, but political humor has long been one of the most common ways that politics and entertainment meet on television. For many years this meant programs like *Saturday Night Live, Politically Incorrect*, or the Leno and Letterman shows. Some of these shows—such as *Saturday Night Live, The Late Show with Stephen Colbert*, and *Jimmy Kimmel Live*—remain important, as Alec Baldwin's 2016 characterizations of Donald Trump on *SNL* and Kimmel's influence on the health care reform debate demonstrate. At the start of the twenty-first century, however, the Comedy Central programs *The Daily Show* and its spin-off *The Colbert Report* took political humor to a different level, mixing real news and commentary with humor and sarcasm. These shows are important, especially among young Americans. Each show affected both politics itself and how the rest of the media covers politics (de Morales 2006; Smolkin 2007). With *The Colbert Report* having ended in December 2014 (Colbert took over CBS's *The Late Show* from David Letterman in September 2015) and Jon Stewart leaving as host of *The Daily Show* in August 2015 and being replaced by Trevor Noah, the impact of these two particular programs disappeared or declined. However, new programs, such as *Last Week Tonight with John Oliver* and *Full Frontal with Samantha Bee* (both Oliver and Bee are *Daily Show* alums) have filled in this space.

Politicians covet appearances on these types of shows, but as with any free media interaction there is a certain amount of risk that goes with the reward of coverage and exposure. In a classic example of this risk/reward situation, Representative Robert Wexler (D-Fla.) appeared on *The Colbert Report* during the 2006 campaign. As he was interviewing Wexler, Colbert asked the congressman to complete the following sentence: "I enjoy cocaine because . . ." Wexler looked directly into the camera and said: "I enjoy cocaine because it's a fun thing to do." Wexler also stated that he enjoyed prostitutes during the interview. The next day Wexler was forced repeatedly to assert that his comments had been in jest, as a number of media outlets reported the story.

The biggest change in the free media in recent years is of course the rise of the Internet. As noted in the introduction to this chapter, an ever increasing number of American regularly get news online. Certainly many of these online Americans get their news from the websites of traditional media outlets such as the three broadcast networks, Fox News and CNN, and major daily newspapers—either from these outlets' websites directly or through aggregators such as Yahoo, Google News, or Reddit. But people are increasingly seeking out news from web-only sources such as *Slate Magazine*, *Salon.com*, *The Drudge Report*, and *Politico* (the last of these does, however, have a print version that is available in the Washington, D.C., area and by mail).

Where we see the biggest change in news consumption (and in some cases, production as well) comes in the rise of social media. Supporters and opponents alike of various candidates now regularly post commentary and other materials on popular websites such as YouTube, Facebook, Instagram, and Twitter. Even more important, candidates themselves use these services to reach out directly to voters. Donald Trump's successful 2016 campaign demonstrates this to perfection. As Trump's 2016 digital director, Brad Parscale, put it to *Wired*, "Facebook and Twitter were the reason we won this thing" (Lapowsky 2016). A look at Americans' social media usage demonstrates its significance. According to the Pew Research Center for the People and the Press (2018), in 2018 73 percent of American adults used YouTube, while 68 used Facebook. Six other social media platforms—Instagram, Pinterest, Snapchat, Linkedin, Twitter, and WhatsApp—were used by 20 percent or more of American adults. Snapchat and Instagram are especially popular among eighteen- to twenty-four-year-olds, perhaps pointing to the next political frontier in social media. Increasingly, Americans are using multiple social media sites in a single day (Pew Research Center 2018). Perhaps more important, many of these people also use their social media accounts to recommend and pass along news to the other users they are connected to. A fair number of these individuals also use their phones to capture video and upload the video to the web. Others go so far as to create flashy, professional-looking videos either for or against candidates and post them on the web. Some of these contributions become what have been termed "viral videos," meaning that they spread around the Internet like a virus as discussions about and links to the video spread from user to user (Marinucci 2007; Parsons and McCormick 2007; Sender 2007). Such viral videos can both benefit and harm candidates for public office. As Mark McKinnon, chief media adviser for the 2000 and 2004 Bush campaigns, stated, in many ways today anyone with a camera can be in control of the message, and to a certain extent the news. Americans are also more able than ever before to craft a news menu suited to their own individual tastes and

desires. As Pew has stated in a number of reports and presentations, "People's relationship to news is becoming portable, personalized, and participatory" (Pew Research Center 2010a).

The Role of the Free/Earned Media

Perhaps there is another way to view the role of the free media in political contexts. Rather than look at the number of media and the ways in which they communicate information, perhaps we can concentrate on the role that they should theoretically be playing in American campaigns and elections. That is, what is it we hope free media do in order to make our political processes function more effectively?

Informed Consent of the Governed

A representative democracy rests not just on the consent of the governed but on the **informed consent of the governed**. The role that the media should play in our political system is to permit those who choose our elected officials to do so in an informed way. That answer, however, oversimplifies a complex situation. As noted earlier, one important question deals with how much information citizens need to make an informed judgment. That obviously reflects on what kind of information we should expect the media to provide.

Let's look at the question from a slightly different perspective. The media are an intermediary institution in our system. That is, they link other important actors; in the case we are interested in, they link those seeking elective office (including those currently holding office) with those who will make the electoral choice. In an earlier era, political parties performed this role for almost all offices. Today, many citizens reject the automatic link between themselves and political parties, even if they assume the link between parties and candidates. The media fill that void.

But we still need to explore what kinds of information should be provided. Should citizens be concerned only about candidates' policy positions? Should they be concerned about personalities? Should they be concerned about personal lifestyle, about "youthful indiscretions," and about families? Do the media have an obligation to provide all of this information? In what form? The briefest answer is that the media can be expected to provide the information that citizens seek.

How that definition is reached still poses difficult questions. For instance, we claimed earlier that the media today do provide virtually any information that a citizen could want about officeholders and candidates for office. But the citizen must play an active role in finding that information. On the other hand, information that may not be relevant to citizens' needs reaches many "automatically." Certainly in recent years the media have delved more deeply into highly personal aspects of candidates' lives than was true in the past. Many complain that they are learning things they do not need to know, that candidates' private lives should remain just that, private. Some claim that this kind of intrusive media information changes the political scene by discouraging strong candidates.

Speaking before an informal meeting of senators during the heat of the Senate trial on the impeachment of President Clinton, former president George H. W. Bush echoed this view: "I worry too about sleaze, about excessive intrusion into private lives. I worry about once great news organizations that seem to resort to tabloid journalism, giving us sensationalism at best and smut at worst" (Dewar 1999, A16).

On that very same day, the former president's daughter-in-law Laura told a group of journalists in Austin that she was very reticent to have her husband seek the presidency, owing to the loss of privacy such a campaign would entail (Neal and Duggan 1999, A8). Of course, she overcame that reticence as her husband began his successful campaign.

Why do the media insist on presenting stories that cause these concerns? Simply put, because the public buys them. They sell newspapers and magazines; they produce large Nielsen ratings; they increase site visits and page views. The public expresses its desires in a number of ways. The media react to the cash register, to the public's demonstrating its real desire by what it purchases.

Window on the Candidates

The media should play other roles as well—and these too may be controversial. As noted already, it is impossible for every citizen to see every candidate. But many voters want to "experience" the candidates they are supporting or opposing. The media should let them have this experience. These windows should be free from outside manipulation; they should be free from candidate manipulation. And in searching for this lack of interference, controversy arises. It is clear that candidates know when the media are covering them—and they act accordingly. It is thus difficult for the media to provide a clear picture. In the most recent electoral cycles, C-SPAN has played this role probably as well as it can be played, following candidates for various offices for extended periods of time, making it more difficult for candidates to perform for the camera in ways different from how they act when not under such scrutiny.

Referee between Candidates

We have all seen campaigns in which candidates get involved in a "'He said. . . ,' 'No, I didn't'" kind of dispute. In recent years these battles have often been fought through competing television advertisements. A relatively new role for the media is serving as a referee in these battles and thus raising the chances that candidate advertisements will be honest. During the 1988 presidential campaign, the record of Democratic candidate Michael Dukakis as governor of Massachusetts was attacked in a series of negative ads that many observers felt were unfair. Following suggestions by veteran campaign watchers David Broder of the *Washington Post* and Ken Bode, then-host of Public Television's *Washington Week in Review*, largely as a result of this experience, many newspapers and television stations took on the role of monitoring political advertisements for truthfulness, so-called **adwatch campaigns**. "For the first time in most places, a referee in the form of political reporters showing up in the campaign arena with the savvy to call fouls and a voice that's being heard [is present]. A game with a referee is a different kind of game" (Monroe 1990, 6).

Adwatches "force campaigns to issue extensive documentation *before* the ad is aired—instead of waiting until the other side has complained" (Alter 1992, 37). Adwatches have even spread to small-town newspapers. Most feel that their impact has been positive, reducing the likelihood of campaign ads being false or misleading (Gottfried et al. 2013; Milburn and Brown 1997). Adwatches can be particularly important in analyzing third-party ads, which tend to have a higher number of misleading statements than ads produced and put out by the candidates themselves (Winneg et al. 2014). That the referee's role in the rough-and-tumble of political campaigns is an appropriate one for the media, however, is now well accepted. It is also a role that the American public very much supports (Pew Research Center 2013b).

The Actual Role That the Media Play

It should come as little surprise that analysis of the role that the media actually do play in the political process differs significantly from the role observers theoretically feel they should play. Much of the work on this topic has looked at presidential campaigns and the role that the media have played in them, but the findings apply almost as directly to campaigns for other offices in which candidates must rely on the media to communicate with potential voters (see Iyengar and Reeves 1997; Norris 1997; Davis 1996; Seib 1994). Based on this work, it is possible to characterize the role actually played by the media in modern campaigns according to a number of different categories.[3]

The Great Mentioner

How did George W. Bush become the front-runner for the 2000 Republican presidential nomination so early in the preprimary process? Bush became a front-runner before he announced his candidacy for the White House or even formed an exploratory committee. How did he get to be a front-runner? The press dubbed him one. To be sure, Bush had enormous political assets—his name and family connections, his ability to raise money, and his popularity in a large state. But he was not the only Republican governor reelected in 1998, and many of the others were not "mentioned" as leading contenders for their party's nomination.

Thus one role that the press has come to play is to raise some potential candidates above others in the months before a campaign really starts. This kind of mention can give momentum to a nascent campaign, whereas the lack of such recognition can stop a campaign in its tracks. One key to a candidate's being taken seriously is having his or her name recognized by large numbers of citizens. Early preference polls are often nothing more than name recognition polls. Candidates who do not do well in them are not taken seriously by influential politicians. Thus the media role at this early stage is a most critical one.

Image Creator

Think for a moment about what you know about any major political figure. How did you acquire that image? Where did it come from? The simple answer is that most images of that type are media created. For example, in 2000 George W. Bush was personable and grounded, while

Al Gore was stiff and aloof. In 2008, Barack Obama was young, hip, and energetic, while John McCain was old, square, and tired. Each picture was oversimplified but widely accepted. Obama in 2012 might not have been as young and hip any more, but neither was he the square and aristocratic Mitt Romney. Donald Trump came into the 2016 campaign with an image honed and sharpened from decades in the media spotlight and in front of the camera, but the media amplified this image exponentially in the 2016 campaign.

The press has the ability to portray such an image because members of the press tend to read each other's writing, talk with each other, and follow each other's lead. The concept of **pack journalism**, in which "one reporter's story becomes every reporter's story" (Seib 1994, 60–61), has been expounded for almost forty years (see Sabato 1991; Crouse 1973; Thompson 1973). Although reporters strive for independence, the news of the day is often dictated by the schedules set by the campaigns themselves. Events are planned in order to create good visual effects for television and to meet deadlines for the print media. Candidates rush from event to event; so too must those covering them. As a result there is little time for reflection, and stories tend to be similar from one reporter to the next.

Expectation Setter

Commentator after commentator, as well as media critic after media critic, has pointed to the role that the media play in setting expectations for candidates at various early stages in campaigns.

When looking at presidential campaigns, the media note how much money each candidate raises at the times of various Federal Election Commission reports. They comment on candidate performance in debates vis-à-vis their opponents. They examine poll results, noting who is doing better than predicted and whose ratings are not so high. And, most important, they lay out in advance how each candidate is likely to do in an upcoming primary and weigh that candidate's performance and standing in the polls in terms of how well he or she fared in comparison to those expectations. State and local media play similar roles in the campaigns they cover. And evaluations about whether a candidate is meeting expectations are important as a campaign progresses.

The **expectation game** is also the primary reason for the outsized importance of the Iowa caucus and the New Hampshire primary in presidential nominating contests. In 2004, when Senator John Kerry followed up his win in Iowa with a victory in New Hampshire, the race for the 2004 Democratic presidential nomination was over. Barack Obama vaulted to front-runner status with his victory in Iowa in 2008, while Hillary Clinton temporarily saved her campaign with her victory in New Hampshire. In 2012, Romney's strong second place showing in Iowa (he was not expected to do well there and initially was announced as the winner of the caucuses) coupled with his convincing win in New Hampshire upheld the media's view of him as front-runner and began his inexorable march to the Republican nomination. In 2016 Donald Trump's strong performance in Iowa (second place) followed by his resounding victory in New Hampshire firmly established him as the Republican front-runner, whether people wanted to believe it or not.

Where did the expectations come from? From the media—often prodded by candidates who tried to set low standards for themselves so that they could exceed those standards. But in each case, the popular view of the expectations—and of whether they were met—was put forth by the media covering the campaign.

Issue Identifier

The media determine what is important in a campaign. That is, they determine which of the items that candidates mention are transmitted to the public. Every candidate for a major office discusses a large number of issues during a campaign. All develop position papers. All give speeches on many topics. All make a sincere attempt to tell the public what they stand for. Often, however, it is the media who determine what the agenda for the public will be. The agenda might well be the personal characteristics of a candidate. It might be how competing candidates stand on contentious issues. It might be which candidate in a primary election is likely to poll better in the general election.

In primary elections the agenda is frequently related to the game of politics, not to the business of governing. The journalists covering a campaign are concerned about who is likely to win, what techniques are in use to push a campaign forward, what groups or key individuals favor which candidates. Even in general elections, the media frequently concentrate more on the nuts and bolts of the campaign than they do on differences among candidates. Consequently, that is what the public knows about the campaign. That is what is discussed over the water cooler, at the mall, on the subway, at the dinner table. Citizens are more likely to view campaigns in terms of the latest poll results, debate strategy, or advertising gambits than they are to know about substantive differences in candidates' stands on key issues, since citizen knowledge reflects media presentation.

Field Narrower

When all of these roles are combined, one result is that the press plays an important role in narrowing multicandidate fields. This role, also known as **field winnower**, has long been recognized in presidential primaries (Barber 1978) and is just as apparent in statewide and other highly visible primaries.

When the media stop mentioning a candidate, when the image associated with a candidate is an unflattering one, when a candidate does not meet expectations, or when the agenda discussed in the media excludes issues raised by a candidate or his or her role in a campaign, a signal goes out that this individual's candidacy has lost viability. This role is an important one in primary campaigns, particularly in presidential primary campaigns, in which it is necessary to present the public with a set of choices with which it can cope. But this role is not necessarily one that the media are best suited to play.

In primaries below the level of the presidency, this role is often played either by political parties in a formal way (when state laws or party rules permit it; chapter 6) or by party leaders in an informal way. Some candidates are supported by party regulars; others are not. Some find encouragement from those who typically fund campaigns; others cannot raise money. While these "winnowers" are not always part of the formal process, they have a certain legitimacy within the process. Below the presidential level, the extent to which the media have assumed this role varies from state to state. Like at the level of presidential nominations, the extent to which the media's playing such an important role is accepted often depends on the perspective of the person evaluating the process. Not surprisingly, those who are "winnowed out" tend to be less satisfied than those who are "winnowed in."

Campaign Critic

The media have also assumed the role of critic, judging the performance of those seeking office. Some patterns have become clear in recent elections.

First, the media tend to view themselves as watchdogs of the public good, a role strongly supported by the public even as the public has become more distrustful and less convinced of the accuracy of the news media (Pew Research Center 2016, 2009b; Sullivan 2017; Swift 2016). Thus the media are particularly vigilant in observing and commenting on the character and performance of individuals who are likely to be elected, or who are serious contenders to be elected. Much of what is reported is negative. Rarely does one read a story that is full of praise for all aspects of a front-running candidate's qualities (Davis 1996, 187–89). On the other hand, underdog candidates are often afforded much kinder treatment. In 1992, when Texas billionaire H. Ross Perot was seeking the presidency, the press treated him as something of a darling early in the campaign season. He was photogenic, funny, willing to take controversial stands, and he was polling better than was expected. However, once Perot started to receive serious consideration from voters, the press turned more critical, raising questions about his electability and the extent to which his solutions were more simplistic than the problems they addressed (Germond and Witcover 1993).

Of course, the result of this kind of treatment has a certain impact not only on the campaigns but also on the public officials subsequently elected. Winners appear in a less-favorable light than do losers, who frequently emerge from elections as figures deserving of sympathy. Certainly this kind of media treatment contributes to public cynicism.

Documenter of Elections

It is also true that the media play the role of documenting elections for the public. That is, we know what happens in an election because the media tell us.

In some instances, this role is played because the election events themselves take place on or in front of the media. Thus debates among or between candidates for many offices are aired on and closely covered by the various media. The public has the opportunity to observe these events as they happen, to read transcripts, to absorb analysis, or to follow others' reactions.

In other instances, the role involves media documentation of what is happening. Media polls tell the public how the various campaigns are doing. Whereas media polls were intermittent during the elections of the 1960s, by the 1990s national and statewide polls were so frequent that individual voters began to wonder how so many polls could be published without their opinions having been sought.[4] These polls have proven accurate as predictors of outcomes, to be sure, but they are also important to provide an understanding of which voters are supporting which candidate and for what reasons. Even with all of the controversy surrounding the polls in the 2016 presidential cycle, academic polling experts have shown that the national polls were quite accurate, although there were a few problems with some state polls, particularly in the upper Midwest (AAPOR 2017).

These polls have also been criticized. In most recent presidential elections, pollsters have known the results well in advance of the actual voting; for instance, President Clinton's lead over Senator Dole was so large in 1996—and his lead in so many states was so overwhelming—that his reelection was assured well before election day. Critics claim not only that these polls remove the drama from a campaign but also that they deflate turnout and may impact elections lower on the ballot. Although they may be documenting one election, they can alter the results of another. The media have been sensitive to this charge—changing the ways in which they use exit polls on election night, as one example—but they also feel an obligation to provide such information about a campaign as they are able to garner. The example of adwatches was noted earlier. In these and other ways, the media ensure that the public knows what is happening in an election. But the line between "news" and "analysis" can blur in these circumstances. The media are certainly a documenter of what is happening during an election—but in playing that role, they become a participant as well.

Purveyor of Results

Many of us stay up late on election night, our eyes glued to our favorite analysts as they give us the results of the elections. The networks are our respected source—fast and accurate, up to the minute. And then there was Election Night 2000, the night that would never end.

But first let's take a step back, for giving results on election night has been controversial for some time. For years networks predicted winners based on results in sample precincts. They were conservative in their estimates, but they were often very early in giving results. The controversy arose when networks gave "results" before the polls were all closed. They were able to do so with great accuracy, based on exit polls, surveys taken of voters as they were leaving the poll booths. The problem was that many politicians felt that early predictions affected races lower down on the ballot, because voters who had not yet gone to their polling places might be dissuaded from doing so if they knew the results of the top-of-the-ticket races.

The situation was exacerbated in 1980 when President Carter conceded to his challenger, Ronald Reagan, well before the polls closed on the West Coast. To be fair to the networks, Carter did so based on the advice of his own pollster, Patrick Caddell, not based on network predictions, though those predictions were in place. Many observers felt that the results of congressional and senatorial races—as well as state and local races—on the West Coast were affected; there was anecdotal evidence of citizens getting out of voting lines when they heard that Carter had conceded the race to Reagan.

As a result, the networks decided to police themselves, not to release predictions based on exit polls until all polls in a jurisdiction have closed. But they still do exit polling, and they still race to be first with their predictions. And thus arose the problem on Election Night 2000. The networks, rushing to be first and then not to fall behind the opposition, declared Florida for Vice President Gore early in the evening. The Bush campaign, confident that the candidate's brother, Florida governor Jeb Bush, would carry the state for the Republicans and in possession of data running counter to the exit polls, cried foul, noting that some polling places in western Florida had yet to close. As more results came in, the networks first withdrew their prediction of a Gore victory, calling the state too close to call, then gave it to Bush, and then withdrew that prediction as the contentiousness of the vote tallying became apparent.

It is difficult to imagine network news executives more chagrined. The purveyors of truth had missed badly and given false information not once, but twice, to the public. In a rush to be first, they had failed in their most important task—to be accurate. The major news organizations have undertaken internal analyses of how they went so badly wrong; they have pledged to avoid such disasters in the future. But their reputations were damaged nonetheless.

The failing here, of course, was a result of the closeness of the race in Florida and the confusion concerning how voters cast their ballots in relation to how they meant to cast those votes. The exit polls might well have reflected how voters intended to vote, but the actual vote count was something else. Florida as a state—and we as a nation, and the networks as news gatherers—did not have a means sufficiently sophisticated to know the result in a timely and accurate manner. The networks' failure was not that they did not give us an accurate count; it was that they purported to do so when subsequent events proved that to be impossible.

An Assessment of the Role of Free Media

Leaving aside the delicious controversy caused by election night reporting, it is clear that the role that the free media play in the electoral process itself differs from theories propounded by political scientists about that role. Two questions remain: Why is it different? Is this good or bad?

Why Do the Media Play the Roles They Do?

No journalist feels compelled to play a role dictated by electoral theories. That should go without saying. Journalists follow the dictates of their profession. They cover stories. They write about events in what they perceive to be an evenhanded way.

But their efforts are by necessity constrained. They must meet deadlines. They can only cover so many campaigns in so much detail. They have limited access to some sources. They must be aware of the costs to their owners of their efforts, a concern that has dramatically increased with the combination of the recent changes to the media environment discussed earlier and the economic downturn that began in 2008 (Project for Excellence in Journalism 2010). Publishers and editors, and executives in electronic media outlets, are concerned about audience share.

Many journalists would like to cover every aspect of a certain campaign in great depth. But they must also cover other campaigns. They must compete for space in their newspaper or time on the air. They must be certain that their stories are accurate and fair, that one candidate is not advantaged over another. Thus they follow certain patterns. Their access is dictated largely by campaign staff. Their ability to file complete stories is compromised at times by deadlines. They compete with fellow journalists covering a campaign, but they also do not want to be too far away from what most of their colleagues are saying, for fear that they will be proven wrong or that they will have missed the "real story." In short, media coverage of campaigns evolves the way it does because of the norms of the journalists' profession, the demands of their employers, and the constraints on their efforts. This all being said, it is clear that the media covered Donald Trump far more than all of the other candidates in the 2016 presidential contest, during both the nominating phase and the general election phase. As we discussed in chapter 5, this presented Trump with a huge edge in free/earned media coverage, allowing him to spend less on advertising (Harris 2016; Francia 2017; Stewart 2016). Did Trump merit such an edge in coverage? Did the media tilt the election toward Trump through its coverage, as some critics claim? These are important questions to consider.

How Should We Evaluate That Role?

In a sense, it does not matter how the role is evaluated because it is largely inevitable. But the media do have an impact on campaigns. Is it good or bad? By what standards should that impact be judged?

In general, the answer is that the media role contributes positively to the electoral process as long as that role is played openly, honestly, and fairly. In the overwhelming majority of American elections, these criteria are met. The electoral process is relatively well served by the free media. Given constraints, the media cover campaigns quite well. Citizens can get what information they need. Journalists look carefully at how they practice their own craft and seek to correct obvious flaws. Thus, for instance, the major networks now routinely rotate reporters among various campaign assignments so that no reporter becomes too close to one campaign and loses objectivity. Campaigns attempt to get the best publicity that they can—for that is the nature of their enterprise—but they also permit journalists to do their job. And the public picks and chooses what it watches and reads, as another example of citizens' participating in the process to the extent that they desire to be involved.

PAID MEDIA: THE CANDIDATE PROVIDES THE MESSAGE

The difference between free media and paid media could not be starker. With free media, candidates put their best face forward, but someone else communicates the message to the public. There is an intermediary—the journalists who determine how the message will reach the public. With paid media, candidates determine their message and pay to communicate it directly to potential voters. No intermediary. Straight shot. In this section, we will explore who produces paid advertisements for political campaigns (and what types of advertisements they produce); we will then look at controversies surrounding the ways in which paid media impact political campaigns. We will conclude by looking at the impact of paid media on the electoral process.

Types of Paid Media

Paid commercials for political campaigns in this country come from three sources—candidates and their campaigns, the political parties, and interest groups. In fact, the producers of these advertisements are frequently paid consultants to the candidates, parties, or groups; but the message is determined in conjunction with strategies set by campaign committees.

Broadly speaking, political advertisements on television fall into two categories—spot advertisements and longer advertisements. Internet, radio, and print media advertisements frequently follow the same themes as do the television ads we discuss here. But television consumes the overwhelming majority of campaign advertising budgets (Steel 2009), so we will focus on those ads here. The spots are equivalent to the ads used by commercial enterprises to sell their products or services (Diamond and Bates 1984). They tend to be short—always under one minute in length—colorful, and polished. The longer commercials, most recently known as infomercials, are often thirty minutes in length or even longer. Some believe that H. Ross Perot invented infomercials for his presidential campaigns, but in fact their history is much longer. Many of the original television commercials were longer attempts by candidates to explain their campaigns to the citizens. These messages were shortened because consultants felt that viewer attention span was too short, that citizens turned off longer commercials and sought entertainment television. Perot resurrected the genre to great effect, as Nielsen ratings demonstrated that citizens were willing to spend the time to become informed. Barack Obama used a variation in 2008 that was also widely viewed.

What purposes are served by political advertisements? The purpose clearly depends on the candidate—and the state of his or her candidacy (Seib 1994). For candidates who are not well known to the public, early in a campaign the purpose of ads is to improve name recognition, essentially to prove that a candidacy is viable. For statewide campaigns and even for congressional campaigns, this kind of advertising can be quite expensive. Quality ads must be produced and repeated over and over in order to make an impression on prospective voters. Of course, incumbents, who have by definition run in the past, do not need to spend money in this way. However, incumbents often run biographical ads early in a campaign to cement a positive image in the public's mind.

Once a candidacy has achieved viability, advertisements are used for one of two purposes. Either they are intended to convince citizens to vote for the candidate, or they are designed to denigrate an opponent.[5] These ads have been characterized as **positive ads** or **negative ads**, though there is a great deal of disagreement about how these terms should be defined.

Positive ads state the case for a candidate. The goal is to convince the public that the candidate is the right person for the job, has the right qualities to do the job effectively, or is on the right side of the crucial issues. Negative ads try to convince voters that they should vote against the sponsoring candidate's opponent. Some feel that all negative ads have a deleterious effect on the system; this view will be discussed later. At this point, let it suffice to state that all negative ads are not alike. Most analysts would claim that it is perfectly legitimate for a challenger to point to his or her opponent's record in office and to question whether citizens approve of that record. Most would also agree that it is inappropriate to distort that record or to present it in a confusing manner. The first of these ads are often called **contrast ads,** and they make up an important part of legitimate campaign discourse. But truly negative ads, ads aimed solely at destroying an opponent's image, are another matter. Furthermore, the appropriateness of other ads raises questions. What about ads discussing a candidate's moral fitness for office? Some claim that such personal matters should not be part of the political discourse. Others claim that they are at the heart of a candidate's qualifications for office. No consensus exists on this point. In addition, disagreement exists on how all of these points can or should be made.

The purpose of ads that are run during the heat of a campaign is to ensure that the voters consider the views of the candidate sponsoring the ads. In so doing, paid commercials create an impression of the candidate and go a long way toward setting the agenda for a campaign. As was pointed out in chapter 7, candidates coordinate their media message with the message they are transmitting throughout the campaign.

Much like free media, paid media are also evolving due to the Internet. All serious candidates for federal office, and many state and even local candidates as well, now have websites, sometimes more than one. Many of these websites are elaborate productions that cost a good deal of money to create and maintain. Contemporary candidates also must pay serious attention to their presence on and use of social media such as Facebook, Instagram, and Twitter. But the payoff can be well worth the effort; as John McCain (in the 2000 campaign), Howard Dean (in 2004), and especially Barack Obama (in both 2008 and 2012) demonstrated, serious money can be raised on the web, and the Internet can also be a valuable tool in informing and rallying supporters. President Obama's 2008 campaign reported that it raised a little more than $500 million via online donations, a figure that rose to about $690 million in the 2012 campaign. In the 2012 campaign the Obama team had twenty people on staff just to write e-mails (Sutton 2013). In October of 2012, Obama had 31.1 million Facebook "likes" compared to 10.2 million for Romney. Followers for Obama on other prominent social media sites included 21.2 million on Twitter, 233,000 on YouTube, and 1.4 million on Instagram. The same numbers for Romney were 1.5 million, 21,000, and 38,000 (The Week 2012). The Obama campaign's efforts in this area in both 2008 and 2012 were unprecedented, and they obviously paid off on election day both times. It remains the case that younger voters utilize these technological advances far more than older voters, but usage among older voters is on the rise (Pew Research Center 2015, 2014c). While Donald Trump did not raise as much money as Obama did online (as discussed in chapter 5, Trump's campaign was an outlier in terms of financing), his campaign did use Facebook to raise a significant amount of money (Lapowsky 2016). And Trump does very well in terms of followers on social media, with over 70 million followers on Twitter (between both his personal and the POTUS account), 23.1 million followers on Facebook, and 8.5 million followers on Instagram (as impressive as these numbers are, it should be noted that former President Barack Obama has over 101 million followers on his personal Twitter account). Additionally, while the use of social media in campaigns has been most prevalent at the presidential level, it is rapidly being adopted in non-presidential campaigns as well (Williams and Gulati 2013).

Controversies Caused by the Use of Paid Media

Paid political advertisements have become the principal means through which candidates for national and statewide office, and those for other offices with large constituencies, communicate with the voters. But they are not without controversy. The first bone of contention involves the question of balance—of whether it is fair if one candidate dominates the political discussion because his or her campaign has been able to raise much more money than opponents' campaigns. That question was considered in chapter 5. But two important controversies remain to be explored. In the following sections we will examine the questions surrounding negative advertising and those raised by so-called issue advocacy advertisements.

Negative Advertising

As noted earlier, no consensus exists on the question of negative advertising. While most agree that it is appropriate to raise questions about an opponent's record and to contrast one candidate's record with another's, most also agree that the practice of attacking an opponent can, at times, go too far. The controversy in the use of paid advertising relates to negative **attack ads** that are either personal in nature or presented in a way that invites criticism as unfair, deceptive, or in other ways inappropriate in political discourse.

Former *Washington Post* media commentator Howard Kurtz examined this issue in an analysis of advertising in a series of statewide campaigns during the 1998 election cycle. Kurtz's article appeared under the headline, "Attack Ads Carpet TV; High Road Swept Away." In that article, which focused on campaigns in California, Florida, Georgia, New York, and Texas, Kurtz concluded that

> America is again being carpet-bombed by political ads, many of them fiercely negative. . . . The themes vary from race to race, from education to the environment to health care to gun control, but many of [them] oversimplify and distort the opponent's record. (Kurtz 1998, A1)

Why do candidates engage in negative advertising? The answer is quite simple. They believe—and they have evidence from recent electoral experience—that such techniques are effective. They work. The point is to win, not to be seen as a nice person or a good sport. But there is also a counterargument—with some supporting evidence—that going negative can sometimes backfire. If this happens, a candidate's unfavorable ratings can soar while at the same time his or her opponent becomes viewed in a more sympathetic light as the victim of an unseemly and unprovoked attack. The question of whether to go negative is one that a campaign must consider very carefully.

Strategists have debated the efficacy of negative attack ads in terms of their contribution to electoral outcomes, but others are concerned about their broader impact on the electoral process. One line of argument holds that the negativity of campaigns has kept qualified citizens from seeking elective office (Maisel, Stone, and Maestas 1999). Another concern is that citizens have become turned off to the political process because they view it as unnecessarily negative. Ansolabehere and Iyengar (1995, 101, 107–10) have demonstrated that positive political advertisements encourage people to vote, whereas negative advertisements reduce voter turnout. According to their analysis, citizens exposed to relentless negative advertising aimed at candidates they favor find that "dropping out may be easier than switching to the attacker" (Ansolabehere and Iyengar 1995, 109–10). On the other hand, Geer (2006) presents compelling evidence that negative advertising actually presents meaningful information to voters, and thus represents a positive contribution to representative democracy. Daniel Stevens (2005) qualifies this argument with findings that while those who are highly politically sophisticated do get a wealth of information from negative ads, those of low sophistication get little or no meaningful information from negative spots. More recent experimental research by Stevens (2012) indicates that the tone of advertisements has much less effect on voters than does the amount of information in the ad.

Whether viewed in a favorable or unfavorable light, negative advertising is not likely to go away. The right of candidates to press their political cause as they see fit is a fundamental aspect of freedom of speech; it is unimaginable that the content of political advertising would be restricted in a way that would survive a legal challenge on constitutional grounds.

That certainty has not deterred reformers from seeking a means of ameliorating the impact of negative attack ads. One proposal that has been seriously floated requires candidates who name their opponents in a political advertisement to do so themselves; that is, any negative attack on an opponent must come from the attacking candidate in his or her own words. The theory behind this reform is that it is more difficult to make outlandish statements personally than it is to do so through a third party, or through clever media presentations.

Whether this or any similar reform effort could pass either Congress or a state legislature, and whether it would pass a constitutional challenge, is highly debatable. However, the mere existence of proposals such as this one suggests that the issue of negative advertising is of enough concern to keep efforts to restrain such practices high on reformers' agendas.

Issue Advocacy Advertisements

Political groups have used a variety of means to further their policy agendas (see chapter 4). One technique used by wealthier groups on critical issues has been to advertise to the public, seeking to gain popular support for their positions. In 1994 opponents of President Clinton's health care reform package ran a very successful set of commercials—the "Harry and Louise" commercials, named after the characters portrayed in the ads—that were given credit for turning public opinion against the president's plan.

Noting the success of the "Harry and Louise" commercials, a number of interest groups decided to tie their issue concerns to particular candidacies in the 1996 election. In so doing, they were taking advantage of a judicial interpretation that the right of groups to advertise on behalf of issues with which they were concerned was constitutionally protected, and could not be restricted by campaign finance regulations as long as the advertisements did not explicitly call for the election or defeat of a particular candidate.

Organized labor was the first to exploit this interpretation of the law. In 1996 they ran a $35 million campaign targeting particular Republican candidates running for reelection to the House of Representatives. Entering the relevant media markets very early in these campaigns, the labor advertisements were successful in raising doubts in voters' minds about their representatives in Congress. Later in the campaign, a coalition of business groups including the National Federation of Independent Businesses and the National Association of Manufacturers countered the labor campaign with a multimillion-dollar effort of their own, targeted at the same contested districts. This trend has increased unabated in the elections that followed, gaining additional strength and momentum in the aftermath of *Citizens United* (see chapter 5). It is also the case that these ads from outside groups tend to be more negative (Fowler and Ridout 2014).

Impact of Paid Media on Election Campaigns

Obviously, modern campaigns have spent such a high percentage of their resources on paid media advertising because candidates, campaign managers, and consultants feel that such expenditures pay electoral dividends. At the most basic level, campaigning through the media allows a candidacy to reach the largest possible audience with a message that is designed by the campaign strategists, not interpreted by journalists. But it is possible to be slightly more explicit, to be clear about what effects campaign commercials are designed to produce.

Intended Consequences of Paid Media Campaigns

Campaign strategists have at least four separate goals for paid media campaigns. The first goal is to establish a positive image for the candidate. If the candidate is an incumbent, that image is of a hardworking, effective public servant. If the candidate is a challenger, the goal is to depict the candidate as one who can do the job well. If the candidate is not well known, the first aspect of this strategy is merely to create name recognition. Tactics vary. Some candidacies stress personal characteristics: He is a family man who is loyal to his friends. Others emphasize connections between the candidate and the electorate: She went to high school here and has always lived here; she knows our people. Still others might talk about job qualifications: She has been successful on the city council and will be a great representative in Sacramento. But whatever the tactic, the strategic premise is to build a positive image. Typically commercials of this type run early in a campaign.

The second goal is to set the agenda for the campaign. Through saturating the airwaves (and now the web as well) with commercials, campaigns hope to affect how potential voters see the entire campaign. If all commercials talk about local issues, voters are likely to think of the candidate and the campaign in those terms. If the paid media stress a candidate's work in Washington or in a state capital, those issues are likely to be at the forefront. The discussions may be very concrete (e.g., about specific legislation) or diffuse (e.g., about the state of the local economy), but the goal is the same—to concentrate public attention on items that play well for the candidate sponsoring the ads and put his or her candidacy in the most positive light. The advanced data mining and microtargeting techniques referenced in this chapter allow modern campaigns—at least at the presidential level—to tailor their agendas and messages to increasingly fine degrees. Indeed, Bimber (2014) argues that the 2012 Obama campaign's ability to craft and deliver highly personalized messages to voters was crucial to its success on election day.

The third goal of a campaign is to reinforce the loyalties of party members and others who should logically support a candidate. These ads often link the candidate to popular figures in the same party; congressional candidates appear with the governor or senator of their party to remind voters where their loyalty should lie. One strategy in any campaign is to protect one's base, to be sure that those who are your most likely supporters turn out to vote. Paid media is used to further this effort.

Finally, some (many observers would say most) campaigns use paid media to attack their opponents. Even critics of negative advertising admit that it is appropriate for a candidate to point to flaws in the record of his or her opponent. A challenger has to provide a reason for replacing the incumbent. As discussed above, the question here revolves around the specific points that are attacked and the way in which the message is presented. From a strategic point of view, the goal is clear—to convince voters that there are reasons not to vote for one candidate—and presumably therefore to vote for the other candidate. While we have much still to learn about how exactly political advertisement affects vote choice (Goldstein and Ridout 2004), we can say with absolute certainty that paid media is the overwhelming weapon of choice used by modern campaigns.

AN UNEASY YET NECESSARY RELATIONSHIP IN TRANSITION

Without meaning to belittle politicians, one could say that their relationship to the media resembles that familiar lament offered by Rowlf the Dog to Kermit the Frog in *The Muppet Movie*: "You can't live with 'em; you can't live without 'em." Politicians complain frequently about how unfairly they are treated in the media, about how difficult it is to talk about issues, about how paid advertising presents distorted images, about how they wish they could talk about issues at length, not in sound bites.

But their actions tell another story. Virtually every politician in Washington has a press secretary whose job is to guarantee that the politician is seen frequently in the media, particularly in the media that serves the elected official's constituents. Every campaign has a press secretary who is charged with the care and feeding (in two senses of that word) of journalists covering the campaign. Candidates treat the press well so that journalists are inclined to treat them favorably, and they want to influence the substance of the stories that are reported. Every campaign for a major office hires political consultants to design and place advertisements. Few candidates fret about the length of the ads, only about their effectiveness. None of the politicians described herein sound like they cannot stand the media.

And of course, the reason is the other side of the equation. They cannot live without them. And this is not all bad. After all, elected officials and candidates for office need to communicate with large numbers of citizens. Mass media—free and paid—are the only effective means of doing this. Journalists, in legitimately and professionally pursuing their craft, cover politicians. Politicians have a clear stake in trying to influence what is said so that their message is heard as they intend it to be delivered. Advertisements do not produce themselves. Candidates, if they want to win, have an obligation to work with professional media consultants who can produce effective ads. They must effectively reach out to voters in the digital world, using both media they control and media they do not. There is nothing evil in any of this.

The problem that thoughtful politicians really worry about is balance. What happens when the press reaction to one set of circumstances impacts another? Examples abound. Potential candidates worry about private matters from their past being raised during campaigns. Some even decide not to run for office, based on such worries (Maisel, Stone, and Maestas 1999). Officeholders worry that principled positions taken forcibly on one set of salient issues might well define their image for some time to come.

The media is an important part of politics, but it is one that is only partially controlled by politicians. They must accept that constraint if they are going to enter the public arena. The positive contributions of the media to our polity were considered so important that the press was given a uniquely privileged position in the Constitution. Nothing in our political experience since the founding has led even the harshest critic of the media to think that the judgment of the founders regarding the sanctity of a free press should be questioned. Many would argue—and we would strongly agree—that loss of a free press will sooner or later (probably sooner) result in the loss of a free society. The importance of a free press has become even more evident as we evaluate the 2016 election cycle and our current political climate. Donald Trump has been a longtime critic of the American media, even as he has used the media to become an international celebrity. But now Trump is president of the United States, and his regular attacks on the news media as purveyors of lies and "fake news" (Kelly 2018) have the potential to cause real damage to American civil society. Americans' trust in the media has been on the decline for quite some time, as noted earlier in this chapter. However, since Trump entered the presidential race in 2015 and almost immediately stepped up his attacks on the media, a major partisan gap in media trust has developed. Republicans' trust in the media has plummeted over the past two years, while Democrats' trust has actually gone up a bit (Dugan and Auter 2017; Dupuy 2018; Pew Research Center 2016; Sullivan 2017; Swift 2016; Wasko 2017). This development—problematic in and of itself—is highly concerning in a society already marked by high levels of partisan polarization.

The growth of social media has presented some particular problems. Some have argued that politicians' use of social media is further increasing partisan polarization (Bump 2017). The ease of creation and dissemination allowed for by social media along with little accountability and the ease in disguising one's identity has allowed for the rise of *real* fake news online. Indeed, a recent study by a group of researchers at MIT clearly demonstrates that falsehoods spread far more quickly than truths on social media (Aral 2018; Lazer et al. 2018). We also know without any doubt—despite what President Trump might say or believe—that the Russian government used social media (Facebook in particular) in an explicit attempt to influence the outcome of the 2016 American election cycle (Bump 2018a, b; Dilanian 2017; Frenkel and Benner 2018; Musil 2018; Oates 2017; Rosenberg 2017; Timberg 2018). U.S. intelligence agencies have testified before Congress that the Russians are already at work trying to influence the 2018 election cycle (Riechmann 2018). As a result of this the FEC has proposed rules increasing the transparency of online political advertising (Lee and Romm 2018b). The FEC is also considering expanding some online advertising disclaimers currently applicable to websites to mobile apps as well (Lee and Romm 2018a). As we go to press with this edition it has been revealed that Cambridge Analytica, a datamining and voter targeting firm that worked on the 2016 Trump campaign (as well as the 2016 Brexit campaign), harvested the private data of over 50 million Facebook users that the company then used to target voters. Cambridge Analytica is currently under investigation in both the United States and the UK (Bump 2018a; Rosenberg, Confessore, and Cadwalladr 2018).

Media in the United States is changing rapidly, especially in regard to how it intersects with politics. While there can be no doubt that a free press is absolutely critical to a free society, there is also no doubt that the American polity currently face some challenges in this area.

CRITICAL THINKING QUESTIONS

1. How have social media changed American campaigns and elections?
2. Do American political campaigns result in educated voters?
3. Do the American media devote adequate time, attention, and resources to covering politics and government?
4. Should negative advertisements be banned in American campaigns and elections?

KEY TERMS

social media
free or earned media
paid media
penny press
informed consent of the governed
adwatch campaigns
pack journalism
expectation game
field winnower
positive ads
negative ads
contrast ads
attack ads

NOTES

1. Radio has never had the same impact on politics that newspapers and television have had, though local politicians do spend a good deal of time making sure that their views are aired on that medium as well and recent GOP success is due in no small part to talk radio.

2. In fairness, it should be noted that the two parties' nominees were known well in advance of these conventions. Thus, even in the absence of party orchestration, there would have been very little drama.

3. What follows draws heavily on Richard Davis (1996), though similar categories have been used in other earlier works. See, for example, Barber (1978).

4. In fact, this very question has been asked of many pollsters. Sampling techniques allow pollsters to obtain accurate assessments of the mood of the nation (always within a specified margin of error) by asking questions to relatively few citizens (under fifteen hundred). The same is true for polling within the various states.

5. The discussion to this point deals with candidate advertisements. Party advertisements have similar goals, either for one candidate or for a group of candidates running under the party label. Interest group advertisements are somewhat more complex and are discussed below.

Chapter 11

Party in Government

From left to right: Speaker of the House Paul Ryan, Senate Majority Leader Mitch McConnell, Senate Minority Leader Charles Schumer, and House Minority Leader Nancy Pelosi prepare to face the media. Greater partisan tension both between and within parties have made it increasingly difficult for Congress to get things done in recent years.

Republicans had every reason to feel great as Election Day 2016 came to a close. Their party's presidential candidate—Donald Trump—had just won an election that most (including him, according to some accounts) thought he had no chance of winning. The party had also maintained its control of both chambers of Congress, giving the party unified control of the federal government for the first time since the 2006 election cycle. Now, after ten long years, including eight frustrating years of having to deal with Democratic president Barack Obama, Republicans were poised to deliver on long-standing policy goals and promises. Atop the list—repealing the hated Affordable Care Act (popularly known as Obamacare) and tax reform, perhaps the most fundamental, bedrock principle of the Republican Party.

But things did not get off to a very good start. The inexperienced Trump administration stumbled out of the gate, making headlines with various gaffes, self-inflicted wounds, and a seemingly endless parade of controversies. Staffing the new administration also proved far more difficult than normal, thus further slowing down the policy-making process. Finally, by summer of 2017, the GOP appeared to be getting serious about one of its top two goals—the repeal and replacement of Obamacare. But no sooner had the process started than red flags began appearing. It soon became clear that the party could not agree on what a replacement (if any) should look like, so that portion was tossed aside to concentrate solely on repeal. But even here congressional Republicans (especially in the Senate) were split by strenuous internal differences. By all accounts, President Trump and his administration were of little help. Nonetheless, a bill was finally put together and scheduled for a vote. Finally, in the early morning hours of July 28, 2017, Arizona Republican senator John McCain, having just returned to Washington from his home in Arizona where he was being treated for a brain tumor, strode to the front of the Senate chamber and with a dramatic "thumbs down" motion indicated his no vote on the repeal of the Affordable Care Act, stunning his fellow Republicans. Another last-ditch effort at repeal in September 2017 also failed. The GOP had swung and missed on a bill to repeal Obamacare, something the party had spent the last eight years saying it would do (Bacon 2017; BBC 2017; Cunningham 2017; Everett, Haberkorn, and Dawsey 2017; Lee et al. 2017; Roubein 2017).

Shortly thereafter, Congress went into recess and members went home to their states and districts. Republicans heard displeasure from both their constituents and their donors. How could they have failed on health care? Indeed, how could the party have zero to show for six months of unified control? At that point, GOP leadership—and rank-and-file members as well—knew they needed to produce a win when they returned to Washington, and the place they decided to seek victory was their other top issue: tax reform. In November GOP leaders in each chamber began putting their tax reform plans in place and building support among their party members. As was the case with the failed health care reform, little assistance could be expected from Democrats. But unlike the health care failure, this time the Republicans had a well-thought-out plan, and they more or less stuck to it. Republican leadership made sure to discuss the plan with all members of the party, and indicated they were very willing to cut deals in exchange for support. President Trump and members of his administration were engaged and helpful in the effort. On tax reform the Republicans were wildly successful. Less than thirty days from when the tax reform plans were officially introduced, the Tax Cuts and Jobs Act passed both chambers of Congress and was signed by President Trump. The biggest tax overhaul in thirty years had been passed in a month. The GOP had gone from the gang that couldn't shoot straight to a well-oiled policy machine. Republicans, from the president on down, said that they had delivered the American people one big Christmas present (Faler and Kim 2017; Faler, Kim, and Wilhelm 2017; Mattingly and Fox 2017; Paletta and Stein 2017).

Before thinking such dramatic swings of partisan performance are solely a function of today's GOP, think back to when Barack Obama first took office. Democrats were riding high in the aftermath of the 2008 election cycle. Barack Obama had convincingly won the presidency, becoming the first Democratic candidate to attain a majority of the popular vote since Jimmy Carter in 1976. The Democrats had also added twenty-one seats to their existing House majority, and although it would ultimately take until July 2009 for it to become official with the swearing in of Al Franken as the junior senator from Minnesota, the party felt relatively confident it had reached the magic number of sixty seats in the Senate, creating a filibuster-proof majority, assuming that all sixty Democrats could stick together. Yes, it was good to be a Democrat.

Given these circumstances, it is not surprising that Obama promised to take swift action on his top legislative priority—a complete overhaul of health care policy in the United States with the ultimate goal of attaining health care coverage for all Americans, or something very close to it. Universal health insurance was regarded by many Democrats as the final, unachieved piece of the New Deal, and for the last almost sixty years a number of Democratic leaders—including former presidents Harry Truman and Bill Clinton—had tried and failed to get the policy enacted into law (Wayne and Epstein 2010; Wilson 2010). Given Obama's impressive electoral victory, his high approval rating, and the Democrats' sizable majorities in both houses of Congress, Obama and his fellow Democrats were sure that finally their time had come; universal health care coverage would become the law of the land.

Despite such favorable circumstances and their high levels of confidence, the Democrats got off to a relatively slow start on health care. The ongoing economic meltdown continued to dominate American politics, and Obama spent a good deal of political energy and capital in getting his $787 billion financial stimulus package—officially the American Recovery and Reinvestment Act of 2009—through Congress. And the seemingly endless legal wrangling over the Minnesota Senate seat prevented the Democrats from being able to overcome a **filibuster**, at least without some help from at least one Republican. Still, in May 2009 President Obama appeared outside the White House with Speaker Pelosi and other Democratic House leaders and stated to the American people that health care reform would get done, and done soon. Pelosi promised a vote in her chamber no later than August 2009, and while no senators were present and no date for a Senate vote was offered, Obama bluntly stated that reform had to be completed "this year" (Condon 2009). Most Democratic leaders believed that they could meet Obama's timeline; they felt that once they seriously turned their attention to health care they would be able to enact reform with little more than the average hiccups and roadblocks faced by all major successful legislative efforts. This was not to be the case.

As spring turned into summer, it became obvious that Pelosi's promise of a health care vote by August would not come to pass. Instead, members of Congress left Washington for August recess and headed home to their states and districts. As they attended town hall forums and other public events back home, many members—especially Democrats—were shocked at what they encountered. Members arrived at town halls and other events and were met with very angry constituents who proceeded to castigate their representatives for the evils they were about to unleash with health care reform. As the number of such events increased, video of angry shouting matches, implied or direct threats of physical violence, and befuddled and sometimes even scared members of Congress became common fare on Americans' televisions and computer monitors. Such images were surprising, but perhaps they should not have been. Complete reform of the American health care system—one-sixth of the American economy and something that directly affects every American—was a truly monumental feat to contemplate. Public discontent with the proposed health care reform had been slowly building; Obama and his fellow Democrats had done little to provide specifics on the plan or make their case to the people, while at the same time Republican leaders and various groups opposed to reform were offering dire warnings about what the consequences of Democratic reform would ultimately be. Sarah Palin, for example, first presented her soon-to-be-famous claim about the "death panels" reform would create in an August 7 Facebook post. High-profile Republican members of Congress such as Michele Bachmann and Minority Leader John Boehner vociferously made their arguments against health care reform, and conservative commentators such as Rush Limbaugh and Glenn Beck informed their vast audiences of the evils of the Democrats' intended reform. By the time Congress returned from its August recess, Republican opponents of health care reform clearly had the upper hand, and the Democrats' momentum toward reform had evaporated (Murray and Montgomery 2009).

Democratic leaders, however, were not about to give up. President Obama continued to believe he could attract some Republican support for health care reform, and along with Senate Majority Leader Harry Reid he tried to reach out to a few GOP senators, most prominently Olympia Snowe of Maine. At the same time, Reid was working overtime trying to ensure the support of a handful of more moderate senators within his own party, such as Ben Nelson of Nebraska and Mary Landrieu of Louisiana. All of this was being done in the Senate at the same time that Senator Ted Kennedy and after his death Senator Christopher Dodd were writing their version of the health care reform bill as chairs of the Senate Committee on Health, Education, Labor, and Pensions, and Senator Max Baucus was compiling his as the chair of the Senate Finance Committee. Clearly there were a lot of moving parts in the Senate.

Meanwhile, in the House, Nancy Pelosi was taking a somewhat different approach in the attempt to get reform through her chamber. Pelosi determined early on that she would likely have to rely solely on Democrats to pass health care reform. As a group of long-tenured, loyal House Democrats—including John Dingell (Mich.), Charlie Rangel (N.Y.), Henry Waxman (Calif.), Pete Stark (Calif.), and George Miller (Calif.), among others—worked at crafting the House version of health care reform, Pelosi, Majority Leader Steny Hoyer, and the Democratic whips assiduously courted their fellow Democrats, trying to figure out exactly what they would need to do to get the 218 votes needed for passage. Given that the Democrats controlled 258 seats in the House, one might think that getting those 218 votes would be easy for Pelosi. But that was not true. Liberal House Democrats were insistent on the inclusion of a "public option," a plan where the federal government would directly provide health insurance to Americans; moderate Democrats—including many so-called Blue Dogs—worried about the huge price tag of reform, as did conservative Democrats, many of whom were also concerned about the treatment of abortion in reform proposals. Many of the House Democrats in these latter two groups were also from swing districts, meaning that they faced reelection concerns that their colleagues from safe Democratic districts did not.

But slowly, largely behind the scenes, Pelosi overcame obstacles and collected votes. Only the abortion barrier could not be dealt with. A number of pro-life Democrats, most of whom were Catholics from the Midwest, would not support reform unless it included an ironclad guarantee that federal dollars could not be used for abortions under the plan. Finally, in a series of closed-door meetings on November 7, Pelosi brokered one more compromise. In a tense meeting with staunch pro-choice members, many of whom were Pelosi's female colleagues in the House, Pelosi made it clear that in order for reform to pass she would have to allow a vote on an amendment explicitly barring the use of federal funds for abortion. According to an insider account of this meeting published by the *Washington Post*, many of the women became furious at this point, and Rep. Louise Slaughter (D-N.Y.), a longtime close friend and ally of Pelosi, raged about "all the women we were just throwing under the bus." Pelosi, reportedly with tears in her eyes, responded that without such a clause they simply did not have the votes for passage (Connolly 2010). Pelosi allowed the antiabortion amendment—dubbed the Stupak Amendment after the leader of the antiabortion Democrats, Bart Stupak (D-Mich.) —and it passed, 240 to 194, with 64 Democrats voting in favor. That was the only amendment Pelosi would allow. On November 7, 2009, in a rare late-Saturday vote, the House approved its version of health care reform 220 to 215, a margin of two votes to spare, 219 Democrats and 1 lonely Republican (Bacon 2009; Montgomery and Murray 2009).

But the House was only half the battle. Progress in the Senate was proving to be more difficult. Despite expending a tremendous amount of time and effort, neither Obama nor Reid was able to attract even a single Republican vote. Passing the measure with only Democrats was difficult as well. A handful of moderate Democrats steadfastly refused to support the "public option" included in the House version of reform, and some of these same moderates were concerned about the cost of the program and how it would be paid for. Even a closed-door meeting with former president Bill Clinton seemingly could not unite all Democrats behind reform. Ultimately, Reid seemingly cut deals with a few of these moderates in exchange for their support. Senator Ben Nelson (D-Nebr.) got the soon-to-be-infamous "Cornhusker Kickback," which would have paid 100 percent of Nebraska's Medicaid premiums for the foreseeable future, and Senator Mary Landrieu got the "Louisiana Purchase," an additional $100–$300 million in Medicaid for her state. Florida senator Bill Nelson received a provision dubbed "Gator Aid," which would have allowed Medicare recipients in his state to keep benefits that Medicare recipients in other states would be losing. In the end, Reid's efforts proved just enough. Just after sunrise on the day before Christmas, the Senate approved its version of health care reform by a vote of 60 to 39 (Murray and Montgomery 2009).

After the Senate vote, members of Congress headed home for the holiday recess, and President Obama left for Hawaii with his family. While there were significant differences between the House and Senate versions of health care reform, Democratic leaders were confident those differences could be worked out in a conference committee, and that each house would then vote in favor of the final bill. The House was scheduled to reconvene on January 12, 2010, with the Senate slated to follow suit on January 19. Although the Senate did reconvene as scheduled on that date, something else happened on January 19, 2010, that threw the future of health care reform into immediate and serious doubt. January 19 was the date of the special election to fill the Massachusetts Senate seat held for forty-seven years by the late Ted Kennedy. Massachusetts being an overwhelmingly Democratic state, no one had considered the possibility that the Democrats would lose that seat. But before the polls even closed on January 19, it was clear that the impossible had indeed happened: Republican Scott Brown had defeated Democrat Martha Coakley for Kennedy's old seat. The Democrats' filibuster-proof majority was gone. Shortly after 6:00 p.m. that evening, President Obama called Speaker Pelosi and Majority Leader Reid to the Oval Office for an emergency meeting (Connolly 2010). There was only one item on the agenda: What now?

No answers were arrived at that evening. Over the next few days and weeks, as Democrats dealt with their shock and worked to overcome disappointment and anger, often directed at their fellow partisans, multiple possible ways forward were mulled over. Some called for action before Brown could be sworn in; such a move was quickly rejected. Others called for the passage of a scaled-back reform. Many Democrats, including President Obama, steadfastly refused. Reid wanted the House to simply pass the Senate version of reform. In that case no further Senate action would be needed and the bill would go directly to Obama to be signed into law. Pelosi initially and repeatedly refused this option, saying she simply did not have the votes to pass the Senate bill. No one doubted her, but Obama kept persistently asking her to try to get them. This urging would ultimately prove critical.

One thing that did occur quickly after Brown's victory in the Massachusetts special election was the determination on the part of the White House that its number one failure in the push for health care reform had been ceding too much control to Congress. The public needed to see the president in charge and driving the bus of reform. As part of the attempt to get Obama out in front on reform, the president went to Baltimore on January 29 for a televised health care forum with House Republicans. While the forum did little to sway Republicans, it did serve to signal to congressional Democrats that Obama was now all in on health care. Obama held a similar televised meeting with Senate Democrats on February 3 and a more than seven-hour summit with a bipartisan group of twenty-eight members of Congress on February 25. In late February and early March Obama and his then chief of staff Rahm Emanuel worked tirelessly to court individual members of Congress over the phone, in meetings on Capitol Hill, and at meetings and parties at the White House. Pelosi was also working hard in the House. Slowly, Obama and Pelosi collected additional votes in favor of the Senate version of reform, with some slight revisions. Obama was able to convert Ohio Democrat and former presidential candidate Dennis Kucinich in a one-on-one conversation aboard Air Force One (Connolly 2010). More conversions followed (Kane, Montgomery, and Pershing 2010).

By the third week of March, Pelosi was confident that her efforts, along with those of President Obama and numerous other Democratic leaders, had finally paid off. After one final address to House Democrats from President Obama, a day filled with checking and rechecking to make sure she had the votes she needed, and intense demonstrations against reform outside the Capitol Building where some black and homosexual Democratic members were bombarded with racial and antigay slurs from protestors, Speaker Pelosi decided to put health care up for a vote on Sunday, March 21 (Montgomery and Kane 2010). Actually, Pelosi would need two separate votes; the first on the original Senate bill and a second on proposed changes to the Senate bill. If successful, the bill with the changes would have to be approved by the Senate, but under a process known as **reconciliation**—a provision of the Congressional Budget Act of 1974 that allows Congress to operate under special rules when dealing with budget-related matters—it could not be filibustered and therefore would need only a simple majority to pass.

In a rare Sunday evening vote on March 21, Pelosi got the results she had long sought. First the House passed the Senate version of health care reform by a vote of 219 to 212; no Republican supported the bill and 34 Democrats voted against it. Once the vote was final, Democrats erupted into cheers on the House floor and hugged their colleagues, while Republicans looked disgusted and forlorn. Soon after the first vote, the House passed its package of fixes to the Senate bill 220 to 211, again without a single Republican vote. Pelosi congratulated her Democratic colleagues on this historic action, sentiments echoed by President Obama (Murray and Montgomery 2010). The primary health care bill, now having been passed in identical form by both chambers, went off to President Obama for his signature while the second bill amending the original headed to the Senate, again under special reconciliation rules that prevented a filibuster. Most now assumed that health care reform was finally accomplished, for good or for ill. While such assumptions were ultimately correct, there were still a few more obstacles to be overcome before the policy would finally become law.

Obama's signature of the original bill was the easy—and celebratory—part. On March 23, Obama gathered a number of high-profile Democratic lawmakers (past and present) who had worked on health care into the elegant East Room of the White House to witness the historic event. Obama was introduced by Vice President Joe Biden, who after making the introduction leaned into Obama and noted "This is a big fucking deal," which of course open microphones picked up. Obama used twenty-two different pens to sign the measure before an audience that appeared awestruck by what had been accomplished, in an atmosphere that sometimes resembled a raucous college football pep rally (Wayne and Epstein 2010; Wilson 2010).

The remaining actions did not go as smoothly, but ultimately produced the same result. Soon after the signing ceremony a number of House Democrats reported being the targets of attacks and threats. A voicemail message for Congressman Stupak stated: "You're dead. We know where you live. We'll get you." Security was stepped up immediately (Rucker 2010a). On March 24, President Obama signed another piece of paper, this one much more quietly: an executive order reiterating and guaranteeing that no federal money could be used for abortion unless the situation met the traditional federal exemptions: rape, incest, or life of the mother in danger. This order, which infuriated many women's groups that were normally very supportive of the president, was a crucial part of convincing some House Democrats to continue with the plan of passing the original Senate bill followed by a separate bill altering the original (Stein 2010). The offer of such an executive order in exchange for the support of these members was first made by Rahm Emanuel to Bart Stupak when they ran into each other at the House gym (Murray and Montgomery 2010).

The Senate took up the House bill containing the alterations on March 24 with Republicans hoping to find some way to argue that the bill violated reconciliation rules and thus open it up to a filibuster, and if this was not possible to amend it in some way that would force the House to act again. After a series of debates and votes (forty-one, to be exact) that lasted over twenty-one straight hours—a process dubbed vote-a-rama by some participants—the bill finally passed the Senate 56–43 on March 25. In one last small glimmer of hope for the Republicans, the Senate parliamentarian did identify twenty words that violated procedural rules, and the alteration of these words did force one more House vote. But later that day the House approved the amended bill 220–207, and President Obama signed it into law on March 30 (Murray 2010).

Health care reform was finally law, but for many Democrats—in and out of government—it seemed that the process was much more difficult than it should have been. As noted earlier, universal health insurance has long been among the Democrats' most cherished goals, if not at the very top of the list. Obama won the 2008 presidential election easily, had very high approval ratings (at least initially), and the Democrats controlled both Houses by bulletproof margins. Yet by spring of 2010 passage of health care reform was in serious doubt, and the fact that the effort was ultimately successful after the events of January–March 2010 still comes as somewhat of a surprise. The same can be said of Republicans' 2017 failure to repeal Obama's signature achievement and their success in achieving major tax reform. These were all fundamental matters to the party in question. So why was passage so difficult? The answer is very simple: The American institutional arrangement of separated institutions sharing powers combined with the federated nature of the American electoral system makes it very difficult for even the most unified party to exert its will over all of its members.

The Republicans' success on tax reform and the Democrats' hard-fought achievement of health care reform are less a demonstration of the power of parties in American government than a demonstration of the constraints on that power, constraints imposed by the very nature of the American political system. These constraints were in full view on the GOP's failure to repeal Obamacare.

A closer look at the convoluted health care reform efforts pursued by both parties here as well as the GOP tax reform effort reveals not a strong majority party organization whipping its members into line but a majority party leadership constrained in its ability to exert its will over members. In the American political system, members of Congress are hired and fired by their constituents, not by the national parties. Representatives and senators owe their seats to the people of their district or state, not to the leaders of their party. Without a hold on the electoral careers of its members, parties in Congress derive their power less from coercion than from persuasion and the wishes of its members. Parties in Congress are only as strong—or weak—as their members want them to be.

Although parties are not mentioned in the Constitution, they are certainly constrained by the governmental structure established by it. Federalism ensures that ideological, social, and economic differences are built into the two-party system from the local level up; that is, the two major parties in the United States can look significantly different from state to state. A Massachusetts Democrat may find little in common with a Georgia Democrat; Republicans from Maine and Texas may vary greatly on legislative priorities. Because members of Congress are elected by local party members on the basis of local issues, these regional, state, and local interests are reflected at the national level. Members responsible to, and punishable by, local electorates tend to be responsive to constituents, not necessarily to party leadership. Thus, the American federal system and a national legislature made up of members elected by plurality in relatively small single-member districts (House) or at the state level (Senate) work against strong parties in Congress.

Furthermore, unlike their European counterparts in parliamentary democracies, American parties operate in a context of the separation of powers and of checks and balances, or "separated institutions sharing powers" (Neustadt 1960). The legislative process is shared by both the House and the Senate, with the Constitution requiring the two to forge a final agreement on policy; yet these institutions differ in their organization, procedures, rules, and norms. As established at the founding, majority rule governs the House, while minority rights are protected in the Senate. Partisanship and disciplined leadership are trademarks of the House as the majority party works to bring together what a fragmented, decentralized committee system pulls apart. In the more individualized Senate, majority party leadership cannot push the party position through the chamber but must forge unanimous consent agreements, always aware of obstructionist tools available to the opposition, such as the filibuster—the right to unlimited debate[1]—and **senatorial holds**—a practice that allows an individual senator to prevent a presidential nominee from coming up for a confirmation vote simply by asking that such vote be held up. These differences across governmental institutions make coordination, organization, and "responsible party" governance all the more difficult for American parties.

Thus, we come to a surprising realization. Political parties are the most important, dominating element in organizing the government of the United States, but they do not control legislative outcomes. Even with the White House and Congress firmly unified under Democratic control after the 2008 election cycle, the Democrats had to scratch and claw to enact sweeping health care reform, arguably their number one goal of the past fifty years. With their unified control in 2017, the Republicans failed on health care reform and barely succeeded on tax reform. More than a half century ago, E. E. Schattschneider (1942, 1), a preeminent theorist of political parties asked, "What kind of party is it that, having won control of the government, is unable to govern?" That question remains as relevant now as it was at the beginning of World War II.

THEORETICAL AND HISTORICAL CONTEXT: IS STRONG PARTY GOVERNMENT POSSIBLE IN THE UNITED STATES?

In his classic text *Politics, Parties, and Pressure Groups* (1964), V. O. Key Jr., his generation's most prominent analyst of American politics, divides his discussion of party into the party organization, the party in the electorate, and the party in government. The basis for that division is the classic notion that partisans, once elected to office, should be able to implement the programs on which they ran. This normative "responsible party" idea is an old and revered one in the study of the American polity. As far back as 1885, Woodrow Wilson (1885), in his pre-presidential days as a political scientist, lamented what he viewed as "committee government"—strong committees, weak parties, and no effective party leaders in Congress. Impressed by the strength of parties in the electorate at the time, Wilson wished for the same in Congress. His solution: "The great need is, not to get rid of parties, but to find and use some expedient by which they can be managed and made amenable from day to day to public opinion" (79–80). In his view, strong parties were the best mechanism through which a democracy could convert public opinion into policy alternatives. Congressional parties must be strong to govern.

Sixty-five years after Wilson's *Congressional Government*, the Committee on Political Parties of the American Political Science Association prescribed stronger parties in its influential report "Toward a More Responsible Two-Party System" (1950), a report frequently referred to as the "Schattschneider report" (after the committee's chair). Again the complaint was familiar. American parties were too weak to form a link between the electorate and the elected. Parties did not stand firmly on issues; candidates did not feel bound to implement party programs once in office. Essentially the norm espoused in the report was a parliamentary system—that is, a government specifically structured to enact the majority party's agenda. In the parliamentary model, implicit in responsible party arguments, the individual who leads a party in the election (e.g., the British prime minister) is the same person who leads that party in government. Programmatic parties stand for opposing policies, enabling voters to cast ballots for or against a distinct party platform. In the legislature, party leaders are strong; party members are loyal; and party unity is high. Certainly, there was little evidence of responsible congressional parties by this definition at the time of the Schattschneider report.

So under what circumstances can we expect party leaders to exert control over the legislative process in the American system? Joseph Cooper and David Brady (1981), in their seminal article on congressional leadership, note the importance of context in examining the ways in which Speakers of the House have led their body. More specifically, they delineate the circumstances under which Speakers have led disciplined, hierarchical, strong party organizations, much like those in parliamentary systems. They point to the turn of the century, not long after Wilson wrote *Congressional Government*, when the two major parties stood for opposing policies and represented distinct electoral bases. During this period of relative homogeneity within each congressional party, Speakers ruled—in particular, two powerful Republican Speakers, Thomas Brackett Reed (Maine, 1889–1890; 1895–1899) and Joseph G. Cannon (Ill., 1903–1911). The tenures of "Boss" Reed and "Czar" Cannon marked the transformation from the committee government of Wilson's observations to the party government characterized by centralized leadership, hierarchal party organization, and strict party line voting (Brady 1973). The party and committee systems were essentially fused to maintain party discipline. Committee seats and chair positions were doled out by the Speaker according to party loyalty, while the top echelon of the party leadership—the Speaker, the majority leader, and the majority whip—chaired the Rules Committee, the Appropriations Committee, and the Ways and Means Committee, respectively.

But division within the Republican party began to surface. With the rise of the Progressive movement in the electorate, preferences within the majority party in the House shifted from homogeneous to heterogeneous. Speaker Cannon, however, refused to acknowledge the new wing within his party. He wielded his exclusive power to appoint committee seats and chair positions (power granted to the Speaker under the "Reed rules"), and he exercised his power as the chair of the Rules Committee to reward loyalists and punish traitors. Cannon denied the Progressive Republicans chairmanships and committee seats, and he refused to recognize them on the floor. Under the "Czar" system, the Speaker effectively controlled the policy process in the House—if he opposed legislation, such as any Progressive policy, he would not let it reach the floor. To the Progressives and Democrats, it was tyrannical rule; to Cannon, it was responsible party government:

> This is a government by the people acting through the representatives of a majority of the people. Results cannot be had except by a majority, and in the House of Representatives a majority, being responsible, should have full power and should exercise that power; otherwise the majority is inefficient and does not perform its function. (Speaker Cannon, *Congressional Record*, March 19, 1910, 3436)

In March 1910, Progressive Republicans joined forces with Democrats to strip the Republican Speaker Joe Cannon of his position on the Rules Committee, to expand the committee, and to vote for its members on the floor. The following year, the Democrats took over the House, voting to turn the committee appointment process over to the House as a whole, further decentralizing party control and weakening the Speaker's hold over members' careers (Galloway 1961; Peters 1990; Sinclair 1998).

What can explain this shift away from strong party government? Cooper and Brady (1981) argue that parties and party leadership are strong (and active) only when their members' policy preferences are relatively homogeneous—for example, the Republicans at the turn of the century. Rising heterogeneity in the party in the electorate (such as the impact of the Progressive movement) is reflected in rising heterogeneity in the party in government (such as the election of Progressive Republicans to the U.S. House of Representatives). The more diverse the member preferences are within a party, the tougher it is to lead it, and the stronger the incentives are for members to build cross-party coalitions—such as Progressive Republicans and Democrats—and decentralize party organization (see also Brady and Epstein 1997; Rohde 1991).

This matter of homogeneity versus heterogeneity also relates to a major dispute in the literature over how to understand the significance of parties in Congress. Krehbiel's (1993, 1998, 1999) view, in extreme form, is that party is the mere aggregation of induced preferences. Thus, on any given policy, when legislators' preferences within the parties are separate or distinct, we call the parties *strong*; when they overlap, we call the parties *weak*. For Aldrich (1995), Aldrich and Rohde (1997), Cox and McCubbins (1993, 2005), Ladewig (2005), Lebo, McGlynn, and Koger (2007), Rohde (1991), Stonecash, Brewer, and Mariani (2003), and Volden and Bergman (2006), parties are, roughly speaking, more than aggregations of preferences. The parties tie together voters, elections, institutions, and strategy. For example, Cox and McCubbins describe the congressional parties as "legislative cartels," far more powerful than others would surmise. With the structural deck stacked in its favor, the majority party can dole out leadership positions in exchange for loyalty (see also Kolodny 1999).

But Rohde[2] (1991, 2013) does not expect party leaders to dominate on all issues; rather, they are expected to utilize the institutional tools available to them if and only if there is widespread agreement within the party caucus or conference on the policy. Rohde has developed this concept of "conditional party government" to explain the higher levels of party cohesion found in the House in the late 1980s. He explains that parties are conditionally active coalitions: If there is preference homogeneity within the party on an issue, then leaders take action.

All would agree that homogeneity within the parties certainly facilitates strong party leadership. When members of the same party share similar views, they are more likely to give more power to their congressional leaders because the party position does not conflict with their electoral interests. Conversely, members of heterogeneous parties have less incentive to follow the party leaders' agenda, especially when it could be electorally damaging (Sinclair 1995). Yet, as Rohde (1991) points out, the power of party leaders can vary from issue to issue, depending on the distribution of its members' preferences on a given piece of legislation.

Taking this argument one step further, in policy arenas with more heterogeneous preference distributions, we would then expect votes cast with members' respective parties to be indicative of strong party leadership.

So if the strength of parties in Congress is variable by time and context, what does this say about the ability of the majority party to achieve its policy goals in situations of **unified control** (one party controls both the legislative and executive branches) versus those of **divided government** (when control of these two branches is distributed between the two major parties)? Political scientists have long examined this question. Inherent in the debate over unified versus divided government is the assumption that party matters. In a party-oriented interpretation of gridlock, the president bargains with the median of the majority party in Congress; when the two are of different parties, it is difficult to pass legislation to move policy away from the status quo (see Fiorina 1996; Jacobson 1990a; Mayhew 1991; Cox and Kernell 1991; Brady and Volden 1998). In such a scenario, unified party control would result in inherently less gridlock and more party-sponsored legislation, a sure positive for advocates of responsible party government.

But what if legislative impasses are not solely party-driven phenomena? The heterogeneity of preferences in the electorate and in Congress, and the complexity of policy areas, may be the sources of legislative stalemates, regardless of divided or unified control. In *Divided We Govern*, David Mayhew (1991, 2005) compares periods of divided and unified party government in terms of the amount of legislation passed, vetoes sustained, congressional hearings held, presidential treaties signed, and judicial appointments approved. Excluding the number of vetoes, he concludes that there is no significant difference in these variables under divided versus unified control. In fact, "the number of laws per Congress varies more *within* universes of unified or divided times than it does between them" (Mayhew 1991, 76; emphasis added). Clearly more is at work than two parties butting heads over policy across institutions.

In sum, when they exist, heterogeneous policy preferences within the parties create barriers to legislation in times of both unified and divided party control. If we think of parties as aggregates of their members' preferences and if these preferences are heterogeneous within a party on a particular policy, then unified party control of the government does not guarantee legislative harmony. Stalemates may simply be the result of legislation proposed that is too far from the median members in Congress, regardless of their party. On the other hand, when preferences within the respective parties are relatively homogeneous on a specific issue, then parties and divided or unified partisan control of government will matter a great deal. Given the constitutional and institutional constraints on party in government, electoral majorities in the United States do not always translate into policy majorities (Brady and Buckley 2002).

MEASURING PARTY STRENGTH IN CONGRESS

So how do we measure party strength in government? One method is to look at patterns of party voting in Congress. Political scientists use three measures to do so. First, party unity votes are votes in which a majority of the Democrats voting cast their votes on one side of an issue and the majority of Republicans on the other side. Party unity scores are the percentage of times that an individual legislator votes with his or her party on party unity votes. Thus, if every Democrat voted aye on a particular vote while 75 percent of the Republicans voted nay and 25 percent voted aye, that would be a party unity vote (a majority of Democrats voting on one side and a majority of Republicans on the other). That vote would be included in a computation of the legislators' party unity score. Political systems in which parties structure legislative decisions tend to have more party unity votes and higher party unity scores.

Figure 11.1 depicts the percentage of party unity votes in the House and Senate since 1954. Even from these rudimentary data, a number of conclusions follow. First, the number of party unity votes fell during the middle years of this period, but just as significant, partisan voting has increased since the mid-1980s. The percentage of party unity votes has been at or near a majority of all votes in both houses of Congress since the beginning of the second Reagan term, with the sole exception of the Senate in 1989. Since the 2000 election cycle, the relatively even partisan split in the nation after the 2000 election and the slim margins held by majorities in Congress have promoted even greater partisanship in House and Senate votes. *Congressional Quarterly* reports that the period 2011–2013 represents the most consistently high partisanship in Congress seen since the World War II era.

Figures 11.2 and 11.3 reveal the truly remarkable extent to which party voting has again become an important factor in Congress, and they give some clues to the reasons. First, claiming that party voting is not important is difficult when the average party unity scores of Democrats and Republicans in both houses of Congress have been well above 80 percent for the last decade. The Republican party, always assumed to be the more ideologically homogeneous, has shown remarkable unity throughout the period under study, but most particularly in the most recent years.

Democratic party scores declined in the mid-1960s and into the 1970s, particularly in the House of Representatives. However, David Rohde (1991, 50–58) has demonstrated that much of the decline in the Democratic party scores was in fact a decline in the party unity scores of *Southern* Democrats. The Democratic scores rebounded—to astoundingly high levels—during the Reagan administration and have stayed high ever since.

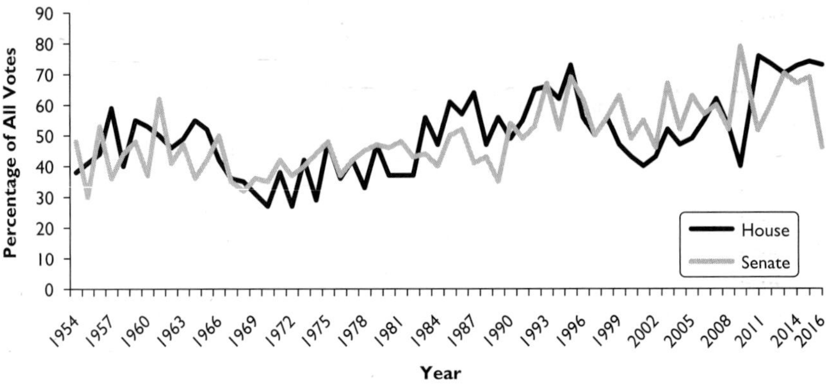

Figure 11.1. Party Unity Votes in Congress, 1954–2016
Source: CQ Almanac and *CQ Roll Call's Vote Studies.*

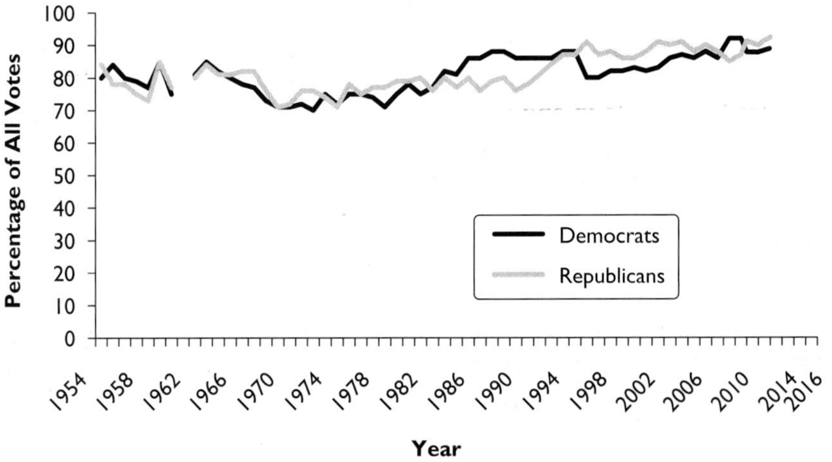

Figure 11.2. Party Unity Scores in the House, 1954–2016
Source: CQ Almanac and *CQ Roll Call's Vote Studies.*

Party unity scores are clearly much higher today than they were thirty years ago, yet that leaves us with the same important questions raised previously: Does greater party unity in Congress reflect effective party leadership or greater homogeneity within the parties? Do party unity scores increase as a result of strong whip organizations, or would members have voted this way regardless of party pressure? It is likely that both dynamics are at work here, but at the end of the day greater homogeneity

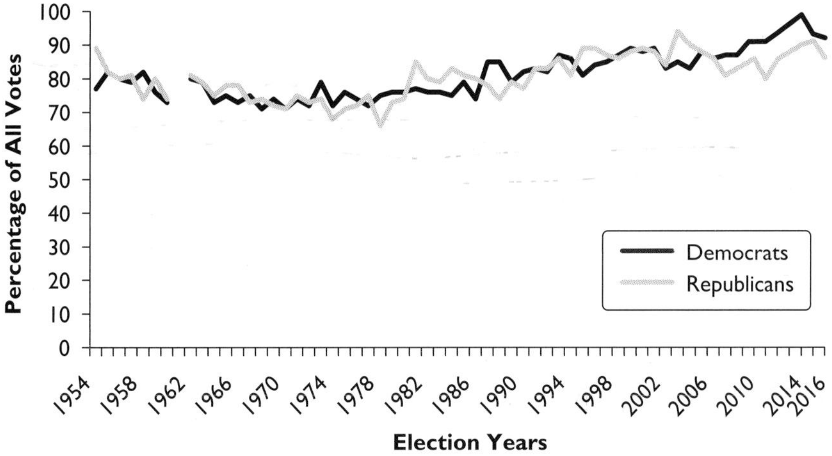

Figure 11.3. Party Unity Scores in the Senate, 1954–2016
Source: CQ Almanac and *CQ Roll Call's Vote Studies*.

within parties plays a more important role than anything the parties and their leaders can do in and of themselves. In a political system in which constituents, not the parties, hire and fire members, party leadership must offer incentives to members in exchange for their loyalty. Leadership can schedule (or block) a vote important to the member, designate (or deny) committee seats and chair positions, and dole out (or withhold) contributions to reelection campaigns from their own PACs. Thus, the party hierarchy can influence the effectiveness of a member's legislative capabilities, but it has limited ability to cajole, and practically no ability to force, members to vote with the party. The reality is that members of Congress who are elected on their own owe little to the party leaders on the Hill. As long as members can please their constituents, neither the national party nor the congressional party can affect members' electoral careers. At best, the leadership can coordinate the preferences of its party members—a job made more difficult when these preferences are diverse. But preference distributions can sometimes be difficult to predict, especially before a vote. The party leadership must know where any given member's constituent and ideology-driven preferences lie across policy areas, a complicated and at times unpredictable endeavor. Many variables can come into play once a bill is on the floor, creating greater uncertainty and increased tensions both within and between the parties.

So what does all this mean for the state of partisanship within Congress? On the one hand, down-to-the-wire, contentious party line votes have become business as usual in recent congresses. The congressional wings of both parties have grown farther apart in the past thirty years, reflecting greater homogeneity within their rank and file. Congressional Republicans have grown more conservative and Democrats more liberal—as many of the conservative Southern Democrats have been replaced by Republican members of Congress. The shift is even evident in the Americans for Democratic Action (ADA) scores in the House: In 2016 the average ADA score for Democrats was ninety-one while the Republican average was two. Comparable scores for 2016 in the Senate were eighty-nine for the Democrats and seven for the Republicans. Such rising homogeneity within the parties combined with greater differences between the parties clearly facilitates strong party leadership.

Yet on the other hand, there is only so much leadership can do to rein in the troops and influence the final tally. There is still some degree of heterogeneity present within both parties in both houses of Congress. To further complicate matters, preferences within the party can shift according to policy area; thus, we are left with the conclusion that party leaders in the American political system can only lead as far and as fast as their followers want them to. Leadership has its privileges, to be sure, but rank-and-file members still exert those independent judgments that constrain leadership prerogatives. In the next section, we see how the unique history, rules, norms, and traditions in each chamber of Congress place further constraints on party leadership.

PARTY ORGANIZATION IN CONGRESS: THE LEADERSHIP HIERARCHY IN THE HOUSE AND SENATE

The major political parties are quite elaborately organized to coordinate their work in Congress. They have to be. Given the enormous workload confronting members and given the complicated committee system developed to tackle that workload, parties must be the integrative mechanisms that bring together what the division of labor pulls apart; yet the ability of House and Senate leaders to coordinate party positions and legislate party policies is constrained by the two very different institutions in which they serve.

Leadership positions in Congress are partisan positions. Although party positions are not mentioned in the Constitution (the document is in fact silent on parties), Article 2, Section 2, does mandate an institutional leader for the House of Representatives. Members must elect their own leader, known as the **Speaker**, and since the earliest days of the Republic, the Speaker has always been partisan, the highest-ranking party leader of the House (Peters 1990). In fact, in the period from Reconstruction to the turn of the century, Speakers were recognized more than presidents as the leaders of their party, rivaling presidential power to set and execute the party agenda and even rivaling the president in recognition among the electorate. At this time the party organization became more structured. The party leadership roles of **majority leader** and **minority leader** (and **majority whip** and **minority whip**, their assistants charged with tracking the vote intentions of individual members and attempting to persuade reluctant members to vote the party line) developed out of the intense partisan conflict of the period, appearing in the House in the late nineteenth century and in the Senate in the first decade of the twentieth century. The institutional development of the organizational support for these leaders followed slowly (Sinclair 1983).

House Leadership

Although Speakers are officially elected by the entire House, the vote to elect them is essentially party line. Each party's caucus (i.e., a meeting of all party members) nominates a candidate for Speaker. Generally all the Republicans vote for their candidate, and all the Democrats for their candidate. The current Speaker of the House, Wisconsin congressman Paul Ryan, was elected Speaker at the beginning of the 115th Congress with all but one Republican vote.

The Speaker's "right hand" is the majority leader. Elected by party members to handle the day-to-day leadership of the party, the majority leader schedules legislation; coordinates committee work; and negotiates with the president, the House minority leader, and the Senate leadership. The goal of a majority leader is to build and maintain voting coalitions and essentially to keep peace in the family (Sinclair 1983).

Next in line in the party hierarchy are the whips—named after the "whippers-in" of the hounds, in the traditional English fox hunt. Their job is to link the rank and file to the party leadership. They are the information disseminators, in-house pollsters, and vote counters. They make the party position known to all members of the party caucus; assess who is for, against, or on the fence on any given piece of legislation; try to persuade reluctant members to follow the party line; and report back to the Speaker and the majority leader or to the minority leaders with the expected vote tallies. Consequently, the whip organization for both parties is extensive, comprising a chief deputy whip and the deputy whips, assistant whips, regional whips, and zone whips. Such a large whip organization allows for many members to participate in party leadership. In addition, members can also serve on the party committees—the Democratic and Republican Steering and Policy committees—which establish each party's legislative priorities, develop tactical strategies for passage of the party agenda, and nominate members for committees.

Over the past forty years the Democrats and Republicans have each had their turns at being the majority party, and thus each has also had turns at being in the minority. The next section looks briefly at how House party leadership has evolved during this period.

Democratic Hegemony

Democratic leadership before the 1970s had much to do with decentralization of power. The desire to strip the Speaker of authoritarian power had been in evidence ever since the revolt against Speaker Cannon in 1910. During the first forty years of Democratic hegemony in the House—Democrats controlled the House for all but four years from the 72nd Congress (1931–1933) through the 103rd Congress (1993–1995)—party leaders shared power with, and often were at the mercy of, committee leaders. Speakers had to rely heavily on their relationships with powerful and independent committee chairs to pass legislation—that is, they relied on those who owed their positions to the safety of their seats and to their seniority on their committees, not to the party or to the Speaker. Committee chairs were chosen strictly by their seniority, not by party loyalty; the Democratic member who had served longest on a committee was the chair (Hinckley 1971).

But all of this began to change in the early 1970s. A group of new Democratic members, frustrated by the seniority system and their inability to pass legislation important to them and their constituents, initiated a period of reform aimed at restructuring power in the House. The reform movement took power away from the committee chairs and spread it more evenly among the members. For a time, power was seemingly fragmented, and no one appeared to be able to formulate a party position in the House (Oleszek 1989; Ornstein 1975; Sheppard 1985; Smith and Deering 1990). Yet the decentralization of power to subcommittees and their leaders, and the empowerment of rank-and-file (and thus junior) members of Congress, would eventually strengthen the party; in fact, in the long run, the movement would reinvigorate the caucus and empower party leadership (Rohde 1974, 1991).

Although the committee system became more decentralized, the party leadership became more centralized. The 1970s reforms saw the first efforts aimed at centralizing party leadership, as party leaders were seen as more likely to be responsive to rank-and-file members than committee chairs protective of their legislative turf. More power was given to the Democratic Steering and Policy Committee (which is one committee for the Democrats but two separate committees for the Republicans), and the Speaker was given more control over that committee. Thus, Steering and

Policy (Steering for the Republicans) became the committee that recommended committee assignments for all House Democrats and subcommittee chairs for the important Appropriations Committee. Composed of the key members of the party hierarchy—the party leader is the chair, the whip is vice chair, and caucus chair is second vice chair—the Steering and Policy Committee (or separate Steering and Policy Committees for the GOP) sets the party priorities and strategy.[3]

Due to these centralizing reforms, during the last roughly two decades of this period of Democratic rule the Speaker stood atop a party hierarchy that had the potential not only to present party positions effectively but also to induce allegiance from rank-and-file members.[4] During the last years of Democratic party rule in the House, Speakers Tip O'Neill (D-Mass.) and Jim Wright (D-Tex.) claimed more power than their predecessors. For example, they had the power to appoint (with caucus approval) the Democratic members of the powerful Rules Committee. They had also been given the power to refer bills to more than one committee, either simultaneously or sequentially, and to control other aspects of the flow of legislation (Bach and Smith 1988; Collie and Cooper 1989). Thus, the clear trend was for the Speaker to become more of a true party leader, and party and House rules were shifting to give him the potential to exercise leadership powers in an effective way. Newt Gingrich's changes at the beginning of the 104th Congress can therefore be seen as long steps in a progression, but steps that clearly had precedents in the actions of his Democratic predecessors.

Republican Revolution

Many of Gingrich's Republican predecessors, the former minority leaders during the period of Democratic hegemony, had a strategy of attacking the opposing party publicly while working with Democratic leaders cooperatively in private. This style rankled a group of younger, more ideologically conservative Republicans at the time that Ronald Reagan assumed the presidency. Robert Michel (R-Ill.; minority leader, 1983–1995), for example, would castigate the vociferous Speaker Wright for overt partisanship, yet he would temper his actions and forge compromises within and across parties to achieve some (albeit limited) legislative goals. By the mid-1980s, a growing number of his increasingly conservative (and also increasingly Southern) troops wanted more forceful leadership. The ascension of Trent Lott (R-Miss.) to the position of minority whip was the first manifestation of this desire, and Lott's replacement by Richard Cheney (R-Wyo.) after Lott moved on to the Senate also was done to appease the growing ranks of Southern conservatives. But after Cheney left the House to become President H. W. Bush's secretary of defense,

Minority Leader Michel endorsed the candidacy of his friend and fellow Illinoisan Edward Madigan (R-Ill.) to succeed Cheney as minority whip. The House GOP conference, however, had other ideas. Despite Michel's popularity as a leader, the Republican membership chose Newt Gingrich, an outspoken conservative and the leading critic of deposed Speaker Wright. Pressure from the conservative wing of the GOP under the leadership of Gingrich led Michel to announce his retirement, after the 103rd Congress.

Gingrich's ascent from relatively obscure backbencher to party whip to party leader can be attributed to his leadership in the 1994 midterm election campaign. It was Gingrich who was credited with formulating the idea of a **Contract with America**, a pact on which all Republican candidates would stand as they fought to take over the House. In an attempt to finally return the Republicans to power in the House, Gingrich designed a plan to nationalize the 1994 congressional elections. Gingrich engineered a short statement of Republican policy goals, gathered all of the Republican candidates for the House on the steps of the Capitol, had them sign the contract, and proclaimed that they would guarantee a vote on the issues in the Contract within the first hundred days of the 104th Congress. Very few observers gave Gingrich and the GOP much chance of actually taking control of the House. But take control the Republicans did, and it was Gingrich to whom the new members of that Congress, in the Republican majority for the first time in forty years and grateful to Gingrich for being there, looked for continued leadership (Kolodny 1996).

Not only did Gingrich become the Speaker of the House at the beginning of the 104th Congress, but he also brought with him an entire leadership team. Dick Armey of Texas became the new majority leader; if Gingrich conceived the Contract with America, Armey was its primary draftsman, a true doctrinaire conservative on the issues that defined the Republican party in the 1994 election. Armey was one of those least happy about compromises that House Republicans had wrought with those in the White House of President George H. W. Bush, much less with conservative Democrats. The rest of the leadership team—including Majority Whip Tom DeLay (Tex.)—were all Gingrich loyalists. No room was left for dissenters within the party hierarchy.

Gingrich clearly understood the need to solidify his organizational power base if he wanted to implement the Contract with America. Thus, he moved quickly to consolidate his power through the whip organization, which comprised members appointed by DeLay (but all acceptable to Gingrich). Built on the model developed by the Democrats some years earlier, the Republican whip organization consisted of a chief deputy whip (considered part of the leadership's inner circle), thirteen deputy whips, and forty assistant whips—the most extensive in the history of the

House. Using sophisticated computer and communications technology, the whip organization could contact every Republican member in a matter of minutes, guaranteeing efficient scheduling and the maximization of Republican support for party proposals.

The Steering Committee, headed by the Speaker and comprising members of the leadership team plus seven selected committee chairs, was given the power to make all committee assignments—a critical change from how Republicans secured their committee seats prior to the 104th Congress. No aspect of the organization of the House is more important to members than the committee appointment process. Members' prestige within the institution, their ability to pass legislation that is most important to them, and their opportunities to serve their constituents are all determined by the standing legislative committees to which they are assigned (Fenno 1973). Prior to the 1994 election, Republican assignments were made by a Committee on Committees composed of the senior GOP members of each state's delegation. Most of the work was done by an executive committee—senior members of the Committee on Committees—with each region of the nation guaranteed representation. Votes for the committee seats were allotted according to the number of Republican members elected from each region. During the forty-year period in the minority, the GOP-ranking minority members of each standing committee were those with the longest service on the committees; seniority was not violated.

Led and dominated by Gingrich, the Steering Committee made the committee assignments. Furthermore, the Steering Committee recommended committee chairs to the Republican Conference. In 1995, seniority was violated in three instances to guarantee that Gingrich loyalists, members well versed in the party agenda and in fund-raising, were in key committee positions. The result was not only a leadership team but also a cadre of committee chairs who were loyal to Gingrich and dedicated to the same conservative cause. Gingrich also stripped committee chairs of some of their powers—control over their own budgets, staff allocations, and scheduling of events—assuming those powers for himself and his lieutenants, in an effort to get the Contract with America through the House. He instituted the use of leadership task forces to draft some of the GOP-sponsored bills and to move legislation through committees that might be recalcitrant, essentially bypassing committee chair jurisdiction. Gingrich supervised aggressive use of the House rules to ensure the timing of legislation that came to the floor.

The picture was a clear one—a dominating Speaker and a loyal party. Gingrich assumed powers that were more evident than those of any Speaker of the House since "Czar" Joe Cannon (deposed in the famous revolt of 1910). Under Gingrich's leadership, at the beginning of the 104th

Congress, party rule dominated once again. In fact, every item on the Contract with America did come out of committee and was voted on by the House within the promised one hundred days. If the contract items did not all become law, it had to do with a less-committed group of Republicans in the Senate and of course a Democratic president, rather than any lack of effective leadership by Speaker Gingrich and his allies.

To be sure, Gingrich's power did not remain absolute. In the winter of 1995/1996, Gingrich and the GOP came out on the wrong end of public opinion as a result of a budget showdown with President Clinton that resulted in two separate shutdowns of the federal government. As a result, the Republican majority in the House was pared to a mere eleven seats in the 1996 elections. In July 1997, a mere two-and-a-half years after the Republicans returned to power, a group of dissidents plotted against the leader who had brought them to the promised land of majority status. Gingrich was able to beat back this attempted coup, but after the Republicans lost seats in the 1998 midterm elections as well, Gingrich decided to resign from the Speakership and the House of Representatives itself. But most of the Gingrich-era reforms lived on even after his departure. The Republican majorities under the leadership of Speaker Dennis Hastert (Ill., 1997–2007) and majority leaders Dick Armey (Tex., 1995–2003) and Tom DeLay (Tex., 2003–2005) operated largely under the rubrics established by Gingrich.

The Democrats Briefly Bounce Back and the Resurgence of the GOP: 2006–2018

The strong majority party organization during the years of Republican control necessitated minority party cohesion, a difficult task for the Democrats given the wide spectrum of ideological, geographical, and ethnic constituencies in their caucus. Much of the blame for the Democrats' losses in the 2002 midterms was directed at the minority party's leaders for their failure to build consensus in the heterogeneous caucus and to put forth a clear, united, and coherent party platform. The question after the 2002 election was: What exactly do the House Democrats stand for? Not: What do they stand against? One reaction to this question was replacing outgoing majority leader Richard Gephardt with Nancy Pelosi, the party whip who had represented San Francisco, one of the most liberal districts in the country, since 1987.

When Pelosi won election to what was then the highest leadership position held by a woman in Congress, defeating centrists Martin Frost (Tex.) and Harold Ford (Tenn.), political pundits and the media portrayed her as the "liberal's liberal," an easy target for conservative critics and the Bush White House—Karl Rove's dream come true. Yet the new minority leader's liberalness was not nearly as much of an outlier in her party as some made it out to be. In addition, Pelosi made it clear that she understood that as minority leader she must appeal not only to her liberal base but to Democratic centrists as well.

Pelosi and the Democrats illustrated how well they understood this need to go beyond the liberal base in the 2006 cycle. Pelosi, along with then DCCC chair Rahm Emanuel (Ill.), actively sought out and gave strong support to more centrist Democratic candidates in districts where it would have been very difficult, if not impossible, for a liberal Democrat to win (Dewan and Kornblut 2006). This move paid handsome dividends as the party took back the House for the first time since 1995. Pelosi and the Democrats built on this success in 2008, reelecting many of these more centrist officeholders and adding additional ones; the party added twenty-one seats to its House majority.

Democrats' control of the House obviously came to an abrupt halt as a result of the 2010 election cycle. The Republicans recaptured control of the House by picking up a net gain of sixty-four seats, the largest figure since 1948. The new Republican leadership promised a change in the way that the House conducts its business, and they established new rules for the House. Republicans maintained their control of the House through the 2016 election cycle. Indeed, many pundits were claiming that the GOP—largely through gerrymandering and natural population movement trends—had a near lock on the House for the foreseeable future, although the upcoming 2018 cycle is drawing such claims into question. Regardless, it is most certainly true that the current House electoral situation stacks up much more favorably for the Republican party than it does for the Democrats.

The Backbone of House Leadership: The Whip Systems

Both the majority and minority leaders rely heavily on their respective whips to garner support for party policies. As former minority whip (and current Republican senator from Missouri) Roy Blunt explains, "The whip should know the members better than anybody else in the leadership and know the whole conference better than anybody else in the building" (Allen 2003a, 750). Whips build majorities by knowing each and every district and by understanding the needs of members—a seat on a specific committee, a project of importance back home, or even a spot in the whip organization. Whips can come under fire, as Blunt knows well. Fingers were pointed at him when a GOP-sponsored bill that allowed companies to offer workers compensatory time off instead of extra pay had to be pulled from its floor debut for lack of votes. Unions had lobbied heavily against the bill. Misjudgment on where Republican members stood on the issue (the job of the whip) led to an embarrassing defeat for GOP leaders (Martinez 2003).[5]

The responsibilities of this demanding job—from polling to persuasion—necessitate an extensive organization, the development of which is only recent. Although the majority and minority whips have been in operation since the late nineteenth century (having emerged out of the intense partisanship of the era), the whip organization has not been an integral part of the leadership structure until recent times (This section draws on Rohde 1991, 82–93; Ripley 1964, 1967; Sinclair 1983). During the New Deal period, the sectional and ideological conflicts within the Democratic party necessitated the addition of a phalanx of regional whips to assist the majority whip. Yet Speaker Sam Rayburn rarely relied on the new whips, instead relying on his personal relationships with the rank and file to rally support for legislation. Either appointed or elected by the members from their area, the regional whips owed little loyalty to the Speaker and the majority leader. In fact, during the Kennedy and Johnson administrations (when New Frontier and Great Society programs split the party, on both ideological and regional grounds), these whips often went against the party leader's policy preferences.

Much of this rebellious individualism changed during the Nixon administration, when the majority Democrats saw the need to organize in opposition to Republican policy initiatives. They enlarged their whip organization to include a chief deputy; three deputies; and at-large whips representing the Women's Caucus, the Black Caucus, and the first-year members. The whip and the chief deputy whip were given ex officio seats on the Steering and Policy Committee. With increased numbers, status, and visibility, the whip organization began to play both the role of persuading members to support the party and the traditional role of informing members of the party position, counting votes, and reporting back to leadership. With continued expansion throughout the 1980s, the majority whip organization at the end of the Democratic period of hegemonic rule in the House included 40 percent of the members of the caucus.[6] When the Republicans rose to majority status in 1994, they based their leadership structure on this Democratic model, and made it even more muscular. The party leadership for the 115th Congress is presented in Tables 11.1 and 11.2.

The greatest challenge to party leadership for both Democrats and Republicans in the House remains the electoral connection—given that members owe their seats to constituents back home, they are inevitably more loyal to their districts than to their parties when conflicting interests arise. Thus, the leadership structure, in particular the whip system, has developed over time to accommodate the electoral, constituent-driven needs of members. Remember, the extent of party control in the House is contingent upon the value members place on participation in the party hierarchy and in deference to its leadership.

Table 11.1. Party Leadership in the House, March 2018

Republicans	
Speaker of the House	Paul Ryan (Wis.)
Majority Leader	Kevin McCarthy (Calif.)
Majority Whip	Steve Scalise (La.)
Conference Chair	Cathy McMorris Rogers (Wash.)
Vice Chair	Doug Collins (Ga.)
National Republican Congressional Committee Chair	Steve Stivers (Ohio)
Policy Committee Chair	Luke Messer (Ind.)
Democrats	
Minority Leader	Nancy Pelosi (Calif.)
Minority Whip	Steny Hoyer (Md.)
Assistant Democratic Leader	James Clyburn (S.C.)
Caucus Chair	Joe Crowley (N.Y.)
Vice Chair	Linda Sanchez (Calif.)
Democratic Congressional Campaign Committee Chair	Ben Ray Lujan (N.Mex.)
Steering and Policy Committee Co-Chairs	Rose DeLauro (Conn.)
	Eric Swalwell (Calif.)

Source: www.house.gov.

Table 11.2. Party Leadership in the Senate, March 2018

Republicans	
President	Mike Pence (Ind.)
President Pro Tempore	Orrin Hatch (Utah)
Majority Leader	Mitch McConnell (Ky.)
Assistant Majority Leader (Republican Whip)	John Cornyn (Tex.)
Conference Chair	John Thune (S.Dak.)
Vice Chair	Roy Blunt (Mo.)
Policy Committee Chair	John Barrasso (Wyo.)
National Republican Senatorial Committee Chair	Cory Gardner (Colo.)
Democrats	
Minority Leader	Charles Schumer (N.Y.)
Democratic Whip	Richard Durbin (Ill.)
Assistant Minority Leader	Patty Murray (Wash.)
Caucus Chair	Charles Schumer (N.Y.)
Vice Chair	Elizabeth Warren (Mass.)
Policy Committee Chair	Debbie Stabenow (Mich.)
Democratic Senatorial Campaign Committee Chair	Chris Van Hollen (Md.)

Source: www.senate.gov.

The constraints on strong party leadership in the House are even greater in the more heterogeneous, individualized Senate. The Senate's norms, traditions, and unique historical development preclude strong party control. Thus, the institutional differences between the House and Senate limit the cohesiveness of party leadership across the two chambers.

Senate Leadership

"The purpose of the Senate is entirely different from the purpose of the House of Representatives. From the beginning it was intended to be a deliberative body where the expenditure of time and the exchange of views should determine judgment in any pending matter" (quoted in Binder and Smith, 1997, 29). Senator Royal Copeland's 1926 analysis of the founders' intent dovetails well with George Washington's classic analogy that the Senate was to be the "saucer" to cool the passions of the more popular House. A slow, deliberative body created to temper majority rule, characterized by consensus and compromise—not exactly the makings for strong party government.

While majorities work their will in the House, minorities wield far greater power in the Senate.[7] For example, in the 108th Congress, a small group of senators blocked drilling in the Arctic National Wildlife Refuge (ANWR) even though the House had already passed the legislation in its energy bill. A single senator blocked the promotions of more than 850 air force officers in an effort to secure four cargo planes for the National Guard back home.[8] In the 111th Congress, Senator Jim Bunning (R-Ky.) single-handedly held up a thirty-day extension of unemployment benefits for days, even in the face of strident criticism from across the political spectrum. Such obstructionist and dilatory tactics available to individual senators are unheard of in the majority-minded House.

Perhaps the most important constraint on strong party governance in the Senate is the tradition of unlimited debate—the filibuster. Any single senator can prevent a vote on a bill or a resolution by speaking indefinitely or by offering amendments or motions to delay. According to Senate Rule 22 (the rule on the cloture vote), sixty members are needed to break a filibuster, end debate, and bring the bill up for consideration. Thus, the Senate majority leader cannot move any controversial legislation through the chamber if a mere forty-one senators oppose it.[9]

Traditionally, the filibuster has been employed to prevent the majority party from enacting their preferred legislation without accounting for the preferences of the minority on major policy issues. But in the 108th Senate, Democrats employed the filibuster for a new purpose: to prevent conservative judicial nominees from being voted on. Battles over controversial judicial nominees are intensely partisan, namely, because the ideological makeup of the courts can affect such hot-button policy issues as abortion, gun control, and states' rights. For this reason, the partisan core of a member's constituency pays close attention to judicial nominations, and it is this core that consistently turns up to vote in primary elections. Thus, partisan confirmation hearings in the Senate translate into vote mobilization on election day (Dlouhy 2002).

Historically, however, no nominee approved by the Senate Judiciary Committee had ever been prevented from a floor vote by the minority party (Dlouhy 2003, 1078). Senate Republicans did put holds on some of Clinton's lower-court nominees to prevent them from advancing out of the Judicial Committee, but no filibusters were employed to block a vote on their confirmation. Thus, the Democratic filibusters of Bush's appeals court nominees, Priscilla Owen, Miguel Estrada (who eventually removed his name from consideration), and William Pryor, infuriated the Republicans. GOP senators argued that the constitutional duty of the Senate to advise and give consent to the president on nominations implied a vote to approve or reject a nominee—the filibuster should not be used to block judicial nominations. In fact, in February 2004, President Bush used his recess appointment power to place Pryor on the bench without Senate confirmation. Though the appointment circumvented the Democratic filibuster, recess appointees can serve only until the beginning of the next session of Congress, which in this case would have been about nine months.

Not able to garner enough support to end the Democratic filibusters, then majority leader Bill Frist (R-Tenn.) in spring 2005 moved to change the rules and employ the so-called nuclear option—amend the Senate rules to allow a filibuster on a judicial nominee to be ended by a simple majority, rather than a sixty-vote supermajority. This option was averted when a bipartisan group of senators—termed "The Gang of 14"—worked out a compromise in which they agreed to allow a vote on three of President Bush's nominees, effectively agreed to allow votes to be blocked on two others, and agreed to limit the use of the filibuster on future judicial nominees to "extraordinary circumstances." But this compromise was tenuous at best, and only applied to judicial nominees. One of the accomplishments of the Gang of 14 was to ensure a vote on the above-noted Judge Pryor, who was eventually confirmed to the U.S. Court of Appeals, 11th Circuit.

Because of the ever-present threat of filibusters and the fact that one senator can place a hold on legislation, nominations, and even military promotions, the primary job of the Senate majority leader is that of chief negotiator. As the Senate does not have a powerful Rules Committee to schedule floor debate, the flow of legislation onto the floor is arranged through unanimous consent agreements. These decrees are hammered out by the majority leader and negotiated by the party leadership in consultation with committee leaders and other concerned senators. Unanimous consent agreements outline the terms of debate and the amendments to be offered, their order, and even how long to debate each one. The majority leader must constantly confer with allies, to be certain that they are all on board; and, at the same time, the majority leader must work closely with the minority leader, to be certain the other party will not disrupt agreed-upon arrangements. The legislative schedule is even changed to accommodate, say, an individual senator who cares about a particular vote but cannot attend the Senate session on a certain day. Individual egos must be stroked, with individual personalities taken into account and individual agendas accommodated. Senate party leaders must be managers and persuaders—they must cajole and coax, negotiate and compromise (On these aspects of the role of the majority leader, see Sinclair 1990).

Gone are the days when the Senate was an intimate club with its own social hierarchy and culture, characterized by unequal power distribution; gone are the days when a freshman was "expected to keep his mouth shut, not to take the lead in floor fights, to listen and learn" (Matthews 1960, 93; Sinclair 1989, 18). The transformation of the Senate from an institution dominated by powerful senior committee chairs with deferential junior members resulted much in part from the similar pressures that prompted institutional change in the House. An influx of newly elected northern liberal Democratic senators in the 1958 and 1964 elections infused the Senate with more heterogeneous policy preferences. Conservative chairs and apprentice norms presented formidable barriers to the advancement of the more liberal newcomers and the more liberal majority policy preferences. In addition, the rise in complex issue areas from the 1970s on meant senators could no longer afford to specialize. Committees and subcommittee positions expanded, staff resources increased, and there was greater access to media. The result was a Senate where everyone was influential (Sinclair 1989). Mitch McConnell is no Lyndon Baines Johnson, the intimidating Texan Democratic majority leader from 1955 to 1961, but in the modern Senate, LBJ's tactics would not necessarily work. Senators are more autonomous and difficult to control; modern Senate leadership is about management, not strong-arm tactics. Parties do "organize" the Senate (e.g., make committee assignments), but their leaders are not given the powers and resources held by their counterparts in the House. The majority leader is responsible for scheduling floor debate and for providing leadership for the majority party's positions, but that person is not given the tools to do so without significant cooperation from colleagues. Therefore partisanship is less influential in the Senate than it is in the House.

THE PRESIDENT AS LEADER OF PARTY IN GOVERNMENT

In such a political system where party leadership is constrained by the institutions in which it operates, what role exactly does the president play as the leader of his party in government? Political analysts are virtually unanimous in agreeing that presidents play the primary role in setting the congressional agenda (Fishel 1985; Jones 1988a, 1988b; Kingdon 1984; Light 1983). It is the president's program that is presented to Congress, the president's budget to which Congress responds, and the president's cabinet that defends his proposals in hearings on Capitol Hill. The president clearly serves as the leader of his party in government, by setting the agenda and defining the issues—a process that begins as early as the presidential campaigns, when candidates make promises and set goals for their administrations.

To illustrate this point we return to the examples we used to open this chapter—the 2017 Affordable Care Act repeal effort, the 2017 tax reform effort, and the 2009–2010 health care reform effort. After his victory in 2016, Donald Trump made it known that he would keep his campaign promises in the areas of repealing Obamacare and reforming taxes. He was able to get both brought up for a vote in less than a year, although only one passed. In 2008 candidate Barack Obama made it clear to Americans that health care reform would be his top priority as president. Once in office, President Obama bluntly told Americans the promised reform would get done, and then directed his fellow Democrats in both houses of Congress to get to work on the issue. The road was not an easy one, but Obama eventually got the outcome he desired.

Obama's experiences to this point in his presidency, along with those of both Clinton and George W. Bush before him, demonstrate a very important point: As much as agenda setting is important, getting that agenda from the White House through the House and Senate and back is the president's greatest challenge. A president cannot simply dictate terms to Congress, even when Congress is controlled by his own party. Thus, a president leads his party in government by convincing legislators that following the chief executive's lead is in their best interest. For this reason, Richard Neustadt describes presidential power as essentially the "power to persuade" (Neustadt 1960, 1976), a description as accurate in the twenty-first century as when Neustadt wrote his seminal book on the presidency almost six decades ago. But, as demonstrated by the difficulties faced by Obama on obtaining health care reform, persuasion is a formidable and complicated task in a political system where members of

Congress are more beholden to their constituencies than to their president or their party.

Hesitant legislators, weighing out the costs to their own careers of supporting controversial presidential proposals, require a president who is willing to go the extra mile for them. President Bush made enormous efforts in the 2002 midterm elections to do just that, becoming personally involved in the reelection campaigns of his fellow Republicans, even traveling to fifteen states in the last five days before the election, to support GOP candidates in tough races. Bush's goal, as party leader, was to get as many Republicans in Congress as possible to support his agenda while demonstrating his commitment to campaign for members in their districts and states if position-taking on presidential priorities had placed them at odds with their constituents. This paid off well for President Bush, as his party gained seats in a midterm election (a rarity), and many members were beholden to the president for his efforts. He was obviously not in such an advantageous position during the 2006 elections, when many GOP members were not eager to have the increasingly unpopular President Bush in their states or districts. The GOP lost control of Congress, and many members laid the blame for this development, rightly or wrongly, at the feet of the president. This failure, combined with his lame-duck status and his lack of popularity, eventually emboldened an increasing number of Republicans in both houses to publicly oppose the president. Consider this comment from Senator Jeff Sessions (R-Ala.) on CNN's *American Morning* regarding President Bush's lobbying efforts for his immigration reform plan, which ultimately died in the Senate on June 28, 2007:

> I think the president is wrong to push this piece of legislation so hard after we've demonstrated the flaws that are in it. He needs to back off. He needs to help us write a better bill and not push a bill that so many of us can't support. (June 12, 2007)

President Obama found himself in a similar position during the 2010 election cycle. While some Democratic candidates—such as Nevada senator Harry Reid and California senator Barbara Boxer—openly and warmly embraced visits by and assistance from Obama, other Democratic candidates—such as Missouri Senate candidate Robin Carnahan—were much more reluctant to appear with Obama, even though the president could raise large sums of money for their campaigns. When Carnahan did appear with Obama, her opponent (and eventual election day winner) Roy Blunt used their joint appearance to attack Carnahan, telling *Politico*, "I think President Obama's policies help me more than her" (Lee and Catanese 2010). Thus far congressional Republicans have had a somewhat rocky relationship with President Trump (Davis 2017; Flegenheimer 2017; Phillips 2017), and certainly many of them are trying to decide how closely to embrace the president for the 2018 election cycle or how far to run away from him.

America is not a parliamentary democracy. We do not elect presidents and give them a mandate to push their policy alternatives through Congress. Congress is a separate branch of the government: Representatives and senators have separate electoral bases from the president. Therefore, the ability of the president to lead his party in Congress will depend on two criteria: first, institutional constraints, where his agenda falls relative to the preferences of his party's majority in the House and of the moderates who can uphold or defeat a filibuster in the Senate; and second, external factors—from scandal to war to the economy—all of which affect the ability of a president to persuade even members of his own party to follow his lead. A president can be a party leader, but nothing in our system guarantees that he will play that role, much less that he will play it effectively.

CRITICAL THINKING QUESTIONS

1. Should the filibuster be eliminated in the U.S. Senate?
2. Should a member of Congress give first priority to her or his party or to constituents when deciding how to vote?
3. Would the United States be better served by a unicameral legislature?
4. Should all congressional elections be made nonpartisan?

KEY TERMS

filibuster	unified control	minority leader
reconciliation	divided government	majority whip
cloture	Speaker	minority whip
senatorial holds	majority leader	Contract with America

NOTES

1. A filibuster can be ended by a vote of **cloture,** which requires a supermajority of 60 votes if the Senate is at its full contingent of 100 members. Even a successful cloture vote does not immediately end debate; it limits debate to an additional thirty hours.

2. Rohde's colleague John Aldrich has also heavily contributed to the development of this theoretical perspective.

3. Other party leaders have seats on this committee (or committees) because of the offices they hold—the chief deputy, the chair of the DCCC, and the vice chair of the caucus. Based on their region of the country, twelve rank-and-file members are elected to the committee by fellow Democrats. The minority leader appoints nine additional members; these members, with the members of the leadership team, ensure dominance over the committee. It is equally important to note that the ranking members of the four most powerful committees in the House—Appropriations, Budget, Rules, and Ways and Means—are also members of the committee.

4. The Democrats have developed a fairly routine path of succession. Richard Gephardt, first elected to the House in 1976, worked his way up the party hierarchy before becoming minority leader in 1995. His predecessor, Thomas S. Foley from Washington, had served in the House for a quarter century before his election as Speaker, in 1989; he had served as chair of the Agriculture Committee (1975–1981), as majority whip (1981–1987), and as majority leader (1987–1989). His predecessors, Jim Wright (Tex., 1954–1989; Speaker 1987–1989) and Thomas P. (Tip) O'Neill Jr. (Mass., 1952–1987; Speaker 1977–1987), had served thirty-three and twenty-five years, respectively, before their elections as Speaker.

5. In July 2003, the bill passed in the House by a narrow margin but was blocked in September by Senate Democrats and six Senate Republicans. In an amendment to a spending bill, the Senate voted 54–45 to oppose the new overtime revision. Bush threatened to veto the final appropriations package if it included the amendment.

6. The first elected whip was Tony Coelho (D-Calif., 1978–1989). Coelho's election says a good deal about the connections among party in government, party organization, and party in the electorate. Coelho had sought and received appointment as chairman of the Democratic Congressional Campaign Committee (DCCC) in 1980. The DCCC had never been a base of power in the House; indeed, it seemed only a poor imitation of its Republican counterpart. But Coelho saw potential and grabbed it. He raised unprecedented sums of money by emulating the methods of the National Republican Congressional Committee (NRCC) and reminding political action committees of which party controlled the House. He won the DCCC chair (and thus himself) a position in the House leadership hierarchy by virtue of the increasingly important role that the DCCC played in maintaining majority status. Although he could not match the NRCC's dollar totals, he built a first-class operation and earned the admiration of (and accumulated political IOUs from) those whose campaigns he supported (B. Jackson 1988). When the whip's seat opened with Foley's ascent on the leadership ladder, Coelho was ready. He drew on his reputation, called in his chits, and won the election.

7. For an analysis of the differences between the House and Senate—in terms of the size of the two bodies, the electoral environments, the prominence of the members, and the partisan contexts—see Baker (1989).

8. In the 108th Congress, the practice of holds made front page when Larry Craig (R-Idaho) blocked the promotions of more than 850 air force officers, many of whom served in Iraq, until the air force agreed to assign four additional C-130

cargo planes to the Idaho National Guard (he had been promised eight planes seven years earlier but only received four to date). Craig's GOP colleagues pressured him to back down, fearing alienation of some of their ardent supporters: young military officers (see Schmitt 2003).

9. Members who choose to employ the filibuster must weigh the benefits of their opposition against the costs of appearing too obstructionist. In 2002, Senate Democrats filibustered the GOP version of the Homeland Security Department Act, on the principle that it infringed upon employees' civil service protections (organized labor opposed the Senate bill). After the November midterm elections, the Democrats backed down: it was evident that the filibuster had little effect on the Republicans; in fact, it had negative repercussions on one of their own. Senator Max Cleland (D-Ga.), a decorated Vietnam vet, was defeated in his reelection bid, much in part for his opposition to the act and regardless of his military service.

Chapter 12

The Role of Political Parties

Republican presidential nominee Donald Trump and Democratic presidential nominee Hillary Clinton on stage during the second 2016 presidential debate at Washington University in St. Louis, Missouri. Political parties and elections are critical in managing conflict and giving voice to the concerns of the public in the American political system.

Modern political parties were in their infancy at the dawn of the nineteenth century. They were dominating the American political landscape at the dawn of the twentieth century. What can be said of them as we approach the end of the second decade of the twenty-first century?

To this point, we have examined the historical development of political parties and the electoral process, and the context in which they currently exist, from an empirical point of view. That is, we have analyzed the role played by parties in nominations and elections, explored why elections have been decided as they were, described the processes, and explained how variations in processes influence results. Then we looked at the implications of some of the aspects of those processes and of institutional linkages for politics and for governance.

In this final chapter, we move from empirical analysis to evaluation. Specifically, we look at how well the electoral process and political parties within that process play the roles that have been assigned to them in the American system of government.

THE ROLE OF ELECTIONS

Recall Professor Finer's definition of the role that elections must play if a democracy is to function effectively:

> The real question . . . is not whether the government deigns to take notice of popular criticisms and votes, but whether it can be voted out of office or forced by some machinery or procedures to change its policy, above all against its own will. (Finer 1949, 219)

In the most theoretical terms, the answer to Professor Finer's question with regard to the American system is that the government can be forced to change its policies against its own will; the government can be voted out of office. But in an empirical sense, is that what elections mean in the United States? Do elections today give the citizenry a chance to decide on the course of action that their government will take? These questions are more easily posed than answered.

The Context of Federalism

It should come as no surprise that the answer to the basic question will vary depending upon whether one is analyzing federal, state, or local elections. Once again, we must be alert not to generalize about the electoral process in the United States, when the process at the federal level is different from that at the state level (and states differ significantly from each other), and the processes in the various states are different from those in localities throughout the country.

Presidential Elections

Presidential elections have come closest to meeting the criterion set forth above. The American public has shown that it is willing and able to remove presidents when the policies of the government have consequences that displease the citizenry. And, of course, it has shown that it will retain presidents and policies with which it is in agreement. These facts may make us infer, at first glance, a number of linkages.

First, we may assume that the policies of the president and those of the government are the same. We know, however, that this assumption is false, in part because the principle of separation of powers ensures that nearly all policies are the result of compromise. But we also know that the public routinely makes this linkage, even if it is not in fact accurate.

Second, we may assume that the consequences of governmental policies were the ones desired or at least foreseen when those policies were implemented. Again, we know that this linkage is partial at best. For example, the success or failure of an administration's agricultural policies is dependent on the weather, advances in technology, and the actions of other nations as well as on the wisdom of the policies put forth. We also know that even the best-thought-out public policies often result in unintended consequences (Lindblom 1959). Again, however, we know that the public holds the president accountable for the consequences of his (and often others') actions, not for the intentions of those actions, and so the assumed linkage has the effect hypothesized.

Third, we may assume that all citizens view all policies in the same way and vote accordingly. Again, we know that this linkage does not hold completely. From the time of Madison, American politicians have recognized and dealt with the diversity of interests throughout this land. Even in landslide presidential elections, approximately two out of every five voters support the losing candidate. In any election those supporting a particular candidate do not all do so for the same reasons. Thus, what is necessary for a change in administration or policies is for a critical mass of citizens to express dissatisfaction with those policies and with the performance (either general or specific) of the administration and to translate those feelings into support for a different candidate.

Given the standard stipulated above, a number of the presidential elections discussed in chapter 9 meet the criterion of serving as an appropriate expression of the views of the citizenry in opposition to the actions of the government. In the election of 1992, for example, the Clinton campaign emphasized the economy using the slogan, "the economy, stupid."

The voters agreed with the Democratic candidate that the Republican incumbent had not been successful in economic terms. Candidate Clinton portrayed himself as an agent of change; the public chose him on that basis.

The elections of 1932, 1952, 1960, 1968, 1976, 1980, 2008, and 2016 can also be interpreted as examples of elections in which citizens chose to change the direction of policy. Obvious differences exist among these examples. The election of 1932 is described as a critical election in which public attachment to the major political parties underwent major changes. In 1952 and 1968, dissatisfaction with the policies of incumbent administrations was strong enough to convince Presidents Truman and Johnson not to seek reelection. The nominees of their parties were unable to dissociate themselves sufficiently to avoid defeat. In 1976 and again in 1980, sitting presidents lost to challengers whose campaigns emphasized the policies that were in place. In 2008, the public was highly dissatisfied with outgoing Republican president George W. Bush, making it almost impossible for GOP nominee John McCain to win the presidential election. In 2016 outgoing two-term president Barack Obama remained quite popular among some voters, but nonetheless the public chose to radically change direction by electing Donald Trump. In each case, the public chose to replace a government whose policies it disapproved of.

The elections of 1964, 1972, 1984, 1996, 2004, and 2012—elections in which incumbents were reelected—can be seen as cases in which the public said, in effect, that it preferred policies enacted by the sitting president to those proposed by the challenger.[1] In the first three elections, in 1964, 1972, and 1984, challengers proposed truly radical changes in the policies in place—and those radical changes were rousingly rejected (Converse, Clausen, and Miller 1965; Miller et al. 1976; Wayne 1984; Shanks and Miller 1990). In the 1996 election Republican candidate Dole attacked President Clinton on issues of character as much as policy; the public voted to stay the course with a president whose policies had proven to be popular. Multiple interpretations of the 2004 presidential election have been offered, but the most plausible seems to be that George W. Bush made the election primarily about terrorism and security, and was able to convince a majority of voters that based on past performance he was better equipped to handle those issues than was Senator Kerry. While Barack Obama's reelection in 2012 was certainly not a given heading into the summer of that year, an improving economy, the campaign's highly successful use of big data and social media, and some missteps by Mitt Romney and his team were enough to clinch a second term for Obama (Jamieson 2013).

In each of these cases, the claim that the electorate expressed its views on the policies of the day through the ballot box can be supported. Presidential elections are highly salient. Although incumbents have some advantages and it can be argued that the "right" issues are not discussed and that the electorate lacks requisite sophistication, the argument can also be sustained that presidential elections fulfill the role they were designed to play in American politics. Despite relatively common complaints to the contrary, presidential elections in the United States offer Americans a real, meaningful choice on election day. And at least on the high salience issues of the day, Americans appear to be relatively well equipped to make that choice.

Congressional Elections

What about elections to other federal offices—to the Senate and the House of Representatives—when the campaigns, the candidates, and the issues are not as visible to the public as they are in presidential elections?

In these cases, the findings are mixed, as are the views of political scientists. In chapters 6 and 7 we presented a good deal of evidence demonstrating incumbent advantages in House elections (but see Stonecash 2008 for a different view of incumbency). Senate incumbents have fewer advantages—and challengers have greater assets—but recent Senate elections suggest that incumbents in those races are not without strengths. Do these elections serve to link the views of the public with the policies of the government? Or are incumbents so protected as to erase the connection between elections and outcomes that Professor Finer defines as necessary?

On their face, elections in many individual districts and/or states do not seem to demonstrate the prescribed connection. Yet there are a few cases in which key issues have led to the defeat of an incumbent and thus indirectly to a representative's reflecting the views of constituents in a different manner. For instance, the defeat of Congresswoman Marjorie Margolies-Mezvinsky (D-Pa., 1993–1995), who cast the deciding vote in favor of President Clinton's budget and tax package in 1993, is generally attributed to that vote. She had barely won election in 1992 in wealthy Montgomery County. In 1994 she lost to the same Republican candidate, John Fox, who used the vote over and over in the campaign to show that Margolies-Mezvinsky opposed tax cuts, an unpopular position among voters.[2]

But more frequently incumbents seeking reelection are sent back to Washington. In 2016, 97 percent of House incumbents seeking reelection were successful, as were 93 percent of senators seeking a return to Washington, figures that are about the norm for the House and slightly higher than usual for the Senate. And when incumbents do lose, more frequently personal scandals, not stands on policies, play a key role in those defeats. There is evidence that campaign discourse in House and Senate elections does not effectively present citizens with informed presentations on the differences between candidates on the issues of the day (Maisel and West 2004).

However, the case that elections allow the electorate to hold its representatives accountable can still be made in a number of less direct ways. First, one could simply talk to incumbent members of Congress. As anyone who has ever worked with an elected official can tell you, the majority of incumbents are genuinely concerned about their reelection. Certainly some are more concerned than others, but the majority of members do not believe they are safe from defeat on election day. They worry about how the media or a future opponent will portray a policy stand or specific vote, and they act accordingly. If an incumbent behaves in such a fashion, accountability can be reasonably assumed to exist, regardless of the fact that the representative or senator gets 65 percent of the vote in election after election. Additionally, sometimes this concern over their reelection chances causes some incumbents to choose retirement rather than facing possibly unhappy voters. This appears to be happening quite often as we head toward Election Day 2018 (Pew Research Center 2018). The high incumbent reelection rates cited earlier are only for incumbents who actually run for reelection; it does not take into account those who willingly retire or otherwise step down. A member of Congress deciding against seeking reelection because they are concerned about their chances for victory certainly seems like accountability.

Second, high reelection rates for incumbents could simply be due to the fact that constituents are happy with what their members of Congress are doing. Under this scenario, reelection is simply a reward for and recognition of good and faithful public service. There is a reason, after all, why one regularly hears that Americans hate Congress as a whole, but love their individual members of Congress.

A third reason for the high rate of incumbency reelection could be all about partisanship. At least in the House of Representatives, the majority of districts are reliably Democrat or reliably Republican (Bishop 2004; Stonecash, Brewer, and Mariani 2003). In such districts, one could argue that it doesn't really matter who the specific candidate in question is; as long as the dominant party in the district manages to put forward a reasonably qualified, reasonably competent, scandal-free candidate, that candidate will win, and will keep on winning as long as she or he remains reasonably competent and scandal-free and generally follows the party line. This scenario too presents a picture of accountability, although here it is accountability rooted mostly in partisanship rather than individual behavior.

Fourth, look at the role of interest groups and their use of soft money (chapter 5; Cigler 2006; Magleby and Holt 1999). Groups tend to invest heavily in campaigns in competitive congressional districts when the major party candidates differ on the issues that the groups feel are most critical. Organized labor, business and industry groups, environmentalists, those on both sides of the abortion issue, and those favoring term limits are all obvious examples of groups that strive to hold representatives accountable for their actions in Washington. Even when these groups are not successful in defeating incumbents, they often define the issue agenda for a campaign, with two consequences: (1) voters do in fact have an opportunity to focus on key issues and to express their preference; and (2) representatives often moderate positions in order to accommodate the views of more of their constituents. Whatever one concludes about the role of money in campaigns—an issue of never-ending controversy—it is difficult not to see that campaign spending often raises the issue content of certain campaigns, allowing for better informed voters (Geer 2006).

A fifth argument in favor of the proposition that congressional elections serve the purpose of holding representatives accountable for their actions rests on observing the results of these elections at the macro level—that is, looking at all elections held in one year together rather than at individual elections separately. There is a good deal of evidence that these elections reflect the views of the voters, at least on the major economic issues of the day (Jacobson and Kernell 1983; Tufte 1975, 1978). At times when there has been massive public discontent with governmental policies, changes wrought on the composition of the legislature as a result of congressional elections have been sufficient to lead to changes in those policies (Brady, Bullock, and Maisel 1988). The election of 1966, generally interpreted as a reaction to excesses in social welfare policies passed by the so-called Great Society Democrat–dominated 89th Congress, is one clear example of this linkage. Certainly it could be argued that the election of 1994, in which Republicans regained control of both houses of Congress for the first time since 1954, had the same impact. The 2006 election had a similar, although lesser, impact as well. The most recent example, of course, of this type of election is the 2010 election cycle. The out-party Republicans were able to rally voters by feeding off the discontent due to the sour economy and with some of the policies of the Obama administration and the majority Democrats in Congress. In so doing the Republicans were able to nationalize the 2010 congressional elections, perhaps to an even greater degree than they were able to do in 1994. This paid off handsomely for the GOP; in 2010 fifty-eight sitting members of the House seeking reelection lost their seats, as did four sitting senators. The overwhelming majority of these losers were Democrats. But even here we must be careful not to go too far. While there is no doubt that the 2010 congressional election cycle produced more turnover than normal, the incumbency reelection rate was still 87 percent in the House and 84 percent in the Senate. Such figures hardly represent "throwing the bums out" at anything even remotely resembling a high rate.

State and Local Elections

While most states now see some level of two-party competition for at least some offices (Bibby et al. 1983; Brown and Bruce 2002; Jewell and Olson 1988; Holbrook and Van Dunk 1993), levels of two-party competitiveness have increased in recent years (Hinchcliffe and Lee 2016), and Democrats are running candidates in more state legislative districts than they have in decades (Rogers 2018), one party or the other still has a decided advantage in statewide elections in many states. Moreover, in legislative districts in virtually every state, true two-party competition remains the exception, not the rule (Crotty 1985; Jewell and Morehouse 2001). The difficulty here is the same in some ways as it is for finding competition in congressional elections. When districts are redrawn after each ten-year census, it seems clear that one criterion used by mapmakers is protection of incumbents. Districts dominated by one party are the norm for state legislative races to an even greater extent than is the case for congressional races. How can citizens effect policy change if the result of the election is known in advance and will have virtually no impact on who governs? Under such a scenario, citizens would have to rely on competition in the primary election.

Local elections have the same types of problems that state elections have, only even more so. Many localities are now and have been for some time dominated by one political party or the other. We read often about the strength of the Democratic party organization in Cook County, Illinois, the area including and surrounding Chicago. In the city of Chicago, Democratic party nomination is all but tantamount to election. Other organizations are not as strong as that in Cook County, but one-party rule in local elections remains very common (see Gibson et al. 1985; Schlesinger 1985).

Nonpartisan Politics

Even more common than one-party rule in local governing units is nonpartisan government. This text has dealt only with partisan elections because those are the elections that see the most competition in the American system. Yet nonpartisan elections merit comment.

Approximately two-thirds to three-fourths of U.S. municipalities hold nonpartisan elections to determine who will hold local offices (Crotty 1985; Schaffner, Streb, and Wright 2001). The movement toward nonpartisan government was part of Progressive Era reforms; advocates of nonpartisan local government feel that running a local government should be more like administering a business than playing partisan politics. Frequently they cite the corruption and the inefficiency of partisan politics. "There is no Republican and no Democratic way to clean a street."

On the other hand, those concerned with democratic control over the means of governing have not been overly impressed with the experience of nonpartisan elections. Critics contend that nonpartisan elections tend to draw fewer voters because citizens do not care who wins these elections and because elections without the cue of party often confuse voters. The voters are less informed about the issues than is the case in partisan elections. Fewer races are competitive in the sense of close elections; in fact, in many races only one candidate runs. The advantages of incumbency are increased over those in heavily one-party areas with partisan elections, since the opposition is deprived of its chance to organize.

The result is less serious, less issue-oriented campaigning, more domination by those with well-recognized names, an increase in domination by single-issue groups that have the ability to mobilize their supporters, and generally less representative and less accountable government.

If the goal of reformers was to establish a system in which democracy functions more effectively, and if democracy for this purpose is defined as a system in which the views of the voters on policy matters are converted into government policy, then nonpartisan elections represent a regressive step. Only someone who believes that local government involves only administration, with no policy implications, can view the results of the nonpartisan movement as a movement toward more democracy. Given the nature of citizen concerns about local issues, about education and crime and growth policies, as well as about street repair and garbage collection, that argument is difficult to sustain, if not downright irresponsible to make.

VOTERS, PARTIES, AND ELECTIONS

In evaluating the effectiveness of elections, it is also important to look at how voters are deciding for whom they will vote. The *American Voter* model (Campbell et al. 1960, focused on the electoral politics of 1950s America) stipulated that most voters used political party as a cue in determining their electoral choices during the decade of the 1950s. The *Changing American Voter* analysis (Nie, Verba, and Petrocik 1979, examining the 1960s to the mid-1970s) revealed that issue orientation was more important in determining vote than had been the case when the earlier study was undertaken. The *New American Voter* (Miller and Shanks 1996, analysis through 1992) argued that the importance of the concept of party identification should not be underestimated, even as we enter the twenty-first century and many voters view politics cynically. Much recent work supports this latter view, presenting evidence that partisanship is once again strongly affecting electoral behavior (Bartels 2000; Green, Palmquist, and Schickler 2002; Hetherington 2001; Stonecash 2006).

So where does this leave us? Clearly the world has changed since the era of the 1950s described by *The American Voter*. While the sources of this change are numerous, perhaps none has been larger or more important than the changes in communications technology and the media. As discussed in chapter 10, the media plays a central role in American electoral politics, and both this role and the media have changed radically over the past five decades.

The Electronic Revolution: Television and Digital Media

The media have always been influential in politics and government in the United States. Perhaps more important, every time there has been a major media change driven by technological advance, it isn't long before the change in question significantly impacts American politics, particularly in the area of parties and elections. This was true of the penny press in the American founding era, the telegraph in the first half of the nineteenth century, the rise of objective journalism in the second half of the nineteenth century, and radio in the early decades of the twentieth century. However, arguably no changes have been as large and significant as those brought about first by television and now by the Internet, especially social media. When discussing the media and contemporary American politics, one must begin with television. Even with the ongoing communications revolution in the United States television is still the news source most relied on by the American voting public, although as noted in chapter 10 its lead over the Internet is slipping relatively fast. But 50 percent of Americans still regularly get their news from television (Pew Research Center 2018), which makes the medium a major player in American politics and government.

Television is a visual medium and emphasizes stories that can be presented visually. Celebrated scholar Doris Graber studied television coverage of presidential elections for many years. Her conclusions support the commonly held view that television presents the news and covers campaigns in a simplified manner. In every election that she studied, save that of 1968, the media in general and television journalists in particular presented stories on campaign events more than analyses of domestic politics, foreign affairs, economic policy, or social problems (Graber 1982, 2005, 2006; see also Buchanan 1991; Crouse 1973; Patterson 1980, 1993; Robinson and Sheehan 1983). Think about how television has covered the major economic policy crises that have dominated the governmental agenda in recent years. How many times can the network news anchors show bar graphs that describe the growth of the federal debt? How many times can they depict the federal budget with pie charts? How can a two-minute story adequately explain the complicated issues of Social Security and Medicare solvency? These economic issues—and the important issues of domestic politics, foreign affairs, and social problems—are complex problems that do not translate easily into two-minute spots on the network news (Graber 1980; see also Kerbel 1998; Buchanan 1991; Gans 1979). Yet these are undoubtedly the important issues of the day. And television, which cannot and does not cover these issues very well, is the medium most relied on by the voting public for its political information. The necessary conclusion we must draw here is that voters are making decisions based on a grossly oversimplified view of the important issues of the day.

The discussion thus far has focused on national news events and presidential elections because that is the only context that has been studied in depth by social scientists. It does not take much intuition, however, to extend this discussion to the state and local contexts. Think for a moment about the quality of news coverage in local newspapers and on local television news broadcasts. Let us assume for the moment that most citizens gain their political information about events at the state and local level from television, just as they do for events at the national level.[3]

The average local news program spends nearly as much time on weather and sports as it does on all news. The news segment frequently carries one story about national news and at least one human interest story. Then, of course, there is the obligatory story about the latest local disaster—fire, murder, automobile accident. But how often is there in-depth coverage of a state house hearing on workers' compensation, of a city council debate on zoning ordinances, of a school board discussion on resource allocation? When state and local elections are held, how often are the candidates seen on local television?

Example after example could be mounted, but the point would remain the same. It should be emphasized, however, that all the blame does not rest with television journalists (nor with newspaper reporters, for much the same argument would apply to most local papers). In point of fact, they are faced with a nearly impossible task. Local journalists for all media have very few resources with which to cover a vast amount of material. They do not have large staffs or large budgets; they have limited space and/or time; they have many localities and issues to cover.

And they are under tremendous pressure to draw an audience. It is difficult to imagine how most issues that face state and local governments—or most issues that distinguish candidates for state and local offices—could be covered in a way that would excite the public. Yet if newspapers do not sell and if television broadcasts do not achieve high ratings, the business end of these enterprises fails and the public is even less well served (Kerbel 1998; Berkman and Kitch 1986; Gans 1979). As a consequence, local journalists do what they can to cover state and local government and politics; in most instances what they can do is very little. And again, very little is what the public is left to rely on in making its decisions.

There is, of course, the possibility that the Internet could solve many of the ills described above. The potential of the web in terms of providing information is virtually limitless. With an increasingly cheap piece of machinery, a high-speed connection, and a little bit of working knowledge, an individual can quickly and easily access virtually any bit of political information he or she desires. And while many Americans (especially older Americans [Pew Research Center 2014b]) still lack at least one of these three necessary components, the number of such Americans is declining every day. As we write these words, there are media institutions doing wonderful things on the web, and modern campaigns are using the Internet and social networking tools to engage and inform voters. But it is far too early to place too much hope in an online salvation. Early research shows that rather than using the web to expose themselves to a greater diversity of political information, Americans use it to access only that information that supports their preexisting views and ideologies (Lawrence, Sides, and Farrell 2010; Pew Research Center 2014a, 2014b; Prior 2007). This research has also found that those who make heavy use of the web for news are more ideologically extreme, more politically polarized, and more interested in so-called niche issues than non-web users (Lawrence, Sides, and Farrell 2010; Nie et al. 2010; Pew Research Center 2014a, 2014b). There are also the growing concerns we discussed in chapter 10 over the ease with which untrue information is spread online and how vulnerable at least some elements of the web are to manipulation, both of which are important matters. Privacy concerns are also in play here, as the unfolding Cambridge Analytica situation (also discussed in chapter 10) demonstrates.

On the plus side there is some research showing that the web is fulfilling at least some of its promise, such as the fact that the Internet is serving to close the long-standing age gap in political participation in the United States by bringing more young people into the process (Schlozman, Verba, and Brady 2010). Recent research also shows that smartphones are making it easier for Americans (especially those in the eighteen-to-twenty-nine and thirty-to-forty-nine-year-old age groups) to follow politics (Pew Research Center 2014e), that Americans are increasingly using social media to not only follow but share news (Pew Research Center

2015, 2018), and that Americans feel better informed because of the Internet (Pew Research Center 2014f). But it is still too early in the digital age to say with any certainty whether or not the Internet will produce a new golden age of a fully informed American polity. Indeed, the events of the past two years make us skeptical of such claims.

The Parties in the Modern Election

Today one regularly is told that contemporary American elections are "candidate centered." Let's be certain we understand what that term means. Candidate-centered campaigns are to be distinguished from party-centered campaigns. A candidate-centered campaign is directed by the candidate and his or her staff. They are in control. A party-centered campaign is directed by the party organization and its leaders. They dictate to the candidate how to run the campaign. Saying that American elections are now candidate centered is to say that the political parties have lost control of their own candidates.

To a large degree this is true. Why? Two reasons stand out. First, parties lost control of the nominating process. The major cause for this change was the advent of the direct primary system. Although state law and state party rules vary, the norm is that the party organization cannot be involved in determining who will be the party's nominees. In a sense, that is ludicrous on its face. A well-meaning reform, aimed at restoring intraparty democracy and lessening the influence of party bosses making decisions out of public view, essentially removed political parties' raison d'être. Parties exist to run candidates who will carry forth the programs supported by party adherents into government. The primary system removed from party control the selection of candidates whom party officials feel could carry out that task. From a practical point of view, the imposition of primary elections as the principal way of nominating candidates meant that those candidates had to set up their own organizations, separate from the party organization, in order to run a primary campaign. This requirement went a long way toward focusing campaigns on candidates and not parties.

Obviously the impact of this reform was not felt everywhere in the nation at the same time. Some states adopted the primary system essentially as a means of weakening political parties—and that effect was felt. In other states, party organizations resisted and developed coping mechanisms; preprimary endorsements is one example. At the national level, party organizations remained important in determining presidential nominees until after the 1968 reforms. But certainly by the end of the century, the role of party in the nominating process had been reduced from a once-prominent position to a much lesser one, everywhere in the nation. Variation still exists, but a pattern is clear.

The second reason for the replacement of party-centered campaigns with candidate-centered campaigns relates to campaign techniques, particularly the revolution in communications avenues discussed earlier in this chapter. Parties were strongest when the most valuable resource in a campaign was manpower. Party organizations, often building on material incentives, could command the troops who would go door-to-door and bring the voters to the polls. Men and women literally worked hour upon hour to turn out the loyal voters, many of whom were also committed to the party because of material benefits that they had received.

With the advent of television advertising and of computer-generated, targeted direct mail, the role of dedicated, loyal campaign workers diminished. These techniques required skilled professionals to design campaigns and raise money to pay for them. Political party organizations responded to this changing environment, but they did so in competition with others who could also provide these resources. Candidates could hire their own consultants and raise their own money. Party organization became one of many players in a game orchestrated by candidate organizations (Kolodny 2000). The rise of big data, complicated analytical techniques, and the microtargeting of voters these allow have provided candidates even greater control over their campaigns, at least at the presidential level (Brennan 2012; Duhigg 2012; Jamieson 2013). Social media have further empowered candidates, who can now reach potential voters entirely on their own, and the 2016 presidential campaign demonstrated that candidates were prioritizing such an approach (Pew Research Center 2016).

As critical as these changes are, it is important not to push the candidate-centered argument too far. It is true that because parties no longer control nominations for office and because candidates can now speak to voters without the assistance of parties, individual candidates now control the direction of their campaigns. The candidate for office is now at the center of the campaign. But it is also true that the candidate is not able to do whatever he or she wants. Candidates must run for office in an environment that for the most part is beyond their control, and they must deal with reality (or at least the perception of reality) as they find it. In many ways that environment and that reality are both partisan in nature. Almost all candidates with a legitimate shot at winning office, at least at the federal and state level, run under a partisan banner. These banners are meaningful to voters, and conjure up certain mental images of the candidates regardless of the candidates' individual characteristics (Brewer 2009). Even Donald Trump—a candidate with extremely high star power—chose to run for president as a partisan. Could Trump have won the 2016 election running as an independent? Perhaps, but it would have been far more difficult. The vast majority of Americans identify with or at least lean toward the Democrats or the Republicans, and no other factor even comes close to party identification in determining individual vote choice. Candidates today are indeed at the center of their own campaigns for public office, but their success or failure in these campaigns more often than not still comes down to partisan factors.

The common description of elections as candidate centered to a certain extent also ignores how successfully parties have adapted to the changes that American electoral politics have seen since the 1950s (Aldrich 1995). Today both national party organizations are staffed with campaign professionals, skilled at aiding their copartisans with all aspects of electioneering (Herrnson 1998b, 2002). This is increasingly true at the state level as well (Bibby 1998, 2002). Parties are now crucial service providers, and as is the case with any service, the individual or organization doing the providing retains a certain degree of control over the service. This is especially true for data mining and microtargeting services that most candidates outside of presidential elections cannot provide on their own. Modern American parties have become what Paul Herrnson (2009) calls "multilayered coalitions," made up not only of the formal party organizations but also party members' leadership PACs and allied interest groups. To a high degree these coalition partners coordinate their resources and activities to help the party's candidates win on election day. In addition, over the past few election cycles we have increasingly seen parties turn to the past in a search for future success. As we've discussed in this book, party organizations at all levels are returning to traditional roles, though implementing them in new ways. Both the state and national parties have rediscovered the value in mobilizing their supporters and turning them out on election day. Some of these efforts are almost traditional registration and get-out-the-vote drives, similar to those run in the heyday of party organizations. But much more frequently they are sophisticated targeting and get-out-the-vote drives using modern techniques to identify and increase turnout among specific segments of the population thought to favor their candidates. The "microtargeting" and seventy-two-hour strategy used by Karl Rove and the Republican party from 2000 to 2006 and the multiple techniques utilized by the Obama campaign in 2008 and 2012 are currently the state of the art here. It is important to note that it would be virtually impossible for all but the wealthiest of candidates to carry out these types of activities on their own. Again, Trump is a useful example here. Despite being the first billionaire ever elected to the American presidency, Trump relied on the RNC for at least some of his voter targeting and especially GOTV efforts. Finally, Chadwick and Stromer-Galley (2016) have recently argued that the rise of digital media will allow parties to be "renewed from the outside in" as participatory and engaged citizens will come into parties by way of their digital engagement and strengthen them as institutions. While it is far too early to empirically evaluate this argument, it would certainly fit with parties' long history of successful adaptation to change.

Parties' Appeal to the Electorate

If there is one constant about American political parties, at least since the introduction of universal white male suffrage, it is that the parties are constantly engaged in the process of defining themselves. A crucial part of this process for each party involves determining what the party stands for; what are its core principles and where does it stand on the issues of the day, and which of those issues are likely to be important in the future? Central in making these determinations are questions about which groups in American society the parties can attract and how each party will go about the critical process of constructing a winning electoral coalition. Parties approach this process strategically, but with less than perfect information. Sometimes parties are successful and sometimes they are not. But either way, it is this process that often leads to partisan, and eventually policy, change (Brewer and Stonecash 2009). Given the current close partisan division that exists in American politics, combined with the high level of citizen discontent—both parties are presently considering these questions very carefully. The stakes, for the parties and for Americans as well, are high.

The Tone of Twenty-first-Century Politics

One further question about the future of American politics in the decade ahead remains to be discussed. It is directly related to the tone and nature of contemporary partisan politics. Citizens and politicians alike have become increasingly distressed about the tone of the political debate. Politicians who are frustrated by a lack of effective compromising have taken to personal attacks on one another. Comity—even in the Senate, once known for just such an atmosphere—seems to have disappeared (Packer 2010), and the public does not like what it sees. Concern regarding the tenor of American politics has reached a fever pitch as we enter the second year of the Trump presidency.

Evidence of this concern and dissatisfaction is rampant. Citizens respond to poll questions saying they are cynical, that they do not like the tone of campaigns, and that they will not vote because of how candidates come across. Potential candidates decide not to run, in part at least because they do not want to face the negativity of a campaign and because they do not want to be associated with that negativity. Many Americans also say they are increasingly turned off by the negative tone of American politics. On the other hand, at least some Trump supporters voted for him in 2016 out of frustration with what they saw as slick politicians practicing politics as usual, with the hope that a brash, outspoken outsider like Donald Trump would shake up the system and shatter the status quo. While thus far President Trump has certainly shaken up the system, he seems to have only added to the bitterness, acrimony, and division of contemporary American politics. When those in the media discuss or write about current American politics, the only thing more frequent than statements about political polarization is condemnation of this polarized state.

All of these factors point in one direction, a negative one. The health of the polity and the efficacy of the roles played by the electoral process and political parties within that process depend on citizen commitment to America's democracy. Alienation from politics has the potential to reduce participation and trust in government, which could raise issues about government's legitimacy. Cynical reactions to negative campaigns that depress turnout and lower the probability that those who might best lead the nation will even enter political life are a cancer on the body politic. Additionally, Mason (2013) and Miller and Conover (2015) found that while strong partisans are the most likely to participate in politics, they also tend to have the most hostile views of members of the opposing party and be the least willing to compromise. On the other hand, weak partisans and independents tend to be turned off by partisan bickering and polarization, and they are less inclined to participate under such circumstances (Klar et al. 2018; Robison and Mullinix 2015).

On the other hand, these types of reactions could be somewhat overheated. There could certainly be some benefits from the current tone of American politics. In experimental work Matthew Levendusky (2010) demonstrates that high levels of elite polarization cause citizens to hold more consistent political views and also increases the percentage of citizens who vote "correctly" based on their preferences. We might also take the view that our politics should be heated and tense, at least to a certain degree. Politics, after all, is conflict. The stakes are high. High-stakes conflict almost by necessity results in certain levels of negativity and animosity. American politics has never been a pursuit for those whose sensibilities are easily offended, and much of the tenor and tone of contemporary American politics can be found in the politics of nineteenth-century America as well. Conflict and tension can promote alienation and withdrawal, but they can also promote engagement and participation. Certainly recent election cycles going back to 2004 have been marked by high levels of interest and participation. They have also produced significant policy consequences. It will be interesting to see what the years ahead hold.

CONCLUDING REMARKS

It is of more than passing interest to some that the political scientists who are vocal advocates for stronger political party organizations have themselves been active in politics (Sam Eldersveld, Bill Crotty, David Price, Tom Cronin, Bob Huckshorn, John Bibby, Kay Lawson, the late Larry Longley, Paul Herrnson, and the senior author of this text, to name a few). That link is not coincidental. Those who become involved in the political process are acutely aware that many citizens simply do not care. They are also aware that policies pursued by government officials often have direct and immediate impact on those citizens. Further, it is difficult to know how the people feel on lots of issues, certainly in advance of the time at which decisions must be made. Politicians hear from the citizens who are most concerned, but not from a wide variety of citizens.

So the search begins for a mechanism to involve more people in the political process, particularly in the electoral process, because it is the vital link between the citizens and their government. And the institution of party readily stands out. For all its imperfections, so vividly described by political analysts and journalists of all types, party remains the vital linking institution. When parties are weak, the linkage role of the electoral process is not played well. When they are strong, a possibility exists that representation and accountability will follow. Other institutions—the media, interest groups—have tried to pick up the slack, but they have done so without notable success. And thus we are drawn back to the conclusion that if political parties did not exist, someone would have to invent them. Our parties are critical to our system of government, whether we like them or not. They are not going anywhere. So the key would seem to be to try to get America's political parties to play their optimum role in our system of representative democracy.

CRITICAL THINKING QUESTIONS

1. Do you know enough about American parties and elections to understand contemporary American politics?
2. Do Americans have an adequate degree of choice on election day?
3. Is American politics broken?

4. Are political parties good or bad for American representative democracy?

NOTES

1. It could be argued that the election of 1988 is another example of this kind of election. In that election, the voters elected a president of the same party as a retiring incumbent. This election is generally interpreted as a reaffirmation of the Reagan legacy, though definitions of that legacy vary. Even with that caveat accepted, the election of George H. W. Bush, Ronald Reagan's vice president and designated heir, as Reagan's successor reinforces the point that presidential elections can serve as an effective means to allow citizens to express their view of the policies of the day (Jones 1988a; Pomper 1989; Shanks and Miller 1989).

2. Margolies (she is now divorced) attempted to win back her old seat in 2014 but was defeated in the Democratic primary. This defeat came despite the fact that former President Bill Clinton—whose daughter Chelsea is now married to Margolies's son Marc—did an ad, a robocall, and a fund-raiser for Margolies over the course of her campaign (Klein 2014).

3. Although this assumption is untested in the professional literature, it seems reasonable. One piece of evidence comes from a Pew Research Center poll conducted right after the 1998 election in which voters responded that they had obtained much more of their information about the election from local news broadcasts than had been the case in 1992 or 1996, when presidential elections were being held.

Glossary

1974 amendments to the FECA The significant changes to the 1971 FECA that structure most of campaign finance law today.

501(c) group A social welfare organization, labor union, or trade association that has tax exempt status, named after the provision of the tax code that governs the activities of these types of organizations. Under current tax and election law, these 501(c) groups can raise and spend soft money in virtually unlimited fashion, as long as campaign activity is not their "primary activity" or "major purpose."

527 group A political organization with a primary purpose of affecting elections, named after the provision of the tax code that governs the activities of these types of organizations. Such groups are tax exempt (except for investment income) and are not subject to any limits in terms of the amounts of money they raise or spend, or the size of donations they receive.

adwatch campaigns Efforts by newspapers and some television stations to monitor political advertising for accuracy.

Air Force One The official air traffic control sign of the United State Air Force aircraft carrying the President of the United States.

attack ads Political advertisements that attack the sponsoring candidate's opponent, often on personal and not political grounds; viewed by many as contributing to citizen cynicism.

Australian ballot The form of secret ballot that came into use in the United States during the Progressive Era.

battleground states Those states that are viewed as winnable by either major party's candidate in a presidential election.

Bipartisan Campaign Reform Act (BCRA), or **McCain-Feingold** Bipartisan campaign finance legislation proposed and debated in the last congresses of the 1990s and finally passed in 2002.

blanket primary Primary election in which all names appear on one ballot, and each voter selects one candidate running for each race on the ballot; the candidates with the highest totals in each party qualify for the general election ballot.

brokered convention When no candidate for a party's nomination obtains the necessary number of votes to secure victory, party leaders and convention delegates make a series of deals that enable one candidate to eventually secure the party's nomination.

Buckley v. Valeo Supreme Court decision overturning certain aspects of the 1974 Amendments to the FECA that remains the ruling precedent for challenges to reform in campaign finance laws today.

cadre parties Parties dominated by politically elite groups of activists.

candidate-centered The focus of a campaign or an organization on a particular candidate, not on a party or a group of candidates running together.

canvassing The practice of campaign officials initiating direct (e.g., door-to door, telephone call, etc.) contact with citizens with the goal of obtaining their vote on election day.

caucuses Meetings of party members at which presidential preferences are expressed and those representing preferred candidates are selected to reflect those views.

challenge primary Primary election held after a nominating convention at which the convention's nominee can be challenged by a defeated candidate who must meet some specified criteria.

Citizens United v. Federal Election Commission A 2010 Supreme Court decision in which the Court ruled that the ban on corporate (and presumably union as well) funding of independent electioneering communications was unconstitutional due to the fact that it violated the First Amendment protection of freedom of speech.

Civil Rights Act of 1964 An important piece of legislation, passed as a tribute to President Kennedy after his assassination, that included among its major provisions equal access to public accommodations without regard to race.

civil service system The system of filling government positions through tests of merit rather than allegiance to a political party, instituted in the United States after the assassination of President Garfield.

closed primaries Primaries in which only voters enrolled in a particular party may participate.

cloture Rule 22 in the U.S. Senate, which states that sixty votes are necessary to end a filibuster and thereby end debate on the bill in question.

competitive two-party system A system dominated by the two main political parties, Republicans and Democrats.

Contract with America Campaign pledges made by Republican candidates for the House of Representatives prior to the 1994 election.

contrast ads Campaign advertisements that offer both an attack and a defense of a candidate's position; more than 30 percent but less than 70 percent attack.

conventions Meetings of party members to endorse or nominate candidates for office, adopt platforms, and establish party rules.

"corrupt bargain" The claim that Henry Clay threw his support in the House of Representatives in the 1824 presidential election to John Quincy Adams, thereby ensuring Adams's election, in exchange for Clay's appointment as secretary of state.

credentials challenges Disputes at a party convention where the legitimacy of a delegate or group of delegates is formally questioned by other delegates or party leadership.

critical elections Elections in which there is a sharp and durable alteration of preexisting cleavages within the electorate.

critical realignment A sharp and durable alteration of preexisting cleavages within the electorate that comes about due to a critical election or elections.

cross-filing Nominating system that permits a candidate to seek the nomination of more than one political party.

crossover or strategic voting Practice of members of one political party voting in the other party's primary, presumably to nominate the weaker candidate.

delegates Party members who are elected to a convention to participate in doing the party's business.

demographic representation Representation based on demographic characteristics such as gender, race, or age.

direct mail A campaign technique through which voters are contacted by mail because of a campaign's prior knowledge concerning those voters' views.

direct primary elections A preliminary election where delegates or nominees are chosen directly by voters.

divided government The situation in which one elected branch of government is under the partisan control of one party and the other branch under the partisan control of the other party.

electioneering communications According to the Federal Election Commission, "An electioneering communication is any broadcast, cable, or satellite communication that fulfills **each** of the following conditions: (1) The communication refers to a clearly identified candidate for federal office; (2) The communication is publicly distributed shortly before an election for the office that candidate is seeking; (3) The communication is targeted to the relevant electorate (U.S. House and Senate candidates only)."

electoral college The indirect means through which U.S. presidents and vice presidents are chosen.

electoral votes The votes cast by electors in the indirect system used for choosing the president of the United States; each state is allotted a number of electors equivalent to the number of representatives in Congress plus the number of senators; states determine how the electors will be selected; the winner is the candidate with a majority of the electoral votes.

equal protection clause The phrase in section 1 of the Fourteenth Amendment to the U.S. Constitution that guarantees that no state may deny any person within its jurisdiction the "equal protection of the laws."

equal time provision Regulation requiring that regulated media provide an equal amount of time to any candidate in an election in which they have given time to another candidate.

expectation game The strategy of setting expectations of performance low so that results will be viewed in a favorable light.

factions Divisions within the population, forming at first over economic interests, which were the precursors of American political parties.

Federal Corrupt Practices Act of 1925 The campaign finance act in place prior to the reforms of the 1970s; honored more in breach than in practice.

Federal Election Campaign Act (FECA) Reform act passed in 1971, amended significantly in 1974 and in less important ways thereafter, which sets the rules for funding federal elections.

Federal Election Commission (FEC) The regulatory body charged with implementing the Federal Election Campaign Act.

federal groups Interest groups whose structure reflects a decentralized organization with local, state, or regional units contributing policy views to the federal unit.

Federalist party One of the first American political parties, composed of the followers of George Washington and the architect of his administration's policies, Alexander Hamilton.

field winnower Playing the role of eliminating some candidates from a multicandidate competition.

Fifteenth Amendment Amendment to the U.S. Constitution that explicitly states that individuals could not be denied the right to vote based on "race, color, or previous condition of servitude."

filibuster Exercising the right to unlimited debate in the Senate; used literally "to talk a bill to death."

filing deadlines The dates by which candidates must fulfill whatever requirements exist to gain a place on a ballot.

focus groups Technique used by pollsters to explore deeper aspects of public opinion.

franchise The right to vote.

free or earned media Media exposure that a candidate receives without having to pay for it, for example, coverage in newspapers or on television news shows.

front-loaded The situation created when multiple states all place their presidential primaries or caucuses as early as possible in the nominating process.

geographic representation Representation based on the geographic area in which a person resides.

gerrymandering Drawing district lines to achieve certain political purposes.

grassroots The rank-and-file voters or party members.

group consciousness Concept that certain attitudes and opinions are adopted because they reflect the views of those in a group with which one associates.

group ratings When organized groups "rate" representatives and senators in terms of the degree to which they support or oppose legislation favored by those groups. These ratings, which usually range from 0 (no support) to 100 (total support), are computed by the groups after they select the issues most important to them.

hard money Political money that is raised and spent under federal guidelines monitored by the Federal Election Commission.

Hatch Act of 1940 Legislation aimed at preventing political abuse of and by federal employees.

Hill committees The name applied to the four party committees, one for each party in each house, charged with aiding candidates for Congress.

hybrid primary A primary election system that has elements of both closed and open primary systems.

ideological representation Representation based on how individuals stand on the issues under debate.

ideology A coherent set of beliefs that structure one's thinking about political issues.

independent expenditures Money spent during an election year that is not coordinated with or controlled by a candidate's campaign.

independents Those who do not identify with one major party or the other.

infomercial Long television commercials, exemplified by those used by H. Ross Perot, that purport to provide voters with enough information to make informed choices.

informed consent of the governed A minimal requirement for an effectively functioning representative democracy.

initiative The process through which citizens can bring a proposed law to a vote by the electorate without legislative approval.

instant runoff voting See **ranked choice voting.**

issue advocacy advertisements Advertisements in which the sponsor's primary interest is in forwarding an issue position, not supporting a particular candidate; money spent in this way is unregulated as long as it is separate and distinct from candidate efforts.

Jeffersonian (or Democratic) republican party The party of Thomas Jefferson that formed around opposition to many of the policies proposed by Alexander Hamilton.

Jim Crow laws Laws designed to restrict the activities of former slaves in the South; included provisions that kept black citizens from voting.

King Caucus The domination of the nominating process by the legislative caucus.

legislative term limits Fixed limitations on the number of terms of office that members of a legislature may serve.

legitimacy Acceptance of the right of public officials to hold office and to promulgate policies because of the means by which they were chosen.

lobbying Taking actions to persuade legislators or those in government to pursue policies favored by one's group.

majority Receiving one-half plus at least one of the votes cast.

majority leader The floor leader for the majority party in a legislature.

majority rule An election system in which a candidate must receive one-half plus at least one of the votes cast in order to be declared the victor.

majority whip The majority party official in a legislature charged with aiding the floor leader, informing members of party positions, tracking the intentions of individual members, and attempting to persuade reluctant members to follow the party stance (when appropriate).

mandates Instructions or directions from the electorate to adopt certain policy alternatives based on what the electorate meant to say in an election.

marginal seats Seats which either major party has a legitimate chance of winning.

mass membership parties Political parties characterized by large memberships that determine party direction; tend to have ideological positions and play an educational role in the system; concern is with governing more than electing.

McGovern-Fraser Commission The first of a series of reform commissions that have restructured the way in which the Democratic party nominates candidates for president and vice president.

minority leader The floor leader for the minority party in a legislature.

minority whip The minority party official in a legislature charged with aiding the floor leader, informing members of party positions, tracking the intentions of individual members, and attempting to persuade reluctant members to follow the party stance (when appropriate).

Motor Voter Bill Officially the National Voter Registration Act of 1993, this law set various conditions for allowing individuals to register to vote, most notably automatically registering an individual to vote when she or he applied for or renewed a driver's license and also requiring individuals be provided the opportunity to register at public assistance and disability services offices.

multicandidate political committee Committee that supports more than one candidate for a federal office.

multipurpose groups Interest groups that reflect the views on a variety of issues on which their members express concern.

national committees The pinnacle of the national party organizations, comprised of delegates from the states and from groups important to the political parties.

national groups Interest groups whose structure is centralized, without powerful local, state, or regional component units.

national party convention A means of nominating presidential candidates by delegates from each state; replaced the congressional caucus as part of democratizing reforms of the Jacksonian era.

negative ads Political advertising that points to perceived flaws in the record of the sponsoring candidate's opponent.

New Deal Coalition A diverse collection of groups of voters who supported the U.S. Democratic party from 1932 until 1964, making it the majority party at that time.

Nineteenth Amendment Amendment to the U.S. Constitution granting women the right to vote in all elections.

one person–one vote Principle that reapportionment and redistricting must be accomplished in such a manner that each district has, to the extent possible, the same population and, therefore, each person's vote counts equally.

open primaries Primary in which each voter may choose one party's ballot or the other.

pack journalism The phenomenon of all journalists covering an event following the lead of one of their colleagues instead of pursuing their own angles on the story.

paid media Media exposure that a candidate's campaign pays for and thus controls.

partisan elections Elections in which those on the ballot are identified by their political party affiliation; by contrast, in nonpartisan elections no designation appears next to a candidate's name.

party identification Self-assessment of a person's allegiance to one or the other of the major political parties.

party in government Members of a political party who are serving in an official capacity in the government.

party in the electorate Those who support a political party at the polls—the loyal followers.

party organization The formal structure of a political party's professional and volunteer workers.

party platform A political party's formal statement of its beliefs, values, and positions.

party renewal The effort to change the way in which political parties operate so that they can play a more important role in the electoral process.

party systems Electoral arrangements in which two or more parties compete for support of the electorate and control of the government and take each other into account as they set various electoral and governing strategies.

party unity scores The percentage of times that an individual legislator votes with his or her party on those votes in which a majority of one party votes against a majority of the other party (party unity votes).

party unity vote A vote in a legislature in which a majority of one party votes in opposition to a majority in the other party.

patronage or spoils system An incentive-and-reward system through which those loyal to, and working for, a political party benefit materially when that party wins elections and holds office.

penny press Newspapers and leaflets in the early years of the republic, so named because they sold for a penny.

plurality Receiving more votes than any other candidate.

plurality rule An election system in which a candidate receiving a plurality of the votes is declared the winner.

political action committee (PAC) An organization that receives contributions from fifty or more individuals and contribute money to at least ten candidates for federal office; often, but not always, affiliated with lobbying organizations.

political culture Norms, expectations, and values concerning political life in a particular polity or region.

political machine A group that controls the activities of a political party.

poll tax A tax paid by each person as he or she exercised the right to vote; the tax weighed especially heavily on poorer citizens, as marginal dollars meant more to them.

popular vote Direct vote for a candidate as opposed to an indirect method such as the electoral college.

positive ads Political advertising that stresses the record of the sponsoring candidate, not that of his or her opponent.

preprimary conventions Party conventions held in advance of a primary to endorse one of the candidates running in that primary.

presidential preference primaries Primary elections in which voters cast their votes for presidential candidates or for delegates who will support specified presidential candidates.

pressure groups Descriptive name by which interest groups were known in the past.

proportional representation A method of assigning seats in a legislative or other representative body whereby the number of seats a party receives is determined by the percentage of the vote the party obtained in the election.

prospective (future) voting Casting a vote based on what the voter thinks candidates for office are likely to do after the election.

public financing Any of the various schemes used to fund state or federal campaigns with taxpayer dollars.

public interest groups Organizations that lobby the government and work for a political agenda that is not defined by economic or other narrowly defined interests.

qualified candidates Candidates who are thought by experts to have the characteristics necessary to run a strong campaign.

Ralph Nader Consumer advocate who has pressured government for reform since the 1960s.

ranked choice voting or **instant runoff voting** A system of casting a ballot that allows a voter to rank candidates in order of preference. After the first vote tally, if one candidate gets a majority of the vote, she or he is declared the winner. If no candidate gets a majority, the candidate with the lowest vote total is dropped from the ballot, and voters who chose the dropped candidate as their first selection then have their votes allotted to their second choice. This process continues until one candidate achieves a majority.

reapportionment The reallocation of districts among the states after each census so that each state receives at least one representative in Congress and all other state delegation sizes reflect population.

recall A procedure through which citizens by petition can call for a vote on removing an elected official from office before the end of his or her term.

reconciliation A provision of the Congressional Budget Act of 1974 that allows Congress to operate under special rules when dealing with budget-related matters. The most important of these special rules involve time limits on debate and approval by simple majority in the Senate.

redistricting The redrawing of the lines for legislative districts that takes place after decennial censuses.

referendum An election in which the citizens are asked to vote directly on passage of a piece of legislation.

regional primaries Presidential primaries scheduled so that those in any one region of the country are held on the same day.

Republican party The political party, formed in 1854, that emerged as the major alternative to the Democrats on the issue of the spread of slavery and has remained one of the two parties dominating American politics since that time.

residency requirements Requirement that a citizen live in a community for a specified period of time before becoming eligible to vote.

retrospective (past) voting Casting a vote based on the records that candidates have built prior to the time of an election.

Revenue Act The 1971 law that encouraged small contributions to political campaigns through tax incentives.

rolling sample Technique used by pollsters to gauge public opinion by continuously replacing one portion of the group they are polling each night with a newly selected group.

runoff primary Primary between the top two finishers in states that require majority votes in order to nominate.

secular realignment Long-term, gradual shift in the partisan attachments of groups of voters, which eventually results in a new party system.

self-identification Responses that individuals give about their own sense of who they are or to what groups they belong.

senatorial courtesy The right of any U.S. senator to veto (and as a practical matter to approve) any appointee from that senator's state if the appointment requires senatorial confirmation.

senatorial holds The practice through which a U.S. senator keeps a nomination from coming to a vote by asking for it to be held up until he or she is ready to vote.

separate segregated fund The way in which a corporation or other entity must maintain a distinction between corporate funds and money raised and spent for political purposes.

Seventeenth Amendment The amendment to the U.S. Constitution that calls for the direct election of U.S. senators; prior to its adoption in 1913, senators had been appointed by state legislatures.

single-purpose groups Interest groups that concentrate their efforts on one particular issue.

single transferable vote A balloting system where voters rank the choices on the ballot. If one candidate receives 50 percent plus one of the votes cast, that candidate is declared the winner. If no candidate receives more than half of the votes, the lowest-achieving candidate is eliminated and her or his votes are reassigned to other candidates based on the voters' second-ranked choice. This process continues until a candidate reaches 50 percent plus one of the vote.

social media Digital content services that use the Internet to allow users to create and instantly share content with others who are also connected.

socializing elements of American society Institutions that teach those in a social grouping its norms, expectations, values, ideas, and so on.

soft money Money raised for political purposes that is outside of the constraints specified under the Federal Election Campaign Act, unregulated money not to be used directly for federal campaigns.

Speaker The leader of the House of Representatives, who, in addition to being the leader of the majority party, has administrative duties.

split-ticket voting Casting votes for candidates of more than one party in the same election—for example, voting for the Democratic candidate for president and the Republican candidate for the U.S. House.

strategy The overall design of a campaign.

SUN PAC The political action committee set up by the Sun Oil Corporation that tested the principle that corporations could establish PACs.

Super PAC Unlike traditional PACs, Super PACs are independent expenditure-only committees, meaning they are not allowed to contribute directly to candidates or parties—in other words, they only raise and spend soft money. However, unlike regular PACs, Super PACs are allowed to raise unlimited amounts of money from unlimited sources. They must disclose the identity of their donors, the same as a traditional PAC.

Super Tuesday The Tuesday during the primary season on which the most delegates are chosen.

superdelegates Delegates to the Democratic National Convention who hold their seats by virtue of their office—for example, members of Congress, senators, and governors.

tactics The specific techniques used to implement the overall strategic design.

tax checkoff The means through which citizens can contribute money to support the public funding of campaigns.

term limits Statutory limits on the number of successive terms an elected office-holder may serve.

third-party candidates Candidates on the ballot representing any parties other than the two major parties.

Tillman Act Early twentieth-century legislation designed to curb political abuse by corporations.

top two system A primary system where all candidates—regardless of political party affiliation—run together on one ballot, with the first and second place vote-getters advancing to the general election.

triangulation The effort to position oneself between extreme positions so as to draw support from both sides.

Twenty-Fourth Amendment The amendment to the U.S. Constitution that prohibited the use of the poll tax or any other tax as a requirement for voting.

Twenty-Sixth Amendment Amendment to the U.S. Constitution setting eighteen as the minimum age for voting.

unified control The situation in which one political party controls both elected branches of government.

Voting Rights Act of 1965 Critical piece of civil rights legislation that permitted the federal government to impose federal registrars on voting districts in which a minority of black citizens were registered to vote.

Whig party Political party that succeeded the Federalists and competed with the Democratic-Republicans through much of the pre–Civil War period.

"whites only" primaries An example of a Jim Crow law by which Southern Democratic parties established themselves as private organizations open only to whites and then nominated candidates for office in elections normally not contested by Republicans, thus effectively denying black citizens the right to vote.

winner-take-all primaries Primary elections in which the plurality winner receives all of the delegates at stake.

References

Abrajano, Marisa A., and R. Michael Alvarez. 2010. *New Faces, New Voices: The Hispanic Electorate in America*. Princeton, N.J.: Princeton University Press.

Abramowitz, Alan I. 1975. "Name Familiarity, Reputation, and the Incumbency Effect in a Congressional Election." *Western Political Quarterly* 28:668–84.

———. 1981. "Party and Individual Accountability in the 1978 Congressional Election." In *Congressional Elections*, edited by L. Sandy Maisel and Joseph Cooper. Beverly Hills, Calif.: Sage.

———. 2010. *The Disappearing Center: Engaged Citizens, Polarization, and American Democracy*. New Haven, Conn.: Yale University Press.

———. 2013. *The Polarized Public? Why American Government Is So Dysfunctional*. Boston: Pearson.

Abramowitz, Alan I., Brad Alexander, and Matthew Gunning. 2006. "Incumbency, Redistricting, and the Decline of Competition in U.S. House Elections." *Journal of Politics* 68:75–88.

Abramowitz, Alan I., and Kyle L. Saunders. 1998. "Ideological Realignment in the U.S. Electorate." *Journal of Politics* 6:634–53.

———. 2005. "Why Can't We All Just Get Along? The Reality of a Polarized America." *The Forum* 3:1–19.

Abrams, Abigail. 2017. "Elizabeth Warren Thinks the DNC System Was Rigged to Help Hillary Clinton." *TIME*, November 3.

Abramson, Paul R., John H. Aldrich, Phil Paolino, and David W. Rohde. 1995. "Third Party and Independent Candidates in American Politics: Wallace, Anderson, and Perot." *Political Science Quarterly* 110:347–67.

Abramson, Paul R., John H. Aldrich, and David W. Rohde. 1995. *Change and Continuity in the 1992 Elections*. Rev. ed. Washington, D.C.: Congressional Quarterly Press.

———. 1998. *Change and Continuity in the 1996 Elections*. Washington, D.C.: Congressional Quarterly Press.

———. 2005. *Change and Continuity in the 2004 Elections*. Washington, D.C.: Congressional Quarterly Press.

———. 2007. *Change and Continuity in the 2004 and 2006 Elections*. Washington, D.C.: Congressional Quarterly Press.

Adamany, David. 1984. "Political Parties in the 1980s." In *Money and Politics in the United States*, edited by Michael J. Malbin. Washington, D.C.: American Enterprise Institute/Chatham House.

Adams, William C. 1982. "Media Power in Presidential Elections: An Exploratory Analysis, 1960–1980." In *The President and the Public*, edited by Doris A. Graber. Philadelphia: Institute for the Study of Human Issues.

Agranoff, Robert. 1972. *The Management of Election Campaigns*. Boston: Holbrook.

———. 1976. *The New Style in Election Campaigns*. Boston: Holbrook.

Ahrens, Frank. 2009. "The Accelerating Decline of Newspapers." *Washington Post*, October 27, online edition.

Aistrup, Joseph D. 1996. *The Southern Strategy Revisited*. Lexington: University of Kentucky Press.

Aldrich, John. 1980. *Before the Convention: Strategies and Choices in Presidential Nomination Campaigns*. Chicago: University of Chicago Press.

———. 1995. *Why Parties? The Origin and Transformation of Political Parties in America*. Chicago: University of Chicago Press.

Aldrich, John, and Richard G. Niemi. 1990. "The Sixth American Party System: The 1960s Realignment and Candidate-Centered Parties." Unpublished manuscript, University of Rochester, New York.

Aldrich, John H., and David W. Rohde. 1997. "The Transition to Republican Rule in the House: Implications for Theories of Congressional Politics." *Political Science Quarterly* 112:541–67.

Alexander, Herbert E. 1976. *Financing Politics: Money, Elections, and Political Reform*. Lexington, Mass.: Lexington Books.

———. 1979. *Political Finance*. Beverly Hills, Calif.: Sage.

———. 1984. "Making Sense about Dollars in the 1980 Presidential Campaigns." In *Money and Politics in the United States: Financing Elections in the 1980s*, edited by Michael J. Malbin. Washington, D.C.: American Enterprise Institute/Chatham House.

Alexander, Herbert E., and Monica Bauer. 1991. *Financing the 1988 Election*. Boulder, Colo.: Westview.

Allen, Jonathan. 2003a. "House GOP's 'Stealth Whip' Knows the Power of Listening." *Congressional Quarterly Weekly*, March 29, 750.

———. 2003b. "Effective House Leadership Makes the Most of Majority." *Congressional Quarterly Weekly*, March 29, 746–50.

Allen, Jonathan, and Adam Graham-Silverman. 2003. "Hour by Hour, Vote by Vote, GOP Breaks Tense Tie." *Congressional Quarterly Weekly*, June 28, 1614–15.

Allen, Mike, and Jim VandeHei. 2012. "Inside the Campaign: How Mitt Romney Stumbled." *Politico*, September 16.

Allison, Bill. 2011. "FEC Surrenders in Hybrid Super PAC Case." *Sunlight Foundation*, August 24.

Almond, Gabriel A., and Sidney Verba. 1965. *The Civic Culture*. Boston: Little, Brown.

Alt, James E. 1994. *The Impact of the Voting Rights Act on Black and White Voter Registration in the South*. Princeton, N.J.: Princeton University Press.

Alter, Jonathan. 1992. "The Media Mud Squad." *Newsweek*, October 29, 37.

American Association of Public Opinion Research (AAPOR). 2017. "An Evaluation of the 2016 Election Polls in the U.S." Oakbrook Terrace, IL: May 4.

American Political Science Association. Committee on Political Parties. 1950. "Toward a More Responsible Two-Party System." *American Political Science Review* 44, no. 3, part 2, supplement (September): v–ix, 1–96.

American Press Institute. 2014. "The Personal News Cycle: How Americans Choose to Get Their News." March 17.

Andres, Gary J. 2009. *Lobbying Reconsidered: Under the Influence*. New York: Pearson/Longman.

Ansolabehere, Stephen, and Shanto Iyengar. 1995. *Going Negative: How Political Advertisements Shrink and Polarize the Electorate*. New York: Free Press.

Ansolabehere, Stephen, and James M. Snyder Jr. 2008. *The End of Inequality: One Person, One Vote and the Transformation of American Politics*. New York: Norton.

Anzia, Sarah. 2014. *Timing and Turnout: How Off-Cycle Elections Favor Organized Groups*. Chicago: University of Chicago Press.

Aoki, Andrew L., and Mark Rom. 1985. "Financing a Comeback: Campaign Finance Laws and Prospects for Political Party Resurgence." Paper presented at the annual meeting of the American Political Science Association, New Orleans, La.

Appelbaum, Yoni. 2016. "The Ingenious Marketing Strategies behind Trump's Success." *The Atlantic*, November 28.

Appleton, Andrew M., and Daniel S. Ward. 1997. *State Party Profits: A Fifty-State Guide to Development, Organization, and Resources*. Washington, D.C.: Congressional Quarterly Press.

Aral, Sinan. 2018. "How Lies Spread Online." *New York Times*, March 11.

Aronsen, Gavin. 2012. "How Dark-Money Groups Sneak by the Taxman. *Mother Jones*, June.

Arsenau, Robert B., and Raymond E. Wolfinger. 1973. "Voting Behavior in Congressional Elections." Paper presented at the annual meeting of the American Political Science Association, New Orleans, La.

Arterton, F. Christopher. 1982. "Political Money and Party Strength." In *The Future of American Political Parties*, edited by Joel L. Fleishman. Englewood Cliffs, N.J.: Prentice-Hall.

———. 1993. "Campaign '92: Strategies and Tactics of the Candidates." In *The Election of 1992: Reports and Interpretation*, edited by Gerald M. Pomper. Chatham, N.J.: Chatham House.

Associated Press. 1998. "Democrats Assail Republicans for Attack Ads." October 28.

Ayres, Drummond. 1998. "Political Briefing: Greens Abandon One of Their Own." *New York Times*, September 29, online edition.

Bach, Stanley, and Steven S. Smith. 1988. *Managing Uncertainty in the House of Representatives: Adaptation and Innovation in Special Rules*. Washington, D.C.: Brookings Institution.

Backer, Dan. 2012. "Why Hybrid PACs Matter." *Campaigns and Elections*, May 20.

Bacon, Perry, Jr. 2009. "A Vote to Make or Break a Career: Lone House Republican Backed Health Bill after Abortion Was Limited." *Washington Post*, November 9, A9.

———. 2017. "Why the Senate's Obamacare Repeal Failed." *FiveThirtyEight*, July 28.

Baker, Ross K. 1989. *House and Senate*. New York: Norton.

Balz, Dan, and Haynes Johnson. 2009. *The Battle for America 2008: The Story of an Extraordinary Election*. New York: Penguin.

Balz, Dan, and Jim VandeHei. 2006. "Amid the Last-Minute Blitz, Some Polls Hold Positive Signs for Republicans." *Washington Post*, November 6, A1.

Banfield, Edward C., and James Q. Wilson. 1963. *City Politics*. Cambridge, Mass.: Harvard University Press.

Banning, Lance, ed. 2004. *Liberty and Order: The First American Party Struggle*. Indianapolis, Ind.: Liberty Fund.

Barber, James David. 1978. *The Race for the Presidency: The Media and the Nominating Process*. Englewood Cliffs, N.J.: Prentice-Hall.

Barker, Lucius J., and Ronald Walter, eds. 1989. *Jesse Jackson and the 1984 Presidential Campaign*. Urbana: University of Illinois Press.

Barnes, Robert. 2017. "Supreme Court Will Take Up a Second Gerrymandering Case This Term." *Washingon Post*, December 8.

———. 2018. "Even on Second Look, Supreme Court Seems Stumped on Gerrymandering Issue." *Washington Post*, March 28.

Bartels, Larry M. 2000. "Partisanship and Voting Behavior, 1952–1996." *American Journal of Political Science* 44 (January): 35–50.

———. 2008. *Unequal Democracy: The Political Economy of the New Gilded Age*. New York and Princeton, NJ: The Russell Sage Foundation and Princeton University Press.

Basehart, Harry, and John Comer. 1991. "Partisan and Incumbent Effects in State Legislative Redistricting." *Legislative Studies Quarterly* 16:65–79.

Battaglio, Stephen. 2016a. "35 Million TV Viewers Watch Trump's Speech." *Los Angeles Times*, July 23.

———. 2016b. "Clinton Speech Ratings Fall Short." *Los Angeles Times*, July 30.

BBC. 2017. "Republican Attempts to Replace Obamacare Fail." *BBC*, July 18.

Beck, John H., and Kevin E. Henrickson. 2013. "The Effect of the Top Two Primary on the Number of Primary Candidates." *Social Science Quarterly* 94: 777–94.

Beck, Paul Allen. 1984. "The Dealignment Era in America." In *Electoral Change in Advanced Industrial Democracies*, edited by Russell J. Dalton, Scott C. Flanagan, and Paul Allen Beck. Princeton, N.J.: Princeton University Press.

Bennett, Stephen E. 1990. "The Uses and Abuses of Registration and Turnout Data." *PS: Political Science and Politics* 23:166–71.

Bennett, Stephen E., and David Resnick. 1991. "The Implications for Nonvoting for Democracy in the United States." *American Journal of Political Science* 34:771–803.

Berelson, Bernard, Paul F. Lazarsfeld, and William N. McPhee. 1954. *Voting*. Chicago: University of Chicago Press.

Berkman, Ronald, and Laura Kitch. 1986. *Politics in the Media Age*. New York: McGraw-Hill.

Berry, Jeffrey M. 1999. *The New Liberalism: The Rising Power of Citizen Groups*. Washington, D.C.: Brookings Institution.

Berry, Jeffrey M., and Clyde Wilcox. 2009. *The Interest Group Society*. 5th ed. New York: Pearson/Longman.

Bianco, William T., and Itai Sened. 2005. "Uncovering Evidence of Conditional Party Government: Reassessing Majority Party Influence in Congress and State Legislatures." *American Political Science Review* 99:361–71.

Bibby, John F. 1981. "Party Renewal in the National Republican Party." In *Party Renewal in America*, edited by Gerald Pomper. New York: Praeger.

———. 1986. "Party Trends in 1985: Constrained Advance of the National Party." *Publius* 16:79–91.

———. 1990. "Party Organization at the State Level." In *The Parties Respond: Changes in the American Party System*, edited by L. Sandy Maisel. Boulder, Colo.: Westview.

———. 1991. "Republican National Committee." In *Political Parties and Elections in the United States: An Encyclopedia*, edited by L. Sandy Maisel. New York: Garland.

———. 1998. "State Party Organizations: Coping and Adapting to Candidate-Centered Politics and Nationalization." In *The Parties Respond*, edited by L. Sandy Maisel. 3rd ed. Boulder, Colo.: Westview.

———. 2002. "State Party Organizations: Strengthened and Adapting to Candidate-Centered Politics and Nationalization." In *The Parties Respond*, edited by L. Sandy Maisel. 4th ed. Boulder, Colo.: Westview.

Bibby, John F., Cornelius P. Cotter, James L. Gibson, and Robert J. Huckshorn. 1983. "Political Parties." In *Politics in the American States*, edited by Virginia Gray, Herbert Jacob, and Kenneth N. Vines. 4th ed. Boston: Little, Brown.

Bibby, John F., and Thomas M. Holbrook. 1996. "Parties and Elections." In *Politics in the American States: A Comparative Analysis*, edited by Virginia Gray and Herbert Jacob. 6th ed. Washington, D.C.: Congressional Quarterly Press.

Bibby, John F., and L. Sandy Maisel. 2003. *Two Parties or More?* 2nd ed. Boulder, Colo.: Westview.

Bimber, Bruce. 2014. "Digital Media and the Obama Campaigns of 2008 and 2012: Adaptation to the Personalized Political Communication Environment." *Journal of Information Technology and Politics* 11:130–50.

Binder, Sarah, and Steven Smith. 1997. *Politics or Principle? Filibustering in the U.S. Senate*. Washington, D.C.: Brookings Institution.

Bishop, Bill. 2004. "The Great Divide." Series in *Austin American-Statesman*.

———. 2008. *The Big Sort: Why the Clustering of Like-Minded America Is Tearing Us Apart*. Boston: Houghton-Mifflin.

Black, Christine M., and Thomas Oliphant. 1989. *All by Myself: The Unmaking of a Presidential Campaign*. Chester, Conn.: Globe Pequot Press.

Black, Earl, and Merle Black. 1987. *Politics and Society in the South*. Cambridge, Mass.: Harvard University Press.

———. 2002. *The Rise of Southern Republicans*. Cambridge, Mass.: Harvard University Press.

Black, Gordon S., and Benjamin D. Black. 1993. "Perot Wins: The Election That Could Have Been." *Public Perspective* 4:15–16.

Blake, Aaron. 2018. "The Trump Administration Is Adding a Citizenship Question to the Census. Here's Why That's Bad for Democrats." *Washington Post*, March 26.

Bloom, Howard S., and H. Douglas Price. 1975. "Voter Response to Short-Run Economic Conditions: The Asymmetric Effect of Prosperity and Recession." *American Political Science Review* 69:1240–54.

Blum, John M., William McFeely, Edmund Morgan, Arthur Schlesinger Jr., Kenneth Stampp, and C. Vann Woodward. 1993. *The National Experience: A History of the United States*. 8th ed. New York: Harcourt.

Bohn, Kevin. 2012. "Romney Campaign Did Not Expect Obama's Turn-Out-the-Vote Results." *CNN*, December 4.

Bone, Hugh A., and Austin Ranney. 1976. *Politics and Voters*. 4th ed. New York: McGraw-Hill.

Born, Richard. 1985. "Partisan Intentions and Election Day Realities in the Congressional Redistricting Process." *American Political Science Review* 79:305–19.

Bougher, Lori D. 2017. "The Correlates of Discord: Identity, Issue Alignment, and Political Hostility in Polarized America." *Political Behavior* 39 (3): 731–62.

Bradner, Eric. 2018. "Democrats' Superdelegates Debate Left Unresolved, Will Continue into the Summer." *CNN Wire Service*, March 10.

Brady, David W. 1973. *Congressional Voting in a Partisan Era*. Lawrence: University Press of Kansas.

Brady, David W., and Kara Z. Buckley. 2002. "Governing by Coalition: Policymaking in the U.S. Congress." In *The Parties Respond*, edited by L. Sandy Maisel. 4th ed. Boulder, Colo.: Westview.

Brady, David W., Charles S. Bullock III, and L. Sandy Maisel. 1988. "The Electoral Antecedents of Policy Innovations: A Comparative Analysis." *Comparative Political Studies* 20:395–422.

Brady, David W., and David Epstein. 1997. "Intra-party Preferences, Heterogeneity, and the Origins of the Modern Congress: Progressive Reformers in the House and Senate, 1890–1970." *Journal of Law, Economics, and Organization* 13:26–49.

Brady, David W., L. Sandy Maisel, and Kevin M. Warsh. 1994. "An Opportunity Cost Model of the Decision to Run for Congress: Another Contributor to Democratic Hegemony." Paper presented at the annual meeting of the American Political Science Association, New York.

Brady, David W., and Joseph Stewart Jr. 1986. "When Elections Really Matter: Realignment and Changes in Public Policy." In *Do Elections Matter?* edited by Benjamin Ginsberg and Alan Stone. Armonk, N.Y.: Sharpe.

Brady, David W., and Craig Volden. 1998. *Revolving Gridlock: Politics and Policy from Carter to Clinton*. Boulder, Colo.: Westview.

Brazile, Donna. 2017. "Inside Hillary Clinton's Secret Takeover of the DNC." *Politico*, November 2.

Brennan, Allison. 2012. "Microtargeting: How Campaigns Know You Better than You Know Yourself." *CNN*, November 5.

Brennan Center for Justice. 2017. *Voting Laws Roundup 2017*. New York: New York University School of Law.

———. 2018. *Voting Rights Restoration Efforts in Florida*. New York: New York University School of Law.

Brewer, Mark D. 2003. *Relevant No More? The Catholic/Protestant Divide in American Electoral Politics*. Lanham, Md.: Lexington Books.

———. 2005. "The Rise of Partisanship and the Expansion of Partisan Conflict within the American Electorate." *Political Research Quarterly* 58:219–29.

———. 2009. *Party Images in the American Electorate*. New York: Routledge.
Brewer, Mark D., and Jeffrey M. Stonecash. 2007. *Split: Class and Cultural Divides in American Politics*. Washington, D.C.: Congressional Quarterly Press.
———. 2009. *Dynamics of American Political Parties*. New York: Cambridge University Press.
———. 2015. *Polarization and the Politics of Personal Responsibility*. New York: Oxford University Press.
Bridges, Amy. 1984. *A City in the Republic: Antebellum New York and the Origins of Machine Politics*. New York: Cambridge University Press.
Broder, David S. 1971. *The Party's Over*. New York: Harper and Row.
———. 2010. "California Switch Could Affect Elections Nationally." *Washington Post*, June 13, A10.
Brody, Richard A., and Benjamin I. Page. 1972. "Policy Voting and the Electoral Process: The Vietnam War Issue." *American Political Science Review* 66:979–95.
Brown, Robert D., and John M. Bruce. 2002. "Political Parties in State and Nation: Party Advantage and Party Competition in a Federal Setting." *Party Politics* 8:635–56.
Brunell, Thomas L. 2008. *Redistricting and Representation: Why Competitive Elections Are Bad for America*. New York: Routledge.
Brunell, Thomas L., and Bernard Grofman. 1998. "Explaining Divided U.S. Senate Delegations, 1788–1996: A Realignment Approach." *American Political Science Review* 92:391–99.
Bruno, Jerry, and Jeff Greenfield. 1971. *The Advance Man*. New York: Morrow.
Buchanan, Bruce. 1991. *Electing a President: The Markle Commission Research on Campaign '88*. Austin: University of Texas Press.
Buell, Emmett H., Jr., and Lee Sigelman. 1991. *Nominating the President*. Knoxville: University of Tennessee Press.
Bullock, Charles S., III. 1988. "Regional Realignment from an Officeholding Perspective." *Journal of Politics* 50:553–74.
Bullock, Charles S., and Loch K. Johnson. 1992. *Runoff Elections in the United States*. Chapel Hill: University of North Carolina Press.
Bumiller, Elisabeth, and David E. Sanger. 2002. "Republicans Say Rove Was Mastermind of Big Victory." *New York Times*, November 7, B1.
Bump, Philip. 2017. "How Politicians' Use of Social Media Is Reinforcing a Partisan Media Divide." WP Company LLC d/b/a The Washington Post, last modified December 18.
———. 2018a. "Everything You Need to Know about the Cambridge Analytica–Facebook Debacle." WP Company LLC d/b/a The Washington Post, last modified March 19.
———. 2018b. "Timeline: How Russian Trolls Allegedly Tried to Throw the 2016 Election to Trump." *Washington Post*, February 16.
Burke, Samuel. 2017. "How Many Social Followers Does Trump Actually have?" *CNN Wire Service*, June 17.
Burnett, Sara, and John O'Connor. 2018. "Illinois Primary Could Set Up Most Expensive Governor's Race." *Washington Post*, March 20.
Burnham, Walter Dean. 1965. "The Changing Shape of the American Political Universe." *American Political Science Review* 59:7–28.

———. 1970. *Critical Elections and the Mainsprings of American Democracy*. New York: Norton.

———. 1991. "Critical Realignment: Dead or Alive?" In *The End of Realignment*, edited by Byron E. Shafer. Madison: University of Wisconsin Press.

Butler, David, and Bruce E. Cain. 1991. *Congressional Redistricting: Comparative and Theoretical Perspectives*. New York: Macmillan.

Caddell, Patrick H. 1981. "The Democratic Strategy and Its Electoral Consequences." In *Party Coalitions in the 1980s*, edited by Seymour Martin Lipset. San Francisco: Institute for Contemporary Studies.

Cahn, Emily. 2013. "Old-School Politics Reign in California's New Primary." *Roll Call*, June 10.

Cain, Bruce E. 1984. *The Reapportionment Puzzle*. Berkeley: University of California Press.

———. 1985. "Assessing the Partisan Effects of Redistricting." *American Political Science Review* 79:320–33.

Cain, Bruce E., and David Butler. 1991. "Redrawing District Lines: What's Going On and What's at Stake?" *American Enterprise* 2 (July/August): 28–39.

Cain, Bruce E., John Ferejohn, and Morris Fiorina. 1987. *The Personal Vote: Constituency Service and Electoral Independence*. Cambridge, Mass.: Harvard University Press.

Calvert, Jerry W. 1979. "Revolving Doors: Volunteerism in State Legislatures." *State Government* 52:174.

Campbell, Angus, Philip E. Converse, Warren E. Miller, and Donald A. Stokes. 1960. *The American Voter*. New York: Wiley.

Campbell, James E. 2010. "The Midterm Landslide of 2010: A Triple Wave Election." *The Forum* 8, no. 4, article 3.

Canon, David T. 1990. *Actors, Athletes, and Astronauts: Political Amateurs in the United States Congress*. Chicago: University of Chicago Press.

Carlisle, John K. 2004. "George Soros: His Plan to Defeat George Bush, Part I." Foundation Watch, Capital Research Center, February.

Carmines, Edward G., John P. McIver, and James A. Stimson. 1987. "Unrealized Partisanship: A Theory of Dealignment." *Journal of Politics* 49:376–400.

Carmines, Edward G., and James A. Stimson. 1989. *Issue Evolution: Race and the Transformation of American Politics*. Princeton, N.J.: Princeton University Press.

Carney, Eliza Newlin. 2013a. "States Target Politically Active Nonprofits." *Roll Call*, January 3.

———. 2013b. "Hate Congress? Blame the (Sharply Divided) Voters." *Roll Call*, September 10.

———. 2014. "Firewall between Candidates and Super PACs Breaking Down." *Roll Call*, February 18.

Carr, Craig L., and Gary L. Scott. 1984. "The Logic of State Primary Classification Schemes." *American Politics Quarterly* 12:465–76.

Carter, Jimmy. 1982. *Public Papers of the President*. Washington, D.C.: U.S. Government Printing Office.

Cassel, Carol A., and Robert C. Luskin. 1988. "Simple Explanations of Voter Turnout." *American Political Science Review* 82:1321–30.

Cassidy, John. 2016. "Three Reasons Why Hillary Clinton Chose Tim Kaine." *New Yorker*. July 23.

Catanese, David. 2017. "Donald Trump and the Disintegration of the Republican Party." *U.S. News*, October 24.

Catt, Carrie C., and Nettie R. Shuler. 1969. *Woman Suffrage and Politics*. Seattle: University of Washington Press.

Ceaser, James. 2017. "The Nomination Game." *Journal of Democracy* 28 (2): 45–49.

Ceaser, James, and Andrew Busch. 1993. *Upside-Down and Inside-Out: The 1992 Elections and American Politics*. Lanham, Md.: Rowman & Littlefield.

———. 1997. *Losing to Win: The 1996 Election and American Politics*. Lanham, Md.: Rowman & Littlefield.

Center for Responsive Politics. 1985. *Soft Money: A Loophole for the '80s*. Washington, D.C.: Center for Responsive Politics.

Chadwick, Andrew, and Jennifer Stromer-Galley. 2016. "Digital Media, Power, and Democracy in Parties and Election Campaigns." *International Journal of Press/Politics* 21 (3): 283–93.

Chambers, William N. 1963. *Political Parties in a New Nation: The American Experience, 1776–1809*. New York: Oxford University Press.

———. 1975. "Party Development in the American Mainstream." In *The American Party Systems: Stages of Political Development*, edited by William N. Chambers and Walter D. Burnham. 2nd ed. New York: Oxford University Press.

Chambers, William N., and Walter D. Burnham. 1975. *The American Party Systems: Stages of Political Development*. 2nd ed. New York: Oxford University Press.

Chang, Jack. 2011. "Meg Whitman's Campaign Spending Totals $178.5 Million." *Sacramento Bee*, February 1.

Cigler, Allan J. 2006. "Interest Groups and Financing the 2004 Elections." In *Financing the 2004 Election*, edited by David B. Magleby, Anthony J. Corrado, and Kelly D. Patterson. Washington, D.C.: Brookings Institution.

Cigler, Allan J., and Burdett A. Loomis, eds. 2007. *Interest Group Politics*. 7th ed. Washington, D.C.: Congressional Quarterly Press.

Citizens' Research Foundation. 1997. *New Realities, New Thinking: Report of the Task Force on Campaign Finance Reform*. Los Angeles: Citizens' Research Foundation, University of Southern California.

Clayworth, Jason. 2016. "Caucus Turnout: Robust, Record-Setting and Surprising." *Des Moines Register*, February 2.

Clymer, Adam. 2003a. "Buoyed by Resurgence, GOP Strives for an Era of Dominance," *New York Times*, May 25, section 1, p. 1.

———. 2003b. "Washington Talk: Campaign Finance Muddle Recalls Election of '76." *New York Times*, May 6, A28.

Clymer, Adam, and David E. Rosenbaum. 2002. "Republicans Hold the House." *New York Times*, November 6, B5.

Cohen, Marty, David Karol, Hans Noel, and John Zaller. 2008. *The Party Decides: Presidential Nominations before and after Reform*. Chicago: University of Chicago Press.

———. 2016. "Party versus Faction in the Reformed Presidential Nominating System." *PS: Political Science & Politics* 49 (4): 701–8.

Collie, Melissa P., and Joseph Cooper. 1989. "Multiple Referral and the 'New' Committee System in the House of Representatives." In *Congress Reconsidered*, edited by Lawrence C. Dodd and Bruce I. Oppenheimer. 4th ed. Washington, D.C.: Congressional Quarterly Press.

Collinson, Stephen. 2016. "Super Tuesday: Clinton, Trump Win Big; Cruz Takes Texas; Rubio Scores First Win." *CNN Wire Service*, March 1.

Common Cause. 1986. *Financing the Finance Committee*. Washington, D.C.: Common Cause.

Condon, Stephanie. 2009. "Obama, House Leaders Promise Health Care Bill by August." CBS News Political Hotsheet, May 13.

Confessore, Nicholas. 2015. "Koch Brothers' Budget of $889 Million for 2016 is on Par with Both Parties' Spending." *New York Times*, January 26.

———. 2016. "Beneath Hillary Clinton's Super Tuesday Wins, Signs of Turnout Trouble." New York Times Company, last modified March 2.

Confessore, Nicholas, and Rachel Shorey. 2016. "Donald Trump, with Bare-Bones Campaign, Relies on G.O.P. for Vital Tasks." New York Times Company, last modified August 21.

Confessore, Nicholas, and Karen Yourish. 2016. "$2 Billion Worth of Free Media for Donald Trump." New York Times Company, last modified March 15.

Congressional Quarterly Almanac. 1971–2010. Washington, D.C.: Congressional Quarterly.

Congressional Quarterly Weekly. 1984. "Today's House Freshmen Getting Started Quickly." December 22, 3137.

———. 2003. "Sharp Divide on Highest Court Revealed in Disparate Opinions." December 13, 3078.

Connolly, Ceci. 2010. "61 Days from Near Defeat to Victory: How Obama Revived His Health-Care Bill." *Washington Post*, March 23, A1.

Converse, Philip E., Aage R. Clausen, and Warren E. Miller. 1965. "Electoral Myth and Reality: The 1964 Election." *American Political Science Review* 59:321–36.

Converse, Philip E., and Richard G. Niemi. 1971. "Nonvoting among Young Adults in the United States." In *Political Parties and Political Behavior*, edited by William J. Crotty, Donald M. Freeman, and Douglas S. Gatlin. 2nd ed. Boston: Allyn and Bacon.

Converse, Philip E., and Roy Pierce. 1992. "Partisanship and the Party System." *Political Behavior* 14:239–59.

Cook, Charlie. 2013. "The Republican Advantage." *National Journal*, April 12.

Cook, Rhodes. 2010. "The Rhodes Cook Letter." December.

Cooper, Joseph, and David W. Brady. 1981. "Institutional Context and Leadership Style: The House from Cannon to Rayburn." *American Political Science Review* 75:411–25.

Cooper, Joseph, and William West. 1981. "The Congressional Career in the '70's." In *Congress Reconsidered*, edited by Lawrence Dodd and Bruce I. Oppenheimer. 2nd ed. Washington, D.C.: Congressional Quarterly Press.

Corrado, Anthony J. 1991a. "Federal Election Campaign Act of 1971." In *Political Parties and Elections in the United States: An Encyclopedia*, edited by L. Sandy Maisel. New York: Garland.

———. 1991b. "Federal Election Campaign Act Amendments of 1974." In *Political Parties and Elections in the United States: An Encyclopedia*, edited by L. Sandy Maisel. New York: Garland.

———. 1992. *Creative Campaigning: PACs and the Presidential Selection Process*. Boulder, Colo.: Westview.

———. 2006a. "The Regulatory Environment: Uncertainty in the Wake of Change." In *Financing the 2004 Election*, edited by David B. Magleby, Anthony J. Corrado, and Kelly D. Patterson. Washington, D.C.: Brookings Institution.

———. 2006b. "Financing the 2004 Presidential General Election." In *Financing the 2004 Election*, edited by David B. Magleby, Anthony J. Corrado, and Kelly D. Patterson. Washington, D.C.: Brookings Institution.

Corrado, Anthony J., and L. Sandy Maisel. 1988. "Campaigning for Presidential Nominations: The Experience with State Spending Ceilings, 1976–1984." Paper presented at the annual meeting of the Western Political Science Association, San Francisco. Occasional Paper nos. 88–84, Center for American Political Studies Harvard University, Cambridge, Mass.

Corrado, Anthony J., Thomas E. Mann, Daniel R. Ortiz, and Trevor Potter. 2005. *The New Campaign Finance Sourcebook*. Washington, D.C.: Brookings Institution.

Cotter, Cornelius P., and John F. Bibby. 1980. "Institutional Developments of Parties and the Thesis of Party Decline." *Political Science Quarterly* 1:95.

Cotter, Cornelius P., James L. Gibson, John F. Bibby, and Robert J. Huckshorn. 1982. "Party–Government Linkages in the States." Paper delivered at the annual meeting of the American Political Science Association, Washington, D.C.

———. 1984. *Party Organization in American Politics*. New York: Praeger.

———. 1989. *Party Organization in American Politics*. 2nd ed. New York: Praeger.

Cotter, Cornelius P., and Bernard C. Hennessy. 1964. *Politics without Power: The National Party Committees*. New York: Atherton.

Courser, Zachary. 2007. "Mugwumps and Goo-Goos: American Democracy and Nineteenth-Century Anti-Partisanship." Paper presented at the annual meeting of the Midwest Political Science Association, Chicago, Ill.

Coval, Michael. 1984. "The Impact of the 1980 Election on Liberal Political Organization." Honors project presented at Colby College, Waterville, Maine.

Cover, Albert D. 1977. "One Good Term Deserves Another: The Advantages of Incumbency in Congressional Elections." *American Journal of Political Science* 21:523–41.

Cox, Gary, and Samuel Kernell, eds. 1991. *The Politics of Divided Government*. Boulder, Colo.: Westview.

Cox, Gary, and Mathew D. McCubbins. 1993. *Legislative Leviathan: Party Government in the House*. Berkeley: University of California Press.

———. 2005. *Setting the Agenda: Responsible Party Government in the U.S. House of Representatives*. New York: Cambridge University Press.

Cox, Gary W., and Scott Morgenstern. 1993. "The Increasing Advantage of Incumbency in the U.S. States." *Legislative Studies Quarterly* 18:495–514.

———. 1995. "The Incumbency Advantage in Multimember Districts: Evidence from the U.S. States." *Legislative Studies Quarterly* 20:329–49.

CQ Magazine. 2018. "CQ Vote Studies: Party Unity." *CQ Magazine*, February 12.

Crespi, Irving. 1988. *Pre-election Polling: Sources of Accuracy and Error*. New York: Russell Sage Foundation.
———. 1989. *Public Opinion, Polls, and Democracy*. Boulder, Colo.: Westview.
Crosby, Stephen. 1998. Correspondence, September 2.
Crotty, William J. 1984. *American Political Parties in Decline*, 2nd ed. Boston: Little, Brown.
———. 1985. *The Party Game*. New York: Freeman.
Crouse, Timothy. 1973. *The Boys on the Bus*. New York: Ballantine.
Cummings, Norman, and Grace Cummings. 2004. "Strategy and Tactics for Campaign Fundraising." In *Campaigns and Elections American Style*, 2nd ed., edited by James A. Thurber and Candice J. Nelson. Boulder, Colo.: Westview.
Cunningham, Noble E. 1965. *The Making of the American Party System, 1789–1809*. Englewood Cliffs, N.J.: Prentice-Hall.
Cunningham, Paige Winfield. 2017. *The Health 202: Five Lessons from the GOP's Failed Effort to Repeal Obamacare*. WP Company LLC d/b/a The Washington Post.
Dahl, Robert. 1961. *Who Governs? Democracy and Power in an American City*. New Haven, Conn.: Yale University Press.
Dahlgaard, Jens Olav. 2018. *The Surprising Consequence of Lowering the Voting Age*. WP Company LLC d/b/a The Washington Post.
Davis, James W. 1983. *National Conventions in an Age of Party Reform*. Westport, Conn.: Greenwood.
Davis, Richard. 1996. *The Press and American Politics: The New Mediator*. 2nd ed. Upper Saddle River, N.J.: Prentice-Hall.
Davis, Susan. 2017. "Trump's Fractured Relationship with Congress Causes GOP Dread." *NPR*, August 24.
DeCosta-Klipa, Nik. 2016. "Maine Became the First State in the Country Tuesday to Pass Ranked Choice Voting." *Boston*, November 10.
de Morales, Lisa. 2006. "Colbert, Still Digesting His Correspondents' Dinner Reception." *Washington Post*, May 2, C07.
Desmarais, Bruce A., Raymond J. La Raja, and Michael S. Kowal. 2015. "The Fates of Challengers in U.S. House Elections: The Role of Extended Party Networks in Supporting Candidates and Shaping Electoral Outcomes." *American Journal of Political Science* 59 (1): 194–211.
Dewan, Shaila, and Anne E. Kornblut. 2006. "In Key House Races, Democrats Run to the Right." *New York Times*, October 30, A1.
Dewar, Helen. 1999. "Senate Democrats Seek an Early Vote on Articles." *Washington Post*, January 21, A1, A16.
DeWitt, Darin Dion. 2013. "Party Formation in the United States." PhD diss., University of California, Los Angeles. Order No. AAI3564429.
Diamond, Edwin, and Stephen Bates. 1984. *The Spot: The Rise of Political Advertising on Television*. Cambridge, Mass.: MIT Press.
Dickinson, Tim. 2010. "No We Can't." *Rolling Stone*, February 2.
Dilanian, Ken. 2017. "Intelligence Director Says Agencies Agree on Russian Meddling." *NBC News*, July 21.
Dlouhy, Jennifer A. 2002. "Parties Use Judicial Standoff to Play to Core Constituents." *Congressional Quarterly Weekly*, October 19, 2722–27.

———. 2003. "A New Level of Acrimony in Parties' War of Procedure." *Congressional Quarterly Weekly*, May 10, 1078–84.

Dobson, John M. 1972. *Politics in the Gilded Age*. New York: Praeger.

Doherty, Carroll, Scott Keeter, and Rachel Weisel. 2014. "The Party of Nonvoters." *Pew Research Center*. October 31.

Downs, Anthony. 1957. *An Economic Theory of Democracy*. New York: Harper and Row.

Drew, Elizabeth. 1981. *Portrait of an Election: The 1980 Presidential Campaign*. New York: Simon and Schuster.

———. 1983. *Politics and Money: The New Road to Corruption*. New York: Macmillan.

Druckman, James N., Martin J. Kifer, and Michael Parkin. 2010. "Timeless Strategy Meets New Medium: Going Negative on Congressional Campaign Websites, 2002–2006." *Political Communication* 27: 88–103.

Drutman, Lee. 2016. "Donald Trump Will Dramatically Realign America's Political Parties." foreignpolicy.com, November 2016.

Dudnick, Laura. 2015. "SF Seeks to Become First Major City to Lower Voting Age to 16." *San Francisco Examiner*, March 17.

Dugan, Andrew, and Zac Auter. 2017. "Republicans', Democrats' Views of Media Accuracy Diverge." *Gallup*, August 25.

Duhigg, Charles. 2012. "Campaigns Mine Personal Lives to Get Out Vote." *New York Times*, October 13.

Dupuy, Beatrice. 2018. "Nearly Half of Republicans Think Negative Stories Are 'Fake News' While Trust in Media Hits All-Time Low, Poll Shows." *Newsweek*, January 16.

Duverger, Maurice. 1951. *Political Parties*. New York: Wiley.

Dwyer, Diana, and Robin Kolodny. 2006. "The Parties' Congressional Campaign Committees in 2004." In *The Election after Reform*, edited by Michael J. Malbin. Lanham, Md.: Rowman & Littlefield.

Edsall, Thomas B. 1986. "Conservative Fund-Raisers Hit Hard Times." *Washington Post*.

———. 2006. *Building Red America*. New York: Basic Books.

Edsall, Thomas B., and James V. Grimaldi. 2004. "How the Two Parties Split Their Millions." *Washington Post*, December 30, A7.

Eismeier, Theodore J., and Philip H. Pollock III. 1984. "Political Action Committees: Varieties of Organization and Strategy." In *Money and Politics in the United States*, edited by Michael J. Malbin. Washington, D.C.: American Enterprise Institute/Chatham House.

———. 1985a. "The Microeconomy of PACs." Paper delivered at the annual meeting of the American Political Science Association, Washington, D.C.

———. 1985b. "An Organizational Analysis of Political Action Committees." *Political Behavior* 7:192–216.

———. 1986. "Strategy and Choice in Congressional Elections: The Role of Political Action Committees." *American Journal of Political Science* 30:197–213.

Eldersveld, Samuel J. 1982. *Political Parties in American Society*. New York: Basic Books.

Elshtain, Jean Bethke, and Christopher Beem. 1997. "Issues and Themes: Economics, Culture, and 'Small-Party' Politics." In *The Elections of 1996*, edited by Michael Nelson. Washington, D.C.: Congressional Quarterly Press.

Ember, Sydney. 2017. "New York Times Reports Strong Quarter on Digital Revenue Growth." *New York Times*, July 27.

Epstein, Edwin M. 1980. "Business and Labor under the Federal Election Campaign Act of 1971." In *Parties, Interest Groups, and Campaign Finance Laws*, edited by Michael J. Malbin. Washington, D.C.: American Enterprise Institute for Public Policy Research.

Epstein, Leon D. 1967. *Political Parties in Western Democracies*. New York: Praeger.

———. 1986. *Political Parties in the American Mold*. Madison: University of Wisconsin Press.

———. 1989. "Will American Political Parties Be Privatized?" *Journal of Law and Politics* 5:239.

———. 1991. "The Regulation of State Political Parties." In *Political Parties and Elections in the United States: An Encyclopedia*, edited by L. Sandy Maisel. New York: Garland.

Epstein, Reid J., and Janet Hook. 2017. "Bernie Sanders Loyalists Are Taking Over the Democratic Party One County Office at a Time." *Wall Street Journal*, February 22.

Erie, Steven. 1988. *Rainbow's End: Irish-Americans and the Dilemmas of Urban Machine Politics, 1840–1985*. Berkeley: University of California Press.

Erikson, Robert S. 1981. "Why Do People Vote? Because They Are Registered." *American Politics Quarterly* 9:259.

Evans, Diana. 1986. "PAC Contributions and Roll-Call Voting." In *Interest Groups and Politics*, edited by Allan Cigler and Burdett A. Loomis. Washington, D.C.: Congressional Quarterly Press.

Everett, Burgess, Jennifer Haberkorn, and John Dawsey. 2017. "Collins' Opposition Dooms Latest Obamacare Repeal Effort." *Politico*, September 25.

Faler, Brian, and Seung Min Kim. 2017. "Republicans Strike Deal on Sweeping Tax Overhaul." *Politico*, December 13.

Faler, Brian, Seung Min Kim, and Colin Wilhelm. 2017. "Historic Tax Reform Vote Lined Up with GOP Bill Finalized." *Politico*, December 15.

Farnam, T. W., and Dan Eggen. 2011. "Lax Internal Revenue Service Rules Help Groups Shield Campaign Donor Identities." *Washington Post*, March 9, online edition.

Federal Election Commission. 2017. *Contribution Limits for 2017–2018 Federal Elections*. Washington, D.C.: Federal Election Commission.

Fenno, Richard F., Jr. 1973. *Congressmen in Committees*. Boston: Little, Brown.

———. 1978. *Home Style: House Members in Their Own Districts*. Boston: Little, Brown.

———. 1984. *The United States Senate: A Bicameral Perspective*. Washington, D.C.: American Enterprise Institute for Public Policy Research.

Ferejohn, John A. 1977. "On the Decline of Competition in Congressional Elections." *American Political Science Review* 71:166–76.

Finer, Herman. 1949. *The Theory and Practice of Modern Government*. New York: Holt.

Fink, Leon. 1983. *Workingmen's Democracy: The Knights of Labor and American Politics*. Urbana: University of Illinois Press.
Finkel, Steven E., and Howard A. Scarrow. 1985. "Party Identification and Party Enrollment: The Difference and the Consequence." *Journal of Politics* 47:620–42.
Fiorina, Morris P. 1977a. "The Case of the Vanishing Marginals: The Bureaucracy Did It." *American Political Science Review* 71:177–81.
———. 1977b. "An Outline for a Model of Party Choice." *American Journal of Political Science* 21:601–25.
———. 1978. *Congress: Keystone of the Washington Establishment*. 4th ed. New Haven, Conn.: Yale University Press.
———. 1981. *Retrospective Voting in American National Elections*. New Haven, Conn.: Yale University Press.
———. 1996. *Divided Government*. 2nd ed. Boston: Allyn and Bacon.
Fiorina, Morris P., Samuel J. Abrams, and Jeremy C. Pope. 2011. *Culture War? The Myth of a Polarized America*. 3rd ed. New York: Pearson/Longman.
Fishel, Jeff. 1985. *Presidents and Promises*. Washington, D.C.: Congressional Quarterly Press.
Flegenheimer, Matt. 2017. "Republicans in Congress May Be Stuck in a Relationship with Trump." New York Times Company, last modified August 17.
Flynn, Hillary, and Rachael Bade. 2015. "IRS May Broaden Rule to Police Political Nonprofits." *Politico*, March 19.
Foerstel, Karen. 2002. "Campaign Finance Passage Ends a Political Odyssey." *Congressional Quarterly Weekly*, March 23, 799–803.
Forgette, Richard, and Glenn Platt. 2005. "Redistricting Principles and Incumbency Protection in the U.S. Congress." *Political Geography* 24: 934–51.
Forgette, Richard, and John W. Winkle III. 2006. "Partisan Gerrymandering and the Voting Rights Act." *Social Science Quarterly* 87:155–73.
Formisano, Ronald P. 1974. "Deferential-Participant Politics: The Early Republic's Political Culture, 1789–1890." *American Political Science Review* 68:473–87.
Fowler, Erika Franklin, and Travis N. Ridout. 2014. "Political Advertising in 2014: The Year of the Outside Group." *The Forum* 10: 51–56.
Fowler, Linda L. 1982. "How Interest Groups Select Issues for Rating Voting Records of Members of the U.S. Congress." *Legislative Studies Quarterly* 7:401–13.
Fowler, Linda L., and Robert McClure. 1989. *Political Ambition: Who Decides to Run for Congress*. New Haven, Conn.: Yale University Press.
Fox, Richard L., and Jennifer L. Lawless. 2011. "Gaining and Losing Interest for Public Office: The Concept of Dynamic Political Ambition." *Journal of Politics* 73:443–62.
Francia, Peter L. 2017. "Free Media and Twitter in the 2016 Presidential Election: The Unconventional Campaign of Donald Trump." *Social Science Computer Review*. First Published September 27, 2017.
Francia, Peter L., John C. Green, Paul S. Herrnson, Lynda W. Powell, and Clyde Wilcox. 2003. *The Financiers of Congressional Elections*. New York: Columbia University Press.
Frank, Barney. 1985. Personal Interview.

———. 2015. *Frank: A Life in Politics from the Great Society to Same-Sex Marriage*. New York: Farrar, Straus, and Giroux

Frank, Thomas. 2004. *What's the Matter with Kansas? How Conservatives Won the Heart of America*. New York: Metropolitan Books.

Franklin, Charles H. 1984. "Issues, Preferences, Socialization, and the Evolution of Party Identification." *American Journal of Political Science* 28:459–78.

Franklin, Charles H., and John E. Jackson. 1983. "The Dynamics of Party Identification." *American Political Science Review* 77:957–73.

Frederickson, Kari. 2001. *The Dixiecrat Revolt and the End of the Solid South, 1932–1968*. Chapel Hill: University of North Carolina Press.

Frendeis, John P., James L. Gibson, and Laura L. Vertz. 1990. "The Electoral Relevance of Local Party Organization." *American Political Science Review* 84:225–35.

Frendeis, John P., and Richard Waterman. 1985. "PAC Contributions and Legislative Behavior: Senate Voting on Trucking Deregulation." *Social Science Quarterly* 66:401–12.

Frenkel, Sheera, and Katie Benner. 2018. "To Stir Discord in 2016, Russians Turned Most Often to Facebook." New York Times Company, last modified February 17.

Fuller, Jaime. 2014. "Why Voting Rights Is the Democrats' Most Important Project in 2014." *Washington Post*, April 10.

Gabriel, Trip. 2017. "Virginia Voting Mess Was Never Supposed to Happen after Bush v. Gore." *New York Times*, December 28.

Gaddie, Robert Keith, and Charles S. Bullock III. 2000. *Elections to Open Seats in the U.S. House: Where the Action Is*. Lanham, Md.: Rowman & Littlefield.

Galderisi, Peter F., ed. 2005. *Redistricting in the New Millennium*. Lanham, Md.: Lexington Books.

Galdieri, Christopher J., and Kevin Parsneau. 2016. "The Party Stands Aside: Elite Party Actor Endorsements during Presidential Primary and Caucus Voting, 2004–2016." *New England Journal of Political Science* 9 (1): 46–73.

Gale Cengage Learning. 2017. *Encyclopedia of Associations: National Organization*. 55th ed. Gale Cengage Learning.

Galloway, George B. 1961. *A History of the House of Representatives*. New York: Crowell.

Gallup, Inc. 2016. "Americans Increasingly Turn to Specific Sources for News." *Gallup*, July 8.

Gans, Curtis B. 1990. "A Rejoinder to Piven and Cloward." *PS: Political Science and Politics* 23:175–78.

Gans, Herbert J. 1979. *Deciding What's News*. New York: Random House.

Gant, Michael M., and Norman R. Luttbeg. 1991. *American Electoral Behavior*. Itasca, Ill.: F. E. Peacock.

Garand, James C. 1991. "Electoral Marginality in State Legislative Elections, 1968–86." *Legislative Studies Quarterly* 16:7–28.

Garrett, R. Sam. 2017. "Proposals to Eliminate Public Financing of Presidential Campaigns." Washington, D.C.: Congressional Research Service, February 7.

Geer, John G. 2006. *In Defense of Negativity*. Chicago: University of Chicago Press.

Gelman, Andrew. 2008. *Red State, Blue State, Rich State, Poor State: Why Americans Vote the Way They Do*. Princeton, N.J.: Princeton University Press.

Gelman, Andrew, and Gary King. 1990. "Estimating the Electoral Consequences of Legislative Redistricting." *Journal of the American Statistical Association* 85:274–82.

Germond, Jack, and Jules Witcover. 1985. *Wake Us When It's Over: Presidential Politics of 1984*. New York: Macmillan.

———. 1989. *Whose Broad Stripes and Bright Stars? The Trivial Pursuit of the Presidency, 1988*. New York: Warner Books.

———. 1993. *Mad as Hell: Revolt at the Ballot Box, 1992*. New York: Warner Books.

Gerring, John. 1998. *Party Ideologies in America, 1828–1996*. New York: Cambridge University Press.

Gibson, James L. 1991. "County Party Organizations." In *Political Parties and Elections in the United States: An Encyclopedia*, edited by L. Sandy Maisel. New York: Garland.

Gibson, James L., Cornelius P. Cotter, John F. Bibby, and Robert J. Huckshorn. 1983. "Assessing Party Organizational Strength." *American Journal of Political Science* 27:193–222.

———. 1985. "Whither the Local Parties? A Cross-Sectional Analysis and Longitudinal Analysis of the Strength of Party Organizations." *American Journal of Political Science* 29:139–60.

Gienapp, William E. 1987. *The Origins of the Republican Party, 1852–1856*. New York: Oxford University Press.

———. 1991. "The Formation of the Republican Party." In *The Encyclopedia of American Political Parties and Elections*, edited by L. Sandy Maisel. New York: Garland.

Gierzynski, Anthony. 1992. *Legislative Party Campaign Committees in the American States*. Lexington: University of Kentucky Press.

Gierzynski, Anthony, and David Breaux. 1990. "It's Money That Matters: The Role of Campaign Expenditures in State Legislative Primaries." Paper presented at the annual meeting of the American Political Science Association, San Francisco.

———. 1991. "Money and Votes in State Legislative Elections." *Legislative Studies Quarterly* 16:203–17.

Glaser, James. 1996. *Race, Campaign Politics in Realignment in the South*. New Haven, Conn.: Yale University Press.

Glazer, Amihai, Bernard Grofman, and Marc Robbins. 1987. "Partisan and Incumbency Effects of the 1970s Congressional Redistricting." *American Journal of Political Science* 31:680–707.

Gold, Matea. 2015a. "Why Super PACs Have Moved from Sideshow to Center Stage for Presidential Hopefuls." *Washington Post*, March 12.

———. 2015b. "Big Money in Politics Emerges as a Rising Issue in 2016 Campaign." *Washington Post*, April 19.

Goldenberg, Edie N., and Michael W. Traugott. 1984. *Campaigning for Congress*. Washington, D.C.: Congressional Quarterly Press.

Goldenberg, Edie N., Michael W. Traugott, and Frank R. Baumgartner. 1986. "Preemptive and Reactive Spending in U.S. House Races." *Political Behavior* 8:3–20.

Goldmacher, Shane. 2013. "Why Nearly Everyone in Congress Has a Leadership PAC These Days." *National Journal*, July 22.

Goldmacher, Shane, and Ben Schreckinger. 2016. "Trump Pulls Off Biggest Upset in U.S. History." *Politico*, November 9.

Goldman, Peter, and Tony Fuller. 1985. *The Quest for the Presidency, 1984*. New York: Bantam.

Goldman, Ralph M. 1990. *The National Party Chairmen and Committees: Factionalism at the Top*. Armonk, N.Y.: Sharpe.

Goldstein, Kenneth, and Travis N. Ridout. 2004. "Measuring the Effects of Televised Political Advertising in the United States. *Annual Review of Political Science* 7: 205–26.

Goodwin, Alec, and Emma Baccellieri. 2017. "Number of Registered Lobbyists Plunges as Spending Declines Yet Again." Center for Responsive Politics, August 9.

Goodwyn, Lawrence. 1978. *The Populist Moment: A Short History of the Agrarian Revolt in America*. New York: Oxford University Press.

Gottfried, Jeffrey A., Bruce W. Hardy, Kenneth M. Winneg, and Kathleen Hall Jamieson. 2013. "Did Fact Checking Matter in the 2012 Presidential Campaign?" *American Behavioral Scientist* 11:1558–67.

Gottlieb, Stephen E. 1985. "Fleshing Out the Right of Association: The Problem of the Contribution Limits of the Federal Election Campaign Act." *Albany Law Review* 49:825.

———. 1991. "Buckley v. Valeo." In *Political Parties and Elections in the United States: An Encyclopedia*, edited by L. Sandy Maisel. New York: Garland.

Graber, Doris A. 1980. *Mass Media in American Politics*. Washington, D.C.: Congressional Quarterly Press.

———. 1982. *The President and the Public*. Philadelphia: Institute for the Study of Human Issues.

———. 2005. *Mass Media in American Politics*. 7th ed. Washington, D.C.: Congressional Quarterly Press.

———. 2006. *Media Power in Politics*. 5th ed. Washington, D.C.: Congressional Quarterly Press.

Graham, David A. 2016. "North Carolina's Deliberate Disenfranchisement of Black Voters." *Atlantic*, July.

Grassmuck, George, ed. 1985. *Before Nomination: Our Primary Problem*. Washington, D.C.: American Enterprise Institute for Public Policy Research.

Green, Donald, and Jonathan Krasno. 1988. "Salvation for the Spendthrift Incumbent: Reestimating the Effects of Campaign Spending in House Elections." *American Journal of Political Science* 32:884–907.

Green, Donald, Bradley Palmquist, and Eric Schickler. 2002. *Partisan Hearts and Minds*. New Haven, Conn.: Yale University Press.

Green, John C., Mark J. Rozell, and Clyde Wilcox. 2006. *The Values Campaign? The Christian Right and the 2004 Elections*. Washington, D.C.: Georgetown University Press.

Greenhouse, Steven. 2006. "Labor Movement Dusts Off Agenda as Power Shifts in Congress." *New York Times*, November 11, A13.

Grenzke, Janet. 1989. "PACs in the Congressional Supermarket: The Currency Is Complex." *American Journal of Political Science* 33:1–24.

———. 1990. "Money and Congressional Behavior." In *Money, Elections, and Democracy: Reforming Congressional Campaign Finance*, edited by Margaret Latus Nugent and John R. Johannes. Boulder, Colo.: Westview.

Grofman, Bernard, ed. 1990. *Political Gerrymandering and the Courts*. New York: Agathon.

Grossman, Matt, and Casey B. K. Dominguez. 2009. "Party Coalitions and Interest Group Networks." *American Politics Research*. 37: 767–800.

Gugliotta, Guy. 1998. "Going Where the Money Is." *Washington Post National Weekly Edition*, July 6, 12.

Hadley, Charles D. 1985. "Dual Partisan Identification in the South." *Journal of Politics* 47:254–68.

Halbfinger, David M. 2002. "Bush's Push, Volunteers and Big Turnout Led to Georgia Sweep." *New York Times*, November 10, section 1, 28.

Hamilton, Alexander, and James Madison. 2007. *The Pacificus and Helvidius Debates of 1793–1794*. Morton J. Frisch, ed. Indianapolis, IN: Liberty Fund.

Handlin, Oscar. 1951. *The Uprooted*. New York: Grosset & Dunlap.

Hansen, Wendy L., Michael S. Rocca, and Brittany Leigh Ortiz. 2015. "The Effects of *Citizens United* on Corporate Spending in the 2012 Presidential Election." *Journal of Politics* 77:535–45.

Harris, Mary. 2016. "A Media Post-Mortem on the 2016 Presidential Election." MediaQuant. November 14.

Hassell, Hans J. G., and J. Quin Monson. 2014. "Campaign Targets and Messages in Direct Mail Fundraising." *Political Behavior* 36: 359–76.

Healy, Patrick, and Jeremy W. Peters. 2016. "Donald Trump's Victory Is Met with Shock across a Wide Political Divide." New York Times Company, last modified November 9.

Heard, Alexander. 1960. *The Costs of Democracy*. Chapel Hill: University of North Carolina Press.

Heersink, B. 2017. *No, the DNC Didn't 'Rig' the Democratic Primary for Hillary Clinton*. WP Company LLC d/b/a The Washington Post.

Herrnson, Paul S. 1988. *Party Campaigning in the 1980s*. Cambridge, Mass.: Harvard University Press.

———. 1990. "Reemergent National Party Organizations." In *The Parties Respond: Changes in the American Party System*, edited by L. Sandy Maisel. Boulder, Colo.: Westview.

———. 1991. "Campaign Professionalism and Fundraising in Congressional Elections." Unpublished manuscript, University of Maryland.

———. 1995. "Potential Research Policies for Political Science." *PS: Political Science and Politics* 28:492–94.

———. 1998a. *Congressional Elections: Campaigning at Home and in Washington*. 2nd ed. Washington, D.C.: Congressional Quarterly Press.

———. 1998b. "National Party Organizations at the Century's End." In *The Parties Respond*, edited by L. Sandy Maisel. 3rd ed. Boulder, Colo.: Westview.

———. 2000. *Congressional Elections: Campaigning at Home and in Washington*. 3rd ed. Washington, D.C.: Congressional Quarterly Press.

———. 2002. "National Party Organizations at the Dawn of the 21st Century." In *The Parties Respond*, edited by L. Sandy Maisel. 4th ed. Boulder, Colo.: Westview.

———. 2009. "The Role of Party Organizations, Party-Connected Committees, and Party Allies in Elections." *Journal of Politics* 71:1207–24.

Herrnson, Paul S., Ronald G. Shaiko, and Clyde Wilcox. 2005. *The Interest Group Connection: Engineering, Lobbying, and Policymaking in Washington*. 2nd ed. Washington, D.C.: Congressional Quarterly Press.

Hershey, Marjorie R. 1984. *Running for Office: The Political Education of Campaigners*. Chatham, N.J.: Chatham House.

Hetherington, Marc J. 2001. "Resurgent Mass Partisanship: The Role of Elite Polarization." *American Political Science Review* 95:619–31.

Hetherington, Marc J., and Jonathan D. Weiler. 2009. *Authoritarianism and Polarization in American Politics*. New York: Cambridge University Press.

Hicks, John D. 1931. *The Populist Revolt*. Minneapolis: University of Minnesota Press.

Hicks, Jonathan P. 1998. "Efforts to Get Voters to the Polls Are Feverish for Both Sides." *New York Times*, November 2, online edition.

Highton, Benjamin. 2004. "Voter Registration and Turnout in the United States." *Perspectives on Politics* 2:507–15.

Hill, David. 2006. *American Voter Turnout: An Institutional Perspective*. Boulder, Colo.: Westview.

Hill, David B., and Norman R. Luttbeg. 1980. *Trends in American Electoral Behavior*. Itasca, Ill.: F. E. Peacock.

Hillygus, D. Sunshine. 2011. "The Evolution of Election Polling in the United States." *Public Opinion Quarterly* 75: 962–81.

Hinchliffe, Kelsey L., and Frances E. Lee. 2016. "Party Competition and Conflict in State Legislatures." *State Politics & Policy Quarterly* 16 (2): 172–97.

Hinckley, Barbara. 1971. *The Seniority System in Congress*. Bloomington: Indiana University Press.

———. 1981. *Congressional Elections*. Washington, D.C.: Congressional Quarterly Press.

Hoffman, Kathy Barks. 1998. "Negative Ads Hurt Turnout—Or Increase It." *Detroit News*, October 17, online edition.

Hofstadter, Richard. 1948. *The American Political Tradition*. New York: Knopf.

———. 1955. *The Age of Reform: From Bryan to F. D. R.* New York: Knopf.

Holbrook, Thomas, and Charles Tidmarch. 1991. "Sophomore Surge in State Legislative Elections." *Legislative Studies Quarterly* 16:49–63.

Holbrook, Thomas, and Emily Van Dunk. 1993. "Electoral Competition in the American States." *American Political Science Review* 87 (December): 955–63.

Huckshorn, Robert J. 1991. "State Party Leaders." In *Political Parties and Elections in the United States: An Encyclopedia*, edited by L. Sandy Maisel. New York: Garland.

Huckshorn, Robert J., James L. Gibson, Cornelius P. Cotter, and John F. Bibby. 1986. "Party Integration and Party Organizational Strength." *Journal of Politics* 48:976–91.

Hunter, James Davison. 1991. *Culture Wars: The Struggle to Define America*. New York: Basic Books.

Ingraham, Christopher. 2018. *Pennsylvania Supreme Court Draws 'Much More Competitive' District Map to Overturn Republican Gerrymander*. WP Company LLC d/b/a The Washington Post.

Ingram, Mathew. 2017. "How the *Washington Post* Makes Money from Its Competitors." *Fortune*, March 13.

Issenberg, Sasha. 2012. *The Victory Lab: The Secret Science of Winning Campaigns*. New York: Crown.

Iyengar, Shanto, and Richard Reeves. 1997. *Do the Media Govern? Politicians, Voters, and Reporters in America*. Thousand Oaks, Calif.: Sage.

Jackman, Robert W. 1987. "Political Institutions and Voter Turnout in Industrial Democracies." *American Political Science Review* 81:405–24.

Jackson, Brooks. 1988. *Honest Graft*. New York: Knopf.

Jackson, John E. 1975. "Issues, Party Choices, and Presidential Votes." *American Journal of Political Science* 19:161–85.

Jacobson, Gary C. 1980. *Money in Congressional Elections*. New Haven, Conn.: Yale University Press.

———. 1981. "Congressional Elections, 1978: The Case of the Vanishing Challengers." In *Congressional Elections*, edited by L. Sandy Maisel and Joseph Cooper. Beverly Hills, Calif.: Sage.

———. 1983. *The Politics of Congressional Elections*. Boston: Little, Brown.

———. 1985a. "Congress: Politics after a Landslide without Coattails." In *The Elections of 1984*, edited by Michael Nelson. Washington, D.C.: Congressional Quarterly Press.

———. 1985b. "Parties and PACs in Congressional Elections." In *Congress Reconsidered*, edited by Lawrence D. Dodd and Bruce I. Oppenheimer. 3rd ed. Washington, D.C.: Congressional Quarterly Press.

———. 1985–1986. "Party Organization and Distribution of Campaign Resources, Republicans and Democrats in 1982." *Political Science Quarterly* 100:603–25.

———. 1987a. "The Marginals Never Vanished: Incumbency and Competition in Elections to the U.S. House of Representatives, 1952–1982." *American Journal of Political Science* 31:126–41.

———. 1987b. *The Politics of Congressional Elections*. 2nd ed. Boston: Little, Brown.

———. 1990a. "Divided Government, Strategic Politicians, and the 1990 Congressional Elections." Paper presented at the annual meeting of the Midwest Political Science Association, Chicago.

———. 1990b. "The Effects of Campaign Spending in House Elections: New Evidence for Old Arguments." *American Journal of Political Science* 34:334–62.

———. 1992. *The Politics of Congressional Elections*, 3rd ed. Boston: Little, Brown.

———. 1996. *The Politics of Congressional Elections*. 4th ed. New York: Longman.

———. 2001. *The Politics of Congressional Elections*. 5th ed. New York: Longman.

Jacobson, Gary C., and Samuel Kernell. 1983. *Strategy and Choice in Congressional Elections*. New Haven, Conn.: Yale University Press.

James, Meg. 2012. "Democratic Convention's Final Night Draws 35.7 Million Viewers." *Los Angeles Times*, September 7.

Jamieson, Kathleen Hall, ed. 2013. *Electing the President 2012: The Insiders' View*. Philadelphia: University of Pennsylvania Press.

Jarvie, Jenny. 2018. "Republican Wins Drawing to Decide Virginia House Race, Keeping GOP in Charge." *Los Angeles Times*, January 4.

Jensen, Richard J. 1971. *The Winning of the Midwest: Social and Political Conflict, 1888–1896*. Chicago: University of Chicago Press.

Jewell, Malcolm E. 1984. *Parties and Primaries*. New York: Praeger.
Jewell, Malcolm E., and David Breaux. 1988. "The Effect of Incumbency on State Legislative Elections." *Legislative Studies Quarterly* 13:495–514.
———. 1991. "Southern Primary and Electoral Competition and Incumbent Success." *Legislative Studies Quarterly* 16:129–43.
Jewell, Malcolm E., and Sarah M. Morehouse. 2001. *Political Parties and Elections in American States*. 4th ed. Washington, D.C.: Congressional Quarterly Press.
Jewell, Malcolm E., and David M. Olson. 1988. *Political Parties and Elections in American States*. 3rd ed. Chicago: Dorsey.
Jewell, Malcolm E., and Marcia Lynn Whicker. 1998. *Legislative Leadership in the American States*. Ann Arbor: University of Michigan Press.
Johnson, Jason. 2011. *Political Consultants and Campaigns: One Day to Sell*. New York: Routledge.
Johnson-Cartee, Karen S., and Gary W. Copeland. 1997. *Inside Political Campaigns: Theory and Practice*. Westport, Conn.: Praeger.
Jones, Charles O. 1988a. *The Trusteeship Presidency: Jimmy Carter and the United States Congress*. Baton Rouge: Louisiana State University Press.
———, ed. 1988b. *The Reagan Legacy*. Chatham, N.J.: Chatham House.
Jones, Jeffery M. 2016. "Democratic, Republican Identification Near Historical Lows." *Gallup*, January 11.
———. 2017. "Democratic Party Maintains Edge in Party Affiliation." *Gallup*, December 4.
Jones, Ruth S. 1984. "Financing State Elections." In *Money and Politics in the United States: Financing Elections in the 1980s*, edited by Michael J. Malbin. Washington, D.C.: American Enterprise Institute for Public Policy Research.
———. 1991. "Financing State Campaigns." In *Political Parties and Elections in the United States: An Encyclopedia*, edited by L. Sandy Maisel. New York: Garland.
Jordan, Hamilton. 1982. *Crisis: The Last Year of Carter's Presidency*. New York: Putnam.
Kamarck, Elaine C. 2006. "Assessing Howard Dean's Fifty State Strategy and the 2006 Midterm Elections." *The Forum* 4, no. 3, article 5.
Kane, Paul, Lori Montgomery, and Ben Pershing. 2010. "Late Push Yields More Votes for Health Bill." *Washington Post*, March 20, A1.
Karpf, David. 2013. "The Internet and American Political Campaigns," *The Forum* 11: 413–428.
Kayden, Xandra. 1978. *Campaign Organization*. Lexington, Mass.: D. C. Heath.
Keller, Morton. 1977. *Affairs of State: Public Life in Late Nineteenth Century America*. Cambridge, Mass.: Belknap Press.
———. 2003. "Money and Politics: The Long View." *The Forum* 1, no. 3.
Kelly, Meg. 2018. *President Trump Cries 'Fake News' and the World Follows*. WP Company LLC d/b/a The Washington Post.
Kennedy, Merrit. 2016. "Clinton-Trump Showdown Was the Most-Watched Presidental Debate Ever." *NPR*, September 27.
Kerbel, Matthew Robert. 1998. *Remote and Controlled: Media Politics in a Cynical Age*. 2nd ed. Boulder, Colo.: Westview.
Kernell, Samuel. 1977. "Presidential Popularity and Negative Voting: An Alternative Explanation of Midterm Congressional Decline of the President's Party." *American Political Science Review* 71:44–66.

Kessel, John H. 1992. *Presidential Campaign Politics: Coalition Strategies and Citizen Response*. 4th ed. Homewood, Ill.: Dorsey.

Key, V. O., Jr. 1949. *Southern Politics in State and Nation*. New York: Knopf.

———. 1955. "A Theory of Critical Elections." *Journal of Politics* 17:3–18.

———. 1956. *American State Politics*. New York: Knopf.

———. 1959. "Secular Realignment and the Party System." *Journal of Politics* 21:198–210.

———. 1964. *Politics, Parties, and Pressure Groups*. New York: Crowell.

———. 1966. *The Responsible Electorate*. Cambridge, Mass.: Harvard University Press.

Kimel, T. J., and Kirk A. Randazzo. 2012. "Shaping the Federal Courts: The Obama Nominees." *Social Science Quarterly* (Wiley) 93 (5): 1243–50.

Kinder, Donald R., and P. Roderick Kiewiet. 1979. "Economic Discontent and Political Behavior: The Role of Personal Grievances and Collective Economic Judgments in Congressional Voting." *American Journal of Political Science* 23:495–527.

King, Gary. 1989. "Representation through Legislative Redistricting: A Stochastic Model." *American Journal of Political Science* 33:787–824.

Kingdon, John W. 1984. *Agendas, Alternatives, and Public Policies*. Boston: Little, Brown.

Kirkpatrick, Jeane Jordan. 1976. *The New Presidential Elite: Men and Women in National Politics*. New York: Russell Sage Foundation.

———. 1978. *Dismantling the Parties*. Washington, D.C.: American Enterprise Institute for Public Policy Research.

Klar, Samara, and Yanna Krupnikov. 2016. "The Partisan Underground in an Era of Polarization." In *Independent Politics: How American Disdain for Parties Leads to Political Inaction*, 150–64. New York: Cambridge University Press.

Klar, Samara, Yanna Krupnikov, and John Barry Ryan. 2018. "Affective Polarization or Partisan Disdain? Untangling a Dislike for the Opposing Party from a Dislike of Partisanship." *Public Opinion Quarterly*.

Klein, Betsy. 2014. "Clinton In-Law Marjorie Margolies Toppled in Pennsylvania Race." *ABC News*, May 20.

Knack, Stephen. 1995. "Does 'Motor Voter' Work? Evidence from State-Level Data." *Journal of Politics* 57:796–812.

Koger, Gregory, Seth Masket, and Hans Noel. 2010. "Cooperative Party Factions in American Politics." *American Politics Research* 38 (1): 33–53.

Kolodny, Robin. 1996. "The Contract with America in the 104th Congress." In *The State of the Parties*, edited by John C. Green and Daniel M. Shea. 2nd ed. Lanham, Md.: Rowman & Littlefield.

———. 1998. *Pursuing Majorities: Congressional Campaign Committees in American Politics*. Norman: University of Oklahoma Press.

———. 1999. "Moderate Party Factions in the U.S. House of Representatives." In *The State of the Parties*, edited by John C. Green and Daniel M. Shea. 3rd ed. Lanham, Md.: Rowman & Littlefield.

———. 2000. "Electoral Partnerships: Political Consultants and Political Parties." In *Campaign Warriors: Political Consultants in Elections*, edited by James A. Thurber and Candice J. Nelson. Washington, D.C.: Brookings Institution.

Kornblut, Anne E., and Scott Wilson. 2011. "Obama Weighs Major Reshuffling of Staff." *Washington Post*, January 4, online edition.

Kramer, Gerald L. 1971. "Short-Term Fluctuations in U.S. Voting Behavior, 1896–1964." *American Political Science Review* 65:131–43.

Krasno, Jonathon S., and Donald Philip Green. 1988. "Pre-empting Quality Challengers in House Elections." *Journal of Politics* 50:920–36.

Kraus, Sidney. 1962. *The Great Debates: Kennedy vs. Nixon, 1960*. Bloomington: Indiana University Press.

Krehbiel, Keith. 1993. "Where's the Party?" *British Journal of Political Science* 23:235.

———. 1998. *Pivotal Politics: A Theory of U.S. Lawmaking*. Chicago: University of Chicago Press.

———. 1999. "The Party Effect from A to Z and Beyond." *Journal of Politics* 61:832–40.

Kurtz, Howard. 1998. "Attack Ads Carpet TV; High Road Swept Away." *Washington Post*, October 20, A1.

Ladd, Everett Carll, Jr. 1978. "The Shifting Party Coalitions: 1932–1976." In *Emerging Coalitions in American Politics*, edited by Seymour M. Lipset. San Francisco: Institute for Contemporary Studies.

———. 1991. *The American Polity: The People and Their Government*. New York: Norton.

Ladd, Everett Carll, Jr., and Charles D. Hadley. 1975. *Transformations of the American Party System*. Rev. ed. New York: Norton.

Ladewig, Jeffrey W. 2005. "Conditional Party Government and the Homogeneity of Constituent Interests." *Journal of Politics* 67:1006–29.

Lamis, Alexander. 1984. "The Runoff Primary Controversy: Implications for Southern Politics." *PS: Political Science and Politics* 17:782–87.

Landler, Mark. 2012. "Pushed by Obama, Democrats Alter Platform over Jerusalem." *New York Times*, September 5.

Lane, Robert E. 1959. *Political Life*. New York: Free Press.

Laposwky, Issie. 2016. "Here's How Facebook Actually Won Trump the Presidency." *Wired*, November 15.

Lawless, Jennifer L. 2012. *Becoming a Candidate: Political Ambition and the Decision to Run for Office*. New York: Cambridge University Press.

Lawrence, Eric, John Sides, and Henry Farrell. 2010. "Self-Segregation or Deliberation? Blog Readership, Participation, and Polarization in American Politics." *Perspectives on Politics* 8:141–57.

Layman, Geoffrey. 2001. *The Great Divide: Religious and Cultural Conflict in American Party Politics*. New York: Columbia University Press.

Layman, Geoffrey C., and Thomas M. Carsey. 2002a. "Party Polarization and Party Structuring of Policy Attitudes: A Comparison of Three NES Panel Studies." *Political Behavior* 24:199–236.

———. 2002b. "Party Polarization and 'Conflict Extension' in the American Electorate." *American Journal of Political Science* 46:786–802.

Layman, Geoffrey C., Thomas M. Carsey, John C. Green, Richard Herrera, and Rosalyn Cooperman. 2010. "Activists and Conflict Extension in American Party Politics." *American Political Science Review* 104:324–46.

Lazarsfeld, Paul F., Barnard Berelson, and Hazel Gaudet. 1944. *The People's Choice: How the Voter Makes Up His Mind in a Presidential Campaign*. New York: Columbia University Press.

Lazer, David M. J., Matthew A. Baum, Yochai Benkler, Adam J. Berinsky, Kelly M. Greenhill, Filippo Menczer, Miriam J. Metzger, et al. 2018. "The Science of Fake News." *Science* 359 (6380): 1094–96.

Lebo, Matthew J., Adam T. McGlynn, and Gregory Koger. 2007. "Strategic Party Government: Party Influence in Congress, 1789–2000." *American Journal of Political Science* 51:464–81.

Lee, Carol E., and David Catanese. 2010. "The Obama Campaign-Trail Calculus." *Politico*, July 9, online edition.

Lee, M. J., Lauren Fox, Ted Barrett, Phil Mattingly, and Ashley Killough. 2017. "GOP Obamacare Repeal Bill Fails in Dramatic Late-Night Vote." *CNN Wire Service*, July 27.

Lee, Michelle Y. H., and Tony Romm. 2018a. "FEC Considers Expanding Political Ad Disclaimers to Mobile Apps." WP Company LLC d/b/a The Washington Post, last modified March 14.

———. 2018b. "New Federal Rules on Facebook and Google Ads may Not be in Place for 2018 Midterms." WP Company LLC d/b/a The Washington Post, last modified March 8.

Leege, David C., Kenneth D. Wald, Brian S. Krueger, and Paul D. Mueller. 2002. *The Politics of Cultural Differences*. Princeton, N.J.: Princeton University Press.

Lehman, Daniel G. 2013. "Local Party Organizations and the Mobilization of Latino Voters." PhD diss., Temple University. Order No. 3564823.

Lemongello, Steven. 2018. "Floridians Will Vote This Fall on Restoring Voting Rights to 1.5 Million Felons." *Orlando Sentinel*, January 23.

Lengle, James I., and Byron E. Shafer. 1980. *Presidential Politics*. New York: St. Martin's Press.

Levendusky, Matthew S. 2010. "Clearer Cues, More Consistent Voters: A Benefit of Elite Polarization." *Political Behavior* 32:111–31.

Levinthal, Dave. 2012. "Meet the Super Super PAC." *Politico*, January 21.

Levitt, Justin. 2010. "Confronting the Impact of *Citizens United*." *Yale Law and Policy Review* 29:217–34.

Liasson, Mara. 2012. "Do Political Ads Actually Work?" *NPR*, October 26.

Light, Paul C. 1983. *The President's Agenda*. Baltimore: Johns Hopkins University Press.

Lima, Christiano. 2016. "Trump Accuses Clinton of Rigging Debate Schedule." *Politico*, July 29.

Lindblom, Charles E. 1959. "The Science of Muddling Through." *Public Administration Review* 19:79–88.

Liptak, Adam. 2018. "Supreme Court Won't Block New Pennsylvania Voting Maps." New York Times Company, last modified March 19.

Lopez, Mark Hugo, and Ana Gonzalez-Barrera. 2013. "Inside the 2012 Latino Electorate." *Pew Hispanic Center*, June 3.

Lorber, Janie. 2012. "Tea Party Tries to Sway GOP Platform." *Roll Call*, June 13.

Lowenstein, Daniel Hays. 1991a. "Campaign Finance and the Constitution." In *Political Parties and Elections in the United States: An Encyclopedia*, edited by L. Sandy Maisel. New York: Garland.

———. 1991b. "Legislative Districting." In *Political Parties and Elections in the United States: An Encyclopedia*, edited by L. Sandy Maisel. New York: Garland.

Lucas, Jennifer C., Christopher J. Galdieri, and Tauna S. Sisco. 2018. *Conventional Wisdom, Parties, and Broken Barriers in the 2016 Election*. Lanham, MD: Lexington Books.

Luntz, Frank I. 1988. *Candidates, Consultants, and Campaigns*. Oxford: Blackwell.

Mackenzie, G. Calvin. 2013. "Partisan Presidential Leadership: The Presidents' Appointees." In *The Parties Respond: Changes in American Parties and Campaigns*, edited by Mark D. Brewer and L. Sandy Maisel. 5th ed. Boulder, Colo.: Westview.

MacWilliams, Matthew C. 2016. "Who Decides When the Party Doesn't? Authoritarian Voters and the Rise of Donald Trump." *PS: Political Science & Politics* 49 (4): 716–21.

Maestas, Cherie D., Sarah Fulton, L. Sandy Maisel, and Walter J. Stone. 2006. "When to Risk It? Institutions, Ambitions, and the Decision to Run for the U.S. House." *American Political Science Review* 100:195–208.

Magleby, David B., and Marjorie Holt, eds. 1999. *Outside Money: Soft Money and Issue Ads in Competitive 1998 Congressional Elections*. Provo, Utah: Brigham Young University.

Magleby, David B., and Candice J. Nelson. 1990. *The Money Chase*. Washington, D.C.: Brookings Institution.

Maguire, Robert. 2014. "No Accountability for Crossroads GPS Grantee, Despite 'No Politics' Rule." *Open Secrets*, November 19.

Maine Department of the Secretary of State. 2018. "Ranked-Choice Voting Peoples' Veto Effort Valid with 66,687 Signatures." March 5.

Maisel, L. Sandy. 1986. *From Obscurity to Oblivion: Running in the Congressional Primary*. 2nd ed. Knoxville: University of Tennessee Press.

———. 1988. "Spending Patterns in Presidential Nominating Campaigns, 1976–1988." Paper presented at the annual meeting of the American Political Science Association, Washington, D.C. Occasional Paper no. 88, Center for American Political Studies, Harvard University, Cambridge, Mass.

———. 1989. "Challenger Quality and the Outcome of the 1988 Congressional Elections." Paper presented at the annual meeting of the Midwest Political Science Association, Chicago.

———. 1990a. "Congressional Elections: Quality Candidates in House and Senate Elections, 1982–1988." Paper presented at the Back to the Future: The United States Congress at the Bicentennial Conference, at the Carl Albert Congressional Research and Studies Center, University of Oklahoma, Norman.

———. 1990b. "The Incumbency Advantage." In *Money, Elections, and Democracy: Reforming Congressional Campaign Finance*, edited by Margaret Latus Nugent and John R. Johannes. Boulder, Colo.: Westview.

———. 1990c. *The Parties Respond: Changes in the American Party System*. Boulder, Colo.: Westview.

———. 1991. *Political Parties and Elections in the United States: An Encyclopedia*. New York: Garland.

———. 1994. "The Platform-Writing Process: Candidate Centered Platforms in 1992." *Political Science Quarterly* 108:671–98.

———, ed. 1998. *The Parties Respond*. 3rd ed. Boulder, Colo.: Westview.

———, ed. 2002. *The Parties Respond*. 4th ed. Boulder, Colo.: Westview.

Maisel, L. Sandy, and John F. Bibby. 2002. "Election Laws, Court Rulings, Party Rules and Practices: Steps toward and away from a Stronger Party Role." In *Responsible Partisanship? The Evolution of American Political Parties since 1950*, edited by John C. Green and Paul S. Herrnson. Lawrence: University Press of Kansas.

Maisel, L. Sandy, and Joseph Cooper. 1981. *Congressional Elections*. Beverly Hills, Calif.: Sage.

Maisel, L. Sandy, Linda L. Fowler, Ruth S. Jones, and Walter J. Stone. 1990. "The Naming of Candidates: Recruitment or Emergence." In *The Parties Respond: Changes in the American Party System*, edited by L. Sandy Maisel. Boulder, Colo.: Westview.

Maisel, L. Sandy, and Elizabeth J. Ivry. 1998. "If You Don't Like Our Politics, Wait a Minute: Party Politics in Maine at the Century's End." *Polity*. Supplement to the winter issue.

Maisel, L. Sandy, Cherie Maestas, and Walter J. Stone. 2005. "The Impact of Redistricting on Candidate Emergence." In *Party Lines: Competition, Partisanship, and Congressional Redistricting*, edited by Thomas E. Mann and Bruce E. Cain. Washington, D.C.: Brookings Institution.

Maisel, L. Sandy, Walter J. Stone, and Cherie Maestas. 1999. "Re-evaluating the Definition of Quality Candidates: Evidence from the Candidate Emergence Study." Paper presented at the annual meeting of the Midwest Political Science Association, Chicago.

Maisel, L. Sandy, and Darrell West. 2004. *Running on Empty? Political Discourse in Congressional Elections*. Lanham, Md.: Rowman & Littlefield.

Malbin, Michael J. 1981. "The Conventions, Platforms, and Issue Activists." In *The American Elections of 1980*, edited by Austin Ranney. Washington, D.C.: American Enterprise Institute for Public Policy Research.

———. 1984a. "Looking Back at the Future of Campaign Finance Reform: Interest Groups and American Elections." In *Money and Politics in the United States: Financing Elections in the 1980s*, edited by Michael J. Malbin. Washington, D.C.: American Enterprise Institute for Public Policy Research.

———, ed. 1984b. *Money and Politics in the United States: Financing Elections in the 1980s*. Washington, D.C.: American Enterprise Institute for Public Policy Research.

———. 1985. "You Get What You Pay For, but Is That What You Want?" In *Before Nomination: Our Primary Problem*, edited by George Grassmuck. Washington, D.C.: American Enterprise Institute for Public Policy Research.

Malbin, Michael J., and Thomas L. Gais. 1998. *The Day after Reform: Sobering Campaign Finance Lessons from the American States*. Albany, N.Y.: Rockefeller Institute Press.

Mann, Thomas E. 1985. "Elected Officials and the Politics of Presidential Selection." In *The American Elections of 1984*, edited by Austin Ranney. Durham, N.C.: Duke University Press.

Mann, Thomas E., and Raymond E. Wolfinger. 1980. "Candidates and Parties in Congressional Elections." *American Political Science Review* 74:617–32.

Marinucci, Carla. 2007. "Political Video Smackdown." *San Francisco Chronicle*. March 18, A1.
Martinez, Gebe. 2003. "Despite Missteps, DeLay and Blunt Close Ranks, Stay Unified." *Congressional Quarterly Weekly*, July 12, 1731.
Mason, Lilliana. 2013. "The Rise of Uncivil Agreement: Issue versus Behavioral Polarization in the American Electorate." *American Behavioral Scientist* 57 (1): 140–59.
Mattei, Franco, and Richard G. Niemi. 1991. "Unrealized Partisans, Realized Independents, and the Intergenerational Transmission of Partisan Identification." *Journal of Politics* 53:161–74.
Matthews, Donald. 1960. *U.S. Senators and Their World*. New York: Vintage Books.
Mattingly, Phil, and Lauren Fox. 2017. "A Fractured GOP Unified to Pass a Landmark Tax Plan: Here's How It Came Together." *CNN Wire Service*, December 20.
May, Ernest R., and Janet Fraser. 1973. *Campaign '72: The Managers Speak*. Cambridge, Mass.: Harvard University Press.
Mayhew, David R. 1974a. *Congress: The Electoral Connection*. New Haven, Conn.: Yale University Press.
———. 1974b. "Congressional Elections: The Case of the Vanishing Marginals." *Polity* 6:295–317.
———. 1986. *Placing Parties in American Politics*. Princeton, N.J.: Princeton University Press.
———. 1991. *Divided We Govern: Party Control, Lawmaking, and Investigations, 1946–1990*. New Haven, Conn.: Yale University Press.
———. 2002. *Electoral Realignments: A Critique of an American Genre*. New Haven, Conn.: Yale University Press.
———. 2005. *Divided We Govern*. 2nd ed. New Haven, Conn.: Yale University Press.
Mazmanian, Daniel A. 1974. *Third Parties in Presidential Elections*. Washington, D.C.: Brookings Institution.
McAdams, John C., and John R. Johannes. 1981. "Does Casework Matter? A Reply to Professor Fiorina." *American Journal of Political Science* 25:581–604.
McClain, Paula D., and Joseph Stewart Jr. 2010. *"Can We All Get Along?" Racial and Ethnic Minorities in American Politics*. 5th ed. Boulder, Colo.: Westview.
McCormick, Richard L. 1986. *The Party Period and Public Policy: American Politics from the Age of Jackson to the Progressive Era*. New York: Oxford University Press.
McDonald, Michael P. 2016. "Iowa's Caucus Turnout and What It Means from Now until November." February 2.
McDonald, Michael P., and Samuel L. Popkin. 2001. "The Myth of the Vanishing Voter." *American Political Science Review* 95:963–74.
McFarland, Andrew S. 1984. *Common Cause*. Chatham, N.J.: Chatham House.
McGerr, Michael E. 1986. *The Decline of Popular Politics*. New York: Oxford University Press.
McGinniss, Joe. 1969. *The Selling of the President 1968*. New York: Trident.
McKee, Seth C. 2010. *Republican Ascendancy in Southern U.S. House Elections*. Boulder, Colo.: Westview.

McKenna, Elizabeth, and Hahrie Han. 2014. *Groundbreakers: How Obama's 2.2 Million Volunteers Transformed Campaigning in America*. New York: Oxford University Press.

Medvic, Stephen K. 2001. *Political Consultants in U.S. Congressional Elections*. Columbus, OH: Ohio State University Press.

———. 2003. "Professional Political Consultants: An Operational Definition." *Politics* 23: 119–27.

Medvic, Stephen K., and Silvio Lenart. 1997. "The Influence of Political Consultants in the 1992 Congressional Elections." *Legislative Studies Quarterly* 22:61–77.

Mellow, Nicole. 2008. *The State of Disunion: Regional Sources of Modern American Partisanship*. Baltimore: Johns Hopkins University Press.

Merton, Robert K. 1957. *Social Theory and Social Structure*. New York: Free Press.

Milbrath, Lester W., and M. L. Goel. 1977. *Political Participation: How and Why Do People Get Involved in Politics?* Chicago: Rand McNally.

Milburn, Michael, and Justin Brown. 1997. "Adwatch: Covering Campaign Ads." In *Politics and the Press: The News Media and Their Influence*, edited by Pippa Norris. Boulder, Colo.: Lynne Rienner.

Miller, Arthur H. 1978. "The Majority Party Reunited? A Comparison of the 1972 and 1976 Elections." In *Parties and Elections in an Anti-Party Age*, edited by Jeff Fishel. Bloomington: Indiana University Press.

Miller, Arthur H., and Warren E. Miller. 1977. "Partisanship and Performance: 'Rational' Choice in the 1976 Presidential Elections." Paper presented at the annual meeting of the American Political Science Association, Washington, D.C.

Miller, Arthur H., Warren E. Miller, Aldern S. Raine, and Thad E. Brown. 1976. "A Majority Party in Disarray: Policy Polarization in the 1972 Election." *American Political Science Review* 70:753–78.

Miller, Arthur H., and Martin P. Wattenberg. 1985. "Throwing the Rascals Out: Policy and Performance Evaluations of Presidential Candidates, 1952–1980." *American Political Science Review* 79:359–72.

Miller, Patrick R., and Pamela Johnston Conover. 2015. "Red and Blue States of Mind: Partisan Hostility and Voting in the United States." *Political Research Quarterly* 68 (2): 225–39.

Miller, Warren E. 1990. "The Electorate's View of the Parties." In *The Parties Respond: Changes in the American Party System*, edited by L. Sandy Maisel. Boulder, Colo.: Westview.

———. 1991. "Party Identification, Realignment, and Party Voting: Back to Basics." *American Political Science Review* 85:557–68.

———. 1992. "The Puzzle Transformed: Explaining Declining Turnout." *Political Behavior* 14:1–43.

———. 1998. "Party Identification and the Electorate of the 1990s." In *The Parties Respond*, edited by L. Sandy Maisel. 3rd ed. Boulder, Colo.: Westview.

Miller, Warren E., and J. Merrill Shanks. 1996. *The New American Voter*. Cambridge, Mass.: Harvard University Press.

Miller, Warren E., and Donald S. Stokes. 1963. "Constituency Influence in Congress." *American Political Science Review* 57:45–56.

Moberg, David. 1998. "Grass-Roots Politics in Comeback—with Winning Results." *Boston Sunday Globe*, June 14, A11.

Moncrief, Gary F., Peverill Squire, and Karl Kurtz. 1998. "Gateways to the Statehouse: Recruitment Patterns among State Legislative Candidates." Paper presented at the annual meeting of the American Political Science Association, Boston.

Mondak, Jeffrey J. 1995. "Competence, Integrity, and the Electoral Success of Congressional Incumbents." *Journal of Politics* 57:1043–69.

Mondak, Jeffrey J., and Dona-Gene Mitchell, eds. 2008. *Fault Lines: Why the Republicans Lost Congress*. London: Routledge.

Monroe, Bill. 1990. "Covering the Real Campaign: TV Sports." *Washington Journalism Review*, October 6, 6.

Montgomery, Lori, and Paul Kane. 2010. "Obama Switches Kucinich to a 'Yes.'" *Washington Post*, March 18, A1.

Montgomery, Lori, and Shailagh Murray. 2009. "House Democrats Pass Health-Care Bill; One Republican Votes for Plan; Senate Will Act Next on Legislation." *Washington Post*, November 8, A1.

Moore, Jonathan. 1981. *The Campaign for President: 1980 in Retrospect*. Cambridge, Mass.: Ballinger.

Moore, Jonathan, and Janet Fraser, eds. 1977. *Campaign for President: The Managers Look at 1976*. Cambridge, Mass.: Ballinger.

Morehouse, Sarah McCally, and Malcolm E. Jewell. 2003. *State Politics, Parties, and Policy*. 2nd ed. Lanham, Md.: Rowman & Littlefield.

Morton, John. 1991. "40 Years of Death in the Afternoon." *American Journalism Review*, November.

Moschella, Michael. 2012. "The Obama Team's 5 Best Strategic Decisions." *Campaigns and Elections*, December 26.

Murray, Shailagh. 2010. "Senate, House Approve 'Fixes' to Health-Care Law." *Washington Post*, March 26, A1.

Murray, Shailagh, and Lori Montgomery. 2009. "Senate Passes Health-Care Bill on 60–39 Vote; Republicans All Dissent; Differences with House Must Be Worked Out." *Washington Post*, December 25, A1.

———. 2010. "Divided House Passes Health-Care Bill." *Washington Post*, March 22, A1.

Musil, Steven. 2018. "Facebook Proved Popular with Russian Election Trolls." *CNET*, February 18.

Mutch, Robert E. 1988. *Campaigns, Congress, and Courts: The Making of Federal Campaign Finance Laws*. New York: Praeger.

Myers, John. 2016. "Unusual Election Outcomes Are the New Normal with California's Top-Two Primary Rules." *Los Angeles Times*, June 8.

———. 2017. "The Political Parties Would Like Voters to Kill California's Top-Two Primary System in 2018." *Los Angeles Times*, September 10.

Nader, Ralph. 1965. *Unsafe at Any Speed: The Designed-In Dangers of the American Automobile*. New York: Grossman.

Nagourney, Adam. 2008a. "McCain Orders Shake-Up of His Campaign." *New York Times*, July 3, online edition.

———. 2008b. "In Debating McCain, Obama's Real Opponent Was Voter Doubt." *New York Times*, October 15, online edition.

Narula, Svati Kirsten, Ryan Jacobs, and Judith Ohikuare. 2013. "32 Republicans Who Caused the Government Shutdown." *Atlantic Monthly*, October.

National Institute on Money in State Politics. 2005. *State Elections Overview 2004*. Helena, Mont.: National Institute on Money in State Politics.

———. 2010. *Competitiveness in 2007–2008 State Legislative Races*. Helena, Mont.: National Institute on Money in State Politics.

Neal, Terry M., and Paul Duggan. 1999. "Concerns in Bush Household." *Washington Post*, January 21, A8.

Nelson, Michael, ed. 1997. *The Elections of 1996*. Washington, D.C.: Congressional Quarterly Press.

———. 2005. *The Elections of 2004*. Washington, D.C.: Congressional Quarterly Press.

———. 2009. *The Elections of 2008*. Washington, D.C.: Congressional Quarterly Press.

Neumann, Sigmund, ed. 1956. *Modern Political Parties: Approaches to Comparative Politics*. Chicago: University of Chicago Press.

Neustadt, Richard E. 1960. *Presidential Power: The Politics of Leadership*. New York: Wiley.

———. 1976. *Presidential Power: The Politics of Leadership with Reflections on Johnson and Nixon*. New York: Wiley.

Newkirk, Vann R., II. 2017a. "The Department of Justice Stands by Texas's Voter ID Law." *Atlantic*, July 8.

———. 2017b. "What's Missing from Reports on Alabama's Black Turnout." *Atlantic*, December 7.

New York State Board of Elections. 2017. "State of New York 2017 Election Law." https://www.elections.ny.gov/NYSBOE/download/law/2017NYElectionLaw.pdf.

New York Times. 2018. "A Flurry of Courts Have Ruled on Election Maps. Here's What They've Said." *New York Times*, February 19.

Nie, Norman H., Darwin W. Miller III, Saar Golde, Daniel M. Butler, and Kenneth Winneg. 2010. "The World Wide Web and the U.S. Political News Market." *American Journal of Political Science* 54:428–39.

Nie, Norman H., Sidney Verba, and John R. Petrocik. 1979. *The Changing American Voter*. Enl. ed. Cambridge, Mass.: Harvard University Press.

Niemi, Richard G., and Simon Jackson. 1991. "Bias and Responsiveness in State Legislative Districting." *Legislative Studies Quarterly* 16:183–202.

Niemi, Richard G., and Herbert F. Weisberg, eds. 1993. *Controversies in Voting Behavior*. 3rd ed. Washington, D.C.: Congressional Quarterly Press.

———. 2001. *Controversies in Voting Behavior*. 4th ed. Washington, D.C.: Congressional Quarterly Press.

Niemi, Richard G., Stephen Wright, and Linda W. Powell. 1987. "Multiple Party Identifiers and the Measurement of Party Identification." *Journal of Politics* 49:1093–103.

Noel, Hans. 2013. *Political Ideologies and Political Parties in America*. New York: Cambridge University Press.

Noguchi, Yuki. 2017. "At 'Washington Post,' Tech Is Increasingly Boosting Financial Performance." *NPR*, June 13.

Norrander, Barbara. 2010. *The Imperfect Primary*. New York: Routledge.

Norris, Pippa, ed. 1997. *Politics and the Press: The News Media and Their Influence*. Boulder, Colo.: Lynne Rienner.

Nyhan, Brendan, and Jacob M. Montgomery. 2015. "Connecting the Candidates: Consultant Networks and the Diffusion of Campaign Strategy in American Congressional Elections." *American Journal of Political Science* 59 (2): 292–308.

Oates, Sarah. 2017. "A Perfect Storm: American Media, Russian Propaganda." *Current History* 116 (792): 282–84.

Oleszek, Walter J. 1989. *Congressional Procedures and the Policy Process*. 3rd ed. Washington, D.C.: Congressional Quarterly Press.

Ornstein, Norman J. 1975. "Causes and Consequences of Congressional Change: Subcommittee Reforms in the House of Representatives." In *Congress in Change*. New York: Praeger.

Ornstein, Norman J., Thomas E. Mann, and Michael J. Malbin. 1998. *Vital Statistics on Congress*. Washington, D.C.: Congressional Quarterly Press.

Ornstein, Norman J., Thomas E. Mann, Michael J. Malbin, and John F. Bibby. 1982. *Vital Statistics on Congress*. Washington, D.C.: American Enterprise Institute.

Ornstein, Norman J., Thomas E. Mann, Michael J. Malbin, Andrew Rugg, and Raffaela Wakeman. 2014. *Vital Statistics on Congress*. Washington, D.C.: Brookings Institution.

Orren, Gary R., and Nelson W. Polsby. 1987. *Media and Momentum: The New Hampshire Primary and Nomination Politics*. Chatham, N.J.: Chatham House.

Overacker, Louise. 1932. *Money in Elections*. New York: Macmillan.

Packer, George. 2010. "The Empty Chamber." *New Yorker*, August 9, online edition.

Paletta, Damian, and Jeff Stein. 2017. "Sweeping Tax Overhaul Clears Congress." WP Company LLC d/b/a The Washington Post, last modified December 20.

Parnes, Amie, and Kevin Cahill. 2015. "The $5 Billion Presidential Campaign?" *The Hill*, January 21.

Parris, Judith. 1972. *The Convention Problem*. Washington, D.C.: Brookings Institution.

Parsons, Christi, and John McCormick. 2007. " 'Crush on Obama' Is You-Tube Hit." *Chicago Tribune*, June 14, 1.

Patterson, James T. 1967. *Congressional Conservatism and the New Deal: The Growth of the Conservative Coalition in Congress, 1933–1939*. Lexington: University of Kentucky Press.

Patterson, Thomas E. 1980. *The Mass Media Election: How Americans Choose Their President*. New York: Praeger.

———. 1990. *The American Democracy*. New York: McGraw-Hill.

———. 1993. *Out of Order*. New York: Alfred A. Knopf.

———. 2016. *Pre-Primary News Coverage of the 2016 Presidential Race: Trump's Rise, Sanders' Emergence, Clinton's Struggle*. Harvard University, John F. Kennedy School of Government, Working Paper Series.

Patterson, Thomas E., and Robert D. McClure. 1976. *The Unseeing Eye: The Myth of Television Power in National Politics*. New York: Putnam.

Perry, H. W., Jr. 1991. "Racial Vote Dilution Cases." In *Political Parties and Elections in the United States: An Encyclopedia*, edited by L. Sandy Maisel. New York: Garland.

Persily, Nathaniel, et al. 2014. *The American Voting Experience: Report and Recommendations of the Presidential Commission on Election Administration.*

———. 2017. "Can Democracy Survive the Internet?" *Journal of Democracy* 28 (2): 63–76.

Peters, Jeremy W. 2014. "Building Legacy, Obama Reshapes Appellate Bench." *New York Times*, September 13.

———. 2016. "Reeling from 2016 Chaos, G.O.P. Mulls Overhaul of Primaries." New York Times Company, last modified May 24.

———. 2018. "A Romney Who Is Unfailingly Loyal to Trump." *New York Times*, January 13.

Peters, Ronald M., Jr. 1990. *The American Speakership: The Office in Historical Perspective.* Baltimore: Johns Hopkins University Press.

Petracca, Mark P. 1989. "Political Consultants and Democratic Governance." *PS: Political Science and Politics* 22:11–14.

Petrocik, John R. 2004. "Hard Facts: The Media and Elections with a Look at 2000 and 2002." In *Campaigns and Elections American Style*, 2nd ed., edited by James A. Thurber and Candice J. Nelson. Boulder, Colo.: Westview.

Pew Research Center. 2007a. "Election 2006 Online." Pew Internet and American Life Project, Washington, D.C.

———. 2007b. "What Americans Know: 1989–2007." Washington, D.C., April 15.

———. 2009a. "Newspapers Face a Challenging Crisis." Washington, D.C., February 26.

———. 2009b. "Strong Support for Watchdog Role, despite Public Criticism of News Media." Washington, D.C., October 2.

———. 2009c. "Partisanship and Cable News Audiences." Washington, D.C., October 30.

———. 2010a. "Understanding the Participatory News Consumer." Washington, D.C., March 1.

———. 2010b. "Ideological News Sources: Who Watches and Why." Washington, D.C., September 12.

———. 2011. "Internet Gains on Television as Public's Main News Source." Washington, D.C., January 4.

———. 2012. "In Changing News Landscape, Even Television Is Vulnerable." Washington, D.C., September 27.

———. 2013a. "The State of the News Media 2013." Washington, D.C.

———. 2013b. "Amid Criticism, Support for Media's 'Watchdog' Role Stands Out." Washington, D.C., August 8.

———. 2014a. "State of the News Media." Washington, D.C., March 26.

———. 2014b. "Older Adults and Technology Use." Washington, D.C., April 3.

———. 2014c. "Political Polarization and Media Habits." Washington, D.C., October 21.

———. 2014d. "The Party of Nonvoters: Younger, More Racially Diverse, More Financially Strapped." Washington, D.C., October 31.

———. 2014e. "Cell Phones, Social Media and Campaign 2014." Washington, D.C., November 3.

———. 2014f. "American Feel Better Informed Thanks to the Internet." Washington, D.C., December 8.

———. 2015. "Social Media Update 2014." Washington, D.C., January 9.

———. 2016. "The Modern News Consumer." Washington, D.C., July 7.

———. 2017a. "Trump, Clinton Voters Divided in Their Main Source for Election News." Washington, D.C., January 18.

———. 2017b. "Despite Subscription Surges for Largest U.S. Newspapers, Circulation and Revenue Fall for Industry Overall." Washington, D.C., June 1.

———. 2017c. "State of the News Media." Washington, D.C.

———. 2018. "Social Media Use in 2018." Washington, D.C., March 1.

Pfau, Michael, and Henry C. Kenski. 1990. *Attack Politics: Strategy and Defense*. New York: Praeger.

Phillips, Amber. 2017. *5 Tough Lessons Congress Learned in the Year of Trump*. Washington: WP Company LLC d/b/a The Washington Post.

Phillips, Cabell B. H. 1966. *The Truman Presidency: The History of a Triumphant Succession*. New York: Macmillan.

Pilkington, Ed, and Adam Gabbatt. 2016. "How Donald Trump Swept to an Unreal, Surreal Presidental Election Win." *Guardian*, November 9.

Piven, Frances Fox, and Richard A. Cloward. 1988. *Why Americans Don't Vote*. New York: Pantheon.

———. 1989. "Governmental Statistics and Conflicting Explanations of Nonvoting." *PS: Political Science and Politics* 22:580–88.

———. 1990. "A Reply to Bennett." *PS: Political Science and Politics* 23:172–73.

———. 2000. *Why Americans Still Don't Vote*. Boston: Beacon Press.

Polsby, Nelson W., ed. 1971. *Reapportionment in the 1970s*. Berkeley: University of California Press.

———. 1983. *Consequences of Party Reform*. New York: Oxford University Press.

Polsby, Nelson W., Aaron Wildavsky, and David A. Hopkins. 2008. *Presidential Elections*. 12th ed. Lanham, Md.: Rowman & Littlefield.

Pomper, Gerald M. 1972. "From Confusion to Clarity: Issues and American Voters, 1952–1968." *American Political Science Review* 66:415–28.

———. 1973. *Elections in America*. New York: Dodd, Mead.

———. 1975. *Voter's Choice: Varieties of American Electoral Behavior*. New York: Dodd, Mead.

———. 1977. "The Nominating Contests and Conventions." In *The Election of 1976: Reports and Interpretations*, edited by Gerald M. Pomper. New York: McKay.

———, ed. 1981. *The Election of 1980: Reports and Interpretations*. Chatham, N.J.: Chatham House.

———, ed. 1985. *The Elections of 1984: Reports and Interpretations*. Chatham, N.J.: Chatham House.

———. 1989. "The Presidential Nominations." In *The Election of 1988: Reports and Interpretations*, edited by Gerald M. Pomper. Chatham, N.J.: Chatham House.

Pomper, Gerald M., with Susan S. Lederman. 1980. *Elections in America*. 2nd ed. New York: Longman.

Pope, Kyle. 2016. "Revolution at the *Washington Post*." *Columbia Journalism Review* (Fall/Winter).

Powell, G. Bingham. 1986. "American Voter Turnout in Comparative Perspective." *American Political Science Review* 80:17–43.

Pramuk, Jacob. 2016. "How Much Does Trump Really Need the Republican Party?" *CNBC*, October 11.

President's Commission on Campaign Costs. 1962. *Financing Presidential Campaigns*. Washington, D.C.: Government Printing Office.

Price, H. Douglas. 1971. "Congressional Careers—Then and Now." In *Congressional Behavior*, edited by Nelson W. Polsby. New York: Random House.

Prior, Markus. 2007. *Post-Broadcast Democracy*. New York: Cambridge University Press.

Project for Excellence in Journalism. 2010. *The State of the News Media 2010*. March 15.

Putnam, Joshua T. 2016. "Rules Changes and the 2016 Presidential Nominations." *Society* 53 (5): 493–97.

Putnam, Robert D. 2000. *Bowling Alone: The Collapse and Revival of American Community*. New York: Simon and Schuster.

Qiu, Linda. 2016. "No, Donald Trump, Bernie Sanders Wouldn't Have Won Even If Super Delegates Were Nixed." *Tampa Bay Times*, July 25.

Quirk, Paul J., and Jon K. Dalager. 1993. "The Election: A 'New Democrat' and a New Kind of Presidential Campaign." In *The Elections of 1996*, edited by Michael Nelson. Washington, D.C.: Congressional Quarterly Press.

Rakove, Milton L. 1975. *Don't Make No Waves . . . Don't Back No Losers*. Bloomington: Indiana University Press.

Ranney, Austin. 1975. *Curing the Mischiefs of Faction: Party Reform in America*. Berkeley: University of California Press.

———. 1979. *The Past and Future of Presidential Debates*. Washington, D.C.: American Enterprise Institute for Public Policy Research.

———, ed. 1985. *The American Elections of 1984*. Durham, N.C.: Duke University Press.

Rapoport, Ronald B., and Walter J. Stone. 2005. *Three's a Crowd: The Dynamic of Third Parties, Ross Perot, and Republican Resurgence*. Ann Arbor: University of Michigan Press.

Reichley, James. 1985. "The Rise of the National Parties." In *The New Directions in American Politics*, edited by John E. Clubb and Paul E. Peterson. Washington, D.C.: Brookings Institution.

———. 1992. *The Life of the Parties*. New York: Free Press.

Reinhard, Beth. 2015. "Southern States Plan New Super Tuesday." *Wall Street Journal*, January 12, A4.

Reuters. 2008. "Obama Infomercial Tops Network Prime-Time Ratings." October 31, online.

Riechmann, Deb. 2018. "US Intel Sees Signs of Russian Meddling in Midterms." *AP Worldstream*, February 14.

Riordon, William L., ed. 1963. *Plunkitt of Tammany Hall*. New York: Dutton.

———. 1995. *Plunkitt of Tammany Hall: A Series of Very Plain Talks on Very Practical Politics*. New York: Signet.

Ripley, Randall B. 1964. "The Whip Organizations in the United States House of Representatives." *American Political Science Review* 58:561–76.

———. 1967. *Party Leaders in the House of Representatives*. Washington, D.C.: Brookings Institution.

Robinson, Michael, and Margaret Sheehan. 1983. *Over the Wire and on TV.* New York: Russell Sage Foundation.

Robison, Joshua, and Kevin J. Mullinix. 2015. "Elite Polarization and Public Opinion: How Polarization Is Communicated and Its Effects." *Political Communication* 33 (2): 261–82.

Rogers, Steven. 2018. *Democrats Are Contesting More State Legislative Seats Than They Have in Decades*. Washington: WP Company LLC d/b/a The Washington Post.

Rohde, David W. 1974. "Committee Reform in the House of Representatives and the 'Subcommittee Bill of Rights.'" *Annals* 411:39–47.

———. 1991. *Parties and Leaders in the Post-Reform House*. Chicago: University of Chicago Press.

———. 2013. "Reflections on the Practice of Theorizing: Conditional Party Government in the Twenty-First Century." *Journal of Politics* 75:849–64.

Rosenberg, Matthew. 2017. "Trump Misleads on Russian Meddling: Why 17 Intelligence Agencies Don't Need to Agree." New York Times Company, last modified July 6.

Rosenberg, Matthew, Nicholas Confessore, and Carole Cadwalladr. 2018. "How Trump Consultants Exploited the Facebook Data of Millions." New York Times Company, last modified March 17.

Rosenstone, Steven J., Roy L. Behr, and Edward H. Lazarus. 1984. *Third Parties in America: Citizen Response to Major Party Failure*. Princeton, N.J.: Princeton University Press.

Rosenstone, Steven J., and Raymond E. Wolfinger. 1978. "The Effect of Registration Laws on Voter Turnout." *American Political Science Review* 72:22–45.

Rothenberg, Stuart. 1983. *Winners and Losers: Campaigns, Candidates, and Congressional Elections*. Washington, D.C.: Free Congress Research and Education Foundation.

Roubein, Rachel. 2017. "Timeline: The GOP's Failed Effort to Repeal ObamaCare." *The Hill*, September 26.

Royko, Mike. 1971. *Boss: Richard J. Daley of Chicago*. New York: Dutton.

Rozell, Mark J., and Clyde Wilcox, eds. 1995. *God at the Grass Roots: The Christian Right in the 1994 Elections*. Lanham, Md.: Rowman & Littlefield.

Rozsa, Matthew. 2016. "Jill Stein Spoiled the 2016 Election for Hillary Clinton." *Salon*, December 2.

Rucker, Philip. 2010a. "Lawmakers Targeted for Vandalism and Threats." *Washington Post*, March 25, A1.

———. 2010b. "Labor Unions Pivot toward Midterm Elections with Jobs Campaign." *Washington Post*, July 12, online edition.

———. 2017. "'He's Not Weak, Is He?': Inside Trump's Quest to Alter the Judiciary." *Washington Post*, December 19.

Runkel, David B., ed. 1989. *Campaign for President: The Managers Look at '88*. Dover, Mass.: Auburn House.

Ruprecht, Louis A., Jr. 2015. "The People versus the Powers; or, On Money and Speech: The Continuing Saga of Campaign Finance Reform." *Soundings: An Interdisciplinary Journal* 98:17–37.

Rusk, Jerrold G. 1970. "The Effect of the Australian Ballot Reform on Split Ticket Voting: 1876–1908." *American Political Science Review* 64:1220–38.

———. 1974. "The American Electoral Universe: Speculation and Evidence." *American Political Science Review* 68:1028–49.

Rutenberg, Jim. 2008. "Obama Infomercial, a Closing Argument to the Everyman." *New York Times*, October 29, online edition.

Sabato, Larry J. 1981. *The Rise of Political Consultants: New Ways of Winning Campaigns*. New York: Basic Books.

———. 1985. *PAC Power: Inside the World of Political Action Committees*. New York: Norton.

———. 1988. *The Party's Just Begun: Shaping Political Parties for America's Future*. Glenview, Ill.: Scott Foresman.

———. 1991. *Feeding Frenzy: How Attack Journalism Has Transformed American Politics*. New York: Free Press.

Salmore, Stephen A., and Barbara G. Salmore. 1985. *Candidates, Parties, and Campaigns*. Washington, D.C.: Congressional Quarterly Press.

Sanchez, Luis. 2018. "Dems Pledge to Reduce 'Perceived Influence' of Superdelegates." *The Hill*, March 10.

Sartori, Giovanni. 1976. *Parties and Party Systems: A Framework for Analysis*. New York: Cambridge University Press.

Schaffner, Brian F., Matthew Streb, and Gerald Wright. 2001. "Teams without Uniforms: The Nonpartisan Ballot in State and Local Elections." *Political Research Quarterly* 54:7–30.

Schattschneider, E. E. 1942. *Party Government*. New York: Holt, Rinehart, and Winston.

———. 1956. "United States: The Functional Approach to Party Government." In *Modern Political Parties*, edited by Sigmund Neumann. Chicago: University of Chicago Press.

———. 1960. *The Semisovereign People*. Hinsdale, Ill.: Dryden.

Scherer, Michael. 2012. "Inside the World of Quants and Data Crunchers Who Helped Obama Win." *Time* 56–60. November 19.

Schlesinger, Joseph A. 1966. *Ambition and Politics: Political Careers in the United States*. Chicago: Rand McNally.

———. 1985. "The New American Political Party." *American Political Science Review* 79:1152–69.

Schlozman, Kay L., and John T. Tierney. 1986. *Organized Interests and American Democracy*. New York: Harper and Row.

Schlozman, Kay L, Sidney Verba, and Henry E. Brady. 2010. "Weapon of the Strong? Participatory Inequality and the Internet." *Perspectives on Politics* 8:487–509.

Schmitt, Eric. 2003. "Pressure on Senator for Blocking Promotions." *New York Times*, June 10, A23.

Schrag, Peter. 2003. "California Revolts, Again." *New York Times*, June 15, section 4, p. 6.

Schram, Martin. 1977. *Running for President, 1976: The Carter Campaign*. New York: Stein and Day.

Schroedel, Jean Reith. 1986. "Campaign Contributions and Legislative Outcomes." *Western Political Quarterly* 39:371–89.

Schuck, Peter H. 1987. "The Thickest Thicket: Partisan Gerrymandering and Judicial Regulation of Politics." *Columbia Law Review* 87:1325–84.

Schwartzman, Paul, and Jenna Johnson. 2015. "It's Not Chaos. It's Trump's Campaign Strategy." *Concord Monitor*, December 10.

Seelye, Katharine Q. 2017. "Ranked-Choice Voting System Violates Maine's Constitution, Court Says." *New York Times*, May 23.

Seib, Philip. 1994. *Campaigns and Conscience: The Ethics of Political Journalism*. Westport, Conn.: Praeger.

Seligman, Lester. 1974. *Patterns of Recruitment: A State Chooses Its Lawmakers*. Chicago: Rand McNally.

Sender, Julie Bergman. 2007. *Viral Video in Politics*. Washington, D.C.: New Politics Institute.

Shafer, Byron E. 1988. *Bifurcated Politics: Evolution and Reform in the National Nominating Convention*. Cambridge, Mass.: Harvard University Press.

Shafer, Byron E., and Richard Johnston. 2006. *The End of Southern Exceptionalism: Class, Race, and Partisan Change in the Postwar South*. Cambridge, Mass.: Harvard University Press.

Shafer, Byron E., and Richard H. Spady. 2014. *The American Political Landscape*. Cambridge, Mass.: Harvard University Press.

Shanks, J. Merrill, and Warren E. Miller. 1989. "Alternative Interpretations of the 1988 Election: Policy Direction, Current Conditions, Presidential Performance, and Candidate Traits." Paper presented at the annual meeting of the American Political Science Association, Atlanta, Ga.

———. 1990. "Policy Direction and Performance Evaluation: Contemporary Explanations of the Reagan Elections." *British Journal of Political Science* 20:143–235.

Shea, Daniel M. 1996. *Campaign Craft: The Strategies, Tactics, and Art of Campaign Management*. Westport, Conn.: Praeger.

———. 1999. "The Passing of Realignment and the Advent of the 'Base-Less' Party System." *American Politics Quarterly* 27:33–57.

Shear, Michael D. 2010. "Republican Immigration Position Likely to Alienate Latinos, Obama Officials Say." *Washington Post*, July 20, A1.

Sheppard, Burton D. 1985. *Rethinking Congressional Reform*. Cambridge, Mass.: Schenkman.

Silbey, Joel H. 1991. *The American Political Nation, 1838–1893*. Stanford, Calif.: Stanford University Press.

———. 1994. *Encyclopedia of the American Legislative System: Studies of the Principal Structures, Processes, and Policies of Congress and the State Legislatures since the Colonial Era*. New York: Scribner's.

———. 1998. "From 'Essential to the Existence of Our Institutions' to 'Rapacious Enemies of Honest and Responsible Government': The Rise and Fall of American Parties, 1790–2000." In *The Parties Respond*, edited by L. Sandy Maisel. 3rd ed. Boulder, Colo.: Westview.

———. 2002a. "From 'Essential to the Existence of Our Institutions' to 'Rapacious Enemies of Honest and Responsible Government': The Rise and Fall of American Parties, 1790–2000." In *The Parties Respond*, edited by L. Sandy Maisel. 4th ed. Boulder, Colo.: Westview.

———. 2002b. *Martin Van Buren and the Emergence of American Popular Politics*. Lanham, Md.: Rowman & Littlefield.

Silver, Nate. 2016. "How Trump Hacked the Media." FiveThirtyEight. March 30.

Simon, Roger. 1998. *Show Time: The American Presidential Circus and the Race for the White House*. New York: Crown.

Sinclair, Barbara. 1983. *Majority Party Leadership in the U.S. House*. Baltimore: Johns Hopkins University Press.

———. 1989. *The Transformation of the U.S. Senate*. Baltimore: Johns Hopkins University Press.

———. 1990. "The Congressional Party: Evolving Organizational, Agenda Setting, and Policy Roles." In *The Parties Respond: Changes in the American Party System*, edited by L. Sandy Maisel. Boulder, Colo.: Westview.

———. 1995. *Legislators, Leaders, and Lawmaking: The U.S. House of Representatives in the Postreform Era*. Baltimore: Johns Hopkins University Press.

———. 1998. "Evolution or Revolution? Policy-Oriented Congressional Parties in the 1990s." In *The Parties Respond*, edited by L. Sandy Maisel. 3rd ed. Boulder, Colo.: Westview.

———. 2006. *Party Wars: Polarization and the Politics of National Policy Making*. Norman: University of Oklahoma Press.

Singer, Paul, and Donovan Slack. 2016. "Tale of the Tape: The 16 Contenders Trump Has Knocked Out." *USA Today*, May 4.

Skinner, Richard, Seth Masket, and David Dulio. 2012. "527 Committees and the Political Party Network." *American Politics Research* 40:60–84.

———. 2013. "527 Committees, Formal Parties, and the Party Networks." *Forum* 11:137–56.

Smith, Aaron, and Maeve Duggan. 2012. "Online Political Videos and Campaign 2012." Washington, D.C.: Pew Research Center, November 12.

Smith, Jeff, and David C. Kimball. 2012. "Barking Louder: Interest Groups in the 2012 Election." *Forum* 10:80–90.

Smith, Steven S., and Christopher J. Deering. 1990. *Committees in Congress*. 2nd ed. Washington, D.C.: Congressional Quarterly Press.

Smolkin, Rachel. 2007. "What the Mainstream Media Can Learn from Jon Stewart." *American Journalism Review*, June/July.

Snowiss, Leo M. 1966. "Congressional Recruitment and Representation." *American Political Science Review* 60:627–39.

Sorauf, Frank J. 1980. *Party Politics in America*. Boston: Little, Brown.

———. 1984. "Political Action Committees in American Politics: An Overview." In *What Price PACs?* New York: Twentieth Century Fund.

———. 1988. *Money in American Elections*. Glenview, Ill.: Scott, Foresman.

———. 1991. "Political Action Committees." In *Political Parties and Elections in the United States: An Encyclopedia*, edited by L. Sandy Maisel. New York: Garland.

———. 1998. "Political Parties and the New World of Campaign Finance." In *The Parties Respond*, edited by L. Sandy Maisel. 3rd ed. Boulder, Colo.: Westview.

Southwell, Priscilla, and Justin Burchett. 1997. "Survey of Vote-by-Mail Senate Election in the State of Oregon." *PS: Political Science and Politics* 30 (March): 53–58.

Sparks, Jared, ed. 1840. *The Writings of George Washington*. Boston: F. Andrews.

Squire, Peverill, Raymond E. Wolfinger, and David P. Glass. 1987. "Residential Mobility and Voter Turnout." *American Political Science Review* 81:45–66.

Stanley, Harold W. 1985. "The Runoff: The Case for Retention." *PS: Political Science and Politics* 18:231–36.

Stanley, Harold W., William T. Bianco, and Richard G. Niemi. 1986. "Partisanship and Group Support over Time: A Multivariate Analysis." *American Political Science Review* 80:969–76.

———. 2006. "Partisanship, Party Coalitions, and Group Support, 1952– 2004." *Presidential Studies Quarterly* 36:172–88.

Stanley, Harold W., and Richard J. Niemi. 2006. *Vital Statistics on American Politics*. Washington, D.C.: Congressional Quarterly Press.

———. 2010. *Vital Statistics on American Politics*. Washington, D.C.: Congressional Quarterly Press.

State of New York. 2017. "State of New York 2017 Election Law." https://www.elections.ny.gov/NYSBOE/download/law/2017NYElectionLaw.pdf.

Steel, Emily. 2009. "For State, Local Office Seekers, Web Ads Present Potential Pitfalls." *Wall Street Journal*, August 3, B6.

Stein, Rob. 2010. "Order on Abortion Angers Core Backers." *Washington Post*, March 25, A8.

Stein, Robert M., and Patricia Garcia-Monet. 1997. "Voting Early but Not Often." *Social Science Quarterly* 78 (September): 657–72.

Steinberg, Alfred. 1972. *The Bosses*. New York: Macmillan.

Stelter, Brian. 2008. "Networks Hope to Find Unique TV Moment at Democratic Convention." *New York Times*, August 25, online edition.

———. 2016. "Debate Breaks Record as Most-Watched in U.S. History." *CNN Wire Service*, September 27.

Stephenson, E. Frank. 2011. "Strategic Voting in Open Primaries: Evidence from Rush Limbaugh's 'Operation Chaos.'" *Public Choice* 148:445–57.

Stern, Philip M. 1988. *The Best Congress Money Can Buy*. New York: Pantheon Books.

Stevens, Allison, and Andrew Taylor. 2003. "Frist Faced with Deep Party Rift after Charge of Double Dealing." *Congressional Quarterly Weekly*, April 19, 931–34.

Stevens, Daniel. 2005. "Separate and Unequal Effects: Information, Political Sophistication and Negative Advertising in American Elections." *Political Research Quarterly* 58: 413–25.

———. 2012. "Tone versus Information: Explaining the Impact of Negative Political Advertising." *Journal of Political Marketing* 11:322–52.

Stewart, Emily. 2016. "Donald Trump Rode $5 Billion in Free Media to the White House." *The Street*. November 20.

Stewart, John G. 1991. "Democratic National Committee." In *Political Parties and Elections in the United States: An Encyclopedia*, edited by L. Sandy Maisel. New York: Garland.

Stokes, Donald E., and Warren E. Miller. 1962. "Party Government and the Saliency of Congress." *Public Opinion Quarterly* 26:531–46.

Stone, Walter J., Sarah Fulton, Cherie Maestas, L. Sandy Maisel. 2010. "Incumbency Reconsidered: Prospects, Strategic Retirement, and Incumbent Quality in U.S. House Elections," *Journal of Politics* 72:178–90.

Stone, Walter J., Nathan J. Hadley, Rolfe D. Peterson, Cherie D. Maestas, and L. Sandy Maisel. 2008. "Candidate Entry, Voter Response, and Partisan Tides in the 2002 and 2006 Elections." In *Fault Lines: Why the Republicans Lost Congress*, edited by Jeffrey L. Mondak and Dona-Gene Mitchell. London: Routledge.

Stone, Walter J., and L. Sandy Maisel. 2003. "The Not-So-Simple Calculus of Winning: Potential U.S. House Candidates' Nomination and General Election Prospects." *Journal of Politics* 65:951–77.

Stone, Walter J., L. Sandy Maisel, and Cherie Maestas. 1998. "Candidate Emergence in U.S. House Elections." Paper presented at the annual meeting of the American Political Science Association, Boston.

———. 2004. "Quality Counts: Extending the Strategic Politician Model of Incumbent Deterrence." *American Journal of Political Science* 48:479–95.

Stone, Walter J., L. Sandy Maisel, Cherie Maestas, and Sean Evans. 1998. "Candidate Quality in U.S. House Elections: Candidate Emergence in the 1998 Elections." Paper presented at the annual meeting of the Midwest Political Science Association, Chicago.

Stonecash, Jeffrey M. 2000. *Class and Party in American Politics*. Boulder, Colo.: Westview.

———. 2003. *Political Polling: Strategic Information in Campaigns*. Lanham, Md.: Rowman & Littlefield.

———. 2006. *Political Parties Matter: Realignment and the Return of Partisan Voting*. Boulder, Colo.: Lynne Rienner.

———. 2008. *Reassessing the Incumbency Effect*. New York: Cambridge University Press.

Stonecash, Jeffrey M., Mark D. Brewer, and Mack D. Mariani. 2003. *Diverging Parties*. Boulder, Colo.: Westview.

Streib, Gregory, James H. Svara, William L. Waugh, Kenneth A. Klase, Donald C. Menzel, Tanis J. Salant, J. Edwin Benton, et al. 2007. "Conducting Research on Counties in the 21st Century: A New Agenda and Database Considerations." *Public Administration Review* 67 (6): 968–83.

Sullivan, Denis G., Robert T. Nakamura, Martha Wagner Weinberg, F. Christopher Arterton, and Jeffrey L. Pressman. 1977–1978. "Exploring the 1976 Republican Convention." *Political Science Quarterly* 92:633–34.

Sullivan, Denis G., Jeffrey L. Pressman, and F. Christopher Arterton. 1976. *Explorations in Convention Decision Making: The Democratic Party in the 1970s*. San Francisco: Freeman.

Sullivan, Denis G., Jeffrey L. Pressman, F. Christopher Arterton, Robert T. Nakamura, and Martha Wagner Weinberg. 1977. "Candidates, Caucuses, and Issues: The Democratic Convention, 1976." In *The Impact of the Electoral Process*, edited by Louis Maisel and Joseph Cooper. Beverly Hills, Calif.: Sage.

Sullivan, Margaret. 2017. "Polls Show Americans Distrust the Media. But Talk to Them, and It's a Very Different Story." WP Company LLC d/b/a The Washington Post, last modified December 27.

Sullivan, Sean, and Robert Costa. 2016. "In Campaign Chaos, Donald Trump Shows His Management Style." WP Company LLC d/b/a The Washington Post, last modified May 28.

Sundquist, James L. 1983. *Dynamics of the Party System: Alignment and Realignment of Political Parties in the United States*. Rev. ed. Washington, D.C.: Brookings Institution.

Sutton, Adam. 2013. "Email Testing: How the Obama Campaign Generated Approximately $500 Million in Donations from Email Marketing." *Marketing Sherpa*, May 7.

Swift, Art. 2016. "Americans' Trust in Mass Media Sinks to New Low." *Gallup*, September 14.

Taggart, William A., and Robert F. Durant. 1985. "Home Style of a U.S. Senator: A Longitudinal Study." *Legislative Studies Quarterly* 10:489–504.

Tarrance, V. Lance. 1978. "Suffrage and Voter Turnout in the United States: The Vanishing Voter." In *Parties and Elections in an Anti-Party Age*, edited by Jeff Fishel. Bloomington: Indiana University Press.

Taylor, Paul. 2013. "Politics and Race: Looking Ahead to 2060." *Pew Research Center*, May 10.

Taylor, Paul, and Mark Hugo Lopez. 2013. "Six Take-Aways from the Census Bureau's Voting Report." *Pew Research Center*, May 8.

Teixeira, Ruy. 1987. *Why Americans Don't Vote*. New York: Greenwood.

———. 1992. *The Disappearing American Voter*. Washington, D.C.: Brookings Institution.

Thayer, George. 1973. *Who Shakes the Money Tree?* New York: Simon and Schuster.

The Cook Political Report. 2018. "2018 House Race Ratings." January 24.

The Week. 2012. "Romney and Obama's Social-Media War: By the Numbers." http://theweek.com/articles/471182/romney-obamas-socialmedia-war-by-numbers. October 22.

Thistle, Scott. 2018. "Voters Will Decide in June Whether Maine Keeps Its Ranked-Choice Voting Law." *Central Maine*, March 5.

Thomas, Evan. 2009. *A Long Time Coming*. New York: Public Affairs.

Thompson, Hunter. 1973. *Fear and Loathing: On the Campaign Trail '72*. New York: Quick Fox.

Thurber, James A., and Candice J. Nelson. 2000. *Campaign Warriors: Political Consultants in Elections*. Washington, D.C.: Brookings Institution.

Timberg, Craig. 2018. "Russians Used Mainstream Media to Manipulate U.S. Voters, Analysis Finds." *Washington Post*, February 16.

Timpone, Richard. 1998. "Structure, Behavior, and Voter Turnout in the United States." *American Political Science Review* 92:145–58.

Tolchin, Martin, and Susan Tolchin. 1971. *To the Victor . . . Political Patronage from the Clubhouse to the White House*. New York: Vintage Books.

Traugott, Michael W. 1985. "The Media and the Nominating Process." In *Before Nomination: Our Primary Problem*, edited by George Grassmuck. Washington, D.C.: American Enterprise Institute for Public Policy Research.

Truman, David B. 1951. *The Governmental Process*. New York: Knopf.

Tufte, Edward E. 1975. "Determinants of the Outcomes of Midterm Congressional Elections." *American Political Science Review* 69:812–26.

———. 1978. *Political Control of the Economy*. Princeton, N.J.: Princeton University Press.

Vaccari, Cristian. 2013. "From Echo Chamber to Persuasive Device? Rethinking the Role of the Internet in Campaigns." *New Media and Society* 15: 109–127.

van Erkel, Patrick F. A. , Peter Thijssen, and Peter Van Aelst. 2017. "One for All or All for One: The Electoral Effects of Personalized Campaign Strategies." *Acta Politica* 52 (3): 384–405.

Vargas, Jose Antonio. 2008. "Obama Raised Half a Billion Online." *Washington Post*, November 20, online edition.

Verba, Sidney, and Norman H. Nie. 1972. *Participation in America: Political Democracy and Social Equality*. New York: Harper and Row.

Verba, Sidney, Kay Lehman Schlozman, and Henry Brady. 1995. *Voice and Equality: Civic Voluntarism in American Politics*. Cambridge, Mass.: Harvard University Press.

Volden, Craig, and Elizabeth Bergman. 2006. "How Strong Should Our Party Be? Member Preferences over Party Cohesion." *Legislative Studies Quarterly* 31:71–104.

Vozzella, Laura. 2017. "Name-Drawing in Tied Va. House Race Delayed after Democrat Announces Court Challenge." *Washington Post*, December 26.

Walker, Jack L. 1983. "The Origins and Maintenance of Interest Groups in America." *American Political Science Review* 77:390–406.

Ware, Alan. 2006. *The Democratic Party Heads North, 1877–1962*. New York: Cambridge University Press.

Warren, Michael. 2017. "White House Watch: Is Trump Changing the Republican Party, or Leaving It?" *Weekly Standard*, September 11.

Wasko, Sarah. 2017. "Democrats Trust the Press and Republicans Don't. What Now?" *Media Matters for America*, December 5.

Wattenberg, Martin P. 1998. *The Decline of American Political Parties, 1952–1996*. Cambridge, Mass.: Harvard University Press.

Wayne, Alex, and Edward Epstein. 2010. "Obama Seals Legislative Legacy with Health Insurance Overhaul." *Congressional Quarterly Weekly*, March 29, 748–53.

Wayne, Stephen J. 1984. *The Road to the White House: The Politics of Presidential Elections*, 2nd ed. New York: St. Martin's Press.

———. 1988. *The Road to the White House: The Politics of Presidential Elections*. 3rd ed. New York: St. Martin's Press.

———. 2000. *The Road to the White House, 2000*. New York: St. Martin's Press.

———. 2008. *The Road to the White House, 2008*. Belmont, Calif.: Wadsworth/ Thomson.

———. 2015. *The Road to the White House, 2016*. 10th ed. Belmont, Calif.: Wadsworth..

Weber, Ronald, Harvey Tucker, and Paul Brace. 1991. "Vanishing Marginals in State Legislative Elections." *Legislative Studies Quarterly* 16:29–47.

Weiland, Noah. 2016. "Everything You Need to Know about Super Tuesday." *Politico*, February 26.

Weisbrot, Robert S. 1990. *Freedom Bound*. New York: Norton.

Weissman, Stephen R. 2005. Remarks at the Campaign Finance Institute Campaign Finance Reform Forum, National Press Club, Washington, D.C., January 14.

Weissman, Stephen R., and Ruth Hassan. 2006. "BCRA and the 527 Groups." In *The Election after Reform*, edited by Michael J. Malbin. Lanham, Md.: Rowman & Littlefield.

Weissman, Stephen R., and Kara D. Ryan. 2007. "Soft Money in the 2006 Election and the Outlook for 2008." Washington, D.C.: Campaign Finance Institute.

Wells, Chris, Dhavan V. Shah, Jon C. Pevehouse, JungHwan Yang, Ayellet Pelled, Frederick Boehm, Josephine Lukito, et al. 2016. "How Trump Drove Coverage to the Nomination: Hybrid Media Campaigning." *Political Communication* 33 (4): 669–76.

West, Geoff. 2017. "Lobbying Spending Hits Historic Lows." Washington, DC: Center for Responsive Politics. October 23.

White, Theodore H. 1961. *The Making of the President, 1960*. New York: Atheneum.

———. 1965. *The Making of the President, 1964*. New York: Atheneum.

———. 1969. *The Making of the President, 1968*. New York: Atheneum.

———. 1973. *The Making of the President, 1972*. New York: Atheneum.

———. 1982. *America in Search of Itself: The Making of the President, 1956–1980*. New York: Harper and Row.

Wihbey, John. 2013. "Negative Political Ads, the 2012 Campaign and Voter Effects: Research Roundup." Journalist's Resource, May 6.

Wilcox, Clyde. 1988. "I Owe It All to Me: Candidates' Investments in Their Own Campaigns." *American Politics Quarterly* 16:266–79.

Wilcox, Clyde, and Carin Robinson. 2011. *Onward Christian Soldiers? The Religious Right in American Politics*. Boulder, Colo.: Westview.

Wilkerson, David D. 2008. "McCain Speech's TV Audience Edges Obama's." *Marketwatch*, September 5, online edition.

Williams, Christine B., and Girish J. "Jeff" Gulati. 2013. "Social Networks in Political Campaigns: Facebook and the Congressional Elections of 2006 and 2008." *New Media Society* 15:52–71.

Williamson, Jonathan. 1999. "Supply-Side of Southern Politics: Candidate Quality and Candidate Emergence in House Elections." Paper presented at the annual meeting of the Midwest Political Science Association, Chicago.

Wilson, James Q. 1962. *The Amateur Democrat*. Chicago: University of Chicago Press.

———. 1973. *Political Organizations*. New York: Basic Books.

Wilson, Scott. 2010. "With a Signature, Obama Seals His Health-Care Victory." *Washington Post*, March 24, A1.

Wilson, Woodrow. 1885. *Congressional Government*. Boston: Houghton Mifflin.

Wines, Michael, and Trip Gabriel. 2018. "Pennsylvania District Map Is Ruled Unconstitutional." *New York Times*, January 23.

Winfrey, Kelly L. 2017. "Crazy for Caucusing: Media Use and Voter Opinions in the 2016 Iowa Caucus." *American Behavioral Scientist* 61 (9): 1002–23.

Winneg, Kenneth M., Bruce W. Hardy, Jeffrey A. Gottfried, and Kathleen Hall Jamieson. 2014. "Deception in Third Party Advertising in the 2012 Presidential Campaign." *American Behavioral Scientist* 58:524–35.

Wirthlin, Richard B. 1981. "The Republican Strategy and Its Electoral Consequences." In *Party Coalitions in the 1980s*, edited by Seymour Martin Lipset. San Francisco: Institute for Contemporary Studies.

Witcover, James. 1977. *Marathon: The Pursuit of the Presidency, 1972– 1976*. New York: Viking.

Wolfinger, Raymond E., and Jonathon Hoffman. 2001. "Registering and Voting with Motor Voter." *PS: Political Science and Politics* 34:85–92.

Wolfinger, Raymond E., and Steven J. Rosenstone. 1980. *Who Votes?* New Haven, Conn.: Yale University Press.

Wolpe, Bruce C., and Bertram J. Levine. 1996. *Lobbying Congress: How the System Works*. 2nd ed. Washington, D.C.: Congressional Quarterly Press.

Wright, John R. 1985. "PACs, Contributions, and Roll Calls: An Organizational Perspective." *American Political Science Review* 79:400–414.

———. 1996. *Interest Groups and Congress: Lobbying, Contributions, and Influence*. Needham Heights, Mass.: Simon and Schuster.

Young, James. 1966. *The Washington Community*. New York: Harcourt, Brace and World.

Zaller, John. 1998. "Politicians as Prize Fighters: Electoral Selection and Incumbency Advantage." In *Politicians and Party Politics*, edited by John G. Gear. Baltimore: Johns Hopkins University Press.

Zeller, Sean. 2011. "2010 Vote Studies: Party Unity." *CQ Weekly*, January 3, 30–35.

Credits

Chapter 1:
1 ©AP Photo.
7 Dave Granlund, Courtesy of Cagle Cartoons.

Chapter 2:
21 Tim Brown / Alamy Stock Photo.
43 Walt Handelsman, Courtesy of Cagle Cartoons.

Chapter 3:
65 Bob Korn / Alamy Stock Photo.

Chapter 4:
111 ZUMA Press Inc / Alamy Stock Photo.
117 Mike Keefe, InToon.com.

Chapter 5:
136 Reinhard Hunger.
148 Adam Zyglis, Courtesy of Cagle Cartoons

Chapter 6:
180 FR170079 AP/©AP Photo.

Chapter 7:
204 Tribune Content Agency LLC / Alamy Stock Photo.

Chapter 8:
246 ©AP Photo.
252 Andy Warner.

Chapter 9:
288 ZUMA Press, Inc. / Alamy Stock Photo.

Chapter 10:
328 Anatolii Babii / Alamy Stock Photo.
338 Tom Stiglich.

Chapter 11:
360 Evan Vucci/©AP Photo.

Chapter 12:
396 Tribune Content Agency LLC / Alamy Stock Photo.

Index

Italicized page numbers locate illustrations and tables; **bold** numbers locate explanations of key terms.

AARP, 114
Abbott, Greg, *204*
abortion: legislation, 281, 364–65, 368, 402; and political groups, 107, 120, 122–23, 133–34, 311; protests, 101, 104, 367; and Supreme Court, 46–47, 389
Adams, John, 25–27
Adams, John Quincy, 28–29
affirmative action, 311
Affordable Care Act (2010), 361–69, 391
AFL-CIO, 114, 121, 162
African-Americans. *See* blacks
age, 71–72, 76–77, *78*, 94, 108, 112–13, 216, 407
Agnew, Spiro, 287n4
Air Force One, **313**
Alaska, 71, 188, 208, 237
Aldrich, John H., 373
Alexander, Herbert, 137, 151–52, 178n3
Alexander, Lamar, 256
The Almanac of American Politics, 124
America Coming Together, 171–72
American Association of University Women, 120
American Bankers Association, 162
American Conservative Union (ACU), 125
American Federation of Labor, 13, 162
American Medical Association (AMA), 114, 162–63
American Morning, 392
American National Election Study (ANES), 112
American party (Know-Nothings), 32
American Realtors Association, 162–63
American Recovery and Reinvestment Act (2009), 363
Americans for Democratic Action (ADA), 114, 121, 124, 377–78
The American Voter (Campbell et al.), 82–95, 404–5
Anderson, John, 13, 19n9, 20n10
An Inconvenient Truth (2006), 324
Ansolabehere, Stephen, 352–53
Anzia, Sarah, 19n1
The Apprentice, 2
Arizona, *6*, 66, 209, 237, 361
Arizona State Legislature v. Arizona Independent Redistricting Commission, 209
Arkansas, *6*
Armey, Dick, 382, 384
Arsenio Hall Show, 336
The Art of the Deal (Trump), 2
associations, 113–16, *115*, 126–28, 131, 162, 166, 171, 173
AT&T, 171
attack ads, **352**. *See also* media
"Attack Ads Carpet TV; High Road Swept Away" (Kurtz), 352
Audubon Society, 116

Australian ballot, **40**
Axelrod, David, 296

Bachmann, Michele, 364
Baker, Howard, *271*, 284
Baker v. Carr (1962), 208
Baldwin, Alec, 336
ballot access: and absentee ballots, 74, 80, 124; and party affiliation, 17, *21*, 38, 40–41, 49, 182, *183*, 233; and primary elections, 186–90, 197, 264, 266; requirements for, 72, 74, 186; and third-party candidates, 14, 33, 237, 245n12, 320, 326–27n8, 327n9
Banfield, Edward C., 36
Bank of the United States, 24
Barrasso, John, *387*
Baton Rouge, La., 3–4, *5*
battleground states, **306**
Battle of the Thames (1813), 30
Battle of Tippecanoe (1811), 30
Baucus, Max, 364
Bauer, Gary, 256
Bayh, Birch, 128, *271*
BCRA. *See* Bipartisan Campaign Reform Act of 2003 (McCain-Feingold)
Beck, Glenn, 364
Beckley, John, 27
Bell, John, 33
Bell Atlantic, 171
Bennett, Bob, 187
Bentsen, Lloyd, 6, 58, *271*
Berelson, Bernard, 82–86
Bibby, John, 413
Biden, Joe, 259, *271*, 276, 283, 287n4, 319, 368
Bipartisan Campaign Reform Act of 2003 (McCain-Feingold), 130, *136*, **137–38,** 144–47, 170–74, 217
Black Lives Matter, 103
blacks: as candidates, 194–95; and Congressional Black Caucus, 268, 386; and Democratic Party, 42, 123, 251, 307; and Jim Crow laws, 35, **68;** and slavery, 30–33, *33*, 44, 63n6; voting behavior, 75–76, 87, 112, 258, 275, 284; and voting rights, 45, **45,** 67–69, *70*, 71, 74, 103
Blair, Tony, 4
blanket primary, **188**. *See also* primary elections
Bliss, Ray, 222–23
Blue Dog Democrats, 364
Blunt, Roy, 385, *387*, 392
Bode, Ken, 340
Boehner, John, 241, 364
Boeing, 16–17
Bowles, Erskine, 158
Boxer, Barbara, 392
Brace, Paul, 230
Bradley, Bill, 256, 265, 324
Brady, David, 371–73
Brady, Henry, 102
Breaux, David, 152
Breckinridge, John C., 33
Brennan, Joseph, 236
Brewer, Mark D., 10, 373, 413
Brexit campaign (2016), 358
Brock, William, 57–58
Broder, David, 340
Brooks, Cornell, *111*
Brown, Jerry, 266, 280
Brown, Scott, 366
Brownback, Sam, *271*
Bryan, William Jennings, 39
Buchanan, Patrick, 179n14, 256, 269, 281, 284
Buckley v. Valeo (1976), **127,** 142–43
Bull Moose party, 39, 320
Bunning, Jim, 388
Burnham, Walter, 90
Burr, Aaron, 26
Bush, George H. W.: and 1988 election, 305, 334; and 1992 election, 269, 280–81, 290, 295, 308, 314, 325, 414n1; career of, 2, 267, 339, 382
Bush, George W.: and 2000 campaign, 11, 256, 267, 280–81, 304; and 2004 campaign, 60, 108, 172, 269–70, 272–73, 308–9, 314, 325, 399; and campaign finance reform, 146; and media, 272–73, 310–11, 341; political background, 203

Bush, Jeb, *246*, *259*, 260, 273, 276, 347
Bush, Laura, 339
Bush, Prescott, 2

Caddell, Patrick, 346
cadre parties, **12**
Cain, Herman, 258
Calhoun, John C., 28
California, *6*, 31, 41, 188–89, 194, 256–58, 263, 352
California Democratic Party v. Jones (2000), 189
Cambridge Analytica, 358, 407
Cameron, Simon, 37–38
campaign finance. *See* finance
Campaign Finance Institute, 171
campaign managers: and presidential elections, 39, 81, 250, 294–96, 319, 354; and state and local elections, 201, 216, 219, 221, 224
Campbell, Angus, 62n1, 82–86, 90, 92
candidate-centered campaigns, **206–7**, 408–11
candidates, 90, 154–58, *155–58*, 228, 241–43. *See also* individual candidates
Cannon, Joseph G. "Czar," 372, 380, 383
canvassing, **227**
Cardin, Benjamin, 74
Carnahan, Robin, 392
Carson, Ben, *246*, *259*
Carter, Jimmy: and 1976 campaign, 57, 143, 266, 276, 282, 290, 305, 362; and 1980 campaign, 58, 92, 314
Carville, James, 276, 295, 316
Cassidy, John, 283
Castile, Philando, *111*
Catholics, 42, 87, 112, 132–33, 283, 365
caucuses, **249–50**, 262, 268, 373, 386
census, 66, 71, 107, 208–9, 233, 240–41, 403
Census Act (1840), 34
Center for Responsive Politics, 116, 137, 149, 160–61, 172–73
centrism, 307–8
Cermak, Anton, 50
Chadwick, Andrew, 410–11
challenge primary, **187**. *See also* primary elections
Chamber of Commerce, 124
Chambers, William N., 14, 62n4
Chambliss, Saxby, 60
Chancellor, John, 333
The Changing American Voter (Nie et al.), 89–92, 404
character, as campaign issue, 108, 265, 270, 273–74, 310–12, 315–16, 325, 344, 399
Checchi, Al 3
checks and balances, 22–23
Cheney, Dick, 283, 287n4, 381–82
Christian Coalition, 60
Christian Right, 50, 112, 256
Christie, Chris, *259*, 260
Church, Frank, 128, *271*
Citizens' Research Foundation, 151–52
Citizens United, *136*, 147
Citizens United v. Federal Election Commission (2010), **124**, 130, *136*, 147–48, 169, 176, 217, 354
Civil Rights Act (1964), **45**, 103
civil rights movement, 44–45, 68–69, 103. *See also* voting rights
civil service system, 40, **61**
Civil War, 33, 35, 44, 63n7, 184
Clay, Henry, 28–30
Clayton, Eva M., 202n5
Cleland, Max, 395n9
Cleveland, Grover, 35, 39
Clinton, Bill: and 1992 campaign, 265–66, 280, 287n6, 293–95, 300, 305, 307–8, 317–18, 326n2, 331; and 1996 campaign, 284, 311–12, 325, 399; and campaign finance reform, 144; and character issue, 108, 270, 273–74, 310–12, 325; and health care reform, 362, 365
Clinton, Hillary, *43* and 2008 campaign, 252–53, 258–59, 268, 300, 342–43; and 2016 campaign, 61, 266–68, 273, 283, 290, 294, 297, 300, 304, 309, 312, *396*; and campaign finance reform, *136*, 147, *259*

closed primaries, **190–92,** 257. *See also* primary elections
Clyburn, James, *387*
CNBC, 331
CNN, 320, *332*, 334, 336–37, 392
Coakley, Martha, 366
Coalition for Government Procurement, 119
coalition strategy, 307–8
Coelho, Tony, 58, 394n6
Cohen, Marty, 255
Cohen, William, 241–42
The Colbert Report, 336
Coleman, Norm, 66
Collins, Doug, *387*
Collins, Susan, 236
Colorado, *6*, 80, 108, 145, 186–88, 263, 306
Colorado Republican Federal Campaign Committee v. Federal Election Commission (1996), 145
Comedy Central, 331
Commission on Party Structure and Delegate Selection, **248–50,** 252, 267
Commission on Presidential Debates, 318, 326n8
Committee on Political Education (AFL-CIO), 162
Committee to Reelect the President, 142, 178n6
Common Cause, 119
competitive two-party system, **14,** 62n4. *See also* parties
Compromise of 1850, 31
conditional party government, 373
Congressional Black Caucus, 268, 386
Congressional Budget Act (1974), 367
Congressional Caucus for Women's Issues, 386
Congressional Committee of the National Women's Suffrage Association, 120
Congressional Government (Wilson), 371
Congress of Industrial Organizations (CIO), 13, 162
Congress Watch, 119
Connally, John, 287n5
Connecticut, 6, 66, 158, 186–88, 190–92, 198, 276
Conover, Pamela Johnston, 412
Conservative Coalition, 44
Conservative party, 189–90
Constitution: and elections, 71, 146, 177, 207–8, 326n5; equal protection clause, 4–6, 68, 209; and freedom of the press, 357; and government structure, 8, 22, 24, 26, 34, 369–70, 378; ratification of, 24. *See also* individual amendments
Constitutional Union party, 33
Contract with America, **97,** 382–84
contrast ads, **350**. *See also* media
Converse, Philip, 82–86, 90, 92
Conyers, John, Jr., 74
Cook, Charlie, 230
Cook County (Illinois), 50, 187–88
The Cook Report, 230
Cooper, Joseph, 371–73
Copeland, Royal, 388
"Cornhusker Kickback," 365
Cornyn, John, *387*
corporations: and campaign finance reform, 138–39, 146–47; and political action committees, *118*, 126–27, *127*, 130–31, 162–66, *164–65*, *167–69*
Corrado, Anthony, 178n3
corrupt bargain, **29**
Corrupt Practices Campaign Act (1925), 126
Corzine, John, 158
Cotter, Cornelius P., 54
Courtney, Joe, 66
Cox, Archibald, 142
Cox, Gary, 373
Craig, Larry, 394n8
Cranston, Alan, *271*
Crawford, William H., 28–29
critical elections, **23**
Critical Mass, 119
critical realignment, **23**
Cronin, Tom, 413

Cronkite, Walter, 284–85
cross-filing, **189,** 193
crossover or strategic voting, **193**. *See also* voter behavior
Crotty, Bill, 413
Crowley, Joe, *387*
Crump, Ed, 50
Cruz, Ted, 158, *259,* 260, 267, *271*
C-SPAN, 334, 340
cult of personality, 88
cultural issues, 44, 46–47, 94, 107, 281, 312. *See also* abortion; gay rights
Culver, John, 128
Cummings, Milton, 86
Cuomo, Mario, 284
Curley, James Michael, 49

The Daily Show, 331, 336
Daley, Richard J., 50, 187–88, 333
Daley, Richard M., 187
data mining, 331, 355, 358, 409–10. *See also* public opinion polling
Davis, John W., 277
Davis v. Bandemer (1986), 209
Dean, Howard, 161, 175, 212, 268, 273–75, 286n2, 297, 351
de la Torre, Hector, 194
DeLauro, Rose, *387*
Delaware, 186–88
DeLay, Tom, 60, 166, 169, 382, 384
delegates, **184**
The Democracy Restoration Act (2017), 74
Democratic Congressional Campaign Committee (DCCC), 56–58, 170, 385, 394n3, 394n6
Democratic Governors' Association, 55
Democratic Leadership Council (DLC), 307, 324
Democratic National Committee (DNC), 55–61, 123, 145, 169, 212, 249, 253, 293–94, 297
Democratic national conventions, 247–48, 251, **251–53,** 267–69, 277, 333
Democratic party: and congressional leadership, 378–81, 384–85, *387;* and finance, 57–59, 166–70, *167–69;* and health care reform, 362–70; and labor unions, 123–24; and minorities, 32, *33,* 42, 123, 251, 307; and nominations, 36–37, 248–49, 251–53, 286n1; and party unity votes and scores, **10–11,** 375, *376–77;* and Southern politics, 44–46, 184; and two-party competition, *15–16;* and voting, 59–61, 68
Democratic-Republican party, 22, 28, 30
Democratic Senatorial Campaign Committee (DSCC), 56–59, 170
demographic representation, **251,** 284
Dewey, Thomas, 324
Dewhurst, David, 158
digital media. *See* media
Dingell, John, 364
direct mail, **161,** 222–23, 225, *328*
District of Columbia, 31, 63n10, 74, 80, 185, 214, 261, 304
divided government, **374**
Divided We Govern (Mayhew), 374
Dixiecrats (States' Rights party), 322
Dodd, Christopher, *271,* 276, 364
Dolan, John T., 128
Dole, Bob, 81, 267, *271,* 276, 284–85, 289
Dole, Elizabeth, 256
Douglas, Stephen A., 33
Downs, Anthony, 12–13, 89
The Drudge Report, 331, *332,* 337
Dukakis, Michael, 6, 280, 289, 296, 334, 340
Dunham, Ann, 2
Dunn v. Blumstein (1972), 69
Durbin, Richard, *387*
Duverger, Maurice, 12

Eagleton, Thomas, 282
economic interest groups, 117–19
economic issues, 24, 35, 38–39, 94, 182, 228, 311–12, 406
education, 76, 80, 84, 114, 162, 312, 330, 352, 404
Edwards, John, *271,* 289
Eisenhower, Dwight D., 42, 139–40, 314

Eldersveld, Sam, 413
electioneering communications, **147,** 178n7
elections, gubernatorial: nomination, 34, 140, *180,* 196, 199, 216, 223, 230–31; parties, 46, 50, 55, 60, 98, *99,* 178n1, 234–37, 248, 252, 270, 329, 355; terms and succession of, 4, 6–7, 182–83, *183,* 215. *See also* state and local elections
elections, national: in 1796–1900, 14, 25–35, 39; in 1948, 45, 326n7; in 1952–1956, 42; in 1964, 91; in 1966, 140; in 1968, 57, 91, 149, 247–48; in 1972, 91, 141, 149, 250–51; in 1976, 57, 91–92, 143, 145; in 1980, 13, 58, 92; in 1982, 123, 127–28, 152, 194, 274; in 1984, 13, 20n10, 99–100, 159; in 1988, 340, 414n1; in 1992, 13–14, 81, 179n14, 264–65, 311–12; in 1994, 166, 233, 235, 245n9, 307, 382–83, 386, 400; in 1996, media, 330, 334, 345, 354, 399, 414n3; in 1996, parties and nominations, 13–14, 46, 81, 233, 263, 267, 276, 284, 384; in 1996, strategy and organization of, 78, 289, 296, 307, 311–12; in 1998, 59, 122, 218, 233, 236–37, 256, 341, 384; in 2000, campaign finance, 145, 149, 159, 171, 175; in 2000, media, 272, 274–76, 283, 310, 346–47; in 2000, nominations, 255–58, 263, 265–67, 270, 285, 289–90, 302, 341; in 2000, parties, 6, 47, 66, 105, 108, 189, 304, 315–16, 321–22, 375; in 2002, 53, 56, 59–60, 171, 194, 384, 392; in 2004, campaign finance, 53, 128, 149, 158–60, 166, 175; in 2004, parties and nominations, 4, 47, 60, 105, 108, 169, 171–73, 257–58, 263, 268–70, 273–74, 289; in 2004, strategy and organization of, 306, 308, 310, 316, 342, 399; in 2006, media, 336, 402, 410; in 2006, parties and nominations, 47, 60–61, 66, 68, 97–98, 169, 199, 232, 324; in 2008, media, 274, 316–19, 331, 349, 351; in 2008, nominations, 252, 258–59, 262, 264–68, 276, 285, 289–90, 326n1; in 2008, parties, 47, 61, 66, 75, 77–81, 89, 98, 105, 198, 229, 362, 369–70, 399; in 2008, strategy and organization of, 269–70, 274, 283, 293–97, 306, 308–12; in 2010, 66, 97–99, 106, 108, 178n1, 187, 198, 216–17, 229–32, 402; and 2012, media, 316–17, 319, 330, 355; and 2012, parties and nominations, 47, 61, 106–6, 231, 236, 253, 258–60, 266–67, 293–94, 297, 399; and 2012, strategy and organization of, 137, 290, 311–12; in 2012, campaign finance, 141, 149, 160, 174, 272, 351; in 2014, 47, 66, 137, 149, 173–74, *204,* 215, 230, 233, 237; in 2016, campaign finance, 53, 137, 147, 153, 160–61, 174–75; in 2016, media, 319, 329–37, 342–45, 357–58, *396,* 409–10; in 2016, nominations, 2, 106, *246,* 247, 253–55, 259–60, 263–73, 276, 283–85, 326n1, 326n6; in 2016, parties, *1,* 7–8, *21, 43,* 43–44, 46, 50, 61, 66, 74–77, 97, 124–25, 190, 230, 233–35; in 2016, strategy and organization of, 280, *288,* 290–91, 293–94, 297, 300, 304, 307, 309, 312; deviating, 62n1; direct vs indirect, **18;** maintaining, 62n1; nonpartisan, 7–8, 19n7, 20n14, 41, 245n10, 403–4; realigning, 23, *32–33,* 33, 39, 43–46
electoral coalitions, 410–11
electoral college: and campaign tactics, **234–38,** 303–6, 315; and election results, 26, 28–29, 34, 45, 320, 324, 326n6; structure and rules, 9, 42, 252, 291, **291–92,** 326n1; and third-party candidates, 319–20
Emanuel, Rahm, 367—368, 385
EMILY's List, 147, 222
EMILY's List v. Federal Election Commission (2009), 147
Enron Corporation, 146
environmental movement, 116, 125, 223, 237, 322, 324

equal protection clause, 4–6, **4–6,** 19n3, 68, 208–10, 217. *See also* Constitution; Supreme Court
Equal Rights Amendment (ERA), 119
equal time provision, **318**. *See also* media
Erikson, Robert, 72
Ervin Committee, 142
Estrada, Miguel, 389
expectation game, **342**

Facebook, *332*, 337, 351, 358. *See also* social media
factions, **22**
Fairbank, Maslin, Maullin and Associates, 220
fair housing legislation, 44
Fair Labor Standards Act (1938), 44
FairVote: The Center for Voting and Democracy, 195
family values, 312. *See also* cultural issues
farmers, 38–39, 42, 112, 117
Farmers' Alliance, 38
Farrakhan, Louis, 275
Federal Corrupt Practices Act (1925), **139**
Federal Election Campaign Act (FECA, 1971 and 1974), 125–27, 141–44, **142,** 149, 163, 170–71
Federal Election Commission (FEC), 13, 116–17, 126, **138,** 143, 147, 154, 159, 163–64, 342, 357–58
Federal Election Commission v. National Conservative Political Action Committee (1985), 159
Federal Election Commission v. Wisconsin Right to Life (2007), 147
federal groups, **121**. *See also* groups, organized
federalism, 369–70, 397–404
Federalist No. 10, 8, 22
Federalist party, **22,** 25, 27–28
federal matching funds, 259, 270–72
Feingold, Russ, 137, 144–47
feminist movement, 46–47. *See also* women's rights
Fenno, Richard, 20n13
Ferraro, Geraldine, 284, 289
field winnower, **344**
Fifteenth Amendment, **68**
50/50 nation, 47
50-State Strategy, 212, 297
filibuster and cloture, **363,** 370, 388–90, 393n1, 395n9
filing deadlines, **264**
finance: campaign finance reform, 137–48, *148,* 160–61, 176–77, 178nn3–4; campaign fundraising, 57–59, 128–35, *129,* 148–77, *154–58,* 222–23, 257, *259,* 260, 289; 501(c) and 527 groups, 130, **148,** 160, 169, 172–74, **173,** 174, *175;* hard and soft money, **138,** 144–47, 170–74, 179n11; and independent expenditures, **143;** and political action committees (PACs), *118,* 125–30, *127,* 144–45, 154–58, *155–58,* 161–69, *167–69, 175,* 394n6; and presidential nominations, *150,* 270–72; public campaign funding, **141,** 142–43, 154–60, *155–58,* 163, 174–76, 179n8, 259, 270–72, 286n2, 322; Super PACS, 130, 169, *175;* and third-party candidates, 13
Finer, Herman, 3, 7, 397
Fiorina, Carly, *259*
Fiorina, Morris, 89, 92
First Amendment, 104, 147, *148,* 191
First Congress, 24
501(c) and 527 groups, 130, **148,** 160, 169, 172–74, **173**
FiveThirtyEight, 333
Florida, *6,* 66, 74, 109nn2–3, 262–64, 304, 306, 322, 324, 346–47
Flowers, Gennifer, 273–74
focus groups, **301**. *See also* public opinion polling
Foley, Thomas S., 394n4
food stamps, 45
Forbes, Steve, 175, 256–57, 270–72
Ford, Betty, 277
Ford, Gerald, 57, 91–92, 143, 278–79, 314

Ford, Harold, 384
foreign policy, 25, 124, 207, 283, 312, 314
4-H clubs, 114
Fourteenth Amendment, 4, 19, 417
Fox, John, 400
Fox News, 331, *332*, 336–37
franchise, **67–74**. *See also* voting rights
Frank (Frank), 241
Frank, Barney, 240–41
Franken, Al, 66, 199, 362–63
Fraser, Donald, 248
free or earned media, **334–48**. *See also* media
Free Soil party, 31–32
free speech and association, 104, 137, 142–43, 147, *148*, 191, 209–10
Fremont, John C., 32–33
Frendeis, John P., 51–52
Frett, Deborah, 120
Frist, Bill, 389
From, Al, 307
front-loaded primaries, **255–56,** 258, 261–64, 272. *See also* primary elections
Full Frontal with Samanth Bee, 336

Gais, Thomas, 152
Gallup Poll, 233
Gardner, John, 119, *387*
Garfield, James, 35, 40
GarinHart-Yang Strategic Research Group, 220
gay rights, 46, 105, 107, 112–13, 241, 311, 367
Geer, John, 353
gender, 67, 78–79, *79*
General Motors, **119**
geographic representation, **251**
Georgia, 60, 71, 202n4, 263–64, 352, 2248
Gephardt, Richard, 60, 384, 394n4
gerrymandering, **208–10**. *See also* redistricting and reapportionment
Gibbs, Robert, 296
Gienapp, William E., 63n6
Gierzynski, Anthony, 152
Gilded Age, 34–40, 49, 52, 64n12
Gilmore, James, *259*
Gingrich, Newt, 258, 381–84
Giuliani, Rudolph, 258
Glenn, John, *271*
Goel, M.L., 103
Goldwater, Barry, 91, 161, 333
Google, *332*, 337
Gore, Al: and 2000 campaign, 6, 145, 256, *271*, 302, 304, 315, 322, 342, 346–47; career of, 284–85, 323–24; and character issue, 108, 310–11
Government Accountability Office, 142, 178n6
The Governmental Process (Truman), 132–33
Graber, Doris, 405
Graham, Bob, *271*
Graham, Lindsey, *259, 271*
Gramm, Phil, *271*, 276
Granger movement, 38
Grant, Ulysses S., 26, 35
grassroots politics, 12, **28–29,** 49–50, 297–98
Gray v. Sanders (1963), 208
Great Depression (1929), 41–43, 85
Great Society, 386, 402
Greenberg Quinlan Rosner Research, 220
Green party, 237, 321–22
Grocery Manufacturers of America, 121
group consciousness, **112–13**
group ratings, **124–25,** 131
groups, organized, 87, *111*, 111–35, *175*, 213–14, 224
Guiteau, Charles J., 40
gun control, *65*, 132, 134, 223, 352, 389

Hague, Frank, 49
Hamilton, Alexander, 22, 24–25, 27
Hanna, Marcus A., 39
Hanna, Mark, 139
hard money, **138**. *See also* finance
Harkin, Tom, *271*
Harris, Fred, 248, *271*
Harrison, William Henry, 30

Hart, Gary, 250, 264, 268, *271*, 274, 276
Hartke, Vance, *271*
Hastert, Dennis, 384
Hatch, Orrin, 256, *271*, 276, *387*
Hatch Acts (1939 and 1940), 126, **139**
Hathaway, William, 235
Hawaii, 2, 6, 71, 74, 208
health care: Medicare and Medicaid, 44, 365, 406; policy and reform, 108, 119, 312, 336, 353, 361–70, 391–92
Health Research Group, 119
Heard, Alexander, 178n3
Heckler, Margaret, 240
Heinz, John, 158
Hennessy, Bernard C., 54
Herrnson, Paul, 54, 170, 410, 413
Hillary: The Movie (2008), *136*, 147
Hill committees, **56–58,** 170
Hispanics, 76, *77*, 79, 107, 112, 195, 258, 284, 298
Hofstadter, Richard, 36
Hogue, Ilyse, 120
Hollings, Ernest, *271*
Homeland Security Department Act, 395n9
Hoover, Herbert, 42, 88
House of Representatives: redistricting and reapportionment, 19n3, 199, **207–11,** 208, 210, 233, 403; structure and leadership, 4, 9, *16*, 285, 370–73, *376*, 378–91, *387*, 394nn3–4; whip system, 280, 372, **379,** 382–83, 385–86, *387*, 394n6
Hoyer, Steny, 364, *387*
Huckabee, Mike, *246*, 258, *259*
Huckshorn, Bob, 413
Hull, Blair, 158
Humphrey, Hubert, 91, 140, 169, 242, 247–48, 250–51, *271*, 324–25
hybrid primary, **190–91**. *See also* primary elections

ideological representation, **251**
ideology, 62n5, 63, **84,** 86, 91, 100, 377
"I Have a Dream" (King), 45
Illinois, 50, 121, 158, 178n1, 187–88, 249, 403
immigration, 32, 35–36, 107, 134, 182, 312, 392
in-and-outers, 86–88, *87*
incumbency: and campaign finance, 144, *154*, 169, 176; and campaign strategy, 16–17, 269, 313–15; and reelection, 20n13, 95–99, *96–97*, *99*, 182, 198–99, 228–31, 244n4, 399–404
independent candidates, 236, 327n10
independent expenditures, **143**
independents (voters), **85**
industrialization, 35, 38–39
infomercials, **321,** 327n11, 349. *See also* television
informed consent of the governed, **338**
initiatives, **41**
instant runoff voting (IRV), **195**
Institute on Money in State Politics, 53
interest groups, 111–35
Internal Revenue Service (IRS), 116, 141, 173–74
Internet, 214–17, 223, 225, 257, 330–31, 349–51, 405–8. *See also* media
Iowa: caucuses, *106*, 181, 257–58, 261–64, 272, 274–75; elections, 74, 105, *106*, 306, 342–43
Iranian hostage crisis (1979–1981), 314
issue advocacy advertisements, **129,** 216–17, 353–54. *See also* media
Iyengar, Shanto, 352–53

Jackson, Andrew, 28–30
Jackson, Henry, 16–17, *271*
Jackson, Jesse, 194, 268, 275, 284–85
Jacobson, Gary, 170, 181–82, 228, 242
Jarrett, Valerie, 296
Jaworski, Leon, 142
Jay, John, 25
Jay Treaty (1795), 25
Jefferson, Thomas, 22, 24–27
Jeffersonian (or Democratic) republican party, **25**
Jewell, Malcolm, 188
Jim Crow laws, 35, **68**. *See also* blacks
Jimmy Kimmel Live, 336
Jindal, Bobby, *259*
Johnson, Hiram, 41

Johnson, Lyndon B., 91, 247, 314, 325, 386, 390
Joint Labor Management Committee of the Retail Food Industry, 119
Jones, Ruth, 152, 179n10
Jones, Walter, 202n5
judicial nominations, 11, 389

Kaine, Tim, 283
Kansas, 31–32, 49–50, 152
Kansas-Nebraska Act (1854), 31
Kasich, John, *246*, 256, *259*, 260, 267, 326n6
Kefauver, Estes, 281
Kemp, Jack, 281, 289
Kennedy, Edward M. "Ted," 258, *271*, 276, 364, 366
Kennedy, John F., 139–40, 169, 280–81, 287n5, 301, 318, 386
Kennedy, Robert, 247, *271*
Kentucky, 71, 74, 106, 152
Kernell, Samuel, 181–82, 228, 242
Kerry, John: and 2004 campaign, 268, *271*, 273, 289–90, 306, 308–11, 316, 342, 399; and campaign finance, 159–60, 169, 175, 258, 270, 286n2
Kessel, John, 310
Key, V.O., Jr., **10,** 13, 23, 62n1, 86–89, *87*, 92, 113, 370–71
Keyes, Alan, 257
King, Angus, 235–36
King, Larry, 320
King, Martin Luther, Jr., 45, 247
King Caucus, **29**
Know-Nothing party (American party), 32
Koch brothers, 177
Koppel, Ted, 334
Krehbiel, Keith, 373
Kucinich, Dennis, 367
Kurtz, Howard, 352

labor, organized, 44, 112, 117, 123–24, 126, 130, 132–33, 162–64, 354
Landrieu, Mary, 364–65
LaRaja, Ray, 178n3
The Last Hurrah (O'Connor), 49
Last Week Tonight with John Oliver, 336
The Late Show with Stephen Colbert, 336
Latinos. *See* Hispanics
Lawson, Kay, 413
Lazarsfeld, Paul, 82–86
League of Conservation Voters, 125, 237
League of Latin American Citizens v. Perry (2006), 209
League of Women Voters, 114, 120, 326n8
legislative term limits, **4,** 5–7, *6*. *See also* term limits
legitimacy, of public officials, **3,** 7, 17, **18,** 26–27, 304, 412
Lehman Schlozman, Kay, 102
Leno, Jay, 336
Lessig, Lawrence, *259*
Letterman, David, 336
Levendusky, Matthew, 412
Lewinsky, Monica, 315
Libertarian party, 189
Liberty party, 31
Lieberman, Joseph, 6, 66, 198, *271*, 284, 315
Limbaugh, Rush, 364
Lincoln, Abraham, 33
lobbying, **116,** *117*, 121
Longley, James, 235
Longley, Larry, 413
Lott, Trent, 381
Louisiana, 3–4, *5–6*, 20n14, 188, 202n4, 248, 365
Lugar, Richard, 198, *271*
Lujan, Ben Ray, *387*

Machinists Nonpartisan Political League, 165
Madigan, Edward, 382
Madison, James, 8, 22, 24–25, 62n5
Maine: and nominating process, 34, 272, 291, 326n1, 369; and slavery, 31; voter turnout and voting rights, *6*, 72, 74, 106, 110n7, 196, 235–37
majority leader, 372, **379,** 382, 384, 386, *387*, 388–91
majority rule, **194**

majority whip, 372, 379, **379,** 382, 386, *387*
The Making of the President 1961 (White), 140
Malbin, Michael, 152, 178n3
Manatt, Charles, 58
Mandate for Reform (McGovern-Fraser Commission), 249
mandates, **85**
March on Washington (1963), 45
marginal seats, **230**
Margolies-Mezvinsky, Marjorie, 400, 414n2
Marjorie Stoneman Douglas High School (Parkland, Florida), *65*
Maryland, 214–15, 263
Mason, Liliana, 412
Massachusetts, *6,* 108, 187, 202n2, 241, 263, 366
mass membership parties, **12**
matching funds. *See* finance
Mayhew, David, 63n8, 374
McAuliffe, Terry, 56, *180*
McCain, John: and 2000 campaign, 89, 256–57, 274, 351; and 2008 campaign, 161, 169, 175, 257, 265, 270, *271,* 274, 289–90, 296, 312, 342; and campaign finance reform, 137, 144–47; and health care reform, 361
McCarthy, Eugene, 247, *271*
McCarthy, Kevin, *387*
McConnell, Mitch, 138, 145–47, *360, 387,* 390
McConnell v. Federal Election Commission (2003), 138, 146–47
McCubbins, Mathew D., 373
McCutcheon v. Federal Election Commission (2014), 138, 148, 160
McGinniss, Joe, 140, 302
McGovern, George, 91, 128, 248–50, 265, *271,* 282, 333
McGovern-Fraser Commission. *See* Commission on Party Structure and Delegate Selection
McKinley, William, 39
McKinney, Cynthia, 199
McKinnon, Mark, 337
McMahon, Linda, 158
media: adwatch campaigns, **340–41;** and campaign finance reform, 141, 145; and freedom of the press, 357; free or earned, **334–48;** impact of digital, 206–7, 216–17, 405–8; paid, 321, **334,** 349–55, 359n5; and presidential elections, 290, 298, 302–3, 308, 315–17, 321, *332,* 341–47; and presidential primaries, 262–63, 272–75; radio, 225, 331, *332,* 336, 349–50, 358n1; role in electoral process, *328,* 356–58; and state and local elections, 207–10, 214–17, *220,* 221–25, 234; targeting, 214–17, 316–17, 358, 409–10. *See also* newspapers and magazines; social media; television
Medicare and Medicaid, 44, 365, 406
Meehan, Marty, 137, 145
Messer, Luke, *387*
Mexican-American War (1846–1848), 31
Michaux, H.M. Mickey Jr., 194–95
Michel, Robert, 381–82
Michigan, *6,* 143, 305–7, 322
Milbrath, Lester W., 103
Miller, Carol, 90, 92, 237
Miller, George, 364
Miller, Patrick R., 412
Miller, Warren, 82–86, 94–95, 99–100
Mills, Wilbur, 276
Minnesota, 50, 66, 72, *111,* 187, 199, 236, 245n11, 362–63
minority leader, **379,** 385, *387,* 390, 394nn3–4
minority whip, 379, **379,** 381, 385, *387*
Mississippi Freedom Democratic party, 278
Missouri, *6,* 31, 49–50, 392, *396*
Missouri Compromise (1820), 31
Mitchell, George, 58
Mondale, Walter, 264, 268–69, 284–85, 289
Monroe, James, 27–28

Montana, *6*
Morehouse, Sarah, 188
Mormons, 258
Morris, Richard, 307
Motor Voter Bill, **72–73**
Mott, Stewart R., 160
MoveOn.org, 171–72
MSNBC, *332*, 336
MTV, 331
multi-candidate political committee, **162**. *See also* political action committees (PACs)
multipurpose groups, **120**. *See also* groups, organized
Murkowski, Lisa, 198, 231
Murray, Patty, *387*
Muskie, Edmund, 250, *271*, 276

NAACP (National Association for the Advancement of Colored People), *111*
Nader, Ralph, **119,** 321–22
Nagourney, Adam, 319
Napolitan, Joseph, 140
NARAL Pro-Choice America, 120, 123, 133
narrowcasting, 215–16. *See also* media
Nash, Pat, 50
National American Women's Suffrage Association, 120
National Association of Manufacturers, 119, 354
national committees, **54–56,** 58, 293–95. *See also* Democratic National Committee (DNC); Republican National Committee (RNC)
National Conference of State Legislatures, 74, 202n3
National Conservative Political Action Committee (NCPAC), 127–28
national conventions: brokered convention, **269;** credentials challenges, **278;** funding of, 175, 270; history of, **29,** 32, 34, 184; media coverage, 333–34; and nomination process, **184,** 248–52, *254*, **269,** 277–86, 287n7, 358n2. *See also* Democratic National Conventions; Republican National Conventions
National Election Study (NES), 89–92
National Federation of Democratic Women, 55
National Federation of Independent Businesses, 114, 123, 130, 354
National Football League Players' Association, 114
national groups, **121**
National Organization for Women (NOW), 120, 123
National Pro-Life Alliance, 120
National Public Radio (NPR), 331, *332*
National Republican Congressional Committee (NRCC), 56–58, 170, 394n6
National Republican Senatorial Committee (NRSC), 56–58, 145, 170
National Rifle Association (NRA), 114, 123, 132, 223
National School Walkout (2018), *65*
Native Americans, 30
Nebraska, *6*, 34, 245n10, 326n1, 365
negative ads, **350,** 352–53. *See also* media
Nelson, Ben, 364–65
Nelson, Bill, 365
Neumann, Sigmund, 12–13
Neustadt, Richard, 391
Neutrality Proclamation, 62n3
Nevada, *6*, 106, 224, 262–63
The New American Voter (Miller et al), 94, 404–5
New Deal, 386
New Deal coalition, **42–43,** 44, 63n7
New Frontier, 386
New Hampshire, 66, 181, 256–58, 261–65, 272–75, 306, 322, 342–43
New Jersey, 49, 158, 249
New Mexico, 31, 187, 237–38
newspapers and magazines: as free news source, 224, 302, 326n3, *328*, *332*, 335, 337, 339–40, 348, 405–7; and paid ads, 215, 349–50; relevance of, 205, 215, 329–31. *See also* media

Newsweek, 335
new voters, 86–88, *87*
New York State, 36–37, 49, 103, 186–90, 245n12, 256–60, 263, 305
New York Times, 224, 326n3, 331, *332*, 335
Nicholson, Jim, 123
Nie, Norman H., 89–92
Nightline, 334
9/11, 103, 308
Nineteenth Amendment, **69–70**
Nixon, Richard, 140–42, 159, 178n6, 302, 314, 318, 324–25, 386
Noah, Trevor, 336
Northam, Ralph, *180*
North Carolina, 45, 137, 158, 202nn4–5, 306
North Dakota, 72, 186–88, 215
NRA (National Rifle Association), 114, 123, 132, 223
nuclear weapons, 280, 282

Obama, Barack: and 2008 campaign, 61, 75, 77, 258, *271*, 289, 293–94, 296–97, 300, 306, 309, 311, 318–19; and 2012 campaign, 280, 314, 325; and campaign finance, 137, 141, 149, 161, 175, 270; and economy, 229–30; and health care reform, 361–69; and media, 274–75, 284–85, 316–17, 327n11, 331, 342, 349, 351, 355, 410–11; nomination, 252–53, 268; policy changes, 11, 69, 233, 399; political background, 203
Obama, Barack, Sr., 2
Obamacare. *See* Affordable Care Act (2010)
O'Connell, Dan, Edward, and John, 49
O'Connor, Edwin, 49
O'Connor, Sandra Day, 146
Ohio, *6*, 60, 257–58, 263, 305–6, 367
Oklahoma, *6*, 19n5, 202n4
old politics, 205–7, 224–28
O'Malley, Martin, *259*
O'Neill, Thomas P. (Tip), 108, 381, 394n4
one-party rule, 302
one-party system, 184
one person-one vote, **208**
open primaries, **190–93,** 257. *See also* primary elections
Open Society Institute, 171–72
Oregon, 19n5, 57, 68, 71–72, 80, 249, 322
Oregon v. Mitchell (1970), 68, 71
Organizing for America, 216
Owen, Priscilla, 389

pack journalism, **342**. *See also* media
Packwood, Robert, 57–58
PACs. *See* political action committees (PACs)
paid media, 321, **334,** 349–55, 359n5. *See also* media
Palin, Sarah, 267, 283, 289
parliamentary system, 10, 371
Parscale, Brad, 337
parties: candidate-centered, 206–7; definition and types of, 12–14; and finance, 13, *150*, 154–58, *155–58*, 169–70, 270–72; in government, 10–12, *360*, 360–93, *396*, 396–413; history of, 22–44, 64n12; national organization, 10, 54–61; and new and old politics, 205–28; and partisanship, 99–100, *360;* programmatic, 371; and realignment of the South, 44–47; state and local organization, **50–53,** 50–54, 59, 203n7, 211–13, 226–28, 233–34; unity votes and scores, 10–11, 375–76, *376–77*. *See also* national committees; national conventions; individual party names
partisan elections, party, **7–8, 19n7, 48–49**
party-centered campaigns, 408–11
party identification, *83*, **84,** *93*, 94, 213, 404–5, 410
party in government, **10**
party in the electorate, **10**
party leadership, *360* majority leader, 372, **379,** 382, 384, 386, *387*, 388–91; minority leader, **379,** 385, *387*, 390, 394nn3–4; in Senate, 56–58, *377*,

387, 388–91; Speaker of the House, **371–73,** 378–80, 394n4; whip system, 280, 372, 379, 381-83, 385–86, *387,* 394n6
party organization, **10**
party platform, 10, 122–23, 181, **279–81,** 322, 384
party systems, **14,** 14–15, 17, 20n12, 23–49, *33*
Party Transformation Study (Institute on Money in State Politics), 53
party unity votes and scores, **10–11,** 371, 375–77, *376–77*
Pataki, George, *259*
patriotism, 102–3
patronage or spoils system, **29–30,** 36–38, 40, 52, 61, 63n8
Paul, Rand, *259, 271*
Paul, Ron, 77, 258, 326n6
PBS (Public Broadcasting Service), *332,* 334
Peace and Freedom party, 189
Pelosi, Nancy, *360,* 363–67, 384–85, *387*
Pence, Mike, 283, *387*
Pendergast, Tom, 49–50
Pendleton Civil Service Reform Act (1883), 40
Penn, Schoen, and Berland, 220
Pennsylvania, 210, 249, 322
Pennsylvania Supreme Court, 210
penny press, **335**. *See also* media
Perdue, Sonny, 60
Perez, Tom, 55–56
Perot, H. Ross, 13–14, 81, 179n15, 236, 305, 320–21, 323, 327n11, 344–45, 349
Perry, Bob, 172
Perry, Rick, *259*
Persian Gulf War, 4, 97, 311–12
Petrocik, John, 89–92
Pew Research Center for the People and the Press, 337
Phi Beta Kappa, 115
Philip Morris Co., 171
Pinckney, Charles Cotesworth, 26
Plouffe, David, 276, 296
Plunkitt, George Washington, 36–37, 59
plurality rule, **194**
political action committees (PACs): and campaign finance, *118,* 125–30, *127,* 144–45, 154–58, *155–58,* 161–69, *167–69, 175;* ideology of, 166–67, 179n13; and organized groups, **116,** 121–25, 130–31; SUN PAC, **164;** Super PACS, 130, 169, 173, *175*
political culture, **3**
Politically Incorrect, 336
political machines, **35–38,** 40, 49–50, 52, 63n8, 181, 187–88
political participation: and civil rights movement, 68–69; and groups, 116–21; and non-voting behavior, 101–5; and polarization, 412–13; and protest movements, 44–45, *65,* 68–69, 103–5, 333, 367; recent changes in, 105–9; and voting, 65–100; and women's suffrage movement, 69–71. *See also* volunteers
Political Parties (Duverger), 12
politicians, careers, 202n1, 244n1
Politico, 337
Politics, Parties, and Pressure Groups (Key), 113, 370–71
Politics in America, 124
Politics without Power (Cotter et al.), 54
polls. *See* public opinion polling
poll tax, **67**. *See also* voting rights
Pomper, Gerald M., 62n1, 279
Poor Peoples Campaign party
popular vote, **291–92**
Populist party, 38–40
positive ads, **350**. *See also* media
Powell, Colin, 316
preprimary conventions, 187, **191**
Presidential Campaign Fund, 141
Presidential Commission on Election Administration, 73–74
presidential elections: and candidates, *271,* 323–25; contingency election, 326n5; debates, *246,* 318–19, 326n8, 345, *396;* and finance, 148–49, *150,*

163, *288;* and geography, 17–18, 108–9, 304–7, 315–16; nomination process, 34, *246,* 246–86, *252, 254, 259,* 286n1, 291–92; organization and party leadership, 289–303, 391–93; strategy, *15,* **292,** 303–15; tactics, 315–19, 326n3; and third-party candidates, 319–23; voting behavior in, 82–94
President's Commission on Campaign Costs (1962), 139–40
pressure groups, **113**. *See also* interest groups
Price, David, 413
primary elections: and candidate choices, 203n8; direct, 9, **40–41;** front-loaded, **255–56,** 258, 261–64, 272; open and closed, **190–93,** 257; presidential preference, **247–49,** *252, 254;* and state and local offices, 184–96, **185,** 191–96, 200–201, 202n2–202n3, 202n6, 203n8; and Super Tuesday, **257,** 263–64; top two system, **187–89;** whites only, **68;** winner-take-all, 34, **251–52,** 265–67
prison reform, 70
privacy, 339, 356, 358, 407
Progressive Bull Moose party, 39, 320
Progressive Era, 40–41, 50, 52, 184, 372–73
Project for Excellence in Journalism (2010), 329
proportional representation, **266**
Proposition 14 (California), 188–89
prospective (future) voting, **88–89,** 92. *See also* voter behavior
protest movements, 44–45, *65,* 68–69, 103–5, 333, 367
Pryor, William, 389
Public Citizen, 119
Public Citizen Litigation Group, 119
Public Disclosure, 171
public interest groups, **119**
public opinion polling: importance of, 51, 54, 212, 220–22, 225, 234; techniques, 301, 308–9, 319, 342, 345–46, 359n4
qualified candidates, **182**
Quay, Matt, 37–38
Quayle, Dan, 256

race and ethnicity: and Democratic Party, 42, 45, 123; and groups, 112–13; Hispanics, 76, *77,* 79, 107, 112, 195, 258, 284, 298; Jim Crow laws, 35, **68;** and voting behavior, 75–76, *77,* 87, 107, 195; and voting rights, 67–69. *See also* blacks
radio, 225, 336, 349–50, 358n1. *See also* media
Rainbow Coalition, 275
Rangel, Charles, 364
ranked choice voting (RCV), **195**
Rayburn, Sam, 386
Reagan, Nancy, 277
Reagan, Ronald: and 1976 convention, 278–79; and 1980 campaign, 11, 58, 92, 99–100, 159, 164, 303, 314, 317; and 1984 campaign, 100, 284, 325, 414n1; conservative legacy, 269, 414; and cultural issues, 47, 132, 269
recall, **41**
reconciliation, **367**
Reconstruction, 44, 63n7, 184
redistricting and reapportionment, 19n3, 34, 198–99, **207–11,** 233, 403
Redmond, Bill, 237
Reed, Ralph, 60
Reed, Thomas Brackett "Boss," 372
referendum, **41**
Reform party, 13–14, 236, 245n11, 257, 323
regional divisions, 94, 100, 108–9
regional primaries, **263**
Reid, Harry, 364–66, 392
religion: Catholics, 42, 87, 112, 132–33, 283, 365; and party, 42, 107–8, 123, 258, 283; and political influence, 46, 105, 107, 258; and political participation, 87, 102, 112–13, 119, 133; and religious right, 50, 105, 107–8, 112, 123, 256, 283
Republican National Committee (RNC), 55–60, 63n11, 63nn10–11, 123, 263, 294, 410

Republican national conventions, *1*, 32, 253–55, 257–60, 277, 287n5, 333. *See also* national conventions
Republican party: and cultural issues, 47, 107; and economy and tax reform, 229, 312, 361–62, 370, 391; and finance, 57–59; and health care reform, 361–69; history of, **31–33,** 41, 63n6; and interest groups, 114, 122–23; and party leadership, 245n9, 372, *387;* and party unity votes and scores, **10–11,** 375, *376–77;* and political action committees, 166–69, *167–69;* and Proposition 14, 189; and realignment of South, 44–46; and Tea Party movement, 103, 106, 112, 198, 229; and two-party competition, *15–16;* vote mobilization and voter registration, 59–61, 73–74
The Responsible Electorate (Key), 86–88
retrospective voting, **88–89,** 91–92. *See also* voter behavior
Revenue Act (1971), **141**
Revolt of 1910, 383
Rhode Island, 19, 186–87, 263
Ribicoff, Abraham, 333
Rice, Condoleezza, 300
Rice, Donna, 274
Richardson, Bill, 280
Ricketts, Pete, 158
RJR Nabisco, 171
Roberts, John, 147
Rockefeller, Nelson, 140, 178n5, 287n4
Roe v. Wade (1973), 47
Rogers, Cathy McMorris, *387*
Rohde, David W., 373–75
rolling sample, **301**. *See also* public opinion polling
Romney, Mitt, 258–60, 272, 283, 285, 296, 306, 342–43, 351
Romney McDaniel, Ronna, 55–56
Roosevelt, Franklin D., 26, 42, 44, 88, 282, 314
Roosevelt, Theodore, 39, 138–39, 320
Rove, Karl, 59–60, 276, 384, 410
Rubio, Marco, *246*, *259*, 260, *271*
runoff primary, **194**
Ryan, Paul, 260, 283, *360*, *387*

Salon.com, 337
Sanchez, Linda, 194, *387*
Sanchez, Loretta, 194
Sanders, Bernie, 50, 235, 253, *259*, 259–60, *271*, 272
Santorum, Rick, *259*
Sartori, Giovanni, 13
Saturday Night Live, 310–11, 336
Scalise, Steve, *387*
Schattschneider, E.E., 370
Schlozman, Kay Lehman, 102
Schmidt, Steve, 296
Schumer, Charles, *360*, *387*
Schwarz, Joe, 199
Schwarzenegger, Arnold, 199
Schweiker, Richard, 278
secular realignment, **23,** 43, 109nn2–3
self-identification, **112**
The Selling of the President 1968 (McGinniss), 140, 302
Senate: filibuster and cloture, 144–45, **363,** 370, 388–90, 393n1, 395n9; and finance, *153–54*, 154, 158–59; senatorial courtesy, **52;** senatorial holds, **370,** 394n8; structure and leadership, 9, *15*, 52, 56–58, *360*, *377*, *387*, 388–91; terms, 4, 19n2
Senate Select Committee on Presidential Campaign Activities (Ervin Committee), 142
Seneca Falls conference (1848), 69–70
Sentencing Project, 74
separate segregated fund, **162**
separation of powers, 22–23, 370
Sessions, Jeff, 392
Seventeenth Amendment, **41,** 52, 56
72-Hour Task Force, 59–60
Shanks, Merrill, 94
Shapp, Milton, 178n5
Shays, Chris, 137, 145
Shays-Meehan bill, 145
Shelby County v. Holder (2013), 69
Shriver, Sargent, 282
Sierra Club, 116

Silbey, Joel, 20n12, 64n12
Silver, Nate, 333
Simmons, Rob, 66
Simon, Paul, *271*
single purpose groups, **120**
single transferable vote (STV), **195**
The Sister Fund, 123
60 Minutes, 274
Slate Magazine, 337
Slaughter, Louise, 365
slavery, 30–33, *33,* 44, 63n6. *See also* blacks
Smith, Bob, *271*
Smith-Connally Act (1944), 126
Smith v. Allwright (1944), 68
Snowe, Olympia, 236, 364
socializing elements of American society, **84–85**
social media: Facebook, *332,* 337, 351, 358; and fundraising, 351; and new politics, 205–7; and partisan polarization, *338,* 357–58; and political news, 275, *328,* **330–31,** 332, 337–38, 399, 405–9; and state and local elections, 214–16, 221–22, 225; Twitter, 205, 216, 317, 330–31, *332,* 337, 351
social security, 108, 406
soft money, **138,** 144–47, 170–74, 179n11. *See also* finance
Sorauf, Frank J., 13, 170
Soros, George, 171–72
South, realignment of, 43–46, 63n7
South Carolina, 34, 45, 202n4, 262–63
South Dakota, *6,* 202n4
Southern Pacific Railroad, 41
Speaker of the House, **371–73,** 378–80, 394n4. *See also* House of Representatives
Specter, Arlen, *271*
SpeechNow.org v. Federal Election Commission (2010), 148
split-ticket voting, **40**. *See also* voter behavior
Spotted Eagle, Faith, 326n6
Stabenow, Debbie, *387*
standpatters, 86–88, *87*
Stark, Pete, 364
state and local elections: candidate-centered, 205–7; competition in, 228–34, 302; and media, 207, 214–17, 225, 406–7; nonpartisan, 403–4; and policy, *204;* and politicians, 238–43; redistricting and reapportionment, 207–11; and role of parties, 14–15, 52–54, 211–13, 226–28, 234–38; structure and organization of, 19n1, 50–53, 179n10, 180–202, 219–26, *220;* term limits, 182–83, *183;* voting behavior in, 94–99. *See also* elections, gubernatorial
states' rights, 45, 389
States' Rights party "Dixiecrats," 45, 322
Stein, Jill, 322
Stephanopoulos, George, 311
Stevens, Daniel, 353
Stevens, John Paul, 146
Stevens, Stuart, 296
Stevenson, Adlai, 42, 281, 324
Stewart, Jon, 336
Steyer, Tom, 177
Stivers, Steve, *387*
Stokes, Donald, 82–86, 90, 92, 95
Stonecash, Jeffrey M., 10, 49
strategy, campaign, **292**
Stromer-Galley, Jennifer, 410–11
students, *65*
Stupak, Bart, 365, 368
Stupak Amendment (health care reform bill), 365
succession, 6–7
Sundquist, James L., 62n2
Sun Oil Company, 126, 163–64
superdelegates, **251–53,** 267–69. *See also* Democratic National Conventions
Super PACS, **130,** 169, 173, *175. See also* political action committees (PACs)
Super Tuesday, **257,** 263–64. *See also* primary elections
Supreme Court: and 2000 election, 304; and campaign finance, 127, 130, *136,* 137–38, 142–43, 145–46, 159, 166,

176; and cultural issues, 46–47; and equal protection clause, 4–6, 19n3, 208–10, 217; and freedom of association, 191; and voting rights, 68–69, 71
Swalwell, Eric, *387*
Swift Boat Veterans for Truth, 172, 316
switchers, 86–88, *87*. *See also* voter behavior

tactics, campaign, **292,** 315–19
Taft-Hartley act (1947), 126
Tammany Hall, 36–37, 49, 181
Tarrance Group, 220
Tashjian v. Republican Party of Connecticut (1986), 191
tax checkoff, **141**. *See also* finance
Tax Cuts and Jobs Act (2017), 362
taxes, 24, 116, 173, 361–62, 369, 391
Tax Reform Research Group, 119
Tea Party movement, 103, 106, 198, 229
telephones, 215–16, 218, 289
television: and electoral process, 284, 302, *328,* 329–30, 335–36; infomercials and paid advertising, 273, 321, 327n11, 340, 349–50; and new politics, 206–7; as news source, 316–17, *332,* 405–7, 414n3; and state and local elections, 207, 214–17, 225, 406–7. *See also* media
Tennessee, 50, 186, 208
Terkel, Studs, 92
term limits: legislative, **4,** 5–7, *6,* 19n4, 26, 242nn2–3, 245nn8–9; and state and local elections, 182–83, *183;* term limit movement, 231–32
Texas, 50, 80, 202n4, *204,* 209, 352, 369
The Theory and Practice of Modern Government (Finer), 3
third parties, 31, 33, 36, 38, 234–38, 245n12. *See also* individual parties
third-party candidates, **13–14,** 19n9, 238, 303, 319–23, 326–27n8, 327nn9–10. *See also* independent candidates
Thune, John, *387*
Thurmond, Strom, 45, 319
Tillman Act (1907), **126,** 139
Time, 335
The Tonight Show with Jimmy Fallon, 331
top two system, **187–89**. *See also* primary elections
"Toward a More Responsible Two-Party System" (American Political Science Association), 371
trade associations, 127–28, 131, 162, 166, 171, 173
triangulation, **307**
Trippi, Joe, 276
Truman, David B., 132–33
Truman, Harry, 50, 139–40, 282, 314, 325, 326n7, 362
Trump, Donald J.: and 2016 campaign, *1, 246,* 260, 285, *288,* 293–96, 300, 304, 309, 326n6, *396,* 409–10, 412; and character issue, 310–11; and economy and tax reform, 312, 361–62, 369–70, 391; and fundraising, *259,* 272; and media, 216, 275–76, 317, 332–33, 337, *338,* 342, 348, 351, 357, 410–11; nomination, 253, 255; and party affiliation, 11, *43,* 43–44, 56, 61; political background, 203
Trump, Fred and Mary, 2
Tsongas, Paul, 240, 284
Tucker, Harvey, 230
Tweed, William Marcy ("Boss"), 49, 181
Tweed, William Marcy "Boss," 36–37
Twelfth Amendment, 326n5
Twenty-Fourth Amendment, **67**
Twenty-Second Amendment, 326n5
Twenty-Sixth Amendment, **71,** 76
Twitter, 205, 216, 317, 330, *332,* 337, 351. *See also* social media
two-party competition, *15–16,* 25, 34, 403
two-party system, 14–15, **18,** 31, 38, 234–35, 319, 369–71

Udall, Morris, 237, 285
Udall, Stewart, 237
Udall, Tom, 237
unified control, **374**

unions. *See* labor, organized
United Auto Workers, 119
United We Stand, 321
University of Michigan Survey Research Center, 89–92
Univision, *332*
Utah, 31, 106, 186–88, 287n3

Valentine, Tim, 194–95
Van Buren, Martin, 29
Vander Jagt, Guy, 57–58
Van Hollen, Chris, *387*
Ventura, Jesse "The Body," 236, 245n11
Verba, Sidney, 89–92, 102
vice president: nomination process, 28, 278, 281–83, 287n4, 291, 324, 326n5; presidential campaigns of, 108, 140, 247, 256–57, 259, 269–70, 275, 287n4, 302–3; role in campaigns, 315, 319, 321; succession of, 6–7, 314
Vietnam War, 44, 71, 76, 91, 103
Viguerie, Richard, 222–23
Vitter, David, 101
Voice and Equality (Verba et al.), 102
volunteers: and presidential elections, 56, 60, 317, 320–21; and state and local elections, 51, 144, 200, 217–19, 224–25. *See also* political participation
voter behavior, 40, 65–100, *83, 87,* 105–9, 130–35, 193
voter registration: party organization of, 51, 54, 205, 207, 213, 225, 227, 289; requirements for, *70,* 72–74, *73*
voter turnout: and ballot options, *21;* factors in, 66, 72–75, *73, 75, 78,* 78–82, *79;* and party organization, 59–61, *106,* 213; and race, 45, 68–69, *70,* 75–76, *77*
voting rights: and franchise, 25, **67–74;** and literacy tests, 68; and race, 45, 67–69, *70,* 74; and residency requirements, **68–69;** and restrictions on, 67–68, 72, 74, 76, 109nn2–3
Voting Rights Act (1965, 1970, 1975), **45,** 68–69, 71, 103

Walker, Bill, 237
Walker, Scott, *259,* 260
Wallace, George, 161, 319, 323
Warren, Elizabeth, *387*
The War Room (1994), 326n2
Washington, George, 9, 22, 24–27, 62n3, 388
Washington Post, 332, 335, 340, 365
Washington State Grange et al. v. Washington State Democratic Party, 189
Washington Week in Review, 340
Watergate scandal, 57, 91–92, 314
Waxman, Henry, 241, 364
Webb, Jim, *259*
Weber, Ronald, 230
Webster, Daniel, 30
Weissman, Stephen, 171
welfare policies, 44–45
Wesberry v. Sanders (1964), 208
Wexler, Robert, 336
WhatsApp, 337
Whig party, **30,** 31, *33,* 63n6
White, Theodore, 140
whites only primaries, **68,** *See also* primary elections
Whitman, Meg, 137, 216
Wilmot Proviso, 31
Wilson, James Q., 36
Wilson, Woodrow, 39, 70, 184, 371
winner-take-all primaries, 34, **251–52,** 265–67, *See also* primary elections
Wisconsin, 249, 322
Wolfinger, Raymond E., 72, 76, 80
women's rights, 46–47, 107, 112, 119–20, 133, 222, 364–65
women's suffrage, 67, 69–71, 78–79
Workers party, 189
Working Families party, 190
Wright, Jim, 381–82, 394n4

Yahoo, 337
Young, James, 27
Young Democrats, 55